VICTORIAN LITERATURE

AND CULTURE

Volume 23

ADVISORY BOARD

VICTORIAN LITERATURE AND CULTURE

Volume 23

EDITORS

JOHN MAYNARD
ADRIENNE AUSLANDER MUNICH

Associate Editor: Sandra Donaldson
Managing Editor: Abigail Burnham Bloom

Review Editor: Winifred Hughes
Assistant Review Editor: Susan Katz

Special Effects Editor: Jeffrey Spear
Assistant Special Effects Editor: Pearl Hochstadt

AMS PRESS
1995

Copyright © 1996 by AMS PRESS, Inc.

ISSN 1060-1503

Series ISBN 0-404-64200-4

Vol. 23 ISBN 0-404-64223-3

Library of Congress Catalog Card Number: 73-80684

For current subscription information or back orders for volumes 1–22, write to AMS Press, Inc., 56 East 13th Street, New York, NY 10003, USA.

VICTORIAN LITERATURE AND CULTURE is a publication of the Browning Institute, Inc., a nonprofit organization. It is published through the generous support of New York University, the State University of New York at Stony Brook, and the University of North Dakota. The editors gratefully acknowledge our indebtedness to our editorial assistants Corinne Abate, Lisa Golmitz, Martha Heller, and Maria Jerenic.

Manuscripts and editorial correspondence can be addressed to either editor: Adrienne Munich, Department of English, SUNY/Stony Brook, Stony Brook, NY 11794 (516 632 9176; fax: 516 632 7302);
John Maynard, Department of English, NYU, 19 University Pl., Rm. 235, N.Y., NY 10003 (212 998 8835; fax: 212 995 4019).

Please submit two copies of manuscripts; articles should be double-spaced throughout and follow the new MLA style (with a list of Works Cited at the conclusion). Chapters of books submitted for the *Works in Progress* section may follow the author's chosen style in the book project.

Correspondence concerning review essays should be addressed to Winifred Hughes, 50 Wheatsheaf Lane, Princeton, NJ 08540 (609 921 1489).

Suggestions for reprints of Victorian materials, texts or illustrations, should be addressed to Jeffrey Spear, Department of English, NYU, 19 University Pl., Rm. 200, N.Y., NY 10003 (212 998 8820; fax: 212 995 4019).

All AMS Books are printed on acid-free paper that meets the guidelines for performance and durability of the Committee on Production Guidelines for Book Longevity of the Council on Library Resources.

Manufactured in the United States of America

CONTENTS

WORKS IN PROGRESS

REVIEW ESSAYS

BROWNING BIBLIOGRAPHY

ILLUSTRATIONS

2. Ford Madox Brown, *Carrying Corn.*

3. Dante Gabriel Rossetti, *The Maids of Elfin-Mere.*

THE METAPHORS OF HOMOSEXUAL COLONIALISM AND TOURISM

By Chris White

"Women for breeding, boys for pleasure, and melons for sheer delight"[1]

THE COLONIZED COUNTRIES OF the Empire and the countries of the Mediterranean and North Africa provided a source both of homosexual experience and experimentation and also of sexual metaphors for British writers concerned to develop a language and framework in which to write about homosexuality and homosexual desire. These countries and cultures were a place (singular, homogenized) where the white colonialist/traveller could look for and "discover" (a sex-power metaphor) sexual experiences which were unavailable and unobtainable in northern Europe. The objects of desire, the boys, are not so homogenized, racial and cultural differences applying in the representation of Venetian, Arab, and Indian boys. The texts discussed here display a concern with and a partial reproduction of what Edward Said calls "a complex array of 'Oriental' ideas (Oriental despotism, Oriental splendour, cruelty, sensuality)" (4), a set of ideas about the nature of non-Western cultures which incorporates discourses about sexuality. The fetish-object of the Orientalist boy is constructed out of this set of "Oriental" ideas and includes within it Arab boys, boys living under the Raj, and Venetian boys, especially gondoliers. What is marked about the construction is that the powerful terms of Said's definition are removed, leaving only sensuality and the cruelty of the fickle lover, with occasional references to the impotent desire of colonized cultures to overthrow the power of the colonizer.

The purpose of this essay is to discuss a range of late nineteenth-century texts that construct and organize a discourse of homosexual pleasure in relation to ideological structures and institutions of imperialism and colonialism. The majority of texts date from the 1890s and include writings by Aleister Crowley, John Addington Symonds, and Frederick Rolfe, a group whose eclecticism in itself serves to demonstrate the relative homogeneity of the ideas about the Orientalist fetish object.[2]

1

The fetish-object represents the delineation of a precisely defined sex-object, classified very exactly as to age or role or physical appearance or race or activity, or all or any combination of the above.

> We all have our little hobbies. Some men like soldiers, others sailors; some are fond of tight-rope dancers, others of dandies. There are men who, though in love with their own sex, only care for them in women's clothing. (*Teleny* 142)[3]

In Frederick Rolfe's (Baron Corvo's) Venice correspondence, which celebrates the gondoliers and boys of Venice and his relationships with them, he enters into a debate with Fox[4] over his preference for older, bigger-built boys, while Fox favors younger, slighter boys:

> A soft little body is all very well to lie in one's arms all night: but it cannot give me furious joys. I want one long enough to be face to face with me while I thrust through its thighs, and strong enough to struggle and to give as much joy as I take. (46)

The fetish-object is described as "it," not he, an object, not a subject. In depersonizing the fetish-object, Rolfe makes it into a functional object, which is designed to enable certain acts to be performed with ease and effectiveness. This practice of generalization and depersonization, in which the specific individual becomes a representation of an entire class of beings, and in which the erotic value of the individual is dependent upon the fullness with which he achieves all the prerequisites ascribed to that class of being, runs through the vast majority of texts considered here. Intrinsic to many of the fetish-objects is their positioning within class and race structures, but equally ideological in usage are the inequalities of age. It is necessary for there to be a real difference in status between fetish-object and desirer for the desirer to be able to achieve his pleasures, given that it is for the fetish-object to do the fulfilling, and not to have his own desires fulfilled. He is an object in the field of desire of the desiring subject and as such is not a coherent subject in his own right but is subjected to another's subjectivity. The fetish-object does not have desires of his own but has them built into the object-identity given to him by someone with more objective and objectifying power, the repository of sexual practice. He functions as a site of sexual practice, as a functional space of eroticism, not as an equal partner and not as mutually desirous of the subject.

Where the imperialist project and practices of imperialism were justified in terms of their presumed beneficial effects to the colonized peoples, the reverse formation was applied by the colonizer to the sexual relationships between colonizer and colonized, so that sexual imperialism is construed as being beneficial for the sexual imperialist. In the adage of the epigraph, the merely functional (heterosexuality) is opposed to the pederastic (homosexuality) and the exotic pleasure-for-pleasure's-sake (masturbation with fruit that is, in Britain, either an imported commodity or grown in the greenhouses of the rich).[5] The sensuality ascribed to the Orient extends to and incorporates the material and marketable products of the colonized countries.

The metaphors of the marketplace that appear in many of the texts discussed below have an associated form in imperialist, missionary texts, summed up by this passage from David Livingstone's *Missionary Travels and Researches in South Africa*:

> When converts are made from heathenism it becomes an interesting question whether their faith has the elements of permanence, or is only an exotic too tender for self-propagation when the fostering care of the foreign cultivators is withdrawn. If habits of self-reliance are not encouraged the most promising converts are apt to become like spoiled children. (84)

There is a conflation here of the metaphors of plants and children that need to be taken care of by the gardener/adult-missionary. In addition, the functional/utilitarian perennial, transplanted to another country, is contrasted with the exotic, growing in its home soil, that cannot reproduce itself — a paradox that is revealing. The metaphors connect with the ascribed sensuality which is at the root of the conceptions of the sexual relationship between Oriental and Occidental. The tastes, flavors, textures of the commodified Orient, which are represented as exotic and excessive, as opposed to the merely functional and pragmatic Occident, are reproduced in the fetish-object. In Livingstone's terms, the exotic is non-(re)productive and requires the intervention of the foreigner to sustain it. The implication, amazingly, seems to be that the exotic (melon, fetish-object, heathen-turned-Christian) is a creation/production of the foreigner (remembering that it would never be his fault, since he is working on foreign, therefore unknown and unreliable, soil). This turn of thought is apparently supported by Livingstone's later reference to the condition of the non-Christianized, non-colonized peoples, who experience "the hard struggle for the necessaries of life" (113), barely succeeding in a functional existence.

Underlying the production of the Orient's role as provider of "licentious sex" is the imperialist project of turning colonized countries into means of production. The association between imperialist practice and sexual discourse is repeatedly reproduced in the texts discussed below, obfuscating the a priori of racism and economic exploitation with the a posteriori of sexual exploitation. The fetish-object of the Oriental boy always contains both the exotic and the economic in its delineation. The discursive surface of the exotic simultaneously conceals the economic power underlying it, making it a "commonsense" category, desirable in itself, and exposes that economic power through the rendering of the fetish-object into metaphors of fruit and representations of the country or culture from which they emerge. Hegemonic justification for the status quo exists in cooperation and conflict with the explicit, "naked" expression of the power/economic relationship between Occidental and Oriental. Literal power over colonized peoples is so total and so transparently "natural" that the necessity to conceal the operations of power is less than obvious. What is necessary is to suspend the transparently "unnatural" discourses about the practices of homosexuality through making the Oriental boy simultaneously pure commodity and actively seductive (exotic). The common-sense seductiveness of exotic fruit (the melon, the hot climate) becomes the common-sense seductiveness of the exotic boy (boy as fruit). The Oriental boy is the paradoxical site of active seduction and passive purchase as commodity. These contradictions are an integral part of the discourse of imperialism and are clearly manifested in the homosexual colonialist texts.

Sexual practice itself is encoded in terms of military conquest and the body in terms of weapons. This metaphor is taken to extremes in Kenneth Searight's "Paidikion, volume I: an anthology or the book of Hyakinthos and Narkissos," which includes an extended poem 2,706 lines long entitled "The Furnace: an autobiography in which is set forth the secret diversions of a paiderast"; "Nel Bagno: A Neapolitan Tale" in which our hero visits a Turkish bath in Naples, is seduced by the sixteen-year-old attendant, and participates in an orgy which includes masturbation, fellatio, coprolagnia, and urolagnia; "Floreat Etona: or, where Waterloo was Won," in which the narrator tells the story of his visiting another Etonian and participating in an orgy with foreign boys and animals; and a catalogue, "Paidology," of Searight's sexual encounters with boys between 1897 and 1917, almost all of whom were Indian. In this catalogue, Searight awards all of his sexual "partners" a number between one and ninety-three, the meaning of which ranking is obscure, though it appears to act as some kind of rating figure.[6] Searight was posted to India as an officer in the *Queens* Own Royal West Kent Regiment, and his different postings in India brought him into contact with many different races in the subcontinent. The record of his sex life ceases in 1917, on his posting to Iraq.[7] The shape of the fetish-object is sketched by "Nel Bagno" and "Floreat Etona" in their rendering of the foreign boys as animalistic, where the boys and animals are placed on the same level for the purposes of sexual experimentation, and are wholly defined by their sexual relationship to the white tourist/narrator.

What appears to be, in "Nel Bagno," a statement of oppression and resistance really serves more fully to delineate the fetish-object, when the narrator declares:

> Yes, you may shudder, you may turn from me in loathing, in disgust. But we are all of us God and brute beast. I was learning to what depths the lusts of human nature could descend. (Hammond 35)

The man goes to a school (Turkish bath) where he learns the (natural/unnatural) limits of the body's capacities. The necessity to remain in control (retain mastery, not to be a pupil) involves the reproduction of the relationships of imperialism, enforced submission, and power differentials. The sixteen-year-old bath attendant may be the seducer, but he remains subordinate by virtue of his status and through his knowledge of the full gamut of perversions that depart ever further from any connection with reproductive sexuality. Knowledge does not equate with power here. Power is rather contained in metaphors of military weaponry and imperialist endeavor:

> And when his luscious bottom-hole would brim
> Full of my impoured essences, we'd change
> The role of firing point (but not the range)
> Until his catapult, e'er strongly charged,
> The target with a hail of sperm enlarged,
> Then half an hour . . . and back again I'd come
> To plunge my weapon in his drenching bum. (Hyam 131)

The metaphor is a story of imperialism and of the army, where Searight as narrator and his sex partner are engaged in armed-combat sex, a confrontation between conquerer and conquered. The sex partner, as a member of the imperialized race, has a catapult-penis, a "primitive weapon," and Searight seems to have a rifle-penis with a bayonet fixed. The process of imperialism becomes sex, and sex becomes the process of imperialization. The penetration of the conquered country becomes the penetration of the individual conquered by the conquerer.

The uses of the Oriental to construct images and practices of illicit sex often appear entirely incidental and casual, as in an episode in the anonymous and probably multi-authored novel, *Teleny, or the Reverse of the Medal.* In a discussion during the orgy scene in *Teleny,* concerning the use of a bottle for anal penetration, an exchange takes place in which "the physician smiling" says "It is a crime against nature," and the host, Briancourt, replies "in fact, it would be worse than buggery, it would be bottlery" (*Teleny* 153). In *Teleny* the meanings of sodomy are played with, the categories of the natural and unnatural being brought into question through parody, and the performance of fetish acts with gusto. It is significant that "bottlery" is committed on the character known only as the Spahi, to his great pleasure, and is couched in terms of the militaristic metaphor:

> The Spahi's face expressed a mixture of acute pain and intense pleasure; all the nerves of his body seemed stretched and quivering, as if under the action of a strong battery. (154)

The "bottlery" incident ends with the bottle breaking and the Spahi dying, which is arguably a violent return of the norm. The meaning of this scene, at least for the purpose of this essay, is dependent upon the reader knowing that a Spahi is (or was) a cavalryman, either up to the mid 1850s in the Turkish army, or from the 1850s onwards a native Algerian serving under the French government. From this context the resonances of the moment are produced. The Spahi is both soldier and Orientalist (though not Oriental), a paradox that places him firmly on the battlefield, on the receiving end of a battery assault (the mechanized war machine against the traditional horse-borne soldier), a poor soldier, a victim conquered by the greater power of the white Briancourt. The tension between pleasure and retribution for pleasure that appears elsewhere is a non-event in *Teleny*. The death is effectively covered up by the other participants, because the Spahi is to all intents and purposes a foreigner, as opposed to an Orientalist tourist, and as such does not count as an individual. He is given no name, only the title of his military occupation. He is expendable and expended by the experimentation of a group of westerners, in marked contrast to the anxious attempts to preserve the life of the eponymous hero. With no apparent weight of color, identity, class, or race behind him, there is no danger of legal or social retribution resulting from his death. The twist is that the Spahi is only a member of this social circle because he is a white aristocrat who has spent his inheritance and joined the cavalry as a sexual adventure. One identity, that of white westerner, is succeeded and effectively replaced by the second, that of Orientalist sex/fetish-object. He is not Oriental, but Orientalist, displaying those desires and attitudes that distinguish Orientalism. This annihilates his previous identity, the "lower" identity taking precedence over the "higher" in determining his subject position.

Hellas v. Arabia

THE SHAPE OF THE ORIENTAL fetish becomes clearer when compared with the erotic value attached to the texts and metaphors of ancient Greece, a locus of precedent and legitimation for homosexuality that appears in many forms, variations, and texts but with one predominating theme, the social acceptability, centrality, and *healthiness* of males desiring and loving other males. Integral to the structuring of a space for encounters between men and boys in these texts is a refusal or rejection of urban life or Britain or both. In "Sonnet" by S. S. Saale, industrialized society is contrasted with the golden age of Greece as embodied in the bodies of a group of boys. It is the act of stripping naked and jumping into the river running through an urban-industrial world that results in the boys being "changed by a miracle" (Reade 5); without the trappings of modern culture, "olden days return" (10). The river the boys jump into is linked to the river that Narcissus gazed into, and the boys are compared to Daphnis; they become shepherds in the city, fond of rural employments. The sight of the boys thus transformed makes "new

pulses throb and burn'' (14), which implicitly suggests that an introduction
to the shape of male beauty mediated through an older culture makes others
appreciate and desire them.

The pleasure of the scene is encoded in metaphors for sex acts. Transformation occurs between the plunging into the river and the rising from the water:

> They strip and plunge into the stream below;
> Changed by a miracle, they rise as though
> The youth of Greece burst on this latter day. (4–6)

This seems an embedded — though not deeply embedded — reference to
sodomy. The innocence of these boys is not dependent upon sexual innocence:
instead it is a cultural innocence that does not require sexual innocence to be
pure. They are the modern remains of classic manhood, ''fragrant ashes from
a classic urn'' (11).

''Saloninus'' deploys a similar metaphorical shift in his 1893 poem, ''By
the Aegean'' (Reade 305). The pseudonym used here refers to the son of
Asinius Pollio, who was supposed to be the subject of Virgil's fourth Eclogue,
where the return of the golden age is warmly anticipated. The poem of ''Saloninus'' draws on a set of ideas about the Mediterranean. Mediterranean
boys are sexy, uncorrupted, earthy, harking back to an older culture; they are
on display at their sensual best in the water, in the sun. The liberating of the
energies of the boy in the water is integrally related to the liberating of the
sexual energies of the tourist visiting the Med. This poem plays with images
of birth and rebirth and with the realization of the ideal of adolescent manhood
previously only seen ''in marble serenely quiescent'' (2). The ''you'' who
is addressed ''waywardly impetuously leapt into being'' (3) as a physical
embodiment of the spirit and practices of an earlier culture. The embodiment
is young, naked, unashamed, delicate, and vigorous. Against this adolescent
Greek spirit is set the rigidity and ''all the yearnings of twilight'' (13) that
mean concealment and the absence of ''beauty long sought for'' (1).

These boys, and the Orientalist boys too, are *selected* as fetishes. The boys
operate as fetish because they (temporarily) conceal what male adult sexuality
knows: the threat of female desires; the guilt of homosexual desire; a childhood containing repressed desires and identity; an economic and political
relationship. To equate the Mediterranean boys with Greek youth and mythic
masculinity is to work to conceal, ideologically and discursively, all of those
forms of knowledge. By making it a desire for the classical past, the desire
is simultaneously rendered respectable (academic) and distant/impossible, an
unfulfillable desire for what is dead, not for flesh-and-blood boys. It is no
accident that, while texts about Greek boys and Greek love usually appear in
mainstream publications, texts concerned with the Orientalist fetish more
often appear as private publications, letters, and unpublished manuscripts.

As is evident in several of the accounts, there are structures in place in the countries to which the middle- and upper-class men go, where the currency of young male bodies is bartered for and bought. The cultures in which these boys live produce them as available sexual objects for the sexual colonialists. Frederick Rolfe describes the Venetians as "the slaves of 'Custom.' They fear 'Scorn' — (which only means the Charge of being Singular) more than anything else in Nature" (*Venice Letters* 17). If anything, he argues, is shown to be not singular but commonplace, including homosexuality, then the Venetian boys willingly embrace it. The apparent lack of morality as it is described by Rolfe is the condition of innocence, the mark of unsophisticated peoples aware not of absolute structures but only of relative ones, of public opinion and appearance. This relativism makes the southern boys less human than the white northerners, in the sense that they have less of an identity and less culture than the northerners, and what there is can easily be remolded by the stronger, more developed culture and identity of the north.

The lack of morality, and often the presence of amorality, ascribed to Arab boys, is one object of perversity running through *Teleny*. The principal narrator of the text, Des Grieux, contrasts his own indoctrination with morality—and his subsequent self-disgust at his desire for men — with the animal instincts of young Arabs:

> Unlike poodles, or young Arabs, I had been inculcated with all kinds of wrong ideas, so when I understood what my natural feelings for Teleny were, I was staggered, horrified. (*Teleny* 70)

The absence of moral teaching produces Arab boys as sexually free and natural as dogs, without inhibitions. The choice of the poodle as a parallel implies something that is both exotic/foreign and also implicitly something or someone submissive, who seeks to serve for their own gain. Later in the novel, during the orgy scene, the Spahi discourses on the pleasures of sex with Arabs. The figure of the Spahi functions as the complete engagement of the westerner with the exotic pleasures of the east and the south. He is described as "a young man who having spent his fortune in the most unbridled debauchery," "has enlisted in the Spahis to see what new pleasures Algiers could afford him" (146). The sexual tourist is the man who has exhausted the sexual possibilities of his own culture and goes on to seek more extreme and ritualized pleasures in other cultures. Included in the Spahi's disquisition is the following passage:

> The Arabs are right. They are our masters in this art. . . . They — unlike ourselves — know by long practice how to prolong this pleasure for an everlasting time. . . . They are skilled in enhancing their own pleasure by the satisfaction they afford to others. . . . How smooth and glossy their skin is! What a lava is

bubbling in their veins! They are not men, they are lions; and they roar to lusty purpose. (*Teleny* 152–53)

The animal metaphor is remade, but the assertion is the same. Arabs are not human but animalistic in their sex lives. They are animals, but they are simultaneously feminine, with smooth hairless skin. They are also inhuman but natural, like a volcano, a natural force that cannot be controlled by human will. Their sexuality defines them, from the appearance of their bodies, which are wholly sexualized, to the power relations between sex object and tourist, where they give satisfaction as the primary activity, and their own pleasure is only a secondary effect, an afterthought that indicates a differential in status and rights. All of these things are derived from racial characteristics and identity, where their origins are structured into a sexual identity and a lived practice, these two becoming synonymous.

This structuring is exemplified in André Gide's account of Lord Alfred Douglas's attempt to run away with an Arab boy.

To run away with an Arab is not such an easy thing as he had thought at first; he had to get the parents' consent, sign papers at the Arab office, at the police station, etc.; there was work enough to keep him at Bildah for several days. (278)

Implicit in this account are two things: Douglas's assumption that he can elope with the boy without any social or legal structure intervening, and the actual social and legal structures that are in place to permit the sexual colonialist to remove the child from his family and community. What is at stake with those structures is the institutionalized position of the colonialist, who confers economic advantage on the boy chosen, which in turn maintains the power differential between white and Black.

John Addington Symonds's account in his memoirs of his relationship with a gondolier, while explicitly rejecting the economic basis of the north-south eroticism, implicitly maps its shape:

I gradually strove to persuade him that I was no mere light-o-love, but a man on whom he could rely — whose honour, though rooted in dishonour, might be trusted. I gave him a gondola and a good deal of money. He seemed to be greedy, and I was mortified by noticing that he spent his cash in what I thought a foolish way. . . . Yet there were almost insurmountable obstacles to be overcome. These arose mainly from the false position in which we found ourselves from the beginning. He not unnaturally classed me with those other men to whose caprices he had sold his beauty. (*Memoirs* 9–10)

Symonds views the economically determined relationship and the truly emotional relationship as mutually exclusive, but the version of it that he has and the version that he wants are both based upon a differentiation of class and power. In the desired version, Symonds wants to be a kind of father-figure to the boy or older, wiser friend, to bring him along in the world, to be his mainstay and support. The position which gives money and then seeks to control its use is no different in effect from the position which Symonds sees as a true love between northern man and southern youth.

The South as Sexual Metaphor

SUMMER IS THE TIME of sexual life and desire in A. E. Housman's "Ho, every-one that thirsteth" and the south a place of sexual safety and emotional recuperation for the homosexual in Rennell Rodd's poem, "If Any One Return" (qtd. in Reade 155). In Housman's poem the waters of summer, when drunk, grant life and youth:

> Come to the stolen waters,
> Drink and your soul shall live. (3–4)

"He that drinks in season / Shall live before he dies" (11–12). The warmth of June provides a source of life which is unobtainable in the winter in England and life is equated with "desire" (8) and vitality, implying that cold England is a place where there is no desire and no life, only restraint and death.

Rodd's text is a poem of longing, positing a what-if "we had carried him far away / To the light of this south sun land" (1–2), against the deleterious effect of remaining in the north. Here the difference between life and death must also refer to the sending of sick and diseased wealthy northerners to recuperate or live in the south. The south is defined against a north which is stormy and cloudy and which "the winds deface!" (6). The life the south offers is one of homosexual love as well as literal life.

> And if ever the souls of the loved, set free,
>   Come back to the souls that stay,
> I could dream he would sit for a while with me
> Where I sit by this wonderful tideless sea
>   And look at the red-rocked bay.
>
> By the high cliff's edge where the wild weeds twine,
>   And he would not speak or move,
> But his eyes would gaze from his soul at mine,
> My eyes that would answer without one sign,
>   And that were enough for love. (11–20)

The south is a "flowerful place" (8) in which this love can take place in silence and complete mutual understanding, an ideal condition for a love and desire which are normally dependent upon the deciphering of codes, of a tension of understanding/misunderstanding in the making of contact. The south constructs the appropriate space for this relationship, a still environment (set against the storms and winds of the north) where there is no tide, and becomes, if not an erotic space, then an emotional one.

A much more ambivalent attitude toward the south and the southern lover appears in John Addington Symonds's poem, "The South Wind," from his privately published volume, *Fragilia Labilia*, which contrasts the sexual oppression of the north with the sexual freedom of the south:

> Lay Hope's tired head
> In some south garden,
> Where Youth is warden,
> And gates are barred on
> The North wind's tread!

The metaphor of wind and weather produces the north as cold, snow-bound, a land of "stout pines" (39), and the south as a garden, a "vale" (39), the south wind as "O light land-rover / O soft sea-lover" (36). The south wind is the lover/lover-like which disports itself in the garden that is governed by youth and represents a place where homosexual desire and love can exist in freedom and sensual pleasure. In colonialist terms, this text establishes the south as a region without the north's chilly morality and rejection of sex but with the virtues of youthfulness, beauty, and the open air. However, both the south and the south wind are fragile in face of the strength of the north and the north wind:

> Haste, haste, sea-lover!
> Lest snowflakes cover
> Thy wings that hover
>   Above our vale!
> For the North winds whistle;
> The stout pines bristle:
> Soul of the South, thou art frail and pale! (39)

This is more than the nastiness of the north: the south wind in itself (and hence the southern lovers that it represents) is metaphorically and literally flighty.

> Thou fickle stranger,
> Blithe ocean-ranger
> From dread and danger
>   And man's doubt free! (36)

The south is unreliable, unknown, and unknowable because foreign, and the southerner as lover is fickle and inscrutable. This "thrills faster and faster / Thy yearning strain!" but holds the potential for "disaster" (38).

The Southern Boy

A COMPOSITE PORTRAIT OF the ideal foreign object of desire may be constructed. He is slender and young, is not white but does not have very dark skin, is uneducated, does not speak more than a few words of English, if any, comes from an impoverished background, and is submissive and willing to serve or be servile to the Englishman. The sexuality of the Arab and Mediterranean boy is, according to these texts, naive, uninhibited, experimental, unemotional (in the sense that it is bought and paid for and therefore does not involve the colonialist in emotional contracts), and active or passive as required. But, significantly, he does not take the initiative in making sexual contracts: the white man goes looking for him and negotiates for his favors; the boy does not "hawk his wares" on the street, is not a "common" prostitute, but is a naive and innocent sexual being — innocent in the way that an animal is, without a sense of there being anything wrong in the activity. In part, this construction depends upon the imperialist discourse surrounding Black peoples, that their identity and therefore their sexuality are closely akin to the animals'.

This boy is both the fantasy figure made out of the authors' beliefs about racial characteristics and also is the actual site of racial and economic oppression. Versions of cultural history are brought to bear in the construction of the object of desire, as in Charles Kains-Jackson's "Antinous" (qtd. in Reade 247), which takes the original myth and identifies its contemporaneous equivalent in flesh and blood Asian boys.

> Glory throughout the world thy conquering name
>   Has celebrated, and through ages sung
> The Asian youth whose cult's melodious flame
>   Lends bitter-sweetness to the poet's tongue.
> Thy love's keen darts strike languor through the frame,
>   The aromatic odours of the south
>   Breathe from the half-shut lotus of thy mouth,
> Thy smile's strange power, our conquered hearts proclaim. (1–8)

All the exoticism and eroticism ascribed to the Arab and Oriental boy are contained in the metaphors of this text as odors, hot-house flowers, and strangeness which is not western. The boy's sexuality incites the westerner to desire in the face of the natural, unintellectual pleasure of the exotic. The power given to the object of desire is not political or intellectual but is only the power to create erotic pleasure in another, a mirroring effect which does not result in equal status but which reinforces the sexuality and sensuality reposited with the Arab and Oriental boy, taking away the responsibility for the desire from the westerner and giving it to the boy.

The lack of integrated subjectivity which adult male sexuality conceals, or holds the promise of concealing, in the selection of the boy as fetish constructs a non-contradictory viewing position of the fetish-object. This construction produces a viewing position which is masculine and phallic. And a viewed position that is feminine and non-phallic. Antinous is rendered metaphorically as a flower, as scented, as passively seductive, as dangerous to the masculine. The genderedness of the boys as feminine is constructed from sexual immaturity and purity and from the placing of the boys as the object of desire of masculine, adult, and sexually mature men. The contradiction of a sex object that must retain its sexual innocence in order to remain a sex object hides the fact that, in order to become the fetish-object, the boys have already been selected, arranged, and thoroughly mediated. They are presented as the authentic experience, the real thing, but they are constructed to fit a type, an image, and an arrangement.

The racial characteristics ascribed to the southern boy by Frederick Rolfe in his *Venice Letters* include vanity ("Their weak spot is their vanity," 14) and simplicity ("The simple little devils that they are!" 49):

> I watched him. Such a lovely figure, young, muscular, splendidly strong, big black eyes, rosy face, round black head, scented like an angel. (27)

In part, the narrative is one of a search for the perfect boy, of the type indicated in the quotation. The moment of perfection is awaited and short-lived when it arrives. "I saw one whom I am going to watch as likely to be ready next spring." (27) Ready for Rolfe's sexual desires and practices, that is. The change from one condition to the other is achieved both through the inevitable processes of growing up and through the effects of hard, physical labour.

> A year ago that day when he came to take the 3rd oar in my *pupparin*, he was a lanky uninteresting wafer. Since then, the work of dancing up and down planks with heavy sacks has filled him out, clothed him with most lovely pads of muscular sweet flesh, sweated his skin into rosy satin fineness and softness. (36)

The form of perfection is a kind of fruition of sexual appeal where the identity of the boy has been shaped into the object of desire, whereas his "rough edges" of lower-class status have been smoothed to turn him from a "ragamuffin" (27) into a "comically naive" (28) "intelligent and faithful" (15) servant. The condition is a paradoxical one, both transitory and acquired through effort.

The boy does not exist in a static condition outside all societal involvement but exists precisely within a set of labor relations and racial characteristics which determine his status as fetish-object. The transitoriness of this condition is not determined by age or innocence. Instead it is limited by external factors, primarily heterosexuality:

> He'll be like this till Spring, say 3 months more. Then some great fat slow cow of a girl will just open herself wide, and lie quite still, and drain him dry. First the rich bloom of him will go. Then he'll get hard and hairy. And, by July, he'll have a moustache, a hairy breast for his present great boyish bosom, brushes in his milky armpits, brooms on his splendid young thighs, and be just the ordinary stevedore found by the scores on the quays. (Rolfe, *Venice Letters* 37)

The shift from adolescent boyhood to manhood is here presented as the direct consequence of heterosexual sex and predatory women, where the original effeminacy of the boy becomes the masculinity of the man, the bosom becomes the breast, through the corrupting influence of the female. The language of this extract indicates clearly what is valued in the object — not adult masculinity, a mature body, but an immature body that lacks male secondary sexual characteristics, the signifiers of maturity. The object of desire is not a self-determining person and is instead a figure on the margins between adulthood and childhood, with concomitant dependency and innocence. The fetish is for smooth, muscular flesh, which works as fetish because it wards off the threat of adult (hairy) masculinity. At the same time this mystifies the relation of labor through detaching the body from the degenerating effects of hard, physical labor.

The limits of what is desirable in the fetish-object are very precise in this text:

> Of course one can't admire the slavish tendency. But I firmly maintain that the best method is to begin with slaves and educate them out of slavery into intelligent and faithful servants. (Rolfe, *Venice Letters* 15)

It is necessary for the boy to be willing in his relationship with Rolfe without being his possession but sufficiently servile and conscious of the difference in status. Alongside the class consciousness Rolfe displays in these letters is the sense of buying the boys through the giving of clothes and presents. They are innocent and naive creatures, not mercenary, and are dazzled through the buying-power of the white northerner.

> Dear simple creatures! And then, also, new clothes and money were given, and there was an opportunity of spending a day or two at Burano. So, as I imagine, they instantly threw all scruples over the windmill and were ready and eager and simply blazing to oblige us and themselves. (17)

The boys' innocence consists of gratitude and responsiveness to the generosity of the white northerner, while in response they give of themselves to repay the gift. This exchange is also constructed as a source of pleasure for the boys themselves and is not presented as a form of prostitution. The pleasure resides on both sides, while keeping in place the distinction between classes and racial status.

The Exotic and the Erotic

THEODORE WRATISLAW'S "To a Sicilian Boy," one of two poems excised from the first publication of his *Caprices* and originally published in *The Artist and Journal of Home Culture*, deploys the same type of boy as fetish-object rendered through metaphors of fruitfulness and Mediterranean nature:

> Love, I adore the contours of thy shape,
> Thine exquisite breasts and arms adorable;
> The wonders of thy heavenly throat compel
> Such fire of love as even my dreams escape: . . .
> In sweets the blossoms of thy mouth excel
> The tenderest bloom of peach or purple grape. (1–4, 7–8)

The Sicilian boy is pure physicality without a distinct identity since he is "a" Sicilian boy, any Sicilian boy. He is the object of the white sexual colonialist and simultaneously on a level with the products of nature that can be bought and sold or enjoyed through appetite.

Sicilian boys and Venetian boys display a strong degree of similarity in the erotic discourses at this time. Rolfe's novel *The Desire and Pursuit of the Whole* includes the main protagonist, Crabbe, turning an Italian village girl into a boy gondolier, or, more accurately, an oarsman for his *pupparin*, through the canals of Venice. Crabbe fits out Zildo with a new wardrobe, making him look "like an unpretending junior officer of the mercantile marine in mufti" (52). The new clothes and role turn Zildo into a type, a fixed identity based on service and juvenile masculinity. The erotic interest of *The Desire and Pursuit* lies both in the ambiguity of Zildo's gender identity and also in the figure of the gondolier, a generalized (stereo)type whose fetish value is delineated in this passage:

> Young Venice has as superb a physique as can be found anywhere. In a city where everyone swims from his cradle and almost everyone above five years old has rowed (poised and pushing more than pulling) for twenty or thirty generations — a movement which includes balance with force thrust forward and incessant adaptation to fluent circumstances. (94)

Rolfe makes of this description of the culture of Venice an erotic judgment of young male Venetians. The activity of propelling the gondola becomes the incitement to sexual desire. The thrusting is perhaps a rather crude metaphor, but the adaptation to circumstance implies a flexible identity, an integral responsiveness of sexual desire which has been put into the gondolier through the activities of Venice. The quotation continues:

> You may see (without search) the keen, prompt, level eyes, the noble firm necks, the opulent shoulders, the stalwart arms, the utterly magnificent breasts, the lithely muscular bodies inserted in (and springing from) the well-compacted hips, the long, slim, sinewy-rounded legs, the large, agile, sensible feet. (94)

The action of propelling the gondola develops both the ideal physical type of male body for Crabbe/Rolfe and an entire class of these perfect bodily beings. The honing of the body of the gondolier into an object of desire as a mediation of working-class labor is also emphasized by Symonds in his memoirs, in writing of Angelo Fusato, the youth he had a relationship with.

> He was tall and sinewy, but very slender — for these Venetian gondoliers are rarely massive in their strength. Each part of the man is equally developed in the exercise of rowing; and their bodies are elastically supple, with free sway from the hips and a Mercurial poise upon the ankle. (272)

The gondoliers' identity (singular, homogenous) is determined by the physical effect of their work and their posture, which puts them on display for the viewer. The rhythm of the language here creates the impression of a dynamic masculinity engaged in physical, rhythmic work, in the insertion into and springing from the hips. A variation on the theme of Italian masculinity appears in Rolfe's novel *Hadrian the Seventh*, in which an outcast English priest becomes Pope. Among the Catholic politics and theology, the novel has a homoerotic subtext, exemplified by the following passage:

> . . . some scarlet gentlemen began to bring in tables with the sealed dishes of the pontifical supper. Hadrian's eyes lingered on the intruders for a moment. They were so slim, so robust, so deft, so grave, so Roman. He drew the bishop into the embrasure of a window.
> "Aren't they lovely?" He said. "Isn't the world full of lovely things, lovely live things?" (107–8)

Again, here is the Englishman looking upon and desiring the southerner, the latter generalized into a representation of his race and of a fetish-object which is both unmistakably masculine and marginally "feminine." In *Hadrian the Seventh* this generalization takes the shape of a combination of ancient and civilized wisdom (Rome), slender and graceful "femininity," and (robust) masculinity. The Englishman can, therefore, occupy the position of uncompli-cated masculinity with its associated state of complete authority, while the

"Oriental" is ambivalently masculine, lacks authority, and is the object of scrutiny/desire for the Englishman.

The same constructions appear in Searight's "The Furnace," in which he records his fascination with skin color — "my rod of ivory between the mons / Of buttocks fashioned out of gleaming bronze" (Hyam 130) — with the sexual license of the boys he encountered — "I groaned: the boy's untamed ferocity / So different to the young Bengali's love, / Filled me with anguish" — and his preference for boys between the ages of twelve and fourteen. His desires were not limited to Indian boys. Of Neapolitan boys he wrote, "Paiderastic love in flame unchecked / Is what these Neapolitans expect" (130).

Searight's poem displays two crucial elements: a sexual tour, which includes sampling the wares of different racial groups — "thus encouraged at once began / To explore the amorous realms of Hindustan"; and a breaking of all and every taboo, including race and class barriers, and such sexual practices as flagellation, urolagnia, coprolagnia, and analingus. His construction of the Indian boys is clearly seen in the following passage:

> ... I passed
> From sensuous Bengal to fierce Peshawar
> An Asiatic stronghold where each flower
> Of boyhood planted in its restless soil
> Is — ipso facto — ready to despoil
> (Or be despoiled by) someone else; the yarn
> Indeed so has it that the young Pathan
> Thinks it peculiar if you would pass
> Him by without some reference to his arse.
> Each boy of certain age will let on hire
> His charms to indiscriminate desire,
> To wholesome Buggery and perverse letches. . . .
> To get a boy was easier than to pick
> The flowers by the wayside; for as quick
> As one went out another one came in. . . .
> Scarce passed a night but I in rapturous joy
> Indulged in mutual sodomy, the boy
> Fierce-eyed, entrancing . . . (1490 ff.)

Where Wratislaw's Sicilian boy was like fruit, Searight's is like a wild flower, free to anyone who wishes to pick it, but even more available, since there is a never-ending supply of these anonymous boys. The availability of the boys, and their complete lack of identity outside of their race identity (and its consequent sexual identity), is more extreme in Searight's text. This lack of identity is a comment upon the status of children in non-Christian, non-Western cultures, where they are not seen by Europeans as unique individuals but one of many products on a conveyer belt of copulation. Searight makes the sexual availability an essential and integral part of the boy's racial identity. His role as fetish-object is bound up with the cultural norms that Searight ascribes to his — this generalized boy's — behavior. The boy wants the sexual attention and would be culturally and racially offended if he does not get it, thereby making the boy's availability as sex object the foundation of his cultural and racial identity for Searight.

Searight's boy is "of a certain age," again on that threshold between childhood and maturity, and the product of "restless soil," not rooted in stable, civilized, and permanent structures but the result of the shifting social and meaning systems of a young, ungrounded culture. It is this cultural difference that makes him sexually available and in possession of this sexual consciousness in a way that, in Searight's text, white boys and men are not. White boys exist in a social structure defined by class, school, and the assumption of heterosexuality unless otherwise proved. Indian boys exist in a culture where they are pre-defined as sex objects and sexual practitioners but never pre-defining, since this would imply a linear progress and sense of destination that does not cohere with the fetish-object. Searight constructs himself as distinguishing between the wholesome and the perverse, whereas the boys are "indiscriminate" in their availability to sexual demands. The use of these boys for buggery is direct and simple, a wholesome response to these boys offering themselves.

The foreign boy as sex object reaches its zenith in Aleister Crowley's sonnet, "Go into the Highways and Hedges and compel them *to come in*." Here it is precisely the exotic, the shape and nature of Arab culture as perceived by Crowley, that constitute the fetish-object:

> Let my fond lips but drink thy golden wine,
>   My bright-eyed Arab, only let me eat
>   The rich brown globes of sacramental meat
> Steaming and firm, hot from their home divine,
> And let me linger with thy hands in mine,
>   And lick the sweat from dainty dirty feet
>   Fresh with the loose aroma of the street,
> And then anon I'll glue my mouth to thine.
>
> This is the height of joy, to lie and feel
>   Thy spicèd spittle trickle down my throat;
> This is more pleasant than at dawn to steal
>   Towards lawns and sunny brooklets, and to gloat
>   Over earth's peace, and hear in ether float
> Songs of soft spirits into rapture peal.

The north here is rendered as that which is safe and tame, as lawns and brooks, as peace and spirit, as a quiet, regulated form of nature, as pastoral;

moreover it is a place where the northerner gloats, looks down from a position of authority and complacency at the way in which the world is organized. This perspective is rejected, and the relationship with the Arab is deemed much superior to this northern position of control and smugness. The Arab functions in the text as the radically other, as that which comes from the street and has bare feet and which has nothing to do with civilized lawns.

The spiritual nature of the north is contrasted with the physical nature of the Arab, who is constructed through metaphors of food and drink, a construction which appears also in Rolfe's *Venice Letters*. The penis in this latter text has a life of its own, to be simultaneously under control and in control, to lead the possessor and dominate the sex object. In Rolfe's *Venice Letters* the following description appears in letter 6:

> He crossed his ankles, ground his thighs together with a gentle rippling motion, writhed his groins and hips once or twice and stiffened into the most inviting mass of fresh meat conceivable, laughing in my face as he made his offering of lively flesh. (31)

The erection at will here is represented as food, an equation that crops up repeatedly. The act of sex becomes the act of making the penis-meat ready to eat. The Venetian boy, as the object of sexual tourism, becomes a commodity offered to the tourist to taste and eat. Here it is literally an offering of wares by the boy to the man, since the boy shows "my person" to Rolfe, and immediately after the extract quoted above he dresses again. Active sexuality on the part of the colonized must be construed in terms of commodity, of food, rather than in terms of desire/seduction for the power differential to be maintained.

The body and body products of the Arab in Crowley's poem become things to eat: they are exotic and highly spiced foods for the palate of the northerner to eat, literally as part of tabooed sexual activity, and metaphorically in the colonization of the south, getting excitement and pleasure from the act of taking the products of the south. What is ostensibly a giving up of cultural and social power/authority, as in the licking of the feet, actually results in the appropriation of the Arab for the mere pleasure of the northerner, expressed by Said as the "flexible *positional* superiority" of the Westerner, which allows him to adopt a series of relationships with the Orient(al) "without losing him the relative upper hand"(7). The dangerous (taboo) exoticism (food) of the Arab is made safe through the continued functioning of the power differential of the races under the pretence of its suspension (abasement) against the class-based imagery of the last lines of the sonnet. Race becomes fetish-object becomes sex object becomes food, sustenance, and pleasure, as well as the annihilation of the colonized and exploited other, the Arab, his body pillaged for its fruits, celebrated for its strangeness and exoticness.

Health and Wealth

THESE TEXTS CONCERNED WITH homosexual desire for the Oriental boy are not necessarily radical or liberatory texts but can be seen here as adapting and reproducing the discourses and institutional practices of dominant culture. The Orientalist fetish-object is both co-essential with the discourses of imperialism and in direct contradiction to it, as can be seen in these remarks about the relationship between moral and physical health and the proper pursuit of imperialism. Lord Rosebery, writing in 1900, delineated a Darwinian health-model of the proper relationship between colonizer and colonized.

> An empire such as ours requires as its first condition an Imperial Race — a race vigorous and industrious and intrepid. Health of mind and body exalt a nation in the competition of the universe. The survival of the fittest is an absolute truth in the conditions of the modern world. (Hyam 74)

What is asserted here is that imperialism is dependent upon moral and physical health, and moral and physical health are in some sense dependent upon imperialist endeavor, upon the processes and actions of constructing the world to fit what is identified and ideologically maintained as health of body and mind. In the absence of the drive to conquer other peoples and claim land for the economic exploitation of the Empire, the race and the individual are emasculated and *lose* the initiative/competition for pre-eminence over the *universe*.

The alternative to Rosebery's vision of the ideal is described by Sir Hugh Clifford, writing in 1898:

> Viewed at the right time, and seen in this deceptive light [the glamour which will always hang about the rags of the East while our world lasts], all manner of things in themselves hopelessly evil and unlovely have the power to fascinate as far more attractive objects too often fail to do. . . . The atmosphere is apt to destroy a man's ability to scale things accurately; it deprives him of his sense of proportion. (Hyam 18)

Clifford's reference to the glamor of the East acknowledges the exoticism contained within the Orientalist attitude that is deployed in the fetish of the Oriental boy by the Orientalist, while he sees it as a deception which will blind the colonialists to the truth of their role and their rightness. The East is corrosive of the West's masculinity and implicit plainness/lack of glamor. That metaphor of "glamour" stands in for a surface that is misleading and implicitly rather flashy, over-stated, not marked by sobriety and understatement. The East's culture is "evil" and "unlovely," whereas the functional and reproductive West is good and lovely. Rosebery takes this line of argument a stage further and constructs a version of Western masculinity diametrically opposed to Eastern lack of healthy and morality. These voices from the dominant conceal the commodification of the culture and individuals of the Orient, where the homosexual eroticization of the Orient works precisely on the contradiction and tension of the relationship between the colonizer and the colonized.

Bolton Institute of Higher Education

NOTES

1. The texts discussed in this essay name the object of desire as "boy" or "youth," and the implied relationship is readable, both then and now, as one of pedophilia. This essay, however, is not concerned with the actual erotic practice of the authors discussed, but with the discourse of homosexual colonialism defined and developed in their texts. The words "boy" and "youth" describe a relationship of economic and political power, in which the object of desire is infantilized, ascribed a limited mental capacity, individually and culturally, on the basis of race, not age, a process marked by the fact that some of these "boys" are in their twenties. There are, however, texts discussed here which do describe relationships between men and boys under the age of fourteen, notably Kenneth Searight's. As a lesbian I vehemently oppose collapsing the categories of "homosexual" and "pedophile" into each other, but such texts reinforce the fact of the racist assumptions of the texts, that any male of color is both always a child, and always already sexually mature by virtue of being "Oriental," in a way that white males could never be within the terms of the Orientalist discourse.

2. The construction of the Orientalist woman shares many of the same features as the male object while displaying significant differences. Where white women's sexuality is purely reproductive and functional, the Orientalist women's sexuality displays the full range of Oriental ideas, retaining the powerful and dangerous terms of Said's definition. Such women are associated with an open and free sexuality (see Charles Fowkes 10–14, in which both Richard Burton, whose translation of the *Kama Sutra* it is, and the modern editor subscribe to a view of Orientalist sexuality as being free from western guilt and sense of sin). They are also associated with "debauchery, violence, and death," and with the "sexual depravity and the overcharged environment of the prince's harem" (Wurgaft 49, 51). Ideas of the harem as the epitome of the Orientalist woman's sexuality appear in Flaubert's *Madame Bovary* (see Said 190), in the paintings of Lawrence Alma-Tadema, particularly *The Women of Amphissa* (see West 90–92), and in novels of the empire (see Showalter 81).

3. The authorship of the text of *Teleny* is in serious doubt, and although the editor describes how it was passed from hand to hand via Charles Hirsch's bookshop in London and claims that one of those involved in writing it was Oscar Wilde (9), this is not absolutely certain, and I therefore refer to the text by its title only.

4. "Fox" is Masson Fox.

5. There is a variant on this adage which reads "A woman for business and a boy for pleasure," which is quoted by Wurgaft from George MacMunn, *The Underworld of India* (London, 1933), 201. The reference to the melon seems to be both metaphorical of an economic relationship and also a literal aid to masturbation, in which the penis is inserted into the melon.

6. The manuscript of "Paidikion" is in private hands. My information on the text is taken from Hammond who describes and quotes from several of the texts in the manuscript, including "Ten Little Bugger Boys." My description is a paraphrase of Hammond's work. He does not include anything from "The Furnace." For this work I am dependent upon Hyam's extracts who quotes only from "The Furnace."

7. Searight's "The Furnace, An autobiography in which is set forth the secret diversions of a paiderast" comprises pages 250–381 of unpublished manuscript (c. 1897–1917), quoted in Hyam. Page references are to this work, not to the manuscript.

WORKS CITED

Crowley, Aleister. *White Stains: the Literary Remains of George Archibald Bishop, a Neuropath of the Second Empire.* Private publication, 1898.

Fowkes, Charles, ed. *The Illustrated Kama Sutra, Ananga-Ranga, Perfumed Garden: the Classic Eastern Love Texts. The Sir Richard Burton and F. F. Arbuthnot Translations.* Rochester, Vermont: Park Street Press, 1991.

Gide, André. *If It Die . . .* 1920; rpt. Harmondsworth; Penguin, 1987.

Hammond, Toby. "*Paidikion*: a Paiderastic Manuscript." *International Journal of Greek Love* 1. 2 (November 1966): 30–36.

Housman, A. E. *More Poems.* London: Jonathan Cape, 1936.

Hyam, Ronald. *Empire and Sexuality: the British Experience.* Manchester: Manchester UP, 1990.

Livingstone, David. *Missionary Travels and Researches in South Africa.* London: John Murray, 1912.

Reade, Brian, ed. *Sexual Heretics.* London: Routledge and Kegan Paul, 1970.

Rolfe, Frederick. *The Desire and Pursuit of the Whole: a Romance of Modern Venice.* 1934; Oxford: Oxford UP, 1986.

———. *Hadrian the Seventh.* 1904; rpt. Harmondsworth: Penguin, 1982.

———. *The Venice Letters.* Ed. Cecil Woolf. London: Cecil and Amelia Woolf, 1974.

Said, Edward. *Orientalism.* London: Penguin, 1978.

Showalter, Elaine. *Sexual Anarchy: Gender and Culture at the Fin de Siècle.* London, Bloomsbury Publishing, 1991.

Symonds, John Addington. *Fragilia Labilia.* Private publication, 1884.

———. *The Memoirs of John Addington Symonds: the Secret Homosexual Life of a Leading Nineteenth-Century Man of Letters.* Ed. Phyllis Grosskurth. Chicago: U of Chicago P, 1986.

Teleny, or the Reverse of the Medal. 1893; rpt., ed. John McRae, London: GMP, 1986.

West, Shearer. *Fin de Siècle: Art and Society in an Age of Uncertainty.* London: Bloomsbury Publishing, 1993.

Wurgaft, Lewis D. *The Imperial Imagination: Magic and Myth in Kipling's India.* Middletown: Wesleyan UP, 1983.

Wratislaw, Theodore. *Caprices.* London: Gay & Bird, 1893.

MUSIC-HALL LONDON: THE TOPOGRAPHY OF CLASS SENTIMENT

By Keith Wilson

ONE OF THE DEFINING CHARACTERISTICS of many Victorian and Edwardian music-hall lyrics is the specificity with which they evoke the classed topography of nineteenth-century London. While the feckless victim of moving-day disorientation in "My Old Man Said Follow the Van," Marie Lloyd's most famous song, may have lost her way and not known where to roam — a situation extended into metaphor for one of Gus Elen's Covent Garden porters, who after coming into "a little bit of splosh" develops delusions of grandeur and "Dunno Where 'E Are" — their situations were not representative. Most Victorian and Edwardian music-hall song characters who were given any circumstantial shading at all knew precisely where they were, and with the exception of the occasional cosmopolite who found his way to the continent or the odd yokel brought in to cater to the *soi-disant* knowingness of working-class London, their roaming was done within a five or six-mile radius of Charing Cross.

The symbolic as well as alliterative possibilities of familiar locations had been recognized by Victorian song writers long before Tom Leamore's "Percy from Pimlico" and Vesta Tilley's "Burlington Bertie," with his "Hyde Park drawl" and "Bond Street crawl," or Ella Shields's even more peripatetic "Burlington Bertie from Bow," consolidated them for posterity in the years before the First World War.[1] Shields's down-at-heels boulevardier cuts a substantial swathe through London in the course of his wanderings: Bow, the Strand, Temple Bar, the Burlington, Buckingham Palace, and out to Sandown Park racecourse. But his careless dropping of familiar names was merely one of the last, and most successful, flourishes of a long-established and by then dying tradition. In the 1860s, while Harry Clifton was singing the praises of "Pretty Little Polly Perkins of Paddington Green," George Leybourne's Champagne Charlie was already dazzling girls "From Poplar to

23

Pall Mall,'' among them no doubt ''My friend Arabella'' who ''at Bow was a dweller'' (''The Nice Looking Girl'')[2] even though she worked in a swell-patronized confectionery up west.

London place-names sprinkled liberally through song lyrics functioned as a kind of topographical shorthand. Before the performer had got much further than the end of the first chorus, the semiotics of place-name could be used to establish the economic and in some degree moral credentials of the song's main character, the ironic possibilities of its situations and social judgments, and the sentimental grounds for the expression, maudlin or raucous, of class and community solidarity among the audience. When Harry Rickards, while enduring real-life and very public financial troubles, sang ''I never go east of Temple Bar/I stick to St. James's and Belgravi-ah!'' (Pulling 29), only to be greeted by a voice from the gallery yelling, ''How did you get to Basinghall Street, then?'' (the former site of the bankruptcy court), he was merely being uncomfortably implicated in the reciprocity between the shared terrains of stage character and audience upon which his medium routinely played.

The two most enduring London music-hall personae, the swell or toff and the cockney coster, embodied topographical as well as social extremes. The swell, popularized by Leybourne and Alfred Vance in the 1860s and 70s, lived and strolled in the West End; the coster, also portrayed by Vance but brought most fully to stage life by Albert Chevalier and Gus Elen in the '90s, lived in the East or South East, though by occupational necessity he spent much of his time around Covent Garden market. Between them, swell and coster encouraged in the songs that featured them a tendency to facile locational definition and invited the binary simplifications of West and East End. But there was sufficient role and class cross-over, in part generated by the tendency of the halls themselves to appeal to the unashamedly upper and lower classes rather than a yet-to-be distributed middle, to make for a complex socio-topographical mix.[3]

For the music-hall swell to maintain his typological appeal, long after his mid-century heyday, he needed not only a developed capacity for self-parody but also the flexibility to assimilate and reproduce the equally self-mocking ambitions of a working-class audience.[4] Stage aspirations to toffdom were not limited to those characters on whom fortune suddenly smiled, like Gus Elen's ''Golden Dustman,'' who comes upon a miser's hoard while clearing away his garbage. But his response to sudden wealth reveals the standard attributes of privilege as identified by those who had none:

> But, nah I'm goin' to be a reglar Toff,
>   A-ridin' in my carriage and a pair,
> A top-'at on my 'ead, and fevvers in my bed,
>   And call meself The Dook o' Barnit Fair.

Asterrycan rahnd the bottom o' my coat,
  A Piccadilly winder in my eye,
Oh! fancy all the dustmen a-shoutin' in my yer,
  "Leave us in yer will before yer die." (Elen)

More often the halls were home to those who played the part without possessing the money. Like Arthur Lloyd's "Immensikoff, the Shoreditch Toff," T. W. Barrett's "The Marquis of Camberwell Green"[5] contrived to be "a dooced big toff of a fellow" by night, despite a plebeian daytime existence as an assistant butcher. Only marginally better placed, at least from the perspective of the genuine toff, was Barrett's best known character, "The Nobleman's Son":

I tell them my father's a Marquis,
  But wouldn't Society frown
If they knew that he shaved for a penny a time
  In a little shop down Somers Town?
I tell them he rides in his brougham,
  And is a big swell of the day;
If they knew that my father
Was Knight of the lather
  I wonder whatever they'd say! (Pulling 28)

By the 1880s, when this song was most popular, Somers Town, never the most salubrious of areas, had largely been taken over by Euston, King's Cross, and St. Pancras Stations. One of the few certainties the stylized parody of a recognizable original and his aspiring ragged-cuffed rival could genuinely share was confidence in a London audience's ability, during the fleeting dynamics of actual performance, to effect reflex interpretations of the significance of place.

That significance was often used to defuse the potential disruptiveness of music hall's preoccupation with class. The pretensions of those who, like the Marquis of Camberwell Green, aped the affectations of their superiors without relocating themselves, either socially or topographically, made actual privilege the stuff of comedy rather than class indignation. Percy from Pimlico, a location which gave him a somewhat ambiguous status depending on whether his audience assumed he came from the Belgravia end or from the environs of Victoria Station, was "a slasher, a dasher, the up-to-date masher." But despite being "stony broke" and unable to lunch at Romano's or the "Cri" ("You'll see me munch my sausage and mash / At Harris's, on the sly"), he remains "as happy as the Prince of Wales" (Prentis 75–76). Similarly, Herbert Campbell's successful proprietor of a Shoreditch "hoyster stall" seems more than content with his modest lot, showing no inclination to leave "the ditch," even though he recognizes his old pals "ain't no class" (Prentis

16–17). He can now afford to dress up a bit and exchange his clay pipe and shag for "fags," and he can't help inclining a little more towards the superiors whose status he distantly mimics, even defending the House of Lords against Shoreditch scepticism. But he stays in his own area of London, a contented vindication of enlightened self-interest, and role-model for his less fortunate neighbors.

An audience's instinctive feel for the resonances of place inevitably encouraged its acceptance of the status quo. Despite Bertie's infiltrations from Bow in the East End, Mayfair, Hyde Park, Pall Mall, Bond Street, the Burlington Arcade, and Piccadilly remained, even in song, a preserve of fashion, penetrated by the lower classes only in their roles as shop-assistants, servants, flower-girls, and fallen women. But much of the West End, particularly Leicester Square, Trafalgar Square, the Victoria Embankment, the Strand, and Covent Garden, was shared territory as well as common iconographic ground for both social extremes. The conveniently central Covent Garden, invoked in countless songs because of its association with coster life, was, after all, home to both opera and cabbages, and as Morny Cash's vagrant refugee from the Embankment, whose last digs were "The third seat from Waterloo Bridge," would come to say of his new lodging in Trafalgar Square, "If it's good enough for Nelson, / It's quite good enough for me!" (Davison 129). Despite all the innate class antipathies on which music-hall performers could easily have capitalized, and on many occasions did, an audience's collective self-congratulation in belonging to the world's most important city, and in enjoying intimacy with its regional idiosyncrasies, was productive of a sense of shared identity that a skilled performer could milk to even greater advantage than he could class indignation.

The paradoxical parochialism of an audience that took great pride in being at the center helps to explain the short shrift the notion of "abroad" tended to receive on the halls. For London-based lyricists, as for their audiences, the world did not extend far beyond the "continong," and even that was unlikely to hold much of a candle to London: "The Continong is all très bon / And so is Leicester Square" sang Harry Freeman, and by and large music-hall patrons agreed with him, especially those who had never been anywhere near the continent. Even "The Man Who Broke the Bank at Monte Carlo," whose nouveau riche swagger helped make Charles Coborn's name (taken from Coborn Road in Bow), depended more for its success on regular newspaper reports of the exploits of its subject, the notorious Charles Wells, and the refusal of its singer to stop repeating the chorus until audiences joined in than on any great enthusiasm for foreign parts. Marie Lloyd had a few songs set in Paris or Boulogne, all of a kind summed up in the title of "The Naughty Continong," but her "Coster Girl in Paris" probably expressed the predominant sentiments:

And I'd like to go again
To Paris on the Seine,
For Paris is a proper pantomime,
And if they'd only shift the 'Ackney Road and plant it over there,
I'd like to live in Paris all the time. (Farson 48)

To London eyes, the English countryside was preferable to abroad, although as late as 1910 Tom Clare's Bertie Bright of Bond Street could still take pride in proclaiming "Some idiots love the country, wherever that may be, / I've never been out further West than Kew" ("Absolutely Wrong," Gammond 170–71). Unmediated nature was, even to the most sympathetic urban sensibility, always a little on the uneventful side, which was why so many songs involved the socio-sexual education of country girls who, arriving in London, undergo urban rites of passage, some of them almost before they have left the railway terminus. While few labor under quite such a disabling weight of innuendo as the Euston-bound farmer's daughter in Marie Lloyd's "She'd Never Had Her Ticket Punched Before," most immediately become blowsily familiar with a broad acreage of West End London, or if they do not wish they could. Another "modest little maiden from the country" created by Lloyd may proclaim in choral refrain, "I have never lost my last train yet, Oh No! / I have never lost my last train yet!", but she still looks forward to exchanging "nature's beauty" for "Metropolitan delights":

I am getting somewhat sick of rural beauty,
Or in other words I've had about enough.
I should love to have a flat in Piccadilly
And to go and do exactly as I choose,
    For had I my habitation
    In a West End situation,
Then of course, I would not have a train to lose. (Davison 107)

The town's associational detail was all the more noteworthy for the rustic anonymity from which the girls usually journeyed and which most of them shared. While they were in the main nameless country maidens who came from equally nameless and atemporal rural landscapes dotted with non-specific wildlife, on arrival they located themselves within a contemporary cityscape immediately identifiable to a music-hall audience.[6]

For example, the girl with "a country accent," "captivating glance," and "golden hair . . . hanging down her back," who never does get assigned a name herself, steps out into a London so familiar to an audience that its landmarks are identifiable merely from truncated half-referents, particularly given the year (1894) of the song's greatest popularity:

She wandered out in London for a breath of ev'ning air,

And strayed into a Palace that was fine and large and fair—
It might be in a Circus or it might be in a Square,
But her golden hair was hanging down her back. (Davison 85)

The Palace Theatre of Varieties in Cambridge Circus and the Alhambra in Leicester Square would immediately be conjured up for a London audience, and the next verse makes the referent all the more specific. "Beside a marble bath upon some marble stairs," wearing only her golden hair hanging down her back, the country girl is posing in *tableaux vivants* even more titillating than the "daring Moorish bath scene" that the Palace had recently been forced to withdraw from the shocked gazes of its more sensitive customers (Pennybacker 130). Nor does the local associative detail stop there. The song ends as she meets up with a young philanthropist, "a friend of Missus Chant," the Mrs. Ormiston Chant who had spent much of the early 1890s trying to close down the notorious promenade at the Leicester Square Empire. The philanthropic friend "lived in Peckham Rye with an extremely maiden aunt," and the next day the aunt catches sight of golden hairs hanging down his back. Thus the cycle is completed: corruptive London becomes London corrupted, and suburban lower-middle-class/aspiring working-class Peckham Rye bears witness to the young man's fall, and music hall's vicarious victory over Mrs. Chant.

Nor was this part of South East London arbitrarily chosen, largely unknown territory though it might be to the fashionable world north of the river. Peckham Rye, the South Londoner's poor substitute for Hampstead Heath, was a large area of common ground in the borough of Camberwell, one of a number of sites for demotic jollification that ringed London and were recurrently invoked in music halls as readily recognizable social, sentimental, and in some degree moral emblems of value for working-class London. While Piccadilly and Leicester Square, Covent Garden and the Strand, Bond Street and the Burlington defined a topographical, cultural, and imperial center, whose resonances working-class audiences responded to as jingoistically as any toff or servant of empire home on leave, the economically marginalized also had alternative sketch-maps of significance, fittingly placed at London's circumference: Epsom (primarily on Derby Day), the Welsh Harp lake and pub at Kingsbury near Hendon, Hampstead Heath (particularly on Easter Monday when it was home to a fair, although Florrie Forde's repeated invitations to "come and make eyes at me / Down at the Old Bull and Bush" would help to make the adjacent Heath's appeal less seasonal), Hackney Marshes and Downs, and Peckham Rye itself were all associated with working class leisure and yearnings toward emotional fulfilment, located against an urbanized rusticity usually enjoyable only on holidays and weekends. None of them, with the possible exception of Epsom, home to the classless enticements of the

Derby, had quite the same associations higher up the social scale, but their invocation usually involved the parodying of the comparable pleasures of social superiors. "The toffs may talk of Rotting Row," sang Albert Chevalier, but "There ain't no place on earth / Like . . . 'appy 'Ampstead" ("Oh! 'Ampstead," Gammond 269).

Chevalier defined both the sentimentalized and more comic versions of this distinctive mode of proletarian contentment, in the process making the music-hall coster acceptable even to Mrs. Chant and her fellow evangelists. His most popular song, "My Old Dutch," was a hymn to an aging wife with whom the coster has shared a lifetime of domestic harmony. Its chorus pointedly set cockney contentment and fidelity in the scales against social advantage:

> We've been together now for forty years,
> An' it don't seem a day too much.
> There ain't a lady livin' in the land
> As I'd swop for my dear old Dutch. (Gammond 86)

The connotations of "lady" would not have been lost on Chevalier's audience, any more than they were on the vicar who wrote to congratulate him on his "special 'Grace of God' to awaken in hearts we parsons cannot reach, appreciation of a faithful woman's comradeship in the hard battle of life" (Chevalier 151). But woman or lady, her capacity for comradeship would have been refined by the kind of experience recalled in "The Coster's Serenade," the song with which Chevalier had made his London Pavilion debut in 1891:

> You ain't forgotten 'ow we drove that day
> Down to the Welsh 'Arp in my donkey shay?
> Folks with a "chy-ike" shouted "Ain't they smart?"
> You looked a queen, me every inch a bart.
> Seemed that the moke was saying "Do me proud,
> Mine is the nobbiest turn-out in the crowd";
> Me in my "pearlies" felt a toff that day,
> Down at the Welsh 'Arp, which is 'Endon way.

The last line, with its combination of locational specificity ("the Welsh 'Arp") and gestural vagueness ("'Endon way"), forms the song's refrain, signalling the coster's emotively precise but geographically approximate sense of an area which lies at the very outer edges of his workday experience, however integral it is to his yearnings towards romance and gentility. His grasp of social gradations may be a little approximate, with queen and baronet bundled oddly together in the mutual felicity of their states, but the genuine ennoblement of sensibility generated by the day's magic is not left in doubt, and there is sufficient pride in this secular pilgrimage that even the donkey comes in for its share.

Similar journeys by donkey and shay provided Albert Chevalier with raw material for a number of songs that made as much of costerland's relationship with donkeys as could reasonably be made. They included the tear-jerking lament for a dead donkey, "Jeerusalem's Dead," and the classic statement of South London's self-mocking aspirations to gentility, "Wot Cher!" or "Knocked 'Em in the Old Kent Road":

> Last week down our alley come a toff,
> Nice old geezer with a nasty cough,
> Sees my Missus, takes 'is topper off
>   In a very gentlemanly way!
> "Ma'am," says he, "I 'ave some news to tell,
> Your rich Uncle Tom of Camberwell,
> Popped off recent, which it ain't a sell,
>   Leaving you 'is little Donkey Shay."
>   "Wot cher!" all the neighbours cried.
>   "Who're yer goin' to meet Bill?
>   Have yer bought the street Bill?"
>   Laugh! I thought I should 'ave died,
>   Knock'd 'em in the Old Kent Road! (Gammond 203–04)

The distinction between the relative opulence of Camberwell and the Old Kent Road was likely to be lost on more comfortably located Londoners, but the second verse moves into their territory as it translates implicit comparison with the inherited wealth of West End aristocracy into explicit self-parody that simultaneously debunks the class it pretends to ape:

> Some says nasty things about the moke;
> One cove thinks 'is leg is really broke,
> That's 'is envy, 'cos we're carriage folk,
>   Like the toffs as rides in Rotten Row!
> Straight! it woke the alley up a bit,
> Thought our lodger would 'ave 'ad a fit,
> When my missus, who's a real wit,
>   Says, "I 'ates a Bus because it's low!"

Uncle Tom's Camberwell was home to thousands of costers, their circumstances sniffily adumbrated in his *Survey of London* by Walter Besant:

today the streets off Crown Street are crowded with the vicious and poverty-stricken classes. Costers, hawkers, and labourers herd together in dirty streets which swarm with neglected children. Every available foot of space is used as stabling for ponies and donkeys and standing-room for barrows and small carts. (Besant 127)

They had migrated south in large numbers as a result of the various waves of slum clearance north of the river. In time that diaspora would spread further, and Gus Elen, whose versions of coster life were more palatable to the real cockney than Chevalier's more sentimentalized and sanitized versions, was soon singing about how "We're not a-living where we lived afore we moved away / From the little wooden 'ouse at Peckham Rye," having parlayed upward, or at least outward, mobility into a move back across the river again to the "Pretty Little Villa Down at Barking" (Elen). But it was a long time before the migration of the working-classes into suburbia would render unnecessary the pursuit of rural idylls within a donkey-shay's distance of Camberwell or Holborn.

The knowing Londoner might condescend to the country, but he would also readily reformulate its imagery into ironic expressions of paradise relocated. Marie Lloyd's husband, Alec Hurley, used to sing "My London Country Lane" under a Drury Lane street sign and next to the coster's barrow that indicated it was the market rather than the theatre that he had in mind:

> Oh I loves to take a ramble down my London country lane,
> Where the nippers chuck things at you & it isn't golden grain
> Though the scarlet beans and marrows
> Doesn't grow — they're all on barrows
> Still it's painted up & sez so — it's a real live lane.

Gus Elen gave the fullest expression to this pastoral impulse in one of the most evocative of 90s music-hall songs, "If It Wasn't for the 'Ouses in Between." Elen's attempts to transfer nostalgic rural verities to an East-End backyard — which include invoking "the ploughboy cove what's mizzled o'er the Lea" from Gray's "Elegy" — generate inspired compromises:

> The dustcart, though it seldom comes, is just like 'arvest 'ome
> And we mean to rig a dairy up some 'ow;
> Put the donkey in the washhouse wiv some imitation 'orns,
> For we're teaching 'im to moo just like a cow. (Elen)

But unlike the actual countryside that the golden-haired girl and her stage sisters came from, Elen's "wery pretty garden" is precisely located: Leather Lane market a mile away, Chingford and 'Ackney Marshes to the East, 'Endon and Wembley to the West, all clearly visible to the eye of proprietorial pride "If It Wasn't for the 'Ouses in Between."

The "'Ouses in Between" *were* of course London for vast numbers of East Enders who rarely saw anything else and whose engagement with anywhere outside was likely to be limited to the odd steamer trip to Southend or Margate or a few weeks of back-breaking work each year down in the hopfields of Kent. While the contemporary London of subsistence living and less was on view to the middle classes in the works of George Gissing or Arthur Morrison, George Sims or Walter Besant, it was mediated imaginatively for those who actually lived the experience by the music halls, whose songs became a latter-day folk poetry. When Gus Elen sang of the neighbor overhead who after a fight with his wife had a face "like the map of Clapham Junction" (Elen, "Mrs. Carter"), he was locating familiar emotional experience topographically as surely as Albert Chevalier reminiscing about rites of courtship performed down 'Endon way. Unfashionable London locations were the guarantors of shared experience conveyed through the specificity of shared space, and the songs that mapped them articulated the relationship of cultural, and for that matter personal, identity to territory.

The manifestation of that relationship in popular music did not outlast the halls themselves. While popular songs would continue to invoke London in very generalized terms — as evidenced in Lupino Lane's 1930s invitation to West-End audiences to share the free-and-easy pleasures of South London life by joining in the "Lambeth Walk,"[7] or in a song like "London Pride," Noel Coward's wartime celebration of London and its bomb sites as a repository of national purpose during the blitz — the casual specificity that distinguished references to London on the Victorian and Edwardian music halls did not survive the First World War. Its disappearance probably owed as much to what male East Enders were about to experience in their thousands on the Western Front as to familial displacement down to Barking or anywhere else. London as imperial center rather than proletarian domestic space had already begun to dominate in the imagery of music-hall lyrics at the turn of the century, thanks primarily to the Boer War: even Albert Chevalier's coster found himself celebrating "Mafeking Night" and cheering Baden-Powell, Bobs, and the Dublin Fusiliers. By 1914, the symbolism of London topography had joined an even greater war effort. As Australians, New Zealanders, Canadians, South Africans, and a good few Londoners marched off to France singing their goodbyes to Piccadilly and farewells to Leicester Square, with which many of them had been intimately acquainted for only a few days, they did so in words fittingly put into the mouth of a home-sick Irishman yearning for his Molly at home in Tipperary. And by the time some of them returned, Gus Elen's topographical contentment had the elegiac cadences of another world.

University of Ottawa

NOTES

1. One of the last appearances of the early type was in "Reckless Reggie of the Regent Palace," a Davy Burnaby song performed by Jack Hulbert during the

First World War (see Pulling 39). By the 1930s, a younger generation of alliterative toffs were less exclusively centered on the West End, among them "rollicking Reggie from Richmond" and "Frightfully Freddy, Freddy,/The flame of the flappers" (Gammond 168–69, 176–77).

2. For a discussion of this song and the wider question of class/gender interplay in music-hall lyrics, see Traies.
3. For discussion of the class make-up of music-hall audiences, see Cheshire and Höher.
4. For a full discussion of the swell song of the 1860s and '70s, see Bailey.
5. For a stylistic analysis of this and other music-hall songs, see Bennett 10–22.
6. About the last of the type was not anonymous, nor was her point of origin, and she resisted the metropolitan fleshpots. Little Nell of Gracie Field's "Heaven Will Protect an Honest Girl" did not journey from Oldham to Waterloo until the 1930s, but when she got to London she was as peripatetic as her predecessors, braving Whitehall, the Strand, Piccadilly, Leicester Square, and Camberwell before retreating north in her underwear with virtue still intact (Davison 225–26).
7. Appropriately enough, this late-Depression hit song, which helped to keep *Me and My Girl* in the West End for four years, owed its title to Alec Hurley's most popular song.

SONGS CITED

The variable fortunes of songs, composers, and singers make the dating of music-hall materials notoriously approximate. Some songs were immediately successful, others took hold more gradually. Some remained the property of a single singer, others were taken up by various performers. Some song sheets were dated, others were not. And, of course, dates of early recordings often attest to a song's longevity rather than its conception.

The dates, some of them indicated as tentative, given in the following list indicate the period of the song's emergence into popularity.

"Absolutely Wrong" (1910). Fred Chester and Tom Clare. Sung by Tom Clare.
"And Her Golden Hair Was Hanging Down Her Back" (1894). Felix McGlennon. Sung by Alice Leamar and Seymour Hicks.
"Burlington Bertie" (1912). William Hargreaves. Sung by Vesta Tilley.
"Burlington Bertie from Bow" (1912). William Hargreaves. Sung by Ella Shields.
"Champagne Charlie" (1866). Alfred Lee. Sung by George Leybourne.
"The Coster Girl in Paris" (189[?]). Fred W. Leigh and Orlando Powell. Sung by Marie Lloyd.
"The Coster's Serenade" (1891). Albert Chevalier and John Crook. Sung by Albert Chevalier.
"Down At the Old Bull and Bush" (1903). Russell Hunting, Percy Krone, Andrew B. Sterling, and Harry von Tilzer. Sung by Florrie Forde.
"'E Dunno Where 'E Are" (1893). Fred Eplett and Harry Wright. Sung by Gus Elen.
"Frightfully Freddy" (1932). Wolseley Charles and Greatrex Newman. Sung by Leslie Henson.
"The Golden Dustman" (1893). Eric Graham and George Le Brunn. Sung by Gus Elen.
"Heaven Will Protect an Honest Girl" (1933). Bert Lee and R. P. Weston. Sung by Gracie Fields.

"If It Wasn't for the 'Ouses in Between" (1894). Edgar Bateman and George Le Brunn. Sung by Gus Elen.

"I Live in Trafalgar Square" (1902). C. W. Murphy. Sung by Morny Cash.

"Immensikoff, The Shoreditch Toff" (1873). Sung by Arthur Lloyd.

"It's a Long Way to Tipperary" (1912). Jack Judge and Harry Williams. Sung by Jack Judge and Florrie Forde.

"I've Never Lost My Last Train Yet"(189[?]). George Le Brunn and George Rollit. Sung by Marie Lloyd.

"Jeerusalem's Dead" (1895). John Crook and Brian Daly. Sung by Albert Chevalier.

"Knocked 'Em in the Old Kent Road" (1891). Albert Chevalier and Charles Ingle. Sung by Albert Chevalier.

"The Lambeth Walk" (1937). Douglas Furber, Noel Gay, and L. Arthur Rose. Sung by Lupino Lane.

"Leicester Square" (189[?]). C. M. Rodney. Sung by Harry Freeman.

"London Pride" (1941). Noël Coward. Sung by Noël Coward.

"Mafeking Night" (1900). Albert Chevalier and Alfred H. West. Sung by Albert Chevalier.

"The Man Who Broke the Bank at Monte Carlo" (1892). Fred Gilbert. Sung by Charles Coborn.

"The Marquis of Camberwell Green" (1884). H. Boden and Ed R. Shrosberry. Sung by T. W. Barrett.

"Mrs. Carter" (189[?]). Edgar Bateman and [?] Murphy. Sung by Gus Elen.

"My London Country Lane" (c. 1900). Edgar Bateman and Albert Perry. Sung by Alec Hurley.

"My Old Dutch" (1892). Albert Chevalier and Charles Ingle. Sung by Albert Chevalier.

"My Old Man Said Follow the Van," also known as "Don't Dilly Dally on the Way" (1919). Charles Collins and Fred W. Leigh. Sung by Marie Lloyd.

"The Naughty Continong" (189[?]). Sung by Marie Lloyd.

"The Nice Looking Girl" (1865). Harriet Bowmer and G. W. Hunt. Sung by Harriet Bowmer, Julia Burns, and Ruth Stanley.

"The Nobleman's Son" (188[3?]). Sung by T. W. Barrett.

"Oh! 'Ampstead" (1914). Albert Chevalier and John Crook. Sung by Albert Chevalier.

"Percy from Pimlico" (189[?]). Sung by Tom Leamore.

"Pretty Little Villa Down at Barking" (190[?]). Herman Darewski. Sung by Gus Elen.

"Pretty Polly Perkins of Paddington Green" (186[?]). Harry Clifton. Sung by Harry Clifton.

"Reckless Reggie of the Regent Palace" (1916). Davy Burnaby. Sung by Jack Hulbert.

"Reggie" (1936). Charles Vivian and Fred Stanton.

"She'd Never Had Her Ticket Punched Before," also known as "What Did She Know About Railways" (189[?]). Sung by Marie Lloyd.

"They Ain't No Class" (189[?]). Sung by Herbert Campbell.

WORKS CITED

Bailey, Peter. "Champagne Charlie: Performance and Ideology in the Music-Hall Swell Song." *Music Hall: Performance and Style.* Ed. J. S. Bratton. Milton Keynes: Open UP, 1986. 49–69.

Bennett, Anthony. "Music in the Halls." *Music Hall: Performance and Style*. Ed. J. S. Bratton. Milton Keynes: Open UP, 1986. 1–22.

Besant, Walter. *London South of the Thames*. London: A. & C. Black, 1912.

Cheshire, D. F. *Music Hall in Britain*. Newton Abbot: David & Charles, 1974.

Chevalier, Albert. *Albert Chevalier: A Record By Himself*. London: MacQueen, 1896.

Davison, Peter, ed. *Songs of the British Music Hall*. New York: Oak, 1971.

Elen, Gus. *You Have Made a Nice Old Mess of It*. Topic Records, 12T396, 1979. Includes "'E Dunno Where 'E Are," "The Golden Dustman," "If It Wasn't for the 'Ouses in Between," "Mrs. Carter," and "Pretty Little Villa Down at Barking."

Farson, Daniel. *Marie Lloyd and Music Hall*. London: Stacey, 1972.

Gammond, Peter, ed. *Best Music Hall and Variety Songs*. London: Wolfe, 1972.

The Golden Years of Music Hall. Saydisc, CD-SDL 380, 1990. Includes "Burlington Bertie From Bow," "Down at the Old Bull and Bush," "The Man Who Broke the Bank at Monte Carlo," and "My Old Dutch."

Höher, Dagmar. "The Composition of Music Hall Audiences 1850–1900." *Music Hall: The Business of Pleasure*. Ed. Peter Bailey. Milton Keynes: Open UP, 1986. 73–92.

Mander, Raymond, and Joe Mitchenson. *British Music Hall*. London: Studio Vista, 1965.

Pennybacker, Susan. " 'It was not what she said but the way in which she said it': The London County Council and the Music Halls." *Music Hall: The Business of Pleasure*. Ed. Peter Bailey. Milton Keynes: Open UP, 1986. 118–40.

Prentis, Terence, Ed. *Music-Hall Memories*. London: Selwyn & Blount, [1927].

Pulling, Christopher. *They Were Singing*. London: Harrap, 1952.

Traies, Jane. "Jones and the Working Girl: Class Marginality in Music-Hall Song 1860–1900." *Music Hall: Performance and Style*. Ed. J. S. Bratton. Milton Keynes: Open UP, 1986. 23–48.

HEAT AND MODERN THOUGHT: THE FORCES OF NATURE IN *OUR MUTUAL FRIEND*

by Jonathan Smith

[Y]ou cannot consider heat without glancing at the whole of the
forces of nature, and becoming acquainted with the latest efforts of
modern thought.
— "Is Heat Motion?" *All the Year Round*, 1 July 1865

PRECISELY IN THE MIDDLE of *Our Mutual Friend*, there is a descriptive passage
that echoes the famous opening paragraphs of *Bleak House*. As in the earlier
novel, "Animate London" is "wheezing, and choking" in "a heap of va-
pour," and gaslights burn "with a haggard and unblest air, as knowing themselves to be night-creatures that had no business abroad under the sun (479;
bk. 3, ch. 1). If the world of *Bleak House* appeared to have "gone into
mourning . . . for the death of the sun," in *Our Mutual Friend* "the sun itself,
when it was for a few moments dimly indicated through circling eddies of
fog, showed as if it had gone out and were collapsing flat and cold."

This image of a dying, collapsing sun is no casual reference but a central
concern of *Our Mutual Friend*. Remarking on the *Bleak House* passage,
Gillian Beer calls the death of the sun "another Victorian anxiety" (78).
This anxiety was, perhaps, even more pressing because of its scientific basis:
scientists were calculating the age of the earth and the age of the sun, pre-
dicting with increasing confidence that day when, its energy depleted, the sun
would go out like a candle, leaving the earth in cold and darkness. Such
discussions caught the public imagination, often serving as subject matter for
popular lectures such as John Tyndall's at the Royal Institution, and for
magazine articles like William Thomson's "On the Age of the Sun's Heat"
for *Macmillan's*. The debate over the sun became a focal point through which
Victorian England learned about the newly formulated laws of thermodynamics as well as about the conflicts among physicists, geologists, and biologists
over uniformitarian geology and evolution. It began about the time of *Bleak*

37

House's publication in 1852 (Kelvin's formulation of the second law of thermodynamics appears in the same month as the second installment of *Bleak House*) and was in full swing during the serial publication of *Our Mutual Friend* in 1864–65.

As my epigraph suggests, à study of thermodynamics in *Our Mutual Friend* cannot be undertaken "without glancing at the whole of the forces of nature." And since thermodynamic concepts were not disseminated to the public in an abstruse, mathematically-sophisticated manner but through easily conceptualized issues (like the death of the sun) or matters of practical, everyday importance (like air pollution, the disposal of waste, and the supply of coal), it is essential to approach thermodynamics in the novel via the presentation of thermodynamics and the other "latest efforts of modern thought" contained in Dickens's periodicals, *Household Words* and *All the Year Round*. The range of scientific reference in *Our Mutual Friend* is extensive; geology, paleontology, comparative anatomy, and thermodynamics all have significant places in the novel, thus reflecting the major scientific interests of the periodicals, particularly in the early- and mid-1860s. But these sciences, and the theories competing within and among them, are also connected, often within their own discourses, to differing views of the social and moral world. These views, whether in the periodicals or the productions of the scientists themselves, were inevitably cast in the form of narrative, of stories with a discernable plot. In appropriating them for use in his own view of the social and moral world, Dickens is, I think, aware of these tensions, and sees them as paralleling and lending authority to his simultaneously critical and optimistic social vision. Yet in *Our Mutual Friend*, where the comedy and the criticism of a society dominated by dust and dead people is perhaps sharper than in any of his other novels, Dickens finds, like the thermodynamicists, that hope is a human construction, tenuous but necessary.

Thermodynamic Laws and Thermodynamic Plots

THE FIRST LAW OF thermodynamics is also called the doctrine of the conservation of energy. It affirms that the total energy in the universe is constant — energy can be neither created nor destroyed but can be changed into other forms. As this law was developed during the 1840s, it was called the conservation of force, for it was dependent on the demonstration of what W. R. Grove christened "the correlation of forces," the fact that the six fundamental physical forces — heat, light, electricity, magnetism, chemical affinity, and motion — could all be converted into any of the others.

The second law, first formulated in Britain by Thomson in 1852, asserts that in any expenditure of mechanical energy a certain amount of that energy is forever "lost" as heat. Each transformation of mechanical energy causes some heat to dissipate into the surroundings (for example, through friction), and ultimately this heat disperses throughout the universe. Since the universe contains a finite amount of energy, and the energy available for conversion into work is constantly diminishing, the universe will eventually run out of usable energy. Over time, randomness and disorder increase until the universe reaches a uniform temperature, a point where motion would cease and life would come to an end. British scientists referred to this process as "the dissipation of mechanical energy," the terminology used by Thomson in his initial paper.[1]

These laws were appropriated by supporters of various other scientific theories in competing ways. The first law was readily accommodated to the traditions of natural theology, to a world whose surface of motion and profusion cannot obscure the divinely ordained harmony and design which lies beneath. Yet it also had affinities with Charles Lyell's uniformitarian geology and Darwin's evolutionary biology, both of which envision a world governed by natural law rather than divine design. Lyell used the first law to attack the nebular hypothesis (the theory that the earth had cooled from an original molten state to its present habitable tranquility) and to defend his own view of a planet in a dynamic steady-state, where conflicting geological forces, though in constant flux, operate gradually to maintain an equilibrium. Yet from the 1850s on, Thomson used the second law to discredit Lyell's uniformitarianism, demonstrating mathematically that the earth could be nowhere near as old as Lyell's vague and unlimited time scale allowed (see Burchfield). He calculated the ages of the sun and the earth to show that the earth had both a finite past and a limited future, and he criticized Lyell's steady-state earth as being a violation of basic physical principles ("On the Secular Cooling of the Earth," *Mathematical* 3: 295–311). After the publication of the *Origin of Species*, Thomson led the scientific attack against Darwin from outside Darwin's field, for Darwin, too, depended on the unlimited time scale of uniformitarianism in his model of species change. Successive editions of the *Origin* indicate Darwin's struggle to meet Thomson's criticisms, and in an 1869 letter to Alfred Wallace he admitted that "Thomson's views on the recent age of the world have been for some time one of my sorest troubles" (qtd. in Burchfield 75).

The cosmogony implied by the second law, a cooling universe and a dying sun, gradual degeneration leading to a sort of quiet apocalypse, could be appropriated as in accord with Scripture (Cannon 130). But most physicists — including Thomson — sought to deny or suppress this bleak second law picture. In his initial scientific paper on the second law, "On a Universal Tendency in Nature to the Dissipation of Mechanical Energy," Thomson bluntly stated its implications for the human race: "Within a finite period of time past, the earth must have been, and within a finite period of time to come the earth must again be, unfit for the habitation of man" (*Mathematical* 1: 514). In the more popular forum of *Macmillan's* a decade later, however, Thomson the anti-Darwinist wanted to defend himself from the charge that his theories give "dispiriting views" of the future and of the Creator, and thus attempted to sidestep the earlier conclusion, offering instead the sort of encouraging interpretation made more easily of the first law. In "On the Age of the Sun's Heat," he says:

> The second great law of Thermodynamics involves a certain principle of *irreversible action in nature*. It is thus shown that, although mechanical energy is *indestructible*, there is a universal tendency to its dissipation, which produces gradual augmentation and diffusion of heat, cessation of motion and exhaustion of potential energy through the material universe. The result would inevitably be a state of universal rest and death, if the universe were finite and left to obey existing laws. But it is impossible to conceive a limit to the extent of matter in the universe; and therefore science points rather to an endless progress, through an endless space, of action involving the transformation of potential energy into palpable motion and thence into heat, than to a single finite mechanism, running down like a clock, and stopping forever. . . . [T]herefore, no conclusions of dynamical science regarding the future condition of the earth, can be held to give dispiriting views as to the destiny of the race of intelligent beings by which it is at present inhabited. (388–89)

This passage speaks of "dissipation," "cessation of motion," and "exhaustion," an "inevitable state of universal rest and death," yet it concludes with the assertion of "endless progress" and the denial that thermodynamics gives countenance to "dispiriting views" of human destiny. Thomson is uncomfortable with the Paleyan vision of the world as a watch, but only because he knows that watches eventually run down and stop — unless the watchmaker intervenes. Such intervention is precisely the hope that Thomson extends: the implication is that the universe will *not* be left to obey existing laws, that a greater power will save the human race from the extinction predicted by the second law.

Other physicists shared Thomson's reluctance to face the implicatins of the second law squarely (see Myers, Wilson). John Tyndall's 1862 lecture, "On Force," concentrates primarily on the first law, but he also offers an extensive demonstration on how the meteoric theory — the sun's gravitational pull draws meteors which strike it and impart heat on collision — might account for the maintenance of the sun's heat. In his 1865 *Fortnightly Review* article, "The Constitution of Nature," Tyndall again stresses the first law and the meteoric theory, and, while admitting that as a holder of the nebular hypothesis he believes the earth has radiated most of its heat away, he emphasizes that the earth's remaining store of potential energy is truly vast. Nine years later, in his famous Belfast Address, Tyndall claims that it is the first law that is of "wider grasp and more radical significance" than any of the "grand generalisations" of his day — including Darwin's theory, of which he was an enthusiastic supporter (2: 180–81).

The great German physicist Hermann von Helmholtz, a friend of Tyndall and a frequent lecturer in Britain, also shared this view that the first law, not the second, was the most important theoretical insight of thermodynamics. In a series of six lectures at the Royal Institution in April of 1864, Helmholtz spoke exclusively of the conservation of energy. Like Tyndall, he devoted considerable attention to the mechanisms by which the heat of the cooling sun may be replenished and, although he finds no single mechanism sufficient in itself, comes to a positive conclusion:

> You see, therefore, that we already know processes by which the loss of heat which goes on along the surface of the sun can be made up through a period of time compared with which the length of human history is infinitely small, and that many generations of human beings must succeed each other before the diminution of the heat of the sun is perceptible. ("Lectures" 444)

In a later lecture on the solar system, Helmholtz acknowledges that "we know of no natural process . . . which can spare our sun the fate which has manifestly fallen upon other suns," but, like Thomson, he offers the hope of reprieve for the human race (*Selected Writings* 293). In the meantime, we should not despair or consider life a "purposeless game" but should bear our burden with selflessness, working for the good of humanity:

> in our knowledge, in our civic order and morality, we are living on the heritage which our forefathers gained for us through work, struggle, and sacrifice. We know that what we acquire in the same way will, in the same manner, ennoble the lives of our posterity. The individual who works for the ideal goals of humanity, even if in a modest position and in a limited sphere, may bear without fear the thought that the thread of his own consciousness will one day break. (294–95)

Work, struggle, sacrifice: it is crucial to see that Helmholtz's language is emphatically moral. This moral element can be seen in the terminology of thermodynamics, in words like energy, work, duty, efficiency, power, and force, and especially in the British preference for "dissipation" over "entropy." Although most of these terms were appropriated from common usage and some were already employed in physics, virtually all of them were given precise thermodynamic meanings in the 1850s, meanings which in turn gave a new immediacy to common usage.[2] Paradoxically, to compare the human body to a steam engine — a common trope for explaining both the first and second laws — became not mechanizing but profoundly human. In a world characterized by the second law, the efficient use of energy is a moral imperative: wasting energy literally brings the universe closer to death. Randomness and decay can only be fought off with work, and so everyone must work, and work productively. Power — whether electrical, political, or personal — must be employed judiciously, for all human beings have a duty, as Helmholtz urged, to lighten the burden of their fellows. And these terms had immediate and obvious application to contemporary social problems engendered by industrialization. With the formulation of the second law, the owners of factories were suddenly more concerned with the efficiency of their steam-engines. The pollution of London, especially the soot in the air, was seen as the product of incomplete combustion, a waste of fuel that could be prevented by employing better furnaces. The recycling of waste products — cinders for making bricks and roads, sewage for fertilizer, bones for glue — took on new urgency. Looking back in 1903, Merz remarked that "the great change" wrought in England by the steam engine had occurred because of efforts to solve "the problem of the motive power of heat, . . . the key which would unlock the mysteries of vegetable growth, of animal nutrition, and of human labour, with their economic, industrial, and political aspects" (2: 117). We can see this matrix of issues surfacing together in the works of Dickens, both in the novels and in the articles of *Household Words* and *All the Year Round*.

The articles in Dickens's periodicals have proved to be a rich source of material for the study of the novels. Those critics interested in Dickens's use of science, from Ann Wilkinson to Nancy Metz and George Levine, have mined *Household Words* in particular for the more specifically scientific references in the articles, though always with the assumption that we must not look too closely for consistent parallels between scientific ideas and Dickens's use of them in his novels. In *Little Dorrit*, for example, George Levine explores Dickens's use of the overlapping and often contradictory models of nature based on evolution, thermodynamics, and natural theology, arguing in part that the employment of these conflicting models leads to "creative incoherences in the way Dickens imagines 'character,' self, and the action of the will" (164).

I want to modify this view somewhat by proposing that such "creative incoherences" are present both in the periodical articles and in the scientific discourse on which the articles are based, and I want to suggest that Dickens is at least partly aware of these incoherences. If, in novels like *Bleak House* and *Little Dorrit* and *Our Mutual Friend*, Dickens does portray a world that can be characterized by the dissipation of energy, he also shares with Thomson and Helmholtz and Tyndall the reluctance to carry the implications of that portrait to their logical ends. Yet in *Our Mutual Friend* Dickens seems to use the text to draw attention to the narrator's strategies for avoiding these implications, to the possible delusions involved in the creation of order, whether by scientist or novelist. I want to demonstrate, then, that there are trends in the periodicals' presentation of thermodynamics (as well as other key scientific theories), that these general trends are marked not by consistency but by tension and contradiction, and that *Our Mutual Friend* enacts these tensions and contradictions.

"We Won't Break the Pile Till the Story's Done": Geology

HOUSEHOLD WORDS APPEARED during the heyday of uniformitarian geology, as many of its articles indicate. "Our Phantom Ship on an Antediluvian Cruise" (16 August 1851) takes the reader back through time to see what England was like millions and millions of years ago, and its geology is uniformitarian: "Elevation of one part and depression of another part of the earth's surface is now going on, has always gone on, and probably always will go on" (3: 492). Volcanoes are seen, but these volcanoes are the same as those of the present, and "the vast effects produced by force on the world's crust are not often produced in an instant by a grand catastrophe; they are the results of constant force applied through enormous periods of time" (3: 493). In "What is to Become of Us?" (26 June 1852) — an article about places in Britain where the sea is encroaching on the land — reference is made to Lyell to support the satiric criticism of the catastrophist vision of the earth as currently tranquil:

> Many people, after peeping into a geological book, or listening to a geological lecture, take away the impression that it is all very well for such ups and downs *to have* taken place, . . . but, thank Heaven! all those unpleasant circumstances are over now. The earth is quiet at last, and has subsided into a well-behaved composure. . . . Geological changes in the nineteenth century are out of the question. They would cause great inconvenience. (5: 352)

Uniformitarianism remains in *All the Year Round*, as it was in *Household Words*, the accepted geological theory. In "How Old Are We?" (7 March 1863), a review of Lyell's *Antiquity of Man*, catastrophism is mercilessly lampooned. Lyell is called "the great opponent of sensational geology," in which "the tale of the earth's life is made harrowing with a series of shocks, cataclysms, and vast peril by fire and flood — here, the abrupt sensation header of a continent into the sea, there, the uptossing of an Andes chain as if it were a fritter, followed by a general explosion of volcanoes and unlimited illumination with red fire" (9: 32).

It seems strange to think of Dickens as a novelist interested in the effects of small forces acting over long periods of time, yet uniformitarianism, in its portrait of the present as full of change and motion, has more in common with Dickens's social vision than catastrophic models of a present that is, in the language of *Household Words*, "quiet" and "well-behaved." The dominant *process* of change, whether in the periodical articles or in *Our Mutual*

Friend, is uniformitarian: the worlds of nature and novel are characterized by a Lyellian dynamic steady-state.[3] Although Gillian Beer has argued that uniformitarianism's emphasis on the study of process over the search for beginnings and ends provides "a highly inconvenient shape for fiction" (69) for any novelist, in *Our Mutual Friend* it is only near the end of the novel that we see Dickens abandoning what had earlier been a surprisingly (for Dickens) self-conscious assertion of *Our Mutual Friend*'s uniformitarianism.

The desire to privilege uniformitarian over catastrophist models of change is epitomized by Old Harmon's dust mounds themselves. Harmon, we are told by Mortimer Lightwood, "threw up his own mountain range, like an old volcano, and its geological formation was Dust" (56; bk. 1, ch. 2). Yet this "range of dust mountains," however suddenly "thrown up," takes a long, long time to be sifted through and removed. It is slowly denuded in uniformitarian fashion, for a "train of carts and horses came and went all day from dawn to nightfall, making little or no daily impression on the heap of ashes, though, as the days passed on, the heap was seen to be slowly melting" (565; bk. 3, ch. 8). It is this tearing down of the mounds, not their erection — the redemption of the Harmon estate through its redistribution, not its initial creation — that the novel is concerned with.

At a crucial point in the novel, the narrator asserts that the story of Rokesmith's feigned death is in fact a gradualist one. Having had his first proposal rejected by Bella, and just after telling us the story of the Harmon "mystery," Rokesmith vows to hide his identity: he constructs his own "mounds" by "heap[ing] mounds upon mounds of earth over John Harmon's grave," determined to bury his past "under a whole Alpine range" (435; bk. 2, ch. 13). Yet, at the beginning of the next chapter, Rokesmith reviews the course of events since his "death" and realizes that his deception, though conceived with no malicious intent, has now involved him in circumstances he did not envision. "He had lapsed into the condition in which he found himself," the narrator tells us, "as many a man lapses into many a condition, without perceiving the accumulative power of its separate circumstances" (436; bk. 2, ch. 14). But Rokesmith's "death" and "the accumulative power of its separate circumstances" are of course the very essence of the plot, for he is the mutual friend who provides so many of the connections among the various groups of characters. If Rokesmith's story is a uniformitarian one, then Dickens would seem to be offering a uniformitarian vision of his own art in this novel.

Yet the novel contains, like any Dickens novel, a sizeable share of "catastrophic" events. In her essay on *Bleak House*, Ann Wilkinson argues that such apocalyptic events as the spontaneous combustion of Krook or the death of Richard Carstone reveal when viewed retrospectively the chain of cause and effect that has gradually led up to them. George Levine sees Dickens as fusing the uniform and the catastrophic so successfully that since "all extremes are merely accumulations of the ordinary, all the ordinary is potentially extreme" (135). *Our Mutual Friend* goes beyond these two positions in the Rokesmith plot, however, by emphasizing its uniformitarian nature *while it is underway.* There is no need for retrospective reading to convert catastrophe into uniformity because Dickens goes to considerable lengths to make the Handford-Rokesmith-Harmon connection evident from the very first number. Similarly, although *Our Mutual Friend* begins with the "catastrophic" event (the discovery and misidentification of Radfoot's corpse) that is the catalyst for the whole story, this event, which will itself later be explained in the middle of the novel as the result of the "accumulative power of separate circumstances," both initiates the novel's various uniformitarian storylines and provides the link that connects them.

What upsets this uniformitarian chain is, of course, Dickens's withholding from us the fact that Mr. Boffin's miserliness is an act, and that Rokesmith and Mrs. Boffin are in on that act. We know from Dickens's chapter notes and plot outlines that both plot devices were in his plans from the beginning, and that he intended the one to be "suggested" to the reader while the other was to remain hidden (Boll; Cotsell; Dickens, *Letters* 3: 412, 422). Yet because the Harmon "mystery" is no mystery at all for us, this deception involving Boffin is all the more striking. A contemporary reviewer, in what is otherwise a highly favorable review, notes the way Dickens's gradualist narrative is suddenly "torn open" by the revelation of the Boffin ruse: "The complication of events does not work itself clear by a slow and natural process, but is, so to speak, roughly torn open" (qtd. in Philip Collins 456). The language of the novel sanctions this view of a sudden and violent disruption of the narrative. Bella, who is also unaware of The Golden Dustman's charade, finds the transformation of her former benefactor "bewilderingly wonderful" and "marvellous" (839; bk. 4, ch. 13). That her husband's name is Harmon she initially says is "not possible" (841; bk. 4, ch. 13). And this sudden revelation, for Bella and for us, parallels a similar experience for the Boffins themselves: Mrs. Boffin describes a scene previously withheld in which Rokesmith "chanced to look up with a pleased kind of smile in my company when he saw me, and then in a single moment every grain of the gunpowder that had been lying sprinkled thick about him ever since I first set eyes upon him as a man at the Bower, took fire" (841; bk. 4, ch. 13). Rokesmith's story, a supposedly gradualist account of "the accumulative power of separate circumstances," depends on a sudden explosion hidden only to be exploded a second time, on Bella as well as on us.

"Regarded in a Boney Light": Paleontology and Comparative Anatomy

DURING THE 1850S, articles in *Household Words* endorsed the theories of archetypal form articulated by Richard Owen, the leading comparative anatomist
in Britain and a friend of Dickens. As "Nature's Greatness in Small Things"
(28 November 1857) explains, varieties in nature are the result of slight
changes from a single archetypal form — the vertebra — and thus serve as
an indication of "order amidst confusion" (16: 512). "Common origin" and
"archetypal form" should not be confused with Darwin's ideas about common ancestors, for Owen's views were specifically formulated as an alternative to pre-Darwinian evolutionary theories (see Desmond). As in natural
theology, the emphasis is on order, connection, and design, but Owen's theory
is said to be more comprehensive because it can account for the presence of
rudimentary or useless structures which caused difficulty for arguments from
design. This "grand demonstration of unity in creation" thus provides "a
new bulwark to religion" (16: 512).

After Darwin and Wallace's joint paper on evolution in 1858 and the
publication of *The Origin of Species* in 1859, Owen became a leading critic
of natural selection. One of his earliest responses to Darwin came in a lecture
on the gorilla at the Royal Institution. Having written three articles himself
for *Household Words*, Owen presented Dickens with a copy of his lecture
(Lohrli 393) and almost immediately saw an article based on it, "Our Nearest
Relation" (28 May 1859), appear in *All the Year Round*. The article stresses
the closeness of the relation but also its gaps, implicitly denying (as Owen
did explicitly in the lecture) the possibility of evolution from gorilla to human.
Yet only a year later, after the appearance of the *Origin*, two articles on
Darwin, "Species" (2 June 1860) and "Natural Selection" (7 July 1860),
are, as George Levine has noted, thorough and even-handed, their criticisms
balanced by a tendency to adopt, often without acknowledgment, Darwin's
own prose (128–29). And even the laudatory piece on "Owen's Museum"
(27 September 1862), a description of the Hunterian Museum at the Royal
College of Surgeons, which Owen oversaw, is infused with Darwinian language. Species are not fixed and separate, but part of a genealogy:

> I wondered at the links which make a rat the ancestor of an ape. . . . I saw by
> what beautiful gradations [bats] pass into the lemuridae; and the lemurs are
> degraded monkeys, or, perhaps, monkeys are selected lemurs. . . . [Apes] carica-
> ture humanity so closely, and make one shudder at the theory of "links." And
> yet, what if, in very truth, the grandfather of all life should be a polype [sic],
> and an ape the parent of humanity? (8: 66–67)

The narrator's playful language suggests both approval and criticism of Darwin, but even the possibility of approval is significant in an article about
Owen.

This scenario is evident in *Our Mutual Friend* as well, where the overt presence of Owen is problematized through the use of Darwinian language. And as in the case of uniformitarianism, the Boffin ruse undercuts the Darwinian vision of natural and social history that the rest of the novel has labored to construct.

Owen's name appears early in the novel, when Mrs. Podsnap, with her "quantity of bone," is said to be a "fine woman for Professor Owen" (52; bk. 1, ch. 2). Owen was famous for his ability to reconstruct the skeletons of extinct creatures from their fossils, so this cutting remark introduces the idea of articulation even before the entrance of Mr. Venus. This ability to articulate is a creative power which provides objects both useful and beautiful and which forms order from the disorder of the wasted or unwanted. The association of articulation and art suggests Dickens's role as the "articulator" of this narrative, both as the voice who tells the story and as the author who puts its fragmented monthly pieces together.[4] In Venus's case, though "surrounded by a muddle of objects . . . among which nothing is resolvable into anything distinct" (122; bk. 1, ch. 7), he is able to put together complete human skeletons. Out of his "miscellaneous" and "human warious" Mr. Venus creates skeletons used by surgeons' colleges and by art schools. "I've gone on improving myself in my knowledge of Anatomy," he tells Wegg, "till both by sight and by name I'm perfect. Mr. Wegg, if you was brought here loose in a bag to be articulated, I'd name your smallest bones blindfold equally with your largest, as fast as I could pick 'em out, and I'd sort 'em all, and sort your wertebræ, in a manner that would equally surprise and charm you" (128; bk. 1, ch. 7). This process of naming, sorting, and articulating is as much the task of author and reader as it is of Venus and Owen.

For Owen, the order of nature is not merely a physical order but a moral order: its various elements fit together in a manner that reveals the benevolence and wisdom of its designer. Monstrosities — those things that do not "fit" — are often moral as well as physical aberrations. They are items of curiosity. Their usually short lifespans and difficulty in breeding are evidence of the fixity of species. Extinct animals, though they appear monstrous to us, provide evidence of both fit and monstrosity: they reveal how the Creator once adapted them to the environment in which they were destined to live. When their purpose on the earth had been exhausted, when it was time for a new climate and new environment and new species, these animals were eliminated. For Darwin, on the other hand, monstrosities are the extreme form of the creative principle of variation, the vehicle of species change. Neither the individual appearance of a monstrosity nor the extinction of an entire species has anything to do with the will of a Creator but with the operation of natural selection in the struggle for existence. The moral element in Owen's position is absent in Darwin's, where survival and extinction are morally neutral.

Here again, we can see something to attract Dickens in both positions. Dickens is curious about the monstrous, and physical deformity is often a sign of moral deformity in his characters. More often, though, the determination of correlation between physical and moral monstrosity requires the kind of study that Owen gave to extinct creatures. In Dickens's world, a physically deformed character is truly monstrous only if there is moral monstrosity. Yet, on the other hand, monstrous characters are not simply curiosities for Dickens: they are often vital figures, whether of good or evil, who propel and disrupt the plot. If Owen's reconstructions are seen as reflecting the neoclassical moral concerns of order and typicality so characteristic of the previous century's natural theologians as well as its poets and critics, they are less interesting to Dickens than Venus's more radically romantic fitting together of miscellaneous and ostensibly anomalous parts, his conversion of the monstrous (like Wegg) into the useful and the beautiful in a world where moral order is at least highly problematic.[5]

Like any Dickens novel, *Our Mutual Friend* has its share of "monstrous" characters, but monstrosity is earmarked as being of particular significance in the novel's early exchange between Venus and Wegg. Asked by Wegg why he has not been able to work Wegg's leg into one of his skeletons, Venus answers that "I can't work you into a miscellaneous one, no how. Do what I will, you can't be got to fit. Anybody with a passable knowledge would pick you out at a look and say — 'No go! Don't match!' " (124; bk. 1, ch. 7). When Wegg offers to buy his leg back, however, Venus is reluctant: "you might turn out valuable yet . . . as a Monstrosity" (127; bk. 1, ch. 7). This sort of language permeates the initial descriptions of Jenny Wren (271; bk. 2, ch. 1) and Sloppy (246; bk. 1, ch. 16), and is even used of Mr. Boffin, "[t]he natural curiosity" in Mortimer's "professional museum" (471; bk. 2, ch. 16), declared at one point by Bella to be "a Monster!" (662; bk. 3, ch. 15).

What differentiates these "monsters" are their moral natures: Wegg is selfish and conniving, while Jenny is helpful and industrious. Charley Hexam likens his own rise up the social ladder to the evolution of primitive forms, telling Lizzie of his determination that "after I have climbed up out of the mire, you shall not pull me down" (461; bk. 2, ch. 15). Like his mentor, Bradley Headstone, Charley desires to suppress his "origin," perhaps because he is uneasily aware that there is "enough of what was animal . . . still visible in him" (267; bk. 2, ch. 1) to suggest that origin. The narrator makes clear that they have not progressed, that it is they, not Lizzie, who are overbearing and selfish. Social rise means little if it is accompanied by moral degradation. As Mr. Boffin, concealed behind the alligator in Venus's shop, listens to Wegg describe him as a tyrant and persecutor, the narrator remarks that the "yard or two of smile on the part of the alligator might have been invested with the meaning, 'All about this was quite familiar knowledge down in the depths of the slime, ages ago' " (647; bk. 3, ch. 14).

Such comments suggest the narrator's dissatisfaction with a Darwinian world where survival is often not equated with moral worth, but they also confirm the fact that the world of *Our Mutual Friend is* a Darwinian world. The narrator, like Owen, assumes that moral worth and real physical deformity are connected, only to find that nature does not dispense justice on the basis of these categories. And in fact, through most of the novel, evil is not punished and good not rewarded. The morally monstrous are just as well off as, or better off than, their virtuous counterparts, who are often victims and sufferers. This disjunction can only be corrected by the intervention of the novel's creator in the form of the Boffin ruse, which restores a sense of order by serving as the basis for the ultimate distribution of each character's appropriate legacy. The novel's final book abruptly swerves from the Darwinian vision of an amoral world which the first three books so faithfully depict, to embrace a world more in keeping with the views of Owen, where perfect justice, dispensed by an authorial hand, triumphs.

"The Most Difficult Part of My Design": Natural Theology

THE SUDDEN UNVEILING OF the novelist's designing hand attempts to claim the world of *Our Mutual Friend* for natural theology. Yet the earlier parts of the novel significantly circumscribe the validity of natural theology's account of a benevolently-ordered universe. Here again, the pattern can be compared to the movement of the periodical articles. Numerous references in *Household Words* to a "Great Architect" or a "Sublime Intelligence" or a "Mighty Designer" are part of natural theological arguments like that of "The History of a Coal Cell" (10 December 1853), in which the coal cycle is said to provide "an instance of the beautiful adaptation of the laws of nature to created beings; of the complete subservience to man of the great organic laws of the universe" (8: 355). In the 3 April 1858 article on "Infusoria," the author echoes the subtitle of the Bridgewater Treatises, the eight volumes on natural theology commissioned by the earl of Bridgewater and published in the 1830s, by declaring that "there appear to be no limits to the power, the wisdom, and the goodness, which the Great Creator of nature displays in regard to his creatures" (17: 375). Yet, as we have already seen, articles from *All the Year Round* in the early 1860s move away from such natural theological pronouncements and towards Darwinian explanations.

Christian language and imagery are typically invoked in *Our Mutual Friend* at moments of death or suffering, promising an escape from the pain of this decidedly un-benevolent world. Even in such moments of transcendence as the death of Betty Higden, however, the novel remains linked to the laws of a physical world suffused with suffering and pain, waste and decay. As Hillis Miller has noted, the resurrection and transformation that the novel continually associates with death is local and limited (316–17). The Bower cannot completely shake off the effects of its long years as Harmony Jail, for this fossilized house has "an air of being denuded to the bone," a state the narrator interprets in the language of natural theology: "Whatever is built by man for man's occupation, must, like natural creations, fulfil the intention of its existence, or soon perish" (231; bk. 1, ch. 15). All that is constructed, whether by human or divine hands — including novels — must serve an implicitly moral purpose. And yet the Boffins cannot halt or reverse the process of decay, which is, regardless of anyone's "intention," inevitable. Their "cleanliness" prevents "the dust into which they were all resolving" from lying thick on the floor, but it does not stop the unending decay itself (231–32; bk. 1, ch. 15).

The more obvious place to look for the influence of natural theology is in the relationship of teller and tale, for Dickens conceived of the novelist's role in terms remarkably similar to the natural theologian's conception of God. In a letter to Wilkie Collins defending the withholding of certain information in *A Tale of Two Cities*, Dickens wrote in 1859 that "I think the business of art is to lay all that ground carefully, not with the care that conceals itself — to show, by a backward light, what everything has been working to — but only to *suggest*, until the fulfillment comes. These are the ways of Providence, of which ways all art is but a little imitation" (*Letters* 3: 125). In the Postscript to *Our Mutual Friend*, Dickens uses similar language to defend himself from the charge that "I was at great pains to conceal exactly what I was at great pains to suggest: namely, that Mr. John Harmon was not slain, and that Mr. John Rokesmith was he" (893). He goes on, however, to admit (though without naming it) that he *was* at great pains to conceal the Boffin ruse: "To keep for a long time unsuspected, yet always working itself out, another purpose originating in that leading incident, and turning it to a pleasant and useful account at last, was at once the most interesting and the most difficult part of my design" (893). The novelist is a benevolent God whose ways are rational and ordered, and the reader is the natural theologian confident that mysteries will be solved and a hidden design revealed.

The character who shares this view is Rokesmith, the novel's natural theologian par excellence.[6] He believes in order and design, in his ability to create within his own world a clock-like regularity, and in the ultimate moral coherence of that world. When his first design to help Bella and the Boffins fails, he simply forms a new plan: he will keep his identity a secret until "the method" that he is establishing in their affairs will be "a machine in such working order as that they can keep it going" (430; bk. 2, ch. 13). Rokesmith's "method" is to play the God of natural theologians, using his wisdom and beneficence to create a machine-like system that even the unworldly Boffins can maintain with a minimum of effort. His belief in moral order is such that when he finds himself wandering in circles after departing from Pleasant's Leaving Shop, he says that "[t]his is like what I have read in narratives of escape from prison, . . . where the little track of the fugitives in the night always seems to take the shape of the great round world, on which they wander; as if it were a secret law" (422; bk. 2, ch. 13). In Rokesmith's experience, narratives provide evidence that the world is subject to a secret law of justice that eventually prevails. It is not surprising that the narrative in which he resides, and which he to a significant degree controls, is resolved by that same secret law.

But Rokesmith's comment is also disquieting, for it associates his own wanderings with those of fugitives. Troubled by the consequences of his feigned death, he tries to mitigate his responsibility for them by arguing that he "wandered" into his plan with good intentions. He says that he has "lapsed" into his present condition, that his "first deception" was to be "harmless," but that "the snare into which he fell so outstripped his first intention" (436; bk. 2, ch. 14). However, he merely replaces his first secretive design with a second, equally secretive one. Rokesmith's justification of this plotting, especially in its connections to notions of reading and story-telling, is as quietly disquieting as Eugene's tormenting of Bradley by leading him at night through London. Eugene is of course merely countering Bradley's plot for keeping him away from Lizzie, but there are disturbing implications for the reader not only in the joy Eugene takes in toying with Bradley, but in the way that Eugene's design involves leading the schoolmaster into "abstruse No Thoroughfares" (606; bk. 3, ch. 10) to no purpose. The writing in this brief scene is Dickens at his comic best, yet there is a part of us, even as we laugh, that shares Mortimer's discomfort with this "extraordinary story." It is at such moments, in a novel in which we know "mutuality" is so important and yet so tenuous, where to be someone's mutual friend may very well mean not to be their friend at all, that we are most aware of the vulnerability inherent to being part of someone else's plot or design (see Jaffe).

And the fact remains that Rokesmith, like Dickens, is the possessor of the novel's secrets, some of which he chooses to tell and some to withhold. In his deception of Bella, the emphasis is always on the ends rather than the means: the goal of rescuing Bella from her mercenary motives is seen by everyone (including Bella, when the plot is disclosed) as justification for whatever deception has occurred. This is, however, deliberate on Dickens's part, for the good intentions behind the deception of Bella parallel Dickens's good intentions behind using the Boffin ruse, which he says he merely wants to turn to a "pleasant and useful account" for his readers. Indeed, what I have called "the Boffin ruse," Dickens calls in his working notes "the pious fraud," stressing that the change in Mr. Boffin is to be broken to the reader through Bella (Cotsell 195, 236). That Dickens was willing to use this "pious fraud" on his readers, apparently with great pleasure and with little concern for the relationship of author-reader trust he expects from his readers in the Postscript, is evident in a triple underlined note that he should "Make the most of Bella" (Cotsell 236). The deceptive practices of Dickens and Rokesmith go beyond that of a designing Providence and become disturbingly secretive, arbitrary, and inaccessible. Rather than participating in the process of discovery, we are deliberately excluded, unable to discern the designer's intent in his creation until he reveals it to us. We are at the mercy of "the care that conceals itself."

"A Mine of Purpose and Energy": Thermodynamics

THE REFERENCES TO THERMODYNAMICS in the periodicals follow closely the concerns of the physicists who were popularizing these ideas in the 1850s and 60s. In *All the Year Round* these references are especially prevalent and direct, mirroring the increased public interest spurred by Tyndall's books and lectures and by Thomson's attacks on Darwin and Lyell over the age of the earth. Between May of 1864 and November of 1865, the period when *Our Mutual Friend* appeared, five *All the Year Round* articles are devoted in whole or part to thermodynamics, while two others touch on it. Two related articles appear during the fifteen months preceding the first number of *Our Mutual Friend*, and two others appear within a year of the last number. These thermodynamic articles in *All the Year Round* continue to emphasize the conservation of energy and correlation of forces, but they also begin to explore some of the consequences of the second law.

Household Words articles consistently link the first law with social concerns to create a series of optimistic moral narratives. The "story" and "history" of coal provides a perfect example, for it connects the vegetable cycle — where plants grow, die, and then decay to provide the nutriments out of which new plants can grow — to the conservation of energy. Metz's view that the universe of *Household Words* is characterized by perpetual metamorphosis is clearly true in "The True Story of a Coal Fire" (6 April 1850), where "the bodies of all living things, whether animal or vegetable, fulfil their destinies by undergoing a gradual transformation into other bodies and things of the most opposite kind to their own original being" (1: 28). Human beings are included in this process, for "man lives to-day, not only for himself and those around him, but also that by his death and decay fresh grass may grow in the fields of future years" (1: 28). "Death and decay" are thus placed in a cycle of continual regeneration which gives them meaning. The Biblical dictum of "ashes to ashes, dust to dust" has scientific validity, but science offers its own analogue to the prospect of resurrection in the capacity of the ashes and dust to be again transformed into life. Conservation and correlation, whether applied to the combustion of coal, candles, or food, is what characterizes the natural world.

The most direct enunciation of the correlation of forces and the first law in *Household Words*, however, occurs in "Physical Force" (12 March 1859). The article opens with a passage stressing the constant motion and metamorphosis in nature, the association of "cessation of action" with death — the universe, like "a living creature," would come to an end if this continual motion were ever to come to an end (19: 354). While it is easy to imagine a "dead universe" in which matter is "impassive and still," in which there is "no change, no mutual affinities, no gravitation of one body towards another, ... no mtion forwards or in retreat, no revolutions on axes or in orbits, no radiation of electricity or of whatever constitutes light and heat," the difference between such a world and our own "adorable universe" is "caused by the presence of ... PHYSICAL FORCES" (19: 354). But these physical forces are "really and ultimately one; or, if not one, at least sprung from one source, ... they certainly are correlative ... ; [and] though neither of them, taken abstractedly, can be said to be the essential cause of the others, yet ... either of them may produce, or be converted into, any of the others" (19: 354). The article then goes on to link this correlation of forces to the first law through examples of the "fixed and definite proportions" involved in conversions of one force into another, especially that of heat into motion (19: 357). Predictably, the article notes that first law calculations have "taught us that we burn twenty times too much coal in the furnaces of our present steam-engines, and that we must invent others on a new plan" (19: 358). The second law, however, is nowhere mentioned. The great lesson to be drawn from the "one-birth of all physical or natural forces" (19: 355) is that this "principle of unity" (19: 354) in nature parallels and vindicates the existence of "one Jehovah, the Lord of all" (19: 355).

Such moral application of thermodynamic principles is evident as early as "The True Story of a Coal Fire." In this tale a young man named Flashley is conducted by an Elfin Spirit through the history of coal. Flashley has lived a life of indolence in London, so his father sends him to a family-owned coal mine with the hope of separating him from the friends and pursuits which "dissipate his time" and prevent him from settling into a career (1: 26). Before his tour with the Spirit, Flashley is predictably hostile to the application of thermodynamic principles of dissipation and work to his own situation. He says that

> human time should not be passed in digging and groping, and diving and searching — whether to scrape up coals, or what folks call 'knowledge.' For the fuel of life burns out soon enough of itself, and, therefore, it should not be

wasted over the baser material; for the former is for one's self, while coal-fuel, and the search after it, is just working for other people. (1: 28)

By tour's end, however, Flashley abandons this carpe diem attitude in favor of the value of work, even work for others, the production of useful things with a minimum amount of waste and "dissipation."[7]

In a similar fashion, the numerous articles on dust and sewage and the recycling of waste products become manifestos for the everyday application of thermodynamic laws. They decry the way society wastes its resources and applaud those who put that waste to use. The early confidence in the unlimited store of coal gives way by 1860 to an *All the Year Round* article entitled "How Long Will Our Coal Last?" (2: 488), which admits that the formation of new coal is too slow to replace that being removed and therefore that we are "responsible morally to those who may come after us for the proper use of it. We have no right to waste or destroy it, nor in any way to interfere with the value of what we do not immediately require." Since dust and soot and smoke are all evidence of incomplete combustion, reusing that unspent fuel, or developing more efficient ways to burn it in the first place, become vital aspects both of controlling pollution and of maintaining the energy supplies so essential to Britain's wealth.

Thermodynamic predictions of eventual cosmic collapse through the cooling of earth and sun are also handled in numerous articles as they were handled by their scientific popularizers: acknowledged but then minimized. In "Small-Beer Chronicles" (14 February 1863), the author notes:

> Another rather startling theory has lately been put forward — the earth, it seems, is growing cold. We are told that its internal heat . . . is losing its intensity. Gracious Heaven! What if the globe, like everything upon it, should be mortal! What if it has only an allotted span of life, and is getting past its prime! Suppose, century after century, it should get colder and colder, and weaker and yet more weak. Suppose its inhabitants should do the same, their passions gradually dying out, the race declining first in energy and ultimately in numbers, until at last there is an end of it all; the people extinct, the world dead, but still lingering in the firmament, the pale spectre of its former self — like the moon, which surely looks . . . like the ghost of a dead world, depopulated, and icy cold. (8: 543–44)

The tone of the passage suggests considerable skepticism not of the earth's cooling but of the specific deductions that are impossible to verify and therefore not worth getting overly upset about. The author prefers to offer his own optimistic possibility by drawing an analogy between the earth and the human body, arguing that perhaps the earth contains heat without fire. The article ends on a positive note, with a reminder from Grove's work on the correlation of forces: "there is NOTHING STILL IN THE WORLD. . . . Life and movement everywhere. Everywhere progression" (8: 544).

According to the nebular hypothesis, however, the moon *is* "the icy ghost of a dead world," for the sun, earth, and moon provide evidence of the successive stages in the life of a nebula. "Respecting the Sun" (22 April 1865) sketches this narrative in detail: our sun, once a nebula, has cooled to what is now a long and comparatively stable phase, but subsequent cooling will eventually cause it to solidify and form a crust. The earth and the moon are examples of the later stages of this process. In this nebular narrative, invariably embraced in some form by thermodynamicists, the sun has a finite supply of energy and hence a finite lifetime; some day, if the earth has not already cooled into "a pale spectre of its former self," the crusting over of the sun will leave the earth without light and heat — and life. But if the earth's "future" is represented by the moon, the article consoles us with the fact that that future is "still far distant" and reminds us that this series of "successive transformations" is part of "the eternal harmony of the universe" (13: 299–300).

"Earth" (24 December 1864) also discusses the cooling of both earth and sun, and like earlier articles it turns back to the path of the first law, embracing Grove's dictum of constant movement and transformation, renovation for every dissolution. This cyclical process is connected to human life and divine dispensation in a passage that must echo through our minds when reading *Our Mutual Friend*:

> "Earth to earth, ashes to ashes, dust to dust," the impressive formula of our Burial Service, is a succinct account both of what we are, and of what earth is. . . .
> Earth is ashes, if ashes be the residue of combustion. Every handful of earth on Earth, has been burnt. Besides passing through the great primeval fire, some of it has been burnt over and over again — in the natural fires existing in warm-blooded animals; in the artificial fires kindled for their various uses by the human race. . . .
> Earth is dust. . . . Whether in the shape of impalpable clays and marls, or made up of sand, coarse gravel, and shingle; whether as leaf-mould, mud, or animal remains, we may fairly say that earth is dust. It is a complex mixture of pulverized materials, . . . elaborately and benevolently combined for the support and sustenance of plants, and through them of animals. (12: 471–72)

These articles on the earth and the sun prepare the way for two articles summarizing Tyndall's book on thermodynamics, *Heat: A Mode of Motion*. "Is Heat Motion?" on 1 July 1865 and "Heat and Work" on 5 August 1865 cover the same ground we have already discussed: correlation of forces, respiration as combustion and the physiological application of the conversation law, the sun as the ultimate source of all energy, the transformation but not the creation or destruction of energy. Tyndall's book, which the author of the articles calls "more entertaining than a novel" (13: 534), emphasizes first-law concerns to the exclusion of direct second-law concerns about dissipation: the "grand point" of Tyndall's lectures is said to be "that *nothing new is created*" (14: 33). Suffusing this account are metaphors that link thermodynamics to social and moral concerns. In "Heat and Work," plants are said to be "the economisers," animals "the spendthrifts," of "vital energy derived from the sun" (14: 32). And "the human will" does not have the power "to create strength, energy, and endurance" because, "[p]hysically considered, the law that rules the operation of the steam-engine" applies equally to the "conduct of different individuals, . . . whether moral or physical" (14: 32). Human will cannot, therefore, create energy, but it can (and must) "*apply* and *direct*" the energy already extant (14: 32). And we should not be concerned about the death of the sun, that "great worker who keeps the whole business of life and action going" (14: 30). The sun is, "[m]easured by human standards, . . . an inexhaustible source of physical energy" (14: 32), and there are possible mechanisms for replenishing that energy. Even though the earth is cooling, and even though it radiates away most of the heat it receives from the sun, the light of the sun is "an incessant compensation" (14: 32).

Such thermodynamic language permeates *Our Mutual Friend* almost from the outset.[8] As Mortimer and Eugene go to identify the drowned body of the Man from Somewhere in the first number, the following exchange takes place:

> "Then idiots talk," said Eugene, leaning back, folding his arms, smoking with his eyes shut, and speaking slightly through his nose, "of Energy. If there is a word in the dictionary under any letter from A to Z that I abominate, it is energy. It is such a conventional superstition, such parrot gabble! What the deuce! Am I to rush out into the street, collar the first man of a wealthy appearance that I meet, shake him, and say, 'Go to law upon the spot, you dog, and retain me, or I'll be the death of you'? Yet that would be energy."
>
> "Precisely my view of the case, Eugene. But show me a good opportunity, show me something really worth being energetic about, and I'll show you energy."
>
> "And so will I," said Eugene.
>
> And it is likely enough that ten thousand other young men, within the limits of the London Post-office town delivery, made the same hopeful remark in the course of the same evening. (61–62; bk. 1, ch. 3)

Coupled with the narrator's satiric comment, this conversation introduces what could be called the novel's concern with the morality of energy consumption. Like the language of the articles on Tyndall's lectures, the language of this conversation is simultaneously thermodynamic, economic, and moral. At issue is, as Eugene suggests, not just *whether* one will work, will use energy, but *how* one will work. While Eugene is correct in saying that his example represents a perversion of energy use that would in fact be a waste of energy, the narrator implies that the example is improperly conceived — there are other, better ways to obtain clients — and that it has become an excuse for not doing anything at all. In the world of *Our Mutual Friend*, both extremes, working frenetically but inefficiently or not working at all, are equally unacceptable.

How one consumes energy and applies one's will is crucial because, as in *Bleak House* and *Little Dorrit*, the world shows signs of decay and disorder, manifestations of the second law. London is a "hopeless" (191; bk. 1, ch. 12) city of litter and dust, the center of a world whose sun is dying. On foggy days, the sun, "when it was for a few moments dimly indicated through circling eddies of fog, showed as if it had gone out and were collapsing flat and cold" (479; bk. 3, ch. 1). On a "grey dusty withered evening" in autumn,

> [t]he closed warehouses and offices have an air of death about them, and the national dread of colour has an air of mourning. The towers and steeples of the many house-encompassed churches, dark and dingy as the sky that seems descending on them, are no relief to the general gloom; a sun-dial on a church-wall has the look, in its useless black shade, of having failed in its business enterprise and stopped payment for ever . . . (450; bk. 2, ch. 15)

For a sun-dial to have "failed in its business enterprise" suggests the connection between the death of the sun, the ultimate source of all the world's energy, and the inability to do work. Dickens's metaphor links the sun's fate with the meaning of work in both its thermodynamic and everyday senses, and thus the "air of death" and disorder extends to all places of business and activity, from the decay and rot of the riverfront's wilderness of warehouses and wharves to the legal dust of Clifford's Inn and the Temple. Nor are schools immune. Charley Hexam's is "crowded, noisy, and confusing," an "exceedingly and confoundingly perplexing jumble of a school . . . where black spirits and grey, red spirits and white, jumbled jumbled jumbled jumbled, jumbled every night" (263–64; bk. 2, ch. 1). Bradley's school, though run on a strict system, is threatened by the jumble which lies just beyond its doors:

> a neighbourhood which looked like a toy neighbourhood taken in blocks out of a box by a child of particularly incoherent mind, and set up anyhow; here, one side of a new street; there, a large solitary public-house facing nowhere; here, another unfinished street already in ruins; there, a church; here, an immense new warehouse; there, a dilapidated old country villa; then, a medley of black ditch, sparkling cucumber-frame, rank field, richly cultivated kitchen-garden, brick viaduct, arch-spanned canal, and disorder of frowziness and fog. As if the child had given the table a kick, and gone to sleep. (268; bk. 2, ch. 1)

The structure of this last description reflects the structure, or lack of structure, of what is being described. In a world that is wearing out, decaying, and dissipating, objects are simply juxtaposed in a manner that is "particularly incoherent." Description of such a world involves the linguistic replication of this messy set of juxtapositions: disparate objects are yoked by semicolons, but the "here-there" pattern is not pattern but chaos, for we have no meaningful spatial sense of where "here" and "there" are. We cannot envision a specific scene with the various objects in specific locations relative to each other because the urbanscape being depicted is itself a jumble. Lists, from Young Blight's roster of Mortimer's fictitious clients and callers (131; bk. 1, ch. 8) to Mr Venus's enumeration of the contents of his shop (126; bk. 1, ch. 7), become the only means for providing any linguistic order at all (see Knoepflmacher 147).

Even newness does not provide protection against disorder: in the neighborhood of Bradley's school is "an unfinished street already in ruins." Restoration and repair cannot keep up with decay. This is the case, comically, for Mr. Wilfer, who cannot afford to buy a new suit of clothes at one time and thus always wears something that is "worn out" or "an ancient ruin" (75; bk. 1, ch. 4). That clothes wear to rags would be of no surprise to Mortimer, who tells Mr. Boffin that in this world "everything wears to rags" (136; bk. 1, ch. 8). And this general law extends to human beings, for Mr. Dolls, in his final convulsions, is "rendered a harmless bundle of torn rags" (800; bk. 4, ch. 9).

Eugene and Mortimer take the attitude that if "everything wears to rags" there is little point in trying to prevent or delay the inevitable. Although they are witty and charming, their refusal to work at anything useful is an abrogation of their responsibility to society. Worse, the two men seem to revel in their indolence, thoroughly enjoying the pose that work is something for which they are constitutionally unfit. Eugene claims that his "weariness" is "chronic" (133; bk. 1, ch. 8), and Mortimer tells Lady Tippins that he has "exhausted myself for life" (470; bk. 2, ch. 16). Except for Mr. Boffin's case, Mortimer acknowledges that he has had "no scrap of business" in five years, whereas Eugene says that in seven years he has "had no business at all, and never shall have any. And if I had, I shouldn't know how to do it" (61–62; bk. 1, ch. 3). When Eugene admits to Mr. Boffin that he does not particularly care for the law, Mr. Boffin remarks that "I suppose it wants some years of sticking to, before you master it. But there's nothing like work. Look at the bees" (138; bk. 1, ch. 8). Mr. Boffin offers the traditional image of work from the natural world rather than the mechanical images that dominate the novel, but Eugene, in rejecting the industrious bees as a model, translates Mr. Boffin's image into more thermodynamic terms: " 'Ye-es,' returned Eugene, disparagingly, 'they work; but don't you think they overdo it? They work so much more than they need — they make so much more than they can eat — they are so incessantly boring and buzzing at their one

idea till Death comes upon them — that don't you think they overdo it?' ''
(139; bk. 1, ch. 8).

This attitude of Eugene and Mortimer is a manifestation of "dissipation"
in the sense of "wasteful expenditure." Because they do no work, choosing
instead to devote themselves to the search for pleasure and diversion, they
live a "dissipated" life. Thomson's use of the term incorporates this idea
of wastefulness, but his primary emphasis is on dissipation in the sense of
"dispersion" or "diffusion": the heat produced by the dissipation of mechanical energy disperses throughout the universe until it is evenly distributed.
When we speak of the second law as an expression of the universe's tendency
towards maximum randomness and disorder, we obscure somewhat this result.
Randomness and disorder are at a maximum when the heat is completely
diffused, but this state of maximum entropy (to use the modern term) is in
effect a proliferation of sameness. In such a state, taken as a whole, temperature is constant, and thus there is no motion. This is the state that the second
law predicts for the universe: uniform temperature brings everything, literally,
to a standstill. Thus dissipation is the break-up or decay of that which is
ordered into a homogeneous mass.

The "disorder" that exists in the neighborhood around Bradley's school
is thus a stepping-stone to a more frightening situation — the cessation of
motion. The school that seems to be an island of order in the midst of chaos
is in fact not a refuge at all: the buildings and teachers and pupils are "all
according to pattern and all engendered in the light of the latest Gospel
according to Monotony" (268; bk. 2, ch. 1). The "jumble of a school" is so
jumbled that all its elements have been thrown together into a uniform mass
and cannot be differentiated. Evidence of such a state, so threatening to the
first-law universe portrayed both in the periodical articles and throughout
Dickens's novels, is present elsewhere as well, from the "Gospel of Monotony" that Bella sees in Rokesmith during Mr. Boffin's tyranny (535; bk. 3,
ch. 5) to Eugene's delirious repetition of Lizzie's name (809; bk. 4, ch. 10).
So oppressive is this proliferation of sameness that Eugene suggests that a
form of limited monotony is more bearable and perhaps the best that one can
hope for. When he says to Mortimer that he wishes they were keeping a
lighthouse and Mortimer replies that "there might be a degree of sameness
in the life," Eugene nonetheless contends that such a "defined and limited
monotony" might be "more endurable than the unlimited monotony of one's
fellow-creatures" (192; bk. 1, ch. 12).

Faced with the implications of the second law, Helmholtz urged that we
cannot despair, that we must work selflessly and productively for the good
of others. Dickens adopts the same position. Good workers are those who
work efficiently, who convert a high percentage of their energy into a useful
finished product. They create order out of chaos, often using other people's

waste products as raw material. Characters in *Our Mutual Friend* can thus be differentiated morally by how they use energy.

Jenny Wren, the novel's greatest recycler, obtains Pubsey and Co.'s "damage and waste" (333; bk. 2, ch. 5) for her dolls' clothes and then from her own scraps makes pincushions and pen-wipers "to use up my waste" (272; bk. 2, ch. 1). When she leaves her home, she conserves the precious fuel that recent *All the Year Round* articles had shown to be of large but limited supply, carefully banking her fire "that it might last the longer and waste the less when she was out" (492; bk. 3, ch. 2). Despite their poverty, Jenny and Lizzie maintain a house that is "orderly and clean"(283; bk. 2, ch. 2). Rokesmith is so industrious in his role as the Boffins' secretary that like a machine he does the work of many hands: "He takes more care of my affairs, morning, noon, and night," says Mr Boffin, "than fifty other men put together either could or would" (362; bk. 2, ch. 8). The Boffins themselves are models of order and efficiency and good work in their own unselfconscious and unmechanical way. Mr. Boffin marvels at "[w]hat a thinking steam-ingein" his wife is when she comes up with ideas like the adoptions of Bella and Sloppy, but these ideas are less the result of a mechanical process than the spontaneous expression of Mrs. Boffin's goodness (145; bk. 1, ch. 9; 388; bk. 2, ch. 10). They invariably conceive of their "work" as the good they can do for others, as when they accept the responsibility of helping Sloppy, who is already a mender of broken things, to "an industrious and useful place in life," of making "a man and a workman" of him "in as short a time as ever a man and workman was made yet" (444, 449; bk. 2, ch. 14).

Among the waterside characters, the two great orderers are the police inspector and Abbey Potterson, who work to maintain order and discipline in their respective domains near the otherwise chaotic "wilderness" of the waterfront. The "orderly appearance" of the Police Station is "very unlike that of the surrounding neighbourhood" (833; bk. 4, ch. 12), and the Six Jolly Fellowship Porters, despite its "dropsical appearance," "had outlasted, and clearly would yet outlast, many a better-trimmed building" (104; bk. 1, ch. 6), thanks largely to the work of Miss Abbey. "It has been hard work to establish order here," she tells Lizzie, " . . . and it is daily and nightly hard work to keep it so" (113; bk. 1, ch. 6). The only way to stave off the effects of the second law is by imposing a law of moral discipline and hard work, and Abbey takes this into account even for the future of her establishment. She wants her brother to take over the Porters, warning that otherwise "The House will go to pieces" (835; bk. 4, ch. 12).

My emphasis on the novel's good workers aims to counteract the critical overstatement that Dickens's purpose in *Our Mutual Friend* is to demonstrate that money is filth and hence that Victorian society has been erected on a heap of dung and dust. Although aware of the ease with which money can and does corrupt, Dickens also depicts the ability of work and wealth to produce positive change. So long as money and power are not the ultimate objectives, so long as the efficient expenditure of energy is seen as a moral responsibility towards society in general and certain individuals in particular, work, and the wealth that can be acquired from it, is a constructive social force. Distortions of this concept — miserly hoarding of money, unwillingness to work, abuse of power — are what threaten to rend the social fabric.

Some of the novel's figures of purest evil are therefore those whose "work" is extortion, an effort to minimize physical exertion and maximize profit by exploiting others rather than producing a useful good or service. Riderhood speaks constantly of "the sweat of an honest man's brow," but his sources of income include the collection of rewards for false accusations and the extortions of Bradley and Betty Higden. Like Riderhood, Wegg speaks of "elevating myself by my own independent exertions" (127; bk. 1., ch. 7), but these "exertions" consist of the extortion of Mr. Boffin's property. For Fledgeby, who buys up bills of credit "at waste-paper price" (483; bk. 3, ch. 1) and takes as much pleasure in bankrupting his debtors as he does in receiving their payments, "every bargain . . . representing somebody's ruin or somebody's loss, acquired a peculiar charm" (324; bk. 2, ch. 5).

This perversion of the idea of work is, in Dickens's view, dangerously systemic, for it pervades a variety of social institutions. The economic system as a whole is characterized by the "grinding" of its "money-mills" (667; bk. 3, ch. 16), which is not a slow and steady but a feverish and uncontrolled process. This frenetic grinding contributes to the city's accumulating dust, and it generates an enormous amount of friction that can set all that combustible material on fire. It is exhausting and wasteful of both energy and human lives. As Fledgeby tells Lammle, Pubsey and Co. are "[r]egular flayers and grinders" who will "skin you by the inch, from the nape of your neck to the sole of your foot, and grind every inch of your skin" (486; bk. 3, ch. 1). According to the narrator, Fledgeby's "youthful fire" is itself "composed of sparks from the grindstone" that "flew off, went out, and never warmed anything" (321; bk. 2, ch. 5). Wegg is similarly determined to bring Mr. Boffin's nose "to the grindstone" (646; bk. 3, ch. 14). Those who participate in this flaying and grinding and whirling are always in danger of "smashing," "going to pieces" (619; bk. 3, ch. 12; 684; bk. 3, ch. 17; 869; bk. 4, ch. 15; 886; bk. 4, ch. 17), or "bursting up" — an expression, as Fledgeby explains, "which is adopted in the Money Market" (626; bk. 3, ch. 12).

The supposedly respectable Money Market is also a place where, despite the feverish activity, there is little useful work. The difference between Lammle and Fledgeby —"outlaws" living "in the merry greenwood of Jobbery Forest, lying on the outskirts of the Share-Market and Stock Exchange" (324; bk. 2, ch. 5) — and the members of "Society" is, both morally and economically, very slight. Those who make their money in the Share-Market and Stock Exchange are seen as speculators who do no real work, whose wealth is created on paper and consists not of long-term investing but of short-term buying and selling for quick profits: "As is well known to the wise in their generation," the narrator satirically remarks,

> traffic in Shares is the one thing to have to do with in this world. . . . Where does he come from? Shares. Where is he going to? Shares. What are his tastes? Shares. Has he any principles? Shares. What squeezes him into Parliament? Shares. Perhaps he never of himself achieved success in anything, never originated anything, never produced anything? Sufficient answer to all; Shares. (159–60; bk. 1, ch. 10)

The greatest perversion of work of all is of course the inaptly named workhouse, the creation of a Parliament which itself epitomizes the national obsession with wasteful expenditure of energy. Referred to in *Hard Times* as "the national dust-yard" (222; bk. 2, ch. 9), Parliament is the source of the institutional dust that in *Our Mutual Friend* connects the effects of the Poor Law with the Harmon mounds:

> My lords and gentlemen and honourable boards, when you in the course of your dust-shovelling and cinder-raking have piled up a mountain of pretentious failure, you must off with your honourable coats for the removal of it, and fall to the work with the power of all the queen's horses and all the queen's men, or it will come rushing down and bury us alive. (565; bk. 3, ch. 8)

Yet the prospect for such reform is not encouraging. The chapter describing Veneering's election to Parliament is entitled "A Piece of Work," but the successful result is due not to work but to money. So long as Veneering puts down his five thousand pounds, the borough of Pocket-Breaches is his. The "work" involved amounts to sitting in clubs, driving about town, and talking to friends. Such frenzied and useless activity is the very soul of Parliamentary work in general, in which "nothing is understood to be so effectual as scouring nowhere in a violent hurry — in short, as taking cabs and going about" (301; bk. 2, ch. 3).

So widespread is this distortion of work, energy, and efficiency that even the first law can be interpreted by "Society" in a disturbingly immoral way. According to the narrator, when the Veneerings' friend the Contractor is asked his opinion of the propriety of Eugene marrying Lizzie,

> It appears to this potentate, that what the man in question should have done, would have been, to buy the young woman a boat and a small annuity, and set her up for herself. These things are a question of beefsteaks and porter. You buy the young woman a boat. Very good. You buy her, at the same time, a

small annuity. You speak of that annuity in pounds sterling, but it is in reality so many pounds of beefsteaks and so many pints of porter. On the one hand, the young woman has the boat. On the other hand, she consumes so many pounds of beefsteaks and so many pints of porter. Those beefsteaks and that porter are the fuel to that young woman's engine. She derives therefrom a certain amount of power to row the boat; that power will produce so much money; you add that to the small annuity; and thus you get at the young woman's income. (890; bk. 4, ch. 17)

This statement reproduces the notion so common in the periodical articles that the body is like an engine, using the food that is its fuel to perform work. Thermodynamicists typically used the analogy of the human "engine" as a heuristic device for demonstrating the superior efficiency of the body in comparison to mechanical engines, but the Contractor effaces the human entirely. His comparison reduces the unnamed Lizzie to a machine that converts beefsteaks and porter into work and then into money. Coming near the end of this long novel, it is an absurdly distant and abstract response to a narrative of such moral complexity and immediacy as the story of Lizzie and Eugene.

The Fiction of Order

DESPITE THE NOVEL'S BLEAK picture of a world in which dissipation can lead to stasis and death, Eugene, Mortimer, and Bella exhibit the possibility of rejecting indolence on the one hand and mercenary motives on the other, of embracing a life as a useful and efficient worker in the service of others. As Nancy Metz puts it, "*Our Mutual Friend* is about the relationship between work and the realization of self, about the necessity to be 'useful' before one can be 'happy' " ("Artistic Reclamation" 59). Thus when Eugene takes an interest in improving Lizzie's education, he evinces for the first time a concern for others, a desire to put some of his money to work on a useful scheme: "I propose to be of use to somebody — which I never was in this world" (286; bk. 2, ch. 2). Later, sitting by Eugene's sick bed, Lizzie predicts that "my husband has a mine of purpose and energy, and will turn it to the best account" (825; bk. 4, ch. 11), while Eugene looks back on "such a trifling wasted youth as mine" (825; bk. 4, ch. 11) and vows to "turn to in earnest" (885; bk. 4, ch. 16). The prospect that Eugene will prove himself a "mine of energy" is enhanced by Mortimer's example: in language that recalls Jenny Wren's occupation, Mortimer is said to have "laid about him professionally with such unwonted despatch and intention, that a piece of work was vigorously pursued as soon as cut out" (875; bk. 4, ch. 16). Bella's conversion follows a similar pattern: after developing a sense of her own uselessness, she abandons her mercenary goals, marries Rokesmith, and transforms herself into a model of domestic efficiency. Once married, Bella turns their little cottage into the same kind of orderly system that her husband had previously made of Mr. Boffin's papers. She makes "amazing progress in her domestic efficiency" and tells her mother and sister that "we are economical and orderly, and do everything by clockwork" (746, 750; bk. 4, ch. 5).

These transformations help to reestablish a first-law world where motion is constant and reversible, where individuals can achieve some success against the forces of social dissipation and decay. Like the physicists of his day, Dickens is willing to depict the implications of the second law in vivid terms, but he also shares with them the view that the second law reinforces the moral necessity of working efficiently for the betterment of one's fellow creatures. If Dickens's fiction ultimately retreats from endorsing the inevitability of second law predictions, implying instead that the first law is the overriding thermodynamic truth, he again has the model of men like Thomson and Tyndall and Helmholtz.

Perhaps more than *Bleak House* and *Little Dorrit*, however, *Our Mutual Friend* calls attention to the tenuous nature of its closing order by suggesting that this order, this rejection of the second law in favor of the first, is a fiction. Indeed, fiction may be the only escape available to us as inhabitants of a world whose sun is slowly dying, a world where dissipation and disorder will ultimately prevail over forces of centralization and order. Young Blight, for example, maintains his "strict system" because "his mind would have been shattered to pieces without this fiction of an occupation" (131; bk. 1, ch. 8). Without any work to do, without any human contact, Young Blight can only give meaning to his meaningless existence by creating a system that is solely the product of his own imagination.[9] The rags into which everything tends are ultimately converted by the mill where Lizzie works into paper, that article on which novels are written. What, then, about the system and order created out of Dickens's imagination?

It is difficult first of all not to speculate on the points of contact between the laws of thermodynamics and Dickens's own "work." He found *Our Mutual Friend* enormously difficult to write; it drained him physically, mentally, and artistically. Deaths of friends, as well as intimations of his own mortality, pressed upon him. The letters of this period speak urgently about "work," "industry," "break down," being "overworked," and the fear that he may have "quite lost the power" (*Letters* 3: 394, 422, 432, 438, 459–60, 404; Angus Collins). Then of course there was the horrible railway accident in which Dickens was involved just a few months before the completion of the novel. Alluding to this in his Postscript, Dickens blurs the lines between his own life and the fictional lives of his characters:

> On Friday the Ninth of June in the present year, Mr. and Mrs. Boffin (in their manuscript dress of receiving Mr. and Mrs. Lammle at breakfast) were on the

South Eastern Railway with me, in a terribly destructive accident. When I had done what I could to help others, I climbed back into my carriage — nearly turned over a viaduct, and caught aslant upon the turn — to extricate the worthy couple. They were much soiled, but otherwise unhurt. (894)

The horrors of the accident (vividly described in *Letters* 3: 423–29) are partially transformed into a comedy with a happy ending, the Boffins rescued like the other passengers, "soiled, but . . . unhurt." But the horrors are only partially deferred, for Dickens closes the Postscript thus: "I remember with devout thankfulness that I can never be much nearer parting company with my readers for ever, than I was then, until there shall be written against my life, the two words with which I have this day closed this book: — THE END" (894). Endings, whether of novels, of life, or of the world, are for Dickens enormously disquieting, but especially so when, like the dissipation of the universe, they cannot be predicted precisely or they come unexpectedly, catching us unawares and unprepared. But if novels and lives must end, Dickens minimizes the effects of such closure by returning us at the end of this novel to a first-law vision that reasserts the primacy of transformation rather than dissipation. In the rescue of the Boffins is a denial of decline in Dickens's own physical and artistic health, for the story — and when it is complete, the next one — can go on.

J. Hillis Miller says that *Our Mutual Friend* "reminds us constantly of its fictitious character," that "all of the characters and all of the scenes are permeated by this overtly fictive quality, reminding us constantly of the presence of the consciousness of Dickens creating the reality of his novel out of the insubstantial stuff of words'" (304, 306). Mortimer's comments about his narration of the story of the Man from Somewhere, for example, can invariably be applied to the improbable coincidences and intricate structure of Dickens's narration as well. When news of John Harmon's drowning arrives at the Veneering dinner party, Mortimer remarks that "[t]his arrives in an extraordinarily opportune manner," as what seemed to Mortimer a rather boring tale is suddenly rendered "completer and rather more exciting than I supposed" (59; bk. 1, ch. 2). Characters also attempt to pass off as chance or coincidence what they know to be part of a design or plan. When Mrs. Lammle tells Georgiana that there is a man who loves her, for example, Mr. Lammle walks in and announces the same thing. This, says Lammle, "shows the accidental combinations that there are in things!" (310; bk. 2, ch. 4), but it is of course no accident at all, but part of their scheme.

The winks exchanged by the Lammles invite us to look behind the numerous remarks that assert the accidental and unconnected nature of the social world. What we find is the designing hand of the novelist. The greatest such claim occurs when Mrs. Boffin explains to Bella who her husband is. To

Bella's statement that it is "not possible" that her husband is John Harmon, Mrs. Boffin asks, "Why not possible, deary, when so many things are possible?" (841; bk. 4, ch. 13). Since so many things are possible, any coincidence, any chance event, anything at all in the narrative, including Mr. Boffin's feigned miserliness, becomes, on the one hand, a realistic depiction of the way the world is, and, on the other, part of the gradually revealed narrative design.

George Levine argues that in Dickens's fiction, as in natural theology, chance is "part of a larger moral design, thus effectively denying its chanciness by making it rationally explicable in terms of a larger structure" (138), a "dramatic expression of the value and ultimate order in nature. . . . Each coincidence leads characters appropriately to catastrophe or triumph and suggests a designing hand that sets things right in the course of nature" (137). Levine goes on to note, however, that "even where [Dickens] persists in the contrivances of coincidence, their discontinuity with the worlds he is creating is disturbing. Such discontinuity is particularly striking in *Little Dorrit* and *Our Mutual Friend*. In most cases . . . coincidence feels too often like a matter of the conventions of narrative." This discontinuity "begin[s] to suggest a chasm between event and meaning . . . away from the natural-theological tradition that had dominated [Dickens's] imaginative vision" (142). While this chasm seems, in Levine's formulation, to arise naturally or even against Dickens's intent, I would argue that the reliance on, and the calling attention to, the "conventions of narrative" represents in *Our Mutual Friend* a partially conscious expression of uneasiness at the secretive intervention necessary to force an unruly second-law universe back into a comfortable, optimistic, ordered first-law mold. Helmholtz was right: a universe dominated by Darwin and the second law is not a comforting place; we must erect like young Blight "the fiction of an occupation" if we are not to be "shattered to pieces." But Dickens is so successful at depicting a world depleting its energy supplies, a world full of people and institutions who do not work to lighten the burden of others, that the gradually revealed connections among the characters is only partly capable of reinstating a first-law world. The coincidences and contrivances necessary to complete this reinstatement impose only a thin veneer of order, for they are clearly a work of fiction, a means of survival rather than triumph.

The fiction of order, however, is our only recourse. We have to act as though we live in a first-law world, a world amenable to natural theological interpretations of order and meaning and the centrality of the human, even if we know our world is dominated by the second law. It is unlikely that "all the queen's horses and all the queen's men" will be able to put this humpty-dumpty world back together again, but the inevitability of "decline and fall" — and the presence of Gibbon's book provides the novel with a powerful historical model of the second law — does not obviate the need for individuals to act in a manner that resists that trend. More even than in *Bleak House* or *Little Dorrit*, Dickens in *Our Mutual Friend* employs the language and the theories of the first law, of conservation and correlation and ceaseless motion, to provide meaning for a society that often seems to be dominated by dissipation, disjunction, and stasis. But by *Our Mutual Friend* this reading has become, with the dissemination of the second law and concern for a dying sun, difficult to sustain. In retreating to the comparative safety of the first law in *Our Mutual Friend*, Dickens covertly acknowledges that this order is a fiction, a work of articulation that cannot put off death but can make some use of the bones.

University of Michigan–Dearborn

NOTES

1. We refer to the measurement of this state of randomness and disorder as entropy, but the term was only coined on the Continent in 1865 by Clausius and was not adopted immediately in Britain. See Merz 2: 119–31; Gillispie 404; Thomson, "On a Universal Tendency"; and Wise and Smith.
2. See Gillispie 400–01; Merz 2: 115–16, 131, 139–40. The *OED*, incidentally, associates energy with action and efficiency, whether of an individual or a machine, and uses an example from *Our Mutual Friend*.
3. Metz, "Science in *Household Words*," argues that "Perpetual metamorphosis . . . is the law of the physical universe in *Household Words*. . . . [L]ife is presented not as an end or a state of being, but as a process continually unfolding itself to the receptive viewer, just as in Dickens' fictional worlds images are fluid and interconnective" (127).
4. For more on the significance of articulation in the novel, and especially for its connection with literacy, see Baker, Kennedy, and Friedman.
5. I am indebted to Robert Patten for this suggestion.
6. Kiely calls attention to the numerous fictional designs that emanate from the novel's characters and argues that the moral issue of the book is not whether to plot and design, but how and to what ends. Kiely, however, sees very little moral ambiguity in the plotting either of Rokesmith or of Dickens.
7. Hayles notes that many Victorian physicists, in their efforts to deny the inevitability of the implications of the second law, invoked some version of the prodigal son story (218). Flashley is clearly one in that tradition, as is Eugene Wrayburn in *Our Mutual Friend*.
8. Levine says that "[a]lthough it would be absurd to claim that Dickens had in mind the developments in thermodynamics of the 1840s and 1850s" while writing *Little Dorrit*, those developments provide "an appropriate metaphor" for talking about that novel (156). I believe Dickens did have these developments in mind, especially for *Our Mutual Friend*.
9. Kiely also sees the episode with Young Blight as paradigmatic: such fictions are matters of survival, for "behind them all is the universally shared dread of no story at all" (272).

WORKS CITED

Baker, Robert S. "Imagination and Literacy in Dickens' *Our Mutual Friend*." *Criticism* 18 (1976): 57–72.

Beer, Gillian. "Origins and Oblivion in Victorian Narrative." *Sex, Politics, and Science in the Nineteenth-Century Novel*. Ed. Ruth Bernard Yeazell. Baltimore: Johns Hopkins UP, 1986. 63–87.

Boll, Ernest. "The Plotting of *Our Mutual Friend*." *Modern Philology* 421. (August 1944): 96–122.

Brantlinger, Patrick, ed. *Energy and Entropy: Science and Culture in Victorian Britain*. Bloomington: Indiana UP, 1989.

Burchfield, Joe D. *Lord Kelvin and the Age of the Earth*. London: Macmillan, 1975.

Cannon, Susan F. *Science in Culture: The Early Victorian Period*. New York: Science History Publications, 1978.

Collins, Angus. "Dickens and *Our Mutual Friend*: Fancy as Self-Preservation." *Etudes Anglaises* 38 (1985): 257–65.

Collins, Philip, ed. *Dickens: The Critical Heritage*. New York: Barnes, 1971.

Cotsell, Michael. *The Companion to Our Mutual Friend*. London: Allen, 1986.

Desmond, Adrian. *The Politics of Evolution*. Chicago: U of Chicago P, 1989.

Dickens, Charles. *Hard Times*. Ed. David Craig. Harmondsworth: Penguin, 1969.

———. *The Letters of Charles Dickens*. Ed. Walter Dexter. 3 vols. London: Nonesuch, 1938.

———. *Our Mutual Friend*. Ed. Stephen Gill. Harmondsworth: Penguin, 1971.

Friedman, Stanley. "The Motif of Reading in *Our Mutual Friend*." *Nineteenth-Century Fiction* 28.1 (June 1973): 38–61.

Gillispie, Charles Coulston. *The Edge of Objectivity: An Essay in the History of Scientific Ideas*. Princeton: Princeton UP, 1960.

Hayles, Katherine. "Self-Reflexive Metaphors in Maxwell's Demon and Shannon's Choice." *Literature and Science: Theory and Practice*. Ed. Stuart Peterfreund. Boston: Northeastern UP, 1990. 209–37.

Helmholtz, Hermann von. "Lectures on the Conservation of Energy." *Medical Times and Gazette* (January–June 1864): 443–46.

———. *The Selected Writings of Hermann von Helmholtz*. Ed. Russell Kahl. Middletown, CT: Wesleyan UP, 1971.

Jaffe, Audrey. "Omniscience in *Our Mutual Friend*: On Taking the Reader by Surprise." *Journal of Narrative Technique* 17 (1987): 91–101.

Kennedy, G. W. "Naming and Language in *Our Mutual Friend*." *Nineteenth-Century Fiction* 28. 2 (September 1973): 165–78.

Kiely, Robert. "Plotting and Scheming: The Design of Design in *Our Mutual Friend*." *Dickens Studies Annual* 12 (1983): 267–83.

Knoepflmacher, U. C. *Laughter and Despair: Readings in Ten Novels of the Victorian Era*. Berkeley: U of California P, 1971.

Levine, George. *Darwin and the Novelists*. Cambridge: Harvard UP, 1988.

Lohrli, Anne, ed. *Household Words: A Weekly Journal 1850–1859 Conducted by Charles Dickens*. Toronto: U of Toronto P, 1973.

Merz, John Theodore. *A History of European Thought in the Nineteenth Century*. 4th ed. 4 vols. London: Blackwood, 1923.

Metz, Nancy Aycock. "The Artistic Reclamation of Waste in *Our Mutual Friend*." *Nineteenth-Century Fiction* 34 (1979): 59–72.

————. "Science in *Household Words*: 'The Poetic . . . Passed Into Our Common Life.' " *Victorian Periodicals Newsletter* 11. 4 (Winter 1978): 121–33.

Miller, J. Hillis. *Charles Dickens: The World of His Novels.* Cambridge: Harvard UP, 1958.

Myers, Greg. "Nineteenth-Century Popularizations of Thermodynamics and the Rhetoric of Social Prophecy." Brantlinger 307–38.

Thomson, William. *Mathematical and Physical Papers.* 6 vols. Cambridge: Cambridge UP, 1882–1911.

————. "On the Age of the Sun's Heat." *Macmillan's* 5 (1862–63): 388–93.

————. "On the Secular Cooling of the Earth." *Mathematical and Physical Papers* 3: 295–311.

————. "On a Universal Tendency in Nature to the Dissipation of Mechanical Energy." *Mathematical and Physical Papers* 1: 511–514.

Tyndall, John. *Fragments of Science.* 6th ed. 2 vols. New York: Appleton, 1898.

Wilkinson, Ann Y. "*Bleak House*: From Faraday to Judgment Day." *ELH* 34. 2 (June 1967): 225–47.

Wilson, David B. "A Physicist's Alternative to Materialism: The Religious Thought of George Gabriel Stokes." Brantlinger 177–204.

Wise, M. Norton, and Crosbie Smith. "Measurement, Work, and Industry in Lord Kelvin's Britain." *Historical Studies in the Physical and Biological Sciences* 17.1 (1987): 147–73.

————. "Work and Waste: Political Economy and Natural Philosophy in Nineteenth-Century Britain." *History of Science* 27 (1989): 263–301, 391–449.

GOOD COPY: GEORGE MOORE AND THE ART OF THE LITERARY CONTROVERSY

By Adrian Frazier

GEORGE MOORE WAS ONE OF the fine literary journalists in the great age of such journalism, the late Victorian period. He did not work in the genre of the literary causerie, that column or two of small talk about authors and books, diced up into paragraphs of gossip and erudition. Moore used this form sometimes, but not so often nor so well as Andrew Lang, Edmund Gosse, and George Saintsbury, the most successful arbiters of the common taste in the period. What Moore did best is to turn himself and his books into good copy for the causeries of others. He did this by mastering the art of the literary controversy — thus the title of this essay.[1]

Moore was perfectly conscious of his power as a controversialist. Years after this period, in 1914, when he was bringing out chapters of *Vale* in the *English Review* (to prepare a public for the complete edition of all three volumes of *Hail and Farewell!*), Moore received through his publisher, W. H. Heinemann, a letter from Lady Gregory, outraged by what Moore had written of her youth. Moore first tried to placate her, or at least stymie her, by saying he only meant to engage in banter when he compared her collection of folklore with Yeats to her distribution of Bibles in her youth with her mother — concluding, once a proselytizer, always a proselytizer; it was horrible, he sympathized with breathtaking hypocrisy, that she should be persecuted on this point; he, of course, hated Catholicism, so for him, to convert anyone to Protestantism could only be a good thing. Why, he had never thought, so long had he been out of Ireland, what the effect would be: he would be sure to send a revise for the American edition of *Hail and Farewell!*.[2]

This did not satisfy Lady Gregory, who next threatened to take legal action against Heinemann and to protest to the papers unless changes were made in the text of the book for English publication. This time Moore went further than fetching up a treacherous simulacrum of condolence: if she publishes a letter repudiating Moore's account, then she will, he says, "bring about an endless controversy [that] will do you no good. I am an old controversialist," he reminds her, "and it seems to me you give yourself away to your enemies in almost every sentence." She admits, he points out, that she had been present when her mother and sisters read the Bible in peasants' cottages, and that would be interpreted "by Moran and his like" that "you distributed tea and sugar" while they indoctrinated the tenants.[3] With this little flick of his lash, he leaves her, apologizing for not signing the letter, as he had to "rush away for an appointment with his solicitor."

Many of the long acquired skills of the literary controversialist are present in this incident: to start the whole affair off, Moore makes use of a periodical read by all who wrote for the other journals; there he publishes pages both perfectly written and totally inflammatory, matter that he knew would fill the letters pages and gossip columns. In the inevitable exchanges with Lady Gregory, he promises her that any controversy she enters will be endless, giving her a glimpse of a long train of consequence, in which her final word will never be final, letters will be printed from all those who ever had cause to wish to give her a kick, and from people with no known cause to seek this chance, when she is in the stocks, to spit in her face — people who just hate the idea of her. The controversy will do her no good, and his own book a world of good: she will be defending her name, he will be defending his art; she must assume the stance of a dignified reticence, whereas he is able to take up the character of scornful audacity, more dignified still; she will threaten legal action, but he will be sure to conduct his controversy with the advice of a solicitor, doing everything that can be done without violating the law of libel, and, should it go to court, he can be confident the trial will be widely reported in the papers; she can of course write a letter of protest to the *Times*, but she will be, paradoxically, writing to the papers to keep her name out of the papers, and he will be proceeding on the understanding that there is no such thing, for him, as bad press — all copy is good copy.

It all will make a great story, the story around the story of *Hail and Farewell!*, and Moore, working from within it, will make sure that he is its author and its genre remains comedy. Moore probably considered himself a gentleman for letting her off with a warning and accepting some very small changes in the text of his book.

Considering the risks Moore ran in losing his own good name, one might imagine that he learned from Wilde, as Ellmann puts it, that to be derided could be part of one's plan, that notoriety was fame's wicked twin, and Moore could reasonably court the first in the hope that the second would favor him too (136–37). Or one might surmise that Moore took his cues from Wilde's own master, James McNeill Whistler. Certainly, one could add a chapter to the *Gentle Art of Making Enemies* from incidents like those with Lady Gregory: after all, Whistler did inscribe a copy of this book to Moore, "For furtive reading" (Balderston 172). A few months after receiving his presentation copy, Moore showed himself an able student. Julia Davis Frankau (nom de plume: "Frank Danby") published a fairly defamatory notice of Moore's collection of stories, *Celibates*: Davis said the characters were nasty, obsessed with sex, and not celibates at all. Moore's reply in the *Saturday Review* begins, as all his many replies of the kind begin, by saying he never replies to literary critics. In a formal, haughty, and very witty manner, he confides that Julia Davis was his "unfortunate pupil," that he had helped her write her two novels. He sighs at the thought that any pupil of his should prove so "unskillful at polemics." He then very pedantically explains to her the etymology of the term *celibates*, that it derives from the Latin for "unmarried," not "heavenly," as she had appeared to believe. And he concludes, as he always concludes, with a very interesting description of the theme of his book, one that will instruct reviewers and entice book-buyers (Moore, *Saturday Review*). In this letter, there are a number of feathers plucked from Whistler's cap: the seigneurial manner, the lecturing to pupils, the condescension, the detection of treachery in others, and, perhaps above all, the readiness to go public with the details of a private dispute. But in fact, Moore had already studied the art of controversy, before the flourishes of Whistler and Wilde: his first masters in journalism were Emile Zola, James Davis, and W. K. Stead.

BY THE TIME MOORE first wrote to Zola in April 1881 offering his services as Zola's London agent, literary advisor, and translator (Becker 215–17), he had already sized up the English literary market and its readiness for works like those of Zola. As he explained to Zola's friend Paul Alexis in November 1879 (Becker 198), in England the condition of the libraries and book-reading public was entirely different from that in France: the middle class read few books; it did not have the time; and the reading of journals, dispatches, and commerical news sufficed them. The novel proper, that is in three-volume form, was a deluxe commodity. For the first edition, five or six hundred copies was often the complete run, and those 600 copies were not purchased by the public; they were stocked in the reading shops, or circulating libraries, like those of Mudie and W. H. Smith, from which they were rented by the aristocracy. Since Mudie and Smith claimed to be "select libraries" — only stocking those volumes any member of a county family might pick up and read without a blush — no publisher would risk publishing Zola, for fear, Moore concluded, of inflaming the national *pudibonderie*.

After Moore and Zola entered into a working relationship, with Moore always addressing the French novelist as "My dear Master" and signing himself, "your devoted student," Zola took this problem in hand: how to get around the English circulating library system and its institutionalization of the *pudibonderie nationale*, in order to establish in England the Naturalist movement. Between them, they found a publisher, Herman Vizetelly, formerly a French journalist and now a wine-trader in England, willing to publish realistic novels. Next, in the autumn of 1884, on Zola's advice (Becker 257), Vizetelly broke the traditions of publication by issuing Moore's second novel, *A Mummer's Wife*, in a cheap one-volume edition, like those common in France — a 6/ novel, as opposed to the standard 33/ triple-decker.

Fully anticipating resistance from the circulating libraries and all those beholden to them, Zola advised Moore to carry the fight to the enemy,[4] making use of England's seething activity in periodicals — magazine articles could serve as a sort of lighted *marquee*, advertizing the theatrical excitements inside, just past the ticket window (there were, by the way, some 25,000 Victorian periodicals, including several hundred literary reviews, magazines, and weeklies) (Houghton 3). Moore prepared a frontal assault on the English library system. First on 10 December 1884, in the *Pall Mall Gazette*, and three days later in the *Saturday Review*, Moore mauled Smith and Mudie as the "circulating censorship," that make the scruples of the weakest the standard for the strongest, that turn the novel into a guide to marriage and the drawingroom, a sort of advanced schoolbook. This controversy, Moore explained to a friend, "marked the whole affair up" (Becker 269). Soon dozens of articles were written about the case. Many attacked the morality of Moore, and especially that of Zola; others called for freedom from censorship, or at least a free market in novels, without fixed pricing. And everyone bought *A Mummer's Wife*: it went through seven editions in four years. Moore did not care that the *Academy* spoke of the book as "the most repulsive tale ever told" and the *Athenaeum* called it "wearisome as well as painful" (Hone 110). For him, discussion in the press was enthusiasm by the press.

It was not long after the publication of *A Mummer's Wife*, Moore's first and only thoroughgoing imitation of Zola, that he began to chafe under the Naturalist school uniform. He soon was confiding to everyone but Zola himself that he did not believe that literature could be scientific, or that humanity was in need of improvement, or that progress and democracy were good things; he wanted to achieve style, and a new style with each book; Zola's own writing was going, he thought, from bad to worse.[5] But he did learn five enduring lessons from Zola about literary controversy:

first, design a novel as a strike upon new fictional territory, never being peaceable, never staying within the boundaries of the already mapped, so that the novel itself is militantly polemical;

second, "mark up" or highlight the points of interest by means of articles in the periodicals, timed for the release of the book, January being, Zola told him, "the best month to boom books" (Zola 99);

third, when challenged on moral ground, seize the still higher ground, connecting your defense to something like truth, sincerity, or artistic freedom;

fourth, take up a polemical attitude with respect to majority opinion, regarded as philistine or oppressive, and appeal directly to discerning readers. In short, Moore dropped, one by one, the fictional methods of Naturalism, and ultimately he foreswore its progressive politics altogether; but he kept the methods of campaign — invasive, provocative, high-toned, and abusive — in the name of his new cause: the expression of personality in art. Zola's most lasting lesson for Moore was the fifth: "Audacity, audacity, and still more audacity!"[6] (Little did Zola then know that even as he gave this advice, Moore was beginning *Confessions of a Young Man*, in which the now indevoted pupil audaciously ridiculed his once-dear master.)

THE SECOND WRITER TO teach Moore the business of literary controversy was James Davis, an English Jew about Moore's age, also from a wealthy family, and, by the early 1880s, a journalist writing a column called "Playhouses without Plays," for a magazine variously called the *Sporting Times*, the *Pink 'Un*, the *Bat*, and the *Hawk*.[7] These weeklies were all basically scandal-sheets, covering the theater and the track, each one a sort of house-journal for the younger sons of landed county families, living the life in London. One typical article was "How to write a letter to an actress," that is, a request for a private dinner after the performance; another article would advise aspiring actresses to accept such dinner-dates with men of culture. And a regular feature was "Things We Wish We'd Never Done, By the People Who Did Them."

In an opening issue of the *Bat* (7 April 1885), Davis explained to potential contributors the house style: not something absurdly pompous and respectable, as if by Hazlitt and G. H. Lewes, but "smart" and "clever" — but not unprintable. He was not very good at following his own advice, at least not the last bit: time and again, he put himself at the mercy of the court for violating the libel laws (Becker 498–501). It would begin, perhaps, with gossip: he would report what he had overheard a minister say about the Sudan, during the intermission at a music hall, or he would fall into a feud with a theater-manager, such as Gus Hare, and say Hare's business was bust, a libel which gave grounds for a 150 pound fine and costs. Davis was brilliant at being annoying, flippant, and naughty, but he did not know when to stop: after four lawsuits, all lost, he fled to Monte Carlo in August 1888 to avoid the inevitable outcome of the fifth.

Moore's letters to Davis have not survived, so the nature of the influence depends more on inference than in the case of Zola. It is known that Moore dedicated *A Mummer's Wife* to Davis; that Davis permitted Moore to advertise himself and other Vizetelly authors in the *Bat*, and that Davis collaborated in creating a public personality for Moore: nicknaming him "the Pagan," reporting his attendance at plays along with that of other celebrities, and serving as a Boswell to his antics at Whistler's parties and in fights with nuns, MPs, Dublin Castle functionaries, Royal Academicians, shocked parents, and, of course, book reviewers.[8] So, as editor, Davis helped Moore turn his literary life into good copy, but as a writer, Davis served him as well. For instance, Moore learned from Davis, I think, two basic lessons:

a) the very nearly unprintable was often the most easily publishable;
b) the actually unprintable — that is, the indefensibly obscene or libellous — was no good at all for one's plans.

This is also the lesson of Wilde's life to the next generation: playing with that tiger life may be spectacular, beautiful, and heroic; getting mauled in the courts and sent to prison, however, is no joke.

But, not to mince words, Davis was also an absolute cad, even a scoundrel, and he gave Moore column after column in which to develop his own very considerable caddishness. I am thinking, for instance, of an article Moore wrote for the *Hawk* in which he explains how to pick up women on trains (6:379–80).[9] Or one could point to *Confessions of a Young Man*, both a complete expression of caddishness, and — for the discerning reader — a triumphantly farcical mockery of it.

WHILE I BELIEVE IT to be true that Moore learned a great deal from both Zola and Davis about how to become an author, he was initially both an imprudent and overly zealous student of the art of publicity. His public campaign on behalf of the Naturalist *A Mummer's Wife* against the circulating libraries led to large sales and considerable notoriety, but it also earned him strong enemies and a type of name-identification (as a "realis[t] of the clothes-hook, man-milliner, hairdresser, and *décolletege* order") that he would thereafter find hard to shake (Wallace 39–40). For his next book, *A Drama in Muslin*, he brought into play a remarkable but finally discordant array of publicity gimmicks. Originally, he had conceived of this novel as his "girl book" about the Irish marriage-market, the *donée* taken from Jane Austen, the treatment from Emile Zola. With the book underway, but still a year from completion, he began to lay a fire of controversy to boil the pot. In late January, 1885, he tried without success to get a London editor to publish an essay on the radical changes through which young women were passing, being pushed "into professions, examinations, etc.," but held back also by "the old grooves." He frankly confided to the editor that he designed his article to start "a glorious polemic" between those who "cry for emancipation" and those who "cry from the bulwarks of society" (Becker 274–75). In short, he was trying to insert *Drama in Muslin* into social debate on "the Woman Question," as

Meredith (*The Egoist*, 1879) and Olive Schreiner (*Story of An African Farm*, 1883) had done before him.[10] The feminist frame of reference is not inappropriate for this novel: it does treat in an original way a conflict between the sexual desires of the debutantes and the social ambitions of their mothers,[11] and there is an evaluation of alternative destinies — Violet gets a Lord, May gets pregnant, Alice gets a job and a dispensary doctor, and the beautiful, brainless, and ambitious Olive gets nothing. The simplicity of the "This Little Piggy" plot enables Moore to examine the moral worth of his heroines and to show that the rational, independent, atheist, considerate, and sexually honest Alice deserves the reader's admiration.[12]

However, no sooner was Moore done with his attempt to frame the novel as a treatment of "the woman-problem" — Ibsen, with a difference[13]— than he trailed his coat in public to create a defining controversy of a very different kind. This time he published in the *Freeman's Journal* (9 February 1885), the leading Dublin organ of parliamentary nationalism, the whole of his extended correspondence with two officials of Dublin Castle, Colonel Dease and Lord Fingal, the State Steward. Moore had written Dease asking for an invitation to a State Dinner. Moore said he had already attended, two years running, the Levee, the Drawing Rooms, the Castle Balls, and other highlights of the debutante season, but he had not yet been a guest at the Viceroy's table. He was, he wrote the Castle officials, in the process of writing a novel that would give as true and vivid a picture as possible of "the social and political power of the Castle in Modern Ireland," and he could not do this without seeing everything with his own eyes, those of "the passionless observer, who, unbiased by any political creed, comments impartially on the matter submitted to him for analysis." The Castle officials did not wish to abet More's plan to expose the private ceremonies of the Viceroy's dinner-table, and they tried to put him off, saying first it was too early for invitations, and then it was too late — no chair left at all, not even for one solitary, observant novelist, even if he was a landowning Irish bachelor. The *Freeman's Journal* letters make a triumphant piece of ironically pretentious ridicule: they flap the unflappable British and inspect what will not bear inspection. Moore received a letter from an Irish member of Parliament saying that Moore was "our best ally against that stronghold of shame," Dublin Castle (Hone 109).

But was that what Moore wanted his novel to be — an attack on the British presence in Ireland? A piece of Parnellite propaganda? If so, what played well in Dublin would be panned in London. The imperialist W. T. Stead, for instance, picked up the *Freeman's Journal* story and retold it to Moore's discredit and with approval of the Chamberlain's "infinite politeness" in dealing with his worshipper of "the great god Realism." It is true that *A Drama in Muslin* tracks the progress of Mrs. Barton's marriage schemes for her two daughters against the major Irish political events of 1881 and '82:

assassinations, intimidation, and evictions, as well as the Phoenix Park Murders, the 1882 bill for the prevention of crime, the No-Rent manifesto of the imprisoned leaders of the Land League, and the Land Act judicially fixing the rents, which led "the lurid phantom of the League" to vanish "suddenly as a card up the sleeve of a skillful conjurer" (*Drama in Muslin* 264). And in the middle of the novel (which may not be the thematic center), Moore staged the promenade of debutante carriages through dark, wet Dublin streets lined with "vagrants, patriots, waifs, idlers of all sorts and kinds . . . [p]oor little things in battered bonnets and draggled skirts, who would dream upon ten shillings a week; a drunken mother striving to hush a child that dies beneath a dripping shawl," and so on, as poverty and wealth are brought together in plainest proximity (171). At the Castle Ball, Moore does not neglect to place Colonel Dease and Lord Fingal in his Irish Pandemonium:

> The first to appear were the A. D. C.s. They were followed by the Medical Department, by the Private Secretary, the Military Private Secretary . . . the Gentleman Usher, the Comptroller, the State Steward, walking with a wand, like a doge in an opera bouffe; then came another secretary, and another band of the underlings who swarm about this mock court like flies about a choice pile of excrement. (181)

In fact, the novel can be read as a political, even as a Home Rule, novel, indicting, with a sort of merciless, inward sympathy, "an entire race, a whole caste, [who] saw themselves driven from their soft, warm couches of idleness, and forced into the struggle for life. . . . What could they do with their empty brains? What could they do with their feeble hands?" (95).

Furthermore, the novel can also be read, and I think best read, as about both "the Woman Question" and "the Irish Question" (the two major matters for which the British did not have answers). Irish landlords and European bourgeois women both had idle hands and empty brains, and both will have now to join "the struggle for life." This comparison of class with gender is formally implied though never explicitly made by the novel. Its most distinctive and famous feature is the fugal treatment of Mr. Barton negotiating with tenants on the gravel drive, while inside the house Mrs. Barton negotiates with an unsuitable suitor; this montage effect is repeated with varitions frequently in the novel, most commonly by moving the focus from dialogue among named gentry characters in the foreground, seeking profitable alliances, to description of unnamed peasant characters in the background, seething with grievance. In a crucial moment near the end of the story, foreground and background, plot and subplot, marriage and politics, all come together when Alice, departing with her husband, notices — usually the poor are either unsightly or completely invisible to the gentry — a family of peasants just evicted from their cottage and asks, "Is it not terrible that human creatures should endure such misery?'' (323). And her husband offers to do something for them: he pays their rent and talks with them. This is no ''solution'' to the Irish question — as sardonic land-agents immediately point out, there are plenty more peasants over the hill if the couple wish to give away their money, and Alice and Dr. Reed then leave Ireland, resolving, somewhat fatuously, that they can best serve humanity ''by learning to love each other.'' But the incident does shatter the glass walls of isolation around the Irish classes with a short-lived act of coming to consciousness.[14]

While the novel will support both a political and a gender reading, Moore opportunistically accented the political reading when it first came out in the *Court and Society Review* in December 1885. The Conservative/Irish Party alliance was then collapsing, to be replaced by a Liberal/Irish Party government, with Gladstone now openly in favor of Home Rule. Moore wrote the editor, Henry Barnett, explaining to him why this ''picture of Ireland, all complete, castle, landlords and landleaguers, and painted by an Irishman'' would prove ''a saleable article'' during the next six months, when Parnell would be holding his demand for Home Rule ''like a red-hot poker at the throat of England.'' He also reviews his *Freeman's Journal* dispute with Lord Salisbury, calling attention to a correspondence the high society readership of Barnett's journal might otherwise have missed. Now the Woman Question has diminished in importance: ''the shrill wail of virgins'' is just something ''heard through the thunder of a people marching to nationhood.''

Even this strongly nationalist way of framing the novel might have been effective,[15] if Moore had not allowed himself to be drawn aside into a dispute with ''An Amazed Parent'' of a child at the Convent of the Holy Child, the scene of the opening chapter of the novel. Moore revelled in the publicity, as his letters and those of the ''amazed'' Catholic parent, Catholic MP Charles Russell, Canon Wenham, and a Mother Superior, all defending the confidences of the nuns and the purity of their students, appeared in the *Tablet*, the *Weekly Register*, the *Bat*, and, at Moore's urging, alongside his novel in the *Court and Society Review*.[16] Moore was always good at settling scores, and he does so effectively here — while parading the moral glamor of documentary accuracy — but it did not leave a good impression to win a ringing victory in a battle with nuns.

At this point, Moore had three kinds of self-promotion going: he is a feminist, a nationalist, and a Naturalist. In early February 1886, he added another: he is an atheist. He sent a copy of the novel to an editor, along with a cover letter meant to instruct a reviewer:

> I have attempted to paint the portrait of a virtuous woman, — I have attempted the supremely difficult task of using the realistic method as a means not of imposing vice but exposing the mechanism of the virtuous mind. My heroine

is an atheist: she is an atheist on the first page, she is an atheist on the last; she is neither prude nor prostitute but a woman endowed with much common sense and a deep rooted belief in the practical rectitudes of life.

This is not an inaccurate description of Alice Barton, and maybe Moore believed that there were enough genteel Darwinians or sympathetic Spencerians to make this an acceptably daring subject for fiction. However, Moore is confused about his readership. Victorian readers on the whole were not going to like any one of his subjects — not feminism, nor Irish nationalism, nor ethical atheism. And when they opened the novel itself, they were going to find more than these three unpleasant matters. The heroine's Catholic mother is engaged in adultery with Protestant Lord Dungory, apparently for money, while her husband turns a blind eye. The heroine's best friend, the Protestant Cecelia, is a lesbian who converts to Catholicism and becomes a nun. Her next best friend, May, gets pregnant by a young cad, has the baby out of wedlock, sees with little sorrow the baby die, returns to have sex with an old sod, and throughout it all remains the heroine's dear friend! Of course, such things happen in life, but they are not supposed to happen in Victorian fiction. William Wallace, the *Academy* reviewer, ignoring all Moore's (somewhat contradictory) urgings about how to read the novel, told his readers that *A Drama in Muslin* was "daringly and disgustingly suggestive, and descriptive of what ordinary writers of fiction leave undescribed"; he hoped such stuff did not have a market (Wallace 39–40). As a matter of fact, it did not. Moore tried to be pleased with a somewhat censorious review in the *Athenaeum*, but, writing to his brother in August 1886, he had to admit that "the book has been very much misunderstood" (Becker 368). When he learned that this book, like *A Modern Lover* and *A Mummer's Wife*, was to be banned by the circulating libraries, he petulantly wrote to the *Times* bidding goodbye to the English novel-reading public; henceforth, he would write in French.

BY THE END OF THE decade Moore's various literary controversies and *succès d'scandale* amounted to a total career failure. The English public regarded him as a Frenchified Irish cad, without manners or morals, as they are understood in England (Hone 91). In England, one did not question in a light-hearted way God's existence or woman's virtue; in Paris, one could, and Moore did. In February 1888, when Moore's new publisher, Swan Sonnenschein, went round with Moore's latest to the booksellers, he was told by one, "Wouldn't have his books in my establishment, not for any consideration!" and by another, "No thank you! We had his last." Furthermore, W. K. Stead's lurid exposé of child-prostitution in London, with the sensational title, "The Maiden Tribute of Modern Babylon," led to the creation of the National Vigilance Association. One of its first aims was to prosecute publishers of

Naturalist fiction, beginning with Vizetelly — the old man landed in prison, and bankrupt to boot (Keating 241–57). Meanwhile, Moore's planned trilogy on Don Juanism (*A Mere Accident, Spring Days,* and *Mike Fletcher*) was being half-botched by Moore himself,[17] mutilated by editors, then banned by circulating libraries, and finally refused by booksellers. This was a serious state of affairs, both for Moore's art and his ability to get along in the world. After deductions for the support of his mother, brother Julian, and Moore Hall, he only had a hundred and fifty pounds a year from his Mayo estates, no more than an ordinary subsistence at the time. If he could not publish books that would sell five thousand copies, he would ultimately have to stop writing novels.

And for a time, Moore turned from fiction to high-brow journalism (Gilcher 182–98).[18] Meanwhile, I think Moore learned about how to approach the British public from his natural enemy, a man who would seem his opposite, W. K. Stead, the editor of the *Pall Mall Gazette*, and principal wire-puller of the National Vigilance Association. Stead is credited with having invented a particular kind of investigative journalism that still sells tabloids in London: a richly hypocritical combination of Zolaesque accounts of scabrous environments and instinctual drives, *combined with* a very English form of moral puritanism. Writing to Zola in August 1885, Moore at first regarded Stead's *Maiden Tribute of Modern Babylon*, once it sold 100,000 copies, as proof that there was a public in England for a more realistic, truthful depiction of contemporary life (Becker 305–06). Three years later, in 1888, with Stead's juggernaut against obscene literature routing his own publishers and friends, Moore began to realize that crusading morality will always win in England over crusading immorality.

In a series of admirable letters, followed by meetings behind closed doors in Stead's office, on a window seat facing the Thames, Moore at first remonstrated with Stead, addressing the editor out of the fullness of his mind.[19] Moore told him straight out that "in all concerning morals," Stead was mistaken. "Women are lustful," he wrote in September 1888, "and the preservation of the race depends on the lust instinct." "To rage against immorality seems to me like going down to the sea and asking the waves to retire, no good can be done in this direction for as I have said lust is life and life is lust. . . . Your bullets flatten against thr rock of the desire of the will to live. I am talking Schopenhauer, his book is a sad book but . . . a terribly true one" (Becker 538–39). Stead was never quick to understand what he did not wish to agree with, and he turned very grim at the idea that life is lust. As the vigilante campaign continued, Moore tried to persuade Stead that it was beneath him to allow the association to prosecute publishers of books like those of Flaubert and de Gourmont — surely, he could see that these were works of consummate art.[20]

But all his remonstrations having failed, in *Esther Waters* Moore succeeded instead in learning from the tactics of his enemy. It is important, of course, that he took immense pains with this novel about the life of a servant and abandoned mother: the narrative is perfectly conducted; no one could say this book was not art. In addition, one might say that Moore deliberately stifled his urge to experiment stylistically; if *A Drama in Muslin* is five or six possible novels within the covers of one, *Esther Waters* has one single gravid note; it is almost boringly monotonic.[21] But it is most crucial to the book's success that it celebrates motherhood, expresses a strong sentiment for home, and could be interpreted (incorrectly) as making a case for the control of gambling among the lower classes. In brief, by English standards, *Esther Waters* looked very much like a moral book; by Moore's own lights, of course, it was an impersonal study of the life-lust, "the assertion of the will to live," that he defended in his rebuke to Stead. Is there an element of hypocrisy here, in Moore's alowing for English readings of his novel that would lead to the founding of the Anti-Gambling League? Absolutely. Earlier, with *A Drama in Muslin* he plausibly but imprudently awakened readers to the many themes and many voices in his book; now he was going to let the English hear what they liked. Indeed, just as he was completing *Esther Waters* in August 1893, he wrote to his brother Maurice that he had finally come to understand "the dull Saxon," and he next wanted to paint his portrait "in his habit of instinctive hypocracy [sic] ... Pecksniff done seriously, and, if the feat does not seem impossible, with love." The Englishman's hypocrisy was, he said, an "extraordinary civilizing agency" (Becker 828). There is a difference, of course, between the hypocrisy of Moore and that of Stead: Moore's was self-conscious, funny, and cynical; Stead's was blind, serious, and quite dangerous. In the event, Moore's plans went off to perfection: *Esther Waters*, like all his books, was first automatically banned by the circulating libraries but then defended by high-brow critics, low-brow moral crusaders, and even a former prime minister. It made him a fortune and established his reputation ... a great victory, really, over his enemies.

A READER MIGHT WELL ASK, having come to the end of this essay, if I have not just explained how Moore learned the commonest tricks of self-promotion, the sort of thing Madonna is now good at, and nothing to do with real art at all. In part, I think Moore's best defense would be to plagiarize Oscar Wilde in *De Profundis*, where he states as part of his achievement that he not only summed up existence in an epigram and perfected the forms of literature, but also created legends around himself, that he, in short, dominated the public mind. That domination is an essential element in being an artist, it seems to me, especially in the age of frenetic cultural journalism. While Moore showed

from the start a talent for provoking comment in the press, he came to understand after *A Mummer's Wife* that it was not enough to be an object of
widespread derision: scandal ultimately limited sales and cramped his authorial freedom. He also had to learn by his mistakes in the promotion of *A
Drama in Muslin* that one had to be not just the author of a novel, and an
author of stories in the press about that novel, but also the author of the whole
controversy, so that it could be played out in a narrative that one guided
toward conclusions favorable to one's interests. To achieve this end, the
readership of fiction and the periodical press had to be educated about what
to see in a book and left in the dark about what, for the time being, they
should best not see. Eventually, this awareness that a book might best work
upon its audience through several levels — one explicit and publicly acceptable, the other inexplicit and subversive of public morality, implied by his
handling of the reception of *Esther Waters* — led Moore to build into his
fiction, as well as his publicity, multiple levels of irony, as in the solemn
beauty of the surface narrative of *The Brook Kerith* and the profoundly funny
and impious undertones of its rewriting of scripture.

And on the whole, Moore's literary controversies, his ways of making his
life good copy, enabled him to create an art of personality that stands as his
best achievement — the seven volumes of autobiography: *Confessions of a
Young Man, Memoirs of My Dead Life, Ave, Salve, and Vale, Conversations
in Ebury Street,* and *A Communication to My Friends.* These sly, indiscreet,
audacious, and always polemical works had their first instructors in Emile
Zola, James Davis, and W. K. Stead.

Union College

NOTES

1. Just as this article was going to press, Grubgeld's *George Moore and the Autogenous Self* came off the press. It is clearly a book no one writing about Moore in
   the future will wish to ignore. It gives extensive treatment to Moore's "desire to
   create a figure whom readers would associate with the 'George Moore' who
   already existed as an author before the reading public. . . . He sought to connect
   his extratextual performances to his in-text appearances not only through autobiography but in countless self-referential letters to newspapers and, in later life,
   books like *Avowals* or *Conversations in Ebury Street*" (17) — a project which
   is also the subject of this article. Though this article differs from her book in
   focus, sometimes in detail, and obviously in scope, I am in complete sympathy
   with Grubgeld's leading claims about Moore's self-conscious invention of an
   authorial personality.
2. Moore is glibly pretending ignorance: having been born an Irish Catholic, he
   knew perfectly well what would be the upshot of his remarks about Lady Gregory's proselytizing.

3. "Moran" is D. P. Moran, the editor of the Catholic and Nationalist periodical, the *Leader*. Moran was witty, determined, and brutal in his hounding of "West Britons," a term he popularized for Irish followers of English customs and policies.

4. Moore was already a bit worried that in this war, he was a soldier in the first wave, where the losses would be great — his first novel, *A Modern Lover*, had already been withdrawn from circulation by W. H. Smith upon the complaint of "two ladies in the country." But Zola gave him courage, and with *A Mummer's Wife*, Moore deliberately aimed to "knock the *école sentimentale* over the head," as he told his mother; he'd plant a dagger in the heart of the sentimental novel, he went on to Zola; why, he'd be "a ricochet of Zola in England." So he knew, and Zola knew, that reviews would soon speak of him again as one of the hogs in Zola's sty.

5. See, for example, Moore's [26 July and 10 August 1886] letters to Francis Netscher, a Dutch Naturalist and avid follower of Zola (Becker 366–67, 370). However, Moore for some time kept a secret of his disenchantment from the French businessman and art critic Theodore Duret, who was a close friend of Zola's (Moore to Duret, Oct. 1886; Becker 387).

6. Moore to Emile Zola, [20 August 1886]; Becker 378–79. The politics of Moore's *A Drama in Muslin* are addressed below. While for the sake of promotion, Moore sometimes highlighted for readers the nationalist elements in that novel, he did not himself view the novel in that light. In this exchange of letters, Zola urges Moore to immediately write a novel on Ireland that is alive, audacious, revolutionary, and the life of liberty. Moore replies that Zola is correct that historically this is a perfect time to move a whole people, but he himself does not have in his guts a novel of the kind Zola describes. What he had to say on the subject, he had just put into *A Drama in Muslin*, presumably something not quite so revolutionary nor so one-sided. A month earlier, in a reply to William Archer's review of the novel in the *Pall Mall Gazette* (14 July 1886), Moore, complaining about Archer's strictures against the morality of the story, wrote that "a work of art has nothing to do with morality or immorality, human sympathy or a want of human sympathy; it is neither realistic nor idealistic" (Moore to William Archer [July 1886]; ALS British Library; Becker 362–54). This aestheticism remained his position, even as he wrote the apparently progressively humanitarian *Esther Waters*.

7. Davis happened to be the brother of Julia Davis Frankau, Moore's "unfortunate pupil," mentioned above. Throughout the 1880s, he was a good friend to Moore and his brother, as well as to Wilde, and later still to Shaw, all of whom appear to have written unsigned articles for one of his many papers; see Glover.

8. See for instance Moore's sarcastic account of his dispute with Charles Russell, M.P., and the nuns of St. Leonard's Convent over his description of Prize Day at a convent school in *Drama in Muslin*, published in the 26 January 1886 issue of the *Bat*. In the 14 July 1885 issue Davis jokes that at Whistler's weekly soiree in Suffolk Street, Moore was careworn because the *Pall Mall Gazette* had "out-Zolaed Zola" with Stead's exposé of child prostitution in London.

9. To be fair, it must be added that Moore turns the little essay, so crudely caddish in its premise, into something quite sensitive, an appreciation of the personalities of the women, whom he chooses in the end not to seduce.

10. According to the letters of Olive Schreiner and Havelock Ellis, Moore had met Schreiner by 23 June 1885; indeed, by July 13, he was declaring his love for her

(Draznin 363, 369). She found *A Mummer's Wife* admirable; he wrote Francis Netscher in August about "that very remarkable book The story of an african farm" (Becker 302). Moore had *Drama in Muslin* underway in January 1885, but he was still at work on the novel during this period of relations with Schreiner. Grubgeld argues that Schreiner influenced *Drama in Muslin* most particularly in Alive Barton's ideal of marriage as a partnership in labor (Grubgeld 8–10). She may have additionally influenced him by putting him in touch with her friend Eleanor Marx and other young socialists: the analysis of property relations in the novel is sharp-eyed and demystified, with a Marxian edge of lampoon about it.

11. Perhaps the most original thing about this overly experimental novel is its clear indication that women like sex, even good women. Not only does May Gould happily give in to the desires of Fred, but in the next room the heroine Alice Barton, thinking of the novelist Harding, feels "a distinct desire possessing for her an intrinsic value" and envies May for at least knowing "what the rest of them might never know" (*A Drama in Muslin* 204).

12. The plot is not literally taken from that nursery rhyme but from the folktale, "King Cophetua and the Beggar Maid." In chapter 1 of *A Drama in Muslin*, the heroine Alice Barton writes a little play on this motif for Prize Day at her convent: all the main female characters take parts that strongly foreshadow their destinies later in the novel. The device is simple but effective (see *A Drama in Muslin* 1–19).

13. Moore was present at Edward Aveling's house when Eleanor Marx, George Bernard Shaw, and May Morris performed *A Doll's House* in January 1886, just as his novel was being serialized in the *Court and Society Review*. Many years later, Moore was proud of the fact that "as a young man of thirty" he had chosen "the subject instinctively that Ibsen had chosen a few years before," but at the time he was prejudiced against the play because he was himself writing from a different point of view. He did not think it right for a woman to be shown suddenly throwing up "her husband and her children, as has been said, for schoolbooks." His heroine would require both books *and* a lover, because "if women cannot win their freedom without leaving their sex behind they had better remain slaves" (*Muslin* x–xii).

14. Grubgeld takes a strong view of the irony in this passage, arguing that it shows Moore's own fatalism about reform in Ireland and also his skepticism about the integrity of a writer's exile from Ireland, the writer in this case being Alice Barton (14–15). I think Moore's political fatalism at this stage was more limited: it would be fatal, he thought, to attempt a reform that would keep the landlord system in place, and silly to fancy that any reform could soon make Ireland a pleasant place to live. But other kinds of reform were possible, indeed necessary, and he was sufficiently involved to make a case for what he thought ought to be done: clear out Dublin Castle, educate women, put the landed aristocracy to work, gradually enable the peasants to come into ownership of the land, and begin to create a degree of civilization in Ireland.

15. "Effective," that is, as a way of promoting the book, and not utterly wrong as a way of reading the book. Scholarly readings of *A Drama in Muslin* correctly see Moore's political position as quite contradictory: he can see that the landlord class is a "plague spot," but he also can hardly bear the thought of "a country composed exclusively of peasants" (*Parnell and his Island* 6). Malcolm Brown's chapter on "The Irish Landlord" in *George Moore: A Reconsideration* remains an excellent account of the complexity of political attitudes in *A Drama in Muslin*;

see also A. Norman Jeffares's chapter in *George Moore's Mind and Art* and especially Grubgeld's discussion of Moore's "Discourse of Repudiation" in the novel (2–21).

16. See the *Tablet* (23 January 1886) 137; the *Bat* (26 January 1886) 337–38; and the *Court and Society Review* (4 February 1886) supplement 6.

17. As an organized and clinical inquiry into the working of sexual desire in late Victorian males, the trilogy is intelligent and interesting fiction, deserving of republication as a set, especially in light of recent scholarly interest in the Men and Women's Club, an 1880s discussion group on rational relations among the sexes, led by Karl Pearson. Moore, though not himself a member, was familiar with several members of the group, such as Havelock Ellis and Olive Schreiner. The problem with the trilogy is that within each novel there are fine things, but that not one is itself a fine thing.

18. See, for instance, "Some of Balzac's Minor Pieces," *Fortnightly Review*, 1 October 1889; "Our Dramatists and Their Literature," *Fortnightly Review*, November 1889; and his weekly articles on painting, especially on French Impressionism, in the *Speaker*, beginning 21 March 1891.

19. Grant Richards gives an account of such a meeting in *Memories of a Misspent Youth* (265). After the meeting, Richards was told "that George Moore spoiled his chances of becoming one of Stead's favorites by refusing to subscribe to Stead's ideal of sexual morality."

20. Stead made one small concession, promising to call off the attack on *Madame Bovary*, but it is unclear whether or not this promise was fulfilled. At the end of his life, Moore recalled that the "hatred" of the Vigilance Society was "stayed" when "W. T. Stead, an honest heart within him, declared that if it was their intention to prosecute the Heptameron of the Queen of Navarre written in the 16th century, and Flaubert's *Madame Bovary*, he would be forced to resign from the Council of the Society" (*A Communication to My Friends* 77).

21. Ohmann writes very well of the way Esther's drabness "overspread its boundaries" into the style of the novel.

WORKS CITED

Balderston, John Lloyd. "The Dusk of the Gods: A Conversation on Art with George Moore." *Atlantic Monthly* (August 1916): 165–75.

Becker, Robert, ed. "Letters of George Moore, 1863–1901." Diss., U of Reading, 1980.

Brown, Malcolm. *George Moore: A Reconsideration.* Seattle: U of Washington P, 1955.

Draznin, Yaffa Claire, ed. *"My Other Self": The Letters of Olive Schreiner and Havelock Ellis, 1884–1920.* New York: Peter Lang, 1992.

Ellmann, Richard. *Oscar Wilde.* New York: Vintage-Random, 1987.

Frankau, Julia Davis. Rev. of *Celibates. Saturday Review* (27 July 1895): 105–06.

Gilcher, Edwin. *A Bibliography of George Moore.* Dekalb, IL: Northern Illinois UP, 1970.

Glover, James M. *Jimmy Glover: His Book.* London: Methuen, 1911.

Grubgeld, Elizabeth. *George Moore and the Autogenous Self: The Autobiography and the Fiction.* Syracuse: Syracuse UP, 1994.

Hone, Joseph. *The Life of George Moore.* New York: Macmillan, 1936.

Houghton, Walter E. "Periodical Literature and the Articulate Classes." *Victorian Periodical Press: Samplings and Soundings*. Ed. Joan Shattock and Michael Wolff. Toronto: U of Toronto, 1982.

Keating, Peter. *The Haunted Study: A Social History of the English Novel 1875–1914*. London: Secker and Warburg, 1989.

Langenfeld, Robert. "A Reconsideration: *Confessions of a Young Man* as Farce." *Twilight of Dawn: Studies in English Literature in Transition*. Ed. O M Brack, Jr. Tucson: U of Arizona P, 1987. 91–109.

Moore, George. *A Communication to My Friends*. London: Nonesuch P, 1933.

———. *Confessions of a Young Man*. London: Swan Sonnenschein, Lowrey, 1888.

———. *A Drama in Muslin*. London: Vizetelly, 1886.

———. *Esther Waters*. London: Walter Scott, 1894.

———. Letter. *Court and Society Review* (24 December 1885): 511.

———. Letter. *Freeman's Journal* (9 Febraury 1885): 5.

———. Letter. *Saturday Review* (3 August 1895): 143.

———. Letter. *Times* [London] (12 August 1886): 10.

———. Letters to Lady Gregory. 9 January and 15 January 1914. mss. 65B2342; folder 2. Berg Library, New York Public Library.

———. *Muslin*. New York: Boni and Liverwright, 1922.

———. *Parnell and His Island*. London: Swan Sonnenschein, Lowrey, 1887.

Ohmann, Carol. "George Moore's *Esther Waters*." *Nineteenth Century Fiction* (Spring 1970): 174–87.

Owens, Graham, ed. *George Moore's Mind and Art*. Edinburg: Oliver and Boyd, 1968.

Richards, Grant. *Memories of a Misspent Youth 1872–1896*. New York: Harper, 1933.

Stead. W. T. "Occasional Notes." *Pall Mall Gazette* (12 February 1885): 3.

Swan Sonnenschein, William. Letter to George Moore. 8 February 1888. Ms. Allen & Unwin. London.

Wallace, William. Rev. of *A Drama in Muslin* and four other novels. *The Academy* (17 July 1886): 39–40.

Zola, Emile. Letter to George Moore, 15 August 1886. *Bookman's Journal and Print Collector* (December 1924): 98–100.

NARRATIVE DIVERSION IN *SHIRLEY,* OR THE PERVERSION OF FETISHISM

By Ruth D. Johnston

PERHAPS THE MOST STRIKING thing about *Shirley* is that it seems such an anomaly in the Brontë canon: it is not an autobiographical narrative. In fact, it is a critical commonplace that in her third novel Brontë abandons the confessional mode to try her hand at the predominant fictional form of the century — the "classic" omnisciently-narrated realistic novel — in reponse to the pressure of contemporary literary influence, especially Thackeray's. But in this context *Shirley* is no less anomalous, for the novel is very eccentric in its use of "third person" narration: there is an incomplete displacement of previous autobiographical forms by omniscient narration. Therefore, it would be more accurate to say that *Shirley* sets in dialectical relation the internal structures of Brontë's previous autobiographical narratives with their opposite forms the better to make explicit their relation as negatives of each other, as in photography the film and the printed picture are reverse images of each other.[1]

Juxtaposing disparate narrative modes brings to the surface their modus operandi, which is ordinarily concealed through a hierarchy of discourses, that, Colin MacCabe argues, distinguishes the classical realist novel. The characters' discourses are set off by inverted commas and subordinated to the narrative prose, which assumes the guise of transparent reflection:

> In the classical realist novel the narrative prose functions as a metalanguage that can state all the truths in the object language — those words held in inverted commas — and can also explain the relation of this object language to the real. . . . [T]he metalanguage is not regarded as material; it is dematerialized to achieve perfect representation — to let the identity of things shine through the window of words. (MacCabe 8)

Of course, insofar as the material of the metalanguage is language, it cannot achieve pure transparency but is subject to the distortion that inevitably results from the arbitrary relation of word and thing. But even if MacCabe's conception of the narrative prose is too monolithic, his observations about the way hierarchy functions to conceal the mechanics of the text — its status as discourse rather than transparent reflection — remains valid.[2]

A number of critics have linked this structure of representation with the psychoanalytic definition of fetishism. Stephen Heath argues that insofar as the suppression of the narrational level — or "the ideology of directness" (104) — functions to position the subject as a whole and unified self, this structure of representation is a structure of fetishism:

> The structure of representation is a structure of fetishism: the subject is produced in a position of separation from which he is confirmed in an imaginary coherence (the representation is the guarantee of his self-coherence) the condition of which is the ignorance of the structure of his production, of his setting in position. (106)[3]

Since I will be arguing that *Shirley* undoes and displaces this fetishistic structure, various aspects of this definition of representation warrant further elaboration.

The definition draws on certain key passages in Freud's 1927 paper, "Fetishism," in particular the case discussed at the beginning, which involves a young man whose fetish was "a certain kind of 'shine on the nose.' " Freud writes,

> the patient had been first brought up in an English nursery and had later gone to Germany, where he almost completely forgot his mother-tongue. The fetish, which derived from his earliest childhood, had to be deciphered into English, not German; the *"Glanz auf der Nase"* [*shine* on the nose] was really "a *glance* at the nose." (214)

For Heath the play on glance/Glanz describes the fetishistic effect: "The fetish is indeed a brilliance, something lit up, heightened, depicted, as under an arc light, a point of (theatrical) representation; hence the glance: the subject is installed (as at the theatre or at the movies) *for* the representation . . . identity in separation, the very geometry of representation" (107).

Though the perspective that Heath delineates is that of a spectator at the theater or the movies, literature certainly belongs in this discussion of representation. For in literature the fictional world is similarly placed within a frame. The space of representation is the space of an imaginary dialogue "fixed by the glance of speaker and listener, 'author' and 'reader' " (Weber 143). In fact, to the extent that the literary text is presented as though it were visual — made up of images and scenes — it denies its status as language, its production through the interplay of differences.[4]

As the idea of framing implies, separation is crucial to the structure because it permits the reader/spectator to assume a transcendent position not implicated in the representation. What may not be so immediately apparent is that separation works in tandem with identification. As Heath explains, these two poles of the fetishistic structure — separation and identification — are interdependent (107). Identification relies on the force or pull of action and character to direct attention to the story level and away from the narrative process or structure that produces the subject in relation to the text. Thus the coherence of the subject depends upon "the split [that the structure] operates between knowledge and belief" (Heath 107): the subject is situated in a specular relation to the representation oscillating between a knowledge of what transpires within the fictional world and a disavowal of his implication in the representation.[5]

Shirley systematically undoes each of these fetishistic aspects of representation: transparent narration, narrative continuity, identification.

Transparent Narration vs Textuality

SHIRLEY DRAWS ATTENTION TO the transparency of narration and the hierarchy of discourses it supports *as conventions*, thereby making the mechanics of the text visible and explicit. One of the key devices used to call attention to the narration per se is negative affirmation, and a prime example is the passage at the beginning of the novel which compares the narrative to a lenten meal and describes what the narrative discourse will *not* do.

> If you think, from this prelude, that anything like a romance is preparing for you, reader, you *never* were more *mistaken*. Do you anticipate sentiment, and poetry, and reverie? Do you expect passion, and stimulus, and melodrama? Calm your expectations; reduce them to a lowly standard. Something real, cool, and solid, lies before you; something *unromantic* as Monday morning, when all who have work wake with the consciousness that they must rise and betake themselves thereto. It is *not positively affirmed* that you *shall not have* a taste of the exciting, perhaps towards the middle and close of the meal, but it is resolved that the first dish set upon the table shall be one that a Catholic — ay, even an Anglo-Catholic — might eat on Good Friday in Passion Week: it shall be cold lentiles and *vinegar without oil*; it shall be *unleavened* bread with bitter herbs and *no roast lamb*. (7–8; ch. 1; emphasis added)

The meal (which is used repeatedly to mark social or calendar/clock time in the ensuing chapters) functions here as a figure of the kind of narration that will be offered. The fact that the meal is a lenten one indicates that the novel proposes to represent only what is "real" and "solid" (although the narrator, through the use of a double negative, concedes the possibility of more excitingly flavored courses later on in the meal). But this pretense to substantiality, which is one of the conventions of realistic narration, is defined as a restricted diet.

Moreover, the negative presentation of the opposite narrative tendencies circumvents this restricted program. First of all, ingredients designated as absent contribute as much to the definition of the meal as those which are present; the meagerness of what *is* present gets intensified through the use of such negation. "Vinegar without oil" seems more sour than just plain "vinegar." In addition, to specify the missing qualities is in some sense to evoke them and represent them: we think of roast lamb only because the narrator mentions its absence.

Finally, even if the lamb is not "really" there, it exists as fully in the language of the narrative as the cold lentils. Therefore, the explicit, surface distinction between narrative modes drawn according to fidelity to some extra-literary reality is undermined: their equivalence as language marks their equal estrangement from "real" experience and establishes them as reverse images of one another.[6] In other words, the negatives which affirm bring to the surface the way language operates: meaning is produced through a play of differences; it does not exist "outside" of this play. Always, insofar as a sign is defined by what it is not, it exists within a chain of signification in which its negative is inevitably implicated: eating implicates not eating. Brontë foregrounds the signifying chain through negation: not eating implicates eating. For negative affirmation insists on the status of these words as *signifiers*, rather than *images*, whose principle is visible likeness. As Peter Wollen points out, "It is well-known that negation is the founding principle of verbal language, which marks it off both from animal signal-systems and from other kinds of human discourse, such as images" (83). The image can only affirm and indicate presence, hence its role as an element of representation.

Shirley insists not only on the materiality of the narrative prose through negative affirmation but also on its heterogeneity through the multiplication of narrators. Hence the significance of the interpolated narratives or "set pieces."[7] In fact, some interpolated passages specifically address the question of fetishism as a structure of representation. Certainly this is true of Louis's diary and Shirley's vision of the mermaid.

It is highly significant that in the diary Louis's words are represented *as* (not merely *in*) a text.[8] The narrator's invitation to "stoop over his shoulder fearlessly, and read as he scribbles" (591; ch. 29), because it is issued in a direct address to the reader, draws attention to the function of this literary mode to engage readers as voyeurs of Louis's fetishism. The diary format, "intimate" and "confessional," solicits the reader's identification. But to the extent that we are aware of the reading process and of the textuality of the words because they are presented as an interpolated text, we are able to resist identifying with Louis's fetishism and instead analyze it as a process that assigns readers a masculine position.[9] In short, the framing here makes the issue of representation, of representation *as* an issue, paramount by displacing identification with analysis.

The diary presents Louis as a textbook fetishist.[10] Moreover, in keeping with the fetishistic effect, the diary functions to silence Shirley: she is transformed into the object of Louis's narration and a mirror of his desire. Her own conception of herself as Captain Keeldar (224; ch. 11) is denied by his description of her as a "stainless virgin" or young leopardess (592, 596; ch. 29).

Dorothy Kelly writes that this naming is itself fetishistic; the image functions as a veil:

> The fetishistic naming of woman as flower, panther, machine, or other traditional metaphors in nineteenth-century texts covers her up with a metaphorical under-garment through which one cannot see the real woman but can see only one's own symbol of what she is. Substituting metaphors for woman and substituting objects for the maternal phallus amount to the same thing in realist texts. (172–73)

On the other hand, the journal itself is a narrative mode usually coded as feminine. And elsewhere in the text Louis is described in feminine terms: as "an abstraction, not a man" (513; ch. 26), who has nursed Henry "better . . . than any woman could nurse" (718; ch. 36). By so carefully situating Louis's fetishism in the context of his feminine qualities, the novel suggests that his fetishism is an attempt to stabilize his uncertain gender by securing Shirley's.

In this connection it is illuminating to consider Shirley's self-description as Captain Keeldar. Critics disagree about the challenge that androgyny poses to the standard organization of sexuality around a set of paired oppositions. Mary Ann Doane points out that androgyny suggests only a limited play of sexual roles insofar as androgyny and bisexuality tend to be more readily linked with the female figure (153). *Shirley* is an exception to this tendency, however, because Louis is also described in bisexual terms, as noted above. Yet as Samuel Weber argues, androgyny, linked with either male or female figures, may still be considered a reduction of sexual difference because it belongs to the order of antithesis, which reduces ambivalence to mere opposition and reversal (83). In fact, Weber also associates fetishism with the form of antithesis (82). From this perspective, Shirley's androgyny is just the reverse side of Louis's fetishism — governed by the same structure of opposition and inversion. And both androgyny and fetishism function to reduce to a dualistic form what otherwise might be a most destablizing series of differences.

The relation between fetishism and bisexuality becomes clear in Freud's description in "Fetishism" of a fetish object said to be very resilient by virtue of its form, which is exactly that of antithesis:

> In very subtle cases the fetish itself — its structure — has become the vehicle both of the denial as of the assertion of castration. This was the case with a man whose fetish was a suspensory belt such as can also be worn as bathing trunks. This piece of clothing covers the genitals as well as all genital differences. Analysis revealed that it could mean both that the woman is castrated, and that she is not castrated, and moreover it allows the supposition that the man may be castrated as well, for all these possibilities could be equally well concealed beneath the belt. . . . Naturally, a fetish of this kind, constructed out of two opposing ideas is especially resilient. (trans. and qtd. in Weber 82)

Here the fetish object renders the wearer androgynous.

Nevertheless, if androgyny and fetishism as forms of antithesis constrain the play of sexual difference, attention to the manner in which they are constituted destabilizes their reductive oppositional definitions of sexual difference by insisting on their determination according to metonymic logic. More specifically, Shirley's pose is inspired by the arbitrary, non-essential relation between her name and position on the one hand and gender on the other: " 'They gave me a man's name. I hold a man's position: it is enough to inspire me with a touch of manhood' " (224; ch. 11). Earlier we learn that her parents gave her this name because they wished for a son but had only the one daughter. Thus from her parents' perspective she is a fetish, a substitute for the absent male.[11]

But the explanation of Shirley's impersonation diverts attention away from herself as fetish *object* to the displacement process that determines her gender. Her pose as Captain Keeldar insists upon the arbitrariness of that process insofar as she is a substitute for no *thing*, no "original," but for that which never existed in the first place; she is an "original substitute." In short, her pose does *not* refer to a prior sexual identity but to its absence.[12]

The law of metonymy which governs Shirley's assumption of the Captain Keeldar pose is quite consistent with the Freudian conception of fetishism. Freud is quite explicit about this in his discussion of the selection of the fetish. He observes that the choice is not based on a symbolic relation of similarity to the penis. The fetish is whatever object happens to be the last one seen just before the sight of the absence of the penis. Its significance derives not from its visible form but from its location:

> One would expect that the organs or objects selected as substitutes for the penis whose presence is missed in the woman would be such as act as symbols for the penis. . . . This . . . is certainly not the determining factor. It seems rather that when the fetish comes to life, . . . some process has been suddenly interrupted. . . . interest is held up at a certain point — what is possibly the last impression received before the uncanny traumatic one [the lack of a penis in women] is preserved as a fetish. ("Fetishism" 217)

What Freud is here describing, therefore, is a glance that is held in check or fixed, a moment of temporal arrest. Fetishism comes into play as an oscillation only when the play of displacement stops.

It is this focus on the displacement process and the arbitrariness of sexuality rather than on the fixed oscillation between opposite poles that distinguishes Shirley's impersonation from Louis's fetishism. On the other hand, Louis's perspective is defined as that of the moment of temporal arrest or fixity. For Louis, Shirley's sexual identity (and by implication his own) is intrinsic and immutable. Only her wealth and position are arbitrary and extrinsic assets:

> "Take from her her education — take her ornaments, her sumptuous dress — all *extrinsic* advantages — take all grace, but such as the symmetry of her form renders inevitable: present her to me at a cottage-door, in a stuff gown . . . I should like her." (593; ch. 29; emphasis added)[13]

Notice that Louis focuses on Shirley's visible form, which he ties to the stability of her identity. It is precisely by focusing on a determinate form that he can deny difference as a "movement of transference and substitution" (Weber 161).

Shirley's mermaid passage, like her Captain Keeldar pose, raises the question of fetishism as a structure of representation. The mermaid passage is of particular interest because it refers specifically to Thackeray's description of Becky as a mermaid in *Vanity Fair*. Beyond this similarity in content, Brontë also appropriates Thackeray's use of the device of negative affirmation. The two passages deserve detailed examination because they clarify the quality and degree of Thackeray's "influence" on Brontë, which so many critics have noted.

The opening of chapter 64 of *Vanity Fair* mocks prudish readers who advocate the literary convention of silence regarding Becky's sexual transgressions. Here, Thackeray uses the mermaid image to describe the hypocrisy of such literary decorum:

> I defy any one to say that our Becky, who has certainly some vices, *has not been presented* to the public in a perfectly genteel and *inoffensive* manner. In describing this syren, singing and smiling, coaxing and cajoling, the author . . . asks . . . has he once forgotten the laws of politeness, and *showed the monster's hideous tail* above water? *No!* Those who like may peep down under waves that are pretty transparent, and see it writhing and twirling, diabolically hideous and slimy, flapping amongst bones, or curling round corpses; but above the water line, I ask, *has not everything been proper*, agreeable, and decorous, and has any the most squeamish *immoralist* in Vanity Fair a right to cry fie? When, however, the syren disappears and dives below, down among the dead men, the water of course grows turbid over her, and it is *labour lost* to look into it ever so curiously. They look pretty enough when they sit upon a rock,

twanging their harps and combing their hair, and sing, and beckon to you to come and hold the looking-glass; but when they sink into their native element, depend on it those mermaids are about *no good*, and we had best *not examine* the fiendish marine cannibals, revelling and feasting on their wretched pickled victims. And so, when Becky is out of the way, be sure that she is *not* particularly *well employed*, and that *the less that is said* about her doings is in fact the better. (617–18; ch. 64; emphasis added)[14]

It is precisely as a version of affirmation by negation that the passage appealed strongly to Brontë. In a letter to W. S. Williams, she specifically praises Thackeray for his skill in indirect evocation as opposed to explicit representation:

He, I see, keeps the mermaid's tail below water, and only hints at the dead men's bones and noxious slime amidst which it wriggles; *but*, his hint is more vivid than other men's elaborate explanations, and never is his satire whetted to so keen an edge as when with quiet mocking irony he modestly recommends to the approbation of the public his own exemplary discretion and forbearance. (*Correspondence* 2: 244)

So congenial did Brontë apparently find Thackeray's mode of expression that she appropriates his image in *Shirley*:

"I am to be walking by myself on deck, rather late of an August evening, watching and being watched by a full harvest-moon: something is to rise white on the surface of the sea, over which that moon mounts silent, and hangs glorious: the object glitters and sinks. It rises again. I think I hear it cry with an articulate voice: I call you up from the cabin: I show you an image, fair as alabaster, emerging from the dim wave. We both see the long hair, the lifted and foam-white arm, the oval mirror brilliant as a star. It glides nearer: a human face is plainly visible; a face in the style of yours, whose straight, pure (excuse the word, it is appropriate), — whose straight pure lineaments, *paleness does not disfigure*. It looks at us, but *not with your eyes*. I see a preternatural lure in its wily glance: it beckons. *Were we men, we should spring at the sign, the cold billow would be dared for the sake of the colder enchantress*; being women, we stand safe, *though not dreadless*. She comprehends our *unmoved gaze*; she feels herself *powerless*; anger crosses her front; *she cannot charm*, but she will appal us: she rises high, and glides all revealed, on the dark wave-ridge. Temptress-terror! monstrous likeness of ourselves! Are you not glad, Caroline, when at last, and with a wild shriek, she dives?" (276; ch. 13; emphasis is mine and marks what is specified as *not* there)

Both Brontë and Thackeray use the mermaid image to critique convention. But Thackeray's mermaid is his omniscient narrator's image of Becky and designates a conflict neither in Becky herself nor in the narrating consciousness, but between fact (the vice that actually exists) and the conventions that govern its representation. The passage therefore upholds the dualism of the structure of representation. Indeed, it produces the fetishistic effect in exemplary fashion because it operates a split between knowledge and belief on distinct narrative levels. On the level of the story, the knowledge of Becky's vice balances the belief in the subject's separation from the scene of vice by the water line; on the level of the narration, knowledge that the real exceeds its representation (expressed in the narrator's mockery of convention) is balanced with a belief in that very convention (evidenced by the adherence to literary decorum). In other words, the self-reflexiveness of the passage does not undermine but confirms the fetishistic structure. For negative affirmation in the mermaid image constitutes a way of avoiding the explicit and specific description of Becky's activities. The image conceals as much as it reveals insofar as it generalizes. The depiction of Becky's vice as *common* through reference to a *common* image detaches that vice from any specific sociopolitical context and thereby universalizes and essentializes it, which in turn enables the subject's detachment from that vice.

Shirley radically transforms as it appropriates both Thackeray's image and strategy of negative affirmation. Shirley's vision, like Thackeray's, mocks literary convention and raises the question of fetishism on distinct narrative levels. But in Shirley's vision the conflict between fact and its traditional representation is displaced by a discrepancy between two perspectives, which calls into question what *is* fact. For the question of difference in *what* is seen (that is, the partial versus the full revelation of the mermaid) is converted into a question of *who* sees: a conventional "third person," masculine perspective, presented as absent, is juxtaposed with an unconventional, "first person" feminine perspective whose presence negates the power of the mermaid. Negative affirmation describes what does not take place: the men's response, the mermaid's effect on them, and her power over the women.

Thus in Brontë's text negative affirmation functions first of all to represent sexual difference as two disparate modes of seeing and two distinct relations to the mermaid. (In Thackeray's passage, on the other hand, sexual difference is aligned with a subject/object opposition, although this structure remains implicit. The reader's engagement with the text depends on his/her identification with the narrator and the assumption of a masculine subject position at a distance from the feminine object/mermaid.[15])

In *Shirley*, men's response to the beckoning mermaid is pursuit, which depends on and upholds a structure of vision that assumes the separation of subject and object. But Shirley relates to the mermaid through qualified identification: the mermaid's face resembles Caroline's in style but is called a "monstrous likeness of ourselves." The emphasis is on the qualification of her identification with the object. At the same time, Shirley's vision rules out identification with a masculine subject and along with it the subject/object distinction so crucial to the fetishistic structure.

However, it would be erroneous to read this "feminine" image as a corrective to the masculine one, as more truthful or more accurate. Quite aside from the fact that both represent the mermaid as monstrous, both perspectives also suppress the mermaid's tail/tale. (Shirley merely says the mermaid "glides all revealed" on the wave but does not describe what is revealed any more explicitly or specifically than Thackeray. All we hear from the mermaid is a "cry" and a "wild shriek.") In other words, the two visual structures do *not* produce difference as antithesis.

Rather, the doubling of perspectives in Shirley's vision displaces the gendered positions of the fetishistic structure by directing attention to the structure of seeing instead of the object seen, which in turn transforms the mermaid *image* (that is, a reflection of the woman's essence) into a *sign* that can be read by the woman. The passage, therefore, is an instance of masquerade, which Mary Ann Doane defines as the simulation of a gap or distance between the image and the woman that permits a reading (32).[16]

Brontë's appropriation of Thackeray's image and technique also undermines another aspect of the fetishistic structure: it breaks the frame that circumscribes the fictional world through intertextuality, which ruptures that world's self-sufficiency and self-containment through the introduction of disparate "external" discourses. Shirley's mermaid passage demonstrates the impossibility of fixing the meaning of a figure, its susceptibility to transformation through a change in context. It thereby suggests the possibility of a disjunction between text and meaning that ultimately subverts the very idea of intentionality. Since so many other passages refer to pre-existing texts, allusions and quotations become a structural feature within the novel and make considerations of context all important.[17]

Narrative Continuity vs Interruption, Digression, Repetition, and Postponement

NARRATIVE CONTINUITY IMPLIES a causal chain. The effect of narrative, as Heath points out, is "a tightening, action moulded in a *destiny*, an inevitable coherence of the real" (121). Weber ties narrative to fetishism, which seeks to reduce the movement of desire "by giving it the form of an enigma, a secret, or mystery, the *form* of a determinate absence" (161).

The interpolated narratives in *Shirley* not only distribute the function of narration among characters and narrator, they also undermine the fetishistic structure of representation by arresting and interrupting narrative continuity; in some, like Shirley's vision of Milton's Eve or her devoir on "La Première Femme Savante," rhetoric displaces narrative as the principle of composition.[18] But these passages are not the only or even the most significant means used in the novel to transform narrative continuity.

Brontë's strategy is twofold: she undermines the sense of resolution in the final chapter, converting it into a sort of anti-climax as she shifts attention to the time of waiting and deferral that disrupts the emotional spell of the narrative drive.

More specifically, the final chapter in *Shirley* offers conclusion as hyperbole in order to reveal how resolutions in classic narrative suppress differences that emerge in the preceding chapters. The chapter title explicitly names its function and underscores its artifice. Brontë calls it "The Winding-Up." In it the narrator refers to the description of the marriage between Sweeting and Dora Sykes as "varnish" and uses the conventional formula of "they lived long happily together" to sum up their future (723; ch. 37).

The refusal to narrate Malone's final fate and to offer a moral at the end achieve the same effect through a negation of this procedure — a denial rather than an exaggeration of omniscience. Consequently, they *negatively* underscore the artifice of the conventional ending by drawing attention to the conventions they do *not* follow. In addition, the refusal to complete Malone's history is a characteristically Brontëan version of open-endedness: it *explicitly* reveals the arbitrariness of the ending.[19]

This chapter's inappropriateness as an ending is also signalled by its reversal of all the previous representations in the narrative. For one thing, marriage throughout has been described as unhappy. And Shirley repeatedly resists entering that state. She keeps trying to postpone the wedding and turns very cold towards Louis once she has agreed to marry him. As the wedding draws near she grows thin and pale, displaying signs of illness (730; ch. 37). Such reversals indicate the price that resolution of differences at the end always exacts: reconciliation to a narrative system always belies concrete experience. In short, a harmonious ending is regarded as a kind of textual violence.

As for the love scenes between the two couples, though these are presented as alternative resolutions to the final chapter in that they are elaborately delineated, not "wound-up" dismissively, what is crucial from my viewpoint is that they insist on difference at the level of narration. The narrative alternates between the highly dramatic account of Louis and Shirley's courtship and the tamer progress of Caroline's relationship with Robert as it shuttles between different narrative modes, styles, and languages.[20] In the unconventional courtship of Shirley and Louis, as reported in Louis's private journal, the lovers address one another in highly extravagant, erotically charged language matched by violent behavior. (Louis almost throttles Uncle Sympson.) Caroline's seemingly more conventional story is recorded by the omniscient narrator in quieter, almost pedantic language (see the explanation for the use of "effleurer" [664; ch. 33]). The action is more subdued as well. Instead of physical violence, Martin Yorke — a surrogate for and parody of the narrator in this portion of the story — uses trickery to bring the couple together.

But the Caroline-Robert thread assumes melodramatic proportions as Martin exaggerates the "tactics" of the "third person" romance writer, for example putting the house under a spell (659; ch. 33). The narrative explicitly refers to the meeting he contrives as an "adventure," and to the incidents as "chapters" in his romance (667; ch. 34). Furthermore, the analogy between Martin in this episode and the narrator of the novel alerts us to the manipulations that have throughout governed Caroline's story and which are very evident in the astonishing discovery of Mrs. Pryor's identity and here, in the resolution, in the poetic justice of Robert's illness.

Therefore Caroline's story is every bit as exaggerated as Louis's diary account, but it exaggerates a different ("third person") mode. By exaggerating and juxtaposing disparate narrative modes and languages, the text deflects attention from the story level to the narrative procedures themselves and displaces difference from event to that of narration. This disparity in narrative modes cannot be aligned with either the public/private distinction (both depict private love scenes) or a male/female polarity (both diarist and surrogate narrator of the romance are explicitly male).

As the novel undermines the very notion of narrative resolution, attention shifts to the representation of the time of waiting for and deferral of resolution. Jacques Derrida describes the function of deferral: "to temporalize, to resort, consciously or unconsciously, to the temporal and temporalizing mediation of a detour that suspends the accomplishment or fulfillment of 'desire' or 'will,' carries desire or will out in a way that annuls or tempers their effect" (136; qtd. in Lawson 736). Deferral functions, then, to shift attention from effect to the time of waiting and absence, which is conventionally coded as feminine.[21]

More specifically, the novel operates a split between internal, individually determined time and social or clock/calendar time. Significantly, however, this opposition is *not* aligned with the public/private or masculine/feminine dichotomies precisely because *both* temporalities perform the function of deferral.

Psychic time is associated with illness and is represented as repetitive or cyclical and monumental, terms used to describe temporal modalities which Kristeva designates as "hysterical" and which are traditionally linked with feminine subjectivity, although the hysteric may be male or female:

A psychoanalyst would call [linear time] "obsessional time," recognizing in the mastery of time the true structure of the slave. The hysteric (either male or female) who suffers from reminiscences would, rather, recognize his or her self in the anterior temporal modalities: cyclical or monumental. (17)

Caroline's decline illustrates this temporality perfectly. The continuity of Caroline's psychic time derives not from chronology but from repetition and is accordingly represented through the use of the past imperfect tense and such indefinite temporal notations as "once, on a dark, wet Sunday" (191; ch. 10). Moreover, Caroline's measurement of time in large blocks (half centuries) expresses the inadequacy of her social role as a temporal dislocation from clock/calendar time: " 'I have to live, perhaps, till seventy years. . . . [H]alf a century of existence may lie before me. How am I to occupy it?' " (193; ch. 10). Finally, this psychic time scheme is marked by increasing thinness and the gradual onslaught of illess, a form of notation that is the exact opposite of the social time scheme, which is measured by meals. Thus Caroline is repeatedly described as growing thin and losing her color. As her condition worsens, at the low point in her illness, her delirium is described as complete temporal confusion: she thinks the moon is setting just as it is rising (482; ch. 24).[22]

All four main characters — male and female — fall ill and suffer this temporal definition. Louis catches a fever (541–44; ch. 27), Shirley wastes away after she has been bitten by a dog which she fears is rabid (563–88; ch. 28), and Robert suffers from a bullet wound (637–66; chs. 32–33).

However, calendar time is never totally disrupted. Even Caroline's illness is punctuated by Tuesday noons when Robert goes to market. Only the number of Tuesdays remains unspecified. Brontë resists more obtrusive distortions of calendar time because she is concerned with contrasting the two time schemes, which necessitates representing both.

But what is most interesting about the representation of calendar or social time in *Shirley* is that its narrative continuity is not so much interrupted as extended. That is to say, narrative tempo in the novel is conventionally controlled by four basic procedures — ellipsis, descriptive pause, scene, summary.[23] Through formal manipulation of these movements novelists can either emphasize or subordinate particular events. In fact, as readers, we are so accustomed to this sort of rhythmic variation, that a narrative which declines to employ such tactics strikes us as lacking a sense of proportion. But this is precisely the strategy Brontë pursues. She literalizes the representation of time with regard to duration.

Brontë is here experimenting with a narrative time scheme which Julia Kristeva describes as "obsessional time": "[T]ime as project, teleology, linear and prospective unfolding; time as departure, progression, and arrival — in other words, the time of history" (17). To denaturalize the linear and teleological ordering of "obsessional time," Brontë gives an obsessively precise rendering, in duration and detail, of each event, dwelling especially on the time between "events," which is associated with the feminine. Brontë thereby insists upon what classic narrative represses as she calls into question what constitutes an "event."

This strategy is most evident in the account of the Whitsuntide school picnic, the single occasion in the novel that involves the entire community. The feast takes the whole day, and a chapter is devoted to each activity throughout the day: Chapter 16 recounts the morning preparations until the procession, scheduled for noon, chapter 17 the procession itself. Chapter 18 covers the period in which the others attend church while Caroline and Shirley remain outside. Chapter 19, which includes the attack on the mill, gives an account of the whole evening. And since the attack does not last an hour (389; ch. 19), in terms of strict clock time it should not occupy more than one quarter of the narrative of that day. Brontë's refusal to heighten the mill attack by distorting clock time demonstrates that the sense of "proportion" that informs realistic narratives has no reference to any "reality" outside the literary structure, despite the narrative systems' pretension to continuity of time beyond the covers of the text.

Not only does Brontë make the attack on the mill only a small part of the Whitsuntide celebration, she represents this key moment of "action" from a perspective removed from it — that of the non-participants, Caroline and Shirley (or, more precisely, the narrator's representation of their view). The text underscores the limitation of Caroline's and Shirley's perspective, literal-izes it as a difficulty in seeing resulting from the darkness and their distance from the scene. Furthermore, the text explicitly specifies this limitation as feminine and exposes its distortion when the "bare facts" are revealed the morning after (406–07; ch. 20). On the other hand, the significance of the episode resides precisely in this distortion or limitation. First of all, the wom-en's private viewpoint registers what is ordinarily omitted from more conven-tional narrative accounts of similar events: their exclusion and frustration at being forced into a non-participatory role.

Secondly, the account also registers their failure to see how their concern with Robert and his supporters blinds them to their own relationship to the workers: the mutual dependency on paternalism and patriarchal power, which the text elsewhere formally represents through figures of deprivation, starva-tion, and unemployment used to describe both women and workers (Boumelha 94). Hence Shirley's qualified recognition of the workers' organization, which misses the significance of such organization for her as a woman:

> "How steadily they march in! There is discipline in their ranks — I will not
> say there is courage: hundreds against tens are no proof of that quality; but . . .
> there is suffering and desperation enough amongst them — these goads will
> urge them forwards." (386; ch. 19)

Robert, on the other hand, assumes heroic proportions in his individual stance against the workers: "a cool, brave man: he stood to the defence with unflinching firmness; those who were with him caught his spirit, and copied his demeanour" (388; ch. 19). In short, the scene demonstrates that a private "feminine" perspective is no guarantee against a vision that exalts paternalism and patriarchal power. Despite differences of content, this feminine perspective repeats the oppositions that structure the hierarchical organization of society and reproduces the masculine perspective's structures.

The narration of the attack on the mill therefore displaces the question of sexual difference from the event and biological identity of the viewer to that of the structure of vision or perspective and in the process calls into question the conventional association of the feminine perspective with the private. The private feminine perspective in this instance reflects/complements the "public" middle class male's.[24]

Identification vs Estrangement and Implication of the Reader

BRONTË'S STRATEGY TO GIVE priority to the time of deferral over the moment of action ultimately implicates the reader in the novel's temporality and undermines the mechanisms of identification which support fetishism. For the reader is also made to wait — for an introduction to the protagonists, for instance. Thus Caroline makes her first appearances in chapter 5 of volume I. Shirley appears in the last chapter of volume I, Louis in the last chapter of volume II (Lawson 735). In this case deferral does not merely frustrate the reader's expectations and desire for narrative movement and denouement, it radically transforms the hero from a central consciousness and mediator of the action to an effect of positioning that is subject to a process of displacement. For as each main character is introduced s/he becomes the focus of the story until displaced by the next one.[25]

Nor is the character's designation as hero determined by an introspective psychology that facilitates identification. This is evident in the displacement of the conventional distinction between major and minor characters by the private/public opposition. The former is usually based on degree of psychological complexity, which distinction assumes that access to characters' thought processes is available to the narrator and reader and in turn supports the realistic premise that one consciousness is continuous with another. Brontë's demarcation, on the other hand, implies the imperviousness of the individual consciousness and resists alignment with a gendered polarity. Instead it describes a discrepancy between the individual personality and his/her social role, which is expressed in pervasive figures that define society as "patterned" and the individual (male or female) as "strange." Society is represented as a rigid context at odds with the individual consciousness.

The Whitsuntide celebration underscores the "patterned" nature of this society to the point of parody:

The twelve hundred children were drawn up in three bodies of four hundred souls each: in the rear of each regiment was stationed a band; between every twenty there was an interval, wherein Helstone posted the teachers in pairs. (337; ch. 16)

Two "lady-generals" go to the head of each regiment. And finally, each regiment is headed by one of the three rectors (337; ch. 16). At the feast the patrons of the school are segregated from the students: they are summoned by a bell to take their tea in the schoolroom, where further distinctions set apart certain classes: the female servants and wives of the lower class men serve as waiters while Caroline, Mrs. Boultby, and Margaret Hall officiate at the three tables reserved for the elite of the company (343; ch. 17).

Certainly each of the four protagonists is described in opposition to such pattern. Thus one function of the Rectory tea which Caroline serves to the Sykes ladies (who reply "by one simultaneous bow") is to demonstrate her discomfort in assuming her social role (123–24; ch. 7). If the Sykes ladies cast Caroline's difference into relief, the Misses Sympson perform a similar function vis-à-vis Shirley: they are described as "two pattern yong ladies, in pattern attire, with pattern deportment. Shirley had the air of a black swan, or a white crow, in midst of this party" (439; ch. 22). Louis's isolation is communicated through his relationship with the Sympsons too. He is introduced as a "satellite" of the family: "connected, yet apart"(513; ch. 26). And Robert is as difficult to place in a pattern as his brother. He is described as a "hybrid" and therefore unattached to parties and sects (34; ch. 2). At the market dinner he is not like the other tradesmen (601; ch. 30).

Secondly, as the preceding examples suggest, it is only peripheral characters in whom the conflict between role and personality does not emerge but who are presented exclusively in terms of rigidity and pattern. Otherwise, the distinction applies to all the characters. Less important characters are also presented in a way that articulates their defiance of social labels rather than gives them psychological depth. For instance, Helstone's personality deviates from conventional notions of a clergyman's character. The narrator describes him as a man who was not cut out to be a priest; "he should have been a soldier" (44; ch. 3).[26] In others, the exaggeration of some aspect of their assigned social role registers antagonism to it. Thus Caroline comes to see Miss Ainley as morbid, her resignation like a nun's. In other words, there is no consistent, single way to resist convention.

Moreover, each of these characters resists permanent definition. Unlike the foil characters in Brontë's previous autobiographical narratives, the characters in Shirley do not have fixed personalities. While Bertha Mason consistently represents one component of Jane Eyre's psyche, Helstone is the totally unsympathetic uncle of Caroline who is nevertheless capable of visiting his niece during her illness and bringing her some chicken selected from his own plate as well as the fork Caroline used when she first came to the Rectory. As Helstone says, the fork is "a happy thought — a delicate attention" (496; ch. 24) and just the kind of sentiment he would have spurned before and which might have been considered out of character. In fact, his behavior raises the question of what it means to be "in character."

Nor does the public/private opposition merely describe the conflict between individual characters and their social context. This opposition also exists *within* the individual consciousness (male or female). For instance, both Shirley and Robert have a public side that is inaccessible to their mates. Or characters can have private and public motives for the same action. Thus political or religious opinions may appear to account for certain relationships such as the antagonism between Helstone and Robert Moore (188). However, in each case Brontë supplies an additional and idiosyncratic reason for the antagonism. For example, Helstone forbids Caroline to visit Hollow Cottage not only because he has quarreled violently and publicly with Robert over the war, but also because he has observed Caroline's liking for Robert and his for her and this faint expression of mutual regard annoys him. It is "these private considerations, combined with political reasons, [that] fixed his resolution of separating the cousins" (189; ch. 10). Brontë repeatedly furnishes a public and a private motive that do not interpenetrate. Indeed, these forces are either totally unrelated, as in the case above, or in violent opposition to one another: for example, Robert's attempt to mix business and marriage by proposing to Shirley is treated as a moral lapse.

In addition to the discontinuity between public and private, the use of disparate narrative modes to represent the main characters' consciousnesses also insists upon the singularity and imperviousness of the individual consciousness — most obviously in the indirect presentation of Shirley's and Robert's thoughts but also in the more direct but different representation of Caroline's through "third person" narration and Louis's through his journal. The fact that the narrator's access to the protagonists' thoughts is not uniform but changes with each mode makes manifest the limitations and inconsistency of the narrating consciousness itself and ultimately redefines the relation between the reader and the text as well.

That is, the narrator never reveals to the reader anything that Robert, Shirley, or Mrs. Pryor conceals from the other characters. Thus Mrs. Pryor's true identity remains a secret because the narrator refrains from supplementing Caroline's knowledge of the lady. As a result, instead of fostering an identification between the narrator and the reader by allowing them to share knowledge unavailable to the characters, the relationship formally reverses dramatic irony: it ruptures rather than cements the complicity of narrating and reading consciusnesses and insists upon their discontinuity.

More specifically, the dilemma precipitated on the level of the story by Mrs. Pryor's disclosure is precisely and explicitly expressed by the lady herself. By way of explaining why she kept her identity a secret, she says that she feared that Caroline's physical resemblance to her father indicated a similarity in manner and disposition as well. In other words, she poses the question of what it means to be one's father's daughter. What is the nature of this "natural" relation? Does paternity determine character? Momentarily Mrs. Pryor introduces the possibility of a disjunction between birth and character, for she reveals her own relationship to Caroline only when she ascertains the *lack* of continuity between the temperaments of father and daughter. But then she resolves the conflict for herself by operating a body/mind, surface/depth split on Caroline, who is said to have inherited her father's facial features and her mother's heart and brain (487; ch. 24). This solution leaves intact the assumption that birth determines character.

But this solution is not entirely satisfactory to the reader. For Mrs. Pryor's reluctance to acknowledge the relationship earlier (not to mention her abandonment of the child in the first place) calls into question the nature or naturalness of her own maternal bond to Caroline. (She even calls herself an "unnatural parent" [492; ch. 24]). This criticism was repeated in the early reviews of the novel. Thus G. H. Lewes judged the depiction of Mrs. Pryor a failure because of its inauthenticity: she is an unnatural and therefore implausible mother. His argument subsumes both definitions of maternity — biological and behavioral — under the category of the "natural." For Lewes, Mrs. Pryor's refusal to recognize her child violates "the natural current of maternal instincts" (167). His critique therefore denies the possibility of a disjunction between birth and behavior that Brontë's text briefly opens up.

At the same time, Lewes's critique implies that what is at stake here is the reader's ability to identify with this character. For according to Lewes, Mrs. Pryor is "untrue to the universal laws of our common nature" (167). Insofar as our identification with and comprehension of Mrs. Pryor are blocked and the narrator keeps her secret without explanation, the question of the nature of parenthood is transposed to the level of narration per se, bypassing the narrator (in the absence of a hierarchy based on superior knowledge, the narrator exists on a par with the characters, and the narration itself is simultaneously foregrounded and de-personified).

At this level the issue of identity is transformed into a question of temporality or causality. For in the order of events Caroline's birth precedes the relationship she develops with Mrs. Pryor as an adult and seems to offer an explanation for their unusually strong affinity, as if the natural bond were the origin of the emotional one. However, in the order of narration the pivotal event in Caroline's life is not the birth itself but its disclosure because it revives Caroline, who is seriously ill and likely to die. In fact, one could argue that Mrs. Pryor gives life to Caroline twice (once through her body and once through her words) and that her revelation of the natural bond (the second or re-birth) is meaningful precisely because of the pre-existing emotional bond. For in the narrative the emotional affinity prefigures the genetic one. In other words, the order of significance is a narrative or rhetorical order at odds with so-called "natural" chronological order: it reverses cause and effect. (Mrs. Pryor is well named for she raises the very issue of priority).[27]

Moreover, the reader is implicated in this narrative order insofar as Mrs. Pryor's disclosure motivates a re-reading of her earlier scenes with Caroline in light of this new knowledge. Therefore access to knowledge is *not* a product of identification with the narrator and/or character but of a process of reading that is not conceived as linear inasmuch as it requires retroactive revision. The text thus subjects the reader to a temporal movement that separates knowledge and belief and insists on their non-coincidence. It therefore demonstrates that the reader's knowledge is not given but produced. Through such means it undoes the fixed oscillation of fetishism.[28]

Winding

AS MRS. PRYOR'S DISCLOSURE detaches chronology from linear causality by displacing chronological with narrative order, it exposes identity and causality to be the products of a rhetorical operation, which is to say an arbitrary ordering. This critique of teleology displays with precision the *movement* of fetishism and indicates the strategy that *Shirley* as a whole systematically pursues to dismantle the structure of fetishism.

More specifically, *Shirley* undoes fetishism, not by providing an alternative structure, but by giving full play to the shiftiness inherent in its structure (which is what fetishism disavows through a fixation on the object). This principle of mobility — described below as substitution and detachment — is central to Freud's definition of the perversion:

> The situation only becomes pathological when the longing for the fetish passes beyond the point of being merely a necessary condition attached to the sexual object and actually *takes the place* of the normal aim, and, further, when the fetish becomes *detached* from a particular individual and becomes the *sole* sexual object. (*Three Essays on Sexuality* 154; emphasis of "detached" is mine)

As this definition suggests, fetishism furnishes a model of desire that can detach from one object and move to others related to the first term (which is lost) only by contingency (i.e., through metonymic displacement). The irreducible difference between the fetish object and the missing sexual organ for which it substitutes suggests the enormous diversity of representations that perversion can generate.

At the same time, Freud's definition raises another question: is this principle of mobility necessarily pathological?[29] Interestingly, Freud's association of the process constitutive of perversion with pathology is incompatible with his own elaboration of *anaclisis* elsewhere in *Three Essays on the Theory of Sexuality* to explain the emergence of sexuality per se. Anaclisis designates the movement whereby a natural or vital function (for example, Freud's paradigmatic case of an infant sucking at the mother's breast) is displaced and perverted into sexuality as drive. As Jeffrey Mehlman puts it, "unconscious sexuality is constituted in excess (or in place) of biological instinct. The Freudian wish (*Wunsch*) persists in opposition to its natural support; everything begins with this perversion or disqualification of 'nature' " (455). This sexual/natural opposition cannot be assimilated to the pathological/normal opposition, for the notion of anaclisis indicates that displacement is at the very heart of human sexuality. Another way of saying this is that "normal" human sexuality is fundamentally perverse.

Nor does the concept of anaclisis exclude an Oedipal organization of sexuality. Quite the contrary. According to Mehlman, "Oedipal sexuality is fundamentally linked with the process of anaclisis" (448). In this reading, the Oedipus complex refers to a structure of exchange brought about by the introduction of a third term (not necessarily incarnated in a person or associated with a particular familial configuration). Thus Mehlman argues, "In the mother-child interaction discussed above the third element is the intersubjective fantasy generated in excess of the vital satisfaction: less than a particular structure the Oedipal reference concerns the fact of structure itself" (449). In other words, the heterogeneity introduced by this triangular structure need not be subsumed under gender difference, which depends on the penile symbolization of the phallus.

The final point to be made before we wind up this detour through perversion is that sexual pleasure, as the definition of fetishism with which we began implies, is a pleasure in representation; indeed it is constituted by figural transformations. However, we are not limited to any particular representation. The capacity for a free-floating play from one representation to another is implied by the process (anaclisis) that constitutes not only fetishism but human sexuality per se. This in turn suggests that fetishism may itself be perverted by activating the displacement process at the heart of all human sexuality.

In *Shirley* this displacement process or perversion of fetishism always involves a movement to another register (rather than simply to another object) and concomitantly a textualization of sexual difference that effects a divorce between gender and sexuality.

1. Thus the incomplete displacement of "first person" by "third person" narration undoes the fetishistic hierarchy of discourses and shifts attention from the story to the mechanics of the text (foregrounded by the use of the device of negative affirmation).

2. Attention to narrative context displaces/perverts the fixation on the fetish object in Louis's interpolated text: in the context of Shirley's androgynous pose as Captain Keeldar, attention shifts from the fetish *object* to the arbitrary *process* that governs its selection.

3. Shirley's vision of the mermaid detaches the image from its initial context and referent and thus opens it up to a different reading in which the representation of sexual difference is projected onto the question of perspective, which in turn transforms the image into a sign.

4. The artifice of the conclusion of the novel draws attention to the conventions of closure and displaces resolution from the final chapter to the love scenes between the two couples. In these scenes interest in differences between narrative modes, styles, and languages supplants the concern with the formation of the heterosexual couples on the level of the story.

5. Insofar as the text undermines the notion of resolution, it diverts attention to the time of waiting for and deferral of resolution, or, more precisely, to the manner in which time is represented, that is, to the procedures which control narrative tempo — ellipsis, descriptive pause, scene, and summary. The refusal to use these means to heighten the attack on the mill and the representation of the action from Caroline's and Shirley's limited point of view displaces attention from the action or event to the perspective and the question of sexual difference that it poses.

6. Deferral transforms the notion of the hero as central consciousness and mediator of the action to his/her definition as an effect of positioning subject to the process of displacement.

7. The displacement of the major/minor distinction between characters by the public/private opposition insists on the imperviousness of the individual consciousness and frustrates the reader's identification with the characters. Attention is thereby directed from the characters to the mechanisms of identification per se.

8. The use of disparate narrative modes to represent the consciousnesses of the four main characters diverts attention from the characters to the inconsistency of the narrator's knowledge, which in turn redefines the relation between

reader and text. In the case of Mrs. Pryor's disclosure, the reader's inability to identify with either the character or the narrator directs attention from the nature of the maternal bond to the temporality of the narration itself and the reader's implication in the production of meaning.

9. Finally, the endless displacement of attention implies a redefinition of narrative pleasure. As the reader/subject is moved by a process that exceeds him/her, ending up in a different position from the expected one, the fascination with privileged scenes and images so crucial to fetishistic representation is transformed into the pleasure of perversion: the diversion of winding displaces the desire for the winding up.

Pace University

NOTES

1. The figure drawn from photography is an attempt to avoid the representation of the text as a palimpsest, which depends on a surface/depth distinction and is a version of the hierarchical structure that *Shirley* systematically undermines. Instead of a palimpsest, *Shirley* is a composite text which uses contradictory codes on the same narrative level.

2. Even in a text where the guise of metalanguage cannot be assumed (i.e., in autobiography, which explicitly identifies the level of narration as the discourse of the writing self and not the reflection of some superhuman "omniscient" consciousness), the subordination of other characters' and the younger self's discourses can be achieved through hierarchical structure. For instance, in *Jane Eyre* different accounts of the past do challenge the narrator's and therefore constitute elements that remain unassimilated to the narrative system, but these challenges to the narrator's authority are, significantly, associated with minor characters and are articulated solely on the level of the story. They remain only hints of another system.

3. Heath's definition is notable in that it defines fetishism as a *structure* rather than an *object*, as in Freud's own formulations of the fetish as a penis substitute or "a substitute for the woman's (mother's) phallus" ("Fetishism" 215). To conceive of a fetish as a substitute object is in fact to enact fetishism, for the fetish object serves as "an original substitution . . . pointing to an original referent" (Weber 82). That is, the fetish object conceals the fact that the phallus is itself already a representation, not the thing itself.

4. Moreover, as Weber points out, the fetish can be both a visible image and an "audible image, the word which appears secure in the unity of sound and sense." The fetishistic denial of difference is present, for instance, in "the identification of the two signifiers, *glance* and *Glanz*, in the reduction of their difference in the homophony"(160).

5. According to Freud, in another passage from "Fetishism," what characterizes the fetishist is a double attitude to the question of castration, the ability to juggle knowledge and belief: "He retains this belief [in the woman having a phallus] but he also gives it up" (216).

6. Brontë uses negatives which affirm in all her narratives, not exclusively in *Shirley*, to express the conflict between meaning and linguistic form. (In this connection see my article on *The Professor*.) But here the device is used to articulate the limitations of "third person" rather than autobiographical narration and to refuse the privileges of omniscience.

7. Many critics, starting with Lewes, have commented on these interpolated narratives: Shirley's vision of the mermaid, Shirley's vision of Milton's Eve, the First Bluestocking, Robert's narration of Shirley's rejection of his proposal, Louis's journal, the attack on the mill.

8. Weber discusses a passage in Arabic in Balzac's *La Peau de Chagrin* in similar terms (46–47).

9. In Freudian theory voyeurism and fetishism are distinctly masculine perversions. In *Three Essays on the Theory of Sexuality* Freud writes, "Little girls do not resort to denial of this kind when they see that boys' genitals are formed differently from their own. They are . . . overcome by envy for the penis" (195). I am arguing that narrative framing in *Shirley* functions to displace identification (which depends on the certainty of this kind of sexual alignment) with analysis.

10. See Rabine's discussion of Louis's fetishism 114–15.

11. See Dupras for a provocative discussion of the multiple readings this passage and others engender, esp. 303–04.

12. I am here following Kofman's argument in *Ça Cloche* that the fetish is a substitute not for the man's penis but for the mother's phallus, that is, a fantasmatic penis which is never *seen* as such but is just believed in. The fetish is therefore an original representation that implies the play of supplementary difference (136–37) and exposes the status of castration as a *fiction*.

Here it is necessary to distinguish my argument from Schor's theorization of "female fetishism" because she also cites Kofman. In the first place this citation is puzzling to me because Kofman does not talk about *female* fetishism but about "un fétishisme généralisé" which is not bound to a single gender. In fact, Apter rejects Kofman's model because it is not exclusively one of female fetishism (Apter 110, 113, 119). Secondly, in her reading of George Sand's use of fetishism, Schor argues that "by appropriating the fetishist's oscillation between castration and denial, women can effectively counter any move to reduce their bisexuality to a single one of its poles" (368). However, this definition of female fetishism keeps the issue in phallic terms. Even Schor wonders, at the conclusion of her essay, if her appropriation is not just "the latest and most subtle form of 'penis-envy' " (371). Kelly, also citing Kofman, but (in my view) to better effect, proposes a fetishism once removed in which the undecidability of the woman's castration itself oscillates with a recognition of castration's groundless, fictional status: "the undecidability of woman's castration (she is and is not castrated in fetishism and in realism) alternates with the undecidable, groundless state in which castration is always already a fiction" (Kelly 178).

This notion of a fetishism once removed enables us to distinguish Shirley's pose from versions of androgyny that are recuperable, according to Doane, because bisexuality is thought to be *inherently* female. Shirley's pose is *not* inherent but the result of metonymic displacement. Even her role as a daughter is regarded as a substitution.

13. My reading therefore differs from Boumelha's (83–84), who regards Shirley's androgyny as a self-indulgent fantasy of transcending social determination, which is enabled by her social privilege and which the text grounds in the context of

realism. In my reading, Shirley acknowledges that her pose is supported by her name and wealth but is subject to an arbitrary logic, while Louis is the one who desires to transcend social determination and strip away her wealth, even her education, in defining her sexual identity.

14. Tillotson (69–70) quotes both this passage and Brontë's comment on it in the letter to Williams, which suggested to me that the mermaid vision in *Shirley* is actually a revision of Thackeray's.

15. The description of this structure of vision and its division of labor according to gender follows Mulvey's psychoanalytic analysis of film spectatorship.

16. In "Masquerade Reconsidered" Doane writes that

    masquerade seemed to provide a feminine counter to the concept of fetishism. . . . Both concepts theorize subjectivity as constituted both spatially and temporally by a gap or distance; but fetishism does so through a scenario which is dependent upon the presence-in-absence of the phallus. . . . Masculinity as measure is not internal to the concept [of masquerade but] . . . is present as the context provoking the patient's reaction-formation. (39)

17. Boumelha observes that contested readings of other texts often give rise to gendered readings in which gender and class become sites of struggle for power (88). Examples she cites include Shirley's vision of Milton's Eve, "discussions of the biblical Eve, Solomon's virtuous woman, Lucretia" (87). Armstrong, however, notes an opposite tendency. Focusing on Caroline's reading of *Coriolanus*, she argues that the reading of literature in *Shirley* functions to transform the social — economic, ethnic, and religious — conflict at the beginning of the novel into a homogeneous community divided exclusively according to gender and generation (divisions within the nuclear family). However, Armstrong's analysis ignores key textual operations: In turning Caroline's interpretive practice into a general model for reading the novel, she makes the character a mouthpiece for the author and thereby ignores the multiplicity of voices in the text. Moreover, to regard the ending of the novel as the fulfillment of the goals of this process of reading is to ignore numerous strategies through which Brontë calls into question that resolution. Finally, the psychologizing tendency which Caroline's mode of reading promotes depends on mechanisms of identification which the novel subverts elsewhere.

18. For this reason, a number of feminist readers regard these interpolated passages as feminine elements which resist the narrative momentum, coded as masculine. See Boumelha (82) and Freeman (562). Though Armstrong focuses on the power rather than the subordination of middle-class women excluded from the work place, the binary oppositions of public/private and male/female remain intact and coincide in her reading (255). In contrast I argue that the hierarchy of discourses implied by all these oppositions is precisely what this novel systematically subverts as it undoes the structures of fetishism.

19. Though Bock and Lundberg also point out the sarcasm and consequent "lack of rapport between narrator and audience" (Bock 233), they rely on a communications model that is hierarchical (makes distinctions among levels of readers) and assumes that the author's intentions can be determined. In contrast, my psychoanalytic approach calls into question structures of intentionality as it focuses on the inscription of a non-biological sexually differentiated place for the

reading subject within the text, which implies involvement in the production of meaning rather than the reception of a preconceived meaning.

20. Thackeray's choreography of Amelia's and Becky's stories may well have served as a model for Brontë since, according to Kroeber, Thackeray invented the multiple plot (108 n. 12). See Tillotson's discussion of the contrast of Becky and Amelia (246). However, the contrast of heroines in *Vanity Fair* does not entail a radical opposition of narrative modes as does the presentation of heroines in *Shirley*.

21. Barthes connects this time with the feminine: "Historically, the discourse of absence is carried on by the Woman: Woman is sedentary, Man hunts, journeys; Woman is faithful (she waits), man is fickle (he sails away, he cruises). It is Woman who gives shape to absence, elaborates its fiction, for she has time to do so . . . " (13–14).

22. Peters discusses such marking of time in the autobiographical novels (28). In *Shirley*, more often than not, social time is marked by meals. The first eight chapters, which cover four days, illustrate this point well. Chapter 1 opens with the curates at dinner. Chapter 2 takes place that evening when Malone visits Robert at the counting house and shares his drink and mutton chops. Chapter 3 takes place later that evening when a rescue party encounters Mr. Yorke. In chapter 4 the whole party retires to Yorke's house for some wine. Chapter 5 describes Hollow's Cottage at breakfast time the next morning. Chapter 6 includes a description of the dinner shared by Hortense and Caroline that day and continues into the evening when Robert returns. Chapter 7 begins with Caroline later that night in her bedroom, followed by an account of breakfast with her uncle the next morning, and the Rectory tea which Caroline serves to the curates and the Sykes ladies later that day. In chapter 8 Moore confronts the unemployed mill workers: he encourages Sykes to stand firm by offering him drink. After the encounter Farren returns to his cottage where his wife tries to quiet the hunger of his children with an inadequate dinner of porridge.

23. Genette defines duration as the proportional relation of the length of the text (measured in lines and pages) and the duration of the story (measured in seconds, minutes, hours, days, months) (87–88, 94).

24. Rabine argues that not only do Caroline and Shirley identify with the men of their own class, but so does the narrator (130–31). More persuasive is Bodenheimer's argument that contradictions in the presentation of both Moore and the workers complicate any simple reading of their opposition (44–45).

25. This explains the disagreement over just which one is the hero. For example Gubar favors the women over the men (6). But Peters designates Louis the hero (121, n.9), and Heilman calls Robert the romantic hero (103).

26. Similarly, the contradictions that compose the description of Hiram Yorke serve to underscore his idiosyncracy rather than give access to his consciousness (Kroeber 30). Freeman points out that not only the main characters but also Yorke, Mr. Sympson, Mary Cave, Miss Mann, and Miss Ainley are said to have faces that are only partially legible (573 n.16).

27. Chase's reading of *Daniel Deronda* in similar terms suggested to me this reading of Mrs. Pryor's disclosure.

28. Note that this plot structure is not at all uncommon in the nineteenth-century novel. In much the same way Jane Eyre's discovery of her kinship with the Rivers family raises the question of whether the genealogical bond is a fulfillment or a precondition of the special affinity she feels with them from their first

meeting. Here too the revelation of a family tie seems too good to be true, especially since Jane learns of her inheritance at the same time. But this implausibility remains confined for the most part to the level of the story because the reader learns of the relation at the same time as Jane, through whom the narrative is focalized and with whom, consequently, the reader strongly identifies. Nor does St. John neglect to inform her of the connection beyond the time required for him to verify it. But in *Shirley* the impact of this plot structure on the reader is different because the implausibility is insisted upon inasmuch as

> 1) Mrs. Pryor deliberately witholds the information for very specious reasons; 2) the novel as a whole is not focalized through Caroline's point of view; instead, a selectively omniscient narrator fails to exercise omniscience just here, which refusal diverts the reader's attention to the level of narration.

29. Adams addresses the same issue as follows:

> The question then is whether all human sexuality is Oedipally organized and whether the perversions which are not so organized are indissociable in principle from pathology. (261)

> Though our arguments both recognize the principle of mobility inherent in fetishism, the "root" or "essence" of the other perversions according to Adams (251), I do not consider Oedipally organized sexuality to be exempt from this metonymic process. Thus our arguments diverge at this point. For Adams it is the lesbian sadomasochist who furnishes a model of perversion without pathology insofar as there is no reference to the paternal phallus in her disavowal of sexual difference (263). In contrast, I argue that the dissociation of sexual difference from gender difference does not require the association of perversion with female sadomasochism.

WORKS CITED

Adams, Parveen. "Of Female Bondage." *Between Feminism and Psychoanalysis*. Ed. Teresa Brennan. London: Routledge, 1989. 247–65.

Apter, Emily. *Feminizing the Fetish: Psychoanalysis and Narrative Obsession in Turn-of-the-Century France*. Ithaca: Cornell UP, 1991.

Armstrong, Nancy. *Desire and Domestic Fiction: A Political History of the Novel*. New York: Oxford UP, 1987.

Barthes, Roland. *A Lover's Discourse*. Trans. Richard Howard. New York: Hill and Wang, 1978.

Bock, Carol A. "Storytelling and the Multiple Audiences of *Shirley*." *Journal of Narrative Technique* 18 (1988): 226–42.

Bodenheimer, Rosemarie. *The Politics of Story in Victorian Social Fiction*. Ithaca: Cornell UP, 1988.

Boumelha, Penny. *Charlotte Brontë*. Bloomington: Indiana UP, 1990.

Brontë, Charlotte. *Shirley*. Ed. Herbert Rosengarten and Margaret Smith. Oxford: Clarendon, 1979.

Brontë, Charlotte. "To W. S. Williams." 14 August, 1848. Letter 385 in *The Brontës: Their Lives, Friendships & Correspondence*. Ed. Thomas James Wise and John Alexander Symington. Vol. 2. Oxford: Shakespeare Head Press, 1932. 243–44.

Chase, Cynthia, "The Decomposition of the Elephants: Double-Reading *Daniel Deronda.*" *Decomposing Figures: Rhetorical Readings in the Romantic Tradition.* Baltimore: Johns Hopkins U P, 1986. 137–74.

Derrida, Jacques. "Differance." *Speech and Phenomena and Other Essays on Husserl's Theory of Signs.* Trans. David B. Allison. Evanston, IL: Northwestern UP, 1973.

Doane, Mary Ann. *Femmes Fatales: Feminism, Film Theory, Psychoanalysis.* New York: Routledge, 1991.

Dupras, Joseph A. "Charlotte Brontë's *Shirley* and Interpretive Engendering." *Papers on Language and Literature* 24. 3 (Summer 1988): 301–16.

Freeman, Janet. "Unity and Diversity in *Shirley.*" *JEGP, Journal of English and Germanic Philology* 874. (October 1988): 558–75.

Freud, Sigmund. "Fetishism." *Sexuality and the Psychology of Love.* Ed. Philip Rieff. New York: Collier, 1963. 214–19.

———. *Three Essays on the Theory of Sexuality.* (1905). *The Standard Edition of the Complete Psychological Works.* Vol. 7. Trans. & ed. James Strachey et al. London: Hogarth, 1953.

Genette, Gérard. *Narrative Discourse: An Essay in Method.* Trans. Jane E. Lewin. Ithaca: Cornell UP, 1980.

Gubar, Susan. "The Genesis of Hunger, According to *Shirley.*" *Feminist Studies* 3. 3/4 (Spring–Summer 1976): 5–21.

Heath, Stephen. "Lessons from Brecht." *Screen* 15.2 (Summer 1974): 103–28.

Heilman, Robert B. "Charlotte Brontë's 'New' Gothic." 1958; rpt. in *The Brontës: A Collection of Critical Essays.* Ed. Ian Gregor. Englewood Cliffs, NJ: Prentice-Hall, 1970. 96–109.

Johnston, Ruth D. "*The Professor*: Charlotte Brontë's Hysterical Text, or Realistic Narrative and the Ideology of the Subject from a Feminist Perspective." *Dickens Studies Annual* 18 (1989): 353–80.

Kelly, Dorothy. *Fictional Genders: Role and Representation in Nineteenth-Century French Narrative.* Lincoln: U of Nebraska P, 1989.

Kofman, Sarah. "Ça cloche." *Lectures de Derrida.* Paris: Galilée, 1981. 115–51.

Kristeva, Julia. "Women's Time." Trans. Alice Jardine and Harry Blake. *Signs: Journal of Women in Culture and Society.* 7.1 (Autumn 1981): 13–35.

Kroeber, Karl. *Styles in Fictional Structure: The Art of Jane Austen, Charlotte Brontë, George Eliot.* Princeton: Princeton UP, 1971.

Lawson, Kate. "The Dissenting Voice: *Shirley*'s Vision of Women and Christianity." *S E L* 29 (1989): 729–43.

[Lewes, G. H.] *Edinburgh Review* 91 (January 1850): 153–73. Partially rpt. in *The Brontës: The Critical Heritage.* Ed. Miriam Allott. Boston: Routledge & Kegan Paul, 1974. 160–70.

Lundberg, Patricia Lorimer. "The Dialogic Search for Community in Charlotte Brontë's Novels." *Journal of Narrative Technique* 20 (1990): 296–317.

MacCabe, Colin. "Realism and the Cinema: Notes on Some Brechtian Theses." *Screen* 15.2 (Summer 1974): 7–27.

Mehlman, Jeffrey. "How to Read Freud on Jokes: The Critic as *Schadchen.*" *New Literary History* 6.2 (Winter 1975): 439–61.

Mulvey, Laura. "Visual Pleasure and Narrative Cinema." *Screen* 16.3 (Autumn 1975): 6–18.

Peters, Margot. *Charolotte Brontë: Style in the Novel.* Madison: U of Wisconsin P, 1973.

Rabine, Leslie W. *Reading the Romantic Heroine: Text, History, Ideology*. Ann Arbor: U of Michigan P, 1985.

Schor, Naomi. "Female Fetishism: the Case of George Sand." *The Female Body in Western Culture: Contemporary Perspectives*. Ed. Susan Rubin Suleiman. Cambridge: Harvard UP, 1986. 363–72.

Thackeray, William Makepeace. *Vanity Fair*. Ed. Geoffrey and Kathleen Tillotson. Boston: Houghton Mifflin, 1963.

Tillotson, Kathleen. *Novels of the Eighteen-Forties*. 1956; rpt. London: Oxford UP, 1961.

Weber, Samuel. *Unwrapping Balzac: A Reading of La Peau de Chagrin*. Toronto: U of Toronto P, 1979.

Wollen, Peter. "Godard and Counter Cinema: *Vent d'Est*." *Readings and Writings: Semiotic Counter–Strategies*. London: New Left Books, 1982. 79–91.

BROWNING AND THE PRE-RAPHAELITES

By Rowena Fowler

WHEN BROWNING PROTESTED TO Ruskin that he should not be classed among those modern artists who are "without God in the world" (Armstrong n.p.), Ruskin at once reassured him: "I consider you a Pre Raphaelite" (DeLaura 330). Other contemporaries of Browning linked his art with that of the Pre-Raphaelites, finding similarities in style or subject and invoking his poetry in response to their paintings. A reviewer of Ford Madox Brown's *The Last of England*, for instance, noted the effect of outdoor light, "the 'everlasting wash of air' as Browning calls it" (Ford Madox Brown 186).[1] The enthusiasm for Browning of the original PRB, especially Thomas Woolner and Dante Gabriel Rossetti, is well documented, and the story of Rossetti's championship of Browning, the development of their friendship, and its eventual cooling has often been told.[2] Although endlessly reciting Browning's poems, however, and pressing them on his friends, Rossetti seldom took them as subjects for paintings or illustrations. Tennyson, who as an "Immortal" rated only two stars to Browning's three, inspired far more and better Pre-Raphaelite pictures, as indeed did Keats, Shakespeare, Chaucer, Boccaccio, Dante, and the Bible. Most Pre-Raphaelite versions of Browning turn out to be partially realized and only intermittently successful. The exceptions, fully-achieved works in their own right, succeed only by "defamiliarizing" the poetry. Why then did these artists respond so keenly to a poet whose style was antithetical to theirs? Or, to pose the question in another form, what is it in Browning that resists translation into the visual terms of the Pre-Raphaelites?

It would be interesting to ask Browning himself, but (ironically, since of all the Victorian poets he was the most interested in and knowledgeable about the visual arts) we know little of his response to the attempts to paint his work. There is no exchange comparable to that between Holman Hunt and Tennyson (whose appreciation of art was rudimentary) over the illustration of the Moxon edition. Browning saw and commented on a few pictures from his poems, briefly and politely. Little is recorded of his reactions to the various

117

Pre-Raphaelite likenesses of himself: the Rossetti and Sandys portraits, the Woolner medallion, the photographs by Eveleen Myers and Julia Margaret Cameron. His well-known objections to Pre-Raphaelite painting and poetry were that it was affected and archaizing, peopled with effeminate or epicene figures;[3] he preferred a more robust, classical, and three-dimensional style, as in Etty, Watts, or Leighton. Two of the most popular Pre-Raphaelite works, Holman Hunt's *The Light of the World* and Millais's *A Huguenot, on St. Bartholomew's day, refusing to shield himself from danger by wearing the Roman Catholic badge*, make an appearance in one of his poems as immediately recognizable clichés, the inevitable furnishings of a shabby-genteel hotel parlor (*The Inn Album*, line 37). Of all the Pre-Raphaelites and their associates his favorite seems to have been Ford Madox Brown, whose *Christ Washing Peter's Feet* (Tate Gallery, 1856), with its massive ideal figures boldly foregrounded and vividly and naturalistically painted, bears a striking resemblance to Browning's *Saul* (1845).[4]

The term "Pre-Raphaelite" is nowadays applied to a variety of artists and works. A rigorously narrow definition would include only those artists who were members of the original PRB, their immediate associates (Brown, Hughes), and the landscape painters (John Brett, A. W. Hunt) who formed a distinct but direct offshoot of the movement. This Pre-Raphaelitism, which lasted only from 1848 to about 1860, can be characterized in terms of a shared vision of the role and value of art and a similar approach to subject, style, technique, and iconography. A broader and more eclectic definition, which I have adopted here, includes Burne-Jones and his followers as well as those romantic painters like J. H. Waterhouse and John Byam Shaw, sometimes described as "post" or "neo" Pre-Raphaelite, who continued throughout the century to find in the earlier movement a source of influence and inspiration.

The first Pre-Raphaelites were not concerned with literal illustration; their scrupulous regard for accuracy of observation and "truth to nature" aimed at artistic authenticity rather than narrative fidelity. The tension in their work between naturalistic detail and symbolic, heightened meanings finds some parallels in Browning, for example in "Saul" or in the nightmare landscape of "Childe Roland," but the hermetic iconography of Pre-Raphaelite art, its emblematic and often claustral quality, contrasts with the style of Browning's imagery, which is vibrant and improvisatory. The Pre-Raphaelites responded to the drama in Browning, which matched their own search for intensity, but their characteristically shallow picture spaces and flat planes tend to frame their subjects in a single "situation," a mood or a moment which finds its counterpart in Tennyson rather than Browning: as John Dixon Hunt has shown, many of Tennyson's poems, like Victorian pictures, "seek to announce the past and future of narrative in the present of their painterly image" (180–81).[5] Browning is shifting and restless where the Pre-Raphaelites are composed; his scenes break up and re-form so that they can be visualized but not pictured. Although his "canvas" is full and authentically detailed, he concentrates on the single figure, group, or action; the ultimate Pre-Raphaelite quality, on the other hand, is a brilliantly unreal emphasis on all the details of a scene, according them equal tonal importance in the overall composition. From the wide range of his work, the Pre-Raphaelites, as might be expected, chose mainly medieval, Italian, or chivalric subjects, avoiding poems of modern life and sifting out the discursive, anecdotal, analytical, and relentlessly *speaking* voice of the poet. Browning's naturalistic psychology was transmogrified into more stylized and decorative evocations of beauty, mystery, and evil. His clogged meter and syntax, the uningratiating phonetic texture of his poetry, may be compared to the early drawings of Rossetti and Holman Hunt, with their intricate cramped compositions and spiky forms (as the mellifluousness of Millais's line pairs him with Tennyson). Browning's verbal dissonance finds no authentic counterpart, however, in the burnished surfaces of Hunt's and Millais's paintings or in the fluent and sumptuous designs of the later Pre-Raphaelites.

Browning's influence on the Pre-Raphaelites, seen first[6] and at its most marked in the early Rossetti and realized in very different ways by Elizabeth Siddal, Arthur Hughes, William Henry Hunt, and J. B. Yeats, finds its most original and inspired interpreter in Burne-Jones, whose creative mis-reading of the poet transforms him into a Pre-Raphaelite magus. Later artists chose subjects from Browning but almost always from the better-known early poems, so that there was an increasing gap between the poet's own development and the more conservative taste of his illustrators. (Not one picture, as far as I have been able to establish, was inspired by *The Ring and the Book*.) At the Grosvenor Gallery, for instance, where Browning was a frequent visitor, several versions of "Childe Roland" were exhibited. The Pre-Raphaelite impulse continued, if in odd and attenuated forms, after Browning's death and into the new century, when "literary" paintings finally went out of fashion in Britain. At the New English Art Club *intimiste* scenes of people reading took the place of pictures from books; a new interest in the psychology of the reader rather than the visualization of the text can be seen in William Rothenstein's *The Browning Readers* (1900).[7]

"Confronted with Browning," Rossetti found, "all else seemed pale and in neutral tint. Here were passion, observation, mediævalism, the dramatic perception of character, act, and incident." He responded to the "sonorous rhythmical effect" of the poetry and "revelled in what, to some other readers, was mere crabbedness" (*Dante* 1: 102). His first picture from Browning, *Taurello's First Sight of Fortune* [fig. 1], is his most successful translation into visual terms of such "perception of character, act, and incident," attempting to concentrate in one scene a complex narrative that encompasses past, present, and future. It takes as its starting-point the passage in *Sordello* where Taurello Salinguerra recollects how he was challenged by his future father-in-law, Heinrich VI of Sicily, to take over the leadership of the Ghibellin faction in Northern Italy and regain land lost to the Guelphs. An aloe, "bloated sprawler" of a plant, which like himself lacks courage to climb upright, brings back the memory of

> The day I came, when Heinrich asked in sport
> If I would pledge my faith to win him back
> His right in Lombardy: "for, once bid pack
> Marauders," he continued, "in my stead
> You rule, Taurello!" and upon this head
> Laid the silk glove of Constance — I see her
> Too, mantled head to foot in miniver,
> Retrude following! (*Sordello* 4. 781–88)

In Rossetti's drawing there is no aloe or other symbolic vegetation. Browning's enclosed setting — "Messina's castle-court" — becomes a bare, stage-like rampart on which Heinrich and his family are grouped in a vertical block high above the backdrop of city and sea. As A. I. Grieve has noted, the composition has a "strange, open symmetry" which, together with the "abruptness of gestures and the uneasiness of the confrontation between the characters," is awkward and disturbing (51). The act of investiture is one of those dramatic moments or significant turning-points which figure so often in Pre-Raphaelite art; here Taurello's youth and obvious reluctance are unexpectedly touching. Constance is posed in the act of drawing off her glove, Heinrich's left hand is cupped to receive it and his right is outstretched to touch Taurello's face with a kind of autocratic playfulness. Retrude, Taurello's future wife (and Sordello's mother), and her brother Ecelin, Taurello's future enemy and rival, look on. Rossetti has added a family dog, Taurello's emblem and counterpart, offering an arrow for his bow. The outlines of the drawing are spiky and hard-edged and the whole design squared off and densely cross-hatched, as if answering to a dryness, even "crabbedness," of style in *Sordello*.

An early experiment in another medium, Rossetti's first completed water-color, *The Laboratory* [fig. 2], offers a very different version of a Browning poem. A Victorian reviewer found *The Laboratory* perfectly "in the spirit of the poet whom it illustrates" and suggested that Rossetti had learnt his method from Browning, the precursor and "spiritual father" of Pre-Raphaelitism who "added thought to romance in the study of the past" and "secured the truth of a situation by perfect knowledge of its details" ("Dante Gabriel Rossetti" 195–96). The picture, for all the drama of its cramped space and arched, leaning figure, is, however, very different in atmosphere from Browning's poem, with its passionate, cold murderousness: "Let death be felt and the proof remain: / Brand, burn up, bite into its grace — / He is sure to remember her dying face!" (38–40). Part of the reason is that Browning's speaker is — literally — masked; the urgency and relish of the poem is carried in her voice. In necessarily removing his characters' masks Rossetti has rendered them less sinister. There is even, as David Sonstroem has suggested, an element of caricature: Rossetti's early *femmes fatales* "are all somewhat playfully depicted . . . [they] lack final seriousness, and their terrors are make-believe ones" (108–09). While bringing out the bright colors and gorgeous details of the woman's jewels and ballgown in the dark room, Rossetti has played down the perverse eroticism of the poem, the "sweet" and "exquisite" poison and the intermingling of gold and youth, dust and death:

> Now, take all my jewels, gorge gold to your fill,
> You may kiss me, old man, on my mouth if you will!
> But brush this dust off me, lest horror it brings
> Ere I know it — next moment I dance at the King's! (45–48)

Rossetti's imagination did not really respond to the worldliness of the *ancien régime* and he could not match Browning's grasp of the urbanity and inventiveness of evil. He was more at home with the medieval setting of the other Browning picture he was working on at the time, from the refrain of Pippa's third song in *Pippa Passes*, " 'Hist!' said Kate the Queen." He may have made rough sketches for this subject as early as the summer of 1847; he returned to it in 1850 having in the meantime worked on and destroyed an unfinished larger design. The composition was altered several times; F. G. Stephens saw a version in three compartments (28), and a tantalizing reference in William Michael's diary suggests that Rossetti's visit to Paris in 1849 had a special influence on his style: "A letter came from Gabriel. . . . He has been to see the working of the Gobelin[s] tapestries, which has so altered his ideas concerning the matter that he says he shall probably make an entirely new design for *Kate the Queen* when he is prepared to paint the subject" (*P.R.B. Journal* 19). The mid-nineteenth century was not an inspiring time at the Gobelins factories, which were turning out "woven pictures" in imitation of Old Masters; but perhaps there was something in the process itself which suggested to Rossetti a more colorful, stylized, and two-dimensional approach to easel painting. Tapestry seems to have made an impact on Rossetti's imagination earlier than medieval pictures, woodcuts, and illuminations. The surviving oil sketch for *Kate the Queen* [fig. 3] crowds nearly thirty figures into three-quarters of the canvas; outside on a terrace the page "carols unseen" while the queen inclines her head to hear him and her ladies pause in the act of brushing her hair, sewing, flirting, or reading aloud from the *Decameron*.

The page is separated from the court by a thick vertical structure and barred from the viewer by the uprights of a colonnade. His extreme youth and awkward pose link him to the figure of the queen who, also very young and rather stiff, seems to be alone at the center of the picture.

The queen bears a striking resemblance to Elizabeth Siddal, though it is not clear whether she had begun modelling for Rossetti at the time the picture was painted. Siddal's own version of *Pippa Passes, Pippa Passing the Loose Women* [fig. 4] illustrates the episode (in scene 3 of Browning's poem) where the innocent Pippa meets three "girls" who are discussing their clients. Her upright pose and simple hair and dress contrast with the "loose" style of the prostitutes, from whom, as Jan Marsh has described, she is "visually separated by an unmistakable barrier of strong vertical lines" (192). The spare, careful drawing seems to show the influence of the wood-engraving techniques which Siddal was studying at the time. Rossetti told Allingham that when he showed it to Browning "he was Delighted beyond measure, and wanted excessively to know her" (*Letters* 1: 281), but when the opportunity arose, in Paris in 1856, Siddal was ill and nothing came of it. Siddal's drawing, her only one from Browning, was also the only Browning subject in the Pre-Raphaelite exhibition of 1857.[8]

Although by the mid-1850s Rossetti's enthusiasm for Browning was as strong as ever, his interest as a painter was tending increasingly towards religious subjects; it was only the failure of his *Ecce Ancilla Domini!* to sell that had kept him working at *Kate the Queen* — "a subject which I have pitched upon principally for its presumptive saleableness. I find unluckily that the class of pictures which has my natural preference is not for the market" (*Letters* 1: 88). Rossetti made only one other Browning picture. When, in 1856, he was asked to contribute to the Rev. R. A. Willmott's *Poets of the Nineteenth Century* he found that "That venerable parson had not, it seems, included Browning, for whose introduction I made an immediate stand, and said in that case I would illustrate him . . . I shall propose . . . *Count Gismond*, — 'Say, hast thou lied?' — which I designed some years ago." The suggestion was not taken up and the two poems which were selected — poems of contemporary life — did not fire Rossetti's imagination: "I had engaged to do Browning; but what could have been done with *Evelyn Hope* or *Two in the Campagna*?" (*Letters* 1: 292, 310).[9] For his design for "Count Gismond" (now lost) Rossetti chose stanza 17, in which Count Gismond confronts the dying Gauthier as his future Countess looks on half-fainting with fear and relief.

The only other Pre-Raphaelite to illustrate the poem, Arthur Hughes, took up the story at stanza 19, with Gismond and his rescued lady alone: "Over my head his arm he flung / Against the world" (109–10). His painting *The Guarded Bower* [fig. 5] is composed in three arched shapes, his favorite curved-top frame echoing the bower of branches behind the lovers and the man's arm (still holding a sword) encircling the woman's head and shoulders. Many of Hughes's best-known works (*April Love, The Long Engagement, The Tryst*) depict lovers posed among or against trees at some moment of tension when love is doomed or innocence threatened. His young women seem virginal and vulnerable. *The Guarded Bower*, however, has some of the ambiguous atmosphere of Browning's poem, with its hint of unresolved memories and half-told secrets. Years after the event Browning's countess confides the violent beginnings of her married life: "Scarce I felt / His sword (that dripped by me and swung) / A little shifted in its belt" (110–12). Hughes plays down these gruesome details and dresses Gismond in soft velvet rather than the unwieldy ironmongery of the poem ("greaves," "hauberk," "ringing gauntlets"). Browning's imagery of falconry, which casts the countess in the role of hunter, not prey — "and have you brought my tercel back?" (124) — is oddly paralleled in Hughes's iconography: a peacock, symbol of vanity, occupies almost the whole of the foreground, its tail repeating the shape and color of the woman's cloak. The male dove at the lovers' feet stretches its wings in a courtship display which looks threatening as well as protective and the scattered petals on the ground draw attention to the bare stem in the woman's hand and compromise the beautifully-embroidered sprigs on the hem of her dress. These details suggest an interpretation of "Count Gismond" which is enigmatic and elegaic rather than dramatic or triumphant. Traces of a heart radiating light can just be made out in the foliage above the lovers' heads, a too-insistent emblem which Hughes fortunately thought better of and painted over. The woman's inscrutable gaze is out of the picture, not quite meeting that of the viewer; it is impossible to say whether her thoughts are tending forward, where "South our home lay many a mile" (114), or guarding the secrets of the past. As in Browning's poem the final meanings remain unexplained.

The Guarded Bower is Hughes's only picture from Robert Browning (two paintings, *Good Night* and *The King's Orchard*, have mottoes from *Pippa Passes* but no real connection with the poem; two others, *The Tryst* and *That Was a Piedmontese* are from Elizabeth Barrett Browning). Hughes's life and work are less well documented than those of other major Pre-Raphaelites, and little is known about the inception and execution of *The Guarded Bower* or about his response to Browning's poetry in general; it is not even clear whether the two men ever met.[10] Browning presumably approved of Hughes's illustrated edition of Tennyson's *Enoch Arden* since he gave a copy as a Christmas present to his sister-in-law Arabella.

In the same year (1866) as *The Guarded Bower* was exhibited at the Royal Academy, a painting from "Childe Roland" was shown at the Society of Painters in Water Colours. The artist, Alfred William Hunt, an associate of the Pre-Raphaelites (no relation to Holman Hunt or William Henry Hunt), sent Browning a ticket to the exhibition. Browning's reply offers a rare glimpse of his reaction to a "realization" of his work:

> I feel proud indeed, and something better, that any poem of mine should have associated itself with the power which conceived and executed so magnificent a picture — I weigh the word and repeat it. My own "marsh" was only made out of my head, — with some recollection of a strange solitary little tower I have come upon more than once in Massa-Carrara, in the midst of low hills, — for I wrote at Paris. (*New Letters* 172–73)

Even allowing for conventional courtesies, Browning's tone seems genuinely enthusiastic; a lifelong friendship with Hunt and his family ensued.[11] Hunt was taking a risk. "Childe Roland" is one of the most powerfully suggestive imaginary landscapes in Victorian literature; seeing it visualized by someone else must have been a strange experience for Browning ("My own 'marsh' was only made out of my head"). Hunt adapted one of his own favorite landscapes, Dolbadarn Castle in North Wales [fig. 6], thus avoiding the pitfalls of excessive literalism or second-hand fantasy. He himself had once hoped to be a poet and, as his career as an artist developed, he allowed the topographical naturalism of his earlier style to give way to a more abstract concern with color, light, and shade. He greatly admired the vision and technique of Turner, especially the "poetical instinct" which Turner brought to his illustrations of Scott. In Hunt's *Childe Roland* swirling clouds envelop the horizon in a dramatic reddish glow, and Turneresque eddies of paint dissolve the form of the landscape, from which only tower, pool, lone horseman, and a frame of stark, ruined undergrowth emerge. The castle itself is softened, distanced, and transformed. Hunt's painting is both intimate and generalized; though it does not limit the poem to any one particular historical period, it anchors "Childe Roland" in the recognizable physical world of the English Romantic landscape.

Where Hunt's Turneresque *Childe Roland* links the poem to a tradition of landscape painting, Burne-Jones's version [fig. 7] re-imagines it as myth and fairy-tale. Roland's pose, the angle of his sword and style of his armor, and the barrier of vegetation recall "The Prince Entering the Rose Thicket" which was designed at the same time, and "The Prince Enters the Wood" and "The Prince Enters the Briar Wood" in the later *Briar Rose* sequences.[12] The resemblance suggests that Burne-Jones interpreted "Childe Roland" as a poem of enchantment. As in his handling of the "sleeping beauty" theme he suggests the possibility of, but stops short of picturing, the moment of disenchantment; Roland's "slug-horn" is raised, taking the place of the shield in the *Briar Rose* scenes, but it is never to be sounded. As John Christian has noted, Browning's work was essentially too dramatic to suit Burne-Jones's conceptual approach: "whereas the mood of the poem is introspective, the drawing is conceived in decorative terms" (123). The Childe's pose, the upward curve of arm and "slug-horn" repeated in the inscription on the title scroll, is set against a flat background with little illusion of depth or distance. W. David Shaw has suggested that, of all Browning's "medieval" poems, "Childe Roland" comes closest to a Pre-Raphaelite atmosphere and style, sharing with some of Rossetti's poems "a kind of etched austerity," and resembling "a two-dimensional landscape of flat forms of the kind common in quattrocento art" (75). Browning's starved, blighted landscape — "ragged thistle-stalk" (67) and "dock's harsh swarth leaves" (70) — is, however, transformed by Burne-Jones into a tangle of sunflowers barring Roland from the tower and seeming to stand for all his lost comrades, ranged "To view the last of me, a living frame / For one more picture!" (200-01). "Did you ever draw a sunflower?" he once wrote, "it is a whole school of drawing and an education in itself," and again, "Do you know what faces they have — how they peep and peer, and look arch and winning, or bold and a little insolent sometimes?" (1: 225). In spite of this rather fanciful tone Burne-Jones studied the flowers minutely; the drawing was first owned by, and possibly commissioned by, Ruskin, whose ideals of accurate observation and imaginative vision it seeks to embody.

"Childe Roland" belongs to the period, early in Burne-Jones's career, when he was most influenced by Rossetti's style and outlook. He had discovered Browning's poetry while still at Oxford and was introduced to him by Rossetti in 1856. Both the Brownings liked Burne-Jones and tried to draw him out, admiring a drawing he had brought with him: "a drawing in the extreme Pre-Raphaelite manner, exquisitely over-elaborated, a work of infinite detail, quaint, but full of real feeling and rare fancy" (Norton 1: 341–42). For his part, Burne-Jones felt that Browning "is the deepest and intensest of all poets — writes lower down in the dark heart of things" (Burne-Jones 1: 153). An album of his favorite poems, illustrated for Sara Prinsep's sister, Sophia Dalrymple, at Little Holland House, includes Browning's early troubadour poem "Rudel to the Lady of Tripoli," chosen, perhaps, for Rudel's device, the sunflower [fig. 8].

Burne-Jones's only other Browning picture, *Love Among the Ruins* [fig. 9] also has an oblique relationship to the poem, which it interprets freely and idiosyncratically. The design of the two lovers had previously been used to illuminate one of Morris's calligraphic versions of *The Rubaíyát of Omar Kháyyám*, and it has also been seen as an illustration of another favorite Pre-Raphaelite text, the fifteenth-century *Hypnerotomachia Polyphilii* or *Strife of Love in a Dreame*.[13] The high-waisted, loose-fitting costumes and the architectural setting, the substantial but imaginary monuments covered in inscriptions, certainly owe something to the *Hypnerotomachia*. The juxtaposition of human figures with crumbling masonry and luxuriant vegetation was a frequent motif in Pre-Raphaelite art, especially after the popular success of Millais's *A Huguenot*. The features and trance-like expressions of the lovers, however (painted from two of his favorite models), and the entwined briars are very much Burne-Jones's own, and the mood of the painting may owe something to the crisis in his affair with Maria Zambaco. Preliminary sketches show that he experimented with the lovers' pose — reclining, turned away from the viewer, or kissing face-to-face — and chose a twisted, curving embrace which becomes part of a larger design taking in thorns and drapery. Though briar roses, with their associations of enchanted beauty, have replaced the homelier fecundity of Browning's caper, gourd, and houseleek, Burne-Jones alludes to the contrast in the poem between the horizontal rhythms of grass and plants and the ruined but still potent vertical allure of pillar, spire, and turret. Past glories compete with present-day love affair for the attention of Browning's shepherd but the poem is in the end a celebration, however wistful, of the possibility of love and the transformation of the hard gold of legendary empires into the "yellow hair" of a living girl. Burne-Jones's lovers remain trapped forever among the ruins, which, while adding piquancy to their situation, also mirror it and doom it to unfulfilment

The other important Browning picture painted at the same time as *Love Among the Ruins* is John B. Yeats's *Pippa Passes* [fig. 10]. Yeats, whose own "Brotherhood" with Edwin J. Ellis, J. T. Nettleship, and George M. Wilson was modelled on the PRB, began his career as a Pre-Raphaelite painter, and his *Pippa* shows the influence of Rossetti in its rich palette and dramatic characterization. The pose of the figure — arms uplifted to emphasize the lines of the body, head tilted backwards, and mouth slightly open — has been compared with the female figures of Frederick Sandys, whose studio Yeats often visited (Cullen 21–22), but his Pippa is less graceful and langorous than Sandys's women. The sense of movement in the composition, the swinging apron and hair, the twisting path and trees make it more dynamic than most Pre-Raphaelite pictures. Pippa's costume is picturesque, reminiscent of an Eastlake brigand painting, but it is also authentic, the peasant dress of early nineteenth-century Italy. (Yeats fortunately rejected his first idea, which was to dress her entirely in white.) Her face and sturdy bare legs and feet are unidealized. Yeats's image seems to have been influential: the pose is echoed, for instance, in Leslie Brooke's illustration for the Porter and Clarke Arno edition of Browning's *Complete Works* (1898), though Brooke's Pippa has been re-clad in turn-of-the century factory uniform and sensible shoes. John Todhunter, who had commissioned *Pippa Passes* from Yeats, also owned his drawing of *In a Gondola* (now lost); Browning was shown both pictures by Todhunter in 1878 and was apparently so impressed that he immediately

1. Dante Gabriel Rossetti, *Taurello's First Sight of Fortune* (1849).
Reproduced by permission of the Tate Gallery, London.

3. Dante Gabriel Rossetti, " 'Hist!' said Kate the Queen" (1851). Reproduced by permission of Eton College Collections, Windsor, England.

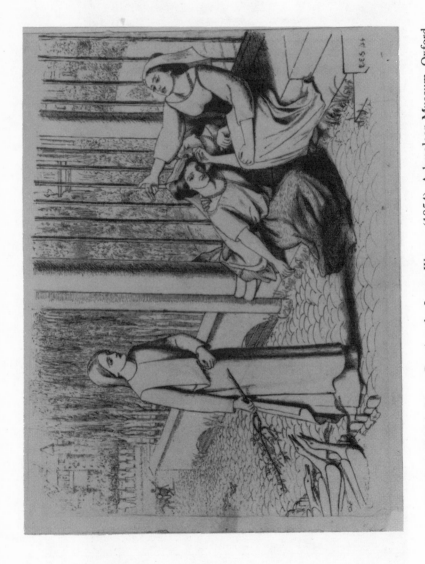

4. Elizabeth Siddal, *Pippa Passing the Loose Women* (1854). Ashmolean Museum, Oxford.

5. Arthur Hughes, *The Guarded Bower* (1866). Reproduced by permission of Bristol Museums and Art Gallery, Bristol, England.

6. Alfred William Hunt, *Childe Roland to the Dark Tower Came* (1866). Private Collection; reproduced by permission.

7. Edward Burne-Jones, *Childe Roland* (1861). Reproduced by permission of the Cecil Higgins Art Gallery, Bedford, England.

8. Edward Burne-Jones, *Rudel to the Lady of Tripoli* (1859), reproduced in *The Little Holland House Album,* with an introduction and notes by John Christian, 1981. Reproduced by permission of the Dalrymple Press, Edinburgh.

9. Edward Burne-Jones, *Love Among the Ruins* (1870–73). Private Collection. Later oil version, 1894. Reproduced by permission of the National Trust, London.

10. John Butler Yeats, *Pippa Passes* (1869-72). Reproduced by permission of the National Gallery of Ireland.

11. John La Farge, *"This was a spray the bird clung to"* (1861). Reproduced by permission of the National Museum of American Art, Washington, D. C.

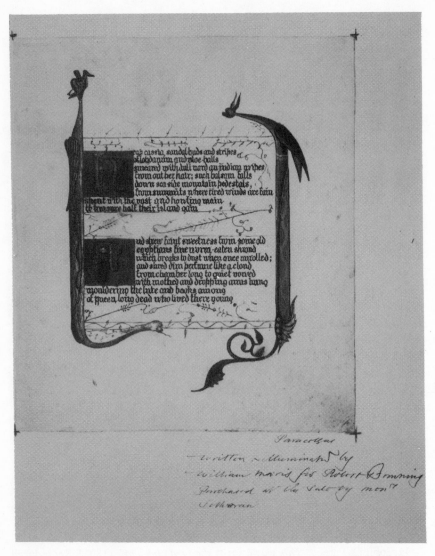

12. William Morris, *"Heap cassia, sandal-buds and stripes"* (1870). Reproduced by permission of The Huntington Library, San Marino, California.

13. John Byam Shaw, *"This is a Heart the Queen Leant On"* (1908). Reproduced by permission of Sotheby's, London.

14. Eleanor Fortescue-Brickdale, *"If I Could Have that Little Head"* (1909).
Courtesy of Russell Cotes Art Gallery and Museum, Bournemouth.

called on Yeats to congratulate him. Yeats was not at home and, with characteristic lethargy, allowed Browning's invitation to visit him to lapse (Murphy 116).

The various strands of later Pre-Raphaelite art deriving from Rossetti and Burne-Jones rarely drew on Browning for their inspiration. In America, the influence of Pre-Raphaelitism was mainly felt in landscape painting — landscape that was free of literary associations. Browning's most enthusiastic illustrator was John La Farge, whose designs for *The Pied Piper* were sent to William Rossetti, who showed them to Browning (*Rossetti Papers* 304, 306).[14] La Farge particularly liked *Men and Women*, which he had read with William and Henry James, and in 1859-61 he made over three hundred illustrations: "For Saul, the number of drawings I could make (if I had the power) is so great — that I could hardly enumerate them and these *outside of the story*" (Weinberg 55).[15] The drawings were in black and white so as to be suitable for printing in the style of the Pre-Raphaelite illustrations in the Moxon Tennyson, which La Farge admired. (He had also seen work by Rossetti, Hunt, Millais, and Brown when he visited England.) Few now survive, though a design for the frontispiece, *"This was a spray the bird clung to,"* is preserved on a *cliché verre* plate [fig. 11]. The spray of blossom of Browning's "Misconceptions" becomes a frame for the title page, balancing the drapery of the woman on the left, who holds a statue of a winged child. More foliage decorates the gorgon's head: a detail very much "outside of the story." The design is imaginative and graceful, but too purely ornamental for an edition of Browning.

As Pre-Raphaelitism shaded into aestheticism and *art nouveau* Browning's poetry was transposed into increasingly distant keys, its angularities and colloquialisms attractively but incongruously framed by the flowing borders and illuminated initials of Charles Ricketts (Vale Press, 1899) or the delicate wood engravings of Lucien Pissaro (Eragny Press, 1904). A notable exception to such a mismatch of styles is William Morris's calligraphic transcription of the song from *Paracelsus*, "Heap cassia, sandal-buds and stripes" [fig. 12]. Here, the Gothic letters, illuminated initials and grotesque borders, together with the robustness of the vellum itself, complement and echo the song's archaic dignity.

The last phase of Pre-Raphaelitism, after Browning's death, coincided with the heyday of the Browning Societies and saw a brief but prolific resurgence of interest in pictures from and of his work. Byam Shaw, for instance, with his penchant for literary and historical subjects, experimented with Browning pictures in a variety of styles and media, though none is as successful as his painting of Rossetti's *Silent Noon* (Leighton House). His sixty-seven illustrations for Browning's *Poems* in the Endymion Series (1897) vary from decorative headpieces to Beardsleyesque designs of naked women at candlelit banquets ("How It Strikes a Contemporary") and more naturalistically-drawn genre scenes in contemporary dress ("The Lost Mistress"). The influence of the original PRB, especially Hunt and Millais, is seen in his cabinet picture, *Notice Neptune, Though*, from "My Last Duchess."[16] Shaw's only major oil painting of a Browning subject, *"This is a Heart the Queen Leant On"* [fig. 13], visualizes Browning's image (from the second stanza of "Misconceptions") in terms of an early Renaissance court, the brightly-colored coronation or wedding procession in the background under the colonnades distanced from the rejected suitor by an expanse of empty grey steps. The canvas is small by Shaw's usual standards (49 × 76 cm) but elaborately painted: the costumes are richly detailed and the figures in the procession individually modelled from his family and colleagues (Cole 151–52).

Shaw's fellow artist Eleanor Fortescue-Brickdale (standing just in front of the queen in his picture) was herself a noted illustrator of Browning: the Chatto & Windus *Pippa Passes and Other Poems* (1908) and *Dramatis Personae and Dramatic Romances and Lyrics* (1909) each have ten of her pastels or watercolors. She also turned to Browning's "Natural Magic" (in *Pacchiarotto*) for a subject for her 1905 exhibition of watercolors "Such Stuff as Dreams are Made Of." Fortescue-Brickdale, unlike Shaw, was interested in techniques and materials and worked in various crafts, notably stained glass design. The decorative background and haloed pose of *"If I Could Have That Little Head"* . . . [fig. 14] resemble stained glass; the gold paint suggests an illuminated manuscript. The rich colors and textures and airless, artificial atmosphere of neo-Pre-Raphaelitism conjure up an eternal and unironic portrait which Browning's speaker never intended and only momentarily desired: "If one could have that little head of hers / Painted upon a background of pale gold, / Such as the Tuscan's early art prefers!" ("A Face" 1–3).

Fortescue-Brickdale's painting is innocent of the ghastly logic of wish-fulfilment that it embodies and remains untouched by Browning's knowledge of the murkier aspects of fantasy and desire. The possibilities of Pre-Raphaelite interpretation were played out once his poetry offered no more than beautiful, timeless, contextless subjects for pictures. The energy of Browning's influence passed in the new century from art to poetry; it is in the poets most indebted to him — Eliot, Pound, and Cavafy — that his work was to be renewed.

University of Bristol

NOTES

1. In "Two in the Campagna," stanza 5.
2. See Cramer, Adrian, Grylls, and Lasner. For Browning's reservations about Rossetti's style see note 3 below.

3. See Browning, *Dearest Isa* 336–37 (on Rossetti); 331 (on Simeon Solomon).
4. For Browning's visit to Brown's studio see *The Diary of Ford Madox Brown* (185); on "Saul" see Edwards. Brown never painted a subject from Browning.
5. See also Stein.
6. David Scott's *The Alchymical Adept Lecturing on the Elixir Vitæ*, 1838 (National Gallery of Scotland) and Richard Redgrave's *The Wonderful Cure by Paracelsus*, 1840 (present whereabouts unknown) are sometimes said to be based on *Paracelsus* (1835), but there is no conclusive internal or external evidence to connect these paintings with Browning's poem. Scott (1806–49), elder brother of William Bell Scott, is more fittingly described as an idiosyncratic history painter than as a Pre-Raphaelite *avant la lettre*. Though Redgrave was later sympathetic to some of the achievements of the PRB, his meticulously-finished landscapes and genre pictures are not Pre-Raphaelite in style or conception.
7. See my "William Rothenstein Reads Browning."
8. The drawing is reproduced in *Letters of Dante Gabriel Rossetti to William Allingham 1854–1870*, facing p. 161. For details of the three versions of Siddal's drawing see David Brown (292).
9. "Two in the Campagna" was illustrated in Willmott's anthology with a rather old-fashioned vignette by E. A. Goodall.
10. Hughes met Browning's uncle Reuben at a party and they talked about the poet (*Letters . . . to William Allingham* 168). The main collections of Hughes's MS letters (to F. G. Stephens, to William Bell Scott and Alice Boyd, and to the Hale-White family) unfortunately do not cover 1866, the year *The Guarded Bower* was exhibited.
11. See Robert Secor. Hunt exhibited two other landscapes with mottoes from Browning: *A North Country Stream* ("Summer redundant, Blueness abundant" from the prologue to *Jocoseria*, RA 1883) and *On the Dangerous Edge* ("Our interest's in [sic] the dangerous edge of things" from "Bishop Blougram's Apology," RA 1887). Seeing the former, Browning wrote gallantly: "For my own motto — glorified by its application — I am properly grateful" (*New Letters* 285). For Hunt's views on illustration and his appreciation of Turner see A. W. Hunt. For the identification of Hunt's landscape as Dolbadarn Castle, see Bernard Richards (226).
12. See Martin Harrison and Bill Waters, pls. 139, 223, color pl. 43.
13. See Harrison and Waters, 82; see also Penelope Fitzgerald (141).
14. William Michael Rossetti, Diary, 13 April and 28 April 1868.
15. Two studies for "Fra Lippo Lippi" and one for "Protus" are reproduced in Russell Sturgis (4, 5, 11).
16. Present whereabouts unknown: reproduced in "Modern British Water-Colour Drawings," *The Studio*, special supplement (London, 1900) 57. This and two other Browning subjects were exhibited at Dowdeswell's Gallery (1899) and the Art Institute of Chicago (1900).

WORKS CITED

Adrian, Arthur A. "The Browning-Rossetti Friendship: Some Unpublished Letters." *PMLA* 73.5 (1958): 538–44.

Armstrong, Mary M. "A Letter from Robert Browning to John Ruskin." *Baylor University Browning Interests* 17 (1958): n.p.

Brown, David. "Pre-Raphaelite Drawings in the Bryson Bequest to the Ashmolean Museum." *Master Drawings* 16 (Autumn 1978): 287–93.

Brown, Ford Madox. *The Diary of Ford Madox Brown*. Ed. Virginia Surtees. New Haven: Yale UP, 1981.

Browning, Robert. *Dearest Isa: Robert Browning's Letters to Isabella Blagden*. Ed. Edward C. McAleer. Austin: U of Texas P, 1951.

———. *New Letters of Robert Browning*. Ed. William Clyde DeVane and Kenneth Leslie Knickerbocker. New Haven: Yale UP, 1950.

———. *The Poems*. Ed. John Pettigrew and Thomas J. Collins. 2 vols. New Haven: Yale UP, 1981.

[Burne-Jones, Georgiana]. *Memorials of Edward Burne-Jones*. London: Macmillan, 1904.

Christian, John. "Burne-Jones's 'Childe Roland'." *National Art-Collections Fund Review* (1984), pp. 122–24.

Cole, Rex Vicat. *The Art and Life of Byam Shaw*. London: Seeley, Service, 1932.

Cramer, Maurice Browning. "What Browning's Literary Reputation Owed to the Pre-Raphaelites 1847–1856." *ELH* 8 (1941): 305–21.

Cullen, Fintan. *The Drawings of John Butler Yeats (1839–1922)*. Albany, NY: Albany Institute of History and Art, 1987.

"Dante Gabriel Rossetti." *Quarterly Review* 184 (July 1896): 195–96.

DeLaura, David J. "Ruskin and the Brownings: Twenty-Five Unpublished Letters." *Bulletin of the John Rylands Library* 54 (Spring 1972): 314–56.

Edwards, Suzanne. "Robert Browning's 'Saul': Pre-Raphaelite Painting in Verse." *Journal of Pre-Raphaelite Studies* 6.2 (1986): 53–59.

Fitzgerald, Penelope. *Edward Burne-Jones: A Biography*. London: Michael Joseph, 1975.

Fowler, Rowena. "William Rothenstein Reads Browning." *Browning Institute Studies* 18 (1990): 1–14.

Grieve, A.I. *The Art of Dante Gabriel Rossetti: The Watercolours and Drawings of 1850–1855*. Norwich: Real World, 1978.

Grylls, Rosalie Glynn. "Rossetti and Browning." *Princeton University Library Chronicle* 33 (1972): 232–50.

Harrison, Martin, and Bill Waters. *Burne-Jones*. 1973. 2nd ed. London: Barrie and Jenkins, 1989.

Hunt, A. W. "Modern English Landscape-Painting." *Nineteenth Century* 39 (May 1880): 778–94.

Hunt, John Dixon. " 'Story Painters and Picture Writers': Tennyson's Idylls and Victorian Painting." *Tennyson*. Ed. D. J. Palmer. Athens, OH: Ohio UP, 1973. 180–202.

Lasner, Mark Samuels. "Browning's First Letter to Rossetti: A Discovery." *Browning Institute Studies* 15 (1987): 79–90.

Marsh, Jan. *The Legend of Elizabeth Siddal*. London: Quartet, 1989.

Murphy, William M. *Prodigal Father: The Life of John Butler Yeats (1839–1922)*. Ithaca: Cornell UP, 1978.

Norton, Charles Eliot. *Letters of Charles Eliot Norton*. 2 vols. Boston: Houghton Mifflin, Riverside Press, 1913.

The P. R. B. Journal: William Michael Rossetti's Diary of the Pre-Raphaelite Brotherhood 1849–1853. Ed. William E. Fredeman. Oxford: Clarendon, 1975.

Richards, Bernard, ed. *English Verse 1830–1890*. London: Longman, 1980.

Rossetti, Dante Gabriel. *Letters of Dante Gabriel Rossetti*. Ed. Oswald Doughty and John Robert Wahl. 4 vols. Oxford: Clarendon, 1965.

———. *Letters of Dante Gabriel Rossetti to William Allingham 1854–1870*. Ed. George Birkbeck Hill. London: T. Fisher Unwin, 1897.

———. *Dante Gabriel Rossetti: His Family-Letters*. Ed. William Michael Rossetti. 2 vols. London: Ellis and Elvey, 1895.

Rossetti Papers: 1862 to 1870. London: Sands, 1903.

Secor, Robert. "Robert Browning and the Hunts of South Kensington." *Browning Institute Studies* 7 (1979): 115–36.

Shaw, W. David. "Browning and Pre-Raphaelite Medievalism: Educated versus Innocent Seeing." *Browning Institute Studies* 8 (1980): 73–83.

Sonstroem, David. *Rossetti and the Fair Lady*. Middletown, CT: Wesleyan UP, 1970.

Stein, Richard L. "The Pre-Raphaelite Tennyson." *Victorian Studies* 24 (1981): 279–301.

Stephens, F.G. *Dante Gabriel Rossetti*. London: Seeley, 1894.

Studio, The. Modern British Water-Colour Drawings Special Supplement (1900), 57.

Sturgis, Russell. "John La Farge." *Scribner's Magazine* 26 (July 1899): 3–19.

Weinberg, H. Barbara. *The Decorative Work of John La Farge*. New York: Garland, 1977.

"SPEAKING LIKENESSES"— AND "DIFFERENCES": THE PROSE FANTASIES OF CHRISTINA ROSSETTI

by Ruth Parkin-Gounelas

CHRISTINA ROSSETTI, OF COURSE, is known almost exclusively as a poet. I want to look at some little-known tales she wrote in the early 1870s as an example of one of the forms women's fantasy writing was taking in its multifarious development throughout the nineteenth century. These tales, which read today as a strange blend of hobgoblin and psychic parable, combined a series of different forms of writing from the earlier Victorian period. There was the tradition of the Christmas tale, developed by writers like Dickens and Gaskell from the 1840s onwards, of which *A Christmas Carol* is the most famous example. There was the vogue of "faery" writing, especially since the English translation of the tales of the Grimm brothers in 1823, and also that of Hans Christian Andersen in 1846. There was the sternly moralistic Evangelical tale such as those by Anna Laetitia Barbauld dating from the late eighteenth century, in whose ethos Rossetti was deeply embedded. At the same time there was the new mode of anti-moralistic fable for children combining psychological parable with nonsense or sophisticated word play — of which Lewis Carroll's two *Alice* books, written around the same time as Rossetti's tales, are the main example. And above all there was Gothic fantasy, particularly attractive to women writers, again from the late eighteenth century and lasting well into the nineteenth.

If all of these modes of writing bore their own conventions, Gothic fiction, especially since Ann Radcliffe, must be *the* conventional genre *par excellence*, written, as David Punter points out (2), for an audience adept at decoding a fixed set of narrative and stylistic formulae. The imaginative geography of the Gothic of Ann Radcliffe which Christina Rossetti inherited is a geography of dark threatening spaces where an immobilised heroine attempts to ward off a series of violating forces. Christina Rossetti, who was the niece of Dr. John Polidori, author of "The Vampyre" (1818), had also been an avid reader of Radcliffe's novels in her early years and in fact did research towards a biography of Radcliffe in 1883 (Jones 200–01). The extent to which Rossetti was initiated in Radcliffe's formulae becomes particularly evident in her tales (and helps explain, incidentally, what seems to be the startlingly original configurations of her famous poem *Goblin Market*).

Fantasy elements in the form of the supernatural (whether actual or imagined) were gradually disinfected out of the novel as it developed from the early Victorian period, and they were dispersed into marginal genres like Christmas tales and children's literature. Ann Radcliffe, in the romantic 1790s, could write extended fables of fear and desire in novelistic form which were consumed by a huge and varied readership. "Phantasmagoria," at least according to one of Radcliffe's admirers, de Sade, was "the inevitable result of the revolutionary shocks which all of Europe [had] suffered" (Sade 109).[1] But by the 1830s, with a growing Victorian sensitivity to the dangers of transgression — what was called "the unnatural" — figurations of psychic disturbance were buried into the symbol or sub-plot of a realistically-framed novel. For a writer to exploit these figurations, then, she needed to resort to the short genres like Christmas or children's tales in order to secure a special dispensation. The three-decker novel, with its comforting solidarity, kept night-time fears in the shadows. With the partial exception, perhaps, of the fiction of "terror" or "sensation" from Bulwer Lytton in the 1840s to Wilkie Collins in the 1860s, it was not until the late 1880s and 1890s that literal representations of fear or desire such as R. L. Stevenson's Hyde or Bram Stoker's Dracula could occupy a central space in the novel in the way that Mary Shelley's monster had done in 1818.[2]

The supernatural was removed, then, out of the everyday adult world and employed to "keep us in the dark," to use Freud's phrase from his essay on "The 'Uncanny' " (251) — in the dark and licence of unrealistic forms intended for merely holiday (or childhood) consumption. Women, culturally classified with children throughout the Victorian period, turned to these forms in large numbers, the result of which was a burgeoning of women's fantasy writing in the genres of Christmas tales and children's fiction, providing women with a fictional outlet previously provided by the Gothic romance. Some, like Elizabeth Gaskell, used the fantasy tale (in her case the Christmas tale) to channel off those strains not tolerated by the realistic novel she so successfully "mastered" (I use the masculine verb advisedly). Her "Old Nurse's Story" is the most well-known of many, written for the Christmas numbers of Dickens's magazine *Household Words* in the 1850s. Other mid-Victorian ghost story writers, who are now beginning to receive critical attention, include Dinah Mulock, Catherine Crowe, Mary Elizabeth Braddon, Rhoda Broughton, Mrs. Henry Wood, Vernon Lee, and Margaret Oliphant.[3]

The Yuletide tradition of the Christmas tale allowed the Victorian bourgeoi-
sie access to an older world of demons and spirits which a pre-industrial and
rural community had taken for granted. As in Gaskell's "Old Nurse's Tale,"
it is the servants and peasants who know about the past and warn the (usually
resisting) proprietor of its ability to haunt the present. This same knowledge
was used by women narrators to bring "dislocation and menace" (Uglow
xiv) to the social structures which constrained their lives. Briefly, on All
Souls' Day or on Christmas Eve, the ghosts could rise to give expression to
the grievances or passion normally kept in the dark.[4]

Christina Rossetti was one of the many women to try her hand in the
Christmas Annuals and release demons under cover of the festive spirit. As
an extra precaution, she wrote one of her most subversive tales for *children*
at Christmas. "Speaking Likenesses" was sent to Macmillan for a children's
Christmas volume in 1874.[5] Like *Goblin Market* of fifteen years earlier, however, its youthful characters belie its simplicity, and, in spite of a characteristically Evangelical frame of moral sentiment which has relegated the tale to
oblivion,[6] "Speaking Likenesses" can be read as a tale of Gothic excess, a
literalization of a sophisticated range of transgressive drives.

Christina Rossetti, in fact, was an adept at the art of subterfuge. Poetry, as
a private and figurative form, gave her some licence to project a stark, emotional voice, but prose fiction proved exceptionally constraining to her. Within
the context of the regimen of renunciation she had imposed upon herself, it
was as inconceivable that she should find a fictional style as that she should
find a life style to represent the rebellion she so passionately needed to express
against this same self-imposed renunciation. So when it came to the choice
of prose forms she might adopt, she turned to quiet, unexposed genres. Her
only attempts at "realism" are a couple of stories in the volume she aptly
entitled *Commonplace, and Other Short Stories*, published in 1870, which
depict scenes of quiet feminine existence in the seaside resorts Rossetti knew
from her rare summer outings from London. The "commonplace" consists
as much in the tone of sanctimonious piety and constraint as in the subject
matter. Rossetti's inheritance, via her mother, of the language of religious
self-denial proved a refuge against the impossibly unfeminine rebelliousness
of her two brothers — the bohemian Dante Gabriel or the atheist William.

The fantasy/fairy tale, and there are two of them in the *Commonplace*
volume, allowed Rossetti the freedom of indirection, the suggestiveness of
the allegorical, releasing her from her adherence to daily forms. The first one,
"Nick," is about an envious old misanthrope who, being granted by a fairy
woman the ability to become everything he wishes suffers a series of transformations — into a sparrow, a dog, a bludgeon, fire, and finally a miser and
village outcast. The second, "Hero," a tale of gems and sea nymphs suggesting both Christian Andersen and the *Arabian Nights*, again employs a

series of metamorphoses as an image of the unattainability of desire. It is significant that the young heroine should be called Hero, for her wish, granted by the fairies, is "to become the supreme object of [masculine] admiration" (Rossetti, *Commonplace* 190), that in her, "every man shall find his taste satisfied" (193). Through metamorphosis, Rossetti explores the implications of the masculinization of women, the shaping of female desire according to masculine contours — what Luce Irigaray punningly calls "a hommosexual imaginary" (*Speculum* 229).

Hero's fate is to be constantly deferred. While her body is held in abeyance by the fairies, her "spirit" enters the form of first a beautiful princess, then a famous opera singer, and finally the shoot of an exquisite rare flower. Rossetti's prose evokes the instability of forms, the repetitiousness of deferral which is the feminine condition. The feminine, Irigaray writes in her 1986 essay "The Three *Genres*," "has yet to find its forms, to flower in accordance with its roots. It has still not been born into its own growth, its subjectivity. The feminine has not yet deployed its *morphology*" (151). If all desire is obsessed by the allure of completion, feminine desire, in Rossetti's mytho-morphologies, is characterized by its necessary incompletability. The "*hysterical fantasmatic*" (Irigaray again)[7] is a result of the fact that women have not come to form, have "not yet taken (a) place": "Woman is still the place, the whole of the place in which she cannot take possession of herself as such" (*Speculum* 227). This "place" where women cannot take form is the site of the female fantastic.

It is, one could argue, one of the reasons why women's narratives have such difficulty with endings. The enforced closure of many nineteenth-century novels by women is notable: Charlotte Brontë's Shirley, from restless rebel to model wife and Jane Eyre, tamed into the perfect marital union; George Eliot's Dorothea Brooke, the compliant helpmeet for Will Ladislaw after a lifetime of irresolution and Maggie Tulliver, drowned. Fictional murder in the first degree was not uncommon at the end of nineteenth-century novels by women. Women's *non*-realistic fiction, freed from the necessity of accommodating female desire to social circumstances, was less hampered by endings. Hero's ever-deferred desire to arouse male admiration ends calamitously with the neglect of the rare flower by new owners of the conservatory. Rossetti does give her tale a realistic frame whereby Hero, being allowed to return to the body, submits to the belief that "only home is happy" (*Commonplace* 211). But the fantastic tale within the frame remains intact, an image of the placelessness or non-locatability of female desire. If home is happy, the female psyche is especially preoccupied with *das unheimliche* (literally "the un-homely" — or, as Freud's phrase is usually translated, "the uncanny").

There is a scene in Lewis Carroll's *Through the Looking-Glass* where Alice finds herself in a shop, and when asked by the Sheep behind the counter what she wants, she finds that though all the shelves around her are full of bright objects, the shelf she looks directly at is always empty (Carroll 207–08). The place where desire *resides*, its locus, is the elusive object of most fantasy writing. Because of its investment in the masculine sexual economy by proxy, women's fantasies are obsessed less with the object itself than with *approaches to* this ever-elusive object. Ann Radcliffe's novels depict a variety of mysterious subspaces: subterranean chambers, descending and ascending staircases, long tortuous passages — all approaching but never reaching the center of suspense.[8] Unlike Matthew Lewis's *The Monk*, where the inner dungeon finally delivers the virgin up to Ambrosio the monk for rape, in Radcliffe's novels, one secret chamber is discovered only to disclose a yet more urgently-desired unknown.

Rossetti's inheritance from Radcliffe is most apparent in "Speaking Likenesses," although the story's initial impact derives from its similarity to Carroll's *Alice* books. Rossetti dismissed it in characteristically self-deprecatory terms as a "trifle, would-be in the *Alice* style" (Knoepflmacher 316). But elsewhere, more shrewdly, she said it was "in the *Alice* style with an eye to the market" (Jones 164). The Carrollean model was clearly the key to success in the early 1870s, with *Alice's Adventures in Wonderland* (of 1865) and *Through the Looking-Glass* (of 1872) at the center of critical attention.[9]

The story consists of "three short stories in a common framework" (Rossetti, qtd. in Jones 163). In the first of these, which is the one I want to focus on, eight-year-old Flora, depicted in Arthur Hughes's illustrations in similar golden-haired, sylph-like form to Tenniel's illustrations for the *Alice* books, enters a dream/fantasy space to experience a series of uncomfortable moments — of deprivation, abuse, illogic, and thwarted expectation. The sadism is more clearly marked in Rossetti's tale than in Carroll's,[10] a quality which made it distasteful to contemporary readers like Ruskin.[11] Flora, like Alice, represents innocence in the hands of irrational violence. Within the Enchanted Room she is confronted by a group of children specially formed for torment:

> Quills with every quill erect tilted against her, . . . Angles whose corners almost cut her, Hooks who caught and slit her frock, Slime who slid against and passed her, Sticky who rubbed off on her neck and plump bare arms, the scowling Queen, and the whole laughing scolding pushing troop, all wielded longest sharpest pins, and all by turns overtook her. (Auerbach and Knoepflmacher 336)

In playing pincushion to these forces, both erect and piercing as well as repulsively slimey, Flora repeats Alice's victimization but not her resistance to it. Unlike Alice, Flora does not answer back. Amidst the wrangling and invective of the battle-play, "The only silent tongue was Flora's" (341). As in Radcliffean Gothic, the heroine's suffering is the only action she can perform, an abundant supply of sensibility the only quality she need possess.[12]

To offset the passivity of her heroine, it is true, Rossetti made the tale realistically accessible by framing it with a scene of specifically mid-Victorian feminity, one where passivity is overlaid by the ethos of feminine industry and self-improvement advocated by Samuel Smiles in his immensely popular book *Self-Help* of 1859.[13] Five girls sit diligently sewing with their aunt, a "spinster" of both tales and stockings. The two (tales and stockings) are inter-dependent, as the aunt's Evangelical tones insist: "story and labour" — "no help no story" (343). Busy fingers, laboring for the poor, keep wandering minds in check, although the aunt, through her opening injunction, suggests that she knows the power of her tale to distract from Evangelical imperatives: "Silence! Attention! All eyes on occupations, not on me lest I should feel shy!" (325).

Writing about contemporary Mills and Boon romances, Joanna Russ notes that "These novels are written for women who cook, who decorate their own houses, who shop for clothing for themselves and their children — in short, for housewives. But [their] Heroines . . . toil not, neither do they spin" (39). "Speaking Likenesses," with its frame and inset tale, repeats this same split between the industrious bourgeois consumer of narratives and their passive heroines. Whereas the frame advocates industry, the tale itself endorses the ethos of fantasy as romance where, in the games of the children, the narrator says, "The boys were players, [and] the girls were played (if I may be allowed such a phrase)" (338).

In pleading for the use of such phrases, the narrator disingenuously postulates a set of gender distinctions. Rossetti's strategy is to mimic the very condition of silence and passivity, at the same time exposing her own mimicry: the girls (as opposed to the boy players), we are told, "all alike seemed well-nigh destitute of invention" (341). The fantasy tale, like the girls, and as its title suggests, "speaks like" the masculine language it caricatures and deforms. Mutism and mimicry, the strategy of the hysteric, constitute Rossetti's version of "the *Alice* style."[14]

Rossetti had originally intended calling the story "Nowhere" (Auerbach and Knoepflmacher 318), its being set, as the narrator states, in the "Land of Nowhere" (338). This title signals the story's participation in a climate which was producing in the early 1870s a whole series of utopian (or dystopian) fictions: Bulwer Lytton's *The Coming Race* (1871), Samuel Butler's *Erewhon* ("Nowhere" backwards, 1872), R. E. Dudgeon's *Colymbia* (1873), and so on. Coming as it did after these utopias in 1874, Rossetti's "Nowhere" announces its difference from them by its enactment of the very condition of placelessness. Feminist critic Annis Pratt has noted that some critics see women's heroines as always being nowhere, their fantasies producing heroines who feel "less authentically feminine than exiles from patriarchy" (205). The exiled status of Rossetti's Flora consists not in her relegation to the periphery of the dominant space, which, in women's fantasy writing or science fiction of the twentieth century would come to constitute a new and empowered space, but in her highlighted submission to it, her complicity with the condition which the Freudian analyst Joan Riviere, writing fifty years before Irigaray, called "womanliness . . . [as] 'masquerade' " (38).

She is exiled, in other words, from the place of her own desire, and desire becomes the missing object, the slipper that is always hunted and never found in Rossetti's enactment of the games played by the young girl on the brink of entry into adolescence. At supper time, strawberries and cream appear miraculously, only to be snatched from her at the moment of tasting, the prohibition coming, significantly, from her own alter ego, the "birthday Queen," who looms over her, anticipating and frustrating her every attempt at pleasure. Of all the girls, Flora suffers most. But, we are told, "even the boys did not as a body extract unmixed pleasure" from the games. Only the Queen, representing the utopian possibility of pleasure's fulfilment, is allowed, "perhaps, [to] taste of mirth unalloyed." "But if so," the narrator continues, "she stood alone in satisfaction as in dignity. In any case, pleasure palls in the long run" (338). Through the ambivalence and evasion here, the Queen's failure stands for desire's inconceivability.

This fragment of narrative, then, is one of a young girl trapped in the apartment of frustrated desire, and unlike Carroll's Wonderland, with its door to the longed-for Garden which Alice eventually finds, the door to Rossetti's Nowhere, or rather the exit from it, is itself nowhere to be found, "If she could only have discovered the door Flora would have fled through it . . . but either the door was gone, or else it was shut to and lost amongst the multitude of mirrors" (334). The apartment is depicted as a hall of mirrors where Flora encounters both the reflection of her own "fifty million-fold face" as well as that of the Queen, "reflected over and over again in five hundred mirrors" (334). The idea of repetition ("over and over again") is one of the dominant motifs in the story, which can be read as a re-enactment of what Freud called the repetition compulsion, "the dominance in the unconscious mind of a 'compulsion to repeat' " ("The 'Uncanny' " 238) in the attempt to master a trauma until it can be incorporated into present experience.[15] The strawberries and cream — this time strawberry ice — return towards the end of the narrative, to be denied Flora again (although the Queen demolishes one quart of it: small wonder that "pleasure palls"). The threatening playmates repeat and multiply themselves — to the number of "a hundred thousand" (339). But most alarming of all, the mirrors, which at first had offered Flora a pleasing opportunity for narcissism,[16] throw back at her an endless series of repeated images of her own torment and thwarted desire. "In such a number of mirrors," the narrator records, "there were not merely simple reflections, but reflections of reflections, and reflections of reflections of reflections, and so on and on and on, over and over again" (334).[17]

In his article on the language of the late eighteenth-century tale of terror called "Language to Infinity," Foucault argues that the function of language is to avert death:

> The gods send disasters to mortals so that they can tell of them, but men speak of them so that misfortunes will never be fully realized, so that their fulfillment will be averted in the distance of words. . . . Before the immanence of death, language rushes forth, but it also starts again, tells of itself, discovers the story of the story and the possibility that this interpenetration might never end.[18] Headed toward death, language turns back upon itself; it encounters something like a mirror; and to stop this death which would stop it, it possesses but a single power: that of giving birth to its own image in a play of mirrors that has no limits. (54)

Rossetti's limitless play of mirrors averts first of all the awful possibility of desire's fulfilment (the Queen): female desire has no topos. But it also signals the impossibility of release from its infinite pursuit — in Flora, whose name suggests nature's infinite proliferation. The female author's pursuit of language has a particular obsessively repetitious urgency. If Ann Radcliffe's romances work towards the pursuit of a homely space, safe from the threat of rape (the feminine literalization of death), Christina Rossetti's mid-Victorian re-play of this drama refines the issue to one of the pursuit of language itself. Rossetti's version of the *Alice* stories, in other words, depicts a game that has to do with deferral to infinity of language's pursuit of female desire. In "speaking like" Carroll, Rossetti can only repeat her "*differance*."

Aristotle University, Thessaloniki

NOTES

1. As Punter points out: "The ending of the long-drawn-out war with France produced a curious kind of cultural Indian summer, and the dominant mode of fiction during the period between 1815 and 1827 was so-called 'silver fork' fiction, which was characterised principally by its exclusive dealing with the world of the aristocracy" (167).
2. This is true of popular fiction (the so-called "penny dreadful") as well as of the fiction intended for a bourgeois readership. Louis James, writing of popular fiction of the 1830s–50s, notes that "the historical, with its claims to authenticity which appealed to the cosmopolitan [working class], knowledge-seeking reader, was increasingly ousting the Gothic traditions. History was respectable . . . " (101).
3. Symptomatic of this recent interest is the appearance in the last five years of several collections such as *The Virago Book of Victorian Ghost Stories*, ed. Dalby,

and *Victorian Ghost Stories: An Oxford Anthology,* ed. Cox and Gilbert; the
second collection reprints several stories by women writers already printed in the
Virago volume.

4. This paragraph owes much to Uglow's short but excellent introduction to *The
Virago Book of Victorian Ghost Stories.*

5. The edition of "Speaking Likenesses" in *Forbidden Journeys* is wrongly dated
as "Christmas of 1873" (Auerbach and Knoepflmacher 318). In an earlier study
(of the relationship between Lewis Carroll and Rossetti), however, Knoepflmacher dates the story as Christmas 1874 (311).

6. One hundred and twenty years after its original publication, "Speaking Likenesses" has just been brought into print again, along with the original illustrations
by Arthur Hughes, in the Auerbach and Knoepflmacher volume.

7. The phrase is translated by Gillian Gill in 1985 as *"hysterical fantasy,"* but I
prefer the translation of this same extract by David Macey on p. 53 of *The
Irigaray Reader* ("The Three *Genres*").

8. Wilt, adapting Eino Raillo, gives a similar description of Gothic space (10).

9. Dusinberre notes that "By the time of Carroll's death in 1898 *Alice* had supplanted
The Pilgrim's Progress in the popular imagination" (1).

10. This is the central thesis of Auerbach and Knoepflmacher, who write of the
tale's "defiant negativism" (318) and Rossetti's "sly dissent from Christmas
paternalism" (133) in her Christmas tales.

11. Surveying a batch of Christmas books in January 1875, Ruskin called Rossetti's
"Speaking Likenesses" "the *worst*": "how could she or Arthur Hughes sink so
low after their pretty nursery rhymes" (qtd. in Knoepflmacher 310).

12. A similar point is made by Russ, in her article on contemporary romance novels,
"Somebody's Trying to Kill Me and I Think it's My Husband: The Modern
Gothic" (50).

13. Characteristic of the self-consciousness of Rossetti's inset tale is its inclusion of
the game called "Self Help" which is played, to the further discomfort of Flora,
by the children. See p. 338.

14. See Irigaray, "Questions," *This Sex Which is Not One* (136–37).

15. Freud expanded on his discussion of the repetition compulsion in the work published a year after "The 'Uncanny,' " "Beyond the Pleasure Principle" (1920),
especially sections II and III. For an interesting discussion of the repetition compulsion in relation to Gothic, see Morris.

16. "[B]oth ceiling and wall were lined throughout with looking-glasses: but at first
this did not strike Flora as any disadvantage; indeed she thought it quite delightful
and took a long look at her little self full length" (Auerbach and Knoepflmacher 332).

17. The same image of reflected repetition occurs in Rossetti's famous poem "In an
Artist's Studio":
> One face looks out from all his canvases,
> One selfsame figure sits or walks or leans:
> We found her hidden just behind those screens,
> That mirror gave back all her loveliness.
> . . . . every canvas means
> The same one meaning, neither more nor less. (*Poetical Works* 330)

18. "This is one of the structures of language which defines fantastic literature for
Borges; see *Labyrinths* (New York: New Directions, 1967), p. xviii." (Foucault's note).

WORKS CITED

Auerbach, Nina, and U. C. Knoepflmacher, eds. *Forbidden Journeys: Fairy Tales and Fantasies by Victorian Women Writers.* Chicago: U of Chicago P, 1992.

Carroll, Lewis. *Alice's Adventures in Wonderland and Through the Looking-Glass.* London: Macmillan, 1975.

Cox, Michael, and R. A. Gilbert, eds. *Victorian Ghost Stories: An Oxford Anthology.* Oxford: Oxford UP, 1992.

Dalby, Richard, ed. *The Virago Book of Victorian Ghost Stories.* London: Virago, 1992.

Dusinberre, Juliet. *Alice to the Lighthouse: Children's Books and Radical Experiments in Art.* Houndmills, Basingstoke: Macmillan, 1987.

Foucault, Michel. "Language to Infinity." *Language, Counter-Memory, Practice: Selected Essays and Interviews.* Trans. Donald F. Bouchard and Sherry Simon. Ed. Donald F. Bouchard. Oxford: Blackwell, 1977. 53–67.

Freud, Sigmund. "Beyond the Pleasure Principle." Vol. 2 of The Pelican Freud Library. *On Metapsychology: The Theory of Psychoanalysis.* Trans. James Strachey. Ed. Angela Richards. Harmondsworth: Penguin, 1986. 275–338.

———. "The 'Uncanny.' " *The Standard Edition of the Complete Psychological Works of Sigmund Freud.* Trans. & ed. James Strachey, Vol. 17. London: Hogarth Press, 1955.

Gaskell, Elizabeth. "The Old Nurse's Story." *Cousin Phillis and Other Tales.* Ed. Angus Easson. Oxford: Oxford UP, 1987. 35–56.

Irigaray, Luce. *Speculum of the Other Woman.* Trans. Gillian C. Gill. Ithaca: Cornell UP, 1985.

———. *This Sex Which is Not One.* Trans. Catherine Porter with Carolyn Burke. Ithaca: Cornell UP, 1985.

———. "The Three *Genres.*" *The Irigaray Reader.* Ed. Margaret Whitford. Oxford: Blackwell, 1992. 140–53.

James, Louis. *Fictions for the Working Man 1830–50.* Harmondsworth, Middlesex: Penguin, 1974.

Jones, Kathleen. *Learning not to be First: The Life of Christina Rossetti.* Moreton-in-Marsh, Gloucestershire: Windrush P, 1991.

Knoepflmacher, U. C. "Avenging Alice: Christina Rossetti and Lewis Carroll." *Nineteenth-Century Literature* 41.3 (Dec. 1986): 299–328.

Morris, David B. "Gothic Sublimity." *New Literary History* 16.2 (Winter 1985): 299–319.

Pratt, Annis. Rev. of four books on women's novels and myth. *Signs* 14.1 (Autumn 1988): 204–09.

Punter, David. *The Literature of Terror: A History of Gothic Fictions from 1765 to the Present Day.* London: Longman, 1980.

Riviere, Joan. "Womanliness as a Masquerade." *Formations of Fantasy.* Ed. Victor Burgin, James Donald, and Cora Kaplan. London: Routledge, 1986. 35–44.

Rossetti, Christina G. *Commonplace, and Other Short Stories.* London: Ellis, 1870.

———. *The Poetical Works of Christina Georgina Rossetti.* Ed. William Michael Rossetti. London: Macmillan, 1928.

Russ, Joanna. "Somebody's Trying to Kill Me and I Think it's my Husband: The Modern Gothic." *The Female Gothic.* Ed. Juliann E. Fleenor. Montreal: Eden Press, 1983. 31–56.

Sade, Marquis de. "Reflections on the Novel." *The 120 Days of Sodom and Other Writings*. Trans. Austryn Wainhouse and Richard Seaver. London: Arrow, 1991. 97–116.

Uglow, Jennifer. Introduction to *The Virago Book of Victorian Ghost Stories*. Ed. Richard Dalby. London: Virago, 1992.

Wilt, Judith. *Ghosts of the Gothic: Austen, Eliot, & Lawrence*. Princeton: Princeton UP, 1980.

THE SOCIALIST "NEW WOMAN" AND WILLIAM MORRIS'S THE WATER OF THE WONDROUS ISLES

By Florence Boos

SEVERAL LITERARY WORKS APPEARED in the 1880s and 1890s which represented female activity and sexuality with growing sympathy and intelligence (George Moore's *Esther Waters*, Mona Caird's *The Daughters of Danaus*, Israel Zangwill's *Children of the Ghetto*), but they were often countered by hostile and phobic literary images of female power and aggression.[1] William Morris's last romances, by contrast, offered a qualified social-pastoral idealization of the "new woman," as projected and imagined by contemporary male socialist-feminists — an idealization whose strengths and limitations were brought into sharper relief by the prose romances' characteristic blend of temporal detachment and visionary emotion.

William Morris's artistic temperament had in fact always included some identification with projected inner emotions and life circumstances of women. Several of his long narratives imagine a woman's adventure, and several more, such as "Gertha's Lovers" and "The Lovers of Gudrun," concern themselves with the effect of an impressive woman on the fates of one or more men. Not surprisingly, most of these female romances are tales of confinement or accounts of the frustrations of a woman's inner life as she seeks or awaits the advent of love. When Morris chose a woman protagonist for one of his late prose romances, socialist-feminist debates about sexuality and oppressive family structures influenced his fashioning of a more complex and sophisticated account of a woman's psychological development and achievements than any he had attempted before.

Each of the last three romances includes an extended account of its heroine's life. Two parallel those of their lovers/husbands: Elfhild's briefer story in *The Sundering Flood* folds into that of Osberne, and Ursula's in *The Well at the World's End* into that of Ralph. Birdalone's complicated and interconnected stories control the narrative of *The Water of the Wondrous*

159

Isles, in which the adventures of her lover Arthur play a subsidiary role. Morris's only woman-centered romance was the last he was able to complete with the loving amplitude of his best work.

Morris wrote *The Water of the Wondrous Isles* in 1895, 27 years after Eliza Lynn Linton attacked "The Girl of the Period"; eight years after the appearance of Eleanor Marx and Edward Aveling's *The Woman Question*; twelve and two years, respectively, after Meredith and Gissing published their ambivalent portraits of self-directed unmarried women in *Diana of the Crossways* (1882) and *The Odd Women* (1893); and a year after the appearance of the disturbing Sue Bridehead in Hardy's *Jude the Obscure*. Against the background of these "realistic" portrayals by other male writers, Morris's Birdalone is an empathetic figure, who embodies several features characteristic of the "new woman." Readers familiar with the ideas of contemporary progressive and socialist reformers who wrote on the family and sexuality would also have recognized in her tale a kind of alchemical residue of their broader aims and ideals.

Among distinguishing features of the fin-de-siècle "new woman" relevant to Morris's female epic were the desire and ability to secure financial and physical freedom and self-support; rejection of "gentlewomanly" behavior for healthy exercise, outdoor labor, and useful work; and determination to demystify notions of "purity" and "family" and to eradicate tolerance of rape, sexual exploitation, battering, and child abuse. The more radical reformers even envisioned a world in which women could express and enact manifold sexual desires without punitive double standards and began to explore conjectures that women's contributions to religion and myth had been distorted or erased from the historical record.[2]

Even more fundamentally, women writers began to explore women's psychology as a subject in itself, apart from possible relationships with men. Reconsideration of mother-daughter relationships, female friends, and female mentors also made possible the creation of new plots, in which women's marriages or failures to marry became one among several aspects of their adult lives, rather than an all-important determinant of plot closure.[3] *The Water of the Wondrous Isles's* presentation of women's psychology and sexual relationships shows the influence of these new possibilities.

In this essay I will examine the figure of Birdalone in *The Water of the Wondrous Isles* against a background of late-century ideals of the socialist "new woman," and compare the tale's presentation of women's affiliations and creativity with accounts of women's lives by several Victorian women. Something of these writers' gynocentrism came to inform Morris's use of a historically-evocative tradition of goddesses, witches, and mother-figures. The extensions and modifications of Morris's earlier temperamental affinities suggest benign psychological changes in his late-middle age as well as continued empathetic alignment with his reformist milieu.

It is unlikely that Morris consciously set out to write a romance about a historically-displaced socialist "new woman" or to formulate ideal models for women's character(s) and social role(s). Morris had responded to an earlier reviewer in the *Spectator*, who plausibly suggested that he had written political allegories into his prose romances, with a firm denial of any such intent.[4] Nevertheless *The Water of the Wondrous Isles* completed a rapprochement with socialist feminism, noticeable in *Pilgrims of Hope* (1888) and *News from Nowhere* (1890). Morris had composed powerful narratives with female protagonists ("The Defence of Guenevere," "The Story of Cupid and Psyche," "The Story of Aslaug") twenty and thirty years before, but *The Water*'s hero Birdalone (whose "bird" may derive from the Middle-English "burde," "maiden" or "embroidress") carries one of his most fully developed (and, critics agree, finest) romance epics from beginning to end. The romance's concern with mobility, sexuality, and eroticism also prompted Morris to engage in thought-experiments about gender roles which explore the limits of women's behavior, and to suggest what women under less constrained circumstances might be able to do.

Morris shifted between two contrasting views of eroticism. On the one hand, he preserved a conventional, idealized, and rather anxious set of associations with the youthful female body's beauty, its power to lure and fix a romantic male "gaze." On the other hand, he also expressed throughout his work a sympathetic and respectful sense of a woman's right to her own (hetero)sexuality — be it romantic (Guenevere), vengeful (Gudrun), or extramarital (the wife in "Pilgrims of Hope"), and when the women of his writings are immured in a variety of confinements (Guenevere, Jehane, Rapunzel, Danae), he clearly identified with their near-intolerable frustrations. As a sixty-year-old man approaching death, he also continued to idealize and romanticize physical youth and its impulses, and sympathize apprehensively with the practical and emotional complications they create. Birdalone is in many ways a romanticized counterpart of Ellen in *News from Nowhere*, detached from Ellen's placement in the anticipated twenty-first century and her role as spokeswoman for socialist ideals, and free to embody other emotions and struggles of psychic independence. Like Ellen, however, Birdalone expresses "socialist-feminist" ideas in ways which are qualified by Morris's lingering presuppositions about women's alleged physical dependence and the centrality of romance-quests to his protagonists' inner lives.

The first aspect of a new ideal of womanhood mentioned above was its demand for female independence and self-support. Birdalone is a socialist and no Victorian gentlewoman in her zest for manual labor. No work is too hard for her, and no useful task too menial. In "The Society of the Future," Morris had noted: "[M]y ideal is first unconstrained life, and next simple and natural life. First you must be free; and next you must learn to take pleasure in all the details of life: which, indeed, will be necessary for you, because, since others will be free, you will have to do your own work" (William Morris 2: 459). The Witch-wife beats the twelve-year-old Birdalone to "learn her swinking" [heavy labor], but the sturdy child "was not slack nor a sluggard, and hated not the toil, even when it pained and wearied her." (*Water* 9). Straining plausibility somewhat, the narrator adds that "busy and toilsome days . . . irked her in nowise, since it eased her of the torment of [her] hopes and fears . . . , and brought her sound sleep and sweet awaking" (*Water* 11).

More specifically, Birdalone's labors for the Witch include a wide array of harvesting and hunting tasks, described in some detail at various points in the story:

> The kine and the goats must she milk, and plough and sow and reap the acreland according to the seasons, and lead the beasts to the woodland pastures when their own were flooded or burned; she must gather the fruits of the orchard, and the hazel nuts up the woodlands, and beat the walnut-trees in September. She must make the butter and the cheese, grind the wheat in the quern, make and bake the bread, and in all ways earn her livelihood hard enough. Moreover, the bowman's craft had she learned, and . . . must fare alone into the wood now and again to slay big deer and little, and win venison: but neither did that irk her at all, for rest and peace were in the woods for her. (11)

At every stage of her journey, moreover, Birdalone manifests an ability to fend for herself and others. When she meets the three gentlewomen who live helplessly on the "Isle of Increase Unsought," and who later become lifelong friends, one of them explains that they cannot use "the fruits of the earth and the wild creatures for our avail, [for] . . . we have not learned how to turn them into dinner and supper." In pointed contrast, Birdalone offers her services: "[F]or in all matters of the house and the byre and the field have I skill" (65). She later leaves the Castle of the Quest at age twenty and spends the next five years as a successful embroideress in the City of the Five Crafts, where she employs at least three workmen and several workwomen, and disperses the workshop's profits and accumulated capital when she leaves the city. When she offers to deed the house in which she and her companions have worked to her friends and assistants Gerard and the Gerardsons, the men graciously decline: "Wherefore we pray thee to give this house that hath been so dear to us unto thy work-woman and her mates; for we need it not, nor the hire thereof, but shall do well enough with what money or good thou mayst give us" (279). The fruit of their common labor thus becomes a legacy to assist the women who have worked with her.

In a period when women's higher education was still a bitterly disputed reformist ideal, Birdalone's eagerness and ability to exploit every opportunity for education also deserves mention. In the Castle of the Quest, Leonard the

Priest offers to teach her to read, and "she yeasaid that joyously; and thence-
forth would she have him with her every day a good while; and an apt scholar
she was. . . . [A]nd she learned her A B C speedily" (139). There is also no
suggestion that Birdalone ever relinquishes rule of her own affairs during her
subsequent married life at Utterhay or sets aside her former occupation to
help Arthur engage in his. Arthur's temperament and predilection for military
roles might conceivably lead him to depart from time to time on "man-like"
adventures. If so, this might leave Birdalone all the freer to practice the
socially needed arts of craftswork, food production, and friendship.

Patricia Vertinsky has shown in *The Eternally Wounded Woman: Women,
Exercise and Doctors in the Late Nineteenth Century* that many members of
the women's movement struggled to demand women's access to physical
exercise. In this respect, at least, Birdalone has a model upbringing. At twelve,
"far stronger and handier than at first sight she looked to be," she had
"learned herself swimming, as the ducks do belike" (8,9), and in order to
investigate the isles she "pushed off into the deep and swam strongly through
the still water" (23). The Witch-wife describes her as "swift-foot as the best
of the deer, [who] mayest over-run any one of them whom thou wilt" (31).
Birdalone also fishes skillfully and, as mentioned, she is a good archer. On
arrival at the Castle of the Quest, she "took the bow in hand, and shot
straighter and well-nigh as hard as the best man there, whereat they marvelled,
and praised her much" (184).

Later, however, in the presence of Arthur and other "Champions of the
Quest," she is unwilling to join in a more open athletic competition:

> Then the young men ran afoot before her for the prize of a belt and knife, and
> forsooth she wotted well that were she to run against them with trussed-up
> skirts she would bear off the prize; but she had no heart thereto, for amidst
> them all, and her new friendships, she had grown shamefast, and might play
> the wood-maiden no longer. (130)

The presence of these men thus forces on Birdalone a partial reversion to
Victorian womanliness, but they are fortunately absent during large parts of
the ensuing narrative.

It was a central socialist-feminist doctrine that bourgeois marriage
amounted to a commodification of women's bodies, a form of sexual slavery,
or in the words of an 1885 Socialist Manifesto which Morris co-authored:
"property-marriage, maintained by its necessary complement, universal venal
prostitution" (Letters 2: 852). In *News from Nowhere*, Ellen identifies the
need to marry one's source of income as capitalism's worst offense to women,
when she observes that as the daughter of a "mere tiller of the soil" she
would have been poor in the nineteenth-century:

my beauty and cleverness and brightness . . . would have been sold to rich men, and my life would have been wasted indeed; for I know enough of that to know that I should have had no choice, no power of will over my life . . . I should have been wrecked and wasted in one way or another, either by penury or by luxury. (*Collected Works* 16: 204)

(This remark also closely echoes several passages in Mill's *Subjection of Women* and Wollstonecraft's *Vindication*)[5]. It is no surprise, then, that Birdalone determines to flee the Witch-wife, when

she saw, that she was not her own, but a chattel and a tool of one who not only used her as a thrall in the passing day, but had it in her mind . . . to bait the trap with her for the taking of the sons of Adam. Forsooth she saw, though dimly, that her mistress was indeed wicked, and that in the bonds of that wickedness was she bound. (10)

The Witch only confirms her apprehensions later, when she attempts to dissuade her from flight with promises of future sexual power:

the time is coming when thou shalt see here a many of the fairest of men, and . . . all those shall love and worship thee, and thou mayst gladden whom thou wilt, and whom thou wilt mayst sadden; and no lack soever shalt thou have of the sweetness of love, or the glory of dominion. (31)

Birdalone is shrewd enough to see quickly through this scenario. The tale ends with the obligatory and much-desired heterosexual union, of course, but it is one in which Birdalone's choice of partner is free of coercion, manipulation, or economic constraint.

Socialist-feminist reformers similarly demanded an utter end to prudery and assertion of women's (hetero)sexual desires. Eleanor Marx had noted with pain that "as our boys and girls grow up, the whole subject of sex relations is made a mystery and a shame. . . . Always understanding by chastity the entire suppression of all instincts connected with the begetting of children, we regard chastity as a crime" (21,24). Less melodramatically, Ellen of *News from Nowhere* speaks openly of her desire for marriage and motherhood, with emphasis on the latter. (Collected Works 16: 94)[6]

Even Birdalone's three friends on the "Isle of Increase Unsought" assert the erotic nature of their responses — or rather, they repudiate the Victorian assumption that women's sexuality is wholly characterized by narcissistic indirection and sublimation. Atra, for example, tells Birdalone that the three women have lovers, and her conventional account of their relationships is bluntly rebuked by her more affectionate and passionate sister Viridis. To Atra's claim that "they desire our bodies, which they deem far fairer than belike they be. And they would bed us, and beget children on us. And all this we let them do with a good will, because we love them for their might, and their truth, and the hotness of their love toward us," Viridis responds with heated annoyance: "[H]er eyes gleamed amidst the flushing of her cheeks, and she said: Sister, Sister! even in such wise, and no other, as they desire us do we desire them; it is no mere good will toward them from us, but longing and hot love" (Water 66). Atra does not dispute the correction.

Birdalone is similarly passionate in her response to Arthur, and her states of sexual longing are explicitly described: she "stood there with her heart beating fast and her flesh quivering, and a strange sweetness of joy took hold of her" (129), and "whiles she looked on her limbs, and felt the sleekness of her sides, . . . she said: O my body! how thou longest!" (141). It is also Birdalone's "new-womanly" desire for therapeutic outdoor activity and more active pursuit of romantic aims which inspires her to explore the surrounding countryside and leads to the adventures which occupy much of the central part of the tale. In the book's penultimate section, Birdalone leaves the City of the Five Crafts to seek Arthur, after a scene in which, after she arises and kneels naked on the window seat; "the sun came round that way, and its beams fell upon her bosom and her arms; and she stood up and looked on the fairness of her body, and a great desire took hold of her heart that it might be loved as it deserved by him whom she desired" (277). Narcissism and the "male gaze" are not exactly absent here.

The narrative likewise emphasizes a strong need for sexual honesty and straightforwardness. Arthur and Birdalone (and the tale's other lovers) declare their love simply and immediately, without reserve, coyness, inflated rhetoric, or affectation, and there is a near-complete absence of flirtation or guile. In their early courtship Arthur "would talk with her almost as one man with another, though with a certain tenderness in his voice, and looking earnestly on her the while" (128). After Birdalone is rescued from the Red Knight, she wavers and asks that Viridis narrate her tale of captivity to Arthur, but Viridis bluntly answers that "I am not a proper minstrel to take the word out of thy mouth. . . . When all is told, then shall we be more bound together again" (201). Viridis is right, for Birdalone's own narration of her story soothes Arthur's anxious fears.

Indirectly, Morris's tale also rewards Birdalone's bold visit to the Valley of the Greywethers to further her love. Left alone while the champions seek Aurea, Viridis, and Atra, she ventures into the Valley, avoided by the other castle-dwellers, to petition the ancient powers of the earth: "O Earth, thou and thy first children, I crave of you that he may come back now at once and loving me" (159). This act does lead to her entrapment by the Black and Red Knights, and thus indirectly to the deaths of Baudoin (one of the three "Champions") and the less vengeful Black Knight, so female autonomy can be dangerous to her and others. Birdalone conscientiously regrets her choice, but Hugh points out that: "we have lost a captain, [but] they have lost their head devil, and their head little devil," and Arthur remarks that "it were unmeet for us to murmur at our loss in our fellow" (212), and in fact "no blame have we to lay on our sister Birdalone" (211). Moreover, Arthur suggests a further campaign to press their immediate advantage and purge the area of the tyrannical and merciless Red Knight, and this decision lays the groundwork for a more peaceful life within the region.

Birdalone's prayer in the valley is also answered, when Arthur returns "at once and loving." They quickly admit their mutual attraction, and the tale never subjects either Birdalone or Arthur to criticism for disruption of Arthur's prior attachment to Atra. Socialist-feminist reformers such as Engels and Eleanor Marx seem similarly to have assumed that virtuous, companionate love which finds sexual expression will endure for life, or if not, will end without rancor — an innocent moment in the history of social thought.

Entrapped and threatened women have always been a staple of romance-plots, of course, since the days of the *Arcadia* and Aphra Behn. Morris first used the literary motif of the coerced woman in his 1858 poem, "The Hay-stack in the Floods" (in which Jehane threatens to strangle her potential rapist, Godmar), and he had always recognized that rape and threats of rape are forms of aggression which block women's access to roles readily accorded men. Josephine Butler, William Stead, and other late-century sexual reformers had often denounced sexual coercion and violence, and Morris may also have been influenced in part by recent publicity of sexual coercion during debates of the Matrimonial Causes Act of 1884 (which abolished the penalty of imprisonment for denial of "conjugal rights") and the Criminal Amendment Bill of 1885 (which raised the age of consent for women from 12 to 13, in an attempt to limit forced prostitution).[7] Whatever the source(s), Morris's treatment of these issues in *The Water of the Wondrous Isles* suggested a deeper understanding of their pervasiveness in women's everyday life.

Rapists and would-be rapists, in fact, are an ever-present danger in the romance's narrative. Birdalone chafes at several points under the requirement that she remain indoors or travel with male companions to prevent attack on her, and she spends quite a bit of time and energy negotiating with and warding off men who embody or express varying degrees of unwanted attraction and aggression. When she wishes to leave the Castle of the Quest alone, for example, the castellan Sir Ameryis restrains and warns her that "If [her female attendants] bring thee back safe, they may chance to sing to the twiggen fiddle-bow, that they may be warned from such folly; but if they come back without thee, by All-hallows the wind of wrath shall sweep their heads off them!"(143). Birdalone is finally convinced of Ameryis's good intentions, but she notes with irony and some bitterness that "Thou art a hard master, lord castellan; but I must needs obey thee. . . . Nay, nay, thou shalt not kneel to me, but I to thee: for thou art verily the master" (144–45).

Even uncoercive male attention can be a weariness of the flesh. Almost all the men who encounter her — the old man on the Isle of the Young and Old; Sir Amyeris the castellan; Leonard the Priest; the Geraldsons, father and two sons; and the alderman Jacobus — become strongly attracted to Birdalone, and she sometimes struggles to remain independent of her own friends and supporters. Again and again, she has to soothe the emotions of infatuated friends and rejected suitors, a source of persistent embarrassment and, in some cases (that of Jacobus, for example) genuine pain and regret.

Birdalone's narrowest escape occurs when she is seized by the Black and Red Knights. No sooner does she offer her prayer to the Earth in the Valley of the Greywethers, than the Black Knight captures her. She manages to ward him off warily for several days and eventually wrests from him a kind of protection against the even more threatening Red Knight, but she remains constantly alert. On first seeing the Black Knight, "she feared him and rued the meeting of him" (161); when he orders her to mount her horse and asserts that she need not be afraid, since he will "watch and ward thy waking," she answers, "Sir, I am now become afraid of the waking" (164).

Indeed, Birdalone eventually owes her survival to her adroit recognition of the Black Knight's many feints. She retains his armor during the night, "lest desire over-master thee" (167), and responds to his many invitations to accompany him elsewhere with equally stubborn demands that they return to the Castle. Consider the tensions and suppressed anger of the following exchange:

> Forsooth she had her bended bow in hand; but . . . she scarce deemed that it behoved her to slay or wound the man because she would be quit of him. Wherefore angrily, and with a flushed face, she answered him: So shall it be then, Sir Knight; or rather so must it be, since thou compellest me. He laughed and said: "Nay, now thou art angry. I compel thee not, I but say that it will not do for thee to compel me to leave thee[1]. . . . Forsooth, damsel, I have said harder words to ladies who have done my pleasure and not deemed themselves compelled." She paled but answered nought. (161–62)

Birdalone also resents the Black Knight's obtrusive "gaze": "she suffered not his hand, [but] his eyes she must needs suffer, as he gazed greedily on the trimness of her feet and legs in her sliding from her horse" (164). Walking beside him, "she, for her part, was silent, partly for fear of the strange man, or, it might be, even for hatred of him, who had thus brought her into such sore trouble" (170). Bitterly, she acknowledges that "thou art stronger than I, and thou mayst break my bow, and wrest this knife out of mine hand; and thou canst bind me and make me fast to the saddle, and so lead my helpless body into thraldom [to the Black Knight's more evil master, the Red Knight] and death" (179).

Compared to his master, however, the Black Knight is an ambivalent and tormented soul, and his reluctant agreement to return her to the castle is an act of defection. Birdalone is understandably alarmed by his bizarrely intense response to her refusals — he rolls on the ground and tears at the grass — and enjoins him, "Rise up, I bid thee, and be a man and not a wild beast" (181). Fear as well as pity prompt her attempts to calm him: "she thought within herself how wild and fierce the man was, and doubted if he might not go stark mad on her hands and destroy her if she thwarted overmuch; and, moreover, frankly she pitied him" (182).

Her wary bargaining with the Black Knight eventually loses precious time, unfortunately, and his master the Red Knight surprises them both. Morris leaves little doubt about this *capo's* gratuitous depravity. After her capture, Birdalone "was tethered to the horse's crupper by a thong that bound her wrists together, so that she had but just room left 'twixt her and the horse that she might walk, and round about her neck was hung a man's head newly hewn off" (195).

The Red Knight does not simply rape women, the Black Knight has warned her — he tortures them. One of his milder suggestions is a final offer to the disloyal Black Knight: "I forgive thee all if thou wilt ride home quietly with me and this damsel-errant to the Red Hold, and let her be mine and not thine so long as I will; and then afterwards, if thou wilt, she shall be thine as long as thou wilt" (208). The Black Knight rushes him instead but is killed, and the Red Knight then continues home with his prey. He threatens the captured Birdalone: "As my foe I might slay thee in any evil way it might like me; as my thrall I might well chastise thee as sharply and as bitterly as I would. But it is not my pleasure to slay thee, rather I will bring thee to the Red Hold, and there see what we may make of thee" (210). In effect, the Red Knight is an allegorical representation of unapologetic male brutality and predation — the ultimate antagonist and Apollyon of a woman's romance epic.

Morris seems to approve of female self-defense, but in the direst circumstances his heroine's efforts seem to fail. Although Birdalone carried with her a knife as well as bow and arrows into the Valley of the Greywethers, she scruples to use them in her uneasy truce with the Black Knight:

> Sir, thou shalt know that beside these shot-weapons, I have a thing here in my girdle that may serve either against thee or against me, if need drive me thereto; wherefore I will pray thee to forbear. Forsooth, thou shalt presently happen on other women, who shall be better unto thee than I can be. (166)

She does use her knife later, however, in a desperate attempt to aid the Black Knight's suicidal attack: "in . . . a flash I bethought me of the knife at my girdlestead, and drew it and ran to the Red Knight, and tore aside his mail hood with one hand and thrust the knife into his shoulder with the other; but so mighty was he that he heeded nought the hurt, but swept his sword back-handed to the Black Knight's unarmed leg. . . . Then arose the Red Knight, and thrust me from him with the left hand" (209). Morris's plot thus seems to suggest that even a physically valiant woman needs male defenders, although it should be recalled that Birdalone's captors have all the heavier weapons, and they have been undefeated by anyone — male or female — for many years.

All the same, such abridgments of a strong (but beautiful) woman's autonomy leads Birdalone to dress as a man called Louis Delahaye during part of her later wanderings. Cross-dressing, of course, is a familiar trope for a woman's escape from Victorian constraints on her behavior.

In none of Morris's earlier narratives is there significant mention of female companionship or friendship. Heroines such as Guenevere, Danae, Psyche, or Aslaug do not benefit from helpful mothers or mother-figures. In *The Water of the Wondrous Isles*, by contrast, female friendship and mentoring relationships are almost as central to the plot as they are in contemporary novels by Edith Johnstone, Mary Chalmondely, Gertrude Dix, Margaret Oliphant, and Mona Caird.[8] Birdalone's friendships with Aurea, Atra, and Viridis (especially the cheerful and sensuous Viridis) are essential to her happiness throughout the work. She reunites these women friends to their lovers, and all four friends experience great sadness each time they part. Their Morrisian sense of "fellowship" and mutual sympathy later survives both the stress of romantic competition (between Atra and Birdalone) and the death of Aurea's partner. Birdalone and Arthur undergo a long period of trial separation and psychological testing of their love, but her women's friendships are essentially immediate, and they transcend wariness, testing, and competition.

Not coincidentally, the now-solitary Atra also becomes a figure of priestess-like wisdom — an honorific, socially useful role which recalls that of the prophetess Hall-Wood in *The House of the Wolfings*. Much of the substance of these young women's confidences remains their longing for their absent male friends, but the tale's celebration of their complementary traits and mutual aid provides an empathetic counterharmony to the adventure-, journey-, and battle-motifs which *The Water* shares with Morris's other prose romances.

It is absolutely typical of Morris's work, moreover, that friendship and trust are expressed in the outer tale through the telling of inner stories, and the most significant of these are the life-histories of Birdalone and other women. When Birdalone meets Atra, Aurea, and Viridis, they exchange stories of their respective pasts. Later, Birdalone describes her friends' situation and narrates her own adventures to the Champions of the Quest. Still later, after the final defeat of the Red Knight, all exchange stories of their respective trials. When separated from her closest women friends, moreover, Birdalone solicits the tales of other women. When the "champions" leave the Castle of the Quest in search of their partners, Birdalone spends her time in "talking with her women, whereof were five now left. . . . All these told her somewhat of their own lives when she asked them; and some withal told of folk whom they had known or heard tell of. And well pleased was Birdalone to hear thereof" (139). Like the Wanderers and Elders' narratives in *The Earthly Paradise*, these imbricated interior narratives make the tale(s) as much a series of interlocking memories as an ongoing adventure, as tale folds into tale. And markedly *un*like the seven monologues of Tennyson's *The Princess*, which are all spoken by men to women, *The Water's* tales of women and men alternate, and the women's tales are unamended and uncensored narratives of their own experiences.

Women's narratives of female maturation typically place great emphasis on women's relationships with older women, including mothers, and reunion with a lost mother (or learning details of her fate) is often an important aspect of feminine identity-formation. Gilbert and Gubar have pointed out the importance of the vision of a tutelary maternal image which appears to the fleeing Jane Eyre, for example, and Caroline Henstone in *Shirley* is reunited with her unknown mother before she becomes engaged to Robert Moore.

Birdalone's brief reunion with her mother similarly gives her a deeper understanding of her past and fulfilled sense of kinship before she leaves the City of the Five Crafts.[9] After her adventures in the Valley, Birdalone earns her living for five years as an embroidress in the City of the Five Crafts, as I mentioned earlier. Shortly after she arrives, the master of the embroidery guild notes the resemblance between her designs and those of an older woman, Audrey, whose needlework "is somewhat after the manner of thine" (265), as is her appearance: "now I look on thee again, she might be somewhat like unto thee, were she young and fresh-looking and strong as thou art" (265). When the widow Audrey comes to visit, Birdalone immediately sympathizes with the gentle older woman, and asks "Why dost thou weep, Mother?" using the term at this point only as an honorific, and the two women exchange stories. Birdalone reminds Audrey of a stolen daughter she has never ceased to mourn, and they suddenly realize that Birdalone is Audrey's deeply-loved daughter, stolen in infancy by the exploitive Witch-wife of the tale's opening scenes. Both are overcome with emotion: "For in good sooth I am thy mother, and it is long since I have seen thee: but hearken, when I come quite to myself I shall pray thee not to leave me yet awhile, and I shall pray thee to love me." Birdalone responds: "I love thee dearly, and never, never shall I leave thee" (271).

Birdalone thus establishes her "proletarian" heritage — as Carole Silver points out, she now knows she is a peasant's daughter — and her origins as daughter of a farmer and needlewoman confirm that she has come naturally by her agricultural and textile-designing skills. Only after Audrey dies five years later does Birdalone turn her mind to the unfinished business of her relationship with Arthur, and at this point she seeks the assistance of a more complex and supra-earthly mother-figure.

Throughout *The Water of the Wondrous Isles*, Birdalone's spiritual mentor and tutelary spirit is the "earth goddess," Habundia. Within the narrative she fulfills many roles: a second and ideal self; an archetype of Birdalone's awakening self-awareness; a source of knowledge, intelligence, and earth-lore; a protectress and guide; and an enfolding source of love in extremity and distress. Their first meeting occurred years earlier when Birdalone was seventeen, and Habundia identified herself as Birdalone's spiritual Other: "As to our likeness, thou hast it now; so alike are we, as if we were cast in one mould. But thy sister of blood I am not; nay, I will tell thee at once that I am not of the children of Adam" (19).

Birdalone returns now to her girlhood home, invokes the presence of her spiritual mother, and opens her heart: "Mother, she said, I am grown older than I should be by the tale of the years . . . and now that the years have worn, the grief abideth and the joy hath departed, save this joy of thee and the day of the meeting I have so often thought of" (322). Habundia responds: "Now I deem thee my daughter again, whereas thou thankest me with such sweet passion for doing to thee as a kind mother needs must without any thought thereof. And I bid thee, my dear, never again to go so far from me as that I may not easily help thee and comfort thee from out of my realm wherein I am mighty. And now tell me all in thy dear speech" (324). Birdalone then tells her tale in full, and Habundia leads her to Arthur. Before the two marry, Birdalone again seeks her counsel, and Habundia offers advice and an extraordinarily generous promise: "And I think I can see that thou and thy man shall do well and happily in Utterhay; and the Green Knight also and thy she-friends. And whatsoever thou wilt of me that I may do for thee or thy friends, ask it freely, and freely shalt thou have it" (378).

There is a close parallel, in fact, between Habundia and a male counterpart in another tale. Steelhead, Osberne's eerily protective "warrior"-spirit in *The Sundering Flood*, Morris's last romance. Osberne continues to seek the elusive Steelhead after his marriage, as he ages, and Steelhead remains unchanged. In *The Water of the Wondrous Isles*, similarly, Birdalone and Arthur continue to visit Habundia for advice together after their marriage, and Habundia remains a tutelary wisdom-figure throughout their lives: "As to the wood of Evilshaw, it was not once a year only that Birdalone and Arthur sought thither and met the Wood-mother, but a half-score of times or more, might be, in the year's circle; and ever was she kind and loving with them, and they with her" (387).

The deepest trait Habundia shares with her human "daughter," moreover, is the one Morris had presented as the most essential quality of the woman of his new society — a deep and instinctive affinity with the natural lore and surfaces of the earth. As Ellen approaches the house at the base of the Thames, in a familiar passage from *News from Nowhere*, she "laid her shapely sun browned hand and arm on the lichened wall as if to embrace it, and cried, 'O me! O me! How I love the earth, and the seasons, and the weather, and all things that deal with it, and all that grows out of it — as this had done!' " Birdalone is similarly marked from girlhood by her kinship with living things: "the very grass and flowers were friends to her, and she made tales of them in her mind; and the wild things feared her in no wise, and the fowl would come to her hand, and play with her and love her" (8).

The designs which spring from her embroidress's fingers, accordingly, are of the plants and animals she knows. To make shoes, for example, Birdalone embroiders a skin with "oak-leaves . . . and flowers, and coneys, and squirrels" (13), and she covers her one new gown with "roses and lilies, and a tall tree springing up from amidmost the hem of the skirt, and a hart on either side thereof, face to face of each other. And the smock she had sewn daintily . . . with fair knots and buds" (14–15).

The gift the adolescent Birdalone seeks most urgently from Habundia is the lore of natural "wisdom," and Habundia gladly offers "to open the book of the earth before [her]. For therein is mine heritage and my dominion." Their communion is too profound to be conveyed or memorialized in language: "Forsooth forgotten is the wisdom, though the tale of its learning abideth, wherefore nought may we tell thereof" (42). Birdalone thus expresses the spirit of her wood-mother when she first rides forth from the Castle of the Quest, and her soul responds to the physical beauty of the land outside its walls: "of a sudden all care left her, and she dropped her rein, and smote her palms together, and cried out: Oh! but thou art beautiful, O earth, thou art beautiful!. . . . Ah! she said, but if I were only amidst it, and a part of it, as once I was of the woodland!" (148). For such a secular religion, one appropriate altar is a Valley, in which Birdalone later addresses a prayer to "Earth, thou and thy first children" (159).

The figure of Habundia is new in Morris's writings, and fin-de-siècle interest in non-classical mythology may have helped inspire her creation.[10] Female characters such as the Psyche in *The Earthly Paradise* are sometimes *subject* to female divinities in Morris's earlier work, but Venus is a harsh rival to Psyche, almost a kind of *domina*, and a rather repellent archetype of Victorian rites of sexual passage. Habundia's name suggests some of the fertility of the classical Venus or Ceres, but her behavior also evokes the benign and intelligent qualities ascribed to Celtic goddesses such as Macha — wise sorceress, prophetess, and mother — and Brigid — patroness of poets, goddess of healing, and smith-goddess of water, fire, and energy. Birdalone's name, too, many resonate slightly with a tradition of bird-women-goddesses.[11]

Morris may or may not have been aware of such parallels, of course, but he read with remarkable depth and range in the folklore and legendary source materials of his generation, and his general awareness of these sources may have blended with an evolving interest in female analogues of the mentor-/father-/brother-figures of his male-centered narratives. The result, in any case, is one of his most benign and original figures: a spiritual and pragmatic guardian-spirit and fitting protectress for Birdalone, as she seeks autonomy and eroticism, selfhood and community.

A similar icon of socialist-feminist allegory might be found in the figures of Birdalone's witch-stepmother or her evil sister-in-spirit, the Lady of the Isle of Increase Unsought. There are many precedents for the Witch in medieval English legend, classical and Scandinavian lore, and Morris's own earlier writings. To the traditional traits of such women — their use of spells, potions, serpent-rings, and the like — Morris added a realistic sense of their particular exemplar's relative indigence and her motives for exploitation of Birdalone's labor. Her power is also limited from the beginning by Habundia's lore and Birdalone's physical endurance and high intelligence, which jointly enable the "bürde" to survive the many perils of her subsequent adventures. As the spiritual daughter of a wise goddess, Birdalone also has a heritage which complements her human one and which befits the numinous status Morris came to accord to an essentially female divinity "of the earth."

In summary, Morris's characterization of Birdalone is remarkably consistent with socialist notions of the "new woman." His romantic plot implausibly makes Birdalone the cynosure of *all* available male "gazes," but the tale's ensuing plot complications are explored with pragmatic insight into the complex circumstances of a woman who is not only beautiful but athletic, and artistically and intellectually gifted. With the help of the tale's numinous archetype of "womanist" competence, the wise and loving Habundia, its female hero slays emblematic dragons of reaction and patriarchy, and begins the narrative of her adult life in a society of equals, lovers, and friends.

University of Iowa

NOTES

1. See Cunningham and Ardis for discussions of these novels and the reactions to them.
2. See Florence and William Boos, and Florence Boos, "A History of Their Own," for discussions of these developments.
3. For a discussion of the qualities and literary pervasiveness of the "new woman," see Jeffreys; Helsinger, Sheets, and Veeder; and Showalter.

4. Morris's letter to the Editor asserted of the reviewer's remarks on *The Wood Beyond the World* that "I had not the least intention of thrusting any allegory in *The Wood Beyond the World*; it is meant for a tale pure and simple, with nothing didactic about it. If I have to write or speak on social problems, I always try to be as direct as I possibly can" (*The Introductions*, 2: 499).

5. See *A Vindication of the Rights of Woman*, chapter 8, "Of the Pernicious Effects Which Arise from the Unnatural Distinctions Established in Society," and chapter 12, "On National Education"; and *The Subjection of Women*, chapter 1.

6. See Florence Boos, "An (Almost-)Egalitarian Sage."

7. See Strachey.

8. See Ardis.

9. For discussions of contemporary British women's contributions to the arts and crafts movement, see Marsh; Marsh and Nunn; Callen; and Burkhauser.

10. See Florence Boos, "Gender Division."

11. See Dexter, 88–93, 164.

12. See Strachey, chapter 10.

Several critics have observed that Morris's post-revolutionary socialist future resembles feminist utopias in a variety of intriguing ways (for example, Levitas, chapters 7 and 8). In *The Water of the Wondrous Isles*, even the female villains — the Lady of Abundance and the Witch — become projections of a socialist feminist's worst enemies: patriarchy (woman idealized as idle and near-mindless siren), and capitalism (exploitation of woman's labor in all its forms). More individually, Birdalone's clear-eyed analysis of the boundaries imposed on her behavior and resistance to them, her friendships with other women and identification with a female mentor, her physical courage and mental independence — all of these exemplify Morris's intense love and respect for intelligence, creativity, and kinship with the earth, and parallel images of female maturation sketched by Morris's reformist female contemporaries.

WORKS CITED

Ardis, Ann L. *New Women, New Novels: Feminism and Early Modernism*. New Brunswick: Rutgers UP, 1990.

Boos, Florence. "An (Almost-)Egalitarian Sage: William Morris and Victorian Socialist Feminism." *Victorian Sages and Cultural Discourse: Renegotiating Gender and Power*. Ed. Thais Morgan. New Brunswick: Rutgers UP, 1990. 187–206, 296–301.

———. "Gender Division and Allegory in William Morris's *The Sundering Flood*" *Journal of Pre-Raphaelite Studies* 1.2 (Fall 1992): 12–23.

———. "A History of Their Own: Late Victorian Feminist Family History." *The Rhetoric of Social History*. Ed. Jeffrey Cox, Linda Kerber, and Shelton Stromquist.

Boos, Florence and William. "Victorian Socialist-Feminism and William Morris's *News from Nowhere*." *Nineteenth Century Contexts* 14.1(1990): 3–32.

Burkhauser, Jude. *Glasgow Girls: Women in Art and Design 1880–1920*. Edinburgh: Canongate, 1990.

Callen, Anthea. *Women Artists of the Arts and Crafts Movement, 1870–1914*. New York: Pantheon, 1979.

Cunningham, Gail. *The New Woman and the Victorian Novel*. New York: Macmillan, 1978.

Dexter, Miriam. *Whence the Goddess.* New York: Pergamon P, 1990.

Faulkner, Peter, ed. *William Morris: The Critical Heritage.* London: Routledge, 1973.

Jeffreys, Sheila. *The Spinster and Her Enemies: Feminism and Sexuality 1880–1930.* London: Pandora, 1985.

Helsinger, Elizabeth K., Robin Lauterbach Sheets, and William Veeder, eds. *The Woman Question: Society and Literature in Britain and America, 1837–1883.* New York: Garland, 1983.

Levitas, Ruth. *The Concept of Utopia.* Syracuse: Syracuse UP, 1990.

Marsh, Jan. *Pre-Raphaelite Women: Images of Femininity in Pre-Raphaelite Art.* London: Weidenfeld and Nicolson, 1987.

Marsh, Jan, and Pamela Nunn. *Women Artists and the Pre-Raphaelite Movement.* London: Virago, 1989.

Marx, Eleanor and Edward Aveling. *The Woman Question.* London: Swann Sonnenschein, 1887. Rpt in *Thoughts on Women and Society.* Ed. Joachim Muller and Edith Schotte. New York: International Publishers, 1987. 21, 24.

Mill, John Stuart. *The Subjection of Women.* New York: Frederick A. Stokes, 1911.

Morris, May. *The Introductions of the Collected Works of William Morris.* Ed. Joseph Riggs Dunlap. 2 vols. New York: Oriele, 1973.

Morris, May, ed. *William Morris: Artist, Writer, Socialist.* 2 vols. Oxford: Blackwell, 1936.

Morris, William. *The Collected Works of William Morris.* 24 vols. London: Longmans, 1910–15.

———. *The Letters of William Morris: 1881–1888.* Ed. Norman Kelvin. Princeton UP, 1987.

———. *The Water of the Wondrous Isles.* Vol. 20 of *The Collected Works of William Morris.* London: Longmans, 1913.

Showalter, Elaine. *Sexual Anarchy: Gender and Culture at the Fin de Siècle.* New York: Viking, 1990.

Silver, Carole. "Socialism Internalized: The Last Romances of William Morris." *Socialism and the Literary Artistry of William Morris.* Ed. Florence Boos and Carole Silver. Columbia: U of Missouri P, 1990. 117–26.

Strachey, Ray. *"The Cause": A Short History of the Women's Movement in Great Britain.* London, 1928. Rpt. Port Washington, NY: Kennikat, 1969.

Vertinsky, Patricia. *The Eternally Wounded Woman: Women, Doctors, and Exercise in the Late Nineteenth Century.* Manchester: Manchester U P, 1990.

Wollstonecraft, Mary. *A Vindication of the Rights of Woman.* London: Johnson, 1792.

MAX BEERBOHM: THE VIOLENCE OF THE WAX MASK

By Franco Buffoni

WRITING IN *THE LONDON MAGAZINE* on "the future of the novel" on the occasion of the death of Max Beerbohm in 1956, Philip Toynbee suggested that it was no longer possible to write in the "exquisite" manner of Beerbohm, because, in contrast to the 1890s, there no longer existed a social group that cultivated the art of polished and witty conversation.

Beerbohm died in 1956, a year which recent literary histories often take as an important turning point.[1] However, 1956 is not a particularly significant year for *his* work, which had been neglected for more than a generation. The turning point for Beerbohm's work can be associated more significantly with 1895, the year of the trial of Oscar Wilde, when Beerbohm was twenty-three (and E. M. Forster sixteen). The reason that *Maurice* was kept from publication until the 1970s was the same that led Beerbohm to compose his short story "William and Mary" in a certain manner: a coercive social situation.

With the delicacy and veiled allusions still felt as necessary when certain themes were mentioned in the late 1940s, Beerbohm's Italian translator, Emilio Cecchi, wrote:

> "William and Mary" is of particular interest . . . , and it is an important clue to Beerbohm's idea of the art of writing. Its nonchalant air, the *divertissements* offered by the text, will not hide from the thoughtful reader one of the subtlest and deepest-felt representations of those renunciations which lie behind all styles and all literary vocations and careers. (*Ipocrita* 15)

Although Cecchi's "renunciations" may only refer to style — to Beerbohm's understatement and verbal self-denial — his remark can be taken as the starting-point for a re-reading of "William and Mary" (from *And Even Now*, 1920) and "James Pethel" (from *Seven Men*, 1919) in the light of the coercive social deterrent mentioned above.

William is an old University acquaintance, "one of the principal pariahs of our College," "[I]t was rather in a spirit of bravado, and to show how sure of myself I was," confesses the narrator, "that I began, in my second year, to cultivate his acquaintance. We had little in common. I could not think Political Economy 'the most exciting thing in the world,' as he used to call it" (268).

But is it only as an act of open defiance that the narrator — apparently a worldly, dandyish, and frivolous figure — decides to further his acquaintance with this "tall, broad, raw-boned fellow, with long brown hair flung back from his forehead" who bores him to death with his reading aloud of "Mr. William Morris' interminable smooth Icelandic Sagas"? Or did the open challenge conceal a stronger though clearer impulse? In short, how would Beerbohm have written the background to the story if he had felt free to reveal the feelings and thoughts that confused the narrator while William, "standing on his hearth-rug" (269), was reading?

An author generally invents imaginary characters and situations and alters his own world and experiences either to create a more interesting narrative or to preserve his own privacy. In the case of Beerbohm's "William and Mary" and "James Pethel," however, we should talk not only of privacy or artistic reasons: in the England of George V, any attempt to narrate what clearly lies behind these stories would have made Beerbohm clash against the rules of "respectable" behavior, and it might even have laid him open to legal prosecution. Such vain gestures did not belong to Max's style, and social ostracism and imprisonment were not among the aims of his life. Hence the creation of "masked" texts. In these two narratives the author gives the impression of inventing nothing, as he declares the situations to be autobiographical in nature; yet he "masks" his own narration by changing the reason the narrator gives for cultivating an unusual friendship.

In both stories the first-person narrator is a frank and fascinating figure of great surface polish who meets by chance another man. After a close description of the meeting, his narrative can be said to consist of four phases, which can be summarized as follows: (1) a disguising of the motive for cultivating the friendship; (2) his encounter with the man's fiancée; (3) his intrusion into their private lives; (4) the modelling of his behavior on that of the woman.

Beerbohm the "uncle," as it were, because he is alone and it is his duty to visit other people, an uncle who, shyly and delicately, becomes the asexual first-person narrator. He seems to be telling the story of the friendly sentiments he increasingly feels for William's wife, Mary (judged at first to be "neat, insignificant, pleasing" and "practical," 271).

The encounter with William, with whom he had lost touch after leaving university, occurs in the customary fatal way: "One afternoon in the spring of '95 I happened to meet him at the corner of Cockspur Street" (270). William tells him straightaway, "I'm married" (the narrator has already told us of William's former, fanatical hostility to marriage while at Oxford), and he invites him to spend the weekend with himself and his wife. It is a carefully-phrased invitation which reminds us of Clive's invitation to Maurice in Forster's novel.

Unlike Maurice, Beerbohm's narrator does not suffer from the new situation. He is detached, nameless, and ironic: " 'You must see her,' he said; and his impatience to show her proudly off to some one was so evident, and so touching, that I could but accept his invitation" (270). It turns out that it is Mary's laugh which overcomes the aesthetic and affective reservations of the narrator: "her laugh was a lovely thing . . . a trill of notes . . . as though she were pulling repeatedly a little silver bell" (271). The narrator's happy, regular visits to their cottage ("An actual cottage, of seventeenth-century workmanship," 273) continue for four years, until Mary's death in childbirth and William's departure for South Africa as a war-correspondent and his death.

Some years later, the narrator walks past their deserted cottage. He yields to temptation, and he goes up to look through the window and rings the bell: "The scrape of the wire — and then . . . a whole quick sequence of notes, faint but clear, playful, yet poignantly sad, like a trill of laughter echoing out of the past" (284–85).

During the frequent visits the narrator pays to the couple in their four happy years of marriage, his function is similar to Mary's: both of them listen to William's readings and praise his literary talent. However, Mary's admiration is simple and sincere, while the narrator's is hypocritical. That is why he feels obliged to justify his visits as a consequence of his liking for Mary, and in particular for her common sense and for the rapt attention with which she listens to her husband. The narrator attempts to imitate her devout respect, although he says: "I sometimes wished this work had some comic relief in it. Publishers, I believe, shared this wish; hence the eternal absence of William's name from among their announcements" (276). Indeed, the narrator's justification is expressed in increasingly extreme forms:

> The main reason why I wished for light passages in what he read to us was that they would have been cues for Mary's laugh. This was a thing always new to me. I was never tired of that little bell-like euphony; those funny little lucid and level trills. (276)

The friendship and affection the narrator so explicitly expresses for the woman loved by "my dear old William" becomes a unilateral fusion with Mary herself. It is not important that glances of love and desire cannot be stolen from William, since the narrator sees Mary as a projection of himself. The narrator is happy when he is given the same attention and the same glances as Mary:

> I cultivated in myself whatever amused her in me; I drew out whatever amused her in William. . . . She used to call me . . . the Gentleman from London. I used

to call her the Brave Little Woman. Whatever either of us said or did could be twisted easily into relation to those two titles; and [to] our bouts . . . William listened with a puzzled, benevolent smile. (276–77)

.* * *

ANOTHER SHORT STORY, "JAMES Pethel," can be interpreted in similar terms. The title, which indicates a single male protagonist, seems to promise less ambiguity. But here too, as in "William and Mary" — where everything apparently hinges on Mary's laugh — the "subject" is to be found in the abstract, in this case, perhaps, the *libido audiendi*. (In Freud's study of Dostoevsky, gambling is defined as a regression to the infantile stage in order to assert superiority over adults — by winning, while freeing the subject from resultant guilty feelings through punishment — by losing.) James Pethel is a "player": "Nobody has so much strength of character as *he* has," (125) and yet he is "the weakest of men" (126). He is weak because he is a slave not only to gambling but also to a diabolic impulse to risk everything whenever possible, jeopardizing even his own and other people's safety. Yet he is strong because he hazards his own life completely though calmly ("those pursed out lips . . . seemed to denote no more than a pensive interest," (109) in order to satisfy the dictates of his "religion."

James is a self-made man in his mid-thirties: "a putative thirty-six, not more. ('Not less,' I would have said in those days)" (109). (Beerbohm always leaves a trace of his own feelings: we are aware that the voice is telling a story from his own past.) James has made a great deal of money through risky investments, of course:

"But there's no knowing the future. A few errors of judgment — a war here, a revolution there, a big strike somewhere else, and —" He blew a jet of smoke from his lips, and looked at me as at one whom he could trust to feel for him in a crash already come. (117)

They strike up an acquaintance in the casino in Dieppe at the height of the season. James risks and wins a great deal of money, and they spend a day together. Their first encounter is followed by a long conversation, an invitation to lunch at the Hotel Royal the following day, and a drive in James's car, where the narrator is greatly shaken by the thoughtless driving of his new friend.[2]

Beerbohm's narrative focuses on a question: what kind of man is James Pethel? The answer is elegantly held in suspense during the frightening car trip until the end of the story:

I understood him. . . . Those pursed-out lips . . . had told me suddenly all that I needed to know about Pethel. . . . I remembered the strange look he had given

when I asked if his gambling were always "a life-and-death affair." Here was
the real thing — the authentic game, for the highest stakes! And here was I, a
little extra-stake tossed on to the board. (130)

The narrator justifies his interest in the new acquaintance as anthropological
curiosity. But let us look more closely at the circumstances of their first
meeting:

> My gaze was held by him for the very reason that he would have passed
> unnoticed elsewhere. . . . Between his lips was a cigar of moderate size, . . . his
> face [had] neither that extreme pallor nor that extreme redness which belongs
> to the faces of seasoned gamblers. . . . And his eyes had neither the unnatural
> brightness nor the unnatural dullness of the eyes around him: they were ordi-
> narily clear eyes, of an ordinary grey. . . . I noticed that the removal of his cigar
> from his mouth made never the least difference to his face, for he kept his lips
> pursed out as steadily as ever when he was not smoking. (108–09)

Right from the start the narrator concentrates on James's features: is this
simply "for the very reason that he would have passed unnoticed elsewhere"?
Or does this Pethel ("a regular all-round sportsman — had gone after big
game all over the world and had a good many narrow shaves," whose wife
"had been a barmaid at Cambridge. Married her when he was nineteen,")
(111) strike him so much at first sight for a more credible reason? Once the
motive has been hidden, the narrator's attraction for the man becomes an easy
narrative development thanks to the Dostoevskian situation: "How easily had
he won in a few minutes more than I . . . could earn in many months!" In
fact, it turns into mere hypocrisy: "I wished I were he. His lucre seemed to
insult me personally." It turns into the natural, understandable reaction to an
unknown person who unwittingly becomes the focus of an exclusive attention:
"I disliked him" (109).

Dislike. Because the Ego defends itself by opposing what the Id desires:
"I hoped he would not take another bank. I hoped he would have the good
sense to pocket his winnings and go home." In its turn, the Superego provides
a rational justification: "Deliberately to risk the loss of all those riches would
intensify the insult to myself" (109).

But then something happens; one of those chance encounters (in fact desired, encouraged encounters), which are almost commonplace in a certain
kind of early twentieth-century narrative (in Gide especially):

> Turning to go, I encountered a friend. . . . "Going to play?" I asked. "Not
> while Jimmy Pethel's taking the bank," he answered, with a laugh. (110)

This go-between character is always laughing. He is detached, relaxed,
superficial, and unconcerned. At this point he is at a zero degree of feeling;

his nonchalance acts in counterpoint to the narrator's state of tension. The latter must nevertheless affect nonchalance ("Is that the man's name?" "Yes. Don't you know him? I thought every one knew 'old Jimmy Pethel.' ") and justify his attraction (to himself? to the reader?) by pretending to be repelled: "I asked what there was so wonderful about 'old Jimmy Pethel' that every one should be supposed to know him" (110). Nevertheless he betrays himself by his instinctive choice of the adjective "wonderful," which is underplayed in the context but is symptomatic of the strength of his feelings.

Henceforth the relationship is a crescendo of potential opportunities: "At the cry of 'Messieurs, la banque est aux enchères' we looked round and saw that the subject of our talk was preparing to rise from his place" (111). And the apparition is baroque, as it were — a vision of Cleopatra, act 2, scene 2:

> With his lips no longer pursed, he had lost his air of gravity, and looked younger. Behind him was an attendant bearing a big wooden bowl — that plain but romantic bowl supplied by the establishment to a banker whose gains are too great to be pocketed. (111–12)

It is remarkable that this human being talks just like everyone else ("He said he had arrived in Dieppe this afternoon — was here for a day or two"), and that he even accepts the interlocutor: "He spoke to me with some *empressement*, saying that he was a 'very great admirer' of my work." The narrator allows himself moments of understated self-irony ("I no longer disliked him"), and he finally obtains evidence of his conquest:

> Pethel, with a wave of his hand towards the tables, said "I suppose you never condescend to this sort of thing?" "Well —" I smiled indulgently. "Awful waste of time," he admitted. (112)

This, then, is the technique used to strike up an acquaintance. All that follows is simply an attempt at moral justification — first of all, contingent justification (to the author's benefit at the moment of the action), then narrative justification (in order to develop the story in an uncompromising manner):

> Pethel asked me to tell him who every one was. I told him no one was any one in particular, and suggested that we should talk about ourselves. (114)

Beerbohm, whose exquisite humor and spellbinding style led many critics to number him among the finest modern artists, masterfully succeeds in hiding the desperate search of the narrator for an illusion consisting of acceptable feelings of friendship and concessions of courtesy:

> As we took our seats in the café, he looked around him with boyish interest and pleasure. Then, squaring his arms on the little table, he asked me what I would drink. (114)

The narrator's state of reverie is translated into actions and gestures:

> He drank his glass of water, and, linking a friendly arm in mine, passed out
> with me into the corridor. He asked what I was writing now. (119)

And the precise recollection seems a sort of philter which brings back re-
lived feelings:

> "I want to get a little sea-air into my lungs now," and he asked with a sort
> of breezy diffidence if I would go with him.... We were not long on the
> terrace ... there was a wind against which you had to stagger.... Against that
> wind acquaintance could make no headway. (113)

Now let us turn to the intrusion of the narrator into the familiar world of
the other person. In this case, it is not the wife who stimulates a protective
behavior. Her existence is not even a surprise, since she is immediately mentioned in the friend's conversation. The narrator says: "I had figured her as
'flaunting,' as golden-haired, as haughty," but he is introduced to "a very
pale small lady whose hair was rather white than grey" (121). The narrator
sees that her husband does not love her anymore; it is even probable "that
he never had loved her — had taken her, in his precocious youth, simply as
a gigantic chance against him" (131). In the story, the woman who owns the
heart of the male protagonist is his adolescent daughter.

The girl — "by the news of whose existence I felt idiotically surprised"
(119) — is as fascinating and defiant of danger as her father: "Whenever he
was looking at her ... the effect ... was that of a very vain man before a
mirror ... the two were so absurdly alike" (133). The more the father takes
risks, even if only while driving his car fast, the more his daughter adores
him. And the narrator shares these feelings, while he only feels commiseration
for the wife ("Poor lady! My heart was with her. As the car glided along the
sea-front ... I wished that her husband inspired in her as much confidence as
he did in me. For me the sight of his clear, firm profile ... was an assurance
in itself" 127). However, he has to show admiration for Jimmy Pethel — an
admiration as boundless as that of the daughter. But the narrator is no hero,
and at the most critical point of the drive he stares straight ahead and then,
with Chaucerian self-irony, admits: "Loth to betray fear, I hadn't turned my
face to Pethel" (129).

It is when the narrator is with both Pethel and his wife, however, that the
most significant scene takes place:

> I explained that I was ... envying her husband's strength of character. She
> smiled too, but wanly, with her eyes on him. "Nobody has so much strength
> of character as *he* has," she said.

"Nonsense!" he laughed. "I'm the weakest of men."
"Yes," she said quietly. "That's true, too, James."
Again he laughed, but he flushed. I saw that Mrs Pethel also had faintly flushed;
and I became horribly conscious of following suit. (125–26)

* * *

THE HAPPY HYPOCRITE,[3] the story of a man who changes as a result of a conscious and consoling reverie, can be read as a metaphor. George Hell is an evil man with an evil face who falls in love with a good young girl able to love only a man with the face of a good man. In order to win her love and to live with her in a hut at the edge of a greenwood, George visits a maker of wax masks and has the mask of a good man fitted to his face. He plays the part of the good man so well that the girl suspects nothing for a long time. Then a former mistress discovers their hideaway, and in a fit of jealousy she falls on him and tears the mask away. George Hell, unmasked, loses everything and is in despair, but then he realizes that his own face has changed into that of a good man. He can stay forever with the girl he loves, and his name is changed to George Heaven.

The event can be read as the dream of a man who feels guilty of not conforming to certain conventional ethical norms and who unconsciously desires to change and conform to them. (In a similar way, Rolfe's friendly gondolier changes into Zilda; the creature in a dinner jacket at the end of Hesse's *Steppenwolf* changes into a "woman.")

Nothing could give a better idea of a most common source of existential anxiety after the *trobar clus* of the subdued narrative of "James Pethel."

The metaphor of the wax mask may show us a kind of subtle violence the author inflicts on his own text when, for example, Proust gives the name "Albertine" to the strong-necked person on the divan whose fingers intertwine with his own. In a social context which excludes and condemns in variable degrees the "unspeakable vice" of the ancient Greeks, the homoerotic artist may find himself exercising on the text what Foucault calls the "power of coercion," thereby manipulating the real object of the narration in some way, until in extreme cases such substitutions and manipulations become Pavlovian reflexes. (After reading Proust's *L'Indifférent*, for example, the reader wonders whether the "ignoble" persons the protagonist meets are really women.)

The alternative to such masked texts is the cathartic confessional text. The best-known example is Forster's *Maurice*, and an Italian example is Umberto Saba's *Ernesto*. In both cases the usually-exercised power of coercion is held in check in the text, but, since both works remained unpublished, this power is anyway exercised over the act of communication (if we exclude the communication of the author with himself as a reader, and perhaps with a narrow circle of close friends). The power of coercion injures the common reader (especially the homoerotic common reader), who is deprived of a document he has the moral right to experience. The author may decide not to manipulate the content of his text and to lay himself open to public criticism. Two such examples (dating from the years just after the Second World War) are Carlo Coccioli's *Fabrizio Lupo* and Roger Peyrefitte's *Les amitiés particulières*. In other cases, such texts are published anonymously or under a pseudonym, like Jean Cocteau's *Le livre blanc*.

Structural analysis will render the discussion easier. The following abbreviations will be used throughout the second part of the essay:[4]

CSC = the coercive social context (which represses the unspeakable vice)
HA = the homoerotic author
HR = the homoerotic reader
HAR = the homoerotic author as reader of himself
MT = the (more-or-less) masked text
ST = the sincere text
DMT = decodable masked text

The intensity of coercion involved in the production of a MT by a HA obviously depends on the force of the CSC. For example, Gore Vidal, who in the United States after the Second World War clearly suffered less coercion, needed in turn to apply less coercion to his text than did Max Beerbohm in Edwardian England.

One might believe that the CSC offers the HA the difficult choice between the production of a ST (leading to self-exposure and to the CSC's consequential violence) and the masking of his own text. A real CSC, however, offers no choice: it simply does not allow the publication of a ST. (In the late Soviet Union and in contemporary China, Gore Vidal would never have obtained permission to publish *The City and the Pillar*.) How shall we judge France between the two World Wars,[5] when Gide was allowed to publish his *Corydon*, but he then became the inevitable victim of reactionary violence? Might we say that there are absolute CSCs and relative CSCs, which retain the option of punishing the HA but, nevertheless, permit the publication of his ST? What transforms a CSC from asbsolute into relative? If we start from the presupposition that a CSC which forbids the publication of the ST will nonetheless allow the publication of the MT, we may see the transition from absolute to relative CSC. Such a transition is achieved by means of the acquired competence of the HR and of readers in general (hence, we may say, of the CSC itself) in the decodification of the MT. This may be achieved either consciously or unconsciously, either voluntarily or involuntarily.

England in the late nineteenth century, an absolute CSC, would never have allowed a ST — yet it accepted the publication of *The Picture of Dorian Gray*, a typical MT that can be decoded by any reader. (Of course, the transition from absolute to relative CSC does not depend on the narrative only, but such investigation beyond the scope of the present paper.) A conspicuous production of DMTs leads to the type of linguistic and ethical infiltration which subsequently allows the HA to choose between ST and MT freely. A conspicuous production of STs, together with other non-literary cultural changes, should finally make the CSC increasingly tolerant of the HA, to the point where the CSC is no longer coercive.

We have now to discuss how and when a text can be decoded and who can decode it. The stories by Beerbohm looked at above were not decodable by the average reader of the time (not decodable by the CSC, therefore). Conversely, *Dorian Gray was* decodable. The only tenable position to adopt in this kind of speculation is the awareness that even if the codes of a period are always unlimited, there is a limitation in the ways of reading that a period can apply to its codes.

Since the author's exercise of coercive power on the text and the text's coercive power on the reader are acts of communication, it is natural to see the CSC as the context in which communication takes place:

$$HA \rightarrow MT \rightarrow HR$$

$$CSC$$

If we consider the results and not the processes and we see the HA as what a person who lives in a certain CSC becomes, then the HA himself, the story of his life and of his interpersonal relationships, can be considered as the context. Indeed, it might be better not to refer to the HA but to a subject with certain characteristics that the CSC has defined as homoerotic.[6] If we could limit the meaning of "context" to the whole set of significant elements belonging to the life of a person, as the individual himself experienced them, we might assert that if the symptom is the signal, and the meaning of the symptom is the message, then *the context is the neurosis*, together with all the elements and the individuals to which it refers.

The consequence is that the lines of communication can be represented as the simple transmission of a message of prohibition/force from an emitter (the CSC) to two receivers: the first of them is the HA, the receiver-decodifier and recodifier of the message of prohibition/force; the second, the indirect receiver, is the HR, the final destination. It should not be forgotten, however, that the HA can also be a HR, that is, a reader of himself.

Jakobson's well-known diagram can be used to describe this communication from CSC to HR.

```
                        CONTEXT
                        MESSAGE
EMITTER ---------------------------------------------------------------- RECEIVER
                        CONTACT
                        CODE
```

(Jakobson 17)

The diagram contains all the elements we have discussed so far: the CSC acts on a *message*, which refers to a *context* expressed in a shared *code* through the medium of physical *contact* (visual perception of the written word). In line with the considerations made above, we will no longer represent the context as the HA, but as any H *Subject*:

```
                        CODE

                      H Subject
        CSC --------------------------------- HR
                        MT
```

If we believe that not all that is expressed is expressed intentionally, we see that this model fails to consider the interaction of message and code. In order to complete our picture of the transmission of the particular power of coercion at present under discussion, let us consider the application of Sebeok's model of communication:

```
                             channel
                               →
        EMITTER                ←             RECEIVER
                             feedback
                             --------
        signal               CODE            noise
                             MESSAGE
                             --------
                             CONTEXT
```

(Sebeok 44)

According to Sebeok, communication takes place in a context that includes every possibility of communication. In such a context, code and message interact and modify each other.

We can see the Context as the H Subject and his individual life story, and the Emitter as the HA, but the picture remains incomplete. Such a scheme does not contain the device that can replace all the subconscious and preconscious processes which inevitably occur to the "HA as HR-of-himself." Using HAR to represent the "HA/HR-of-himself," we can indicate more clearly the existence of such processes:

$$HAR--->MESSAGE--->CSC$$

CODE
H Subject

The Message/Code relationship acts on the linguistic and ethical modes the CSC permits, and therefore on the CSC itself. We can also see how the constraining power, which in the text is represented by M ("masking"), acts in the direction of the HR through the medium of the MT (here the CSC acts as the Emitter). However, the constraining power, still through the medium of the MT, also acts in the direction of the CSC (and here the HAR acts as the Emitter, and the modified CSC as the Receiver). As Message and Code can almost be seen as a single interactive term, every single act of *parole* is not just the simple execution of a possibility allowed by the *langue*, but it carries with itself in greatly variable measure a transformation of the code.

The HA, carrying out an act of *parole* within the *langue*, influences the code and in some way (perhaps even imperceptibly) transforms it. If we accept this hypothesis, it means that the HA can modify the CSC's power of coercion. The CSC, though closed and dogmatic by definition, can never be completely impermeable to infiltrations from the HA, since any SC is naturally modelled on the *langue*. Therefore, the SC transforms as the *langue* itself transforms.

Returning to our original analysis of the situation, it may be said that although the sequence

$$CSC--->HA--->MT--->HR(A)$$

still has a meaning from a static, abstract, and temporally isolated point of view, it is incomplete from a point of view which is dynamic, concrete, and temporally open. The reason is that the CSC will always *change* in time; it may even become a neutral SC if subjected to a powerful series of MTs followed by STs. Its coercive power, the basis of its strength, will probably be shifted to other fields. In other words, when, from *our* point of view, the CSC becomes a simple SC, in some other field the individual will continue to be afraid of not saying what is conventionally said, or of saying something different from what is conventionally accepted. The CSC seeks to exorcise words, to take away their power, making it conform to an established way of thinking, to a permitted ideology.

Our reading of Foucault suggests that the HA will yield to another and more insidious coercion, that is, to play along with the limitations of the CSC. This is not because the HA simply speaks or writes, but because, as Foucault suggests, he inevitably presents himself as a meeting-point of discourses, as a unity, as the source of their meanings, as the fulcrum of their coherence. And this means presenting oneself as the explanatory-I of an event (or a series of events) and not as a narrating-I, who conforms to the events themselves.

Beerbohm clearly yielded to this subtle request and took up the role imposed by the CSC. His playful attitude, his brilliant style, and the situations he wittily constructs by using ethical and linguistic elements considered as acceptable by the CSC demonstrate it. A clear case in point is the brief fable *The Happy Hypocrite*.

But, even while respecting the rules of the CSC, the author follows an imperative dictated by his being different. He is constitutionally incapable of using the communication model of those who are called normal. His imperative allows him to claim power of speech and to say what the CSC — and his own desire to be only an author, not a HA — would forbid. This mechanism balances the Pavlovian reflex of the naturally masked text.

This is not the place to undertake a study of message-code interaction in intra-psychic communication. Limiting our interest to verbal expression, we can suggest that the vital balance which allows the shift from "power of coercion" to "power of transformation" is the relationship between *langue* and *parole*. It is therefore necessary to accept that there is a pre-verbalization process, below the author's consciousness, involving the transmission of a message (the codification of a signal) from the subconscious to the preconscious level. During the process, the first underminings of the common code can be supposed to take place. It is only after a deep reading that such underminings can be seen as structures intimately associated with the verbalization of any act of *parole*.

The author's self-censorship may indeed be weakened until he produces a work that can be seen as a ST. But, since signals from the subconscious cannot be understood as signals by the author himself, and since they will in any case undergo some kind of transformation, the degree to which the author is able to receive the signal from his own subconscious is the degree of ST he is able to produce.

If we look through any of the STs previously mentioned, the low degree of their sincerity is immediately evident. Even if we take a simple definition of the ST ("That product on which the HA does not deliberately place a mask"), we may wonder if we should not consider as mask-like certain typical conclusive turns of the plot, such as those in which the protagonist falls in love with the sister of the beloved. Such a device, which can be found in the works of Jean Cocteau (*Les enfants terribles*) and Yukio Mishima (*Confessions of a Mask*), seems as ingenuous as the other device used to avoid the real ST, the sudden and violent death (especially suicide) of the protagonist (as in *Fabrizio Lupo*) or of the former, adored lover (Peyrefitte's Alexandre). The former devices allow the text to return to the permitted modes of the CSC, the latter lead to a conclusion that is suitably heroic.

The young protagonist is not allowed to grow old in what the CSC would call a squalid reality. Hence the need of the cathartic mask of a permitted love (as in Beerbohm's *Happy Hypocrite*) or of a purifying suicide followed by a moral acceptable for the CSC. Otherwise, other plots would be required — plots hinging on a real truth, which is, as such, neither heroic nor exciting, but only annoying. Here we are reminded of a line at the beginning of Harold Pinter's *No Man's Land*: "Do you often hang about Hampstead Heath?" It is part of an exchange between two men in their sixties — clearly, it is another story.

Università degli Studi di Torino

NOTES

1. One need only consider the uproar created by the production of John Osborne's *Look Back in Anger* in that year.
2. The witty self-irony with which the narrator describes the terrifying drive to Dieppe is reminiscent of Chaucer's description of the perilous flight in the claws of an eagle in *The House of Fame*. While the narration of the eagle is verbose, Chaucer gives brief replies, often monosyllables: *yis, wel, nay, what?, no fors, gladly.*
3. Written by Beerbohm when he was twenty-five.
4. I recognize that the reading and writing experiences of men may operate under a somewhat different dynamic than those of women; it is male authors and readers that I discuss here.
5. Similarly, identifying a CSC with a particular nation in a particular period is an oversimplification, but it is necessary for the present argument.
6. As the context is everything that is implied by the message and to which the message therefore refers, Prieto's definition of context includes "all the data known to the receiver but which are independent of the semic act, when the latter takes place" (17).

WORKS CITED

Beerbohm, Max. *The Happy Hypocrite*. London: Heinemann, 1905.
———. *L'Ipocrita Felice e Altri Racconti*. Trans. Emilio Cecci. Milan: Bompiani, 1947.
———. "James Pethel." *Seven Men and Two Others*. London: Heinemann, 1919. London: Oxford UP, 1966.

————. "William and Mary." *And Even Now*. London: Heinemann, 1920. New York: Dutton, 1921.

Foucault, Michel. *L'Ordre du Discours*. Paris: Gallimard, 1971.

Jakobson, Roman. *Essais de Linguistique Générale*. Paris: Minuit, 1963.

Prieto, Luis. *Messages et Signaux*. Paris: Gallimard, 1966.

Sebeok, Thomas A. *Style in Language*. Cambridge, MA: Technology P, 1960.

Toynbee, Philip. Obituary. *The London Magazine* May 1956.

"MEDICATED MUSIC": ELIZABETH BARRETT BROWNING'S SONNETS FROM THE PORTUGUESE

By Sharon Smulders

"YOU ARE PARACELSUS, AND I am a recluse, with nerves that have been all broken on the rack, & now hang loosely, . . quivering at a step and breath" (Kintner 1: 41).[1] So wrote Elizabeth Barrett two months before her celebrated first meeting with Robert Browning in May of 1845. Although she had become, as she said, "a very byword among the talkers, for a confirmed invalid through months & years" (Kintner 1: 203), she improved dramatically under the influence of Browning's visits that summer and consented in September to pledge her love, if not her hand, to him. Her fear of a relapse, however, prevented her from agreeing to a formal engagement. Indeed, throughout their courtship, her physical weakness posed the greatest impediment, in her mind, to the marriage which finally took place the following September. By this time, she had substantially completed the sonnets recording her romance with Browning. But while her experience of love undoubtedly informs the female speaker's curative restoration in *Sonnets from the Portuguese* (1850), the series also shows the conscious deliberation of a Victorian poet engaged in the task of renovating generic imperatives to release feminine subjectivity — which had been invalidated by the conventions of Renaissance lyricism — into healthy self-expression. Thus, though Barrett Browning claims less for her work than for the "Antidotes / Of medicated music" (sonnet 17) she had found in the verse of her Paracelsus, she yet posits love as cure in *Sonnets from the Portuguese* and so embarks on a project to purge the genre of a pervasive invalidism.[2]

Expressly relating poetry to remedy, the speaker's elaborate compliment to the beloved's "Antidotes / Of medicated music" isolates the major concerns of the sequence. The conceit itself probably draws on Browning's account of J. Baptista Porta's belief "that any musical instrument made out of wood possessed of medicinal properties retains, being put to use, such virtues undiminished" (Kintner 1: 484). However, the compliment is also consonant with Barrett Browning's identification of her correspondent with the Renaissance physician, hero of his own *Paracelsus* (1835), and with her praise of him in "The Book of the Poets," a review published in the *Athenaeum* (1842). In this essay, Barrett Browning doubles the role of medical diagnostician on that of literary critic. Assimilating both roles to herself, she compares the jaded reader to "the hypochondriac" and prescribes to "the hopeful" reader "the Tennysons and the Brownings, and other high-gifted spirits," as an anodyne to that "plague of poems in the land apart from poetry" (*Poetical Works* 650). When she later began to correspond with Browning, she proposed other remedies for the ills of modern verse. In a letter of March 1845, for instance, she rejects a possible return to "the antique moulds . . classical moulds" and instead exhorts both herself and Browning to find "new forms . . . as well as thoughts" for poetry, to "aspire rather to *Life* — & let the dead bury their dead. If," she continues, "we have but courage to face these conventions, to touch this low ground, we shall take strength from it instead of losing it" (Kintner 1: 43). Ironically, in *Sonnets from the Portuguese*, she chooses to communicate this aspiration to life in a genre that, as her remarks in "The Book of the Poets" suggest, had long been exhausted by its own plagues.

Indeed, although she argues that "the natural healthy eye turns toward the light, and the true calling of criticism remains the distinguishing of beauty," the language of contagion infects her discussion of the Elizabethan amatory tradition. "Many poets of an excellent sweetness," she writes of Sidney's contemporaries, "fell poetry-sick, as they might fall love-sick, and knotted associations, far and free enough to girdle the earth withal, into true love-knots of quaintest devices" (*Poetical Works* 631). Interested in the etiology as well as the pathology of love poetry, she characterizes "that plague of over-curious conceits" as "the plague of Italian literature transmitted by contagion, together with better things — together with the love of love-lore, and the sonnet structure, the summer-bower for one fair thought" (*Poetical Works* 628). In *Sonnets from the Portuguese*, she ventures to restore these diseased devices, "together with the love of love-lore, and the sonnet structure," to new health. Such a project of reclamation inevitably affects the form as well as the content of her sonnets. By dissociating love from sickness, moreover, Barrett Browning implicitly contrasts the affectation of a Renaissance sonneteer with the real disabilities of the Victorian woman. In *Sonnets from the Portuguese*, therefore, illness is not a sign of unrequited love, but an obstacle to its consummation. But if, by stipulating the priority of "natural ills" (sonnet 42), she rejects sonnet conventions reifying the effects of desire in physical infirmity, she also rejects cultural conventions hypostatizing genteel illness as a sign of feminine desirability. Setting these conventions in collision, she asserts the female speaker's intrinsic worth as a healthy subject.

Although critics have hitherto suggested a connection between Barrett Browning's illness and *Sonnets from the Portuguese*, they have paid scant attention to the way the sequence positions the female speaker between inherently diseased generic and cultural conventions. For instance, locating the possibilities for "universal communication" in sonnets "written by, or in the character of, a young man," Alethea Hayter implies that Barrett Browning's sonnets possess an idiopathic quality precisely because they "are written by a mature invalid woman" (105). Also distressed by the almost febrile intensity of feminine utterance, Joan Rees maintains that the sonnets suffer from "flaccidity of form" and give "the effect . . . of somebody declaiming aloud . . . all by herself in a small retired room where, to our embarrassment, we have strayed" (151). More fruitfully, Dorothy Mermin contends that Barrett Browning "doubles gender roles" (130) and disturbs amatory conventions by transferring the "signs of male desire" — or love-sickness — to the "object of desire" who is, in fact, "an ill and aging woman" (131). Plainly, the symptoms chronicled in the sequence — a pounding heart (sonnets 28 and 34), pale cheeks (sonnets 11, 18, 39), "trembling knees" (sonnet 11), and trembling hands (sonnets 23 and 28) — are suggestive of both disease and desire. Perversely, these dissonant indicators jeopardize Barrett Browning's project not because, as Mermin suggests, illness repels masculine desire, but because illness encodes feminine desirability.[3]

Sickness, closely associated with what medical historians Barbara Ehrenreich and Deirdre English call "the sexual romanticist ideal of femininity," virtually became "a way of life" for Victorian women of the middle and upper classes (105).[4] While Barrett Browning's own complaint, variously diagnosed in retrospect as pulmonary tuberculosis (Pickering 249) and chronic bronchitis (Forster 133 and 276), was quite certainly organic, she also suffered from the headaches, insomnia, erratic pulse, and muscular convulsions common to women of her station and generation. Although the isolation of the sickroom had procured her "the desolate advantage [. . .] of living a little like a disembodied spirit, & caring less for supposititious criticism than for the black fly buzzing in the pane" (Kintner 1: 263), she had a fine contempt for "medical oracles" (1: 102) whose prescriptions confirmed patients — that is, women — in a general weakness of mind and body. "They never did much more for *me*," she later told Browning, "than . . when my pulse was above a hundred and forty with fever . . to give me digitalis to make me weak, — &, when I could not move without fainting (with weakness) . . to give me quinine to make me feverish again" (1: 102). Particularly ineffectual, in her view, was the expediency decided upon by Dr. Barry, the physician who had attended her in Torquay in 1838. He "thought he had done every-thing," she recalled, "because he had carried the inkstand out of the room" (1: 151). Far from concurring in Barry's opinion that poetry "was a mortal malady & incompatible with any common show of health" in women (1: 151), she believed her work, especially that published in 1844, had done "much for me in giving me stronger roots down into life" (1: 152). Despite this conviction, sonnets such as "Past and Future," "Substitution," "Insufficiency," and "Irreparableness," all included in the 1844 collection, issue a double farewell to poetry and to life. In "Substitution," for example, the speaker calls on Christ "to fill this pause" and to remedy a silence that "Aches [. . .] like a strong disease and new." With *Sonnets from the Portuguese*, however, Barrett Browning enacts other substitutions so as to empower a return from silence to song and from death to life.

Ironically, the female speaker of *Sonnets from the Portuguese* attributes to the beloved's "Antidotes / Of medicated music" the health-giving properties that Barrett Browning had derived from her own excursions into verse. For her part, this speaker, who "once was girt / To climb Aornus, [. . .] can scarce avail / To pipe now 'gainst the valley nightingale / A melancholy music" (sonnet 11). Shaken by sobs, her voice, with its "sink and fall" (sonnet 41), contends even more weakly against that of a "chief musician" (sonnet 3) and dispenser of "medicated music." In fact, she describes herself as "an out of tune / Worn viol" that is "laid down at the first ill-sounding note" (sonnet 32). To redeem this "ill-sounding note," she not only submits to male tutelage but transforms herself into an object for the beloved's "use" (sonnet 17). "For," she writes, "perfect strains may float / 'Neath master-hands, from instruments defaced" (sonnet 32). But although she agrees to yield to his "use," she never actually cedes control of her voice to him. As Angela Leighton explains, Barrett Browning relies on "a language of self-abasement that is paradoxically proud of its imaginative rights" and that asserts, in a deceptively modest fashion, the woman's right of mastery over her own expression (*Elizabeth Barrett Browning* 94). Because the conventional amatory lyric does not feature a female speaker, the woman's attempt to articulate self, much less "to spread wing and fly in the outer air," is seemingly one of "most impossible failure" (sonnet 15). Yet, in daring "To fail so" (15), Barrett Browning's speaker succeeds in vanquishing impossibility. Her success, moreover, wins the male poet's surrender, for he drops his "divinest Art's / Own instrument" (sonnet 41) to listen to her. By compelling his attention in this manner, the speaker claims the right to dictate her destiny to her own rather than another's "use."

The language of modest self-effacement has other uses too, for it allows Barrett Browning to examine the ill-founded assumptions "transmitted by contagion" in forms of speech deemed suitable to love. In the parlance of

Luce Irigaray, she retraverses the rhetoric of the amatory lyric in order to explore "*the discursive mechanism*" of "a masculine logic" which locates the woman as the object of desire (76).[5] Challenging the presumptions of this logic, she appoints "a *disruptive excess*" to "the feminine," otherwise "defined as lack, deficiency, or as imitation and negative image of the subject" (Irigaray 78). In *Sonnets from the Portuguese*, therefore, the speaker not only mimicks but exaggerates the role traditionally ascribed to her in the sonnet to discover how its conventions falsify women's physical and emotional reality. As a result, her "ill-sounding note" reverberates against "the first ill-sounding note" of a moribund genre; her real sickness becomes the excess that disrupts at once the twin conventions of the love-sick poet and the elusive maid.

In the first several sonnets, then, the speaker is a poet, but she also takes the role of a recalcitrant Delia or Diana who strives against the male poet's mastery. In her illness and nearness to death, however, she possesses a rationale for retaining her independence and resisting her lover's entreaties. Exploring the inequities between man and woman, in life and death, in love and grief, she comes to the conclusion that "We are not peers, / So to be lovers." Figuring her renunciation as a refusal to "breathe my poison on thy Venice-glass," she commands the beloved to withdraw. But even as she shields him from contagion, she admits, "I only love thee!" (sonnet 9). This secret acknowledgement of love inaugurates the therapeutic process of transformation and endows the speaker "With conscience of the new rays that proceed / Out of my face toward thine" (sonnet 10). As her physical strength increases, her resolve to retain an autonomy conceived in illness and fostered in renunciation weakens. By sonnet 16, she says, "I at last record, / Here ends my strife." By sonnet 27, moreover, her convalescence advances so far that she is "safe, and strong, and glad" enough to "Make witness, here, between the good and bad, / That Love, as strong as Death, retrieves as well." Appropriately, an understanding of the speaker's progress toward well-being in the sequence as a whole "retrieves as well" the pun contained in this sonnet's concluding words.

Although the speaker's return to health gradually erodes the obstacle to the lovers' union posed by "natural ills," she occasionally wonders whether the beloved's "words have ill availed" (sonnet 28). Consequently, even when "serene / And strong," she experiences "A still renewable fear" that "these enclaspèd hands should never hold" (sonnet 36). "Through sorrow and sickness," however, the beloved persists "to bring souls to touch" (sonnet 40). For Glennis Stephenson, the tactual quality of such imagery "eliminates both the sense of unattainability typically associated with the object of love and the sense of space typically imposed between lovers" (89). Nevertheless, much of the sequence's drama remains with the speaker's attempts to over-come "doubt's pain" (sonnet 21) and to develop strategies to affirm possibilit-ies for individual well-being in a relationship between healthy equals.

One threat to such a relationship resides in the possibility that "natural ills" are in fact responsible for the suitor's attentions. Feeling that her own weakness was unseemly, Barrett Browning initially declined to meet Brow-ning because, she wrote, "it wd be unbecoming to lie here on the sofa & make a company-show of an infirmity, & hold a beggar's hat for sympathy" (Kintner 1: 65). In his discussion of the drama enacted in the love letters, Daniel Karlin notes that her fear that Browning "would be disappointed in her *image*," as opposed to "her *looks*," intensified her anxiety about the proposed visit (71). That he was far from disappointed did little to set her mind at ease. Indeed, as the courtship correspondence reveals, her "most enduring anxiety concerned the very nature of Browning's love — the fact (indubitable to her) that it was based on a false image" (Karlin 132). Finally convinced of his love for her, she later confessed, "I have sometimes felt jealous of myself . . of my own infirmities, . . and thought that you cared for me only because your chivalry touched them with a silver sound — & that, without them, you would pass by on the other side" (Kintner 1: 247). Love's "motive" she subsequently reports, "shd lie in the feeling itself & not in the object of it" (Kintner 1: 266).

In sonnet 14, the speaker considers whether her attractiveness to the beloved owes, as the poet herself feared, to the "accidents" of "adversities" rather than to the "essentials" of being (Kintner 1: 249). Doubling the "accidents" of "sorrow and sickness" upon the "accidents" of countenance and gesture, she addresses a complex set of "adversities" afflicting woman as convention-ally figured in the Renaissance sonnet and in Victorian culture. In so doing, she administers a gentle rebuke to the male poet who would locate love's motive force in its outward object:

> Do not say
> "I love her for her smile . . her look . . her way
> Of speaking gently, . . for a trick of thought
> That falls in well with mine, and certes brought
> A sense of pleasant ease on such a day" —
> For these things in themselves, Belovèd, may
> Be changed, or change for thee, — and love, so wrought,
> May be unwrought so.

Constructing herself under her lover's gaze, the speaker nevertheless remains the subject of her verse and forestalls her transformation into the object of his. Her very resistance to such usage belies the gentle speech and "sense of pleasant ease" that she assigns to herself. Furthermore, while Barrett Brow-ning argued "that the affection which could (if it could) throw itself out on an idiot with a goître would be more admirable than Abelard's" (Kintner 1: 266), she also realized, as the parenthetical aside alone suggests, that such an aberrant affection might itself be diseased. Accordingly, her speaker goes on in sonnet 14 to clarify the distinction between "accidents" and "essentials" as one also between pity and "love's eternity." Because "A creature might forget to weep, who bore / Thy comfort long, and lose thy love thereby," she asks him not to "love me for / Thine own dear pity's wiping my cheeks dry" but "for love's sake only."

Restoring the speaker from the "natural ills" responsible for her pallor as well as her doubt, love's curative power also has a profound impact on the form her expression takes in the sonnets. In part, *Sonnets from the Portuguese* witnesses the actualization of Barrett Browning's belief, related to Mary Mitford some three years before she began to write the sequence, in the fitness of the sonnet's formal discipline to English verse: "The sonnet structure is a very fine one, however imperious, and I never *would* believe that our language is unqualified for the very strictest Italian form" (Raymond and Sullivan 2: 52). Adhering to "the very strictest Italian form" (*abbaabbacdcdcd*), the pattern of rhyme in her sonnets reproduces the sick woman's immurement within "this close room" (sonnet 44). However, as the speaker begins to overcome an invalidism that is as much a response to cultural and generic constraints as it is to organic conditions, she becomes increasingly adept at commanding the sonnet's formal severity to challenge the infirmity of its conventions. Unfortunately, Barrett Browning's effort to disclose as "empty and artifical" the confines of convention has often led, Jerome Mazzaro argues, to charges of "impetuosity, faulty judgment, or misplaced ingenuity" (168). Categorizing her sonnets as either "sublime" or "non-sublime," Mazzaro believes that her technical infractions work "to suggest a release from religious preconceptions" in the former instance and "from social expectations" in the latter (177).[6] In both cases, the paradox of "impossible failure" aligns this "*disruptive excess*" with unparalleled success: for each time the poet deliberately fails to comply with formal protocols she also succeeds inasmuch as she exceeds the established bounds of feminine possibility to include and make compatible love, health, and verse.

Thus, when Barrett Browning moves toward "the infinite / From the dark edges of the sensual ground" ("The Soul's Expression"), the Petrarchan rhymes that define these "dark edges" begin to lose exactness. For instance, in sonnet 13, the speaker rejects her lover's request for some spoken acknowledgement of affection. Rhyme falters as she considers the futility of "finding words enough" for love:

> I cannot teach
> My hand to hold my spirit so far off

> From myself . . me . . that I should bring thee proof
> In words, of love hid in me out of reach.
> Nay, let the silence of my womanhood
> Commend my woman-love to thy belief, —
> Seeing that I stand unwon, however wooed.

Using the convention of feminine silence to literalize the sonneteer's conceit, Barrett Browning shows the tremendous strain experienced by a speaker unaccustomed to seize the prerogative of speech. A dispirited Aurora Leigh, having forfeited love to seize this prerogative, later says, "I am a woman perhaps / And so rhyme ill" (5.503–04). Aurora is also understandably loth, given the amatory sonnet's centrality to a tradition that silences women, to "stand still" (5.89) in it even if she, "Like Atlas," can then "support / [. . .] heavens pregnant with dynastic stars" (5.87–88). Similarly concerned to unite love and poetry, the Portuguese sonneteer rhymes ill in order to mark her struggle against a form that invalidates feminine subjectivity and, consequently, the expression of feminine desire. This struggle emerges in the second quatrain in which "off" and "proof" rhyme in an "ill-sounding" manner with the first quatrain's "enough" and "rough." Likewise, the sestet's "womanhood" rhymes imperfectly with "wooed" and "fortitude." Thus, the near rhymes at the center of the sonnet mirror its concern with words' deficiency, especially for a female speaker.

Because her very passion defeats speech, the speaker is not, like any number of women celebrated in the Renaissance sonnet, an "iron Idol that compassion wants" (Constable, *Diana* 4.4) nor "a senseless stone" (Spenser, *Amoretti* 54).[7] Instead, by converting the impassivity of a desired object into the subject's "dauntless, voiceless fortitude" (sonnet 13), she makes her feebleness as a sonneteer into the sign of her strength as a woman and as a lover. In effect, what Barrett Browning had in 1844 called the poet's "Insufficiency" — "what we best conceive we fail to speak" — becomes in this poem love's superabundance. Thus, although the suffix "less" in "voice*less*" signifies a verbal lack, this lack accompanies emotional excess. For Leighton, therefore, the speaker's silence operates as "a generous kind of restraint" since it shields the beloved from "the very force of her words" (*Elizabeth Barrett Browning* 111). This aphasic stance serves, however, only as an interim tactic to preserve inviolate a hard-won subjectivity. Ultimately, to take her place as a poet and as a lover, in all respects equal to her beloved, the speaker must risk "impossible failure" and "teach" herself to communicate those words hidden "out of reach."

Her achievement of this capacity emerges in the carefully balanced terms of sonnet 43, "How do I love thee? Let me count the ways." Extending her soul's "reach" to "the ends of Being and ideal Grace," she finally grants the request denied in sonnet 13. Again, slant rhymes attend the movement from "the sensual ground" out to the furthest point of the soul's "reach." Like the end-rhymes in the first four lines of the sestet, the imperfect rhymes at the juncture of the octave's two quatrains mark differences in both the sonnet's and "the sequence's associative 'fields' of religion, daily life, and personal history" (Mazzaro 177) as too big to be anything but impossibly harmonized. As a result, sublime "Grace" chimes oddly against the word of familiar life, "everyday's." Marking out love's infinite "depth and breadth and height," these imperfect rhymes argue the failure of the amatory sonnet to match the speaker's experience rather than the poet's failure to match the technical requirements of the form.

As Alice Meynell observed in 1896, Barrett Browning's sonnets are "strictly Petrarchan in rhymes though not in pauses — nor, therefore, in construction" (xiv). Eminently suited to the unconventionality of a female speaker, this "pause of style" (Meynell x) nevertheless finds a precedent in the sonnets of such practitioners as Wordsworth and Milton. Indeed, in "The Book of the Poets," Barrett Browning pays tribute to Milton, that "iconoclast of [. . .] idol rhyme," for "protesting practically against the sequestration of pauses" and creating "the first sonnets of a free rhythm" (*Poetical Works* 641); and she admires Wordsworth's sonnets for their "broad and pouring sluices of various thought, imagery, and emphatic eloquence" (*Poetical Works* 649). Just as Barrett Browning owes a debt to the "emphatic eloquence" of her male precursors, her speaker owes one to the beloved who can "strike up and strike off the general roar / Of the rushing worlds, a melody that floats / In a serene air purely" (sonnet 17). In sonnet 7, for instance, she readily acknowledges that she "Was caught up into love, and taught the whole / Of life in a new rhythm." Using the passive voice, the speaker vividly conveys her status as the object of performed action rather than its agent. Yet, in her sonnets, this "new rhythm" conforms to the idioms of her speech. She is, therefore, the agent of the sonnet's transformation. As Stephenson points out, furthermore, the speaker's utterance not only increases in speed and vigor as she returns to life and health, but incorporates the rhythmic "pounding of the pulses, of the heart beat, of the blood" (85–86). Doubling the heart's rhythm on the rhythm of verse, Barrett Browning returns to a trope she had used before: "When I attain to utter forth in verse / Some inward thought," says the poet of "Insufficiency," "my soul throbs audibly / Along my pulses, yearning to be free." But whereas the 1844 speaker looks beyond death to "seek / Fit peroration" and so to achieve "consummation of right harmony," *Sonnets from the Portuguese* discovers in the "pulses that beat double" (sonnet 6) a "new rhythm" fit to measure "the whole / Of life."

Barrett Browning develops this "new rhythm" through strong medial caesura, phrasal repetition, and frequent enjambment. In the resultant "pause of style,'' her speaker displays a wide range of tones and accents. First, a reader as well as an invalid, she muses languidly over "the sweet years, the dear and wished for years" of a past both literary and personal (sonnet 1). Then, an uncertain speaker, she hesitates over feelings impossible to "fashion into speech" (sonnet 13). Lastly, a woman of assured confidence, she counts love's ways. However, between the reluctance of sonnet 13 and the measured poise of sonnet 43, she discovers another very different register. She, formerly the instrument of "A melancholy music" at best, annexes joy to her repertoire. A testament indeed to the speaker's recovery of spirits, the witty humor evident in so many of the later sonnets remits the sequence's "first ill-sounding note.''

Sonnet 21, with its brief reversion to "doubt's pain," dramatizes this change in the disposition of her verse:

> Say over again, and yet once over again,
> That thou dost love me. Though the word repeated
> Should seem "a cuckoo-song," as thou dost treat it,
> Remember never to the hill or plain,
> Valley and wood, without her cuckoo-strain,
> Comes the fresh Spring in all her green completed.
> Beloved, I, amid the darkness greeted
> By a doubtful spirit-voice, in that doubt's pain
> Cry . . "Speak once more . . thou lovest!" Who can fear
> Too many stars, though each in heaven shall roll, —
> Too many flowers, though each shall crown the year?
> Say thou dost love me, love me, love me — toll
> The silver iterance! — only minding, Dear,
> To love me also in silence, with thy soul.

The sonnet's turns — from joy to pain in line seven, from doubt's dismissal to love's celebration in line twelve, and from speech to silence midway through line thirteen — deviate from the traditional periods inscribed by octave and sestet. Moreover, the line quantities move to excess, suggesting that there can never be "Too many stars," "Too many flowers," nor "Too many" syllables for love. Impersonating an unreserved, artless sincerity, these irregular turns and measures usher in a series of images that transform love, "the word repeated," and that demonstrate thereby the speaker's facility with words.

Because these imagistic transformations seek to penetrate through poetic convention to a source of meaning mutually realized, sonnet 21, for all its apparent trifling, represents an important point in Barrett Browning's recovery of the amatory lyric. As Browning told her, "poetry is not the thing given or taken between us — it is heart and life and *myself*, not *mine*, I give — give? That you glorify and change and, in returning then, give *me*!" (Kintner 1:

278). Exploiting this principle of transformative exchange, the poet borrows her initial image and mood from one of Browning's letters. Impatient with James Russell Lowell's *Conversations on Some of the Old Poets*, he admitted, "when I turn from what is in my mind, and determine to write about anybody's book to avoid writing that I love & love & love again my own, dearest love — because of the cuckoo-song of it, — then, I shall be in no better humour with that book than with Mr. Lowell's!" (Kintner 1: 329). Returning to the "cuckoo-song" Browning would turn from, Barrett Browning imitates its resounding echo in the octave's double rhymes and the poem's numerous verbal repetitions, culminating with "love me, love me, love me." Then, reminding the beloved that this "cuckoo-strain" heralds spring, she glorifies love, the emotion as well as the word, by transforming its sound into the bell's "silver iterance." Like "The silver answer rang . . 'Not Death, but Love' " in sonnet 1, this sound not only describes the beloved's voice but vaguely alludes to "all those bells waiting to be hung!" — Browning's *Bells and Pomegranates* (Kintner 1: 102).

Appropriately, the spoken word's *"silver iterance"* contracts to become the soul's silence as the sonnet itself moves to the silence of closure. Given the primacy of final position, this silence subsumes both love's "cuckoo-strain" and its "silver iterance." In so tempering frivolity with solemnity, the speaker implicitly sets before the beloved the example of her own "dauntless, voiceless fortitude." Indeed, whereas his "example" had "shown [. . .] how" she too might love (sonnet 12), the convalescent speaker increasingly takes the initiative as instructor. Calling forth and giving shape to his response, she teaches the beloved how to speak and feel his love in terms acceptable to her. Consequently, while sonnet 21 reverses the negative injunction ("Do not say") of sonnet 14 and rejoices in the beloved's volubility, it privileges the woman's voice, both the inward "spirit-voice" as well as its outward expression ("Speak once more . . thou lovest!").

Although Browning was initially slow to understand similar instructions in love that his correspondent pressed upon him in her letters, he began to answer her demands for " 'the woman's reason' suitable to the woman" (Kintner 1: 265). So when his "dear 'inverter' " again raised the spectre of an ill-founded attachment, he wrote,

> If there had been a vague aimless feeling in me, turning hither & thither for some object to attach itself to and spend itself on, and you had chanced to be that object . . I should understand you were very little flattered and how a poplar does as well for a vine-prop as a palm tree — but whatever love of mine clings to you was created by you, dearest. (Kintner 2: 656)

The letter's significance lies not only in Browning's response to his lover's doubts but in her appropriation and inversion of his words in sonnet 29.

Making it, like sonnet 21, the scene of a reciprocating imaginative process, she realizes in part the aim of a cooperative poetic effort, the "something in concert" (Kintner 1: 56) that Browning had proposed early in their correspondence.[8]

Positioning the beloved as the palm-tree and her speaker as the clinging vine, the poet investigates in sonnet 29 another "trick of thought" to which she is heir:

> I think of thee! — my thoughts do twine and bud
> About thee, as wild vines, about a tree,
> Put out broad leaves, and soon there's nought to see
> Except the straggling green which hides the wood.
> Yet, O my palm-tree, be it understood
> I will not have my thoughts instead of thee
> Who art dearer, better! rather instantly
> Renew thy presence. As a strong tree should,
> Rustle thy boughs and set thy trunk all bare,
> And let these bands of greenery which insphere thee,
> Drop heavily down, . . burst, shattered, everywhere!
> Because, in this deep joy to see and hear thee
> And breathe within thy shadow a new air,
> I do not think of thee — I am too near thee.

In this poem, Barrett Browning tightens the restrictive pattern of rhyme to which she submits throughout the sequence and underlines her habitual elision of the sonnet's discrete parts by incorporating the masculine *b* rhymes of the octave within the feminine *d* rhymes of the sestet.[9] Reusing the same word — "thee" — four times for these end-rhymes as well as a further three times for internal rhyme, she formally reproduces the way the speaker's thoughts "insphere thee," "twine and bud / About thee." Adapting the sonnet's structural requirements to the extended metaphor of the speaker's twining thought, she realizes her own definition of the sonnet as a "summer-bower for one fair thought" and develops its faint allusion to "Shall I compare thee to a summer's day": "When in eternal lines to time thou grow'st," says Shakespeare, "thy eternal summer shall not fade" (sonnet 18). However, while Barrett Browning's reiterated "thee" represents the sonneteer's "one fair thought," this thought cannot replace the beloved who is "dearer, better."

Flattering Browning, the poet of *Sonnets from the Portuguese* also corrects the unflattering portrayals of the beloved object of Renaissance verse. In so doing, she touches the "low ground" of convention and takes life from diseased tropological devices. Thus, while her inspiration clearly originates in the courtship correspondence, she yet appropriates, like Barnabe Barnes before her, the elm-and-vine *topos* which, following the precedent established in the epithalamies of Theocritus and Catullus, symbolizes the interdependence of man and woman in marriage. The elm reifies masculinity's supportive function; the vine, femininity's procreative function. But when Barnes adapts the classical *topos* to the lyric of desire in sonnet 76 of *Parthenophil and Parthenophe*, he confounds gender roles and reverses the inequities implicit in the figure: the male speaker, emasculated by desire, assumes the weaker position of the clinging vine; the female beloved, the stronger position of the elm. Additionally, he uses verbs connoting enervation and debilitation to represent the pathological effects of desire:

> Pine, Arms! which wished-for sweet embraces miss.
> And upright parts of pleasure! fall you down.
> Waste, wanton tender Thighs! Consume for this;
> To her thigh-elms, that you were not made vines!
> And my long pleasure in her body grafted.
> But, at my pleasure, her sweet thought repines.

Obviously, the failure to graft the elm and the vine dramatizes sexual frustration. In his despair, moreover, Barnes's speaker not only suffers a loss of vitality, but also entertains thoughts of suicide: "Why do I longer live? but me prepare / My life, together with my joys, to finish!" To describe the extent of his frustration, he supplements images of disease and self-mortification — of blinding, wasting, withering, and pining — with other conventional tropes. Thus, for example, the beloved's "stormy frown" buffets the speaker's heart as it sails upon an "ocean of . . . deep despair" (sonnet 76). Because these "knotted associations," as Barrett Browning called them (*Poetical Works* 631), lack aesthetic integrity, a profound dis-ease infects the sonnet.

In the English tradition, the elm-and-vine *topos* shows symptoms of blight even before Barnes transplants it into the alien soil of the amatory sonnet. For instance, when Sidney invokes the *topos* in his third eclogue, he first uses the elm and vine to embody the symbiotic relationship between the sexes; then, by replacing the elm and the vine with the oak and the mistletoe, he subtly reinterprets the gender dynamic of marriage, associates femininity with parasitism, and so anticipates Hardy's subversion of epithalamic convention much later in "The Ivy-Wife." When Barrett Browning recovers the trope, however, her twining vines suggest healthy growth rather than parasitic infestation. Retaining the conventional association of the vine with femininity, she recovers reciprocated love as a fertile source for women's poetry and discovers in the outworn *topos* a metaphor to convey the generative vitality of the feminine imagination rather than the fecundity of the female body. Indeed, the wildness of her vines serves as an interesting counterpoint to the cultivated domesticity suggested by the originating trope.

However, while Barrett Browning creates a metaphor for a strong feminine imagination from the conservative *topos* of feminine dependence, she also realizes that the speaker's self-absorption ("the straggling green") obscures the subject ("the wood") of her thoughts.[10] Thus, she compels the beloved, a strong palm-tree, to assert his virility as well as his independence and to shatter the insphering greenery of her thoughts. Since this independence follows on the speaker's imperative, both cooperate to overthrow the old modes of thought epitomized in the elm-and-vine *topos* itself. Barrett Browning effects, thereby, a double liberation from the confines of convention. Seeking a basis for sexual equality, her female speaker is not merely an object of transformation but a subject who elicits her lover's cooperation to transform the conceptual structures that confine them both. Nevertheless, the conclusion of the poem seems to retain a residual taint of the old sexual economies engrained in the now-shattered *topos*, for the woman stands in the "shadow" of the man. This position, however, reverses the relative roles advanced in sonnet 17. Thus, although she submits to the beloved's "use" and asks whether he would have her for "A shade, in which to sing . . . of palm or pine" (sonnet 17), sonnet 29 witnesses his transformation to her "use" as well as her ultimate rejection of the beloved's reduction through such "use" to a "trick of thought."

Despite Barrett Browning's rather elastic approach to received tropes, Antony Harrison dismisses the sequence on the grounds of its "active collusion with the amatory ideologies" of Victorian England (137) and its failure to engage in "successful competition with the work of the great male poets of the past" (139).[11] Certainly, she is not an absolute iconoclast. But if, as Mermin believes, Barrett Browning eschews irony in order "to take her place in the tradition, not to prove herself an outsider" (144), her ideological displacement of diseased convention yet marks out difference in other ways. For instance, art's eternity, too often a Renaissance substitute for "love's eternity," fares poorly in Barrett Browning's sonnets. So whereas Spenser, whom she revered as a poet of "cheerful ideality" (*Poetical Works* 630), contends "that fairest images / Of hardest marble are of purpose made, / For that they should endure through many ages" (*Amoretti* 51), her speaker does "not build / Upon the event" of first meeting "with marble" (sonnet 36) and asks pardon when tempted to memorialize her beloved in "an image only so / Formed of the sand, and fit to shift and break" (sonnet 37). Indeed, when imaginative excess threatens to obliterate the beloved's true "likeness" and "distort / [. . .] worthiest love to a worthless counterfeit," the poet sees "fit to shift and break" received convention. Likewise, in sonnet 29, thought's idol is "burst, shattered, everywhere!"

As sonnet 29 suggests, Barrett Browning's dissociation of disease from desire moves the sequence from sickness to health, from death to life, from elegy to epithalamion. Looking forward to the "budding" of the speaker's "pilgrim staff" (sonnet 42) and the flowering of "this close room" (sonnet

44), the flourishing vegetation of sonnet 29 anticipates the woman's final recovery from "natural ills" (sonnet 42) and testifies to the poet's ability to remedy "the first ill-sounding note" (sonnet 32) of the genre. These images of natural growth, given impetus with "the fresh Spring in all her green completed" (sonnet 21), not only relieve the wintry desolation of a speaker who describes herself "alone here in the snow" (sonnet 20) but adumbrate the sequence's movement toward physical and emotional well-being. Before the prescient allusion to spring's "blossoms white" in sonnet 20, such images merely function as static poetic emblems: the cypress of death (sonnet 3), the palm of victory, the pine of pity (sonnet 17), the rose and myrtle of love (sonnet 18), and the bay of rewarded merit (sonnet 19).[12] When the palm-tree of sonnet 17 reappears in sonnet 29, however, nature's vitality invigorates its emblematic meaning and broadens its significance. In addition to palm-trees and wild vines, the sonneteer mentions flowers (sonnets 20, 21, 34, 40), lilies (sonnet 24), asphodel (sonnet 27), cowslips (sonnet 33), "green leaves with morning dews impearled" (sonnet 42), rue, eglantine, and ivy (sonnet 44). By contrast, the green world is conspicuously absent from the beginning of the sequence. Instead, Barrett Browning doubles on the courtly décor of the opening sonnets, retrospectively described as "this drear flat of earth" (sonnet 27), the scenery of "Full desertness" ("Grief") described in the 1844 sonnets. Inasmuch as this is the case, "the first ill-sounding note" of *Sonnets from the Portuguese* is also that of *Poems* (1844).

The difference between the sonnets of 1844 and those of 1850 clarifies just how Barrett Browning uses natural imagery to indicate the woman's renewed commitment to life. In her valedictory sonnets, she refigures the Romantic trope of man's alienation from nature for a female speaker and so replaces the open vistas of fields and meadows with images of decay and enclosure.[13] For instance, musing "link by link" over the "chains" of isolation (sonnet 20), the Portuguese sonneteer initially resembles "The Prisoner" who has not "felt the green sward under foot" nor heard "the great breath of all things summer-mute" for "months and years"; but while this speaker, imprisoned "behind this door so closely shut," catches the "strange wild music" of "Nature's lute" ("The Prisoner"), the sound of the invalid woman's "music in its louder parts" attracts the attention of one "Who paused a little near the prison-wall" and who then did drop his "divinest Art's / Own instrument" (sonnet 41). Significantly, the piece that affected Browning most "in its louder parts" was "Past and Future": "How can I put away your poetry from you," he asked, "for is not that sonnet to be loved as a true utterance of yours?" (Kintner 1: 272).

Challenging her lover to "put away" the old work from the new woman, Barrett Browning begins sonnet 42 by quoting from "Past and Future": " '*My future will not copy fair my past*'." The pathos of "Past and Future" lies, of course, in the five words that follow: "On any leaf but Heaven's." Only published with the sequence in 1856, sonnet 42 appeared in 1850 as "Future and Past," a title suggestive of the poem's inversion of 1844 imperatives. In *Sonnets from the Portuguese*, abundant "green leaves" replace the comparative meagreness of Heaven's leaf and "earth's green herbs" ("Past and Future"). As a result, the speaker "seek[s] no copy now of life's first half" (sonnet 42) nor of her resolve to await death patiently. But while she charges the beloved to "write me new my future's epigraph," Barrett Browning in fact undertakes the task of revision herself. Writing anew the 1844 sonnets, she refigures the motif of imprisoning exclusion as one of saving inclusion. Before the lone subject of "absolute exclusion" (sonnet 2), the speaker finds with the beloved "A place to stand and love in for a day" (sonnet 22). Together "In this close hand of Love," they "hear no sound of human strife" after "the world's sharpness like a clasping knife / Shut[s] in upon itself" (sonnet 24).

Although the 1844 lyrics combat the temptation to "overstate the ills of life" ("Exaggeration") and to rebel "Against this work-day world, this ill-spread feast, / As if ourselves were better certainly / Than what we come to" ("Adequacy"), an awareness of these ills nonetheless taints the poet's attempts to secure psychogenic balance. For instance, having gathered flowers "in the meadows all the day," the speaker of "Irreparableness" notices that "decay / Has met them in my hands more fatally / Because more warmly clasped, — and sobs are free / To come instead of songs." The tacit identification of the female poet with her flowers, severed from their roots and "warmly" constrained, is so destructively absolute that a return to the expansive life outdoors is impossible for both. The dead blossoms become, therefore, a funereal bouquet:

> My heart is very tired, my strength is low,
> My hands are full of blossoms plucked before,
> Held dead within them till myself shall die.   ("Irreparableness")

The floral imagery of *Sonnets from the Portuguese*, on the other hand, breathes with life.

While the "blossoms plucked before" suggest the 1844 speaker's irreparable disconnection from youth, song, freedom, and ultimately life, the flowers of *Sonnets from the Portuguese* focus on vital connections and surprising reconnections. Indeed, Barrett Browning, amazed that her lover's flowers "put up with the close room" and did not, like "all other flowers, die of despair," took "*that* for an omen" (Kintner 1: 348). "Plucked in the garden," the "many flowers" that the beloved brings in *Sonnets from the Portuguese* likewise "seemed as if they grew / In this close room, nor missed the sun and showers'' (sonnet 44). Miraculously, even those flowers culled in ''early youth'' with talk of love ''smell still'' (sonnet 40). Despite her confinement, the speaker also blossoms in ''this close room,'' for age, like ''sorrow and sickness,'' is one of those ''natural ills'' that ''Love, as strong as Death, retrieves as well'' (sonnets 44, 40, 42, 27). Shortly after yielding to the beloved's suit, she soberly consents to give a lock of hair to him, but she will not ''plant [. . .] it'' in a token of love ''from rose or myrtle-tree, / As girls do,'' because her ''day of youth went yesterday'' (sonnet 18). However, rejuvenated as well as healed by love, she later directs her suitor to ''Gather the north flowers to complete the south, / And catch the early love up in the late'' (sonnet 33). Thus, gathering the already recollected flowers of memory, he apparently gives back to her the youthful beauty she had abandoned along with ''the cowslips piled.''

In exchange for such gifts, the speaker closes the sequence by presenting the beloved with the ''green leaves'' nurtured in ''this close room'':

> Take back these thoughts which here unfolded too,
> And which on warm and cold days I withdrew
> From my heart's ground. Indeed, those beds and bowers
> Be overgrown with bitter weeds and rue,
> And wait thy weeding; yet there's eglantine,
> Here's ivy! — take them, as I used to do
> Thy flowers, and keep them where they shall not pine.
> Instruct thine eyes to keep the colours true,
> And tell thy soul, their roots are left in mine.

Enshrining more than ''one fair thought'' in this poem's ''beds and bowers,'' Barrett Browning expands her definition of the sonnet in order to restate the key motifs of the sequence. The ''green leaves'' that spring here include ''bitter weeds and rue'' — the remnants of sorrow — as well as eglantine and ivy. Recalling the wild vines of thought in sonnet 29, ivy serves as a conventional emblem for marriage, eglantine for poetry. These twinned ''thoughts'' are bound, moreover, to the speaker's soul, the ''heart's ground,'' in which ''their roots are left.'' But while ''there is a discrepancy'' or ''break,'' as Leighton contends, ''between the flower's expression and the 'heart's ground' from which it comes'' (''Stirring a Dust'' 14), it is not the self-destructive rupture of ''Irreparableness.''[14]

Poetry ''is the flower of me,'' asserts Barrett Browning at one point in her letters: ''I have lived most & been most happy in it, & so it has all my colours; the rest of me is nothing but a root, fit for the ground & the dark'' (Kintner 1: 65). Repealing the deathliness of this self-portrait, she insists on the vital importance of buried roots in *Sonnets from the Portuguese*: ''The lilies of our lives,'' albeit ''Very whitely still,'' ''may reassure / Their blossoms from their roots, accessible / Alone to heavenly dews'' (sonnet 24).

Consequently, the speaker's colours, reduced to "so dead / And pale a stuff" by "frequent tears" (sonnet 8), take on the verdant hues of nature that, in turn, inform her poetry — what Browning had, for his part, called "heart and life and *myself.*" In fact, the final sonnet's integration of "heart and life and *myself*" recalls the flowery prose of Browning's very first letter. "I love your verses with all my heart, dear Miss Barrett," he declared: "so into me has it gone, and part of me has it become, this great living poetry of yours, not a flower of which but took root and grew" (Kintner 1: 3). Ever the "dear 'inverter'," Barrett Browning retrieves the poetry taken into his heart as the poetry taken from her heart.

As Barrett Browning's self-reflexiveness suggests, *Sonnets from the Portuguese* — the "green leaves" that supplant all those "pages with long musing curled" (sonnet 42) — exists in complex relationship with several intertexts: the courtship correspondence, the Renaissance amatory lyric, and *Poems* (1844).[15] Taken from the "heart's ground" rather than "Plucked in the garden," the sonnets become meet return not only for the beloved's "many flowers" but for his "Antidotes / Of medicated music." By so transforming what Wordsworth called "the Sonnet's scanty plot of ground," Barrett Browning makes the "close room" of a sick woman's confinement a place of unexpected largesse. However, she did not again return to the "close room" of the amatory sonnet. For whatever "desolate advantage" accrued to her poetry from her own enforced separation, she began to chafe under the "lamentable disadvantage" of being "shut from most of the outward aspects of life" and denied "full experience" (Kintner 1: 48). Nevertheless, her creation of the persona of a female poet who overcomes her disabilities and who counts over her intellectual, emotional and physical responses to love remains a remarkable achievement. Love — prescribed as a cure rather than diagnosed as a sickness — reprieves her from death, releases her into new life, and provides her with a way to effect the same transformation in a genre plagued by infirmity.

Mount Royal College

NOTES

1. Unless enclosed in square brackets, ellipsis points within quotations from the Brownings' prose and verse reflect the punctuation of the original. For all other quotations, I have followed the standard practice whereby ellipses indicate an omission.
2. Quotations from the sequence, cited by sonnet number rather than line number, derive from *A Variorum Edition of Elizabeth Barrett Browning's* Sonnets from the Portuguese.

3. The idealization of feminine illness, of course, affects novelistic convention. See, for instance, Michie on the valorization of weakness and pallor in her chapter on "Ladylike Anorexia: Hunger, Sexuality, and Etiquette" in *The Flesh Made Word*.
4. Drawing on Olive Schreiner's analysis of "female parasitism," Ehrenreich and English attribute this "vague syndrome" to the definition of feminine gentility in terms of economic dependency and enforced leisure (105).
5. For Irigaray, "mimicry" represents "[a]n interim strategy for dealing with the realm of discourse (where the speaking subject is posited as masculine), in which the woman deliberately assumes the feminine style and posture assigned to her within this discourse in order to uncover the mechanisms by which it exploits her" ("Publisher's Note and Note on Selected Terms," *This Sex Which is Not One* 220). In this respect, mimicry is an adjunct of "retraversal," defined as "[t]he process of going back through social, intellectual, and linguistic practices to reexamine and unravel their conceptual bases" (221).
6. Cooper makes a similar point and unites it specifically, as Mazzaro does tangentially (168–69), to the speaker's gender. She argues that Barrett Browning's union of " 'I' a woman and 'I' the poet" (100) encourages her to substitute the sonnet's "formal discipline . . . for the speaker's imprisonment" (109). For Cooper, this substitution enables the woman poet to transform "a known world . . . into one hitherto unimagined, a world created in art that she can then inhabit (101–02).
7. Citations from the Renaissance sonnet derive from Lee's two volume edition of *Elizabethan Sonnets*. A few other hard substances used to describe the unattainable object of the Renaissance lyricist's desire include marble, steel, frost (*Licia* 8), adamant (*Chloris* 40), stone and flint (*To Delia* 13).
8. The process does not end with the sonnets. Inasmuch as Browning's attempt to reconcile love and art in "Saul" led him back to Barrett Browning's imagery in *Sonnets from the Portuguese*, Sullivan concludes that "much of what he gratefully 'took' from her was essentially a re-working of ideas that had originated with him" (65). Such a statement, however true it may be, nonetheless underestimates the very nature and consequences of Barrett Browning's borrowings for the sonnets themselves.
9. I owe thanks to Loren Macdonald, University of Calgary, for encouraging me to rethink Barrett Browning's use of rhyme in sonnet 29.
10. According to Mermin, this sonnet reveals Barrett Browning's awareness "that desire can conceal the object it transforms" (134). Like Mermin, Leighton argues that "the poem's greenery . . . forces the object out of sight and out of words" (*Elizabeth Barrett Browning* 110). For Leighton, Barrett Browning's refusal to substitute the real pleasure of the beloved's presence for the intellectual pleasure of mere thought therefore "makes the poem both strong and false" (*Elizabeth Barrett Browning* 109).
11. Harrison's attack on *Sonnet from the Portuguese* serves his defence of Christina Rossetti's "Monna Innominata."
12. *The Language and Poetry of Flowers* has been consulted for the emblematic significance of flowers.
13. Arguably, the speaker's sex, often clouded by the use of the plural first person ("we"), is not a central issue of the 1844 sonnets. However, "George Sand: A Recognition" does suggest, in its description of "weaker women in captivity," an integral connection between femininity and forms of imprisonment. This connection Barrett Browning explores more thoroughly in "The Runaway Slave at

Pilgrim's Point" and "Hiram Powers' 'Greek Slave'." Again returning to women's desire for freedom in *Aurora Leigh*, she uses language oddly reminiscent of *Sonnets from the Portuguese*: "We are sepulchred alive in *this close* world, / And want more *room*" (5.1040–41); emphasis added). Aurora's choice of words not only expands the phrasing of sonnet 44 but reverses the meaning.

14. Leighton also discusses "the many shared double meanings of flowers throughout the correspondence" and their importance at the end of the sequence ("Stirring a Dust" 14–15).

15. Of course, *Sonnets from the Portuguese* also interacts with classical and biblical texts. On these intertexts, see Mermin (138–39) and Mazzaro (170–77).

WORKS CITED

Barrett Browning, Elizabeth. *The Poetical Works of Elizabeth Barrett Browning*. Ed. Frederic G. Kenyon. London: Smith, Elder, 1897.

———. *A Variorum Edition of Elizabeth Barrett Browning's Sonnets from the Portuguese*. Ed. Miroslave Wein Dow. Troy, NY: Whitston, 1980.

Cooper, Helen. *Elizabeth Barrett Browning, Woman and Artist*. Chapel Hill: U of North Carolina P, 1988.

Ehrenreich, Barbara, and Deirdre English. *For Her Own Good: 150 Years of the Experts' Advice to Women*. New York: Doubleday, 1979.

Forster, Margaret. *Elizabeth Barrett Browning: A Biography*. New York: Doubleday, 1989.

Harrison, Antony H. *Victorian Poets and Romantic Poems: Intertextuality and Ideology*. Charlottesville: UP of Virginia, 1990.

Hayter, Alethea. *Mrs Browning: A Poet's Work and its Setting*. London: Faber and Faber, 1962.

Irigaray, Luce. *This Sex Which Is Not One*. Trans. Catherine Porter with Carolyn Burke. Ithaca: Cornell UP, 1985.

Karlin, Daniel. *The Courtship of Robert Browning and Elizabeth Barrett*. Oxford: Oxford UP, 1987.

Kintner, Elvan, ed. *The Letters of Robert Browning and Elizabeth Barrett Barrett, 1845-1846*. 2 vols. Cambridge: Harvard UP, 1969.

The Language and Poetry of Flowers, and Poetic Handbook of Wedding Anniversary Pieces, Album Verses, and Valentines. New York: Hurst, nd.

Lee, Sidney, ed. *Elizabethan Sonnets*. 2 vols. 1904. New York: Cooper Square, 1964.

Leighton, Angela. *Elizabeth Barrett Browning*. Bloomington: Indiana UP, 1986.

———. "Stirring a Dust of Figures: Elizabeth Barrett Browning and Love." *Browning Society Notes* 17. 1–3 (1987–1988): 11–24.

Mazzaro, Jerome. "Mapping Sublimity: Elizabeth Barrett Browning's *Sonnets from the Portuguese*." *Essays in Literature* 18.2 (Fall 1991): 166–79.

Mermin, Dorothy. *Elizabeth Barrett Browning: The Origins of a New Poetry*. Chicago: U of Chicago P, 1989.

Meynell, Alice. Introduction. *Prometheus Bound and Other Poems*. By Elizabeth Barrett Browning. London: Ward, Lock and Bowden, 1896.

Michie, Helena. *The Flesh Made Word: Female Figures and Women's Bodies*. Oxford: Oxford UP, 1987.

Pickering, George. *Creative Malady: Illness in the Lives and Minds of Charles Darwin, Florence Nightingale, Mary Baker Eddy, Sigmund Freud, Marcel Proust, Elizabeth Barrett Browning*. London: George Allen and Unwin, 1974.

Raymond, Meredith B., and Mary Rose Sullivan, eds. *The Letters of Elizabeth Barrett Browning to Mary Russell Mitford 1836–1854*. 3 vols. Waco, TX: Armstrong Browning Library, Browning Institute, Wedgestone Press, and Wellesley College, 1983.

Rees, Joan. *The Poetry of Dante Gabriel Rossetti: Modes of Self-Expression*. Cambridge: Cambridge UP, 1981.

Shakespeare, William. *The Complete Works*. Ed. Stanley Wells and Gary Taylor. Oxford: Clarendon P, 1986.

Stephenson, Glennis. *Elizabeth Barrett Browning and the Poetry of Love*. Ann Arbor: UMI Research Press, 1989.

Sullivan, Mary Rose. " 'Some Interchange of Grace': 'Saul' and *Sonnets from the Portuguese*." *Browning Institute Studies* 15 (1987): 55–68.

DISRUPTION AND DISCLOSURE: WOMEN'S ASSOCIATIONS IN HARRIET MARTINEAU'S *DEERBROOK*

By Jacque Kahn

SINCE ITS PUBLICATION in 1839, *Deerbrook* has received relatively little critical attention even though its author, Harriet Martineau, was an unusual Victorian woman. Unique in her role as a celebrated spokesperson for progressive political and economic theories, she was also a lifelong feminist, advocating numerous women's causes, including advanced education and full political representation. Martineau criticized the legal and social inequities of nineteenth-century marriage for the degradation of women and congratulated herself on remaining single. Many of her concepts of equality seem extraordinarily farsighted; her claim that a dairymaid ought to earn the same pay as a farmhand performing equivalent work, for instance, anticipates the late twentieth-century principle of comparable worth. But Martineau's own particular feminism was always contradictory. Like other nineteenth-century feminists, her politics were circumscribed by contemporary beliefs about the nature and role of women. She was convinced that women were inherently suited for and thus enjoyed housekeeping and that monogamy was the only "natural method" of sexuality. She frequently advocated conventional morality, refusing to associate with women like George Eliot or Harriet Taylor because they had transgressed marriage vows. That she continued to meet and correspond with George Henry Lewes and John Stuart Mill indicates the extent to which she accepted the sexual double standard.[1]

Feminist scholars like Gayle Yates have rightly pointed out that the limitations of Martineau's cultural and historical position do not negate her important contribution to the history of women's rights (7). But critics have been less generous when it comes to Martineau's only novel.[2] *Deerbrook* is frequently criticized as an artistic failure; most discussions are biographically based, blaming Martineau's failure as a writer of fiction upon her personal shortcomings, including her flawed feminism.[3] Deirdre David's reading of *Deerbrook*, informed by her analysis of Martineau as a Victorian intellectual, specifically links the depiction of powerless female characters in the novel to Martineau's failure as an artist. Because Martineau's previous writing, such as her work on political economy, was "defined by the propagation of received theories and ideas," David concludes that she was "strangely powerless when it came to the production of a text of her very own and unable to exercise authorial 'authority' to create a world of her own making" (86).

Because *Deerbrook*'s female characters seem rigidly defined by prevailing constructions of Victorian womanhood, and because the romantic plot does not promote alternative or independent roles for women, critical discussions which focus upon her representation of individual women usually diminish Martineau's commitment to women's issues and overlook *Deerbrook*'s implicit feminism. In this article I focus on collective rather than single representations of women in order to argue that *Deerbrook* magnifies and scrutinizes what remains muted in many nineteenth-century novels — the social and formal function of women's relationships in a heterosexual society and in the domestic novel. Martineau's novel emphasizes the interdependence of women, but rather than offering an idealized conception of female friendship or "sisterhood," *Deerbrook* treats these constructions of women's relations with suspicion. Unlike many nineteenth-century novels, *Deerbrook* directly confronts and analyzes sexual and social competition as obstacles to the formation of genuine solidarity among women.[4]

In many ways Martineau's novel engages contemporary feminist debates over formulations of women's solidarity. Many feminists have pointed out that studies which privilege women's friendship or utopian sisterhoods as forms of political solidarity offer a limited literary and historical approach which reinforces established perceptions of what constitutes valuable relationships among women. As Hilda Smith warns in her criticism of Carroll Smith-Rosenberg's study of female friendship in nineteenth-century America, "[t]o concentrate on these emotional ties among women, and especially to discuss only their favorable aspects and isolate them from the restrictions on women's public activities, runs some risk of giving legitimacy to society's acceptance of separate male and female spheres" (281). Studies of Victorian literature concur with Smith's argument: rather than subverting received beliefs about women, female friendship in this period often authorized the conservative ideology about women's nature and her separate sphere. Advocates of female friendship emphasized the common bonds of womanhood, such as motherhood and emotional vulnerability, which drew women to each other.[5] Martineau's novel demonstrates that such bonds are inadequate to the formation of women's friendships and that, in fact, commonality among women may weaken rather than strengthen their associations.

In "Beyond the Search for Sisterhood" Nancy Hewitt also discusses the danger of essentialism implicit in concepts of sisterhood. Her study shows how differing nineteenth-century communities of American women were formed out of their diverse "material conditions and constraints," and she concludes that women's historians must acknowledge that "diversity, discontinuity, and conflict were as much a part of the historical agency of women as of men" (316). This article will explore the power of diversity and conflict among women in Martineau's novel; I use the term "association" to encompass the numerous and often unrecognized ways in which women can be connected to other women without reinscribing the familiar Victorian (and in some ways, modern) notion that women are either friends or enemies, sisters or rivals, united or divided. I also use the word association because of its semantic capacity to bridge the dominant structuring of human relations along the boundaries of public and private. The term association can indicate a casual acquaintance or a full-scale organization, implicating both public and private without suggesting, like the term community, that women create a separate and distinct culture.[6]

Martineau's novel also rejects the conventional polarity between sentimental friendship on the one hand and social rivalry on the other. *Deerbrook* employs the stereotype of a divisive female community which, as Nina Auerbach describes it, is characterized by exclusive but transitory cliques and bitter competition (12).[7] But the novel complicates rather than reinforces this stereotype, locating the source of women's conflicts in the social and cultural forces which circumscribe women's lives. At the same time, the novel refuses the conventional answer to this problem in the ideal of sisterhood and challenges the conservatism inherent in Victorian conceptions of female solidarity.

Deerbrook also exemplifies the importance of women's associations, especially women's conflicts, as the site of other cultural confrontations. In many nineteenth-century novels, literary representations of antagonism between women signify the moral failure of a particular society or community. Class divisiveness and social conflict are often feminized and articulated upon the proverbial hatred of women for their own sex.[8] In Jane Austen's *Emma*, for example, the meaning of social responsibility is epitomized in the troubled associations between women. Emma's manipulation of Harriet Smith evinces her irresponsibility as a member of her society, but she comes face to face with her failure when Mr. Knightley censures her rudeness to Miss Bates. When Austen's heroine neglects the old maid and the widow, she refuses to assume the obligations which come with the privileges of rank and wealth.

In *Emma* women's conflicts are safely contained within the mundane world of female sociality, but in Martineau's novel the enmity among women is no longer just a symbol of social irresponsibility. In *Deerbrook* women's conflicts instigate treacherous, and ultimately dangerous, battles for power, dividing and nearly destroying the community. The working-classes are actually the agents of most of the violence in the novel, but the roots of social unrest are traced to the contention among middle-class women. The menace of class revolt is feminized and contained within a story about the impossibility of female friendship. This impossibility is extended to all women's associations, which are eliminated by the novel's resolution. Women in contact with women form an anarchical threat to Victorian hegemony, and a disruption which betrays the contradictions in the middle-class narrative of love and marriage.

* * *

BRIEFLY SUMMARIZED, *DEERBROOK*'s romantic plot revolves around the courtship and marriage of two orphaned sisters, Hester and Margaret Ibbotson, who come from Birmingham to stay with their cousins, the Greys, in the small provincial village of Deerbrook. The village apothecary, Edward Hope, falls in love with Margaret, but he marries Hester out of a sense of duty when he discovers that she has fallen in love with him. Margaret lives with her sister and her brother-in-law, but she is completely unaware of Hope's unspoken passion. She falls in love with Philip Enderby, who is brother to Mrs. Rowland, the novel's antagonist. Mrs. Rowland, who opposes the engagement, convinces Philip that Margaret returns Edward Hope's love, causing him to renounce their engagement. To make matters even more complicated, Margaret's new friend Maria Young is also in love with Philip Enderby. Maria, who works as a governess for both the Greys and the Rowlands, is also orphaned and crippled as well. After undergoing a number of hardships, including poverty and social ostracism, the story's protagonists are finally rewarded for their endurance; Margaret marries Philip, and Hope, through his righteous adherence to duty, manages to fall in love with his wife. The ''social problem'' subplot provides the violent background to this romantic narrative: economic hard times and crop failures elicit social unrest among the starving rural workers and aggravate political differences among the middle classes. The novel ends with a devastating epidemic which annihilates a large portion of the countryside's working class population, grimly returning the village to its peaceful state.

Deerbrook begins by connecting the intolerance and provincialism of a rural community to the circumscription of women's lives. As the novel opens the reader looks in on Mrs. Grey and her daughter Sophia, who are anxiously waiting to welcome their cousins, Hester and Margaret Ibbotson. In a small rural village the arrival of strangers is an unusual event and thrusts everyone into a ''state of expectation.'' The narrowness of country life, where people "have rarely anything to expect beyond the days of the week, the newspaper, and their dinners," is especially intensified for the women in this town, who find in the most obscure details about each other's lives subjects for conversation and intrigue. The narrator informs us that on this special occasion Mrs. Grey has opened up the drawing-room, too "dull" for everyday use, because it "looked merely into the garden" (2; ch. 1). Mrs. Grey prefers the dining room for sitting, where she can "command" a view of her neighbors' houses, in particular the residence of Mrs. Rowland, wife of Mr. Grey's business partner and Mrs. Grey's arch social rival.

The reader soon detects, however, a vital dependence underlying the hostility between Mrs. Grey and Mrs. Rowland. What gives Mrs. Grey's otherwise insufferably monotonous existence meaning and flavor, what makes her dining room window a perpetual source of interest, is Mrs. Rowland, who is steadfastly dedicated to humiliating and eclipsing her neighbor. Their mutual envy ensures that no circumstances, however small, can be without relevance. Whether their sons go fishing or stay home, whether their daughters go out bare-headed or walk through wet grass, all matter because the other is watching, waiting to define her behavior in opposition to her neighbor's. The Ibbotsons soon learn, to their dismay, that in the Grey household no conversation can be held, no decision made, without reference to Mrs. Rowland. Mrs. Grey is surprised and delighted by Hester's uncommon beauty, primarily because she anticipates Mrs. Rowland's reaction:

> "I hope she will come tomorrow. . . . She will be surprised, I think," she added, looking at Hester, with a very meaning manner of admiration. "I really hope, for her own sake, she will come, though you need not mind if she does not. You will have no great loss. Mr. Grey, I suppose you think she will call?" (8–9, ch. 1)

For Mrs. Grey, Mrs. Rowland's envy intensifies the few available interests in Deerbrook, magnifying them into the semblance of individual achievement. The fact that Mrs. Rowland works steadily to disparage her neighbors, neglecting her children and her aging mother, indicates that this rivalry has become for her, too, the grand purpose in her life.

Locked into a narrow, stagnant, and monotonous existence, these women survive by aggrandizing the details of their lives. Mrs. Rowland apparently has, in a way unspecified by the novel, some indistinct claim to a marginally higher class background, which provides the pretext for her assumed superiority over the Greys. She remodels the outside of her house annually in a desperate effort to distinguish her social position from her neighbors, buttressing a fictionalized identity which threatens to collapse into the ordinary middle-class wife and mother. In fact, Mrs. Grey and Mrs. Rowland magnify their differences *because* they are two of a kind. Both women are married to middle-class businessmen, who, as partners, are socially and economically identical. They employ the same governess, their children attend lessons together in the shared property of the summer house, and their social activities are so similar as to cause inevitable conflicts and duplications which only increase the weariness and repetition of small town life.

At first the sentimental sisterhood between Margaret and Hester Ibbotson seems to pose a direct contrast to the virulent competition between Mrs. Grey and Mrs. Rowland. Left alone together by the death of their parents, the sisters vow to place their faith and confidence in each other, and they imagine their interdependence as an intensely private and sacred bond. Alienated by the provincialism of the Grey family, Margaret and Hester are drawn to each other their first night in Deerbrook. They pledge complete faith in each other, with no secrets, no hidden resentments. Margaret believes that "our confidence must be as full and free, our whole minds as absolutely open, as — as I have read and heard that two minds can never be" (14, ch. 2). Hester assures her sister that she can confide to her what could never be said to any other, and Margaret responds, "If I were to lose you, Hester, there are many, many things that would be shut up in me for ever. There will never be any one on earth to whom I could say the things that I can tell to you. Do you believe this, Hester?" And Hester solemnly responds, "I do" (14; ch. 2). This ceremonial exchange of vows echoes the ritual of an actual marriage as the sisters pledge emotional fidelity and undying trust.

Hester and Margaret's intimate sisterhood appears to be the antithesis of the highly publicized rivalry between Mrs. Grey and Mrs. Rowland. But the narrator informs the reader that this idealized sisterhood is only a "vision," a delusive "scenery of hope." "Such visitations of mercy," the narrator explains, "are the privilege of the innocent, and the support of the infirm. Here were the lonely sisters sustained in bereavement and self-rebuke, by the vision of a friendship which should be unearthly in its depth and freedom . . . " (15; ch. 2). The vision of a paradisiacal sisterhood cannot be sustained; even Margaret intimates that it "can never be." In this same conversation we learn that Hester suffers from obsessive and irrational jealousy; she is so dependent on and possessive of her sister's confidence that she suspects everyone who comes close to Margaret of unsurping her privileged position. Sisterhood has been a burden, rather than a blessing; it is founded upon biological accident and economic necessity, for the sisters have no other family, and their combined inheritance is barely enough to support them. Like Mrs. Rowland and Mrs. Grey, Hester and Margaret are associated by the inevitable social circumstances of their gender, bound by an interdependence which is enforced by their limited social and economic opportunities.

Female conflict, and especially social and sexual rivalry between women, is a familiar comic device in literature, often aimed at ridiculing the narrowness of women's minds and interests. But Martineau's treatment of women's conflicts becomes tragic rather than comic. Hester's jealousy envelopes her sister Margaret in personal despair, while the secret of Edward Hope's misplaced desire continually threatens to forever divide the sisters in the knowledge that their utopian sisterhood has fallen into the world of sexual rivalry. Women's conflicts also create public, as well as private tragedy; in *Deerbrook* social rivalry begins as comedy, but its consequences are developed and magnified until the novel finds the vicious disputes between women ultimately responsible for the ruination of individuals and the community.

But with the burden of guilt comes the privilege of agency. When *Deerbrook* faults women for the town's numerous calamities, including everything from a working-class riot to a deadly epidemic, it grants them — temporarily — the power to govern their community, and the kind of influence which is denied to the capitalistic enterprise of Mr. Grey and Mr. Rowland, or to the privileged status of the aristocratic landlord, Sir William Hunter, or even to the benevolent representative of middle-class paternalism, Mr. Hope. By endowing female associations with so much destructive power, and by magnifying the influence of women's conflicts, the novel weakens the power of men and patriarchy. The men in *Deerbrook*, Edward Hope included, frequently seem ineffectual, physically and emotionally weak. Hope's heroism is mostly passive; he lets his reputation deteriorate and subjects himself and his family to physical danger rather than confront his persecutors.[9] Mr. Grey and Mr. Rowland are even more impotent, helpless to stop the feud between their wives and finally forced to abandon Hope when he needs them most. Moreover, the power of women's conflict erodes the Victorian separation between personal (domestic and female) and political (public and male) interests: Mrs. Rowland's personal malice directly ignites public violence.[10]

Certainly *Deerbrook* condemns the violent power of Mrs. Rowland and feminine tyranny in general, but in doing so it offers a critique of women's oppression. The Rowland-Grey feud provides an outlet for the frustrated intelligence and ambition of two middle-class mothers. Hope acknowledges that in Mrs. Rowland's case "it is a pity so much ingenuity should be wasted on mischief" (284; ch. 26). Both the problem of women's restricted opportunities for action and their struggle to resist the normative middle-class female identity are more fully explored in the character development of Hester Ibbotson.

Margaret and Edward Hope are repeatedly tried by Hester's querulous temper; she is, like Mrs. Rowland, a "domestic torturer" (211; ch. 19), and she too needs some wider horizon in which to exercise her better qualities. Much of Hester's resentment originates from her dislike of the townspeople

and their narrow-minded prejudices. By marrying Edward Hope, Hester resigns herself to becoming a member of the Deerbrook community, but she is
perpetually reminded that she and her husband are culturally and intellectually
superior to the people she must call her neighbors. Hester is not only disillu-
sioned with the town but with her marriage as well. When Hope encourages
her to avoid criticizing her neighbors, telling both sisters that ''[w]e will not
watch our neighbours, and canvass their opinions of us by our own fireside,''
Hester responds angrily to his use of the diplomatic and authoritative ''we'':

> I understand you. . . . I take the lesson home, I assure you. It is clear to me
> through your cautious phrase, — the ''we,'' and ''all of us,'' and ''ourselves.''
> But remember this, — that people are not made alike, and are not able, and not
> intended to feel alike; and if some have less power than others over their sorrow,
> at least over their tears, it does not follow that they cannot bear as well what
> they have to bear. If I cannot sit looking as Margaret does, peeling oranges and
> philosophizing, it may not be that I have less strength at my heart, but that I
> have more at stake. . . . (206; ch. 19)

Not only does Hester find herself imprisoned in a dull, provincial village, she
discovers that even in her own home she is compared unfavorably to her
sister, whom Hope clearly admires (and secretly loves), repeatedly singling
her out as an exemplum of patience for his wife. Hester's angry reminder
that ''people are not made alike'' is a plea for acknowledgement of her
separate and equally valuable identity. Hester has ''strength'' just as Margaret
does, but thus far her only expression of it has been through domestic tyranny.
What makes Hester bitter and jealous, and what fuels the perpetual competition between Mrs. Grey and Mrs. Rowland, is their need to be different from
the ideal domestic woman. Martineau's female ''tyrants'' are women who
need their difference to be recognized and appreciated, who need the opportunity to exercise their own particular strengths. And unlike the other deviant
women in the novel, Hester does get the chance to redeem herself and win
Hope's love; faced with poverty, social exclusion, and persecution, Hester
discovers a larger, more noble self ''on the threshold of a new life'' (296;
ch. 27).

The problem with Hester, with Priscilla Rowland, with Deerbrook itself,
emanates from the historical limitations of gender and class, as articulated by
Maria Young, the governess. When Margaret asks how a woman can earn
money, Maria observes that working-class women actually have more options
than middle-class women:

> . . . for an educated woman, a woman with the powers which God gave her,
> religiously improved, with a reason which lays life open before her, an under-
> standing which surveys science as its appropriate task, and a conscience which
> would make every species of responsibility safe, — for such a woman there is

in all England no chance of subsistence but by teaching . . . for which not one
in a thousand is fit — or by being a superior Miss Nares — the feminine gender
of the tailor and the hatter. (448; ch.39)

The restriction of middle-class women's opportunities for growth and change
also means that their lives will necessarily duplicate each other, denying
essential differences which can free women from the entrapment of class-
and gender-defined roles. Responding to Maria's disquisition, Margaret asks
despondently, "The tutor, the tailor, and the hatter. Is this all?" The three
job titles, ringing with nursery-rhyme simplicity, fully capture the circumscription and trivialization of the correlation between women's lives and wom-
en's identities.

While Hester must passively await the adversity that will exalt her life and
elevate her above the usual middle-class occupations of wife and mother,
Priscilla Rowland aggressively creates it. Almost majestic in her villainy, she
towers over the middling ambitions and interests of Deerbrook society. As
Margaret observes to Philip, "Your sister is as strong a heroine in one direction as mine is in another" (310; ch. 28) and he admits that her "audacity"
makes her "sublime." The narrator compares her to Lear as she longs to effect
some "deed" which "should be the wonder and terror of the place . . . " (52).
Mrs. Rowland does, in fact, create both wonder and terror as she incites the
superstitions of the peasantry, creating stories about Mr. Hope's midnight
expeditions to the graveyard to exhume recently buried bodies and the tortures
he inflicts upon his living patients in the name of medical science. Throughout
Deerbrook gossip reappears as a malignant evil that infects the town, feeding
upon and reproducing ignorance and suspicion; Mrs. Rowland represents the
primary source and symbol of this creative power. Patricia Spacks discusses
the power of gossip as a weapon of the subordinate and describes how gossip
provides agency for its participants, in particular for women, allowing them
to take control of others' experiences (30). In *Deerbrook* Mrs. Rowland, Mrs.
Grey, and an aggressive feminine network cultivate gossip as artillery in a
verbal germ warfare which infects the entire community and disrupts patriarchal order.[11]

The spread of these horrifying stories about Edward Hope, exaggerated
and embellished by the superstitious imaginations of the tellers, incites the
mob violence that threatens the position of the only man in town who represents the potential harmony of community. When the Hope household is
literally invaded by an angry crowd of rural inhabitants, Mrs. Rowland's
malevolent stories become actual agents of violence. Philip recognizes that
"[t]his uproar is all of her making" (310; ch. 28). The antagonism between
women breeds the deadly gossip which resists (male) truth; the stability of
class divisions are in turn infected: anarchy is contagious. For even though

the epidemic that descends upon Deerbrook originates in another town, even though it is exacerbated by both the superstitions of the poor and the neglect of the upper classes for the welfare of those who serve them, and even though poor weather conditions have created a scarcity of food which weakens the resistance of the laborers to infection, the epidemic is metaphorically and literally laid at the door of Mrs. Rowland. Philip Enderby warns his sister that her animosity towards the Hopes is a "bad symptom . . . of a malady which neither Hope nor Mr. Walcot, nor any one but yourself, can cure" (327; ch. 29). She is, in fact, the Typhoid Mary of a community polluted by gossip and rumor. Named for the idyllic pastoral setting which greeted early settlers, Deerbrook has become unhealthy. Edward Hope, the man who attempts to cure the town's moral illness, makes the connection between gossip and disease when he describes how disruptive and dangerous "rumours . . . - rise 'by natural exhalation' from the nooks and crevices of village life" (77; ch. 8).

The "cure," or the defeat of Mrs. Rowland is, however, inflicted by her own hand. The final victim of the epidemic is Mrs. Rowland's eldest daughter Matilda, a girl whose character has already been disfigured by her mother's ambitions. Her death offers a feminine version of the Old Testament retribution upon the Egyptians, for Priscilla Rowland unknowingly sacrifices her daughter to her own desire for power. Determined to oust Hope from his former popularity, she brings a new but incompetent apothecary to Deerbrook. By the time Mrs. Rowland realizes that her daughter is dying and that Hope is indeed, her only hope, it is too late. This is the defeat which evokes Mrs. Rowland's confession, enabling Edward Hope to regain his position and Philip to renew his engagement to Margaret. Mrs. Rowland is humbled before a tribunal of men who make her promise to keep the secret of Hope's initial love for Margaret. She promises to make "reparation," hoping that "then perhaps God will spare my child." Hope despises her last minute attempt to appease God, reflecting "[h]ow alike is the superstition of the ignorant and of the wicked! My poor neighbours stealing to the conjuror's tent in the lane, and this wretched lady, hope alike to bribe Heaven in their extremity — they by gifts and rites, she by remorse and reparation" (508; ch. 44). In the same sentence, Hope collapses the poor (the ignorant) with the public woman (the wicked); both are condemned for their refusal to accept legitimate (middle-class male) authority, as well as for their deluded belief in their own autonomy. The poor refuse Hope's medical advice, choosing to spend their money on fortune-telling; Mrs. Rowland produces her own medical authority, who also fails. Irrational and recalcitrant, both the working classes and Mrs. Rowland pay dearly for authorizing their own knowledge.

The similarities between the injustices suffered by both women and the working class — the lack of education, the denial of work, and the resulting idleness — haunt the novel, becoming most powerfully apparent in the robbery of the Hope household during the famine. On an evening when Edward Hope is away from home, a suspicious looking "extremely tall woman" arrives with her child, asking for the doctor; the maid advises her to seek help elsewhere. The woman, however, is actually a man, a starving worker who returns later to rob an easy target — a household of women. Just prior to this frightening event, however, Margaret and Maria are seated by the fire, discussing the economic hardship faced by the Hope household. Margaret asks Maria to recommend some way for her to earn some money, since Hope, his medical reputation destroyed, has practically no income left at all. Maria suggests that what Margaret "ought to do" is save, rather than earn money. Margaret responds that "earning is so much nobler and more effectual than saving," and just as she asserts that she is "enjoying the prospect" of "labour," she hears footsteps outside the door. Maria whispers that she "heard it a minute or two ago . . . but I did not like to mention it" (449; ch. 39). It is, of course, the "tall woman," a desperate working-class man in disguise who announces that he wants exactly what Margaret wants — money. Exactly what neither middle-class women nor the working classes can earn honestly. The skimpiness of the proceeds from this robbery emphasizes the ironic similarity of their situations: by taking advantage of a household of women, the thief gets next to nothing.

By insisting that Margaret should save rather than earn, Maria consigns her friend to the economic activities of the traditional domestic woman — to organize and economize. Margaret's desire for "labour," to "earn money," threatens to displace her domestic identity, to assign her an ambition that is reserved only for men and the wicked women, like Mrs. Rowland, who reject their domestic responsibilities. It also makes the similarity between the subordination of women and working classes all too apparent — both want to work for their independence, and both are denied that opportunity. What Maria had already heard, echoed in the threatening footsteps of the working class, was Margaret's desire for economic autonomy. The double identity of the "tall woman" who is also a working-class man, who invades the peaceful domestic world demanding money, incorporates both threats, uniting them in one dreadful anarchic figure who violates gender and class boundaries as she/he invades the middle-class home.

* * *

IN THE ASSOCIATION BETWEEN Maria and Margaret, Martineau offers a tentative respite from the prevailing rivalry between women in Deerbrook and an alternative perspective on the meaning of women's interdependence. Their friendship, which is voluntary rather than obligatory, affirms the traditional pleasures of feminine society. Maria and Margaret begin studying German together and their friendship develops throughout the novel, providing an island of contentment in an otherwise turbulent narrative. Like Jane Eyre and her "sisters," Diana and Mary, their study of another language suggests a linguistic hideaway, a shared discourse unavailable to outsiders. The two women share similar intellectual interests, philosophical outlooks, and strong, courageous characters. But in this association difference also fosters friendship. Maria, physically and financially crippled, leads an austere life as a governess; her many disappointments make her an older and wiser counselor to the innocent Margaret. Margaret, child-like in her enthusiasm and devotion, becomes the one joy in Maria's otherwise lonely and tedious life. The friendship between the two women proclaims that women's associations can accommodate difference, that difference may do as much, even more, to enhance female friendship as the fact of identical gender. The problem with women's associations, as we have learned from the rivalry between Mrs. Grey and Mrs. Rowland, is that they have too much in common; the friendship between Margaret and Maria, however, strikes a balance between mutuality and difference.

But this friendship is circumscribed by the social disadvantage of gender, including Margaret's responsibility to her sister and Maria's demanding profession. Maria and Margaret's intimate conversations are limited to a few blissful evenings. In one of these visits Martineau describes in detail the pleasure of informal female companionship; the friends discuss housekeeping and shopping, they engage in gossip about friends and acquaintances, and they entertain each other with singing and drawing. These traditionally feminine occupations have been ridiculed, often vilified throughout the novel. But at this privileged moment they are a source of joyous female communion. Like the social competition between Mrs. Grey and Mrs. Rowland, their friendship maximizes the pleasure and interest of the everyday. For Maria and Margaret the dangerous elements of women's associations — gossip and speculation — are benign forms of entertainment. Shared in the seclusion of a domestic setting, untainted by the social or sexual self-interest which propels public gossip, Margaret and Maria's conversations are confined to intimate interludes marked by their retreat from the rest of the community. They are momentary flights from the reality of female competition, for only by refusing to speak their competing heterosexual desire for Philip Enderby can these friends preserve a mutually satisfying companionship.

Margaret and Maria's unspoken rivalry over Philip Enderby lies at the heart of *Deerbrook*'s final elimination of women's associations. The novel's resolution, which silences the voices of women's conflict and asserts male order over female disruption, is symbolically figured near the end of *Deerbrook*. In a chapter entitled "Rest of the Placable," Margaret and Philip are reconciled to each other. The "Rest" refers not only to the return of Margaret's peace of mind but also to the death of Mrs. Howell, a village shopkeeper. Margaret, who was present at the deathbed, relates the story to Hester. For a moment this event preempts the rapidly approaching resolution of the romance narrative: "even the news that Edward was now in the same house with Philip, could not efface from her mind what she had seen; nor could Hester help listening, though full of anxiety about her husband" (510; ch. 45). The story is not about Mrs. Howell's death, however, but about her betrayal by her friend and business partner, Miss Miskin. Fearful of catching the disease, Miss Miskin remains in her own room throughout her friend's illness, abandoning her to the care of her maid and Margaret's daily visits. Even as Mrs. Howell utters her dying wishes, Miss Miskin refuses to enter the room, kneeling outside the doorway until her partner's last breath; then she instantly withdraws. "What an end to a sentimental friendship of so many years!" exclaims Hester (511; ch. 45). But of course Miss Miskin's fear of female contamination is repeatedly justified by the novel's metaphoric insistence upon women's associations as the site of disease. And while the story of female betrayal seems to offer an inappropriate introduction to a chapter devoted to the fulfillment of a long and difficult courtship, it (like the novel) predicates the possibility of heterosexual fulfillment and the restoration of communal harmony upon the termination of women's associations.

The novel's connection between verbal infection (gossip) and social malady (public violence) provides the narrative clue to *Deerbrook*'s elimination of women's associations. While Mrs. Rowland's rumors are often exaggerated, even false, they contain the seeds of truth, alternative stories which threaten to disrupt the romantic narrative, disclosing the implicit deceptions beneath the "truth" of the happy, heterosexual resolution. What Priscilla Rowland and other women outside the immediate self-interest of the romantic plot know is that Edward Hope did not marry the woman he loved, but her sister, that their marriage is founded upon falsehood, as are, in fact, all the marriages in this novel. Philip will marry Margaret without ever revealing to her the real reason for his temporary rejection of her, without admitting that he once believed her capable of falsehood. More subtly, and more ominously, Margaret never learns that Maria Young believes she was jilted by Philip because of an accident which left her both poor and lame. Philip acquits himself of such an imputation, but Maria maintains it until the very end of the novel, when she somewhat grudgingly concedes that she may have misinterpreted his "looks" and "words." Unless these stories of male betrayal and deceit are suppressed the novel cannot come to the appropriate romantic resolution. Martineau sends Margaret and Philip to live in London, thus breaking up two love triangles and insuring that confidences between women will not expose the truths that would undermine traditional marriage. In *Deerbrook* the proximity of women and the tensions created by their interdependence produces alternative stories which construct men as deceptive and dangerous. Priscilla Rowland's revision of Edward Hope as a small town Victor Frankenstein has no basis in fact; but like Mary Shelley's guilty protagonist, Hope carries a secret which can destroy his family and himself.

Despite the brutal but logical resolution of a troubled romantic narrative, *Deerbrook* mourns the elimination of women's associations, conveying the longing to retain them even in the face of all contrary knowledge. We can read, in the novel's resolution, either the inevitable end of all women's associations or the seeds of their regeneration. In the final chapter the parting of Maria and Margaret overshadows the joy of Margaret's impending wedding. *Deerbrook* does not end on a note of fulfillment but on one of grief — the sorrow of a severed friendship between women:

> Once more the friends sat in the summer-house, by the window, whence they loved to look abroad upon meadow, wood, and stream. Here they had studied together, and cherished each other: here they had eagerly imparted a multitude of thoughts, and carefully concealed a few. Here they were now conversing together for the last time before their approaching separation. (519–20; ch. 46)

Along with the nostalgia belonging to girlhood memories, the passage insists upon the finality of these pleasures. Maria makes an oath to Margaret that echoes the vows of the sisters in the beginning of the novel: "you are, and ever will be, my intimate. There can be no other" (523). She is responding to Margaret's suggestion that some other friend may make up for her absence, but Maria refuses this consolation. As we have seen earlier, such oaths, between sisters and even between heterosexual lovers, are deceptive, at times purely false. Only the visionary future, intimated in the sisters' vows of fidelity, elicits any shared hope:

> When that crowd of new graves in the churchyard shall be waving with grass, and those old woods looking more ancient still, and the grown people of Deerbrook telling their little ones all about the pestilence that swept the place at the end of the great scarcity, when *they* were children, you and yours, and perhaps I, may sit, a knot of grey-headed friends, and hear over again about those good old days of ours, as we shall then call them. (523; ch. 46)

Maria imagines a benign gathering of female friends, reliving and transforming the past, reconstructing the rivalry and dis-ease of women's associations into "good old days." The vision is hopeful, yet oppressive in its serenity. The inactivity of old age, the only safe haven of female associations, seems devitalized next to the turbulent energy and influence of women like

Mrs. Rowland and Mrs. Grey, the vanguard of an unregulated but powerful, feminized society. Maria's vision has the same dream-like, unearthly quality that dooms Margaret and Hester's naive sisterhood. Yet it signals the way in which the novel refuses to completely relinquish the dream of female companionship: if *Deerbrook* is a story which consents to restoration of a heterosexual and patriarchal hegemony, it is also a story that foregrounds the price that women must pay for their enforced obedience to this law. At the same time *Deerbrook* recognizes that women's associations can re-interpret and re-invent the narratives which dominate their lives. The "knot of grey-headed friends" is engaged in the same activity which threatens to undermine male truths; telling stories, revising and enlarging the available past, is Priscilla Rowland's crime, as well as the bond which produces Maria Young's visionary female community.

Throughout *Deerbrook* the ruptures between women unearth and expose hegemonic forces, disclosing the weaknesses of heterosexual marriage, the strategic sacrifice of middle-class women to the maintenance of a class hierarchy, and the double-edged oppression of class and gender that divides women as it binds them. Although women suffer from the pain inflicted by other women, nothing is more agonizing in this novel than the blindness which is forced upon its heroines. In a moment of despair, unable to conceive the reasons behind Philip's abrupt cancellation of their engagement, Margaret cries out:

> Oh! why are we so made that we cannot see into one another's hearts? If we are made to depend on one another so absolutely as we are, so that we hold one another's peace to cherish or to crush, why is it such a blind dependence? Why are we left so helpless? (415; ch. 36)

Critics are right when they complain that Martineau's innocent heroines seem powerless; they are powerless because they are innocent. But Martineau's female antagonists are — and tell — another story. Only those women who are guilty of fracturing the veneer of a unified womanhood in order to look into the "nooks and crevices," — the ruptures created by women's conflicts — have the power not only to see but to alter truth.

Iowa State University

NOTES

1. Yates discusses these and other aspects of Martineau's contradictory feminism.
2. Martineau wrote another book-length fiction entitled *The Hour and The Man* (1841), but according to Thomas, Martineau used the term novel only for *Deerbrook*.

3. Colby emphasizes *Deerbrook*'s historical importance as a possible "archetype" for the domestic love story and suggests that Martineau's "Victorian reticence or her own sexual innocence" caused her to "shrink from acknowledging the real problem" in her representation of a troubled marriage (247). Pichanick makes a similar charge when she claims that Martineau's "freedom from romantic passion" made "her depiction of the emotion stylized and unrealistic" (117). Thomas blames Martineau's lack of self-confidence: "Martineau's modest estimate of her own fictional abilities becomes a kind of self-fulfilling prophecy whereby the power of her writing is undermined by her insecurity about her capabilities" (95).

4. While examining Martineau's own relationship to other women might be relevant to a reading of *Deerbrook*, it is outside the scope and purpose of this paper. Undoubtedly her friendships were of great importance; Webb locates evidence of her "latent lesbianism" but Pichanick claims that Webb has no real evidence for this observation. Martineau's ambivalent relationship to her mother may also be reflected in *Deerbrook*'s censure of domineering, ambitious mothers.

5. Nestor offers an extensive bibliography of contemporary discussions of women's friendships. Another recent study of women's friendships in nineteenth-century England is in Cosslett. Cosslett's argument — that the purpose of woman's friendships in the conventional romantic plot of nineteenth-century fiction was to assimilate characters into traditional womanhood — demonstrates one way in which female friendship served hegemonic interests. In fact, the entire debate over women's friendships helped to codify the commonsense notions of public and private life, with friendship frequently regarded as a means of personal fulfillment and thus suitable for and important to women.

6. Studies like Auerbach's or Smith-Rosenberg's have emphasized the marginalization or insularity of women's societies and communities. It is clear, however, that associations among middle- and upper-class women were often fundamental in forming and maintaining societies and organizations which served hegemonic interests. See, for example, Langland for a discussion of the ways in which middle-class women codified and wielded political power.

7. Auerbach rightly criticizes this but fails to challenge it in her work when she suggests that contention, rivalry, and betrayal are antithetical to community, that such a stereotype means that female communities are "in the true sense nonexistent" (12). Auerbach's "true" community is mythological; a cultural definition of community can incorporate the inevitability of conflict without accepting or reaffirming the stereotype.

8. In Victorian literature, for example, consider the Dodsons in George Eliot's *The Mill On The Floss*, whose squabbles signify the narrowness of provincial life; or the aristocratic Ingrams in Charlotte Brontë's *Jane Eyre*, who, like Mrs. Reed and family, exercise social superiority at the expense of morality. Lady Waldemar's infamous betrayal of Marian in Elizabeth Barrett Browning's *Aurora Leigh* exemplifies the epitome of social intolerance and individual selfishness in a work which tries to reconcile philanthropic duty and artistic ambition.

9. Because the novel uses Hope's last name, I have also chosen to refer to him as Hope, rather than by his given name. Martineau referred to other male characters by their first names, but Hope's has obvious symbolic significance. Edward Hope also has many traditionally feminine characteristics besides passivity, including physical weakness and emotional vulnerability. Martineau magnifies Hope's feminine attributes by referring to him throughout the novel by a woman's name.

10. The exaggeration of the Victorian woman's influence in the public sphere reinforced and consolidated this kind of scapegoating until John Ruskin could proclaim her unqualified guilt: "There is not a war in the world, no, nor an injustice, but you women are answerable for it. . . . There is no suffering, no injustice, no misery in the earth, but the guilt of it lies lastly with you" (75).

11. Martineau often indulged in gossip, sometimes at the cost of her own reputation. George Eliot noted that "[a]mongst her good qualities we certainly cannot reckon zeal for other people's reputation" (qtd. in Pichanick 107).

WORKS CITED

Auerbach, Nina. *Communities of Women: An Idea in Fiction.* Cambridge, MA: Harvard UP, 1978.

Colby, Vineta. *Yesterday's Woman: Domestic Realism in the English Novel.* Princeton: Princeton UP, 1974.

Cosslett, Tess. *Woman to Woman. Female Friendship in Victorian Fiction.* Atlantic Highlands, NJ: Humanities P, 1988.

David, Deirdre. *Intellectual Woman and Victorian Patriarchy: Harriet Martineau, Elizabeth Barrett Browning, George Eliot.* London: Macmillan, 1987.

Hewitt, Nancy. "Beyond the Search for Sisterhood: American Women's History in the 1980's." *Social History* 10 (1985): 299–321.

Langland, Elizabeth. "Nobody's Angels: Domestic Ideology and Middle-Class Women in the Victorian Novel." *PMLA* 107 (1992): 290–304.

Martineau, Harriet. *Deerbrook.* 1839. London: Virago Press, 1983.

Nestor, Pauline. *Female Friendships and Communities; Charlotte Bronte, George Eliot, Elizabeth Gaskell.* Oxford: Clarendon P, 1985.

Pichanick, Valerie Kossew. *Harriet Martineau: The Woman and Her Work, 1802–76.* Ann Arbor: U of Michigan P, 1980.

Ruskin, John. "Sesame and Lilies." *Sesame and Lilies, The Two Paths, and The King of the Golden River.* 1865. London: J. M. Dent, 1907.

Smith, Hilda. "Female Bonds and the Family: Recent Directions in Women's History." *For Alma Mater: Theory and Practice in Feminist Scholarship.* Ed. Paula A. Treichler, Cheris Kramarae, and Beth Stafford. Urbana: U of Illinois P, 1985. 272–91.

Smith-Rosenberg, Carroll. "The Female World of Love and Ritual: Relations Between Women in Nineteenth-Century America." *Signs* 1 (1975): 1–29.

Spacks, Patricia Meyer. *Gossip.* New York: Knopf, 1985.

Thomas, Gillian. *Harriet Martineau.* Boston: Twayne, 1985.

Webb, R. K. *Harriet Martineau: A Radical Victorian.* New York: Columbia UP, 1960.

Yates, Gayle Graham, ed. *Harriet Martineau On Women.* New Brunswick: Rutgers UP, 1985.

BLINDING TEXTS: THE MEDUSOID FACE OF THE SIGNIFIER IN *AURORA LEIGH*

By Caroline Roberts

IN "SEMINAR ON 'THE PURLOINED LETTER,'" one of his most important essays on the relations between literature and the major concepts of his own psychology, Jacques Lacan demonstrates the decisive orientation which the subjects of Poe's tale receive from the itinerary of a signifier, namely the letter that the Queen receives at the story's start. This signifier, he argues, determines the subjects in their acts, fates, destinies, refusals, acquisitions of gifts, and blindnesses. I believe that signifiers have the same function in Elizabeth Barrett Browning's *Aurora Leigh*; books and letters in particular operate as Medusa-like "gazes." Like many "looks" in the text, they attempt to control, limit, castrate, or blind the characters who read them.

In Greek mythology Medusa was one of three Gorgons, daughters of Phorcys and Ceto. Her hair was entwined with serpents, her hands were made of brass, her body was covered with scales, and her teeth were as long as the tusks of a wild boar. What is most significant about Medusa, however, is that she turned anyone she looked at to stone (Lemprière 317). She opposes, then Western culture's construction of the gaze: as the practice of men who objectify women. Medusa sees; and it is, it would seem, precisely this attribute that makes her so threatening. As Beth Newman argues in "The Situation of the Looker-On: Gender, Narration, and Gaze in *Wuthering Heights*," the knowledge of someone else's look, the awareness that another sees, disturbs the pleasure that a subject, traditionally male, takes in gazing. In Lacanian terms, a returning look "from the place of the other" disturbs the sense of completeness associated with the scopophilic pleasures of the mirror stage and implies, consequently, the threat of castration (1031).

Medusa's image is featured at the start of *Aurora Leigh*. As a Child gazing at her mother's portrait, Aurora recognizes Medusa as one of the many masks worn by the painted face which

was by turns
Ghost, fiend, and angel, fairy, witch, and sprite . . .
A still Medusa with mild milky brows
All curdled and all clothed upon with snakes
Whose slime falls fast as sweat will; or anon
Our Lady of the Passion, stabbed with swords
Where the Babe sucked; or Lamia in her first
Moonlighted pallor, ere she shrunk and blinked
And shuddering wriggled down to the unclean;
Or my own mother (1. 153–54, 157–63)

As Gilbert and Gubar have pointed out, the portrait of Aurora's mother is
connected to anxieties about women being "killed into art," about women
being made into icons of male fantasies (18–19). Simultaneously, however,
as D. W. Winnicott observes, following Lacan, the mother's face is a mirror
in which the child sees itself (cited in Rosenblum 326). Such a recognition
suggests that Aurora identifies with the Medusa mask; yet, as she does so,
Aurora sees herself being seen as an object. It is this image of self as object
of another's gaze that Aurora strives to overcome in her development as an
artist. Aurora attempts throughout the novel not only to avoid the medusoid
gaze of others, but, I would argue, to gaze like Medusa upon others through
her writing.

Aurora is a "sight" from the moment she arrives in England. She is conscious not only of the "frosty cliffs" that "looked cold upon [her]," but also
of her Aunt Leigh's gaze (1. 251–52). When Aurora meets her aunt, she is
subjected to a violent inspection: "with two grey-steel naked-bladed eyes /
[she] Searched through my face, — ay, stabbed it through and through"
looking for my mother (1. 327–28, 337). Aurora undergoes a similar ordeal
when she refuses Romney's marriage proposal:

I could not sit,
Nor walk nor take a book, nor lay it down,
Nor sew on steadily, nor drop a stitch,
And a sigh with it, but I felt her looks
Still cleaving to me, like the sucking asp
To Cleopatra's breast. . . . Nay, the very dog
Would watch me from his sun-patch on the floor. . . . (2. 860–65, 886–87)

For Aurora, to be observed "When observation is not sympathy, / Is just
being tortured" (2. 867–68). Aurora is not, however, watched merely by her
aunt's "probing and unscrupulous eyes" (2. 686). Aunt Leigh gives Aurora
books to read which function as an extension of her gaze. These patriarchal
books on "womanhood" are intended to teach Aurora that she must serve
others, that women "do not think at all," but "may teach thinking" (1.

428–29). They are another of Aunt Leigh's attempts to control Aurora, to limit her creativity, to confine her "soul agaze in [her] eyes" (1. 1031). As a budding artist, Aurora resists the role that these signifiers and her aunt prescribe for her, and, instead, gains nurture from "the Unseen . . . as a babe sucks surely in the dark" (1. 473–76). Aurora compares herself to an observed child in her attempt to evade her Aunt Leigh's fixed look.

Aunt Leigh not only attempts to use signifiers to control her niece, she also appears to die as a consequence of signification. Sitting upright in her chair, the dead woman is found holding an unopened letter, which, we discover, is a letter from Romney offering her a gift of thirty thousand pounds for her heir, namely Aurora. It is, I think, possible that although Aunt Leigh had not opened the letter, she was, nonetheless, aware of the letter's meaning (and conversely, that she would not necessarily have known the letter's meaning even if she had unsealed and read it). As Lacan explains in his "Seminar on 'The Purloined Letter,' " the materiality of the signifier is "odd" (53); for the signifier is a unit which, by nature, is a symbol of an absence. As such, Lacan continues, we cannot say of a letter that, like other objects, "it must be *or* not be in a particular place but that unlike them it will be *and* not be where it is, wherever it goes" (54). The circumstances of Aunt Leigh's death suggest that she knew of the letter's always already absent meaning and that the letter's form as manifest organization was therefore more significant to her than the letter's contents. Aunt Leigh is found "open-eyed." "What last sight," Aurora asks, "Had left them blank and flat so, — drawing out / The faculty of vision from the roots?" (2. 932, 942–44) While Aurora fears that she may, in some sense, be responsible for her aunt's fate, it seems that the sight of Romney's Medusa-like letter caused Aunt Leigh's blindness and death. Unlike her aunt, Aurora is, as Lacan might put it, a "realist imbecile" (55). Like the police in Poe's tale, Aurora treats the letter as "real, like any other object," and rips it up. While Lacan argues that a letter cut into small pieces remains a letter, Aurora is clearly unconcerned about the "odd" nature of signifiers' materiality. Unlike Aunt Leigh, Aurora is unwilling to have her destiny oriented by a signifying chain.

Instead of being gazed on by medusoid epistles, Aurora writes such letters, particularly to Lady Waldemar. Like Aurora's aunt, Lady Waldemar tries to control people with her gaze. Marian, for instance, muses:

> *Did* she speak,
> . . . —or did she only sign?
> Or did she put a word into her face
> And look, and so impress you with the word? (6. 963–66).

Lady Waldemar is, as Rosenblum notes, "the other who overwhelms the self" (330): "Leaning on [Marian's] face / Her heavy agate eyes . . . crushed

[her] will'' (6. 1076–77). She too is a Medusa figure, a Lamia, a hag, "preserved / From such a light as [Aurora] could hold to her face / To flare its ugly wrinkles out to shame'' (7. 685–87). Aurora is not, however, blinded by the "woman-serpent'' (6. 1102). Instead, she uses signifiers to return Lady Waldemar's look. Home from Lord Howe's party, Aurora loosens her long hair which, like Medusa's,

> began to burn and creep,
> Alive to the very ends, about my knees. . . .
> "She shall not think
> Her thought of me,'' — and drew my desk and wrote. (5. 1126–27, 1135–36)

Aurora writes to Lady Waldemar to stop her gaze, a gaze that "found *that* in me, she saw *that*, / Her pencil underscored *this* for a fault'' (5. 1058–59). Having listened to Marian's story of Lady Waldemar, Aurora writes to the "Lamia-woman'' (7. 152) warning her that "[she's] . . . Aurora Leigh'' (7. 374). Aurora uses signifiers both to control and to limit Lady Waldemar and to achieve self-recognition.

It is not Aurora's letter, however, but rather her book that "blinds'' Lady Waldemar, insofar as it castrates her love for Romney. After the fire, Romney asks Lady Waldemar to read Aurora's book to him. "I read / your book,'' Lady Waldemar writes (in her "letter, with its twenty stinging snakes'') (9. 175),

> for an hour that day:
> I kept its pauses, marked its emphasis;
> My voice, empaled upon its hooks of rhyme,
> Not once would writhe, nor quiver, nor revolt;
> I read on calmly, — calmly shut it up,
> . . . [And said] Good morning, Mister Leigh;
> You'll find another reader the next time. . . . (9. 50–55, 61–62).

Having read Aurora's book to Romney, Lady Waldemar leaves her betrothed.

In addition to "blinding'' Lady Waldemar, Aurora's book blinds Romney. Initially, it seems as though Romney was blinded by a falling beam that "nicked [him] on the forehead'' (9. 547). Such an explanation is, however, implausible. Barrett Browning herself explains why in a letter (26 December 1856) to her friend, Anna Jameson:

> Not only did he *not* lose his eyes in the fire, but he describes the ruin of his house as no blind man could. He was standing there, a spectator. Afterwards he had a fever, and the eyes, the visual nerve, perished, showing no external stain — perished as Milton's did. I believe that a great shock on the nerves might produce such an effect in certain constitutions . . . it was necessary, I

thought, to the bringing-out of my thought, that Romney should be mulcted in his natural sight. (qtd. in Steinmetz 27–28).

The "great shock" that Romney experiences is Aurora's book, a medusoid book, a book that functions as an extension of Aurora's gaze. As Romney describes it.

> A thousand women have not larger eyes:
> Enough that she alone has looked at him
> With eyes that, large or small, have won his soul.
> And so, this book, Aurora, — so, your book. (8. 294–97)

Romney's blindness was necessary for the "bringing-out" of Barrett Browning's thought because it expresses Aurora's desire to rid herself of the gaze. Romney cannot see Aurora, as she herself recognizes: "You think, perhaps, I am not changed from pride, / And that I chiefly bear to say such words, / Because you cannot shame me with your eyes" (9. 696–98). Romney can, however, like the "blind dial-eyes" (8. 55) that measure the shadow cast by the sun, praise Aurora's art, something that Marian, it seems, cannot do although she too is frequently described as "blind": she looks "blindly" (4. 118) into Romney's face and says in her letter "I am blind" (4. 982), while Aurora draws attention to "the cataracts of her soul" (4. 184). The fact that Aurora needs to share achievement with someone, needs someone to be proud of her is, as Christine Sutphin observes, evident (49). She envies Mark Gage his mother, for instance, who murmurs "Well done" when he lays his book's review on her lap (5. 529). Her own parents dead, "The best verse written by this hand, / Can never reach them" (5. 550–51), and so, Aurora flings herself at Romney's breast "As sword that, after battle, flings to sheath" (9. 834). Aurora, like a Medusa, stabs and blinds Romney with her book, ridding herself of his gaze, but not his approval. No longer does she "[play] at art, [make] thrusts with a toy-sword" (3. 240). It is perhaps with irony that in his final injunction to her, Romney both recognizes and promotes Aurora's Medusa-like art: "Gaze on, with inscient vision toward the sun, / And, from his visceral heat, pluck out the roots / Of light beyond him, Art's a service" (9. 913–15).

Books and letters then determine characters' acts, fates, destinies, and blindnesses throughout the novel, operating as gazes, and, frequently, as medusoid looks. Ultimately, I think that Lacan's quotation and development of the medusoid signifier in "The Purloined Letter" best describes the signifier's role in Barrett Browning's novel. Such is the signifier's answer:

> You think you act when I stir you at the mercy of the bonds through which I knot your desires. Thus do they grow in force and multiply in objects, bringing

you back to the fragmentation of your shattered childhood. So be it: such will be your feast until the return of the stone guest I shall be for you since you call me forth. (71–72)

Trinity College, Oxford

WORKS CITED

Browning, Elizabeth Barrett. *Aurora Leigh*, ed. Margaret Reynolds. Athens: Ohio UP, 1992.

Gilbert, Sandra M., and Susan Gubar. *The Madwoman in the Attic: The Woman Writer and the Nineteenth-Century Literary Imagination*. New Haven: Yale UP, 1979.

Lacan, Jacques. "Seminar on " 'The Purloined Letter.' " *Yale French Studies* 48 (1972): 38–72.

Lemprière, John. *A Classical Dictionary*, 15th edition. London: T. Cadell, 1828.

Newman, Beth. " 'The Situation of the Looker-On': Gender, Narration, and Gaze in *Wuthering Heights*." PMLA 105. 5 (October 1990): 1029–41.

Rosenblum, Dolores. "Face to Face: Elizabeth Barrett Browning's *Aurora Leigh* and Nineteenth-Century Poetry." *Victorian Studies* 26. 3 (Spring 1983): 321–38.

Steinmetz, Virginia. "Beyond the Sun: Patriarchal Images in *Aurora Leigh*." *Studies in Browning and His Circle* 9. 2 (Fall 1981): 18–41.

Sutphin, Christine. "Revising Old Scripts: The Fusion of Independence and Intimacy in *Aurora Leigh*." *Browning Institute Studies* 15 (1987): 43–54.

WORKS IN PROGRESS

Maura Spiegel's essay, "Unfelt Feelings: An Evolving Grammar of Hidden Motives," is excerpted from a forthcoming work on the history of the emotions from the Enlightenment to Modernism.

Monica F. Cohen's essay, "Professing Renunciation: Domesticity in *The Cloister and the Hearth* and *Felix Holt*," is part of a project on professional domestication in Victorian culture.

J. Michael Léger's essay, "Triangulation and Homoeroticism in *David Copperfield*," is from a work on homoerotic tropes in nineteenth-century literature.

UNFELT FEELINGS: AN EVOLVING GRAMMAR OF HIDDEN MOTIVES

By Maura Spiegel

ADAM SMITH grows impatient with Hutcheson's scrupulousness regarding motives of virtuous actions:

> Dr. Hutcheson was so far from allowing self-love to be in any case a motive of virtuous actions, that even a regard to the pleasure of self-approbation, to the comfortable applause of our own consciences, according to him, diminished the merit of a benevolent action. This was a selfish motive, he thought, which, so far as it contributed to any action, demonstrated the weakness of that pure and disinterested benevolence which could alone stamp upon the conduct of man the character of virtue.[1]

Hutcheson's idea is that the mere "regard to the pleasure of self-approbation" taints with selfishness "that pure and disinterested benevolence." Smith, in contrast, does not rule out self-interest as a motive for virtue: "Regard to our own private happiness and interest, too, appear upon many occasions very laudable principles of action" (304). Hutcheson, probes a virtuous motive deeply and thoroughly, plumbs its imagined depths, until it becomes a kind of complex mystery. Like Hutcheson, Dickens applies a rigorous conception of selflessness or disinterestedness, not accepting Smith's dictum that self-interest can be regarded a "laudable principle of action."

Selflessness is a major ingredient of Dickensian benevolence, and Dickens goes a long way to establish it as a trait of his good characters, but it is not established blithely nor in one consistent fashion. We find in fact that Dickens's virtuous characters are held to varying and dissimilar affective requirements from one another in their benevolent feelings. Dickens's ideas about virtuous motives, of the origins or springs of virtuous action, change from one characterization to the next. With regard both to benevolent and egoistic feelings, different theories of the emotions seem at different times to prevail.

In Smith's rendering quoted above, Hutcheson suggests that we should not be motivated to goodness by the gratification of self-approval. But what does this suggest if not that we taint our virtuous motives by taking pleasure in their virtue? Benevolence, therefore, would seem to demand a lack of consciousness, either of the meaning of virtue, or of one's own motives and feelings. We must do good without recognizing or appreciating our own benevolence. This calls either for a radical simplicity, a lack of self-awareness (the kind often attributed to children and the simple-minded, both Dickens's stock in trade) or the exercise, for the sake of virtue, of a selective ignorance of ourselves, or a selective acknowledgment of our feelings. (More on the distinction between awareness and acknowledgment later.) Dickens employs all of these options in his characterizations, inventing endless twists and surprises to accomodate this demand of virtue.

In *Martin Chuzzlewit*, a novel organized around the themes of selfishness and greed, Mark Tapley is offered as a counter-force to egoism. Here is a character who goes in search of hardship in order to challenge his own undauntable good spirits because he believes that under the ordinary "jolly" conditions of life he can accrue no credit for his good cheer and benevolence. Aboard the Screw, a wretched sailing vessel bound for America, Mark, sick himself, tends after the ailing and helps "all parties to achieve something, which left to themselves, they never could have done, and never would have dreamed of" (*MC*, Oxford, 1991, 250–51). The narrator explains and then provides Mark's ideas about his own good works:

> In short, there never was a more popular character than Mark Tapley became on board that noble and fast-sailing line of packet ship, the Screw; and he attained at last to such a pitch of universal admiration, that he began to have grave doubts within himself whether a man might reasonably claim any credit for being jolly under such exciting circumstances. (*MC*, 251)

Mark Tapley is in no danger, in Hutcheson's terms, of weakening his disinterested benevolence by "a regard to the pleasure of self-approbation." Self-approbation is perpetually postponed for Mark as he awaits a circumstance which will relieve him of his lightheartedness so that, presumably, a good deed will cost him more than any has so far. Mark seeks a greater expense of spirit, believing that this is what true virtue demands. Put in other terms, Mark remains unaware of his own goodness by a combination of self-ignorance and an eccentric idea of the demands of virtue.

Characters who do not perceive their own virtues are everywhere to be found in Dickens, and those who do are often parodied as smug or sanctimonious. Dickens chooses not merely to *assert* the unself-conscious virtue of his "good" characters, but rather to *account for* it, to conceive and report the complicated mental maneuvers by which characters remain remote from their own selfless feelings and behaviors; each is provided with his or her own particular system for sustaining the effect.

Benevolent feelings and self-consciousness are at odds, however, not only because recognizing one's good motives can be compromising to one's virtue in the sense proposed by Hutcheson, but because, for Dickens, a virtuous motive is an object of scrutiny and doubt. Dickens often reflects ambivalence in his treatment of selfless feelings. Are they really selfless? If we keep probing, Dickens seems to feel, we may find that sometimes deep within a selfless impulse lies hidden a self-interested motive. In *The Old Curiosity Shop* we find such an instance when Little Nell, on one of her lonely walks, observes two girls, sisters, being reunited after five years separation. Nell watches them embrace as the younger one is helped from the stage-coach, and they "weep with joy." The narrator comments:

> Why were the eyes of Little Nell wet, that night, with tears like those of the two sisters? Why did she bear a grateful heart because they had met, and feel it pain to think that they would shortly part? Let us not believe that any selfish reference — unconscious though it might have been — to her own trials awoke this sympathy, but thank God that the innocent joys of others can strongly move us, and that we, even in our fallen nature, have one source of pure emotion which must be prized in Heaven! (*OCS*, Oxford, 1991, 241)

Here we find Dickens taken up with the question of why it would be that Nell — even the unquestionably virtuous Nell — should feel so deeply for the joys and sorrows of strangers. The virtuous impulses of even Dickens's most exemplary characters may conceal that hint of "selfish reference" that Dickens attaches to Little Nell. In Dickens's treatment of the character Kit in *The Old Curiosity Shop* we find a case of another virtuous character possessed of a hidden self-interested desire.

Kit, a London lad employed by Nell's grandfather, is devoted to Nell, and it is perfectly clear to the reader that his love for her exceeds a servant's proper love for his mistress. Like Nell in the passage quoted above, Kit is portrayed as possessing a feeling that cannot be condoned — in her case, an "unconscious" self-reference that awakens her sympathy; in his case an unconscious desire that prompts his devotion. Unlike Nell's, however, Kit's hidden motive carries a double onus; beyond its "selfish" quotient, Kit's desire crosses class boundaries. (Of course, such boundaries in Dickens' world — until *Our Mutual Friend* — are not named, and are depicted as natural ones, like those that separate unlike species.)

As in the case of Little Nell, Dickens attributes a self-gratifying incentive to an otherwise sentimental characterization, and again the character remains ignorant of his motive. Kit never recognizes his feelings for Nell as those of romantic desire, not even after they have dissipated. It is interesting to pause for a moment to compare Dickens's treatment of Little Nell's devoted servant with that of another character upon whom Dickens's influence is felt, that is,

Harriet Beecher Stowe's Uncle Tom, and specifically the relation between Uncle Tom and Little Eva.

Dickens's sentimentality is quite differently comprised than Stowe's; consider the consequences of Uncle Tom's harboring — like Kit — a secret longing for Little Eva, even one of which he is not aware. Impossible. His fidelity hides no traces of desire, but rather a religious awe that affirms the established rules of racial deference/difference. Uncle Tom's servile love is just what it seems.

As long as Kit does not know that he possesses such ill-placed longings, he is, Dickens suggests, blameless, both to himself and the reader. Now this is not quite the case for Nell. The possibility that her sympathetic tears might have their source in some feeling of self-pity — even unconscious self-pity — redounds upon Nell, and Dickens feels he must reluctantly address it, both to acknowledge and to qualify it. No such moral culpability attaches to Kit. In fact Kit's love augments the pathos of his characterization, while offering the reader a lesson in class relations; we are perfectly aware that it is to Kit's credit that he would never consciously presume to love above his station. Are Kit's and Nell's unconscious feelings treated differently because the one pertains to romantic love and the other to sympathy, or is their difference tied to class? Are the simple folk of the servant class held to a different and less rigorous standard of affective culpability? of purity of motive? One's critical rationality must be presumed sharp in order for blame to fall on the self-deceived. Are the lower orders in possession of adequate critical rationality to be susceptible of this kind of blame? Or is love simply the only self-interested involuntary motive that Dickens will allow because for him the desire to win love is not a selfish one? Or both?

We are here reminded by Dickens of Darwin's efforts to accomodate selflessness in his theory of instinct, and the confusion to which it led. Like Darwin, Dickens seems sometimes to want to argue that certain self-interested goals, certain affective needs that might be classed with Darwin's instincts, should not be judged selfish. One might as well, we imagine Dickens contending, call a flower selfish for seeking the rays of the sun. As Darwin wants to withdraw certain instincts from moral classification, so Dickens would like, conceivably, to withdraw certain emotional needs from such judgments.

Not only does Kit himself never acknowledge the existence of his feelings for Nell, but they receive no direct narrative acknowledgement — except from Barbara, Kit's betrothed, and her acknowledgement is hardly direct. When Kit expresses his excitement at what he believes to be the imminent return of Nell, we are told:

Barbara did not absolutely say that she felt no gratification on this point, but she expressed the sentiment so plainly by one little toss of the head, that Kit was quite disconcerted, and wondered, in his simplicity why she was so cool about it. (*OCS*, 519)

and this is as direct as the narrator gets on the subject; in fact we begin to wonder how *we* the readers are so sure of it. The narrator's complicity in Kit's lack of awareness has the complex but unmistakable effect of adding social approval to his unwitting method of self-regulation. Here the character is ignorant, and the narrator plays along.

IN THESE RATHER complex narrative negotiations, Dickens finds his way into the egoism-sympathy debate, and his position there is not simply or easily charted. On the one hand, he seems to believe that merely being aware of one's own virtue can tarnish a selfless impulse — a high standard of purity is suggested — while on the other hand, he contends that even those most admirable of impulses can contain a selfish motive. What Nell, Kit, and Mark Tapley have in common, despite the vast differences in their characterizations, is some measure of self-ignorance which is treated by their narrators with varying degrees of acknowledgement, and which is provided to protect their virtue.

In contrast to his treatment of the virtuous, Dickens, in these early novels, typically represents villains and hypocrites as aware of their motives. The good, we find, are less self-aware and are moved to action by inchoate feelings and by other and less explicit or unconscious promptings. According to the logic of the sympathetic school, it is rational to be selfish, while the benevolent impulses are conceived to be irrational and involuntary. These involuntary impulses are described as the deeper springs of action, the truer indexes of our human nature. Continuous with this way of thinking, we find that for Dickens's villains, self-interested motives are not involuntary; they are rational.

While villains recognize and acknowledge their self-interested feelings, for the virtuous, even an innocent secret wish is something to be carefully negotiated by character and narrator. Dickens's virtuous, we find, stumble on, unconscious of their own desires or, if they do gain a glimpse of some secret wish burning in their breast, they certainly do not act upon it.[2] Kept away not only from their own virtuous impulses but also from their selfish ones, the virtuous appear to exist in a middle ground between a theory of natural benevolence, and the egoistic view, or one in which benevolence is achieved at the cost of self-scrutiny.

In his early works, Dickens perhaps suggests the proposition that moral sentiments can coexist with, even triumph over egoistic motives, as long as those selfish motives remain unconscious. Perhaps for Dickens, unlike Hume and Smith, the moral *quanta* do not belong to the feeling itself (the involuntary impulse); rather we exercise our moral faculty in our choices about which aspects of ourselves to acknowledge or to heed. This process, I would suggest, is not imagined by Dickens to be a conscious decision-making activity or an exercise of rational judgment as distinct from feeling, but rather it too is an involuntary expression of our moral natures.

If our virtue, as Dickens suggests, resides not in our capacity to contain only what is virtuous, but to determine what should be allowed to enter consciousness, it is not hypocrisy to manage your attentiveness to feelings, or even to deceive yourself or repress your feelings. Rather, this is precisely the function the moral sense is relegated to perform. The odd proximity of moral sentiments and hidden motives (suggesting a nascent idea of unconscious processes) may account for the sense, so long expressed by readers, that a deep hypocrisy is at work in Dickens's renderings of virtue.

If by allowing the virtuous to remain unconscious of certain non-exemplary motives, Dickens suggests that we are not morally responsible for unconscious wishes, it is not because they are — as Freud will suggest — amoral, but rather because we don't *intend* to act upon them. Moral credit is granted for good intentions in Dickens's world. Only when unconscious desires turn to conscious motives are we morally accountable. Of course this proposition would seem to rest on the assumption that unconscious feelings do not produce effects, or that even if they do, these effects are subject to less moral scrutiny than the effects of conscious acts. We return to a morality based on intention (not identical to cause) and not consequence.[3] One further and unexpected ramification here is that a person would seem to lose a greater number of "moral points" for his awareness of his own virtuous motive, than for his *lack* of awareness of a selfish one.

As observed, readers of Dickens have long sniffed hypocrisy in these methods of self-management. The related legacies of Romanticism and psychoanalysis lead us to identify the involuntary and unconscious processes as the "authentic" ones, and any modification of these that involves denial becomes a denial of the authentic, of the truth, or simply of the psyche's most powerful and uncontrollable forces.[4] According to this model, consciousness appears to be either a complicitous partner or a censorious judge, in either case offering a false facade for the subversive forces of the unconscious.[5] Strictly speaking, all conforming or moral behavior becomes according to this model, hypocrisy — a denial, a lie against our deepest natures. Is there then, we can imagine Dickens inquiring, no virtue without hypocrisy?

In Kit's case, and perhaps in Nell's, we observe mechanisms we want to describe as classic Victorian repressions, feelings that are hidden or denied in the service of a moral status quo. Such repressions have come to signify Victorian hypocrisy, sentimentality, and false-feeling. These are the traits that Freud in his early years deemed crucial to his theory of neurosis, and that have come to look like signs of social and sexual pathology to Dickens's readers for almost a century. Dickens, however, saw something else when he looked upon these arrangements. What did he see? Repressions performed by characters and narrators outside of consciousness in order to protect certain moral values, are, for Dickens, distinctly unlike the mechanisms of hypocrisy. Hypocrites are a favored and a repeated subject of Dickens's, and it is interesting to observe that Dickens's hypocrites, like, for example, Pecksniff and Uriah Heep, are not unconscious of or deluded as to their motives; they merely falsify them for others.[6]

IN HIS COMPLEX narratorial treatments of the virtuous, and in their own "unconscious repressions" that hide their selfish impulses, Dickens — in this period — seeks to validate and protect a conception of natural benevolence and of virtue based on selflessness, to protect it perhaps from his own creeping doubts. In his conflicts regarding the springs of virtue, Dickens, like Darwin, will not be led to a Hobbesian view of the matter; rather than concede a greater selfishness in man, Dickens, again like Darwin, chooses to redefine his idea of what constitutes a selfish motive, and to reconceive virtue and its requirements. Having developed a conception of unconscious and conflicting urges, Dickens, in the later works, is led to a larger conception of "emotional need," a less selfless ideal of virtue, and a more self-conscious engagement with the problem of rendering them.

In the later novels, acts of repression performed in the service of virtue by characters comparable to Kit (in class and moral authority) are often accompanied by verbal or gestural tics that seem to suggest that an effort is required to sustain their innocent virtue. Virtue begins, in the later novels, to approach pathology; repression begins to produce symptoms. Dickens wants not to suggest by this that he sees such repression as a form of hypocrisy; rather, that such efforts toward selflessness are emotionally costly. Virtue is no longer an expression of natural benevolence; it is a kind of affective achievement.

The model proposed here, of the achievement of virtue by the exercise of control over hidden or unconscious self-interested motives is certainly a familiar one, hardly revelatory, but it was one at which Dickens arrived slowly, over the course of many years and many novels. A comparison between what we can loosely term a Freudian model of motivation and that of the moral sense philosophers, will help us to define Dickens's evolution and his place in the history of the emotions. Instead of the model whereby our irrational and involuntary impulses represent the interests of uncontrolled self-gratification, the moral sense school suggests that our involuntary impulses represent the interests of sympathy and benevolence.[7] Not only, however, do these two models differ regarding the character of our involuntary impulses, but regarding the force of those impulses. According to this loosely-defined Freudian model, the emotions are not simply at odds with reason, they are the truer and *deeper* reason than reason. This model of motivation is nicely represented in a paper by Joseph Jastrow, entitled "The Place of Emotion in Modern Psychology," delivered at the Wittenberg Symposium on "Feelings and Emotions" in 1928. Speaking of assignation of motive, Jastrow writes:

> Those who answer the "why" with a motive — it may be revenge, it may be sympathy, it may be deviltry — are emotionalists; those who answer it with a reason — it may be to obtain advantage, to save trouble, to avoid disaster — are the emotionalists once removed, whom we call rationalists. They stress the means-to-end relation in its plan and mechanism, its logical device, and do not choose to uncover any *deeper* motivation-level for the choice of behavior or its defense. (My emphasis.)[8]

The "Freudian" view — here represented by Jastrow — proposes a vertical model of "levels of consciousness," and an implicit idea that that which is hidden is DEEPER, and therefore truer.[9] For the moral philosophers, there are no such hidden or deeper motivations.

Throughout this section I have spoken of a lack of self-consciousness, self-ignorance, self-deception, and unconscious motives as if they were interchangeable terms and concepts. Each of these terms might suggest a distinct model of the mind, some entailing a dynamic between manifest and latent or covert impulses, and some not. What we discover in Dickens's introduction of the hidden motive to the discourse of egoism and sympathy is the fluidity of these concepts (of self-deception, unconscious motives, etc.) as Dickens found them.

Of the eighteenth-century moral philosophers, only Hume makes reference to a realm of mental activity of which we are not consciously aware.[10] Of what he terms the "influencing motives of the will," Hume writes, "Now tis certain, there are certain calm desires and tendencies, which, tho' they be real passions, produce little emotion in the mind, and are more known by their effects than by any immediate feeling or sensation.[11] Hume goes on to provide the origins of these unfelt feelings: "These desires are of two kinds; either certain instincts originally implanted in our natures, such as benevolence and resentment, the love of life, and kindness to children' or the general appetite to good and aversion to evil, consider'd merely as such" (417). No conflict with the conscious mind is suggested, and no alternate originating impulse from those of our conscious feelings. Of the prominent nineteenth-century British psychologists, none makes mention of any unconscious processes.[12]

Dickens's own ideas about the uses of repression and denial – in the interest of morality and individual well-being – evolve as his novels record a slowly shifting center from the influence of moral philosophy toward a psychology based upon unconscious processes. Put in other terms, Dickens becomes increasingly aware of a conflict between psychological needs and processes and the demands of virtue.

WE HAVE OBSERVED that novels are routinely credited with providing "psychological motivation," and we have also observed that for Dickens, this was not a ready-made category or set of narrative determinates. When we say that nineteenth-century novels are "psychological," what do we mean? To what characteristics do we refer? The terms psychological and unconscious are both, in this period, being filled up with meaning, and, as is also commonly observed, novelists offered a significant contribution to definitions of both these terms. Why were novelists so "prescient" regarding what would come to be termed our psychological motives, and how do we account for this?

We might begin an answer to these questions with the further question of what distinguishes novelistic narrative from other forms of narrative? and with the observation that the features of Dickens's narrative art are so intricately dependent upon structures of repression and upon the unsaid, that one feels — to paraphrase Voltaire — that he would have had to invent the unconscious if it did not already exist.

In Dickens's renderings of "unfelt feelings," felt-but-unacknowledged feelings, distinctions between conscious motives and hidden desires, one observes a number of discrete and tangible pressures; those of moral didacticism, of class and gender, of liberal and Tory politics, of epistemological weightedness and persuasiveness, *AND* of the specific narrative obligations of his form. The evolution of theories of the emotions, and the evolution of novelistic techniques inform and influence one another.

As I have suggested, Dickens may originally have stumbled upon his technique of narratorial repression — one which is a central feature of his style — in his efforts to protect the virtue (as he then understood it) of his virtuous characters. On the other hand, Dickens's narratorial repressions are employed not only in the service of morality, but of other dimensions of his story-telling. Such repressions nevertheless effect characterization and the presentation of motive. In Dickens's handling of Esther Summerson, his only female narrator,[13] we discover both kinds of narratorial repressions, those enacted to serve her virtue, and those that work toward other ends.

In Esther's first considerations of her feelings for Woodcourt we find an example of an apparently unspeakable — although "meritorious" — love,[14]

For I was so little inclined to sleep, myself, that night, that I sat up working. It would not be worth mentioning for its own sake, but I was wakeful and rather low spirited. I don't know why. At least, I don't think I know why. At least, perhaps I do, but I don't think it matters. (*BH*, Oxford, 1991, 235)

These are hardly considerations at all. If we take into account the peculiar problems Dickens associates with recognizing one's own desires (even virtuous and meritorious ones) that were discussed above, and the restrictions posed by feminine modesty, we have still not exhausted the restraining pressures to which Dickens's only female narrator must respond. Esther faces numerous special problems, including the awkwardness of being herself the subject of her story, of speaking of herself at all. "It seems so curious to me to be obliged to write all this about myself! As if this narrative were the narrative of *my* life! But my little body will soon fall into the background now" (26).

> I don't know how it is, I seem to be always writing about myself. I mean all the time to write about other people, and I try to think about myself as little as possible, and I am sure, when I find myself coming into the story again, I am really vexed and say, 'Dear, dear, you tiresome little creature, I wish you wouldn't!' but it is all of no use. I hope any one who may read what I write, will understand that if these pages contain a great deal about me, I can only suppose it must be because I have really something to do with them, and can't be kept out.(112)[15]

Taking too much interest in oneself requires special pleading, especially for a female. In contrast to Esther, Dickens's other first-person narrators have an easy time of it. David Copperfield will grow up to be a writer; his concern about being the hero of his life has a specialized context. Pip's narrative often functions for him as a confession; he highlights his faults, makes fun of his younger self, records his transformation. Esther, however, is not officially a writer, and unlike Pip, she cannot offer her story as a confession; she has nothing to confess. Often we feel Dickens's difficulty in motivating her act of telling, as well as her acts of *not* telling.

In addition, for Esther the narrator (or half of the narrator), suspense must be listed along with the other pressures to which she must respond. One could argue that the smoke-screening of love is often tied not to prudery or to the delays that establish and intensify the worthiness of the lovers, but to plot concerns. The story, of course, is being told by an older Esther who is married to Woodcourt, a fact which only retroactively informs her evasions. Complicating matters is the fact that Esther is not allowed to keep things back with the intention of creating suspense about herself, that is, she can't be openly secretive, which may account in part for the cryptic acknowledgement quoted. Charlotte Brontë solves this problem in *Villette* by making secrecy and denial, to protect her pride and maintain her self-command, features of Lucy Snowe's character. For Dickens, in contrast, coyness is preferable to cunning as a means of evasion.[16] The representation of emotion and the demands of story, we find, can significantly interact.

One further matter: in her tentative reflections on Woodcourt quoted above, we wonder if Esther is keeping her feelings a secret from herself, from the reader or both? I do not think this is a question easily answered. In this untypical imprecision, Dickens loses ground; the reader remains unclear about Esther's relation to herself, to her own motives and intentions. In Esther's descriptions of her childhood, in contrast, she adopts the voice of the child, and the reader is more clearly situated, recognizing the child's unclarity about her own motives and those of others.[17] Once she no longer perceives with the child's eye, Esther is less manageable for Dickens.

Esther's coyness, her darkness to herself, is commonly cited as a prime example of Dickens' false and hyprocritical treatment of his female characters.[18] While gender and virtue play a large role in Dickens's oblique handling of Esther, other narrative considerations contribute to the workings of her emotions and their relation to consciousness. And sometimes such extraneous narrative demands seem to have contributed to his rendering of motives and feelings and to a logic of unconscious processes.

Dickens's complex operations of keeping characters remote from their own motives leads to both the coyness we have observed in Esther and to the development of what we term "psychological" characterizations. A look at an eighteenth-century narrative, one that responds explicitly to the current debates in moral philosophy and to theories of motive-causality, but does not resemble a "psychological novel" in our understanding of the word, will help to further reveal the mutual dependence of narratorial and psychological innovation.

HENRY MACKENIZIE's *The Man of Feeling* (1771) centers on the character of Harley. Orphaned, educated haphazardly, and financially reduced, Harley, while a descendent of nobility, is something of a rural naif. Nothing has occurred in life to remove the blush of his natural moral, sexual, and social innocence. Employing the convention of "found papers," Mackenzie builds a double frame for his story. The pages we read have been "edited" for us by a disinterested gentleman of the neighborhood who comes upon them by chance; the story is narrated by a deceased friend and neighbor of Harley's who is motivated to write about him by his affection and by his fascination with him as an exemplar of benevolence and sensibility. The narrative, presented in fragments (owing to parts of the manuscript having been "lost"), reports something of Harley's childhood and family circumstances, tells of his silent love for the unspoiled daughter of an affluent neighbor, and then follows him on his first journey from home, as he travels to London in hopes of improving his financial prospects through acquiring a neighboring property. Harley carries a letter of introduction to a baronet who has influence with the lord of treasury. His experiences on the road and in the treacherous city of London — visiting Bedlam, a brothel, and other representative sites, meeting cynics and con-men, as well as people of virtue and generosity — afford Mackenzie the opportunity, not only to reveal and remark upon Harley's unflagging benevolence and sympathy, but to answer in his own way those moral philosophers who adhere to the egoistic theory of motivation.

Taking his position beside those of the sympathetic school, Mackenzie seems eager to assert that the fact that rogues and villains are easily found in the world proves nothing but that rogues and villains are easily found in the world. While self-interest may motivate some, benignity and sympathy, Mackenzie is intent to prove, motivate others. Though taken in by poseurs again and again, Harley does not become cynical or worldly, and while others scoff, he continues to act upon his faith in the good will of people who, more often than not, turn out to be sincere and worthy of his concern.

Mackenzie's narrative is structured to create some suspense regarding the motives of those with whom Harley comes in contact. The reader is commonly placed in a position similar to Harley's; we are given some details about the appearance of those he encounters, and we listen with him to their opinions and stories. While we come to trust that Harley's responses will remain reliably generous, our own reactions, our powers of judgment and sympathy are tested, as we are sometimes encouraged to feel trusting with him, and sometimes to feel suspicious where he does not. Harley allows his sympathy to be the judge, and we, employing our more "rational" faculties, are forced to scrutinize, especially when we judge incorrectly, the cynical tendencies hidden within our "reason."

The novel's two central preoccupations appear to be with encouraging and inducing certain tearful feelings in the reader (and thereby, presumably, affirming man's capacity for disinterested sympathy), and with attaching motives to behavior.[19] While these motives are made a matter of some suspense for the reader (as we try, with Harley, to distinguish the scoundrels from the virtuous), they are not made a matter of great complexity. Characters generally fall into one of two categories of motivation: self-serving or disinterested. One need not enter deeply into the inner workings of characters to discern their moral dispositions; these can be read by their actions and the consequences produced by them. Mackenzie does not wish to open the question of *why* some are motivated in one direction and some in the other.[20]

Let us examine Mackenzie's ideas regarding the springs of virtuous action and his techniques for rendering such impulses in this narrative, which is often described as the prototype of the sentimental novel, and which focuses so steadfastly on the realm of feeling and the philosophical issues at stake in the matter of human motivation. As observed, the story is narrated by a friend of Harley's one who appears with him, however, in a scene only once, at the novel's rather startling conclusion. While Mackenzie has troubled himself regarding the framing of the story, he does not trouble himself over the matter of how this friend knows what he knows. While our narrator is a consistent and frequent commentator on events and behavior, and while he has much detailed knowledge of situations he has not personally observed, he does not have recourse to the convention (not yet a fully developed one) of entering the thoughts of his characters.

Motives to virtue, unlike in Dickens, are provided without ambiguity or ambivalence, although, like Dickens, Mackenzie is highly conscious of the polemical nature of such accounts. The narrator describes, for example, Harley's beloved Miss Walton:

> Her conversation was always cheerful, but rarely witty; and without the smallest affectation of learning, had as much sentiment in it as would have puzzled a Turk, upon his principles of female materialism, to account for. Her beneficence was unbounded; indeed the natural tenderness of her heart might have been argued, by the frigidity of a casuist, as detracting from her virtue in this respect, for her humanity was a feeling, not a principle: but minds like Harley's are not very apt to make this distinction, and generally give our virtue credit for all that benevolence which is instinctive in our nature. (Henry Mackenzie, *The Man of Feeling*, ed. Brian Vickers, [New York: Oxford, 1987] 16.)

Observing that "by the frigidity of a casuist" Miss Walton's beneficence would lose some of its merit in having its source in a "feeling" and not a principle, Mackenzie mocks the idea that a higher virtue attaches to a principled benevolence over a "natural" or "sentimental" one. The narrator reinforces his position on the side of "feelings" by reference to Harley's lack of concern with such distinctions. Miss Walton's benevolence, unlike Little Nell's, is not a matter to be queried, probed, contextualized or explained. It is simply asserted, as is Harley's and that of all the virtuous characters encountered here. Nor does selfishness pose a problem of motivation, although Mackenzie's narrator is less keen to pursue this route. He remarks rather coyly: "From what impulse he did this, we do not mean to inquire; as it has ever been against our nature to search for motives where bad ones are to be found" (48–49).

In this world, unlike Dickens's, we find no evidence of conflict between conscious motives and hidden desires. This is a world of categorical mental operations in which our narrator makes some effort to maintain the clear distinctions between affective spheres found in the writings of moral philosophers. Motives are different from feelings; motives quite simply motivate actions (are goal-oriented), while feelings are reactive — except, of course, that sympathy and benevolence are both motives and feelings. In accounting for a likeable and telling peculiarity of Harley's, his preference for walking over riding or taking a post-chaise (indicative of his unspoiled and natural character), the narrator looks not to Harley's feelings, but his motives: "He did few things without a motive, but his motives were rather eccentric; and the useful and expedient were terms which he held to be very indefinite, and which therefore he did not always apply to the sense in which they are commonly understood" (84). Feelings, Mackenzie seems convinced, do not call or allow for the same kind of accounting as motives, since feelings are natural and involuntary. Love, as both a feeling and a motivator, however, offers some difficulty. In describing the gradations of Harley's feelings for Miss Walton, from esteem to love, the narrator comments: "In times not credulous of inspiration, we should account for this from some natural cause; but we do not mean to account for it at all; it were sufficient to describe its effects"(17) Here Mackenzie pokes fun at empiricism, and its project to account even for love, by "some natural cause," while regretting that the times, which clearly are "not credulous of inspiration" demand this. In this appeal to "inspiration," Mackenzie appears to abandon, for the moment, his own "psychological" project, appealing to images perhaps of Venus and Cupid. He suggests here that feelings are not in need of explanation, not because they are the nature in us, but because they are the *divinity* in us. For Mackenzie, love needs no motive, but, nevertheless, our narrator seems obliged to pointedly deny us one.

In addition, unlike Dickens, Mackenzie's characters' relations to their own motives are unmysterious and direct. Harley's love for Miss Walton, for example, while it is unspoken by him, is not unrecognized by him or by those who surround him (with the exception of his rather preoccupied, elderly maiden aunt). Feelings are felt and motives, both good and ill, are known by Mackenzie's characters.

While Harley's benevolence is too great to survive the world, he is not disallowed consciousness of it. His natural modesty protects him from celebrating it in himself, but, unlike for Hutcheson, and sometimes for Dickens, Harley's awareness of his own virtue does not taint it; his benevolence is, unproblematically, a source of pleasure for him; it is its own reward. After helping to return a prostitute to the protection of her respectable father, Harley accepts their gratitude. His response to their thanks is reflected upon by the narrator: "We would attempt to describe the joy which Harley felt on this occasion, did it not occur to us, that one half of the world could not understand it though we did, and the other half will, by this time, have understood it without any description at all" (69).

Mackenzie's narrator, unlike Dickens's, provides and explains motives at the time of the action and he retains a static relation to characters, which Dickens does not. While Dickens will alter his degree of recognition or delay his acknowledgment of a character's motives for specific effects, Mackenzie's narrator remains consistent in his accounts of motives. Again, the story is not narrated to draw our attention to the complexity, multi-determinacy or revelation of human motive, as it is in Dickens.

As Janet Todd observes, the sentimental novel is "necessarily fragmented — like sensibility that is inevitably expressed in moments" (104). Mackenzie acknowledges this himself, describing his work to his cousin as "a very odd medley,"[21] and the "editor" too addresses this point near the story's end: "[T]o such as may have expected the intricacies of a novel, a few incidents in a life undistinguished, except by some features of the heart, cannot have afforded much entertainment"(125). As Todd notes: "Sensibility does not inevitably learn or develop; if it does, it takes the trajectory of the Man of Feeling or Werther," (105) that is, to death. Such works are not constructed, like the *bildungsroman*, to lead to revelation or self-knowledge. Episodic and fragmentary, *The Man of Feeling* does not trace internal change in characters, nor is the narrative oriented toward the exposure of deep or hidden motives. In this novel, feelings have no histories; causalities are located on an axis of selfish and benevolent motives; they are not traced, as they are in Dickens, according to the specific experiences, syntagmatically and symbolically linked, of individual characters.

Mackenzie activates his narrative both to induce certain feelings in his reader and to exemplify certain principles of moral philosophy. As he put it in a letter of 8 July, 1769:

> The way of introducing these [observations on men and matters] by narrative, I had fallen into in some detached essays, from the notion of its interesting both the memory and the affections deeper than mere argument or moral reasoning. In this way I was somehow led to think of introducing a man of sensibility into different scenes where his feelings might be seen in their effects, and his sentiments occasionally delivered without the stiffness of regular deduction.(xii)

His ideas about psychological causality, like those of the moral philosophers, do not include a theory of unconscious processes, nor do they focus on conflicts between impulses. In Dickens, we find that certain external factors (such as class, in Kit's case) can produce a conflict regarding the recognition of certain feelings. This kind of concern is entirely outside of Mackenzie's purview, where feelings do not exist within a social context, but are meant to signify our natural freedom from such determinates, and where class and economic pressures are simply absent. Mackenzie's narrative art relies on a logical and unparadoxical theory of human motivations. Unbothered by the requirements of plot (since he fragments his text and foregoes all claims to having written a "novel"), Mackenzie need only account for motives and feelings as they apply to a given and localized situation; feelings need not answer to the demands of internal or circumstantial change or development.

His scenarios function as dramatized syllogisms; his rendering of motives and feelings are not dynamic.

This novel, whose popularity was enormous, going through nine editions by 1800, and thirty more by 1824[22], (and the popularity of which is employed as a reliable gauge of the life-span of the "Age of Sensibility") beyond providing an example of the conventions of eighteenth-century sentimentality, offers, in the relation between Mackenzie's narrative methods and his ideas about motivation and psychic causality, a vivid contrast to Dickens, and to the "psychological" causalities and narrative adjustments found in the nineteenth-century novel.

IN CONTRAST TO Mackenzie, Dickens commonly establishes for his characters a kind of zone between what is felt and recognized, or what is felt and acknowledged, and his narrators maneuver around in this place of moral negotiability. Different moral shadings are produced by tiny narrative shifts in a character's or in a narrator's relation to or relative awareness of a feeling. Sometimes the narrator seems to know more about a character's feelings than the character himself knows; sometimes the character is the more cognizant; sometimes both the character and narrator seem to be aware of some feeling that neither is willing to mention; and somehow, nevertheless, the reader is made conscious of each of these dynamics and of its purpose. Frequently one or another motive is tossed out of reach, either by the character or the narrator or both, and a realm is established where feelings exist, have influence and effect, but are kept from consciousness and/or from discourse. In Dickens's narrator's treatment of Arthur Clennam, in *Little Dorrit*, we see not only the distance separating him from Mackenzie, but also from his own earlier renderings of hidden motives.

Clennam, unsurprisingly, is not subject to the same restrictions that applied to Esther. This male protagonist's virtue is differently constructed, as is his relation to himself. In the following passage from *Little Dorrit*, the narrator offers a picture of Clennam's state of mind and heart regarding Miss Pet Meagles:

> If Clennam had not decided against falling in love with Pet; if he had had the weakness to do it; if he had, little by little, persuaded himself to set all the earnestness of his nature, all the might of his hope, and all the wealth of his matured character, on that cast; if he had done this and found that all was lost; he would have been, that night, unutterably miserable. As it was —
> As it was, the rain fell heavily, drearily. (*LD*, Oxford, 1991, 210)

Dickens poignantly handles here an older man's misplaced passion for a young woman, his surprise and bafflement at the failure of judgment and self-control. Dickens's narrator, who almost never reports the thoughts of a character directly, followed by a "he thought," simulates Clennam's efforts at self-repression. Without directly quoting Clennam's thoughts, the narrator gives us a glimpse into what Dorrit Cohn terms the "transparent mind."[23] One feels that the narrator's indirection serves in part to protect Clennam's sense of delicacy in such matters, to convey his scrupulousness. In addition, the narrator's obliqueness reflects Clennam's troubled method of self-management. The theme of Clennam's willessness, the "void in [his] cowed heart," (21) — which can only be healed by the exculpation of his family name and Little Dorrit's love — is developed by the narrator's repeated reference to him as *nobody* (note chapter titles, "Nobody's Weakness," "Nobody's Rival" and "Nobody Disappears) and this motif, of Clennam as absent to himself, is reflected in this rhetorical construction.[24]

Perhaps, however, more than anything else, one experiences in this passage Clennam's acute self-irony (a feature entirely absent from Esther's narrative). The effort to suppress an emotion — in this case desire — through the denial of that emotion is gently parodied here. The persistent reiteration of the rhetorical *IF* drives home the irony, making it clear that *nobody* is being fooled. We are made fully conscious of Clennam's feelings for Pet, and we are aware that Clennam is conscious of them too (differing from the example of Kit above), albeit somewhat shamefacedly. Clennam is, we recognize, all too painfully aware of his folly, and, interestingly, this self-awareness does not detract from his character or the reader's approbation of his character. While Dickens keeps Kit in the dark about his feelings for Nell as a kind of moral requisite, Clennam's awareness of his desire for Pet involves no moral cost.

The "moral outlay" is differently located for Clennam than it is for Kit. Kit is credited for choosing so worthy an object of love as Nell is, but he must remain unconscious of his desires in order for his feelings to maintain their noble character; Clennam's chosen is, the reader feels, unworthy of him, and were he to remain unconscious of his feelings for her, he would be, not a virtuous innocent like Kit, but a fool. Clennam's greater self-consciousness (he *knows* his feelings even if they cannot be overtly acknowledged) demands a *conscious* repression, or the exercise of what Dickens calls "restraint."

> If Arthur Clennam had not arrived at that wise decision firmly to restrain himself from loving Pet, he would have lived on in a state of much perplexity, involving difficult struggles with his own heart. Not the least of these would have been a contention, always waging within it, between a tendency to dislike Mr. Henry Gowan, if not to regard him with positive repugnance, and a whisper that the inclination was unworthy. (306)

In his decision to allow Clennam consciousness of his non-exemplary feelings — while still deferring acknowledgement of them — Dickens makes a new inroad in his treatment of the relation between feelings and virtues — or the psychology of virtue.

Arthur Clennam is a virtuous character whose desires and feelings are not in this instance exemplary,[25] but who sits, as it were, in judgment of his own feelings, who exercises his self-corrective rationality, and whispers to himself that not all of his "inclinations" are worthy of him. In Clennam's "struggles with his own heart" reason appears to be losing. Still, we feel that Clennam is himself the master of the irony; he knows his own heart, but this knowledge appears to him to be somewhat over-rated in its usefulness.

In contrast to Esther, Clennam feels and knows his desires — while she appears ambiguously unaware of her feelings for Woodcourt. In Clennam's case it is not he, but the narrator, who chooses not to acknowledge what is felt. (Esther's role as narrator, as observed, complicates her case.) Clennam's own implied obliqueness with regard to the source of his suffering serves, we feel, to bolster his efforts of restraint. As in the case of Kit, Clennam's narrator's complicity with his reserve confers authorial approval for his method of self-management.

Consistent with the larger movements of the novel, Clennam is moving toward a position of "emotional responsibility" that is dependent upon the idea of uncovering, of bringing to consciousness, and also of taking the blame.[26] In *Little Dorrit* Dickens will go far toward answering the resounding question: "Whose fault is it?" and offering individual responsibility in answer to the vacuums of social, economic, and familial authority. One question, however, will remain unanswered: although Clennam will take conscious responsibility for his feelings for Pet, and he will consciously restrain them, Dickens still wonders, we feel, whose fault are *they*?

IN HIS LATER novels, Dickens's virtuous characters are allowed far more self-scrutiny than we saw in the earlier works. Motives to virtue still require very delicate handling by Dickens's narrators, but repressions do not function to protect an ideal of selfless benevolence; rather, as in Clennam's case, to assist the effort of restraint. We find that Clennam can behave virtuously through the exercise of his judgment; he cannot, however, achieve contentment (or perhaps in our terms, "health") until the family-lie regarding the true identity of his mother is brought to light, until his buried trauma is uncovered. Dickens suggests that his "natural" impulses have been blocked by this unconscious distress. In his final completed novel, *Our Mutual Friend*, Dickens pursues the workings of the unconscious even further, giving the matter a forceful new twist. In Eugene Wrayburn, we find a character not only locked into a state of passivity (resembling Clennam's "willessness"), but one whose natural benevolence is inhibited by his troubled relation to his own motives. The hidden motives and feelings (self-interested and otherwise) that once threatened Dickens's ideal of natural benevolence now require revelation, as virtue itself comes to rely upon self-disclosure. In this new conception, in which the moral and the therapeutic are newly conjoined, Dickens resolves much of the tension between the "psychological" and the "ethical" that was built into the earlier works.

IN *OUR MUTUAL FRIEND*, Bella Wilfer and Eugene Wrayburn are the subjects of the novel's *bildung*; as such they are, to begin with, in the traditional condition of self-misunderstanding, but in this novel this condition is now a theme, not just a given. How feelings and actions are accounted for is made complex in *Our Mutual Friend* in a new way. It is not only the narrator — or treatment of first-person narration — that conveys a character's self-ignorance (the gap between what they understand by a motive and what we are meant to see), but here characters are both consciously and unconsciously engaged in the problem of understanding one another's, as well as their own, motivations. Bella, for example, when confronted by Mr. Rokesmith's (alias John Harmon's) observation that Fortune is not spoiling her, responds:

> "Oh, don't speak of *me*," said Bella, giving herself an impatient little slap with her glove. "You don't know me as well as —"
> "As you know yourself?" suggested the Secretary, finding that she stopped. "*Do* you know yourself?" (*OMF*, Oxford, 1991, 521)

And of course we find that her self-proclaimed avarice, (Bella protests to her father: " 'It's a fact. I am always avariciously scheming . . . I have made up my mind that I must have money, Pa.' " [320]) is not a reflection of her true nature, but that her unselfish love for John Harmon is. Eugene speaks about his lack of self-understanding in a conversation with his friend Mortimer Lightwood who, having sensed some new source of disquiet in Eugene, asks him if he is witholding something from him. Without entirely knowing it, Mortimer probes Eugene's feelings for Lizzie. Eugene responds:

> "I give you my word of honour, Mortimer," returned Eugene, after a serious pause of a few moments, "that I don't know."
> "Don't know, Eugene?"
> "Upon my soul, don't know. I know less about myself than about most people in the world, and I don't know."
> "You have some design in your mind?"
> "Have I? I don't think I have."
> "At any rate, you have some subject of interest there which used not to be there?"
> "I really can't say," replied Eugene, shaking his head blankly, after pausing again to reconsider. "At times I have thought yes; at other times I have thought

no. Now, I have been inclined to pursue such a subject; now, I have felt that it was absurd, and that it tired and embarassed me. Absolutely, I can't say. Frankly and faithfully, I would if I could.'' (285–86)

Eugene's oddly self-conscious darkness to himself is linked, as will be shown below, to his failures of will and of compassion, and these together are implicitly tied to his father's excessive and unnatural dominance; Eugene's irony, impassivity, and apathy are rendered as his somewhat deforming defences against a paternal incursion. Lizzie Hexam will provide the cure: Eugene will be educated from apathy to sympathy, Bella will discover the hidden rewards of selfless love, and both will rely on a newly-emphasized self-recognition. In these two progressions we find a significant evolution in Dickens's ideas of the workings of benevolence in relation to self-consciousness. No longer in conflict, now benevolence would seem to rely upon an achieved self-understanding. Sympathy is not here conceived as an involuntary and innate characteristic; it is a fragile condition of mind that cannot be simply aroused, but must be elaborately achieved.

In addition, Dickens exercises great skill in maneuvering the reader's approbation; his characters are constructed with extreme care according to his ideas about what does and does not arouse the reader's sympathy. In keeping with Shaftesbury, Hume and others of the "sympathetic school," Dickens in his early works seemed convinced of the dependency of sympathy upon a favorable assessment for its inducement, that we feel sympathetic towards that which produces in us what Hume called that "pleasing sentiment of approbation."[27] If Dickens assumes in his early novels that our sympathy relies upon our liking and approving of a character, he offers his first experimentation with this idea in *Bleak House*, in the portrayal of Harold Skimpole, a character thoroughly likeable and yet not worthy of approbation or sympathy. In *Our Mutual Friend* we find this experiment much expanded. Dickens plays more actively with the delicate balance between approbation and sympathy, suggesting that perhaps his confidence in a moral concensus has waned. His once reliable inducements to approbation, respectability and a solid work ethic, are undermined in this novel as the "respectable" and hard-working Bradley Headstone is made entirely unsympathetic to us, while the dubiously motivated and ostentatiously lazy Eugene, Mortimer, and Bella are made eminently likeable. In his handling of Bella and of Eugene, Dickens treats his reader to a lesson in sympathy, asking more now of our tolerance, as it is less simple to like and approve of these consciously self-interested types. His ideas about the relation between judgment and sympathy have evolved, as have his ideas about what makes a character likeable.

Eugene's feelings for and advances toward Lizzie are initially rendered as mysterious to him, but eventually not to others who observe them together

(Mortimer, Jenny, Riah, and Bradley Headstone amongst them), and for Lizzie, the nature of the interest he takes in her is a matter of uncertainty and pain. One Saturday evening Eugene appears at Lizzie's door with no explanation for his appearance beyond his having been strolling with his cigar, and, finding himself in her neighborhood, having the notion that he would look in as he passed. In this brief encounter, a remarkably elaborate exchange takes place, with regard to the question of motives. Lizzie scrutinizes her own and Eugene's while Eugene seems mostly just agitated in the general direction of self-scrutiny.

Having explained to Lizzie that he has nothing new to report regarding Rogue Riderhood, on whom he has promised to keep tabs, Eugene unceremoniously reopens the subject of his repeated offer to pay for Lizzie and Jenny to be taught to read. When Lizzie reveals her disinclination to accept his offer, Eugene, somewhat uncharacteristically, begins to press her. He accuses her of "false pride," pointing out that she knows the value of education, or she would not have gone to such lengths to see to her brother's. "Then why not have it," Eugene demands, "especially when our friend Miss Jenny here would profit by it too?" (235)

Eugene then pulls out the heavy guns, arguing that her refusal does wrong by her dead father by "perpetuating the consequences of his ignorant and blind obstinacy. . . . By determining that the deprivation to which he condemned you, and which he forced upon you, shall always rest upon his head" (236). Lizzie is moved by this argument, but not by the argument alone — also by a new interpretation to which she comes of the spirit of Eugene's offer:

> It chanced to be a subtle string to sound, in her who had so spoken to her brother within the hour. It sounded far more forcibly, because of the change in the speaker for the moment; the passing appearance of earnestness, complete conviction, injured resentment of suspicion, generous and unselfish interest. All these qualities, in him usually so light and careless, she felt to be inseparable from some touch of their opposites in her own breast. She thought, had she, so far below him and so different, rejected this disinterestedness because of some vain misgiving that he sought her out, or heeded any personal attractions that he might descry in her? The poor girl, pure of heart and purpose, could not bear to think it. Sinking before her own eyes, as she suspected herself of it, she drooped her head as though she had done him some wicked and grievous injury, and broke into silent tears. (236)

In this series of exchanges a complex dynamic is described. Lizzie finds in his calculated remark Eugene's disinterested and earnest nature expressed. This is perhaps the puzzle of Eugene to which she is drawn, his casual unconcern in combination with his mostly hidden springs of generosity and warmth. In some respects one finds in Dickens's rendering of Eugene the old model of virtue being held at a distance from itself; Eugene does not recognize his own benevolent urges as such. Unlike, however, the examples of Kit or Mark Tapley examined above, Eugene's self-ignorance is rendered in a more paradoxical mode; his generosity is expressed as unconcern. In fact, in this novel psychological paradox itself (or the idea that "agressive feelings can issue in a caress, or tender feelings in an act of violence"[28]) receives Dickens's special attention, as is consistent with his more paradoxical notion of the workings of sympathy.

In this exchange with Eugene, Lizzie is brought to tears by a number of griefs at once. Eugene revives her fraught desire to somehow make amends for her father's transgressions, and he revives the pain her brother has just caused her in telling her to "let bygones be bygones" (227), that this "fancy" of hers to make amends is selfish in her and injurious to him. In Eugene's "earnestness, complete conviction, injured resentment of suspicion, generous and unselfish interest" she sees something "inseparable from some touch of their opposite in her own breast." The meaning of this clause is not so clear: does she feel herself careworn and ungenerous by contrast, more calculating, more self-interested than he? She has refused his offer in the past believing he was not motivated to it by disinterest, but by some "personal attractions that he might descry in her," and now she feels that she has misjudged and underestimated his character in a vain and unworthy fashion, but perhaps she also feels some disappointment that these higher motives in him may mean the absence of an attraction to her — which of course she should only have cause to dread in the threat it would pose to her virtue. This is quite a muddle: the revelation of his disinterestedness makes her see that she has been selfish and vain to think that he had been selfishly motivated, and she "drooped her head as though she had done him some wicked and grievous injury." In all of this we find some familiar Little-Nellish traits ("The poor girl, pure of heart and purpose could not bear to think of it"), but on the other hand, we see a flicker of self-conscious desire, and although it must be elaborately managed, it is recognized by Lizzie and *consciously* managed by her. For Dickens this is a new development in his handling of a heroine.

Perhaps sensing that she upbraids herself for her readiness to attribute bad motives to him, or perhaps merely trying to make the offer seem, not disinterested, but entirely casual, Eugene remarks in his customary offhand-edness, " 'I hope it is not I who have distressed you. I meant no more than to put the matter in its true light before you; though I acknowledge I did it selfishly enough, for I am disappointed.' " (236) Eugene seems himself to be at a loss regarding his own motives, and here the narrator puts in rather mysteriously, "Disappointed of doing her a service. How else *could* he be disappointed?" The narrator contributes to the distinct unclarity of the matter. Eugene then explains that not only was he being selfish in bringing her father into it — because he was disappointed at her refusal of his offer — but he points out that the offer itself was also motivated selfishly,

> "It won't break my heart," laughed Eugene; "it won't stay by me eight-and-forty hours; but I am genuinely disappointed. I had set my fancy on doing this little thing for you and for our friend Miss Jenny. The novelty of my doing anything in the least useful had its charms. . . . I might have affected to do it wholly for our friend Miss J. I might have got myself up, morally, as Sir Eugene Bountiful. But upon my soul I can't make flourishes, and I would rather be disappointed than try." (236–37)

Eugene disclaims any valor for his good deed, and affects his air of uncon-cern, we feel, in part to let Lizzie off the hook because he is conscious of distressing her — but only in part. Eugene's self-irony is interestingly con-structed; it seems to rest in some measure upon his skepticism about the very possibility in himself of selflessness or sincerity. Eugene assumes that the selfish motive is most probably the truest one, but we also feel that he is hesitant to attempt to make himself appear virtuous when he is unsure himself of his own intentions. His feelings for Lizzie are productive of an earnestness that in his ordinary ironic relation to himself he cannot recognize as genuine. Here, however, there is a first negotiation as he attempts something like honesty, an honesty which, ironically, is not entirely sincere.

Immediately following the "Sir Eugene Bountiful" speech, the narrator comments, "If he meant to follow home what was in Lizzie's thoughts, it was skilfully done. If he followed it by mere fortuitous coincidence, it was done by an evil chance" (237). The narrator's use of the "if" construction, the theme of willessness and the strong presence of self-irony together recall Arthur Clennam in his relation to Pet Meagles. Dickens's handling — and the narrator's — of Eugene is, however, markedly different. Clennam's ironic treatment of his efforts at restraint are mirrored in the narrator's tone and language, and we feel a narratorial approval for, and complicity in, his self-repressions. While Eugene's narrator, like Clennam's, seems to mirror his method of self-management, in Eugene's case the method is not very evolved and the narrator seems as ill-informed about the exact nature of Eugene's motives as he is. The narrator's complicity but not approval is implied here. The narrator sounds an ominous note, suggesting that Eugene has hit the mark with Lizzie, either by his sportsmanlike deftness, or by the most casual lucky stroke, and again we hear a kind of echoing of the character's own discourse, as Eugene is loath, we begin to understand, not only to attribute virtuous motives to himself, but really any motives at all. In the narrator's handling of Eugene, we feel that the entire question of motive as determining of action and plot is somehow suspended and replaced by a rhetoric comprised of words like whim, mood, impulse, inadvertence; Eugene's feelings seem to be sundered — in his own experience of them — both from motives and intentions, but now a distance between motives and consciousness constitutes not a solution, but a problem for his character; one might even say it constitutes a symptom. While much is made of Eugene's failures of self-interpretation, his quick comprehension of Lizzie's thoughts and feelings is also emphasized. As Lizzie begins to succumb to Eugene's persuasion to be tutored, she remarks, "It's not easy for me to talk to you . . . for you see all the consequences of what I say, as soon as I say it" (237). Some time later the narrator tells us that:

> He knew his power over her . . . For all his seeming levity and carelessness, he knew whatever he chose to know of the thoughts of her heart. (406)

And in this perhaps lies his most seductive power over her, and simultaneously the key to his reformation; it will lead to the unlocking of his capacity for empathy and a love based upon a deep understanding. (In this he has his greatest advantage over his would-be rival, Bradley Headstone, who offers not empathic love, but blind obsession.)

Ambiguity surrounds Eugene's motives regarding Lizzie, and the question of whether his intentions are virtuous but unrecognizable to him, or whether his intentions simply change in the course of the novel is not entirely resolved. It is , however, important to point out that a secret or buried benevolence is *NOT* generally implied in Eugene's interactions with other characters. He is not "secretly good" (like Boffin) throughout. Dickens explicitly describes Eugene's failures of sympathy, carefully portraying its slow awakening in him. three small incidents neatly describe Eugene's evolution. Eugene observes an ugly scene between Jenny Wren and her father:

> "There!" said Miss Wren, covering her eyes with her hand. I can't bear to look at you. Go up-stairs and get me my bonnet and shawl. Make yourself useful in some way, bad boy, and let me have your room instead of your company, for one half-minute."
> Obeying her, he shambled out, and Eugene Wrayburn saw the tears exude from between the little creature's fingers as she kept her hand before her eyes. He was sorry, but his sympathy did not move his carelessness to do anything but feel sorry." ((533)

Some two hundred pages later, after Eugene has followed Lizzie to her hiding-place at the paper mill, he registers her mounting distress at his presence and persistence:

> He looked at her with a real sentiment of remorseful tenderness and pity. It was not strong enough to impel him to sacrifice himself and spare her, but it was a strong emotion. (692)

Shortly thereafter, Eugene confesses his love for Lizzie, and she, convinced that it can bring only ruin to her, begs him to leave her alone. His response is:

> "I will try."
> As he spoke the words in a grave voice, she put her hand in his, removed it, and went away by the river-side.
> "Now, could Mortimer believe this?" murmured Eugene, still remaining, after a while, where she had left him. "Can I even believe it myself?"
> He referred to the circumstance that there were tears upon his hand, as he stood covering his eyes. "A most ridiculous position this, to be found out in!" was his next thought. and his next struck its root in a little rising resentment against the cause of the tears. (696)

Eugene's tears, along with his costly brief retort: "I will try" describe his achievement of genuine sympathy. His "next thought," of the ridiculousness of his position, discloses the troubling effect of self-consciousness upon sincerity. His virtue is not deflated by his knowledge of it as such, but by his mental habit of self-distancing, his irony — a very differently aimed irony than Arthur Clennam's. As noted, Dickens allows his characters, at the end of his career, far more self-scrutiny than in his early novels. It is no longer the narrator — as in the case of Little Nell — who asks all the difficult questions about self-interested motives, but the characters themselves who puzzle through their own motives, trying to work their way through the maze of their own deepest desires. The gap between motives and consciousness that Dickens once used to preserve and negotiate virtue is here being filled by characters' self-scrutiny, and the very nature of feelings and their relation to virtue is, as we would suspect, strongly impacted.

Eugene's ironic self-consciousness, his inability to rest comfortably with his own earnestness, seems to call the very notion of sincerity into question. How does sincerity survive the intrusion of a skeptical self-awareness? Lionel Trilling's definition of sincerity as the "congruence between avowal and actual feeling" (Sincerity 2). points to an assumption about the simplicity or directness in the relation between feelings and our experience of them. We find that such mental processes as self-consciousness or reflection upon one's feelings are left out of Trilling's equation. Sincerity, he suggests, is a fragile system, one which we find is difficult to sustain in a narrative where characters feel and react self-consciously. Once Dickens gives his characters room to reflect upon their feelings, sincerity is shifted slightly off balance; the "sincerity" seems now to require a kind of leap of faith with regard to one's motives. In addition, a new channel has opened in Dickens's representation of the workings of love; it is reflected in Eugene's "rising resentment" against Lizzie and in a surprising description of Lizzie's response to his declaration of love:

> She had not been prepared for such passionate expressions, and they awakened some natural sparks of feminine pride and joy in her breast, To consider, wrong as he was, that he could care so much for her, and that she had the power to move him so! (692–93)

We might deduce that self-scrutiny has swept away the old ethic and promise of selflessness; now this lack of pure selflessness is regarded by Dickens, not as a taint to virtue, but as a factor of love that calls for recognition in order for love to be fully realized.

Selflessness is no longer the road, for Dickens, to virtue, and sympathy itself has become the subject of serious reconceptualization. We have come a long way from the notions that involuntary feelings are virtuous, that virtuous feelings are unconscious, and that self-interested feelings — in virtuous characters — must remain unrecognized. Even desires are now allowed entry into the consciousness of Dickens's virtuous characters, and they sometimes receive narratorial acknowledgement as well, but of course they must be *sincere* desires, and this notion is, happily, left unassailed.

In his early novels, Dickens's consistently moralistic treatment of the emotional life may in part be attributed to the demands of plot. In his first, unplotted narrative, *The Pickwick Papers* (1836–37), a benevolence prevails that recalls especially Smollett in whose novels a less "moralistic benevolence" is described. In *Oliver Twist* (1837–38), *Nicholas Nickleby* (1838–39), and *The Old Curiosity Shop* (1840–41) he seems to have adopted the logic and rhetoric of moral philosophy to suit the didactic principles that helped him to organize his novels, to construct his plots. Every reader feels in these highly moralized renderings of motive a conscious protection of what Dickens takes to be goodness, an expression of his understanding of its demands. What Dickens takes to be goodness is constructed with tools provided by a moral psychology that loses its hold on him over time, and which his more evolved narrative ambitions lead him to shed.

IN HIS FINAL completed novel, Dickens offers a revised perspective on the egoism-altriusm debate. We find in the American philosopher John Dewey's *Psychology* (1891) a reformulation of the polemic that seems closest to Dickens's own:

> There are sometimes said to be two distinct *kinds* of feeling for persons; one, feelings for self, egoistic or personal feelings, properly so called; the other, feelings for others, or altruistic or social feelings. This division supposes that, in the first place, feelings belong to our own limited individuality, and are considered only as they affect one's immediate self, but may afterwards be extended to include other individuals. It overlooks the necessary *reciprocal* relations of egoistic and altruistic feelings. There can be no egoistic feelings except as the self is distinguished from others and set over against them; there

can be no altruistic feelings, except as others are recognized in their relations to self, and compared with it. Our first feelings are not personal, in the sense of egoistic.[29]

Dewey underscores the radically individualistic conception of motive offered by the traditional rhetoric of the egoism / altruism debates, of individuals each pre-equipped with a moral faculty oriented first (in some odd temporality) toward self, and then toward others, or vice versa. He attempts to break down the very terms of the debate, to lend them a dialectical aspect and to show up the idiosyncratic conception of self implied by such terms. Dewey adds,

> Personal feelings are such as *arise from the relations of self-conscious beings to each other*. All feeling is the accompaniment of self-realization. No individual can realize himself in impersonal relations — relations of things to each other or to an ideal.'' (282)

Eighteenth- and nineteenth-century discussions of the emotions inherit the discourse of a speculative psychology which, as Amélie Rorty observes, was conceived as a foundation for an idealized epistemology.[30] Dewey moves against this idealized model of psychological functions and toward a more dynamic one. It will be some time before the role of consciousness, let alone that of the unconscious, begins to permeate English psychological writing,[31] but the novel, in its very form and narrative operations has broken from the psychological premises of moral philosophy in its renderings of the workings of the emotions. In his handling of Eugene Wrayburn, Dickens has moved farther from Adam Smith and closer to Freud, who writes:

> In every case . . . the news that reaches your consciousness is incomplete and often not to be relied on. Often enough, too, it happens that you get news of events only when they are over and when you can no longer do anything to change them. Even if you are not ill, who can tell all that is stirring in your mind of which you know nothing or are falsely informed? You behave like an absolute ruler who is content with the information supplied him by his highest officials and never goes among the people to hear their voice. Turn your eyes inward, look into your own depths, learn first to know yourself.[32]

Columbia University

NOTES

1. Adam Smith, *The Theory of Moral Sentiments*, eds. A. L. Macfie and D. D. Raphael (New York: Oxford UP, 1979) 303. Smith may here refer to the following passage in Hutcheson's *An Essay of the Nature and Conduct of the Passions and Affections*:

Some alledge, that Merit supposes, beside *kind Affection*, that the Agent has a *moral sense*, *reflects* upon his own Virtue, *delights* in it, and *chuses* to adhere to it for the *Pleasure* which attends it.* (*See Lord *Shaftesbury's Inquiry concerning Virtue. Part I.*) We need not debate the Use of this Word *Merit*: it is plain, we *approve* a generous kind Action, tho' the Agent had not made this *Reflection*. This Reflection shews to him a Motive of Self-Love, the joint View to which does not increase our *Approbation*. 305, facsimile reproduction of third edition, 1742, (first edition published in 1728) (Gainesville, Fla.: Scholars' Facsimiles and Reprints, 1969)

2. Into the category of those who recognize their desires and attempt to fulfill them promptly fall most of the unhappy lovers in Dickens's canon. There is David in his love for Dora, Pip in his love for Estella, Ada and Richard Carstone, and Arthur Clennam in his attraction to Pet Meagles which will be examined in this paper. Dickens conveys his own rather complicated ideas about how rewards work in relation to recognized or declared desires and goals. It is not strictly that delayed gratification is more meritorious; rather, simply being aware of our motives, even virtuous ones, seems to remind Dickens of the potential Machiavelli in each of us.

3. From precisely this emphasis upon intention as opposed to consequence follows the logic of the stepladder of homicide charges in our criminal justice systems, from murder one to manslaughter, to homicidal negligence, etc. A separate but related matter is that of the distance in Dickens — or lack of distance — between good intentions and actual consequences. Dickens's failure to reckon with the pitfalls that can separate the former from the latter has led to the common criticism of sentimentality. Orwell complains that Dickens seems persuaded that a "change of heart" is all that is needed to improve the world, and that he doesn't, therefore, seriously address the question of social change. This is, I would argue, a feature of Dickens's early work alone, where much that is unintended by characters is expressed and projected out into the world, but what *is* intended generally achieves its aim. In *Bleak House* (1853), Dickens presents his first full-blown rendering of how it is no longer the case that intentions are not compromised, waylaid or distorted upon contact with the world.

4. Much critical attention has been devoted to Dickens's own responses to Romanticism. Recent book-length studies include Lawrence Frank's *Charles Dickens and the Romantic Self* (Lincoln: U of Nebraska P, 1984). Frank proposes that Dickens works with a conception of character that links him to Hume, Rousseau, and Freud, in what he argues is their common Romantic deconstruction of selfhood. Self-ideation and self-narration are explored by Frank as the infrastructure of modern identity, In *Dickens and Romantic Psychology: The Self in Time in Nineteenth-Century Literature* (New York: St. Martin's, 1987), Dirk den Hartog treats Dickens's responses to what he terms Wordsworth's idea of "self-continuity," as well as Wordsworth's treatment of the Romantic opposition of the Promethean and the Stoic. In Dickens, he argues, we find "simultaneously a positive valuing of the subversive and anarchic and an ennoblement of repression as the necessary cost of survival in the struggle of life" (34).

5. Here I am indebted to Lionel Trilling's *Sincerity and Authenticity*, originally delivered at the Charles Eliot Norton Lectures, 1970, and later published by Harvard UP, Cambridge, 1972; especially chapter 6, "The Authentic Unconscious."

6. Dickens's characterization of Silas Wegg in *Our Mutual Friend* as an "impos- ter" — and not a hypocrite — is interesting to note in this connection. Of Wegg the narrator says: "His gravity was unusual, portentous, and immeasurable, not because he admitted any doubt of himself, but because he perceived it necessary to forestall any doubt of himself in others. And herein he ranged with that very numerous class of imposters, who are quite as determined to keep up appearances to themselves, as to their neighbors" (*OMF* 53).

7. On the face of it, this logic would land Romanticism and Freudianism squarely on the egoistic side of the debate, but such is the power of rhetoric that in Romanticism we see the "selfish" drives fashioned into "natural" and therefore "innocent" ones (or sometimes we see in such urges a revolutionary, cleansing fire). Freud, like Darwin before him, moves to sunder what he conceives to be the biological (or instinctive) from the moral realm. Freud's program is less confounded than Darwin's thanks to Hegel's distinction between formal and empirical conditions for experience. Freud also assumes the categories of reflex action and higher thought processes, which Darwin does not. For a discussion of Hegel's transformation of the Kantian unity of science and its impact on emotion theory, see Amélie Oksenberg Rorty, *Mind in Action: Essays in the Philosophy of Mind* (Boston: Beacon Press, 1988), especially "Mind in Action, Action in Context," 1–21.

8. One detects in this passage the notion that while reasons are aim oriented, emo- tions are reactive. See also Alfred Adler's contributions to the symposium, "Feel- ings and Emotions from the Standpoint of Individual Psychology," in which he makes the case that emotions too are aim-oriented. *Feelings and Emotions; the Wittenberg Symposium*, ed. Martin Reymert. Part of the International University Series in Psychology, ed. Carl Murchison (Worcester, Massachusetts: Clark UP, 1928) 24.

9. This is also the logic of literary symbolism — in which the most determining meaning/idea is never stated overtly, only pointed to over and over.

10. One could certainly make a case, although I've not found one, for the idea that in the theory of association, identified with Locke, Berkeley, Hartley, Brown and J. S. Mill, a nascent conception of the unconscious is detectable, that our individ- ual systems of analogy and contiguity, involuntary in nature, perform a function similar to that of the Freudian unconscious.

11. David Hume, *A Treatise of Human Nature*, 2nd ed., ed. L. A. Selby-Bigge (Ox- ford: Oxford UP, 1978) 414.

12. The term "unconscious" appears in Bain's *The Emotions and the Will*, but it refers exclusively to the "suspension of all faculties." (See 539fn) Two English physicians, Thomas Laycock and W. B. Carpenter, in their studies of the brain and the nervous system, defined a separate sphere of mental activity where forgotten memories and impressions are stored and can be recalled by reflex action. See Laycock's *Mind and Brain* (London: Simpkin Marshall, 1859) and Carpenter's *Principles of Mental Physiology* (New York: Appleton, 1884). The thinker most commonly credited with propounding a pre-Freudian theory of the unconscious was Mesmer (1734–1815), whose ideas were of great practical interest to Dickens. For Mesmer's importance in the history of the unconscious, see especially, chap- ter 2 of H. F. Ellenberger's *The Discovery of the Unconscious: The History and Evolution of Dynamic Psychiatry* (New York: Basic Books, 1970), and chapter 11 of D. N. Robinson's *An Intellectual History of Psychology* (Madison: U of Wisconsin P, 1986). For Dickens's attachment to Mesmerism as, intermittently,

a favoured therapeutic resource, see Fred Kaplan's *Dickens and Mesmerism: The Hidden Springs of Fiction* (Princeton: Princeton UP, 1975).

13. In Book II, chapter XXI of *Little Dorrit*, Dickens again speaks in a female voice, this time that of Miss Wade. Her narration takes the form of a letter addressed to Arthur Clennam. As a letter-writer, the narrating Miss Wade has less to account for than has Esther.

14. The term "meritorious" is Dickens's. In his outline for *Bleak House*, at the conclusion of chapter 24, Dickens writes: "Esther's love must be kept in view, to make the coming trial the greater and the victory more meritorious." (Dickens's outline is reproduced in the Penguin edition, ed. Norman Page, 1971, 937–53.)

15. Note here Dickens's extravagant use of exclamation points. No other of his narrators is so equipped, and for Esther they have a complicated tonal effect, as she manages, through her emphases, to mock her own narrative authority, calling repeated and surprised attention to her own assertion-making. While the syntax records her diminutiveness, hesitancy and girlishness, the exclamation points introduce an odd self-consciousness that reflects neither irony nor conviction.

16. From the time of the novel's original publication, critics have expressed their displeasure with Esther's coyness. In 1853, George Brimly commented: "His heroine in *Bleak House* is a model of unconscious goodness; . . . her unconsciousness and sweet humility of disposition are so profound that scarcely a page of her autobiography is free from a record of these admirable qualities" (*The Spectator*, 24 September 1853, 26, 923–25). James Augustine Stothert similarly observed, "as to Esther Summerson, the angelic, self-forgetting young lady, who notes in her journal every thing that a self-forgetting mind would not note, we have found her a prodigious bore, whom we wish the author had consigned to the store-room the moment she was fairly in possession of her housekeeping keys. The manner in which this lady is made to chronicle her own merits, is a proof how unable Dickens is to enter into the real *depths* of a human mind . . ." (*The Rambler*, January, 1854, n.s. i, 41–51). Both are republished in *Dickens: The Critical Heritage*, ed. Philip Collins; London: Routledge and Kegan Paul, 1971 (285, 295). Michael Slater, in *Dickens and Women* (London: J. M. Dent & Sons, 1983), takes an altogether different view of Esther's coyness:

> What is objected to as intolerable coyness on Esther's part — her self-deprecating flutterings . . . — can be taken as very authentic-sounding mimicry of the accents of a certain kind of neurosis, the kind in which the sufferer is always struggling with a crushing sense of his or her own total worthlessness and is virtually paralysed with regard to any conscious assertion of personal needs, desires, beliefs, and feelings. (256)

17. Early in the novel, Esther describes the conditions of her childhood:

> "I was brought up, from my earliest remembrance . . . by my godmother. At least I only knew her as such. She was a good, good woman! She went to church three times every Sunday, and to morning prayers on Wednesday and Fridays, and to lectures whenever there were lectures; and never missed. . . . She was so very good herself, I thought, that the badness of other people made her frown all her life. I felt so different from her . . . I felt so poor, so trifling, and so far off; that I . . . could never even love her as I wished. . . . I never loved my godmother as

I ought to have loved her, and as I felt I must have loved her if I had been a better girl." (*BH* 15)

Through Esther's obliqueness, the portrait is conveyed to the reader of a cold and sanctimonious godmother (later revealed to be Esther's aunt) who repels the love of a restrained child desperate to give love and be loved. The reader is clued to understand that this portrait of her godmother is not consciously or intentionally produced by Esther, neither the child-Esther nor the narrating Esther who, of course, is fully aware of her aunt's blameworthiness. Esther praises where the reader is meant to cast blame because, we understand, she is unwilling to speak bitterly or judge on her own behalf. In having Esther present her own virtues as failings, and the aunt's failings as virtues Dickens is recognizing and perhaps exploiting the pathos of the child's tendency to blame herself for the treatment she receives. Whether Esther here simulates her own childhood perspective, or whether the adult Esther is equally unable or unwilling to pass judgement, the reader is meant to see neither mendacity nor hypocrisy in her obfuscation.

18. In her article, "Charlotte Dickens: The Female Narrator of *Bleak House*" (*Dickens Quarterly*, June, 1992 47–57), Anny Sadrin provides a survey of recent critical intolerance of Esther's coyness. Noting alternative readings that, like Slater's, attribute Esther's narrative strategies to her "neurotic character" — the result of a traumatic childhood — Sadrin contends that the "negation, understatement and equivocation" that mark Esther's style would be read very differently by critics if the novel's author had been a woman. Her "stylistic awkwardness," she argues, would then be attributed to her predicament as an authoress struggling to assert herself. She credits Dickens, not for his portrayal of an authentic neurotic, but for his valiant effort to enter into the crippling anxieties that a woman such as Esther would have experienced in trying to write her own story.

19. Mackenzie's stated ambition, of evoking the sympathetic tears of his readers, as a kind of moral and emotional exercise, have been examined by Janet Todd in her book *Sensibility: An Introduction*. See especially the section "Instruction" in chapter 4. (London: Methuen, 1986). For a treatment of "The Pleasures of Pity," see A. O. Aldridge's essay by that name, *ELH* 16, 1949, 76–87.

20. In accounting for motives, "seduced virtue" poses some special problems for Mackenzie. In perhaps the only instance where he must account for an internal change undergone by a character, in the narrative of the prostitute, he establishes certain causal determinants that are not found elsewhere. In her account, blame is layed not only on the deceiving seducer, but also on her father, whose military-secular morality overpowered the religious values inculcated by her deceased mother.

21. Letter dated 8 July 1769. Quoted in Brian Vickers's Introduction to *The Man of Feeling* xii.

22. These figures are supplied by Brian Vickers in his Introduction to *The Man of Feeling*. Harold W. Thompson, in his biography of Mackenzie, writes: "The facts, so far as I have been able to learn them under the circumstances, are that *The Man of Feeling* has had at least 30 separate editions in Britain, Ireland, and the United States, exclusive of publication in editions of Mackenzie's more or less complete Works, which have appeared in at least 16 editions; this gives us the respectable total of 46 editions in English of whose existence I am certain." *A Scottish Man of Feeling*, (London: Oxford U P, 1931) 152.

23. The narrative technique of quoted interior monologue became conventional, Dorrit Cohn points out, only as late as the middle of the nineteenth century. In the early history of the novel the narrator's omniscience did not, Cohn helps us realize, include a naturalized exploration of characters' thoughts. Although Cohn does not choose to conjecture about what might have stimulated the technical innovations she so wonderfully describes and categories, she paves the way for such a study. Cf. Dorrit Cohn, *Transparent Minds: Narrative Modes for Presenting Consciousness in Fiction* (Princeton: Princeton U P, 1978).

24. The theme introduced here by the idea of absence and the use of the word "nobody," permeates *Little Dorrit*, from the most personal self-abdications to the largest social failures of authority and responsibility. Dickens's Circumlocution Office carries not only a critique of bureaucracy in the abstract, but of the specific and tragic bureaucratic bungling of the Home Office over the course of the Crimean War. The suicide of the fraudulent financier, Merdle, brings the theme of unaccountability to the economic sphere, and points to the need for a stepped-up limited liability act to protect small investors. Dickens's original title for *Little Dorrit* was an ironic one, *Nobody's Fault*.

25. Does Clennam's knowledge, his conscious relation to his feelings, distinguish his desire for Pet from similar emotional errors by others of Dickens's male protagionists? We recall David Copperfield's love for Dora or Pip's for Estella. Such blunders are, for these characters, steps on the road to self-knowledge, to the disciplining of the heart; they describe the development from wrong-desire to right-love. Dickens's heroes are allowed to love unwisely; their romantic feelings are not necessarily indices to virtue. *Finding* their truest and worthiest feelings is at the center of their quests.

26. Clennam's plot is largely motivated by his need to identify and correct some wrong he senses his part in but cannot precisely locate. This idea is reinforced by the letters D.N.F. (Do Not Forget) embroidered on a piece of cloth inserted in his father's watch. Clennam's feelings of free-floating culpability are tied to the novel's themes in a double sense; his guilt is his paternal inheritance in this world where weak and infantilized fathers are everywhere evading responsibility, and Clennam's mission to cast light upon "the shadow of a supposed act of injustice, which hung over him since his father's death" (*LD*, 319) represents his isolated willingness to allow the repressed to return, and, in the novel's terms, to be *at fault*. Clennam becomes a kind of Christ-figure, suffering for the sins of others when he decides to reveal the full measure of his insolvency following the collapse of the Merdle empire and the subsequent ruin of Clennam's small business. Merdle's suicide leaves a public ruined and enraged with nowhere to lay the blame. He is warned that "such a declaration as Clennam's, made at such a time, would certainly draw down upon him a storm of animosity . . . exposing him a solitary target to a straggling cross-fire, which might bring him down from half-a-dozen quarters at once." (*LD* 716) To this Clennam replies: "I must take the consequences of what I have done" (717). The themes of guilt, revelation, and responsibility are woven so closely together in this novel that the idea of responsibility seems to have merged with that of culpability.

27. David Hume, *Enquiries Concerning Human Understanding and Concerning the Principles of Morals*, 3rd ed., ed. L. A. Selby-Bigge, Oxford; Oxford UP, 1975.

28. I am quoting Philip Rieff's characterization of what he terms Freudianism's advantage over less dialectical psychologies. *Freud: The Mind of the Moralist* (Chicago: U of Chicago P, 1959) 54.

29. John Dewey, *Psychology*, 3rd rev. ed., in *The Early Works of John Dewey, 1882–1898* (Carbondale: Southern Illinois UP, 1967) 281–82.
30. Rorty argues that contemporary discussions of the emotions continue to "suffer from their inheritance" from eighteenth-century moral philosophy. "Distinctions between the faculties," she writes, "were designed to substantiate the possibility of an autonomously self-corrective rationality, not only capable of correcting beliefs and inferences, but also (at least in principle) capable of correcting irrational desires and emotions. In this idealized model of psychological activities, the emotions were an embarrassment: on the one hand, they were treated as noncognitive invasions or disturbances; on the other, they were sometimes treated as sound motivational functions, susceptible to a program of rational reform or correction." Amélie Rorty, *Mind* 101.
31. William McDougall's *An Introduction to Social Psychology* (1908) contains a chapter entitled "The Growth of Self-Consciousness and of the Self-Regarding Sentiment" in which he argues: "We cannot consent . . . to escape the difficulty of the problem [of the origins of moral feeling] by accepting any such false assumption as to the normal constitution of human nature, but must seek its solution in the development of the self-regarding sentiment" (65). McDougall contends that the highest developmental stage of human and social conduct is "regulated by an ideal of conduct that enables a man to act in the way that *seems to him* right regardless of the praise or blame of his immediate social environment." (my emphasis) He argues for the importance of "positive self-feeling" as an inducement to moral action, drawing a distinction between "pride" and "self-respect." His developmental account of the growth of the individual's moral capacity bears a resemblance to that later described by Freud as the internalization of the super-ego. See chapter 4, *An Introduction to Social Psychology* (London: Methuen, 1963).
32. Sigmund Freud, "Difficulties of Psychoanalysis" (1917), *Character and Culture*, ed. Philip Rieff (New York: Macmillan, 1963) 189.

PROFESSING RENUNCIATION: DOMESTICITY IN *THE CLOISTER AND THE HEARTH* AND *FELIX HOLT*

By Monica F. Cohen

IT IS ESPECIALLY in connection with George Eliot's work that a brief look at Charles Reade's popular 1861 novel, *The Cloister and the Hearth*, yields a crucial paradigm for Victorian novelistic domesticity. Based on a section of Erasmus's *Compendium* in which the late medieval scholar narrates the history of his parents' courtship and quasi-legitimate marriage *The Cloister and the Hearth* situates the idea of the Home formally in a tale of vocational choice and historically at the heart of the Protestant Reformation.[1] Set in fifteenth-century Holland, Charles Reade's widely acclaimed novel[2] opens when Gerard Eliassoen surrenders his plan of "going into the Church" (5) so that he might marry instead, a decision his family vehemently opposes since Gerard's ecclesiastical career would have provided them with a primary source of income. Betrothed but not yet married to the beloved Margaret, Gerard must quit his Dutch homeland and hearth for Rome. The novel's laborious, quasi-episodic yarn is thus initiated by Gerard's search for the Roman education that would turn his monk-taught skills in penmanship and manuscript illumination into an artistic career by which he might support his now pregnant wife, her father, and a variety of "friends" who have found their way into his household.

After a series of tedious travel anecdotes and picaresque complications, Gerard reaches Rome where he is tricked into believing that Margaret has died. Near despair, he attempts suicide, is saved, enters one of the ubiquitous monasteries that the novel sprinkles along each of its European highways, and finally becomes a Dominican priest sporting a new name, Clement. Due to Clement's oratory talents, the Roman monastery sends him to England, a nation humorously renowned on the novel's continent for its stiff-necked audience. Before crossing the Channel, however, Clement encounters Margaret in Rotterdam, realizes that he had fallen victim to a plot, abandons the journey and confines himself to the Hermit of Gouda's cave, there assuming the hermit's cloistered career of solitude. Margaret, having spent the intervening years supporting a family (that, due to her irresistible charm, now includes Gerard's once disapproving blood kin) by free-lance laundering and adjunct sewing, coaxes the "satanophobic" Clement out of his hermitage by invoking a remarkably Protestant argument: "She showed him," the narrator marvels, "in her own good straightforward Dutch, that his present life was only a higher kind of selfishness, spiritual egotism" (649). Returning him to the community domiciled in his mother's house, Margaret forces him to "eat a good nourishing meal" and rest in "a snowy bed" so that he soon awakes "as from a hideous dream, friar and hermit no more, Clement no more, but Gerard Eliassoen, parson of Gouda" (653), his literal and spiritual homecoming, almost like Lucy Snowe's Auld Lang Syne awakening, thus marked by the falling away of his Roman Catholic delusions as he accepts the connotatively Protestant title of "parson."

Here the novel dilates a peculiar kind of happy ending that lasts for nearly a quarter of the whole story:

> History itself, though a far more daring story teller than romance, presents a few things so strange as the footing on which Gerard and Margaret now lived for many years. United by present affection, past familiarity, and a marriage irregular, but legal; separated by holy Church and by their own consciences which sided unreservedly with holy Church: separated by the Church, but united by a living pledge of affection, lawful in every sense at its date. (660)

History and romance having converged in the "footing" that constitutes Gerard and Margaret's final condition, the couple is depicted at work on negotiating a marriage — what one of Reade's historicizing footnotes calls the "legal betrothal" of an engagement. Their marital home requires such work because, though recognized as legitimate, it must nonetheless be integrated into an ecclesiastical career that is by definition built on its renunciation. Through paired participle phrases linked by a coordinating conjunction, Gerard and Margaret's "footing" seems to require performing a difficult balancing act. Composed in this way of matched predicates pivoting on a "but" axle, each semi-colon-bracketed sentence fragment conveys the sense in which oppositionary tension effects a balance that preserves stasis through a series of concessions, or compromised positions: together but separated, apart from the Church but a part of it, Gerard and Margaret are married but not married. In this way, the passage's syntactical patterning suggests that typical of the domestic situation is a degree of delicate brokering.

This frustrating state of events is important in two ways. From a reader's perspective, such an unlucky twist of events, though based on a historical chronicle, feels embarrassingly cumbersome, the protracted final situation narratively unhinged and aesthetically overwrought: thus it is nearly impossible to avoid hoping that Reade might stage the Reformation at an earlier date as Luther is most clearly the novel's awaited deus ex machina. And in this sense, the Dutch home that so boldly hoards the novel's sympathies, the home whose difficulties would be solved by such a historical imposition, reveals a clearly Protestant disposition. Secondly and more interestingly, however, the novel's relentless artificiality seems generated primarily by a central motivating principle: a need to illustrate the experience of renunciation. Thus wheresoever Gerard turns, he cannot escape renouncing, whether it is the hearth for which he took a marital oath or the priesthood that extracted as powerful a vow.

I should point out here that the novel's diluted Protestantism and heightened degree of artifice may be related. The connection can be seen in how critics describe the popular reception of *The Cloister and the Hearth* among nineteenth-century Englishmen. That Victorians saw in Reade's novel a spiritualization of human life according to a Protestant tradition surfaces in the commonly evoked analogy between the Victorian novel and Dutch and Flemish art. In analyzing Reade's nineteenth-century appeal, for example, Elton Smith ends up explaining the Victorians' taste for Dutch interiors:

> Reade felt quite free to embellish the "musty chronicle" of Erasmus's *Compendium* with fresh motivation, with historical or semi-historical characters, and with complications of plot. In a way, the plot reveals the incredible clutter of his notebooks; but this Victorian failing significantly compares with the Flemish school of painting, which also exulted in exotic possessions such as maps, rugs, pitchers, and flamboyant textures of material. . . . A contemporary journal pointed out the relationship between a Nativity painting by Hans Memling (one of the historical figures introduced for a moment in the burgeoning cast) and the narrative art of Charles Reade. (Smith 143)

Smith implies that Protestant art-forms like Reade's novel humanize the divine; Gerard's reconstructed spiritual family thus becomes a humanized representation of Christian archetypal figures. But when one examines the excerpt Smith cites, it turns out that what the *Blackwood's* reviewer liked so much was how the divinity of Mother and Child is conveyed by a proliferation of background material (Smith 143–44) — superfluous visual details in the painting and extraneous plotlines in the narrative: that is, clutter. It would appear from the context in which such clutter is treasured that the appeal of Dutch and Flemish interiors to Victorians derived not so much from any celebration of material ownership, but from the humanizing of holy ideas to which such material details can be seen to contribute, a subtle but important distinction. Moreover what is peculiarly interesting is that the Victorian reviewer here does not see the numerous things of an interior scene as corresponding simply to the realistic details of the novel's descriptions but rather to its multitudinous narrative conventions and structures: Reade's "infinite variety of scenes," his "paths innumerable" (Smith 144). Whereas the evocations and allusions that so many Victorian domestic novels, particularly George Eliot's, make to Dutch painting is usually ascribed to the commodified nature of the two cultures, the more essential source of attraction appears in the review to be the dispersion of energy each form (genre painting and novel alike) enacts. Rather than focussing on the single figure or groups of figures, Dutch interior painting effects a humanization of religious themes through a deflected lens whereby significance can radiate from a variety of sources. The English novel can be said to develop a comparable structure: as Dorothea Brooke's energies follow a network of rivulets instead of a single current, so do English novels seem to shy away from a concentrated single plot in favor of various melodramatic coincidental story lines. The question should be asked to what extent such dispersion, as a formal characteristic, can be traced to Protestant conceptual paradigms.

Significantly, it is out of Gerard and Margaret's irregular marital condition that the home rises, through a particularly resonant metonymy, as a figure for sociable and societal work: for when Gerard persuades his "wife" to "warm [her]self at the fire that warmeth [him]" by joining him in public service, his metaphor deposits the novel's hearth squarely in Margaret's new job of managing the small district of "twenty housen" (Reade 668), a situation in which the connubial pair are featured as "two saints which meet in secret to plot charity to the poor" and the final home as "a large Xenodochium to receive the victims of flood or fire" (669). In this sense, the renunciative condition that constitutes Gerard and Margaret's happy-home ending evinces the same values that Brontë and Dickens show as proper to domesticity: nonpersonal sociability and spiritually animated work.[3] This is especially evident in Gerard and Margaret's concluding collaboration on the "Xenodochium," a term which, obsolete by the early part of the twentieth century, appears surprisingly common in Victorian historical and archaeological chronicles as designating "A house of reception for strangers and pilgrims" and, as some of the citations indicate, for paupers and needy travellers (OED). Although the term's nineteenth-century popularity can be ascribed to any number of cultural developments — increased travel, increased interest in ancient history and archaeological exploration, increased use of Greek-derived vocabulary, etc. — it is interesting to note in the context of my argument an increased awareness of the Xenodochium as a kind of institution — an asylum or home — whose traces Victorian historiographers claimed to find in the remains of Greek settlements and Medieval monasteries. Thus the *OED*'s citations record attempts to locate Xenodochia of the past ("Many have supposed the xenodochium . . . was placed in this division of the mansion"), to outline the Xenodochium's social function ("Within the precincts of the monastery stood an edifice, distinguished by the Greek name of *Xenodochium*, in which a certain number of paupers received their daily support, and which was gratuitously opened to every traveller who solicited relief"), and to establish it as part of the English contemporary religious inheritance ("Long before the era of persecution had closed, the hospital and the Xenodochion, or refuge for strangers, was known among Christians").

It would seem then from the finale's evocation of a prototypical public housing project and from the metaphorical warmth that such social service fires exude that the novel means to move toward a synthesis between the career and the home. The title's dyad, for instance, and its varied repetition in the novel's three types of chapter titles, "The Cloister," "The Hearth" and "The Cloister and the Hearth" suggest both an antonymic and synonymic relationship for the "career" represented in the cloister and the "home" figured in the hearth. Is the hearth an alternative to the cloister or is the spatial referent both a cloister and a hearth — a meeting of ways, one professional and one domestic, at a kind of crossroads of social work? After all, in the reader's anachronistic wait for such an incisive intrusion of history as the Protestant Reformation, patience for the story's overly contrived personal dilemma wanes. Thus the urge to immerse the self in depersonalized enterprises like social service becomes an increasingly pressing readerly matter.

In this sense, the contortions the plot must perform in order to effect and preserve Gerard and Margaret's renunciatory condition — forged letters, servant foul-ups, evil brother machinations, tavern antics, religious epiphanies, competitive love triangles, the expansion of the printing press into southern Europe, the patronage of Van Eyck's sister (and the list goes on) — serve a purpose other than fueling anti-Popish propaganda. For by engendering what starts to look like what I would call a perversities of renunciation, the plot throws the idea of the selfless life into center court. Faulty as it is, *The Cloister and the Hearth* is therefore interesting in terms of how its depiction of Gerard and Margaret's concluding home, their state of renouncement, departs from the tradition of Tragic genres in which renunciation involves a choice between two incompatible ideals or desires. Exposing the narrative's willingness to go to any length so as to preserve the renunciative condition, Reade's encrusted plot and a byzantine array of narrative devices evidence a structural desire for the selfless state; such awkward pyrotechnics can ultimately be seen as working to mystify any notion of self-sacrifice by focusing on its desirability as a purportedly but perhaps impossibly nonpersonal objective.

Felix Holt *and the Selfless Career*

KEEPING IN MIND the peculiar arrangement of conceptual touchstones that *The Cloister and the Hearth*'s failings divulge, *Felix Holt* can be seen as similarly linking what Felix himself labels his "inward vocation" (367) to an idea of renunciation: in devoting his "life" — as he calls his chosen career path — to the hardly concrete objective of reforming "public opinion" (401), Felix enters the novel as a self-appointed emblem of vocational devotion. Indeed Esther idealizes Felix as the apogee of all "nobleness of character" exclusively in terms of his willingness to "renounce all small selfish motives for the sake of a great and unselfish one" (537). It is therefore no accident that the substitutive symmetry in Esther's pronouncement here, in equating "motives" with "one," avoids specifying that which is "great and unselfish" in the shape of any concrete ideal, work or project, as if the value of vocational devotion stems more from the fact of devotion than from either its contents or its products. The logic of Esther's syntax suggests, moreover, that what Felix actually acquires through his unspecified acts of renunciation is not a deed done, but a "motive"; her grammar intimates that renunciation not only precedes motives, but somehow confers it, motive thus rising as a sign of ennoblement but renunciation featured as its agent.

It would seem then that renunciation does not describe what Felix does so much as it surfaces in the novel as a presence — and a presence valued precisely as a generator of value. Valuable and valuating, its status is curiously complex. For as the slippery idiom, "for the sake of" indicates, the activity of renouncing not only presides over the exchange of small motives *for* the great unselfish one (whatever that may be), but acts *on behalf of* the great unselfish motive — is, in this sense, a substitute for it. Because the "for the sake of" formula yields a notion of renouncing that encompasses the sense of a verb as well as of a noun, renunciation appears to operate as both agency and property, means as well as ends. By thus foregrounding the priority of renunciation in the novel's representation of vocational election, Esther's encomium positions renunciation as the key term in a Victorian vocabulary that fixes on work as a conceptual arena where the meaningfulness of individual life is made manifest.[4] It is therefore not enough to say that work offers a window onto Victorian culture without stressing that there is, at least in George Eliot's novels, an implicit notion of renunciation that invariably qualifies it.

As the *OED* documents, renunciation nearly always entails varying degrees of self-sacrifice. But the list of senses that the *OED* includes provides a repertory for the various permutations that sacrificing a self might take. Thus "renounce" can designate a material divestment as in the formal surrender of the world or of worldly interest "in order to live a spiritual life"; or it can mean, as in Law, the resignation of a right or trust, especially of one's position as heir (and here two of the four citations are taken from George Eliot). But "renounce" can convey an idea of self-sacrifice through an embrace of the worldly as well. In this sense, self-sacrifice can take the shape of abandoning a practice, thought or belief "in open profession" to the world, to the community, or as the disclaiming of a "personal" relationship, usually in the nineteenth century, of a blood kinship.

It follows then that what counts as selfless activity, particularly in the context of how an individual comes to devote him or her self to "a life," emerges as a central complication in the novel's exploration of career and heroism — or what might be called in George Eliot's works, of plot and character. And what her novels structurally and discursively indicate is that it is specifically home life that plays more than simply a participatory role in the battle of conceptual interests whereby individualistic concerns are pitted against socially sanctioned goods. Indeed it is an idea of home that determines how an individual character finds a lifeplot because it is home life that proffers a narrative occasion and evaluative rhetoric for articulating that seemingly paradoxical ideal: the desired selfless career.

A Question of Character: Mr. Lyon's Vocational Crisis

THE FIRST FEW CHAPTERS of *Felix Holt* make this configuration clear in their presentation of Rufus Lyon: for the conventional personal history that backgrounds Lyon's character serves also as a compact paradigm for how domesticity renovates the meaning of vocational selflessness. Thus the central experience of this Dissenting minister's life tells the story of how "marks of a true ministerial vocation" (163) — marks that for Lyon had not only been self-defining, but had provided him with a prestigious job — were overshadowed by another calling — his desire to set up house with a French Catholic woman and her daughter by another man. The difficulty in locating self-sacrifice, and more significantly in conceptualizing personal desire as possibly submerged in the rhetoric of the selfless career rather than in a vocabulary antithetical to it, surfaces when Rufus Lyon resigns his ecclesiastical position in order to take up the domestic mantle by giving Annette and Esther a home:

> Those three years were to Mr Lyon a period of such self-suppression and life in another as few men know. Strange! that the passion for this woman which he felt to have drawn him aside from the right as much as if he had broken the most solemn vows . . . the passion for a being who had no glimpse of his thoughts induced a more thorough renunciation than he had ever known in the time of his complete devotion to his ministerial career. He had no flattery now. . . . The only satisfaction he had was the satisfaction of his tenderness—which meant untiring work, untiring patience, untiring wakefulness. . . .
> (173–74)

That the logistics of Mr Lyon's narrated life posit this home in context with his profession not only invites an equation — however contrapositional — between home and job as both constituting potential occupations or careers, but situates the domestic within a specifically Protestant idea of vocation. That is, Lyon's biographical history represents the apparent opposition between home and profession as more importantly a question of vocational alternative; by stressing that the conflict between home and profession is less an oppositionary relationship than a situation of choice, the Lyon plotline's implied distinction between opposition and alternative allows home life to share the vocabulary not only of professional life but of a spiritually inspired brand of professional life, the Protestant ministry. So it is that Lyon comes to homemaking "as some men have their special genius revealed to them by a tardy concurrence of conditions" (168).[5] So it is that Lyon receives the news of his now Protestant adopted daughter's inheritance as a sign of divine sanction for "the cause of congregational Dissent" (507). So it is that what Lyon finds by building a surrogate household for these virtual strangers is not only that the higher calling is marked by an unexpected coinciding of passion and self-sacrifice — a compound perhaps more superficially recognizable in an ecclesiastical venue — but that there is a sense in which it is the work of homemaking that offers a more thorough fulfillment of such precepts.

By requiring more self-suppression — more renunciation than even his previously "complete" ministerial devotion — Lyon's domestic work in this passage reframes romantic passion and self-gratification as both extracting the price and conferring the privilege of the ultimate sacrifice of self. Thus the gratification home work offers Lyon is more piercing in being less self-centered at the same time that it is more personal: for it is precisely as a consequence of the structural selflessness on which his homemaking rests that Lyon must keep "the satisfaction of his tenderness" to himself, the very category of the personal thereby possible only according to the terms of self-sacrifice. In this way, the passage defines personal satisfaction itself — an experience that would reasonably figure as an objective or result of the domestic work Lyon does — as the work itself: "untiring work, untiring patience, untiring wakefulness." Through anaphorically dilated compounds that yield a sense of active stasis, ongoingness divorced from any idea of progress, and a gerund-accented vision of effort that turns work into a revisitable state of mind or condition of soul, the phrase limns vocational domesticity as what I shall provisionally call a profession — that is, a profession of renunciation.

Domestic Professionalism

TO BE CLEAR, I do not mean to say that homemaking in Victorian England was a profession no different from that of being a surgeon, or lawyer or military officer. But within a historical context, home work does, however, look strikingly similar to the kinds of occupations Victorians were beginning to call "professions." And in fact, the ways in which novels like *Felix Holt* depict homemaking suggest that it can be clearly seen as participating in what Burton Bledstein has identified as a nineteenth-century Anglo-American "culture of professionalism" — a concept which provides the terms for recognizing professionalism as an essential property of domesticity.[6] According to Bledstein, the characteristics associated with the highly developed capitalist environment of Victorian England and America such as increased divisions and specifications of time and space (i.e., breakfast time, weekends, department stores, public parks, private bedrooms, etc.) applied also to the occupations according to which a man or woman might make his or her living: not only were leisure activities such as playing ball organized into "professional sports" whereby a "player" received wages to exercise his talents, but divisions within livelihoods such as medicine or education entailed a heightened degree of specialization whereby doctors or surgeons became, for example, orthopedists or cardiologists or podiatrists. Whereas a "professional gambler" might refer to the amateur cardplayer who showed a marked degree of expertise, the term came to include as well the individual who made playing cards a primary source of income (*OED*); and whereas an "amateur" once designated someone who acted out of love, the word now came to carry a disparaging connotation in the context of professionalism's new scale of value.[7] So it is in this climate of professionalism that the merchants of Treby-Magna criticize Felix's authority to debunk his father's apothecary business on the grounds that such a pronouncement comes from "one who is not a 'professor' " (Eliot 241). Although at this relatively early stage in professionalism's development, it is not specifically a degree or certificate that the townspeople want to see as proof of Felix's apothecariacal knowledge, their objection exemplifies the loose way in which the nineteenth century's vocabulary of professionalism animated so many evaluative statements.

A profession, as Bledstein outlines it, is a full-time occupation that provides a permanent source of income; it requires a lengthy process of education in an "esoteric but useful body of systematic knowledge" by which an individual turns mere talents into trained expertise and at the end of which he receives documentation as proof of his skills (86–87). Most significantly, a professional, particularly in England where those who counted themselves as members of the professional orders were more eager than their American counterparts to distinguish themselves from tradesmen, is marked by his or her devotion to "an ethic of service" — an ethic that underscores the professional's interest in a good other than material personal gain or financial profit.[8]

It is important to note, however, that there are two sides to Bledstein's historicized definition of a profession: descriptive and prescriptive. For in wielding the term "profession" both as a description of certain already recognized nineteenth century careers (like, for example, the law or the military) and as a prescription according to which certain occupations (such as designing a building or teaching a child or commenting on a musical production) attained professional status, Bledstein plies an image of Victorian professionalism as a process — a process not unlike institutionalization. Implicit here, however, is the suggestion that professionalism, in its potential application to each and every human endeavor, functioned not only as a practical means of distinguishing various pursuits, but operated as well as a kind of judicious spectrometer by which a scale of human activities might be glimpsed: art, religion, craft, and service industries alike were subject to its reach, each measured and/or shaped in terms of the degree to which each met "professional" standards. Although such standards grow more concrete as the century progresses, the values they initially measured appear strangely vague, the professional's ascension seemingly predicated on a social function that was curiously divorced from social effect. Consequently, mid-century professionalism can be historicized as something like a rage rather than as, for example, a material means of improvement. Certainly, it can be argued that the increase in professional training and standardization had a significant effect in improving the way in which specific jobs were performed. And certainly the rise of professions played a significant socio-historical role in allowing members of the lower-middle classes to become gentlemen while enabling the younger sons of the aristocracy to remain so despite their need to work for a living. But the purely spiritual dimension of the professional standard, the ethos of professionalism, nevertheless appears to have an almost independent history. Depicting professionalization as a kind of Dickensian fever for example, Bledstein attributes to it an inflated self-perpetuating quality: indiscriminately applied to each and every category of human life, the professional eye exposes "abnormality," irrationality and immorality everywhere, thereby making the job of the specialist that much more crucial to the communal welfare (102).

Yet, the reverence surrounding professionalism derived not only from this potentially universal applicability of its standards, but also from the perceived certainty of its methods: because the professional "excavated nature for its principles," professional expertise was no less than the virtually faultless means of grasping "the concept behind a functional activity" (88). Importantly, however, it is only in the context of the professional's selflessness, as evidenced by his or her remove from moneyed interests, that the surety of methodology evolves into transcendent work:

> The professional did not vend a commodity, or exclusively pursue a self-interest. He did not sell a service by a contract which called for specific results in a specific time or restitution for errors. Rather, through a special understanding

of a segment of the universe, the professional person released nature's potential and rearranged reality on grounds which were neither artificial, arbitrary, faddish, convenient, nor at the mercy of popular whim. Such was the august basis for the authority of the professional. (890)

In its analysis of the professional's social function, the passage makes it clear that the general societal good relies on a compound of specificity and self-sacrifice: for it is only the professional's knowledge of a particular space — a "segment of the universe" — and his or her selfless commitment to that space that ensures the community's well-being. Thus a watered-down kind of positivist emphasis on observed particulars combined with some sign of self-sacrifice, most readily attained through a material surrender, infused professional work with its spiritual purport.

But on what basis Victorian professional standards determined the incorporation and elevation of some practices and some practitioners while barring others remains hazy. At its simplest, the professional tag can be said to amount to a question of training. Thus Casaubon will fail in a career as a philosopher because he has not been educated in German language and literature; Gwendolyn Harleth cannot turn her drawing room talents into an acting career because her voice has not been trained; and Dinah's gift for preaching does not translate into a religious career because she has not received a clerical education. But another salient feature of professionalism, the ethic of service, poses a way in which the professional ethos distinguished activities for which training was actually irrelevant. In its deemphasis on income, English professionalism's ethic of service elevated certain religious, artistic, and political callings as that much more professional, despite the absence of training required for their pursuit. With this in mind, it is possible to identify two strains of Victorian professionalism: a spiritual form, resembling what Max Weber will generally call a vocation developing alongside a more practical form, marked by a quasi-scientific emphasis on specialization. Although these strains are by no means mutually exclusive, it seems possible to trace a predominance of one or the other in a given historical period or culture.

In discussing what he calls George Eliot's novel of vocation, Alan Mintz identifies "the rise of the professions" in the nineteenth century as a sociohistorical medium that "made it possible for the impulse toward self-aggrandizing ambition and the impulse toward selfless contribution to society to be united in a single life" (2). Although he does not directly address renunciation as a crucial ingredient, Mintz follows Weber's lead in tracing Eliot's use of the professions as a spiritualization of work that, in following a secularized Puritan model, combined self-realization and social participation (6). But because characters with ambitious vocations tragically cannot overcome the domestic imperatives of romance and household life, "vocation," according to the argument, "is viewed as a desire that by definition cannot be fulfilled" (7). Setting up domestic ensnarement as a kind of minotaur to whom the best girls and boys are sacrificed,[9] Mintz thus locates the heroism of characters like Dorothea and Lydgate in the tragic surrender of their vocational visions. Ultimately, the "talk of model farms, model hospitals, colonies of workers' cottages, and scientific farming" (63) remains undone as each hero is as well undone by homely realities.

Although Mintz is absolutely right in emphasizing the vocational contest, the question remains why it should always be home life that inevitably wins the battle, what is it about the domestic line of development that makes *its* conquest such a convenient vehicle for representing tragic heroism. After all, it is certainly possible to imagine other *force majeure* "realities" — national events, physical or emotional diseases, wars, environmental catastrophes — that would serve to extract that same surrender of the vocational fantasy. The answer I think lies in a reevaluation of the domestic plotline precisely within, and not outside, the Protestant vocabulary Mintz uses. For it is in this sense that conceptualizing homemaking as a kind of profession changes the significance of the battle: it is not that the vocational path is abandoned, it is simply relocated. As Mintz says, vocation is certainly desire, but I would add that it is not facilely unfulfillable "by definition"; it is simply a particularly subtle kind of desire, the kind that demands nonpersonal gratification. And this is why I would argue that marriage, rather than disrupting the novel of vocation, cannot but be incorporated into it, precisely because the home emerges as the strongest preserve of what is so crucial to authentic vocational choice, renunciation.

If homemaking is like a profession but nevertheless not quite the same as a profession — no quite as close to the superlative pole on the Profession Continuum as a career like law — the question must be asked, why draw attention to the similarity, why place it in the professional bailiwick at all? The answer is that it is only by situating domesticity in this Victorian vocabulary of professionalism, with all its spiritual and self-sacrificial specters still alive, and along the evaluative scale such a vocabulary impresses, that certain truths about what is called domestic ideology can surface. To be clear, I have argued so far that domesticity in novels like *Felix Holt*, regardless of the historical facts concerning domestic ideological imperatives and the false consciousness that the "ideological" label insinuates, can be described as a depiction of a specific category of activity, the work involved in devoting a life to building and maintaining a home — work that is continuous, nonteleological, and self-sacrificial and that therefore constitutes a higher calling in the Protestant tradition. It is important to note then that at the same time that such representations of home making as a spiritually inspired vocation abound in Victorian

culture, there develops as well this spiritually-inflected vocabulary of professionalism. In the context of *this* vocabulary, domesticity is not a leisure pursuit, not an antithesis to industrial production, the home not an antidote to
the capitalist workplace nor a place of material consumption or bourgeois
sport. Rather it is, in nineteenth-century terms, a vocational profession.

The Higher Calling

RETURNING FOR A MOMENT to Mr Lyon, what his foray into homemaking tells
us is that at the heart of an individual's career choice lies this question of
self-sacrifice. By placing such a premium on the renunciation of self-interest
in the context of "choosing a life," the novel questions what kind of relationship links this notion of vocation to what starts to look like a recurrent
professing or profession of self-sacrifice; as Esther's comment on Felix's
nobility indicates, it is not simply that commitment to an ennobling calling
entails renunciation, but that renunciation becomes the condition that is necessary, and perhaps even sufficient, for having a calling in the first place. From
this perspective, it appears that the content of Felix's "character" — and any
action that might demonstrate it — is less important than the fact that he can
be said to have it. After all, what precisely Felix does for a living, how he
intends to fulfill his calling, remains perversely vague: occupied in either
random "watch and clock-cleaning, and teaching one or two little chaps"
(144) or in arbitrary tavern visits to pick up conversation with local workmen,
Felix never explains with what tools or in what sense he will accomplish his
purpose: reforming "the ruling belief in society about what is right and what
is wrong, what is honourable and what is shameful" (401). Never does he
articulate a realizable social vision or plan of action, preferring instead simple
statements of moral distaste for the selfishness that drives political or socio-
economic ambition and for the self-absorption that allows people to be
"ground by wrong and misery, and tainted with pollution" (211). "I go for
educating the non-electors," he tells Esther, "so I put myself in the way of
my pupils — my academy is the beer-house" (155). Despite his propaedeutic
claim, his colloquial idiom and academic metaphor ensure that how and what
he will teach remain inchoate.

But as the Lyon backgrounding episode imparts, the difficulty in recognizing activities like Felix's politicking or Lyon's homemaking as the professions
and higher callings they are derives from the complexities inherent in the
rhetoric of self-sacrifice — a rhetoric with which Felix is particularly enamored. In explaining to Esther, for example, why he has forsworn marriage and
thereby taken a virtual vow of celibacy, he professes, "The old Catholics are
right, with their higher rule and their lower. Some are called to subject themselves to a harder discipline, and renounce things voluntarily . . . It is the old

word — 'necessity is laid upon me' " (363). What Felix means by these
"things" is clear from the novel's onset: the inconvenience of having to
financially support a wife and children, burdens he is certain would force him
to "lie and simper a little, else they'll starve!" (156). Thus evincing a great
deal of self-satisfaction in his self-sacrifice, Felix brandishes the vocabulary
of the domestic life he eschews — marriage, family and livelihood — as
metaphors which, as long as they remain figurative, can turn what he has
renounced into what he has kept: because he has chosen to devote himself to
"a family with more chances in it" rather than a family of fortune (367),
Felix assures himself that no matter what the outcome of his trial, "they can't
rob me of my vocation. With poverty for my bride, and preaching and pedagogy for my business, I am sure of a handsome establishment" (468). In
this sense, the rhetoric of self-sacrifice converts a loss-gain dichotomy into
something more complex when the loss so invariably resounds as a gain:
Felix cannot be robbed because his state of self-sacrifice has already changed
the idea of being without into an idea of possession. Surely it is not accidental
that the tropes Felix finds most apt to convey this retributive rendering of
renunciation and self-sacrifice are connubial, household commonplaces.

In the context of such a renunciation-mathematics, it is not surprising that,
according to the *OED*'s final listing, "renounce" was often used in popular
nineteenth-century card games to refer to playing a card of a different suit
from that which has been led, implying either the possession or want of a
proper card. In other words, Victorian parlor game sociability accommodates
the sense in which renunciation entailed unexpected reverses in loss-gain
ratios. Thus it is not until another instance of parlour sociability, a love scene
with Esther, that it becomes obvious how the "things" renounced and the role
of self in the renunciation economy might have lost their purported clarity:

> "I want you to tell me— once —that you know it would be easier to me to
> give myself up in loving and being loved, as other men do, when they can,
> than to—"
>   This breaking-off in speech was something quite new in Felix. For the first
> time he had lost his self-possession, and turned his eyes away. He was at
> variance with himself . . . "This thing can never come to me twice over. It is
> my knighthood. That was always a business of great cost" . . .
>   Felix reproached himself. . . . He felt that they must not marry—that they
> would ruin each other's lives. But he had longed for her to know fully that his
> will to be always apart from her was renunciation, not an easy preference.
> (418–19)

In prose divided between thought-report and dialogue, aurally fractured
by aposiopetic speech and visually broken by dash-designated qualifiers and
hyphenated compounds, the object of Felix's renunciation materializes simultaneously with the object of his desire: fancying his newly realized passion

for Esther to constitute a test of his heroism — of his knighthood — he loses
"possession" of himself, is "at variance with himself," requires another to
confirm what had until now been an independent inward conviction. Felix
breaks off because the economics of renunciation have gotten too complicated,
the formula that charts what is lost, gained or traded has in fact reversed its
terms: whereas it is clear in Felix's idiolect that taking Esther as his wife
would require him to "give up [him]self" — or what until this point has
amounted to himself, his vocation — it becomes clear in the passage's structure that Felix has sudden doubts as to what falls on which side of the renunciation equation. It would be easier to give himself up than to do what? than
to give up himself? In other words, it is easier to foreswear a home with
Esther than to acknowledge that the conditions securing his supposedly self-
abnegating "vocation" are in actuality self-affirming and thus in some sense
evidence that his celibate vocation is a sham, is nothing more than a product
of false consciousness no matter how well-intentioned. The repressed phrase
that Felix wants Esther to voice — that she recognizes his sacrifice as *self*-
sacrifice — is never confirmed as being the case; it remains at the end of
their dialogue as Felix's unuttered desire for Esther to think that his "will"
to renounce her is different from his desire to have her — and for her to
believe that his passion for his work is not desire. For clearly the question
has become which is the more difficult job? Which requires the most work?
The most sacrifice? Would it really be easier for Felix to give himself up or
is that precisely the cost of this knighthood business — precisely the price
vocational commitment extracts — precisely the ironically sought-after renunciation: giving up the self-sacrificial career in an ironically self-sacrificial
gesture. By the end of their exchange, renunciation itself thus surfaces as the
prize: it is no longer quite something done, but a property that Felix wants
to hear that he has. In this sense, it is the alternative life Esther offers —
presumably a home — and thus the eruption of a marriage plot into Felix's
"career" path that throws into question what possessing selflessness might
mean.

The Work Made Manifest

FOR ALL THE PRIORITY it places on the spirit of the moral work for which Felix
is willing to sacrifice so much, the novel never fully discredits the value of
that work's substance; but it does rely on a domestic storyline of romance,
marriage and home to reveal that Felix's occupation is more than a botched
attempt to halt a riot. The sign that Felix is in fact engaged in something
more than ambling around the countryside exuding righteousness emerges in
the effect he has on Esther, the deeds and choices that compose her own
lifeplot thus serving as the only available proof of Felix's work.[10] So it is that

by claiming not to have been able to "see the meaning of anything fine" until "hearing what Felix Holt said, and seeing that his life was like his words" (537), Esther legitimizes Felix's vocation not only literally by defending him at his trial, but more importantly, in the language of her own psychological character development. But it is ironically this rhetoric of self-denial that animates Esther's epiphany in two important ways: for what it is about Felix that effects the change in Esther and how the novel makes her personal realization manifest pivot on a valuation of nonpersonal categories and the degree to which self-sacrifice as a quality of mind might stand as their expression. After all, what makes an impression on Esther has more to do with Felix's purportedly selfless life than with any compassion for the suffering poor or the unenfranchised laborers he wants to reform: for not only do nearly all of Felix's conversations with Esther either highlight his electing "hardship" and "privation" as a "better lot" (537) or showcase his proud conviction that "the universe has not been arranged for the gratification of his feelings" (556), but Esther never indicates that she has caught his averred concern for social principles. Indeed her heroism relies strictly on the particular moment of her "final choice" (590): whether to marry Harold Transome and assume her rights to the Transome estate or to renounce her claims and hope for a life alongside the selfless and hence morally superior Felix. How it is that the novel situates the right choice in a home with Felix depends precisely on the rhetoric that makes self-sacrifice a vocational property — a good in and of itself. For from a practical point of view, had the social welfare really been Esther's objective, surely her position as mistress of the Transome estate and heiress to its family's wealth would have afforded her a practical means of doing great good: the possibility of a career in philanthropy, a choice that so many wealthy Victorian men and women actually did make.[11]

The rightness of Esther's choice, however, relies — like Felix's — not so much on performing specific good acts, but on her willingness to surrender something (in her case, the estate) and what such an act of surrendering represents. On the one hand, there is in Esther's choice an embrace of renunciation by virtue of the material sacrifices it would entail: marrying Felix, she muses, would mean accepting "the dim life of the back street, the contact with sordid vulgarity the lack of refinement for the sense, the summons to a daily task" (591). Such article-headed nominal clauses, however, offer up a pastiche of abstract static states that makes her future life looks less like an impoverished lifestyle than a collection of spiritual properties: despite the bald qualifying phrases represented in the "back street," the "vulgarity" and the "daily task," the sentence convenes "life," "contact," and "summons" in a quickened visionary triptych that adds a hallowed aura to this version of Esther's future. In this sense, Esther's marriage choice is not a vote for Felix. It is not simply Felix the beloved who figures as the "gain that was to make that life of privation something on which she dreaded to turn her back'' (591), but the idea of renunciation that contact with him has made manifest. Although it is unclear whether Felix will ever really have an effect on any workers, the narrated phrases of Esther's imagination apotheosize him precisely as that force which will check "her self-satisfied pettiness with the suggestion of a wider life" (468). Thus it is here in the workings of a narrated mind that Felix's work evinces itself as a higher calling.

In this sense, the novel uses Esther's psychology as a kind of showcase for an idealized selflessness. And certainly what she gives up by surrendering the "imaginary mansion" of her childish fantasies (500) is the psychologically self-centered Freudian family romance fantasy of noble-birth-after all, thereby embracing a very different kind of personal past: the childhood household of her adopted father's home. Significantly, the novel adumbrates her final rejection of Transome Court with the oblique statement that she began to understand "what it would be to abandon her own past" (496). The question immediately registers, which past does she mean? the childhood experience of Mr. Lyon's home or the childhood fantasy of an aristocratic estate that an older past of blood relations might now legitimize? Through a syntactical ordering that places the future before the past and a subjunctive phrasing that allows biographical time to make the Transome home and the Parish home interchangeable, Esther's statement suggests that the choice of home is a choice of what kind of past will serve as "her own past" — the one of selfish fantasy and familial blood ties or the one of household routines and adopted relations. Her final choice suggests that the right home is the task-filled cottage belonging to a biological stranger, a place gained only if a psychologically delineated personal past of fantasy is renounced.

Interestingly, this personal past of fantasy that the rhetoric of renunciation renders undesirable is linked in an unexpected way to an idea of change. For although the most striking feature of Transome Court is its stillness, such motionless desuetude always conveys a sense that it had not always been so: its "darkened" windows, uncut grass, unswept fallen fir needles, and absence of gardners or servants thus conspire to impress the Transome estate's representation of the past with the signs of change — change which can figure only as devolution. But whereas this renounced home divulges an alliance between stillness and change, motion is found in the changeless activities of "the old-fashioned, grazing, brewing, wool-packing, cheese-loading life of Treby-Magna" (124). Embedded in this montage of cropped, collaterally arranged and anaphorically united scenes, the Dissenting pastor's home is metonymically associated with the gerund-wrought continuity of small town workings. The homey virtues of the right home thus materialize in the home-town details of a past marked by an almost oxymoronic active changelessness.

And this is where the recidivistic leanings characteristic of so many domestically predisposed novels appear in *Felix Holt* to result from the way in which
the tectonics of literary montage can depersonalize the past. That is, the active
changelessness limned in Treby-Magna's hometowniness is the effect of a
technical device: the literary collage; as the right past, this Treby-Magna
home comes to supplant Esther's own personal, imagined past. But because
this right past cannot be separated from the montage technique that presents
it as such and because this technique also presents such a past as actively
changeless, the recidivism of domestically committed plots is more complicated than simply a yearning for the "way things used to be," the world of
the past or the past of personal origins. The Bretton residence in England,
Joe Gagary's Forge, the Marshalsea do not become idealized homes simply
because they represent a lost past, but because they embody a spirit of ongoing
activity that precludes differentiating any notion of the past in the first place.

Meanwhile, change in this novel, when not typified as devolution, seems
either to disappear or to be channeled into a notion of character that can
develop only along domestic lines. Although Esther's choice of the right
home's bustling changelessness results from the fact that she herself has
"changed," this personality conversion crystallizes only through domestic
gestures that carry a heightened sense of significance. When, for example,
Esther demonstrates affection for her adopted father by making his tea, the
minister muses "with wonder of the treasures still left in our fallen nature,"
(214); and when she carries his things upstairs and makes him porridge the
narrative comments, "Very slight words and deeds may have a sacramental
efficacy, if we can cast our self-love behind us" (546). It is not simply that
contact with a domestic implement confers nobility, but that in the context
of a plotline that presents homelife as a career and profession reserved for
the spiritually elect, such domesticities appear charged with meaning. The
novel illustrates the difference when, upon her return from Transome Court,
Esther immediately combs her father's hair and straightens up his study,
inveighing now against Lyddy's false religious enthusiasms because they keep
her from "brushing [Mr Lyon's] clothes and putting out [his] clean cravat"
(504). Although Esther had always criticized Lyddy in a vocabulary of household words, complaining that Lyddy's crying over the soup made it too salty,
the censure now carries the stamp of a critique, of a loftier, perhaps even
more expert, judgment: for it is the selfless concern for another that makes
the details of housework more than matters of convenience or comfort. In this
way, Esther establishes her own housekeeperly authority when she pronounces
upon Lyddy by turning evangelical expressions into domestic metaphors:
"[Lyddy] is always saying her righteousness is filthy rags, and really I don't
think that is a very strong expression for it. I'm sure it's dusty clothes and

furniture'' (504). Good housekeeping thus emerges as the ascendant mode of ethical valuation.

And this is precisely when the structural status of the Lyon vocational crisis episode, once repressed as parenthetical external analepsis meant to gloss Mr. Lyon's character and his relationship with Esther, returns as central to the novel's primary plot line. For the most tangible effect of Felix's exemplary career, besides the domestication of Esther's personality that marks her as the heroine he is destined to marry, is how his influence ultimately breathes life into the surrogate father-daughter relationship lying at the heart of Esther's domestic awakening. In this sense, the ''retribution'' that Felix teasingly calls his future marriage to Esther (603) occurs structurally when the satellite background material of Lyon's foray into homemaking is recovered on a higher narrative plane as a kernel function essential to the meaning of the story as a whole (Barthes). A reconstruction of the plot will then yield the following scenario. The novel marks Esther's ''character development'' by showing her engaged in activities and committed to choices that legitimize a surrogate familial relationship; this surrogate father-daughter relationship, resulting as it does from Mr. Lyon's domestic episode, represents in condensed form a valorization of Lyon's experience of homemaking as a vocation; a legitimization of her adopted father's domestic professions, Esther's household conduct also happens to provide the sign of Felix's hitherto invisible work. Thus her domestic activity shows Felix's vocation itself to be after all, literally, home-making.

Felix the Housekeeper

HOW FELIX ''THE RADICAL,'' whose tremendous physical stature and roughly-hewn carriage constantly code him as virile, finally reveals himself as homemaker par excellence, can be seen in how the novel surreptitiously mines his vocabulary for a pattern of terms that lead to home via a gender neutral vocational corridor. In an early articulation of his inward calling, for example, Felix asserts that he cannot expect to see the results of his ''particular work'' (556) because '' 'Where great things can't happen, I care for very small things, such as will never be known beyond a few garrets and workshops' '' (557). In thus exhibiting what can be called an ethos of particularization, Felix speaks in a Protestant ideolect whereby the summons to worldly engagement can take the shape of involvement in the minutia of daily life. In so far as these Protestant values have been secularized, it follows that Felix should speak Professionalism as well: like the specialist described by Bledstein, Felix concentrates in his worldly work only on that small ''spectrum'' of the universe. Hence Felix's Protestantesque professionalism is established by the way the attention he pays to the small and the narrow play into the novel's spiritually resonant accentuation of the particular.

Showing Felix to have adopted this Protestant elevation of small worldly works, the novel goes on in a different instance to equate wordliness as a quality of mind with domestic expertise, the oddness of Mr Lyon's manners and social behavior thus due to his "unworldliness . . . in small matters". (163). Noteworthy here is that the novel, in its depiction of Mr. Lyon's character, does not cite his sex as the cause of his domestic illiteracy, but stresses instead his absentmindedness, a trait that makes him a comical (however lovable) figure to the townspeople, not to mention a minor minister in a less than prestigious pastorate. Unworldly as he is in the small matters that preoccupy his neighbors, Mr. Lyon is consequently caught off guard when the otherwise historically resonant year of 1812 turns out to be significant primarily as the date on which "romance did befall him" (163). In the metaphorical vanquishment of Mr. Lyon's "fall" before romance and in his consequent lackluster ministerial career there is a shadowy sense that had Mr. Lyon been more domestic, been perhaps as "methodical" as Felix, he would also have been more of "a man."

This is not to say that gender plays no role in novelistic plots centered on domestic storylines; it is only to call attention to how *Felix Holt*, in its severe focus on the Protestant spirit and the formal structures that spin out of it, makes such topics less relevant than they may have been in the real life of its readers. Thus when sexual difference is addressed, as in fact it often is, the novel pointedly uses its ethos of particularization to dismiss it as precisely that veil which hides the higher call. When, for example, Esther and Felix discuss the difference between men and women, Felix presumes that women never choose hardship like his "unless they are Saint Theresa or Elizabeth Frys," to which Esther counters that a woman cannot but choose "hardship as a better lot" because only "meaner things are within her reach" (367). Although superficially commenting on the different socially prescribed destinies that divide the sexes, Esther rhetorically checkmates Felix by translating his idea of hardship into her "meaner things," thereby resituating his apparent Protestant sensibility in a grammar of genderless professional particularization. As a life of these meaner things is presumably what both Esther and Felix seek, it follows that the spirit of specialization that infuses such quotidities with higher meaning also desexualizes the whole process of vocational election. In other words, the banter here is less concerned with sexual differences — whether real or perceived — than with locating the pivotal characteristic of vocational election in the domestic plottings of hearthside meaner things.

What kind of housekeeper Felix represents, however, shows the homewardly developed Victorian novel in a social role different than that which can be seen in either Brontë or Dickens. True, the end of *Felix Holt* pictures

Felix and Esther bound for a spiritually lofty, never-never-land home ostensibly devoted to an abstracted idea of social work and communal imperatives. But the ethos of particularization that professionalizes both Esther and Felix, the spiritually infused methodology that makes them into domestic specialists, shows them not quite as housekeepers at work in preserving arenas of nonpersonal sociability, but as professional keepers of a specific set of communitarian-like ethics. Thus it is through the training Esther receives in Felix's presence that she acquires a certain kind of moral appreciation — what might be called a kind of ethical taste that makes selfish actions not simply wrong, but unpalatable. The aesthetic component mixed in to her ethical epiphany surfaces in the metaphors the novel conjures in describing Esther's moment of romantic choice. Prefacing her final decision, this aesthetic-ethic hybridization first appears when Harold assures himself that "Esther was too clever and tasteful a woman to make a ballad heroine of herself, by bestowing her beauty and her lands on this lowly lover" (536). Relying on a correspondence between aesthetic valuations and class structure, Harold's rhetoric uses the kitchiness of a ballad to invoke an idea of taste as a final arbiter in questions of social correctness.

But Esther overturns his judgment by revealing herself to possess too tasteful a sensibility and too professional a taste to fall from such middle-brow reasoning as that which would define the valuable as no more than economic standing. Demonstrating precisely the refinement Bledstein ascribes to the professionalized intellect, Esther reasons with precision, plumbs what Bledstein calls the "esoteric, but useful body of systematic knowledge," that here one might call ethics, in order to identify those principles" by which the valuable might be glimpsed: half-wishing to be saved "from the effort to find a clue of principle amid the labyrinthine confusions of right and possession," she deliberates on how difficult it was "by any theory of providence, or consideration of results, to see a course which she could call duty" (524). Having received the education of witnessing Felix's exemplary vocational renunciations, however, Esther finally arrives at a scale of valuation that counters Harold's overly literal idea of worth:

> ... this life at Transome ... gave an air of moral mediocrity to all her prospects ... All life seemed cheapened; as it might seem to a young student who, having believed that to gain a certain degree he must write a thesis in which he would bring his powers to bear with memorable effect, suddenly ascertained that no thesis was expected, but the sum (in English money) of twenty-seven pounds ten shillings and sixpence. (524)

By demonstrating her good judgment, Esther's choice of the "right" home spotlights the extent to which her judgment has been contextualized as professional. And here I want to pose a loose parallel between what Freedman

discusses as "aestheticist professionalism" and George Eliot's brand of vocational domesticity, the rise of the professional aesthete as a keeper of culture
thus comparable in a certain sense to the rise of the domestic professional as
a keeper of ethics — a kind of ethicete. According to Freedman's argument,
English aestheticism participated in English professionalist culture by mirroring and generating that "discreet form of professionalism" which I have
called professionalism's spiritual strain; emphatically divorcing themselves
from "the acquisitive, work-oriented ethos of the bourgeois economy"
(Freedman 53), late nineteenth-century aesthetes constituted "a new caste of
professionals who designated themselves as experts in cultural knowledge,
and who defined their own role as that of instructing others in the lineaments
of that knowledge" (55). Indeed Esther evinces in her metaphor's decided
rejection of the moneyed path to scholarly expertise a reliance on a spirit
of specialization that changes the terms according to which the valuable is
determined: value is not an object indiscriminately accessible to any seeker
willing to pay a literal fee, but a whole life of "prospects" available only to
those spiritually correct professionals chosen and trained to fossick for it.
With this in mind, it is particularly interesting that *Felix Holt* closes with
Esther, reminding us that she is a teacher: " 'I mean,' " she tells Felix in
describing what their future home will be like, " 'to go on teaching a great
many things' " (602). Although the prospective Holt home is neither the
literal school room that closes the pages of *Villette* — even though Esther
teases that she will cultivate Felix's French accent — nor the vision of urban
hospitalization that gives *Little Dorrit* its horizon of closure, there is in *Felix
Holt*'s domestic finale a propaedeutic ethic that casts the Victorian home epic
into a complicated relationship with professional social service.

California Institute of Technology

NOTES

1. It is not unreasonable to see in Erasmus's autobiographical association and final
   break with Martin Luther a representation in condensed form of many of the
   Protestant Reformation's central conflicts.
2. Although not a best–seller like his previous novel, *It is Never Too Late to Mend*
   (1856), which sold 65,000 copies in seven years, *The Cloister and the Hearth*
   was popular enough to figure among the first titles Chatto and Windus included
   in its groundbreaking 1893 experiment in less expensive publishing strategies,
   the enterprise they called "sixpenny wonderfuls." After having sold in the thousands since its first publication date, *The Cloister and the Hearth* 6d. edition sold
   380,000 copies over the subsequent fifteen years. See Altick, *The English Common Reader* and *Sixpenny Wonderfuls*.
   It should be noted, however, that *The Cloister and the Hearth* did receive far more
   critical acclaim than Reade's more mass market works. Favorably compared to

George Eliot as well as to Dickens and Thackeray, Reade was lauded by many intellectuals and artists of the period, including William Dean Howells, George Orwell, W. L. Courtney, Sir Walter Besant, Robert Buchanan, and Algernon Charles Swineburne. See Smith, *Charles Reade.*

3. In previous work I have delimited the category of the domestic by arguing that mid-Victorian novels show English homelife to be primarily concerned with nonpersonal sociability: routine, business-like social interaction that is emotionally satisfying precisely because it is focussed not on an internally experienced self, but rather on a self disinterestedly engaged in ongoing activities amid a community often composed of virtual strangers.

4. In *George Eliot and the Novel of Vocation*, Mintz articulates the consensus among Victorianists on work: "The enthusiasm for work is a virtual touchstone of Victorian sensibility. As reason had been to the Enlightenment, work was to the Victorians: an overarching term that sanctioned a multitude of diverse, often antagonistic positions" (1). See also Houghton, *The Victorian Frame of Mind* (242–62) and Welsh, *The City of Dickens* (73–85).

5. I use the term homemaking and homekeeping interchangeably for rhetorical purposes. According to the *OED*, the term "homemaking," though common in Victorian England by the end of the century, was probably an American import as it was more widely used in connection to the nineteenth-century American home economics movement. It would seem plausible nonetheless that during the 1870s and 80s the popular English term "homekeeping" conveyed the same sense as its American version, however more organized and overtly political the American domesticity movement may have been. See Strasser, *Never Done.*

6. See Bledstein, *The Culture of Professionalism* (38 ff).

   Mintz joins Bledstein and others in documenting the rise of professionalism in the nineteenth century:

   The realignment of social forces precipitated by the specialization of function is most evident in the rise and establishment of the professions. Although for centuries there had always been the "ancient three plus two" — the clergy, law, and medicine, in addition to the army and the navy — the nineteenth century saw the rise and establishment of the professional status of many other specialized groups, such as accountants, engineers, surveyors, school teachers, journalists, and under a different set of circumstances, politicians. (14)

   For a more detailed history of English professionalism, see Cannadine, *The Decline and Fall of the British Aristocracy* (391–444); Engel, *From Clergyman to Don*; Perkin, *The Rise of Professional Society*; Reader, *Professional Men*; Rothblatt, *The Revolution of the Dons.*

7. Although its English counterpart remained less developed, the American home economics movement offers an interesting instance of how professionalism extended in a very literal way to the home. Victorians on both sides of the Atlantic saw a proliferation of organizations preaching the rationalization of domestic service whereby managing a home was explicitly compared to running a business, a household of apprentices, servants, boarders, visitors, distant relatives and biological familial members treated no differently than the ranks of men and women comprising a workshop or factory. Late nineteenth-century America, however, appears to have produced a greater variety of official studies on domestic service

(Strasser 169): organizations such as women's clubs, state and federal departments of labor and college alumnae associations financed research, set up conferences, published reports all in an effort to emphasize the parity between the home and the workplace, the same standards used to reform factories thus applied to the domestic household: "The rhetoric of the domestic service reform movement repeated the point incessantly: domestic service must be rationalized according to well-developed principles of capitalist industry" (Strasser 173).

8. Mintz and Freedman both address these aspects of professionalism. Describing the difference between the American and British models of professionalism, Freedman writes in *Professions of Taste*:

It is true that British professionals emphasized the same relation between their social function and an ethic of service as their American counterparts: British and American teachers, bankers, lawyers, and doctors all claimed to be performing a special function in society by using their training, talents, and expertise to aid others . . . But British professionals seem to have been far more intent than their American counterparts to differentiate themselves from what they saw as the acquisitive ethos of mercantile classes or orders, and far more interested in conforming to the codes of behavior appropriate to the "gentleman." (52)

9. The original line is uttered by Ladislaw in *Middlemarch* when he complains that Dorothea has anachronistic notions of self-sacrifice, of martyrdom, "horrible notions that choose the sweetest of women to devour — like Minotaurs." (Eliot 253).

10. Felix's role in the riot demonstrates the sense in which he pursues his calling according to what Weber has called an "ethic of ultimate ends." According to Weber, the professional who follows an "ethic of ultimate ends," as opposed to an "ethic of responsibility," presumes goodness to reside entirely in intention, in something like character judged according to an ultimate moral scheme, rather than in the specific results of specific deeds (Weber 120–27). For such careerists, consequences are, ethically speaking, irrelevant:

The believer in an ethic of ultimate ends feels 'responsible' only for seeing to it that the flame of pure intentions is not quelched: for example, the flame of protesting against the injustice of the social order. To rekindle the flame ever anew is the purpose of his quite irrational deeds, judged in view of their possible success. They are acts that can and shall have only exemplary value. (121)

Favoring work that is exemplary rather than effective in any specific way, the novel seems to construct a system of values around such callings. That the novel allows Felix to remain a righteous man regardless of the consequences of his actions in the riot reveals that it too operates according to an ethic of ultimate ends: although pub-conversing, tea-making and maybe even novel-writing do not allow for tallying the specific goods they produce, the novel registers them all as careers of influence.

11. Certainly this is what remains a question at the end of *Middlemarch*. Although critical consensus seems to hold that Dorothea must channel her vocational visions into a marriage with Will because she is a woman, the novel never explains exactly why she abandons her original plans for a philanthropic housing project. It would seem that Dorothea's position as a wealthy widow would have allowed

her to join the ranks of other female — not to mention male — philanthropists. That she chooses instead to be a housewife to Will (and also a financial help to Lydgate) perhaps suggests less about the status of Victorian women than about the cultural significance of domestic careers.

WORKS CITED

Altick, Richard D. *The English Common Reader: A Social History of the Mass Reading Public 1800–1900*. Chicago: U of Chicago P, 1957.

Barthes, Roland. "Introduction to the Structural Analysis of Narratives." *Image-Music-Text*. London: Collins, 1977 (79–124).

Bledstein, Burton. *The Culture of Professionalism: The Middle Class and the Development of Higher Education in America*. New York: Norton, 1976.

Cannadine, David. *The Decline and Fall of the British Aristocracy*. New Haven: Yale UP, 1990.

Eliot, George. *Felix Holt*. New York: Penguin Books, 1984.

———. *Middlemarch*. New York: Viking-Penguin, 1986.

Engel, A. J. *From Clergyman to Don: The Rise of the Academic Profession in Nineteenth-Century Oxford*. Oxford: Oxford UP, 1983.

Freedman, Jonathan. *Professions of Taste*. Stanford: Stanford UP, 1990.

Houghton, Walter E. *The Victorian Frame of Mind, 1830–1870*. New Haven and London: Yale UP, 1985.

Mintz, Alan. *George Eliot & the Novel of Vocation*. Cambridge and London: Harvard UP, 1978.

Perkin, Harold. *The Rise of Professional Society: England since 1880*. London: Routledge, 1989.

Reade, Charles. *The Cloister and the Hearth*. London: Heron Books, 1968.

Reader, W. J. *Professional Men: The Rise of the Professional Classes in Nineteenth Century England*. New York: Basic Books, 1966.

Rothblatt, Sheldon. *The Revolution of the Dons: Cambridge and Society in Victorian England*. New York: Basic Books, 1968.

Sixpenny Wonderfuls: 60 Gems from the Past. London: Chatto and Windus, 1985.

Smith, Elton E. *Charles Reade*. Boston: Twayne, 1976.

Strasser, Susan. *Never Done: A History of American Housework*. New York: Pantheon, 1982.

Weber, Max. "Politics as a Vocation." *From Max Weber: Essays in Sociology*. Eds. H. H. Gerth and C. Wright Mills. New York: Oxford UP, 1958.

Welsh, Alexander. *The City of Dickens*. Cambridge: Harvard UP, 1986.

TRIANGULATION AND HOMOEROTICISM IN *DAVID COPPERFIELD*

By J. Michael Léger

THE ARTISTRY OF THE CHAPTER recording James Steerforth's death in *David Copperfield*[1] signals David's return, after his grief, to art as vocation, but its Romantic style signals more than a mere return to a profession; here David returns to the dreamy and romantic storytelling of his youth in which he sought his first connection with Steerforth. The chapter returns David to his original state and to his first and lasting love, via the high drama of the storm at sea. There is nothing else like this event in the novel. Its drama need hardly identify itself as central to the text and to the life of the narrator of that text; David Copperfield's emotional engagement with the main character of that drama renders its centrality clear to us, and the preface to the narration of Steerforth's death makes the centrality of the man and his death unmistakable.

If the undisciplined heart is the central theme of Dickens's novel, becoming almost a character in its own right, the theme is resolved or the character is controlled narratively by a murderous discipline; the discipline David discovers in his marriage to Agnes is, as Welsh suggests, death-dealing.[2] More interestingly, however, the attachment we would at first expect to be most severely disciplined or readily condemned — that which at first appears to be merely a homocentric/homosocial attachment of David to a rascally but not despicable rake, Steerforth — is not condemned. Despite the fact that it is disciplined, this attachment is celebrated by its centrality to and superiority in the text, resisting the text's claim of moral movement into the settled state of idealistic Victorian marriage. The central undisciplined heart is unable to usurp the place of Steerforth, even if he and the love he shares with David are disciplined. As Weinstein argues,

> *David Copperfield*'s authenticity — its status as a flawed masterpiece — has
> less to do with the successful "discipline" of a wayward heart than with the

301

compelling imagination of feelings not only undisciplined, but unrecognized. This covert semantics of desire creatively disturbs the authorized script of sublime motives. Together they make something richer than mere coherence: they make a palimpsest that expresses both a mid-Victorian ideal and the gathering forces that ideal was meant to keep at bay.[3] (44)

In this novel, which is ostensibly the autobiographical testament to David's fulfillment of his heterosexual trajectory towards Agnes, the relationship between David and Steerforth reveals itself to involve much deeper attachments than the words homocentric or homosocial imply. The slipperiness of their gender identities in the interactions of David and Steerforth, revealed in their behavioral, subjective, and storytelling "femininity," signals the cultural identification of what today would be identified as homosexual orientation (same-sex object choice).[4] The emotional and situational interactions David experiences with his stepfather and Steerforth neatly fit the literary pattern that Marcus identifies as the (finally homoerotic) flagellation fantasy.[5] The narrative consummation of the relationship between David and Steerforth, providing the dramatic climax of the novel, echoes and anticipates the contexts (literal and later figurative death) in which the narrative consummates the relationships of David with women.[6] Sandwiched between the death of David's first wife and the deadliness of David's second marriage is the intense narrative climax, the scene in which Steerforth dies. The intrusion of this loss even into David's "present" consciousness transcends its self-effacing narrative position and belies the easy assumption and interpretation that such a consummation can only occur in death. The death-transcending reunion of David with Steerforth in the narrative of the latter's death within the autobiography of the former thoroughly upstages the deadly acquiescence, deadly discipline, and narrative deadliness represented by David's conventional marital consummation with Agnes, the ostensibly validated resolution for all the wanderings of this plot. In addition to this strategic upstaging and its flagellatory presentation, the men's reunion in narrative literally returns them to their original gender-transgressive interaction that anticipated the (for them) less satisfactory but, for their culture and ours, more expected erotic triangles they form. In no way is this climax of David's love for Steerforth reducible to supporting status, as Johnson argues.

A word about the issues of consciousness and intention is in order here. Authorial intent may always be finally impossible to discover, particularly in this age after the death of the author, "this break of the covenant between word and world" or "epilogue" as Steiner has it (93, 94). Asserting authorial consciousness and intention may as a project belong to an essentialist or biographical (or even a new-critical) approach to literature, none of which is currently in favor. Nevertheless, there are reasonable speculations we can advance about the issue. Dickens was certainly aware of rigid delineations of gender role and gendered behavior and had definite opinions about the transgression of these. His opinions seem to have coincided with the cultural assessment of such transgressions, an assessment that implicated what we today identify as sexual object choice, behavior, orientation, and identity. Many of Dickens's characters who transgress gender role and gender-behavior guidelines are also involved in intense same-sex emotional relationships, some of which involve close physical proximity and appreciation of physical beauty. Post-Freudian analyses of relational configurations such as these identify such configurations as homoerotic.

Exercising careful discrimination between the sites on the communication trajectory where meaning may light (authorial intention, reader response), and carefully distinguishing among cultural intention, authorial intention, and modern interpretive insight with respect to those narrative and behavioral gestures we (for convenience) label "homosexual," it is possible to read the transgression of gender-role/behavior guidelines and the participation in certain relational configurations as homoerotic transgression and participation without necessarily insisting upon Dickens's conscious and intentional participation in a gay-affirmative project. This is not to say that Dickens or his culture were conscious of creating (in the sense of listing behaviors associated with) the homosexual subject, let alone of creating (in the sense of crystallizing or reifying an amorphous mass of impulses and behaviors into) sexuality of one kind of another, or of asserting this created sexuality to be the focal point (for the understanding) of human identity, gay or non-gay. Nevertheless, the interactive cultural production of descriptive and proscriptive sexuality and identity proceeded apace in the nineteenth century, and *David Copperfield* illuminates the process significantly.

Using the gender and sexual paradigms of Dickens's culture, David produces a text which maps the trajectory of his intimacy with Steerforth, ostensibly to demonstrate his own disciplining of that intimacy by his choice of heterosexual consummations and to reveal Dickens's wish to discipline such emotion by the narrative slaughter of Steerforth. David's appropriation to himself of Murdstone's disciplining prerogative within that text of heterosexual movement allows David both to inscribe his culture's disapproving assumptions about homoeroticism and to subvert that disapproval. For his love story with Steerforth remains the emotional center of David's life and the central impetus and focus of the life of his narrative; his heterosexual arrangements constitute mere stock emotional set-pieces, narrative interruptions, and invitations to death.

Romantic (and sexual) interactions involving two men were ostensibly heterosexual as long as the interaction involved the giving of a woman by one to another, men being the possessors and bestowers of women. Current culture automatically reads more than economics into such an exchange; this modern assessment is based on the folklore of the erotic triangle which ascribes to competition for the female the presence of both men in the triangle, and on the psychoanalytic supposition that the feeling of rivalry with another man for a woman — the feeling of anger and hatred — represents reaction against desire for the other man (see Jones). Such a desire, which Girard reads as preexistent interest in the rival during the choice of a beloved, may be seen as self-evident when the "beloved" female has no excuse for her presence in the triangle except to perpetuate the relationship between the men or is of significantly less importance to the males than they are to each other and is therefore (figuratively) the site for the males' interactions with each other as the sole female is, physically and sexually, in a ménage-à-trois.

In their original and most important triangulation, one to which they are returned by the narrative to consummate their love at the end of the novel, David and Steerforth transgress and inflect the gender-expectations of their culture and obviate the necessity of an actual female mediatrix of their mutual attraction by calling forth the "feminine" in themselves and in each other and by creating a "feminine" subjective space between them in the fictions they construct about and for one another.[7] The "femininity" David and Steerforth both display in their relationship anticipates the deployment of their mutual desire through their eventual interposition of women between them. It is, in fact, imitative of the adult attempt to structure or discipline desire between men into and by means of the presence of a female.

In the femininity of their intersubjectivity a female is truly present, whose sole ontological excuse is that of providing connection between David and Steerforth. In the original relationship of David and Steerforth, including gender-transgressive behavior (mainly on the part of David), and including mutual effeminization in the acts of storytelling, David tells stories *to* Steerforth, but he also tells stories *about* the aristocrat, creating him as object as he uses him as subject matter. And Steerforth also creates a fictional David in David's "sister," one the real David imitates in his feminine persona, Scheherazade.[8] These gender games also allow the boys to anticipate adult triangulations. In their early interactions, the boys bring together what we may view as a conscious choice on Dickens's part to present them as transgressing expectations of gender and orientation or object choice (they effeminize themselves and each other) and a situation of their choosing (they triangulate their desires), the homoerotics of which Dickens may have been unconscious but which post-Freudian readers recognize.

In their later interactions, as well, David and Steerforth attempt to mediate their love, to discipline the passion they feel by channelling it through an acceptable recipient for it — a female. By means of the type of triangulation analyzed by Girard (50) in which the homocentric attachment precedes and creates or augments the heterocentric attachment, Dickens ultimately privileges the homocentric above the heterocentric bond.[9] The triangles through which David and Steerforth mediate their love destroy the actual women they employ, but they neither divert nor destroy the passion of the men for one another. Rather, the deployment of triangles confirms and consummates their passion.

Cultural expectations about gender behavior, cultural assumptions about the gender of subject and object (masculine and feminine, respectively) and about the gender of subjectivity (subjectivity of feeling is feminine, laboring or active subjectivity is masculine), and the cultural deployments of ostensibly heterosexual relational configurations, all inflect David's inscriptions of gender, subjectivity, and romance in this novel. The adult narrator David Copperfield represses (and reveals by the incompleteness of his repression) the sexual desires he and Steerforth share throughout their lives. In recounting the history of his own life and of his love for Agnes, David inadvertently recounts and foregrounds the history of his association with Steerforth and of the ways in which he himself as character and narrator has channelled the eros between himself and Steerforth into more socially-acceptable forms of expression. This repressive channelling is the impulse responsible for the triple triangulation of the erotic desire between David and Steerforth and is the basis for their continued treatment of their attachment as childish. The repression of their true desire forms the basis for David's false judgment of Steerforth and unfair judgement of Em'ly.

Here I will focus on the productions of David's and Steerforth's repressions: the triangles they deploy, the literary work David proffers under cover (the subtitle of the novel reads ''Which He Never Meant To Be Published on Any Account''), and the emotional center of that written life — the love David and Steerforth share that finally reveals itself in that writing, *as* that writing. The writing itself is both a transcendence of individual subjectivity or an attempt to connect subjectivities and an expression of the boundary between them, an implicit admission that subjectivities are separate.[10] The men's storytelling is in fact the delineation and preservation of subjectivity. Expressing their separateness by using words to bridge it, David and Steerforth are also identifying and conserving that which is within it. And what is within their separateness, if not femininity? In this activity of storytelling, David and Steerforth achieve the intimacy that far surpasses the intimacy either attains with any woman in the novel. This intersubjectivity provides the background for the consideration I will make of the narrative choices that reveal other, even romantic and sexual, levels of connection between the males.

The relationship of David and Steerforth resembles at least superficially the cult of romantic friendship, the emotional and erotic interaction of adolescent boys in the public schools, which Sedgwick argues the middle class considered a mere developmental phase. Sedgwick quotes from a twentieth-century letter demonstrating both the continued prevalence of such occurrences in modern public schools and the assumption that such occurrences express a childish phase in sexual development (176).[11] There is a level upon which we may discuss the David-Steerforth relationship as just such a phase. Certainly when it is first established, it is a relationship between children, although the sophisticated interjection of a feminine storytelling persona between the boys, as mediatrix, suggests a clearer understanding (by the adult Copperfield) of the nature of the relationship and of the constraints culture places upon such desire; the more mature Steerforth and David will interpose a real woman between them. In a similar indication that the adult narrator is constructing the scene he claims to be transcribing from memory, it is the adult David who insists that Steerforth's "great power" is the reason the child David obsesses about him; this is clearly editorial afterthought on David Copperfield's part, unreliable as indication of the child's state of mind. A child would not have questioned the attraction here, before Steerforth's cruelty to Mell and Traddles have occurred. Moreover, this assessment is placed between a more realistically childlike observation (that James Steerforth is physically attractive) and a more realistic psychological detail (that the child's unconscious mind idolizes the older boy and dreams of him in a transcendent setting). This narrative emphasis upon Steerforth's "power" rather than either his attractiveness or David's psychological fixation also draws our attention to that which it would seem insistent to deny, namely that there could be another reason for David's mind to run on Steerforth and a more than superficial resemblance of this relationship to the cult of romantic friendship, an insistence the child would not likely feel the necessity of making.

This editorial afterthought is operative in David's and Steerforth's attempts to reconstruct the "childish" register of their mutual attraction when they reunite as adults. It is in adulthood that Steerforth begins to call David by the feminine name "Daisy." Rosa Dartle formalizes the ostensible meaning of this habit in her idiosyncratic questioning: "Is it a nickname? And why does he give it to you? Is it — eh? — because he thinks you young and innocent? . . . I am glad to know it. He thinks you young and innocent, and *so* you are his friend?" (302; ch. 20, emphasis mine). Her interpretation is amazingly perceptive (or baldly reflective of narrative/authorial intent) given that she is present at neither Steerforth's christening of David at the Golden Cross, nor at the toast Steerforth proposes (300; ch. 20). David's innocence and childishness are conflated here in the symbolic name "Daisy." David's "feminine" childishness, and hence his innocence, is stressed here, particularly in the narrator's intrusion in the voice of Rosa; the relationship is returned to its childhood context, to render *it* innocent.[12] Yet the gender-transgressing evocation indicates the presence of other desires.

This adult recasting of David in feminine terms most clearly resembles the childhood recreation of David as female in Steerforth's desire for David to have a sister.[13]

> We, who had remained whispering and listening half-
> undressed, at last betook ourselves to bed, too.
> "Good night, young Copperfield," said Steerforth.
> "I'll take care of you."
> "You're very kind," I gratefully returned. "I am very
> much obliged to you."
> "You haven't a sister, have you?" said Steerforth, yawning.
> "No," I answered.
> "That's a pity," said Steerforth. "If you had had one, I
> should think she would have been a pretty, timid, little,
> bright-eyed sort of girl. I should have liked to know her.
> Good night, young Copperfield."
> "Good night, sir," I replied (97; ch. 6)

Here Steerforth's storytelling anticipates David's self-conscious return to storytelling as a source of reconnection with Steerforth in the chapter entitled "Tempest," which draws all narrative action and emotional reaction to itself. Steerforth's appreciation of David as "Daisy," his appropriation of David's innocence ("and so you are his friend"), and his admission that he is only satisfied with David's "freshness" remind us of the men's tendency to push their love back into childish-phase contexts (328; ch. 22) and of the cultural imperative to isolate homosexual interaction in such a context.

At various points in their relationship, when they are not channelling the attraction they feel for one another through the actual presence of a woman, David and Steerforth call forth femininity from one another in order to posit a figural mediatrix between them. Long before the work of Greenberg and Armstrong, Monod identified David as feminine based upon Dickens's representation of his sensitivity and noted that David's femininity is revealed primarily in his interactions with Steerforth (323–25). But Monod retreats from the implications of his own argument. With unnecessary emphasis if his conclusion is true, Monod interjects:

> Dickens cannot be held to have intended to hint at the existence of unnatural
> feelings — not to speak of intercourse — between David and Steerforth. What
> he was interested in, what he consequently made interesting, was the psycholog-
> ical study of a friendship so vivid and intense, and experienced by such a
> sensitive person, that many of its incidental expressions and manifestations
> resemble those of love. (324)

Monod's interjection, archaic in its rhetoric and panicked in its tone, is less than convincing; it actually alerts us to the strength of the rest of his argument.

Despite its brevity and the disclaimer, Monod offers proof of the love whose name he dare not speak by insistent qualification within almost every discrete statement he makes about David's reactions to Steerforth. Monod wishes to extenuate David's sensitivity by associating it with Dickens's own interpersonal qualities and by associating David with Dickens. But particularly in the context of the work done by socio-cultural critics who have traced the cultural expectations of gendered and capitalistic behavior, the denials of Monod sound hollow, however predictable they are.

Directly expressed sentiment by or between males results, as the unfortunate Traddles discovers, in scathing public ostracism involving the accusation that those involved in expressing such sentiments are effeminate and evoking the cultural assumption that such effeminacy in males represents sodomitical intent. Expressing his moral outrage at what Steerforth has done to Mr. Mell, Traddles is abusively referred to by Steerforth as "you girl," "Miss Traddles," and "Polly" (109; ch. 7). While he is shy of thus publicly exposing his sensitivity and being perceived by Steerforth as "unfriendly" or "undutiful" in this situation, David voluntarily adopts a feminine persona in response to Steerforth's rousing him "like the Sultana Scheherazade" to tell Steerforth stories morning and night (102). David's part in the interaction, he says, is inspired by "no interested or selfish motive, nor . . . by fear. . . . [He] admired and loved him, and [Steerforth's] approval was return enough" (102; ch. 7). David is thus constrained against his relationship with Steerforth. At the same time, he is being drawn to it by Steerforth's handsomeness, power, and transcendental spirituality. So David must become, as Monod recognizes, feminine according to his own perception and that of his culture in order to reach Steerforth. The boys do this in two ways, both centered on storytelling. Interestingly enough, such a transformation itself mediates between the culture's denunciation of sodomitical desire as effeminate and the culture's compromise acceptance of desire between males when it is safely mediated through the (exchange of the) feminine or through a female.

In addition to imitating Steerforth's objectification of David by his voyeurism toward Steerforth awake and asleep, David also releases and affirms that which is "romantic and dreamy," and therefore feminine, in himself; he opts for an anti-pragmatic (and therefore antimasculine) ideal. At once voyeur and "romancier," masculine and feminine, David's adoption of the romantic serves his self-protective end of creating an ideal story about his friend and about their relationship that seeks to leave his own masculinity intact by defusing the homoerotics of his masculine gaze upon the masculine, of his feminine story about the object of his affection. David carries this internal gender-shift to the outside and begins to act the role of a female as the Sultana Scheherazade, a feminine persona performing a feminine task of soothing the dominant male to sleep. This persona becomes the romantic mediatrix through which the two boys can continue their interactions in and out of the bedroom. In this persona David adopts other feminine self-assessments:

> Whatever I had within me that was *romantic* and *dreamy*, was encouraged by so much story-telling in the dark, and in that respect the pursuit may *not* have been very *profitable* to me. But the being cherished as a kind of *plaything* in my room . . . stimulated me to exertion. (103; ch. 7; emphases added)

Character traits and activities that are romantic and dreamy are here being juxtaposed to those that are profitable.[14] The profit-less play of David's story-telling, like the issue-less consummation of homoerotic impulses that it represents, is clearly "anti-masculine" in the context of what David and Steerforth are to be about here at school: David to take his productive place in the middle class and Steerforth to reinforce his aristocratic superiority over those of the middle classes.[15]

David's aesthetic appreciation of Steerforth also reveals the femininity of David and of his homoerotic attachment to the aristocrat. In explaining the rumored love of Miss Creakle for Steerforth, David reveals his own observations of the latter's physical attractiveness: "Miss Creakle was regarded . . . as being in love with Steerforth, and I am sure, as I sat in the dark, thinking of his nice voice, and his fine face, and his easy manner, and his curling hair, I thought it very likely" (96; ch. 6). David's voyeuristic pleasure at the sight of Steerforth here, as he contemplates him with the awareness of Steerforth's romantic attractiveness, prefigures his subsequent obsessive watching of Steerforth while the latter sleeps. David's recollection of his obsession with watching Steerforth sleep makes clear that physical attraction coincides with, and that physical and spiritual attraction enclose, any consideration he might have of Steerforth's socio-economic power or power to aid him in his social climb. This emphasis on Steerforth's physical attractiveness is clearly revealed in the adult David's perspective on the situation of the child David's attraction toward Steerforth, as the adult surveys the child's remembered reactions after the boys' first "good night":

> I thought of him very much after I went to bed, and raised myself, I recollect, to look at him where he lay in the moonlight, with his handsome face turned up, and his head reclining easily on his arm. He was a person of great power in my eyes; that was, of course, the reason of my mind running on on him. No veiled future dimly glanced upon him in the moonbeams. There was no shadowy picture of his footsteps, in the garden that I dreamed of walking in all night. (97; ch. 6)

The assertion that Steerforth's power is what compels David's obsessive thinking about the aristocrat is weakened by its nonemphatic placement within these contexts and by the rhetorical stutter of the double insistence linked by a semi-colon. Whether "no shadowy picture" means no picture at all or simply no shadowed, darkened, ominous picture of Steerforth's footsteps, it is significant that the waking contemplation of Steerforth as he sleeps transports David into an edenic setting in his own dreams. Finally, David may be seen to spiritualize Steerforth by placing him unveiled and unshadowed in that edenic setting. This movement anticipates the responses David makes to Steerforth throughout life and throughout the narrative; physical may give way to economic attraction, but this latter in turn gives way to recognition of Steerforth's spiritual attractiveness and to David's reconnection with him as a spiritual being. The closing, spiritualizing image here reveals again the child's attachment and betrays the narrator's continued emotional enjoyment of Steerforth's memory.

Far from replicating the squeamishness of Monod, Miller points to the homoerotic dimension of the early stage of the boys' friendship. He argues that storytelling by David is intended to divert attention from the true contents of David's subjectivity vis-à-vis Steerforth, and (by quoting the scene that is its center) that Steerforth transfers a quasi-sexual affection for David onto a more respectable narrative object, that is, onto the sister David does not have, who would resemble him (21). Steerforth is the initiator of this fictional arrangement, placing David symbolically into the place of "object" by creating him as a female and so balancing out the subject-object opposition between them. David's final voyeuristic focus in this scene, however, signals his ultimate *subject* status. As *our* "Scheherazade" David is observer and narrator, clearly subject and male, and Steerforth is clearly object and female.[16] But Steerforth not only displays more passionate activity vis-à-vis David, Rosa, and Em'ly and keeps more control; he effeminizes David in a number of ways, beginning with his objectification of the younger boy.[17] So in order to connect, to satisfy the subject demand of each man, they must create between them an object ground on which to interact, to project each other, and to appropriate each other as objects. Miller does not retreat from the implications of the early scene between David and Steerforth and its symbology. Miller's purpose is to demonstrate that narrative or discourse is for the character and narrator David and for Dickens the writer a means of hiding from public view that internal material which is unacceptable. Miller is explicit in discussing what is being obscured in this scene in *Copperfield*:

Here again a powerful affect is evoked, but evacuated of any substantial content. *What* did David think of Steerforth as he looked at him where he lay in the moonlight, his handsome face turned up? In one sense, the question scarcely merits an answer, so eloquently here does the love that dare not speak its name speak its metonyms (the "whispering and listening half-undressed," and so on). Yet in another sense, such an answer is positively averted, since David lapses into distractingly cryptic reverie at just the point where — but for the veil of "no veiled future . . ." — the classic erotics of the scene would have become manifest. And once again, the affect is soon displaced in an experience of fiction: in lieu of the nocturnal sexual episode that — as David might say, "of course" — does not take place between him and Steerforth, they organize the institution of bedtime stories, in which David recounts to Steerforth from memory the novels he has read at home. (21)

This mode of relationship is not confined to the boys' childhood. David's love continues into the storytelling present. He says, "It [Steerforth's approval] was so precious to me that *I look back* on these trifles [of being tired], now, with an aching heart" (102; ch. 7; emphasis added); David's final state will be a return to this "primal" state of the storyteller: looking back and narrating.

The slipperiness in gender-identification of the two males is also not confined to the original voyeuristic scene and the original childhood relationship but reveals itself in every subject-object shift they experience in their collaborative construction of their interactions and of David's autobiography.[18] Their primal scene is evoked later in the novel as David reestablishes his voyeur/ writer relationship with the object/subject Steerforth. David alludes to Steerforth asleep at school three times later in the novel, twice in his narration of his leave-taking from Steerforth, just before the latter seduces Em'ly (the third time is at the discovery of Steerforth's body). At this leave-taking he also reveals, significantly, that he used to touch Steerforth while the latter slept.

> I was up with the dull dawn, and, having dressed as quietly as I could, looked into his room. He was fast asleep, lying, easily, with his head upon his arm, as I had often seen him lie at school.
> The time came in its season, and that was very soon, when I almost wondered that nothing troubled his repose, as I looked at him. But he slept — let me think of him so again — as I had often seen him asleep at school, and thus, in that silent hour, I left him.
> — Never more, O God forgive you, Steerforth! to touch that *passive* hand in love and friendship. Never, never more! (439; ch. 29; emphasis added).

Steerforth is passive on the night before this scene of leavetaking in his reliance upon David's thinking the best of him if anything should separate them and is passive in his (evidently) unconscious reception of David's touch. That David as character continually returns to the allusion to watching Steerforth, that he watches Steerforth die, and that he appropriates Steerforth asleep, Steerforth dying, and Steerforth dead in his role as narrator underscores the masculine-gendered identification of David vis-à-vis Steerforth. His narrative appropriation echoes and confirms the object status of Steerforth as revealed by his sleeping passive reception of David's touching of his hand, which is repeated finally in David's "lift[ing] up the leaden hand, and [holding] it to [his] heart" (797; ch. 56).

The second triangular mediation I am considering almost seems a reaction to the first, in which the feminine angle of the triangle was wholly fictive, merely the evocation of feminine psychic material in both men. In this second triangular configuration, two women, both of whom may be viewed as both middle-class and aristocratic, mirror one another in the feminine corner.[19] Rosa Dartle, ostensibly the sole female in this triangle with David and Steerforth, is monied but not quite enough to be independent, it seems. Dora Spenlow is also ostensibly monied, but the source of that money is the legal profession, rendering her, at best, upper-middle-class and not unequivocally respectable (in the aristocratic perspective). She is, however, trained to imitate the aristocratic woman and is therefore utterly useless as a middle-class managerial wife (see Vanden Bossche). Both Dartle and Dora seem to promise David an improvement in his social condition that will raise him above the middle class. In choosing the "purer" of the two, David ascends morally and imitates his stepfather, who, more cruelly, desires an inexperienced mate that he can train.[20] David also, significantly, falls in love with the decorative Dora at a point in the narrative at which he has reconnected with James Steerforth (ch. 26). We might say that Dora provides a narrative deferment or diversion of the energy of David's love for Steerforth to a woman, so that, even though Steerforth does not know Dora, we have a type of triangulation in that she receives David's love for Steerforth and her behavior mimics that of Steerforth's class. When David meets Dora, he has already dismissed Rosa from her role as substitute for Steerforth and placed her among the women with whom he has been infatuated; Agnes's humorous reception of his confidences about Rosa make this clear (373; ch. 25). In addition, David has already become aware of Agnes as counsellor and as object of Uriah Heep's desire, and he has been put on his brotherly guard with respect to Heep's offensive marital aspirations; he has already introduced Steerforth to Em'ly. He has, it seems, provided a surrogate for Steerforth toward whom he too can divert his inter-male desire. The narrative stage is set for the next chapter, in which David is smitten by Dora.

The relationship of each man to Rosa Dartle in this triangle makes clear that for each man the relationship to the other man is of primary importance. Steerforth's relationship with Rosa Dartle is long past. Yet on the third occasion of David's visiting at the Steerforth home — when David has postponed his trip to Yarmouth to support Peggotty at Barkis's impending death in order to honor Steerforth's explicitly triangulating request to "stand between Rosa Dartle and [him] and keep [them] asunder" (431; ch. 28), just before Steerforth actually elopes with Em'ly—Steerforth plays cruelly at charming Rosa again, only to mock her and dismiss her anew (438; ch. 29). David's love for

Steerforth causes him to adopt Steerforth's willful blindness about the cause of Rosa taking offense at the romantic manipulation and mockery that Steerforth inflicts on her at this last friendly gathering. He even anticipates the mockery when Steerforth asks him to Highgate.

> "Would you love each other too much, without me?"
> "Yes, or hate," laughed Steerforth, "no matter which." (431; ch. 28)

After Steerforth goads Rosa, he laughs about her and invites David to consider her display of anger:

> [H]e laughed about her, and asked me if I had ever seen such a fierce little piece of incomprehensibility. I expressed as much of my astonishment as was then capable of expression, and asked if he could guess what it was that she had taken so much amiss, so suddenly. (438–39; ch. 29)

Both the invitation and the incident of Steerforth's teasing sets Dartle up as the object which the men use as medium for their connection with each other.

Earlier, David, after spending a day with Mrs. Steerforth and Rosa "talk[-ing] about nothing but [Steerforth] all day," admits:

> I felt myself falling a little in love with her. I could not help thinking, several times in the course of the evening, and particularly when I walked home at night, what delightful company she would be in Buckingham Street. (361; ch. 24)

It is of no little significance that David should feel himself "falling a little in love with her" after spending the day talking with her about the man they *both* love. In the Girardian paradigm, David falls "a bit" in love with Dartle because of Steerforth's past love for her. His momentary choice of beloved occurs because he has first chosen the rival for that beloved, the man who has already loved her. And though received warmly by Mrs. Steerforth and Rosa on this occasion, David

> particularly observed . . . the close and attentive watch Miss Dartle kept upon me, and the lurking manner in which she seemed to compare my face with Steerforth's, and Steerforth's with mine, and to lie in wait for something to come out between the two. (433; ch. 29)

Steerforth's cruelty to Rosa and the strange discomfort David is also feeling at this time — his vague disquiet with regard to Rosa's observations of Steerforth and of himself during this visit — reveal her superfluousness to them once they are together.

Dartle is a jealous rival of David's and reveals the rekindling of her love for Steerforth (at his provocation) *because* of the value placed upon him by his other lover — David.

> So surely, as I looked towards her, did I see that eager visage, with its gaunt black eyes and searching brow, intent on mine, or passing suddenly from mine to Steerforth's or comprehending both of us at once. In this lynx-like scrutiny she was so far from faltering when she saw I observed it, that at such a time she only fixed her piercing look upon me with a more intent expression still. Blameless as I was, and knew that I was, in reference to any wrong she could possible suspect me of, I shrunk before her strange eyes, quite unable to endure their hungry lustre. (433; ch. 29)

In her close scrutiny of David and Steerforth together, Miss Dartle reveals her suspicion that David's profession or David himself holds some special fascination for Steerforth that keeps Steerforth from home, a "wrong" to which David's insistent denial draws our closer attention. She questions David closely upon Steerforth's recent activities (434–35) and is incredulous at David's assertion that he has "not seen him this long while, until last night" (434). She seems to think it natural that Steerforth's affection for David would make the latter privy to Steerforth's interiority in a way that she cannot be: "If you are honorable and faithful, I don't ask you to betray your friend. I ask you only to tell me, is it anger, is it hatred, is it pride, is it some wild fancy, is it love, *what is it*, that is leading him?" (435) Herein she recognizes that the place she once held is now being filled by David's friendship. Indeed, what Rosa suspects is no less than the truth: there is very definitely something going on between the men that transcends any bond that either of them may have with her.

In the third significant triangle of the novel, the other actual woman through whom David and Steerforth channel their love for one another is Em'ly, and even in childhood the narrator advances her as a potential pawn to be used in this way. David's precociously mature perception that his culture demands an other in relationships of attraction between males, in addition to encouraging his adoption of a feminine storytelling persona, tempts him, on the night Peggotty and Ham visit him at Salem House and meet Steerforth, to

> tell Steerforth about pretty little Em'ly, but I was too timid of mentioning her name, and too much afraid of his laughing at me. I remember that I thought a good deal, and in an uneasy sort of way, about Mr. Peggotty having said that she was getting on to be a woman, but I decided that was nonsense. (114; ch. 7)

David as a child is here beginning to respond directly to Steerforth's fantasy evocation of David's mediating "sister," Em'ly, just as Steerforth's later request that David stand between him and Dartle evokes the mediation of the erotic triangle. David's panic here echoes the panicked response of David the narrator to *his* narration of the original bedroom dialogue. The source of David's uneasiness is evident even though the text is not explicit; despite his dismissal of that source and that uneasiness as "nonsense," clearly the combination of his friend's handsomeness and of Em'ly's sexual maturation produces David's discomfort and reluctance to mention her.

Confronted with an erotic triangle involving a girl he loves and a boy he loves, David may balk, having already achieved intimacy with Steerforth in the triangle they have created between themselves within the subject/object opposition by exchanging gender roles. When they are adults, and when for all David knows the other attachment has been relinquished forever, then David is certainly eager to introduce Steerforth to the Peggotty household, including Em'ly. He loses no time, in fact, in suggesting that Steerforth meet her, as soon as they reconnect as adults, before the Dartle triangle is created and as quickly relinquished, and immediately preceding his own replacement of Steerforth with Dora (or the narrative's disciplining of his love for the former with the introduction of the latter). The only danger in their adult triangulation, which turns out to be a real danger, is that Steerforth will be swept out of David's life by the action of appropriating the beauty they both appreciate in Em'ly and (by sexual seduction) actualizing his apprehension of it. This causes David's ambivalence on the night he introduces Steerforth to the Peggotty household.

David's ambivalence about the direction of his own sexual desires, about his mutually exclusive loves for Em'ly and for Steerforth, reveals itself in his complicity in Steerforth's seduction of Em'ly. The "pretty little niece" (298; ch. 20) David reveals when he visits Steerforth's house seems to be David's sister as projected by Steerforth in the dormitory at Salem House, "a pretty, timid, little, bright-eyed sort of girl" (97; ch. 6). But Em'ly is much more important as the "pretty little niece" through whom Steerforth can "touch" David in their mutual apprehension of her beauty and appropriation of her as object of desire. In childhood and adulthood Em'ly precedes David in sexual development and in overt sexual response to, and narratively covert sexual interaction with, Steerforth. At their meeting it is clear that Steerforth's presence works unusually upon Em'ly, who has expressed the desire to be a lady, who has glowed when he was described (151; ch. 10), who has just been described as "half-bold and half-shy, and half-a-laughing and half-a-crying" (that is, ambivalent in her acceptance of Ham), in the announcement of her engagement just previous to the arrival of Steerforth and David (319; ch. 21). David may still love Em'ly as an adult, but he may also be confused about sharing her love with Steerforth (and his with her) in the ambivalence he confesses when he introduces Steerforth to the houseboat gathering (320; ch. 21), just as he is shy in childhood about mentioning her to him (114; ch. 7).

If Em'ly is only too likely and vulnerable an object for which Steerforth will turn away from David, choosing the easier and more immediate gratification, Steerforth himself is vulnerable to this girl; his projected description of David's "sister," whom he would desire (97; ch. 6), fits Em'ly particularly well when she is aroused by David's description of Steerforth (151; ch. 10). This is what worries David. Perhaps it is this ambivalence which has brought about the change in David's feelings for Em'ly. He always has been confused by Em'ly as sexual being and at the same time intensely aware of the potential for sexual tension between her and his handsome friend. During his second visit to Yarmouth he has "wondered . . . very much" at her teasing him and has witnessed her reaction to the description of a boy she has never met, and she thereby clearly indicates the awakening of her sexuality (149, 151; ch. 10). Em'ly's desire for Steerforth is clearly and consistently presented by her, Mr. Peggotty, and David Copperfield's narrative as mercenary desire: she is expecting to be made "a lady." Recognition of the relative sincerity of his own love for Steerforth versus Em'ly's probably influences his unflinching judgment of her later in the novel. She has transgressed the bounds David set for her interaction with Steerforth (the latter's apprehension of her beauty, her appreciation of his fine qualities and status as David's friend) and has sought to "write" her own story with the aristocrat. By actually consummating in her own person the love she was to have mediated symbolically for the men, she appropriates the place David wants and so separates the men she was intended to join.

David's unjust condemnation of Em'ly is revealed by several circumstances in the novel, underscoring the primacy of his attachment to Steerforth and his willingness to hide the strength of that attachment under the conventional shaming of a fallen woman. David leaves her suffering under the vitriolic attack of Rosa Dartle. He may decide not to save Em'ly from Rosa's verbal abuse because to do so is Dan'l's place and not his. But he also may not intervene in the Em'ly-Rosa dialogue because he feels the attack is something happening to him. He even suggests as much as he narrates the event: "Would he never come. How long was I to bear this? How long could I bear it?" (718; ch. 50, emphases added). He effectively admits being the lower-class lover preferred by Steerforth and being berated by Rosa for seducing Steerforth's attention from home and from her. If the class disparity between David and Em'ly is clear according to the surface markers we find in the text — the Peggotty's address of David as "Mas'r Davy" and the diminutives of names in the Peggotty family (Em'ly, Dan'l) — the class aspirations of Em'ly and David, the cavalier treatment each receives from Steerforth, and the cruelty of Dartle to each, all speak of class-identification between them.[21] And he also admits collusion with Rosa's belief that Em'ly is the responsible party in the elopement for which Em'ly herself suffers the most punishment by society and by the narrative.[22]

The narrative choices David makes with respect to representing the two characters reveals that there is no ambivalence in his feelings for Steerforth such as David displays towards Em'ly. The power inequities present in the relationship of the two men from childhood onward are least present in Yarmouth, in their sexual interactions, and around the event of the elopement.[23] In Yarmouth, Steerforth most clearly reveals his character to David in his attack on Ham (322–23; ch. 21), in his association with the as-yet-suspicious Miss Mowcher (334–40; ch. 22), and in his attempt to confess his own sense that he is profoundly undisciplined (326–27; ch. 22). For the sake of the middle-class morality he is ostensibly espousing, David pretends to condemn Steerforth as he pretends to forgive and narratively redeem Em'ly, and as he intends the marriage to Dora to replace the attachment to Steerforth. But David stubbornly believes the best of Steerforth at every turn, and the narrative treatment of each makes clear that Em'ly is condemned and Steerforth embraced more closely for his indiscretion. It is after all the only socially-sanctioned romantic and (imaginatively) sexual connection they can make. In the moment of Steerforth's lapse, David loves and cherishes Steerforth to such an extent that he can claim their love was ''never . . . better'' (457; ch. 32). The narrative reveals a more profound and lasting imaginative connection in their original triangle and in David's immortalizing of his friend and their love, in Steerforth's continued presence in David's consciousness and in his dreams, and in David's narrative centralization of Steerforth's death. On the sexual plane, the triangle Steerforth's rakishness forms among them is more palpable and both more and less satisfying to David. Steerforth most clearly demonstrates how little women actually mean to him, since he has never used David in such a way as to destroy his social standing, while Em'ly and possibly Rosa are used in this way. Steerforth demonstrates that his love for David is deeper than ''love'' demanding conventional gratification, sexual or class-powered, yet he is able to appropriate those expressions as its own.[24]

Another indication that David's judgment of Em'ly is based on more than standard middle-class moral codes is the narrative redemption of Martha. Martha has in fact become a prostitute yet is allowed to marry in Australia. Em'ly aspires to be a lady, to transcend her class limitations; Em'ly elopes with a gentleman, believing his promises that she would be made a lady and, most significantly, exposes the undisciplined heart of the person the novel's narrator has most truly loved — a man; Em'ly is punished by the narrator's refusal both to be reconciled to her (he does not wave back) and by Dickens's refusal to provide her with a happy ending (she is not allowed to marry, but must remain ''kiender worn'' with Dan'l). ''She might have married well a mort of times, 'but Uncle' she says to me, 'that's gone for ever' '' Dan'l reports (862; ch. 63). A friend to all, she is denied by Dickens and by David the narrator the "redemption" a marriage would represent, so deep is the "sin" for which the narrative and the narrator/lover, robbed of his beloved, must punish her.[25]

David's judgement of Em'ly explains his refusal to see her before she sails to Australia, even though David suggests other reasons for this refusal. He suggests that to see her might be humiliating or "too painful for her, perhaps"; but he offers to write to her for Ham (732; ch. 51). It seems unlikely that seeing David or David's handwriting would be any less painful to her than reading what the latter conveys: Ham's "words" which she will keep "close to [her] heart" until she dies, which "are sharp thorns, but [which] are such a comfort" (781, ch. 55). The contrivances to make peace between Ham and Em'ly without forcing them to meet seem, nevertheless, humane; those by which David keeps himself away from Em'ly before she sails seem gratuitous, as does his last apostrophe to her: "Aye Em'ly, beautiful and drooping, cling to him with the utmost trust of thy bruised heart, for he has clung to thee, with all the might of his great love!" (807; ch. 57) This judgmental disregard for the truest victim of class oppression, most brutally expressed by Steerforth in his statement of disbelief in the emotional capacity of the lower classes, is prefigured clearly by the narrative in David's apostrophe to Steerforth during the scene of their last leave-taking. Although he signals that his lament is generally for Steerforth's moral transgression, a closer look suggests that that for which David invokes God's forgiveness is not Steerforth's social sin but his withdrawal (particularly the withdrawal of his touch) from David's life: "Never more, oh God forgive you, Steerforth! to touch that passive hand in love and friendship. Never, never more!" (439; ch. 29). Paradoxically, David's unconventional love at once undermines the conventional morality of compulsory heterosexuality and undergirds its sexist double standard for the judgment of transgressive sexual expression.

The narrative climax of the novel allows the men to reattain their triangular attachment and itself functions as a locus of emotional vulnerability in David's case and physical vulnerability in Steerforth's case, connecting both men with an anti-masculine quality (vulnerability) that eternally evokes the feminine and places them within it. This attachment is uncomplicated by the need for an actual woman to mediate their desire for one another. In this it resembles their storytelling mediation earlier; and indeed, here David returns to his self-identification as the teller of Steerforth's story. In narrating Steerforth's death yet resurrecting him as dramatic center of his autobiography, David provides himself safe and eternal emotional access to this his truest lover. This literary repression of his homoerotic desire protects Steerforth's memory, reproduces Steerforth's character, and reincarnates the (ideal) man David loves in a physical text by the actions it performs ostensibly in the interest of killing Steerforth (and Dora) off to make room for the disciplined and disciplinary resolution provided by Agnes. Steerforth's memory and the event of his death seem to impregnate the memory and consciousness of David's character, dictating his focus as subject on this masculine object, fixing the focus of David's emotions and of David's narrative upon Steerforth, and rendering them both trans-gressive:

> I NOW APPROACH AN EVENT IN MY LIFE, SO INDELIBLE, so awful, *so bound by an infinite variety of ties to all that has preceded it, in these pages, that, from the beginning of my narrative, I have seen it growing larger and larger as I advanced like a great tower in a plain, and throwing its forecast shadow even on the incidents of my childish days.*
>
> For years after it occurred, I dreamed of it often. I have started up so vividly impressed by it that its fury has yet seemed raging in my quiet room, in the still night. I dream of it sometimes, though at lengthened and uncertain intervals, to this hour. I have an association between it and a stormy wind, or the lightest mention of a sea-shore, as strong as any of which my mind is conscious. As plainly as I behold what happened, I will try to write it down. *I do not recall it but see it done, for it happens again before me.* (779; ch. 55, emphases added)

The fact that the homocentric climax is played out in voyeuristic narrative underscores David's association with the "romance" of his early storytelling, born in his voyeuristic satisfactions while watching Steerforth awake and asleep, and it links his movement into professional storytelling with his move-ment back to the emotional focus of his first storytelling — Steerforth. In other words, David's professional movement enacts in a public and publiciza-ble way his emotional movement back to Steerforth. Idealized in death and frozen in narrative, Steerforth is now a safe object of David's love.

The narrative connection with Steerforth, born in the drama of his death, in the narrative disciplining reminiscent of the flagellation fantasy and in the narrator's statement that Steerforth is central to the narrative and to the narra-tor's life, is exponentially more compelling than is the narrative climax in which he marries Agnes.

David's love for the idealized (deathlike and deadly) Agnes, narratively revealed only after the narrative has released all its energy in the Steerforth death-scene and after David has released all his passion in grief over the loss of his friend and of his first wife, has no excuse of childish fervor as had his first marriage.[26] Agnes's preternatural calm and goodness and her ill-devel-oped character render her "a vaporous and shadowy attitude rather than a woman" (Kincaid 164). Their single love scene involves a return to their connection in death; they discuss Dora, and the novel closes with Agnes prophesying his own death for David with the same pose she used to announce Dora's death to him.[27] Agnes's non-humanity is too glaring to ignore and becomes clearer as the novel draws to a close. In the last three paragraphs of the novel she becomes even less human, more etherealized as "one face, shining . . . like a Heavenly light" with "its beautiful serenity," a "dear presence," even David's "soul" (870; ch. 64).

The primacy of David's associations with Steerforth are at once willfully hidden and revealed by the strident illogic of his claim that Agnes elicited his earliest hopes. In order to justify his new romantic interest in the woman he has always called "sister," David forces a retrospective romantic tint upon the long association by suggesting that, in his process of grieving for Dora (and Steerforth), he "began to think that I might have set [my heart's] earliest and brightest hopes on Agnes" (811; ch. 58), and he then relates the notion of her loss to the nagging sense of loss he calls "the old unhappy loss or want of something" (812). His statements here are the less convincing when we recall that his association with and affection for Steerforth long antedates his meeting with Agnes, that his immediate childhood responses to Steerforth are romantic while his first impression of Agnes relates her symbolically to stained glass (229; ch. 15), and that this symbology reflects her association, in pointing upward at Dora's death (764; ch. 53) and in her projection of his own (870; ch. 64), with the "spire point[ing] upward from my old playground," the churchyard in which David's parents are buried (161; ch. 10). The enforcement of the heterosexual-romantic ending ultimately fails, then, in its cloying and deadly narrative cast hastily painted over the life of David and Agnes together, to displace the central emotional focus, the true love of David's life, Steerforth. It fails, despite the procreative prescription of compulsory heterosexuality, to convince us that it is anything other than a quiescently deadly choice on David's part. The most convincing hope Agnes may be said to reconnect David to is a hope of death, a hope to which she clearly points, and one which moreover points his way to reunion not just with his mother and his first wife, but also to reunion with his dead friend.[28]

The love of David and Steerforth is narratively productive; it is a creative love, while the heterosexual-romantic ending of this novel is a literal, and literary, "forcing" of David's primary interests in Steerforth into the erotic mold his Oedipalized society ultimately requires. After its denigration as "childish" and its contortion as triangular, David's love for Steerforth is frozen in narrative, frozen as narrative, as past history and therefore safe. But the half-erased focus on the homocentric relationship between David and Steerforth reveals itself in relief under the forced heterocentralization of the ending and in the tenderness underlying David's description of Steerforth's death. Forced into the paradigms his patriarchal society prescribes, all of which are informed by the dominant and oppressive models of compulsory heterosexuality and capitalist manhood, David's love for Steerforth ultimately transcends his culture's constraints and manages to speak many of its names.

University of Texas at Arlington

NOTES

1. References to *David Copperfield* are to the 1962 edition edited by Edgar Johnson.
2. See Needham; Johnson's afterword to *David Copperfield*; and Welsh, chapter ten.
3. The "discipline" of the novel — its insistence on the final contentment of Annie, Em'ly and of David with Agnes, its convenient removal of Dora — permits "the play of disallowed desires," as Weinstein asserts (43–44), and is never quite satisfactory. David's final apotheosis of Steerforth, as well, is a significant palimpsest of the depth of their love, given the judgment and the rejection to which David subjects his friend and given the narrative's slaughter of that friend in the service of disciplining David.
4. The non-sexual but homosocial love of David and Steerforth, inasmuch as it represents an ideal, even a specific ideal like heroic friendship such as Halperin outlines (75–87), may be seen as a deployment "to keep at bay" the gathering forces which were to crystallize in a culture-wide modern self-consciousness of homosexual ontology.
5. See *The Other Victorians*, chapter 6. Inasmuch as the flagellation fantasy employs gender fluidity, a figure Dickens's culture would take as "homosexual," we may say that David and Murdstone and Steerforth self-consciously participate in homoeroticism in this dimension of their interaction. Marcus's interpretation of the flagellation fantasy as ultimately homoerotic relies upon the Victorian conflation of gender identity and object choice, but it interprets the fantasy deployment of that confusion through the screen of Freud. Like Marcus, I argue that both gender theory contemporary to Dickens and post-Freudian sexology allow us to read these and other characters and situations as "homosexual."
6. With a different critical focus, Vanden Bossche points to the progression of David through the "phases" of Em'ly, Dora, and Agnes. Here I am positing a similar movement, but with a romantic rather than a socio-economic impetus behind it.
7. Armstrong both identifies storytelling (particularly novelistic storytelling) as a feminine pursuit (97) and associates subjectivity with social requirements for females and with femininity itself (4). See Greenberg on the association of transgendered behavior with homosexuality (333–37).
8. Manning argues that David, like Scheherazade, tells stories "to secure his sheltered niche — to save his boy's life — in the isolated world of Salem House. The adult David Copperfield tells his story under similar, less comic, compulsion" (332). Miller argues that David and Dickens turn to narrative in order to avoid accurate interpretation of action and desire. What is being held off here, in addition to a vague threat of death to which Manning seems correct to point, is consciousness and consummation of the sexual attraction between the boys, as Miller also argues.
9. See Sedgwick 21.
10. See Kucich (27 and passim), Dickens's male characters are able to use the notion and the motion of repression productively by repressing the public demonstration of impulses, such as the energies of aggression and eros, of which the public disapproves. In this way Dickensian heroes in effect create an interiority for themselves, a separate mental realm. The action meant to join them to society (by diminishing the free-play of individuality) in fact separates them from it and enforces the protection rather than the destruction or even redirection of those impulses. They create a private space deep enough to engulf the sexuality and sexual desire they incorporate, containing and conserving it. According to Kucich,

Dickens characterizes successful interiorizing and subjectivitizing as distinctly male. But he would appear to be doing so in contradiction to the cultural norms that Armstrong and Greenberg identify as prescriptive: that in males subjectivity and storytelling and the expression of emotional bonding are all gender-transgressive (see note 7, above), unless we separate modes of subjectivity and identify the type Kucich calls productive as intellectual subjectivity. David's never-to-be-published autobiography contains many of the mysteries we expect to find in such an enclosed subjectivity, including attempted concealment by linguistic encoding and shaping.

11. The casual attitude expressed by the twentieth-century correspondent Sedgwick quotes may reasonably explain the failure of consistent or logical administrative responses to such activities in nineteenth-century public schools; as Crompton notes, documents by Shelley, Disraeli, and others demonstrate the frequency of adolescent homoerotic encounters in nineteenth-century public schools (Crompton 75–77).

12. Jordan, who refuses to see any but a heterosexual eroticism mediating the males' relationship, argues that Littimer's making David feel "young" and Steerforth's "condescending familiarity" are merely indications of David's social inferiority and the older men's recognition of it (68).

13. See Monod 323.

14. The double message that *Copperfield* ultimately sends about the gender of storytelling may reflect a changing perception in the Victorian era towards that activity. If earlier in history it had been seen as "feminine" (see note 7 above) and if this may be taken as indication of David's and Steerforth's effeminacy, by the end of Dickens's career it was a profession dominated by men, and by the end of the novel David is profiting by it (it becomes a *profitable*, masculine activity, although this particular endeavor — *David Copperfield* — is not meant to be sold as a novel). It is possible, then, to see the final story, the autobiography itself, as representing productive subjectivity and therefore as a masculine project; nevertheless, it becomes the medium for feminine or feeling intersubjectivity between David and Steerforth after the death of the latter.

15. See Greenberg on the pragmatic, capitalist, middle-class, success ideal (overwhelmingly "masculine"), which included proscription of emotional expression between males and prescription of aggression and competitiveness (358–59).

16. For a clear overview of the criticism identifying the "gaze" as subjective, as gendered, and as masculine, whereas the female gaze is transgressive (since to be woman is to be object), see most recently Newman. Jardine identifies the traditions in Western thought that would identify both Steerforth's position as "outside of the conscious subject" (here, David) and David's state of dream (also outside of consciousness) as feminine positions (59).

17. Melnick identifies both as time-honored and as dubious the association of passivity with femininity in Austen's fiction and in her culture. See Monod as well (323–25). By placing emphasis on the behavioral transgressiveness which reveals David's gender-transgressiveness and his failure to honor the middle-class capitalist masculine code, I am suggesting that behavior, cultured as it all is, can reveal that which is within — desire which reveals no gendered subject, though it knows gendered designations in its object choice(s).

18. Just as David, in his first incarnation as storyteller, is feminine, so at first glance, Marcus argues, the flagellator and the victim in the pornographic fantasy appear

to be females; only on second glance does each reveal "her" masculine identity, rendering the fantasy a masculine-homoerotic one (259).

19. See Jordan 69, and note 25 below.

20. While Dora is virtually untouched by adult consciousness, let alone by previous romantic experience, Jordan recognizes the scar on Rosa's mouth as "the mark of Steerforth's sexual violence on her" (69). Monod, too, reveals that Rosa is intended to "have been the mistress — the first one — of [Dickens's] youthful Don Juan, later rejected by him and henceforth repressing her love, which thus turns to hatred" (356; and see 355–59).

21. Dartle's condescension towards David resembles her acerbic condescension towards Em'ly during her verbal attack on the latter. David's failure to respond to the attack underscores his understanding of his class-identification with Em'ly, vis-à-vis Steerforth, and his identification with her as beloved of Steerforth. Jordan argues that Em'ly is enough David's economic contemporary and mirror in class ambition to be viewed as an object of barter by which David may be attempting to improve his own class status. Jordan's cultural-materialist dismissal of the notion that David and Steerforth connect directly in an emotional/sexual manner, based on his insight that David has a socio-political agenda in "exchanging" Dartle and Em'ly with Steerforth, seems short-sighted.

22. I find these to be more plausible explanations for the passivity of David here than are Weinstein's arguments that this passivity is a contrivance to enforce the fact that Em'ly is to be punished for her misconduct against *general* social mores and that the Em'ly/Dan'l bond is the central romantic bond for Em'ly (Weinstein 38–43). In this instance the narrator and the narrative are one. Weinstein argues that the narrative punishes Em'ly, but it seems to me that David, as an injured party in the loss of Steerforth, also punishes her: "This anger . . . expressed in the narrative design of the novel . . . is passed off as a mere irrelevance in a larger scenario that is labelled divinely beneficent. Emily is indeed forgiven, but the form of the forgiveness — a corrosive tongue-lashing followed by a permanent exile with Peggotty — serves also as a disguised punishment for Emily, an illicit reward for Peggotty" (42).

23. These inequities are revealed in Steerforth's sensitivity toward the tenuousness of David's status; he seduces an inconsequential other in place of David himself and in place of a woman truly representative of David's middle class.

24. Steerforth's insensitive statements make clear that to him the members of Em'ly's class are little more than animals (299, 322–23). David's technical innocence in this crime against Em'ly underscores his moral superiority over this gentleman and over this woman who is "born to be a lady" (338).

25. Jordan argues that Em'lys decision against marriage is her choice of "a life of service to the wider community," a productive and independent movement away from David's middle-class conventional vision of what happiness entails for a woman (88). He cites the marriage of Martha as evidence that Dickens was not uncomfortable with such a resolution for "fallen women." But this is wanting to have it both ways. Martha is a stock character, unrealized except as a mirror and a warning for Em'ly; Martha's regeneration serves the middle-class values of David and the philanthropic leanings of Dickens at the time he was writing *Copperfield* (see Welsh 123–40). The resolution and regeneration that Martha is offered is withheld from Em'ly by David as well as by Dickens. It is David whose only true love has been tempted and who has died.

26. Dawson claims for the Alpine experience and its resulting union with Agnes the designation "psychological climax," underplays the importance of the scene of Steerforth's death, and ignores the interest the narrative expresses in the central character of the storm scene, which he calls the "dramatic climax" of the novel (131). Agnes is too focused on David, and for that matter too unrealized as a woman, to respond to Steerforth with anything but judgment, so it would be ludicrous for David to "offer" her to Steerforth in any other way than he does: by ignoring her established counselling role in his life. Unlike Em'ly, who glows at the description the child David makes of Steerforth, Agnes explicitly disapproves of Steerforth from her first meeting with him. But Steerforth's superior attractiveness encourages David to repudiate her warnings about the aristocrat (371, 439).

27. Weinstein notes of the revelation scene between David and Agnes: "suddenly she is for the reader a credible human being, a creature of 'conflicting desires' whose momentary display of feelings serves — *for the only instance in the book* — to transform her admirer into a lover" (34; emphasis mine).

28. As Dawson argues, David's "Alpine episode . . . unites him . . . with his former friends" (139). Den Hartog also presents a very interesting case opposing these two Romantic impulses in Dickens's age and in his oeuvre. He argues that they display engagement with a dialectical dilemma between the opposing and equally immanent Romantic movements of "a psychic continuity with childhood along Wordsworthian lines" (32), that is, hope for a return to a child's perceptions and all-connectedness and consequent dissolution into a broader context than that of the self (Nature, later society), and a Byronic self-assertion, individuation, valuation of adult status/autonomy: the will to commune/connect versus the will to power. Such opposing impulses finally coexist in Pip, den Hartog argues (124); so it is possible to read the regenerated David versus the Byronic Steerforth as emblematic of this struggle in the psyche and narrative of David. Den Hartog reads the development of David as "artificially smooth" based upon Dickens's denial that he contains such impulses as Steerforth displays (32); but for all David's assertion that Nature has restored him to peace and to the love of his childhood, by which he ostensibly means Agnes, the most dramatic event of the narrative, which he calls central and which he says haunts his dreams, is the life and death of Steerforth. From his Wordsworthian peace David writes a narrative the central emotional focuses of which are Byronic in character and in behavior.

WORKS CITED

Armstrong, Nancy. *Desire and Domestic Fiction: A Political History of the Novel.* New York: Oxford UP, 1987.

Crompton, Louis. *Byron and Greek Love: Homophobia in 19th-Century England.* Berkeley: U of California P, 1985.

Dawson, Carl. *Victorian Noon: English Literature in 1850.* Baltimore: Johns Hopkins UP, 1979.

den Hartog, Dirk. *Dickens and Romantic Psychology: The Self in Time in Nineteenth-Century Literature.* New York: St. Martin's, 1987.

Dickens, Charles. *David Copperfield.* Ed. with afterword by Edgar Johnson. New York: Signet, 1962.

Girard, René. *Deceit, Desire, and the Novel: Self and Other in Literary Structure.* Trans. Yvonne Freccero. Baltimore: Johns Hopkins UP, 1965.

Greenberg, David F. *The Construction of Homosexuality*. Chicago: U of Chicago P, 1988.

Halperin, David M. *One Hundred Years of Homosexuality: and other Essays on Greek Love*. New York: Routledge, 1990.

Jardine, Alice. "Gynesis." *Diacritics* 12 (summer 1982): 54–65.

Jones, Ernest. "Jealousy." *Papers on Psychoanalysis*. 5th ed. Baltimore: Williams and Wilkins, 1948. 325–40.

Jordan, John O. "The Social Sub-text of *David Copperfield.*" *Dickens Studies Annual* 14 (1985): 61–92.

Kincaid, James R. *Dickens and the Rhetoric of Laughter*. Oxford: Clarendon, 1971.

Kucich, John. *Repression in Victorian Fiction: Charlotte Brontë, George Eliot and Charles Dickens*. Berkeley: U of California Press, 1987.

Manning, Sylvia. "David Copperfield and Scheherazade: The Necessity of Narrative." *Studies in the Novel* 14 (Winter 1982): 327–36.

Marcus, Steven. *The Other Victorians: A Study of Sexuality and Pornography in Mid-Nineteenth-Century England*. New York: Basic Books, 1966.

Melnick, Burton. "Sexual Identity in *Mansfield Park*: A Freudian Approach." Annual Convention of the MLA. Chicago, December, 1990.

Miller, D. A. "Secret Subjects, Open Secrets." *Dickens Studies Annual* 14 (1985): 17–38.

Monod, Sylvère. *Dickens the Novelist*. Norman: U of Oklahoma P, 1968.

Needham, Gwendolyn B. "The Undisciplined Heart of David Copperfield." *Nineteenth-Century Fiction* 9 (1954): 81–107.

Newman, Beth. " 'The Situation of the Looker-On': Gender, Narration, and Gaze in *Wuthering Heights.*" *PMLA* 105 (October 1990): 1029–41.

Sedgwick, Eve Kosofsky. *Between Men: English Literature and Male Homosocial Desire*. New York: Columbia UP, 1985.

Steiner, George. *Real Presences*. Chicago: U of Chicago P, 1989.

Vanden Bossche, Chris R. "Cookery, not Rookery: Family and Class in *David Copperfield.*" *Dickens Studies Annual* 15 (1986): 87–109.

Weinstein, Philip M. *The Semantics of Desire: Changing Models of Identity from Dickens to Joyce*. Princeton: Princeton UP, 1984.

Welsh, Alexander. *From Copyright to Copperfield: The Identity of Dickens*. Cambridge, MA: Harvard UP, 1987.

REVIEW ESSAYS

IMAGINING THE NATION, INVENTING THE EMPIRE

By Patrick Brantlinger

IN AN *NYRB* REVIEW of recent books on nationalism, historian Tony Judt cautions against those theorists — Marxist, post-Marxist, poststructuralist, postcolonial — who treat nationalism as "a collective hallucination": "In this perspective, nationalism, and nations, are inventions. . . . They are images of an identity that does not 'really' exist, even though the belief that it does so has significantly material consequences" (45). Among other studies that take this view, Judt cites Benedict Anderson's *Imagined Communities: Reflections on the Origin and Spread of Nationalism.* Especially through his treatment of novels as contributing to the "invention" of modern nation-states, Anderson has influenced an array of recent writers — for example, the contributors to Homi K. Bhabha's anthology, *Nation and Narration,* which offers poststructuralist, postcolonial analyses of national identity as a "form of cultural elaboration" (Bhabha 3), or in other words as a sort of fiction-of-state not much different from novels. But granted that Anderson emphasizes and perhaps overemphasizes (as did Marshall McLuhan in *The Gutenberg Galaxy* and elsewhere) the discursive formations — novels, newspapers, museums, maps, and statistics — that contribute to the illusion of a uniform public existing in "homogeneous, empty time" and space, and hence to the modern "imagining" of nationalities, Judt's caveat seems contradictory. *Every* recent commentator on nationalism including Judt recognizes that it is an ideology (though not necessarily in the sense of false consciousness or "collective hallucination") and therefore that nationalism "does not 'really' exist" even though it has "significant material consequences." Judt stresses that "in an attempt to clarify the concept of nation, two features stand out": language and religion (46). But while it is possible to think of belonging to a language community as non- or pre-ideological, religions are clearly ideologies; religions no more " 'really' exist" than do nationalisms, even though no one denies that they have real consequences.

Anyway, while unhappy with analysts who push the fictiveness of nationalism too hard, Judt acknowledges that "many of the most 'ancient' traditions, dates, and ceremonies associated with expressions of national identification in Europe are inventions of the last century" (45). What is true of Europe is equally true or truer of other parts of the world — North and South America, Africa, Australasia, much of Asia — where modern nation-states did not exist before 1776. Both the recentness and the fictiveness of national and imperial identities in the British context were main themes of Eric Hobsbawm and Terence Ranger's influential anthology of a decade ago, *The Invention of Tradition*, which included essays by such well-respected historians as Hugh Trevor-Roper (on the nineteenth-century invention of "the Highland tradition of Scotland"), David Cannadine (on the British monarchy from 1820 to 1977), and Bernard S. Cohn ("Representing Authority in Victorian India"). Paralleling Cohn, Ranger contributed an essay on "The Invention of Tradition in Colonial Africa," while Hobsbawm concluded the volume with "Mass-Producing Traditions: Europe, 1870–1914." In contrast to his negative assessment of Anderson's study, Judt considers the essays in *The Invention of Tradition* "excellent." But the Hobsbawm and Ranger volume, without benefit of either poststructuralism or postcolonialism, gave the theme of the fictiveness of national identities a major boost. Among much else, the essays by Cohn and Ranger in particular demonstrate that, in the imperial context, the exercise of power was inseparable from its symbolic expression.

Hobsbawm pursued these themes in *Nations and Nationalism since 1870: Programme, Myth, Reality*, where he endorses Anderson's "useful phrase, an 'imagined community' " which, he speculates, "no doubt . . . can be made to fill the emotional void left by the retreat or disintegration, or the unavailability of *real* human communities and networks" (46). But here Hobsbawm may be expressing the same epistemological confusion that marks Judt's caveat against theorists of nationalism like Anderson: whatever a "real" community might once have been (and perhaps Hobsbawm has in mind some such contrast as Ferdinand Tönnies's between *Gemeinschaft* and *Gesellschaft*), it would just as surely have consisted of discursive, symbolic, or ideological forms of bonding as the modern nation-state. In any case Hobsbawm's useful, erudite comparative survey stresses the connections between nationalisms and economic and political modernization in Europe over the last two or three centuries, and concludes with the hopeful thought that (despite much evidence to the contrary, which Hobsbawm acknowledges) "nationalism will decline with the decline of the nation-state" (182), opening the way, presumably, for some genuine new world order beyond war and the ravages of capitalism and imperialism.

In passing, Hobsbawm notes the distinctiveness of the "British" as opposed to merely "English" situation. That distinctiveness arises from imperialism, and empires are just as much "imagined communities" or discursive formations as are nation-states. Since Cohn's and Ranger's essays, the symbolic and ritual aspects of British imperialism have been stressed in a number of studies. These are themes in several of the volumes on empire in the series edited by John MacKenzie for the University of Manchester Press, including his own *Propaganda and Empire: The Manipulation of British Public Opinion, 1880–1960*. From about 1870 on, writes MacKenzie, "advertising, bric-a-brac, and packaging all exploited royalty and imperialism, taking symbols of colonial adventures into every home" (5). The aggressive "New Imperialism" of the fin-de-siècle was coterminous with and (though it is difficult to say how) influenced by the new consumerist orientation associated with the second Industrial Revolution. In *The Psychology of Jingoism* (1901) and his classic *Imperialism* (1902), John Hobson identified advertising, along with sensationalistic mass journalism, as one of the main fomenters of the rabid proto-fascism that helped trigger the Boer War. Unlike the novel, however, commercial mass advertising was not a factor in the initial "invention" of modern nation-states and empires. Advertising entered the picture belatedly, with decolonization just over the horizon. Like late-Victorian jingoism in general, the political themes of early mass advertising seem often reactionary, compensatory: "Empire [was] portrayed as a means of arresting national decline" (MacKenzie 10).

Two recent books that also treat imperialism as a "form of cultural elaboration" are Edward Said's *Culture and Imperialism* and Thomas Richards's *The Imperial Archive*. Said's new *magnum opus* replays Raymond Williams's *Culture and Society* by self-consciously attempting to fill a major gap in Williams's work: Williams had little to say about the British imperial experience. Said adapts Williams's generously open-ended, albeit ambiguous, conception of culture to his own analysis of numerous texts, both canonical and noncanonical, and both British and otherwise (*Aida*, for instance), not to indict their authors for being imperialists, nor to discover redeemingly anti-imperialist moments in them, so much as to show the wide variety of resonances and complexities that the imperial experience has introduced into British and other modern cultures, including postcolonial cultures. While Said usually avoids moralizing about texts and authors, his use of Williams's idea of "cultural formations" also keeps him from worrying much about causality, or for that matter about distinguishing the real from the imagined. For Said as for Williams, "culture" is in some sense both cause and effect and also both real and imaginary. Cultural, in other words, is a term that does not demand immediate causal or epistemological explanation.

In regard to being both cause and effect, "cultural formation" echoes another idea, theoretically more fashionable but also closer to Said's earlier *magnum opus Orientalism* (1978): the Foucauldian or poststructuralist idea of a "discursive formation." In *The Imperial Archive*, Richards is both more

Foucauldian and apparently more concerned to develop a causal explanation for the cultural phenomena he explores than is Said. But the explanation (Richards might prefer "theory") involves a strong assertion of the fictiveness or even the phantasmatic basis of empire-building. "An empire is partly a fiction" (1): while "partly" gives Richards an escape from the (merely?) fictive presumably in the direction of Judt's "significant material consequences," Richards mainly analyzes works of fiction — *Kim, Lost Horizon, Dracula, Tono-Bungay, Riddle of the Sands*, and *Gravity's Rainbow* among others. Unlike Anderson, he is not much interested in claiming a specific psychohistorical efficacy for the novel-genre as such, or even for novelistic subgenres like the imperialist adventure story. Rather, Richards demonstrates how literary discourse reflects and reinforces scientific discourse, and especially how the "fantasy" of "universal knowledge" defines the "imperial archive" that was in complex ways both the outcome of Britain's imperial past and the inspiration for the present defense and future expansion of the Empire. The sciences Richards discusses include economics, ethnography, morphology (both pre- and post-Darwin), and thermodynamics (Maxwell's demon and the concept of entropy). Forever chasing "a lost horizon of comprehensive knowledge" (39), scientific discourse collaborated with literature in linking that impossibly encyclopedic knowledge to "national security" (5). In the early twentieth century, the imperialistic dream of universal knowledge grew crazily insupportable and dangerous, in part because of "entropy" or the "epistemological levelling process" (112) that reduces the attempts of nation-states to control information to the paranoia and espionage of modern and now postmodern war-machines.

The overarching discursive formation or, perhaps, supreme fiction of the "imperial archive," Richards suggests, has had all sorts of massively real social and political consequences (war, for instance). The "imperial archive" thus takes on some of the qualities of general cause or primum mobile, like Louis Althusser's Marxist-structuralist conception of Ideology. Richards's term "paranoia," moreover, certainly seems to be the correct diagnosis for the modern, warmaking, empire-building "security state." The day-to-day political decision-making that has led to wars and imperial land-grabs can in general be characterized as variations upon a *Realpolitik* or Machiavellianism that looks manifestly rational, but that, finding rivals or enemies everywhere beyond the borders of the nation-state, always places "national security" at the head of its agenda. In *Myths of Empire: Domestic Politics and International Ambition*, Jack Snyder analyzes the motivations of the political leaders of five modern nation-states as these plunged into "overly aggressive foreign policies" (1) — policies that, while they may have produced imperial aggrandizement and national security for a while, sooner or later became "counterproductive" from the standpoint of the very "political realism" that generated them. Central to the imperialistic decision-making of all of these nation-states has been the idea that "security requires expansion," which is in turn based on a number of "hydra-headed justifications for aggressive policies" (3) — for instance, the thesis that territorial expansion increases power, or the thesis that, in international affairs, offense is the best defense.

Snyder does not diagnose the national leaders whose decisions he analyzes as paranoid, but he does not have to. Their rationalizations for imperialistic ventures may well be correct in the short run, but also draw the nation-states that follow them into ever-increasing conflicts with rivals, including the rival nationalisms that they seem invariably to inspire. Britain, however, avoided the catastrophes that befell Germany and Japan; in his chapter on "social imperialism" in the Victorian era, Snyder asks why that was the case. Were Palmerston and Britain's other leaders *better* "realists" than the leaders of Germany and Japan? In general, Snyder thinks, they were indeed more cautious, more concerned with the economic costs-and-benefits of imperialist expansion, and obviously also more experienced in colonial defense and governance. Palmerston thus emerges as, in "realist" terms, a better (that is, more successful) "realist" than his later counterparts in both Wilhelmine and Nazi Germany.

Although Snyder's own "realist" (empiricist political science) approach does not lend itself to theorizing about the ideological, fictive, or psychological underpinnings or superstructures of modern nation-states and their empires, he nevertheless calls the *Realpolitik* of the politicians whom he surveys "mythical." If their "myths" about national security work out in the short run, then they are less "mythical," perhaps, than they seem invariably to prove in the long run. Snyder does not speculate about either the epistemological or the psychological nature of these "myths." But perhaps the rationalizations for war and expansion espoused by Palmerston, Disraeli, Joseph Chamberlain, and others can be understood as the *parole* to the *langue* of Richards's "imperial archive," constituting the most consequential of the specific, micropolitical *units* of discourse that have been uttered, so to speak, by the macropolitical discursive formations known as modern nation-states and their empires.

In *Imagined Communities*, Anderson quotes Ernst Gellner: "Nationalism is not the awakening of nations to self-consciousness: it *invents* nations where they do not exist" (6). Hobsbawm also says that "with Gellner I would stress the element of artefact, invention and social engineering which enters into the making of nations," and he proceeds to declare that "nationalism comes before nations" (*Nations* 10). Perhaps these are extreme versions of the insistence on the fictiveness of national identities: rather than nation-states giving rise to national identities, certain collectivities based on geographical proximity, language, religion, and/or customs give rise to nationalism which in turn gives rise to modern nations and nation-states. But it is also a thesis that Judt accepts, because the recent book that he praises most highly — Liah Greenfeld's *Nationalism: Five Roads to Modernity* — argues that "the basic framework of modern politics — the world divided into nations — is simply a realization of nationalist imagination; it is created by nationalism" (488). Where most historians including Hobsbawm and Anderson have seen nationalism as an ideological epiphenomenon of (capitalist, industrial) modernization, Greenfeld contends that, if anything, modernity is the effect of nationalism. The inference follows that nationalism is the most "real" causal factor in modern history: instead of class conflict (for instance), nationalism is the engine that drives modern society. But this inference would hardly make nationalism any less fictive or ideological. Indeed, Greenfeld starts with the assertion that "The only foundation of nationalism as such, the only condition, that is, without which no nationalism is possible, is an idea" (3).

In Greenfeld's view, this "idea of the nation" arose first in England (which, according to its own nationalist imagination, is preeminently the land of empiricism, science, and hard facts, free of "collective hallucinations"). Like Snyder, she analyzes five "case histories"; hers illustrate the emergence of nationalism while also exemplifying "five roads to modernity." The five are England, France, Russia, the United States, and Germany, with England by far the earliest: "The original modern idea of the nation emerged in sixteenth-century England, which was the first nation in the world (and the only one, with the possible exception of Holland, for about two hundred years)" (14). England emerged first as a modern nation-state, Greenfeld contends, because of the nation-centeredness of its Reformation. Protestantism then collaborated with commerce, war, and overseas expansion to give England, along with Holland, a competitive edge in the business of empire-building during and after the seventeenth century. While the Spanish, Portuguese, and French monarchies had centralized regimes in the 1500s, they did not have the nationalist glue that officially sponsored religious militancy provided England.

Besides (once again) the fictiveness of nationalism, a further irony of Greenfeld's argument is that "individualistic civic nationalism" — the kind most closely bound up both with Protestantism and with democratic liberalism (10) — was diffused from England via empire-building to America and elsewhere. European imperialism over the last four centuries has everywhere inspired nationalisms, independence movements, and the rush to "modernize," though not always with any impetus toward democratic liberalism. From this perspective, nationalism may seem not so much liberating as, to quote Partha Chatterjee's subtitle from *Nationalist Thought and the Colonial World*, "derivative discourses." Chatterjee stresses the connection between the nationalist impulse to modernize and European Enlightenment thought, or "the bourgeois-rationalist conception of knowledge" (11). Nationalism tends to be essentialist, centralizing, and ruthlessly bent on economic "modernization" to the destruction of local patterns, customs, beliefs, identities. As a "derivative discourse," nationalism in the Indian or African context turns out to be imperialism by other means — less postcolonialism than neocolonialism — and therefore, writes Chatterjee in his final sentence: "The critique of nationalist discourse must find . . . the ideological means to connect the popular strength of [local] struggles with the consciousness of a new universality, to subvert the ideological sway of a state which falsely claims to speak on behalf of the nation and to challenge the presumed sovereignty of a science which puts itself at the service of capital" (170). If imperialism has sown the seeds of its own undoing in nationalism around the globe, those nationalisms have not escaped the maelstrom of modernization, a.k.a. westernization, a.k.a. the capitalist "world system." Nor (though India with its legal and parliamentary system is a *partial* exception, more like the U.S. than like, say, North Korea) have they proven to be necessarily democratic.

Meanwhile, to return to England and (according to Greenfeld's account) the origins of the ideology of nationalism and hence of modernity, it was out of the sixteenth-century process of becoming distinctively English that a subsequent national or, perhaps, supranational identity emerged: from England to Great Britain, and from Englishness to Britishness. The strains and cracks evident in this later "invention" (or construction of national identity, or subject-ness) are largely the results of the contradiction between democracy or civic individualism (liberalism) on the one hand, and imperialism on the other — a contradiction that runs straight through Victorian culture, of course, down to the Thatcher-Major era. This is so because to forge British as opposed to merely English national identity, the differences (and ages-old hostilities) between the English and the Irish, the Welsh, and the Scots had to be smoothed over, mystified, or at least partly resolved.

The "invention" of this modern British togetherness is the theme of Linda Colley's meticulous, ambitious cultural history *Britons: Forging the Nation 1707–1837.* Great Britain was, Colley demonstrates, "an invention forged above all by war" (5). And it was forged in the first instance by war close to home, including the (imperial) subjugation of both Ireland and Scotland. "As a would-be nation, rather than a name, Great Britain was invented in 1707 when the Parliament of Westminster passed the Act of Union linking Scotland to England and Wales. From now on, this document proclaimed, there would be 'one united kingdom by the name of Great Britain' " (11). The end-date in Colley's title, moreover, implies that, by the start of Queen Victoria's reign, the thoroughly modern and modernizing, industrializing and imperializing nation-state of Great Britain had been "forged." For Victorian culture in general, this sense of completion — of being, so to speak, on top of the world — seemed incontestable. And anyway, who would want to contest it? At his trial, the Artful Dodger demands: "I'm an Englishman, ain't I? Where are my priwileges?" Considering that he is about to become a colonist of sorts (and, it may be, a beneficiary of the glorious albeit "invented" British Empire), his questions are just as rational as, for example, the "realistic" "myths of empire" Palmerston and Disraeli espoused to justify their foreign policies.

The fictions of British national identity in the Victorian period seemed so real that, in most Victorian literature, they were taken for granted. Except in emergencies such as the Crimean War and Indian Mutiny, outbursts of patriotic sentiment like Mr. Podsnap's seem ludicrous in part because they seem unnecessary. Contested or embattled ideologies are often noisier than dominant ones; there was nothing moot about most "Englishmen's" sense of national identity between 1815 and 1914. This is in contrast to the ethnic/national identities of the Welsh, the Scottish, and of course the Irish. As an ideology related to but distinct from nationalism, imperialism was a more self-conscious, more debatable affair. One result of this difference is that historians have paid much attention to the emergence of "jingoism" from the 1870s forward, to the relative neglect of patriotic and imperialist beliefs in early and mid-Victorian Britain. A number of recent studies have begun to redress the balance, however, including many of the essays in the three-volume *History Workshop* series edited by Raphael Samuel, *Patriotism: The Making and Unmaking of British National Identity* and also in Roy Porter's anthology, *Myths of the English*. Samuel declares, "The idea of nation, though a potent one, belongs to the realm of the imaginary rather than the real" (1:16), while Porter and his contributors all explore the "ideological constructs" (2) that compose "the peculiarities of the English" genre (4), including such varied items as Mother Goose, Guy Fawkes, the "English Bobby," and Armistice Day. These are all "myths of the English" past which prompt Porter to wonder whether the past itself may not be a "myth," and also whether historians, who "relish demystifying the 'pasts' vaunted by others," may not be "just myth-mongering too, peddling fantasied pasts of their own" (2–3). (Perhaps because he is a professional historian, Porter does not try very hard to answer this troublesome question — he does not, for instance, invoke poststructuralism of the sort evident in Homi Bhabha's anthology.)

Like the earlier contributors to *The Invention of Tradition*, Linda Colley stresses both the recentness and the fragility of the fiction or "invention" called, from 1707, "Great Britain." She implies that this fragile unity was doomed by the very (nationalist, ethnic, particularist) energies it sought to corral: "As an invented nation heavily dependent for its *raison d'être* on a broadly Protestant culture, on the threat and tonic of recurrent war, particularly war with France, and on the triumphs, profits and Otherness represented by a massive overseas empire, Britain is bound now to be under immense pressure" (6). Here Colley strikes a note similar to that of the welter of recent books on the decline and fall of the British Empire, of Great Britain as a world power, and even of England as a special place or of the English as a special race (destined once upon a time — so the story goes — to rule a quarter of the globe). Within the invented "socioscape" (Anderson 32) of Great Britain, in constant friction with the civic-individualistic nationalism that was at first English, are those other, ethnic, particularist nationalisms — Welsh, Scottish, Irish, and more recently East and West Indian — whose dissonance, Tom Nairn declared in 1977, was threatening the downfall of Great Britain. Nairn's *The Break-Up of Britain* (reissued in 1981), was only stating the obvious in relation to Great Britain's relative industrial-economic decline since about 1880 and loss of imperial power and glory since the end of World War I. But as both a Marxist and a champion of Scottish nationalism, Nairn was searching for ways to combine Welsh, Scottish, and Irish nationalisms with class struggle, though he acknowledged that these two forces making for the "break-up" were often pulling against each other.

Whether one national identity is more fictive — more artificial or in some sense less "real" — than another is obviously debatable. But English national identity is older and seems bound to outlast the latecomer of British supranational identity. The latter identity is dependent upon dominion over other, non-English nationalities, both within the circumference of what were once blithely called "the British Isles," and around the world, through possession of an empire upon which, as Macaulay, Tennyson, and other Victorians liked to think, the sun would never set. In much nineteenth-century literature and culture, the only things that seemed more real and more certain to endure forever than the glorious Empire itself were the virtues of the mainly *English* heroes — adventurers, soldiers, rulers — who had "invented" that Empire. These were distinctly *English* virtues, moreover — definitely not Irish, and only occasionally (a bit grudgingly) Scottish.

Of all modern nation-states, Nairn declares, Britain has been "the most profoundly and unalterably imperialist of societies" (69). It is not possible to define English/British nationalism in isolation from imperialism. However defined, the dual ideologies of nationalism and imperialism have been major forces in the shaping of British culture and society over several centuries. If the neoconservatives have their way, the sun will still never set on these ideologies, even if it has already set on Britain's actual industrial and imperial hegemony. These are the fictions whose reality effects, at least, realist historians like Tony Judt want to privilege in their constructions of causality. But as Greenfeld, echoing Max Weber, declares, "Social reality is intrinsically cultural; it is necessarily a symbolic reality, created by the subjective meanings and perceptions of social actors" (18). As does the concept of "cultural formation'' in Said's *Culture and Imperialism*, Greenfeld's use of the adjective "cultural" here provides an alternative to the problematic binaryism that Judt invokes: the "real" on one side; the merely "fictive" or "invented" on the other. To put it mildly, the invented fictions of nationalism and imperialism have had, through the course of modern and now postmodern history, very "significant material consequences."

Indiana University

WORKS CONSIDERED

Anderson, Benedict. *Imagined Communities: Reflections on the Origin and Spread of Nationalism*. London: Verso, 2d ed., 1991.

Bhabha, Homi K., ed. *Nation and Narration*. London and New York: Routledge, 1990.

Chatterjee, Partha. *Nationalist Thought and the Colonial World: A Derivative Discourse*. Minneapolis: U of Minnesota P., 1991.

Colley, Linda. *Britons: Forging the Nation 1707–1837*. New Haven: Yale UP, 1992.

Greenfeld, Liah. *Nationalism: Five Roads to Modernity*. Cambridge: Harvard UP, 1992).

Hobsbawm, Eric. *Nations and Nationalism since 1780: Programme, Myth, Reality*. Cambridge: Cambridge UP, 1990.

Hobsbawm, Eric and Terence Ranger, eds. *The Invention of Tradition*. Cambridge: Cambridge UP, 1983.

Judt, Tony. "The New Old Nationalism." *New York Review of Books* [*NYRB*], 26 May 1994, 44–51.

MacKenzie, John M. *Propaganda and Empire: The Manipulation of British Public Opinion, 1880–1960*. Manchester: U of Manchester P, 1984.

Nairn, Tom. *The Break-Up of Britain: Crisis and Neo-Nationalism*. London: Verso, 1981.

Porter, Roy, ed. *Myths of the English*. Cambridge: Polity Press, 1992.

Richards, Thomas. *The Imperial Archive: Knowledge and the Fantasy of Empire*. London: Verso, 1993.

Said, Edward. *Culture and Imperialism*. New York: Knopf, 1993.

Samuel, Raphael, ed. *Patriotism: The Making and Unmaking of British National Identity*, 3 vols. London and New York: Routledge, 1989.

Snyder, Jack. *Myths of Empire: Domestic Politics and International Ambition*. Ithaca: Cornell UP, 1991.

NORTH BRITAIN, INC.

By Ian Duncan

VICTORIA'S REIGN was the grave of Scottish culture. The fatal blow, the Union of Parliaments of Scotland and England, had been struck in 1707, and despite remissions in the form of cosmopolitan enlightenment (Hume, Smith) and popular genius (Burns), vital signs ceased in 1832, the year of the Reform bill and the death of Sir Walter Scott. Scotland became a ghost nation and a tourist trap: the Queen sat at Balmoral; the public bought souvenirs. Tremors of revival, and a full disclosure of foul play, would not come until the twentieth century.

So goes the modern nationalist story of Scotland, told by Hugh MacDiarmid and Edwin Muir in the 1920s and 30s, and still resonant today. Metaphors of an organic fatality, sickness and decay, inform its central mystery, the Victorian extinction of a literary tradition. Muir's *Scott and Scotland* (1936) diagnosed the fall of a national culture by applying T. S. Eliot's notion of the dissociation of sensibility to the figure of Scottish identity coined in the 1890s by Gregory Smith, the "Caledonian Antisyzygy" or Scottishness as bundle of internal oppositions. In the themes of Presbyterian theology and Scottish fiction Muir found a traumatic splitting of the psyche. Its recursion across a series of historical events — Reformation, Union, Enlightenment — rendered it a constitutional pathology, a national schizophrenia, less historical effect than history's inner cause. Most crippling to literary endeavor was the modern schism between thought and feeling, manifest as a division between writing and speech: while English literature prospered in the absorption of an orality-based stylistics, the dead language of imperial English choked vernacular Scots. David Craig's *Scottish Literature and the Scottish People* (1961) amplified Muir's thesis in a full-scale Leavisite literary history. Scotland's lack of a "great tradition" expressing an ethical unity of national life derived from a deadly class division, established with the Union, between anglicizing elite and disenfranchised populace. The Enlightenment literati sold their inheritance to get ahead in the imperial marketplace of metropolitan English; when a Burns sang out from the hinterland, they patronized him into an early grave.

The resort to English models to measure the defects of a Scottish tradition accounts for much of the fatalism of these histories, and a disabling irony. The colonizing act has already been performed by the critic.

In *The Break-Up of Britain* (1977) Tom Nairn set out to correct this logocentric or idealist cultural history with an analysis of cultural politics, redefining the problem as the lack of a bourgeois nationalist formation in the developmental pattern of Scottish modernization. Nairn argued that the professional-class intelligentsia of the eighteenth-century Enlightenment had no socioeconomic need to generate a separatist nationalism: so far from being disinherited by the Union, they found themselves enfranchised within its imperial networks of patronage and advancement. In short, post-Union Scotland lacked not so much an organic culture as (to use Gramsci's terms) organic intellectuals; the literati from Hume to Scott were "traditional intellectuals" bound to the oligarchy of improving gentry. As Nairn puts it (not entirely accurately), there was no Romantic movement. Although his European reception might have been "Romantic," at home Scott personified the last, overblown stage of a North British Enlightenment which was finally overtaken — in the decades following the Napoleonic wars — by wider historical perturbations, such as industrialization and a new middle-class ascendancy. Confronting the nineteenth century, Nairn repeats after all the scenario of decadence and collapse, with "nationalism," exclusively construed as political separatism, becoming the synecdoche for "culture."

All these accounts converge upon the figure of Scott, whom they arraign for being the agent of a final liquidation of national culture for imperial absorption, the instigator of Victorian Scotland. Both in the Waverley Novels and in his personal conduct Scott is supposed to have pandered to a Tory Unionist establishment, hoodwinked himself as well as others about the nature of Scottish history, reduced national identity to an aesthetic commodity, and so extinguished the last embers that had gleamed in the Enlightenment *philosophes* and in Burns. Devastated by his example, the best the Scottish novel could achieve was exposure of the dissociation of sensibility in allegorical horror fables: Hogg's *Confessions of a Justified Sinner*, Stevenson's *Dr. Jekyll and Mr. Hyde*. It is striking with what regularity the theory of modern Scottish culture condenses into a theory of Scott. His career measures that culture's crisis, his influence its eclipse; again and again Scott's death marks the watershed between overcultivated Enlightenment and Victorian wasteland. A kind of magical thinking prevails: as baneful now as he once seemed provident, Scott remains the Wizard of the North, binding a nation and a century under his spell. (Karl Miller remarks in his autobiography that he spent much of his childhood under the impression that Scotland was named after Scott.) Much like Milton in Eliot's version of English poetic history, Scott effects a collapse of tradition at the same time as his own work seems to have intended its synthetic reconstruction.

The allegorical density of "Scott" compresses two phenomena, both of them important to students of nineteenth-century cultural history. First is the remarkable influence of Edinburgh literary culture in Scott's generation (1802–32), national and indeed imperial in its range and formative of what we think of as characteristically "Victorian" institutions and paradigms; and second, the fall of that culture from metropolitan to provincial status at the onset of Victoria's reign. Scott's own personal and literary authority, undeniably immense, operated in a complex of sites of cultural production unique to Edinburgh at that moment: a regionally dominant professional-class intelligentsia affiliated with distinctively national institutions of cultural identity that had survived the Union (the church, law and education), and a modernizing publishing industry. In both of these respects Edinburgh was far ahead of London, and it was here that some of the genres that would dominate nineteenth-century British literature first took form — not only the national historical romance of the Waverley Novels but the *Edinburgh Review* (first of the mandarin critical quarterlies, 1802) and *Blackwood's Edinburgh Magazine* (prototype of the monthly literary miscellany, 1817).

Yet by the late 1830s the flow of Scotland's cultural capital south to London had become a deluge. In the wake of Lockhart and Jeffrey, transplanted Scotsmen would supply not only the higher ranks of Victorian social criticism (Carlyle, Macaulay, the Mills, Ruskin) but the industrial expansion of journalism throughout Great Britain. The fate of the Scottish novel after Scott, raised by him to be the privileged genre of national tradition, was especially dismal according to those views of the novel that equated it with a realistic representation of social life. The best of the novelists forsook a Scottish for an English domestic realism (Oliphant) or for flights of fantasy (Stevenson, MacDonald, Oliphant again). Those who stayed behind cultivated the Kailyard or cabbage-patch, the metonymy of a sentimental parochialism; George Douglas Brown's anti-Kailyard *The House with the Green Shutters* (1901), a Hardyesque study of the moral squalor of provincial life, was the exception that proved the rule. Hardy's own Donald Farfrae, the emigrant Scot who charms the inhabitants of Casterbridge with the songs "of his dear native country that he loved so well as never to have revisited it," personifies the inauthenticity of a Scottish regionalism exported for sentimental consumption at the end of the century (and sets off the true grit of Hardy's Wessex version).

Victorian Scotland thus presents us with a fascinating problem in cultural history, one that exceeds the specialist concern of Scottish studies. As the problem of national tradition and identity, it has two elements: a diachronic one of periodization and historiographic continuity, and a synchronic one of boundaries and inclusivity. How was it that a powerful Scottish literary culture so suddenly, drastically dissolved into the imperial polity of Great Britain? And what do the shifting relations among the terms, England, Scotland, Britain, tell us about those most nineteenth-century of paradigms, nation and culture? Nairn's argument that the case of Britain in modern national developments was at once exemplary and anomalous makes the case of Scotland still more so. The Victorian figure of Scotland invites us to consider the logic that connects the historical disappearance of a cultural identity, and its unprecedented ideological visibility within the modern state as a phantasm of organic social relations.

The excellent Aberdeen *History of Scottish Literature* devotes the introduction and three opening chapters of its *Nineteenth Century* volume to reckoning with the Victorian fall, and the theme haunts many of the articles that follow. Perhaps Scotland could hardly be expected to have held its own against the decisive ascendancy of London as "world city," metropolis of empire, following the Napoleonic wars. Physically, the distance required to sustain the gravitational integrity of a rival center collapsed with the accelerated development of communications networks and transport technologies; as Lord Cockburn noted at mid-century, the journey between Edinburgh and London could now be measured in hours where a generation ago it had been days. Yet more decisive, perhaps, were the political consequences of Reform, which swept away the quasi-feudal patronage networks that had managed Scottish institutions.

Many of these institutions, distinctively Scottish formations that had survived the loss of political sovereignty as the bearers of national identity, were now subject to rationalization according to English principles. Until recently, historical orthodoxy has cast the pre-reform Tory regime as London's puppet, completing the Unionist sale of Scotland down the river well before 1832. Michael Fry's new political history of the period (1760s–1830s) argues with impressive detail and panache that the oligarchic rule of Scotland by a "Scotch manager" and his clientship, the "Dundas despotism" so automatically reviled by Whigs and moderns, had in fact been remarkably effective in forestalling interference from Westminster. Under Henry Dundas and his son, "the historic Scottish institutions had yet enjoyed a degree of internal autonomy, a vestige of the sovereignty derived from erstwhile nationhood, in short a semi-independence" (384). It was the reforming Whigs, not the Tory old guard, who were the zealous anglicizers.

Less programmatically inclined to denounce cultural life under the Dundas despotism as a decadence that inevitably issued in final dissolution, Fry's analysis helps us to fill out Nairn's account, and correct the fatalism of Craig's and Muir's. If the literati were traditional intellectuals it was because the system worked for the majority of people in Scotland, or at least those who were in any position to say anything about it. (Access to literacy and the professions was far more democratically open than in England; nevertheless, one wonders about this "majority.") In Angus Calder's words, pre-reform Scotland "functioned on republican terms" (8) — even if it was "a comfortably corrupt republic" (20). This reassessment of a polity as not, after all, doomed to reap the consequences of national betrayal has important implications for cultural and literary history, as we shall see.

Perhaps Fry exaggerates the period's political consensus and ideological homogeneity. The anti-Jacobin reaction and war with France undoubtedly helped the old regime to keep the lid on Scottish affairs for longer than it otherwise might have, but after 1815 the social and political energies that flowed with economic modernization could no longer be suppressed. The working out of long-delayed tensions was felt as late as the Great Disruption of 1843, when the contest between government patronage and parochial self-determination within the Church of Scotland, for so long held in check by the patronage party's astute management, finally split down the middle the nation's broadest-based, most reliably popular institution of cultural identity. Meanwhile, English legislation tampered with the Scottish legal system and universities (intellectually far more reputable than the byzantine stagnation of Oxford and Cambridge). Lastly, Scottish book production had been badly shaken by the financial crash of 1825–26, which as well as ruining the most influential of the Edinburgh authors and publishers, Scott and Constable, had the longer-term effect of depressing the trade throughout Great Britain during the 1830s. The industry that recovered was a far more centralized one. In 1840 Blackwood, the remaining major force in Scottish publishing, opened a branch in London, henceforth to be the principal base of operations; in 1847 management of the *Edinburgh Review* was transferred to London (where it was already published by Longman).

These, rather than any inherent fatality, were the main political and economic reasons for the erosion of national institutions and the southward flight of cultural capital that determined the decline of a native literary culture after the 1830s. There remains the important province of cultural criticism, and what I have referred to as magical thinking: the domain of appearances, or apparitions. The vanishing of a national culture coincides with its spectral proliferation in signs, effigies, illusions; Scotland was nowhere more visible than in the distinguished tradition of hallucination and forgery running from Ossian to Balmoral and Fiona MacLeod, if not to Brigadoon and Nessie. The peculiarly Scottish theme of an uncanny encroachment of representations over "reality" has attracted lively critical attention, much of it claiming a more masterful access to that reality than was ever achieved by the superstitious natives of the time. But if the nation is an "imagined community" (according to Benedict Anderson's by now ubiquitous definition), then it must always be ghostly, a regime of images; and its organic form, its corporeal origins, a nostalgic and fearful projection.

The favorite *topos* of Scottish cultural criticism has been the post-Culloden ideological processing of an extirpated Gaelic world into the synecdoche for a primitive, melancholy, but tamed and loyal Scotland. Representative are Hugh Trevor-Roper's essay in *The Invention of Tradition* ("The Invention of Tradition: The Highland Tradition of Scotland," 15–42) and John Prebble's lively narrative of George IV's 1822 Scottish visit, stage-managed by Scott himself as a pageant of clanship and tartanry (*The King's Jaunt*). Both of these tend to ascribe an excessively transparent inauthenticity to the realms of representation: it seems all too easy now to see through the kitsch that duped everybody then. More subtly attuned to trope, Peter Womack's *Improvement and Romance* offers a lucid, usefully programmatic account of the logic of disappearance-and-appearance. Seemingly the contrary of "improvement," "romance" is its dialectical arm, dispensing sentimental recompense for the human costs of progress. Improvement or capitalist restructuring in the Highlands meant first military and then cultural repression, and then (as local economies collapsed) the Clearances, the landlords' forced evacuation of their tenantry for sheep: disappearance at zero degree. The heroic, picturesque and elegiac cult of the Highlands rendered the imperial absorption of Scotland into the political economy of Great Britain a matter for complacency spiced with luxurious aesthetic regret.

Full of acute readings (of Highland romances by women, of *The Lady of the Lake*), the story Womack tells reproduces a little too straightforwardly the logic of Romantic ideology whereby investment in a fantasy measures the loss of something real. The conception of a culture as a psychologically coherent entity makes the imposition of false consciousness from above appear not so much overdetermined as inevitable. In *The Invention of Scotland* Murray Pittock criticizes the notion of a "primitive" historical form, a *destiny*, as the lot of the defeated — a narrative model that turns communities into the passive objects of prefabricated historical meanings. Instead of a geographical topos, the Highlands, Pittock chooses a political one, Jacobitism, usually dismissed as the hollowest token of Scotch reactionary delusion. In a judiciously polemical account of the ways in which mythologies are circulated and consumed — modified, as Auden said of poetry, in the guts of the living — Pittock recuperates the complex, dynamic appeal of Jacobitism to different historical constituencies. Jacobitism is above all a *narrative*, an alternative and thus utopian history, the myth of the once and future king who represents a national identity in the purity of its loss. Such a myth sings to a plurality of the dispossessed; its symbols were taken over and reconstituted by a Radical culture of popular protest in the late eighteenth century, and again by modern nationalism of the Left.

Pittock's study shows how cultural analysis, working with a rigorous empirical historicism, can open up the diversity and contingency of representations and usages rather than shut them down into a single master-plot. It may be that cultural utterances do not invariably converge to produce what we understand as having been destined to happen. That is to say, the current reassessment of such ritually traduced figures as Jacobitism, the Dundas regime, and Scott himself may express something more interesting and useful than a post-cold-war Tory triumphalism. The recent historical revisionism reflects a re-thinking of the categories of culture and nation, as differentially and politically rather than organically constituted, polysemous rather than monolithic, contested and refashioned rather than once-and-for-all received. "Scotland" occupies a series of historically contingent conceptual relations to "England" and "Great Britain," terms that inform one another. The year 1707 meant not simply the digestion of Scotland in the belly of England but the strenuous synthesis of a new entity, Great Britain, in the imperial composition of which Scotland played an active part. Linda Colley's *Britons*, the recent monument of this field of inquiry, insists upon history as cultural history, the collective record of what people felt and imagined; although Colley (whose collective historical subject emerges with brilliant ventriloquism from a wealth of archival sources) professes herself reluctant to interpret so devious an utterance as the literary. Britishness is the positive formation that emerged through the dissolution of local identities in the period of economic modernization; it was made cohesive, above all, by the long world war against France. Aspiring to similar weightiness (but more complacent) is Howard Weinbrot's *Britannia's Issue*, a survey of the rise of Britain as a literary idea in the eighteenth century. Weinbrot documents the representation (indeed exaggeration) of ethnic and cultural heterogeneity — including the poetic and antiquarian vogue for Scotchness — as a positive resource, the virtue of an imperial dynamism.

These studies chart the important prehistory of formations of national and imperial identity that currently preoccupy many readings in Victorian high culture. Scotland occupies a crucial place on the threshold of that prehistory. Empire, the historians agree, is the crucial term in the Scottish equation. The Union provided favorable terms for Scottish access to imperial enterprise, such that Scotch predominance in empire-building was soon a matter of notoriety. The Dundas despotism, to take the most impressive case, effectively controlled the expansion of British interests in India. Empire, in short, replaced political sovereignty as the field of a distinctively Scots identity-formation. The historical argument reinforces recent critical analysis of ways in which the properties of national identity were effects rather than causes of imperial development. Gauri Viswanathan has made the case (in *Masks of Conquest: Literary Study and British Rule in India*, 1989) that the main pedagogical institution of an official national culture, the British literary tradition, was developed in schools in India in the early nineteenth century before being imported to Victorian England: the so-called periphery was driving the so-called core. Viswanathan's analysis might have taken account, however, of the eighteenth-century formation of a literary curriculum in the Scottish universities, which typically produced the men and the systems of knowledge that went to the colonies.

The topic supplies the opening chapter of Robert Crawford's important *Devolving English Literature*. Just as Scottish academics invented "English literature" as a technology of access to the imperial clerisy (the curricular title, "Rhetoric and Belles Lettres," makes the function clear), so did Scottish authors clear space for themselves with the poetic and antiquarian invention of a British literary tradition. In a cunning reversal of the old story, Crawford makes Scotland the dominant imperial agency in the cultural formation of Great Britain — no English colony but the colonizer of "English." This view of an imperialistically mobile and capacious rather than marginal and besieged cultural identity provides for a narratology of continuity and comprehensiveness, in contrast to the Calvinist patterns of rupture and preterition that have obsessed modern accounts of a Scottish literary tradition. We are reminded of the extent (considerable if partial) to which continuity and discontinuity are historiographical artifacts, acts of ideological choice on the part of an interpreter. Crawford goes beyond John MacQueen's erudite demonstration of the distinctive thematic and allusive continuities in Scottish literature between the seventeenth century and the 1830s; for even there, Carlyle (rather than Scott) stands for the end of a tradition. Crawford's version of tradition digests all purported discontinuities, whether between Burns and the literati, or among the hackneyed stages of Enlightenment, Romanticism, Victorianism, Modernism. Its privileged genre is not lyric or novel but anthropology, the quintessentially imperialist discourse, and something of a Scots specialty from the Enlightenment "natural history of man" (Hume, Ferguson, Millar) to the late-Victorian folklorists and mythographers (Lang, McLennan, Frazer).

Devolving English Literature reconfigures the idea of tradition by tracing an imperial periphery rather than reiterating a metropolitan core. In the case of Scotland, Crawford's polemical revaluation of the "provincial" offers a fertile solution to the impasse of Muir and Craig, fixated on the organic centrism of an English Great-Tradition model. In an analogous move, Susan Manning's *The Puritan-Provincial Vision* brackets England to describe an eighteenth- and nineteenth-century common culture of the literatures of the anglophone periphery, united by the medium of Calvinism — H. L. Mencken's "natural theology of the disinherited." If Manning eschews cultural history for a more traditionally thematic kind of literary criticism, this entails no loss of acumen; it would be a pity if readers were to neglect these elegant analyses of an ideological regime of subject-formation, with its typical figures of doubling, self-division, spectatorship and spectralization, predicated on the ontological distance from an inscrutably veiled center.

The province remains, in these accounts, a site of imperial administration rather than of radical dispossession or alterity. (We have only to think of *Middlemarch* to recall the complex ways in which Victorian literature reconstitutes England at the center of the imagined nation through the fiction of "provincial life.") Manning's American canon of Cooper-Poe-Hawthorne-Melville maps an old colonial center after all, according to the subaltern contestations that have enlivened American Studies over the last fifteen years. And while Crawford cites recent deconstructive and postcolonial theorizations of the marginal, his narrative rather tends to reconstitute by displacement a familiar (white, male) high tradition — if the center cannot hold then perhaps the circumference will. Scotland, as the historians have been saying, was well within the pale. I make these remarks not to discredit the valuable work of interpreting high traditions, but to recall that the rhetoric of nationalism is almost always a symptom of class division, whether it emanate from the custodians of high tradition or from some other group. In any case there will always be other groups. In practical terms, perhaps the most drastic revision of nineteenth-century Scottish cultural history is proposed by William Donaldson in *Popular Literature in Victorian Scotland*. Far from a native literary tradition having withered after the 1830s, Donaldson argues, it flourished on a mass-cultural scale in the popular press. Not only regional forms of vernacular Scots but also fiction addressing social issues thrived in the weekly newspapers that proliferated after the 1855 repeal of the Stamp Act. Literary historians have ignored this vast field of evidence because of their characteristic obsession with the expensive commodities of middle-class privilege, such as books.

Donaldson reconnects literary history with a distinguished Scottish tradition of social history (exemplified in the work of T. C. Smout), and redresses habitual assumptions about what must constitute a national culture. The majority of Scots were not, after all, running the empire, but riding the rollercoaster of the industrial economy back home. Interestingly, this redistribution of cultural wealth tends to reassert the familiar theme of a divided national culture; only now a popular renaissance shows up more clearly the immolation of the elite tradition, like a moth in a flame, in the English core.

Such necessary extensions of the map make the varieties of dominant culture no less important a site of interpretation. The historians' reassessment of the imperial republic of the Dundas era coincides with a surge of revisionary interest in its literary culture, inevitably focused on Scott. The vital role of "Scott and his age" in the formation of Victorian literary institutions makes it all the more important that we detach it from its weird posthumous cycle of hagiography and demonization, and establish our own critical relations to its complex contemporaneity. Both Manning and Crawford find in Scott's work a creative resource rather than a burden for their respective constructions of tradition, surely a more plausible view than the still widespread sightings of Scott as a figure of pure influence, like the tail without the comet. A number of recent studies emphasize the imperial rather than local field of Scott's importance, his consequences for a British rather than Scottish literary culture. The books by Ferris, Robertson, and the present reviewer make contextual arguments about how Scott reinvented the novel for the nineteenth century by raising its cultural status (''authority'' seems to be a key concept now in Scott studies) and enlarging its formal and thematic repertoire; while Welsh's *The Hero of the Waverley Novels*, timelier than ever in reissue, examines the invention of a distinctively modern type of masculine bourgeois subject.

Ferris's *The Achievement of Literary Authority* goes furthest towards situating the Waverley Novels in a contemporary milieu of cultural production: here, the *Edinburgh Review* (marking out an elevated domain, masculine and professional, of the literary) and Scott's immediate precursors in the so-called ''National Tale,'' notably Sydney Owenson and Maria Edgeworth. These were predominantly women authors from the Celtic fringe, and they bring Scott's national representation into a particularly sharp, not to say harsh, ideological focus. Katie Trumpener's article (included in the present discussion because it has more matter and argument than most books) stages a militant recuperation of the genre, colonized by Scott as the foundation for his own originality. Perhaps unsurprisingly, the view from the periphery turns out to be less than reassuring in the Irish novels of Owenson and Maturin, which make the frontier rather than the province the site of imperial nation-making. Trumpener is concerned with the political struggles played out in generic and formal diversity, and like Ferris she pits Scott's ascendancy against the predominance of a feminine domestic tradition of the novel, privileged in recent literary histories. (It is worth noting that the precocious professionalization of Edinburgh literary life made it less hospitable to ambitious women authors; the epithet ''bluestocking'' had longer currency there than in London.) Unlike Ferris, Trumpener falls under the familiar compulsion to exorcize Scott, cast once more as the broker of inauthenticity. The gesture risks obscuring the crucial and complex role Scott continues to play in this newly visible literary history of a turmoil of contending currents. Angus Calder's collection of essays and reviews suggests that a critical grasp of Scott's achievement can keep account of its imperial character, as well as its position in the fray of rival and alternative forms, without the false economy of ideological dismissal.

Decomposition of the homogeneity of "Scott and his age" is one of the most fertile enterprises in Scottish studies right now, as scholars retrieve important but neglected figures such as John Galt and James Hogg from the archives. New editions of Hogg's works and of the Waverley Novels, from Edinburgh University Press, are bound to enlarge and complicate our view of the early nineteenth century. Likewise, such projects as the ongoing editorial reassessments of Carlyle and Stevenson, and the overdue critical revaluation of women writers from Mary Brunton to Violet Jacob, promise to restore a "Victorian Scottish literature" that is notably miscellaneous, uneven and accidental in its constitution. If a national tradition meant a dynasty of masterpieces unifying national life, perhaps it is time to celebrate rather than mourn its disappearance.

The current revisionism reflects not simply "the fall of communism" and attendant complacencies about the end of historical alternatives to world capitalism (Calder, for instance, is a republican socialist) but a contentious diversity of claims and interests, along with new arguments about the status of Scotland in a federal Europe. The end of the 1980s meant the fall of Thatcher as well as of the Berlin Wall. The controversy about Scotland's political identity continues to animate literary and cultural studies, as the proliferation of possible futures opens up a new range of possible pasts.

University of Oregon

WORKS CONSIDERED

Calder, Angus. *Revolving Culture: Notes from the Scottish Republic*. London and New York: Tauris, 1994.

Colley, Linda. *Britons: Forging the Nation, 1707–1832*. New Haven: Yale UP, 1992.

Crawford, Robert. *Devolving English Literature*. Oxford: Clarendon P, 1992.

Donaldson, William. *Popular Literature in Victorian Scotland: Language, Fiction and the Press*. Aberdeen: Aberdeen UP, 1986.

Duncan, Ian. *Modern Romance and Transformations of the Novel: The Gothic, Scott, Dickens*. Cambridge: Cambridge UP, 1992.

Ferris, Ina. *The Achievement of Literary Authority: Gender, Genre and the Waverley Novels*. Ithaca: Cornell UP, 1991.

Fry, Michael. *The Dundas Despotism*. Edinburgh: Edinburgh UP, 1992.

Gifford, Douglas, ed. *The History of Scottish Literature, Vol. 3: The Nineteenth Century*. Aberdeen: Aberdeen UP, 1988.

Hobsbawm, E. J., and Terence Ranger, eds. *The Invention of Tradition*. Cambridge: Cambridge UP, 1983.

Manning, Susan. *The Puritan-Provincial Vision: Scottish and American Literature in the Nineteenth Century*. Cambridge: Cambridge UP, 1990.

MacQueen, John. *The Enlightenment and Scottish Literature, Vol. 2: The Rise of the Historical Novel*. Edinburgh: Scottish Academic P, 1989.

Pittock, Murray J. *The Invention of Scotland: The Stuart Myth and the Scottish Identity, 1638 to the Present*. London: Routledge, 1991.

Prebble, John. *The King's Jaunt: George IV in Scotland, 1822*. London: Collins, 1988.

Robertson, Fiona. *Legitimate Histories: Scott, Gothic, and the Authorities of Fiction*. Oxford: Clarendon P, 1994.

Trumpener, Katie. "National Character, Nationalist Plots: National Tale and Historical Novel in the Age of *Waverley*, 1800–1830." *ELH* 60 (1993): 685–731.

Welsh, Alexander. *The Hero of the Waverley Novels: with new essays on Scott*. Princeton: Princeton UP, 1992.

Weinbrot, Howard D. *Britannia's Issue: The Rise of British Literature from Dryden to Ossian*. Cambridge: Cambridge UP, 1993.

Womack, Peter. *Improvement and Romance: Constructing the Myth of the Highlands*. Basingstoke: Macmillan, 1988.

CONTEMPORARY BIOGRAPHERS OF NINETEENTH-CENTURY NOVELISTS

By Frederick R. Karl

RESEARCH HAS IMPROVED, but conceptualization remains shaky or non-existent in the current practice of biography. Strikingly, the latest batch of biographical studies of nineteenth-century novelists reveals how little the genre has moved from what it has been for the last fifty or more years. Of the six books discussed here, only two, Louise DeSalvo's study of Virginia Woolf and Claire Tomalin's of Ellen Lawless Ternan, break with old formulas and attempt something new: the use of biography as a way of reading back into the culture, and the use of culture as a way of reading into biography. I have included DeSalvo's book, *Virginia Woolf: The Impact of Childhood Sexual Abuse on Her Life and Work*, as part of my nineteenth-century roundup because so much of DeSalvo's study focusses on the waning years of Victoria's reign. In many respects, but especially in her emphasis on sexual matters, her handling of Woolf closes out a period. Although she challenges Freud, her biography, in the manner of Freud himself, looks both ways, back to those nineteenth-century dogmas he had to shed, ahead to those twentieth-century views he tried to explain. By the same token, Claire Tomalin's *The Invisible Woman: The Story of Charles Dickens and Nelly Ternan* also breaks the mold, writing the life of an "invisible woman," her story a palimpsest.

The other biographies I have grouped here are certainly workmanlike, lending themselves to individual excellences, but overall they do not contribute to a developing genre. The question re-arises whether biography can remain static, or whether it must reshape itself, just as fiction, poetry, drama, and literary criticism have reshaped themselves periodically. Reshaping does not mean merely the use of better scholarly tools, or greater documentation, or even a greater sense of historical and cultural factors; it surely does not mean only probing more deeply into the subject's disorders. It must involve a rethinking of what biography should be doing in the closing years of the century, if the genre is to be considered as more than a dumping ground for other, related, disciplines; if, in fact, it even has the resources for transformation.

DeSalvo's is a particular kind of biography, in its way a mutant form of the genre. She is not concerned with the full run of Woolf's life; and her book is thesis-driven: to explore through Woolf's sexual abuse as a child how society betrays the child, and how in the larger sense, the entire Victorian practice of child-rearing was a betrayal of children, especially of female children. As she states: "I have explored, through Woolf's life, through the experience of the other members of her family, through her creations, through her nonfiction, and through the work of contemporary researchers into the history of the family, sexual abuse, and patterns of child-rearing, what the effect and experiences were of a childhood like hers" (xiii).

One of DeSalvo's premises is that the exclusion of the father from child-nurturing — indelibly part of Victorian practice — fostered a negative situation in the home. It resulted in an overworked mother, even with servant help; created a father who often himself needed nurturing, becoming more a child in need than the children; and gave over child-rearing, frequently, to uneducated and untrained servants.

From this DeSalvo makes a leap which the reader may or may not accept, however critical it is to her point. She dismisses any question of "inherent madness" and sees Woolf's later behavior as the consequence of sexual abuse and inadequate child-rearing. Woolf herself in her Journal described her condition as living in a frozen state, her metaphor for childhood memories and residue.

The domestic scene was, to say the obvious, a dysfunctional place, in which the children were forced into unnatural roles, especially once the mother died; and criminally dysfunctional in the light of the sexual abuse Woolf suffered over a period of years beginning when she was ten. DeSalvo emphasizes her point: "I now believe that her life, as indeed any life, can be seen as a complex and creative response to many significant conditions of the time in which she grew up, and the family into which she was born, and the special experience she had to endure, and the damaging behavior that was directed at her" (xvii).

Here DeSalvo makes the assumption that what we might call one's primary identity is completely shaped by external conditions, especially those as debilitating (and criminal) as what occurred in the Leslie Stephen home. Yet it is possible that Woolf also manifested some inherent weakness which combined with the dismal domestic situation to send her periodically over the edge. DeSalvo tends to marginalize another component as well — those periods when Woolf could not function, when she required nurturing from her husband. Is it not possible that during those terrible times she was preparing herself for her next artistic venture? That those periods were analogous to

Persephone's descent into the underworld, where she could gather strength for her emergence later — fall and winter giving way, in time, to spring and summer? In this view, Woolf was not undergoing "madness" but was creating for herself the time and space she needed in order to do her work. The periods of illness, severe dependence, even regression, were all means by which she could restore herself creatively; and precisely how this occurred really lies outside of anything the biographer can manage.

Since so much of biographical interpretation works on intuition, speculation, and possibility, it is overdetermining matters to insist on cause and effect. Within the frame of reference she has chosen, DeSalvo makes an excellent case: there is little question that years of sexual abuse seriously affected every aspect of Woolf's adult life; there is no question that her father's needs during her childhood seriously confused Woolf's relationships; there is, further, no question that all of this deeply influenced the kind of fiction she wrote. And DeSalvo does work over the major fiction, demonstrating how these themes find their way into the novels. There is also no question that Victorian child-rearing practices led to the privileging of the father, to the minority status of the mother, to the desexualization of the maternal figure by deeming her the angel in the house, to the blunting or distorting of the emotional lives of the children. But it is equally true that none of this "explains" a figure so creatively generous as Woolf. For in some final sense, DeSalvo separates the woman Woolf, abused and wounded, from the creator Woolf — even while the biographer probes Woolf's fiction for the residue of her childhood anxieties, pains, and fears. In some ultimate sense, Woolf's imaginative processes — clearly the most significant elements — are not linked to the abuse and mistreatment; or else how do we explain that she became a great writer when everything points to a woman who should simply have folded? Apparently, there was another "identity" to her.

None of this will invalidate DeSalvo's type of biographical exploration; it is valuable and serves as a corrective to most previous Woolf biographies, especially Quentin Bell's. But while hers opens up this entire area, not only for Woolf but for Victorian child-rearing practices as a whole, she does require a further extension. That extension is the extremely compelling one in which the biographer sees illness, anxiety, and abuse, as nourishing the mind of a creative writer. Illness and anguish are not necessarily negative for the artist. They may provide time when he or she can stand back, or sustain a reordering of temporal and spatial dimensions. A full-blown biography of Woolf, which has yet to be written, would draw heavily on DeSalvo's work and then move on to the next stage, exploring the ways in which Woolf transformed the worst features of her abusive childhood into imaginative power.

What interests us in Claire Tomalin's *The Invisible Woman* is that both important players are in a sense missing. But they are missing in different ways. Although this is the "story" of Ellen Lawless Ternan, the hovering figure of Dickens makes possible the re-emergence of this woman. Without Dickens, she would have faded into the Victorian scene as just another minor actress from a family of actresses, perhaps cited in some histories for this or that role. Her liaison with Dickens, for thirteen years, from 1857 until his death in 1870, gives her extreme importance; and in a way reveals how women in history have had to gain prominence, in many instances, from their association with famous men — even when the women had interesting or compelling lives of their own.

Related to this is the fact that *because* of her liaison with Dickens, Nelly vanishes from her own life: so low-keyed did she become in order to maintain Dickens's secret that she effaced herself, even in her own story. Claire Tomalin now has to retrieve two vanishing figures and create a scenario for them — one vanishes to protect his name as a solid Victorian paterfamilias, even when he hardly fitted that role; and the other has to disappear in order to play the role consigned to her as the would-be "scarlet woman" who led the famous man astray. Yet several people knew the situation, Wilkie Collins, Dickens's daughter and sister-in-law, Dickens's biographer, John Forster, and Thackeray, who mentioned it to friends. Still, it was in the main kept from the British public. So we have two vanishing points in the book, and Tomalin needed a strategy to bring her two players into focus.

Her method is to recreate the Victorian theatrical scene for the reader; in doing so she can validate Nelly's life, and at the same time, draw in Dickens, an ardent devotee of theatre and theatrical performance, not to speak of the young actresses who performed. Along the way, Tomalin raises some compelling questions for biography itself. How does hers differ from more traditional biographies? What strategies are required to reinforce the differences? Whose "story" is it? Are all conclusions speculations, given the lack of evidence? Is there closure, as in more conventional biographies, or just the perception of closure? Is there a "story" and a "Story" — that is, does the ur-Story blur the lines of the ostensible story? Finally, to what extent did the relationship, just after *Little Dorrit*, shape Dickens's fiction, his portrayal of young women, his attitude toward family, life, society? Can any of this be measured, or does it belong to the shadows — that part which lies beyond language?

The book becomes, accordingly, an exercise in biographical strategies. Even more than she wished to admit, nearly everything Tomalin says falls into a speculative area, the red zone for a biographer. The unvalidated material revolves around whether Nelly had a son with Dickens, who died; perhaps even a second child. But beyond that is an even more fundamental question, a teaser, which is whether or not the affair was even consummated. It is possible — although Tomalin argues differently — that the father-daughter relationship was too strong for Dickens to engage Nelly sexually; or from her point of view, that the disproportion between his fame and her relative insignificance made her reject intercourse. Since any personal reading of Dickens's fiction offers so little guidance here, Tomalin is left in a gray area.

Her argument, which is ingenious and in the main effective, is that Dickens never portrayed a woman who had the complexity of the Ternan actresses; that his fictional women are either wicked or madonnas. And since someone like Nelly — intelligent, shrewd, protective of her virginity, yet willing to form the liaison — never appears in Dickens's fiction, we cannot use *that* as a guide. The affair with Nelly is never fictionally grounded. But the argument can be turned around, in that the writer's very sharp distinction between good and bad women indicates that he hesitated in seducing Nelly — if she permitted it — and putting her in the "bad woman" category. It might be argued that Dickens was so judgmental in his attitude toward women, he would perhaps be impotent or feeble with a young mistress.

Thus while Tomalin can argue the fiction is no real guide, we can counterclaim that the fiction leads to opposite conclusions from the biographer's. We could, in fact, say that Dickens was enamored of the idea of having a mistress — his close friend Wilkie Collins had more than one — but that because of his sharp moral distinctions, he was incapable of moving beyond the fantasy stage. This, too, would be highly speculative, since the liaison lasted for thirteen years, and Dickens's diary indicates how he roved back and forth across England and France in order to see Nelly. The brilliance of the Tomalin book is that it opens up the very question a biographer must try to solve and the reader wants to be solved.

Nowhere more than in the four years covering 1862 through 1865 do we have the mystery which the biographer must unravel. Nelly simply vanishes. "For four years she remains invisible," Tomalin writes (133), even to her absence from her sister Maria's London wedding. Chapter 9, then, becomes a "chapter of guesses and conjectures," and yet this period, when Dickens was himself between books (between *Great Expectations* and *Our Mutual Friend*), is precisely when we would like to know more; as Tomalin recognizes. Nelly disappears, and Dickens does not publish a major novel in this period, even though he was only fifty. This is the period when Tomalin conjectures a son born to Dickens and Nelly, and she cites the writer's son Henry as acknowledging this. "There was a boy, but he died" (143). This "source, however, is secondhand, from Gladys Story, who said Sir Henry Dickens made the remark in 1928. For the biographer, the trail is not exactly evidentiary, and Tomalin moves with cautionary steps. She has found no trace in English or French registers of an illegitimate baby, although this is not final — such registration was not required in England until 1874. Yet a false name was possible especially since in renting residences Dickens used false names and seemed to revel in assuming different identities.

What Tomalin has latched onto, despite the paucity of final proof, is the potential of two people, Nelly and Dickens, who constantly reinvented themselves. The compelling aspect of Tomalin's book is how her two characters in their abilities to reconfigure themselves parallel the biographer's own procedure of resurrecting her subjects, without any assurance of accuracy. Thus Tomalin has created a biography about the act of writing biography. In assessing what occurred to Nelly and Dickens, and their lives before and after their liaison, Tomalin has opened up the biographer's dilemma: a mode in which a great deal is effaced from the subject's life, so that significant elements stand forth in higher relief. As Tomalin says about her subjects: "It was not only Nelly who had to excise a large chunk of her life: all three Ternan sisters effaced their working childhoods and theatrical backgrounds, bowing to a prejudice they were not strong enough to oppose. In the written record they were to exist only within certain particular limits" (235). So, too, Dickens effaced the worst parts of his childhood, hiding them from his wife and children and only divulging them to his biographer, John Forster, to be revealed after his death.

There is the "Story," the main line of Tomalin's book, but there is also the "story," which is the internal drama and which remains concealed, distorted, all but impossible to dredge up. In the writing of biography, that element belonging to the inner story and that pertaining to the outer Story necessarily must connect; and here we have that arrangement, rearrangement, and inherent deception that is at stake in the very conception of biography. With her oddly angled subjects, Tomalin has pushed her way into the very interstices of the biographical process, turning "story" into "Story," and, by necessity, forcing "Story" back into "story." Unlike many biographers, she does not attempt to deceive us about what she is doing; nor does she attempt to provide "filler" for the gaps without warning the reader that she is speculating. For her, the gaps are as significant as the filling, in that the gaps raise possibilities, whereas the filler is much more prosaic. That Nelly and Dickens possibly had a child, even two, is part of the gap, despite the evidence Tomalin offers. What is almost equally interesting is the "gap" between the way Dickens insisted he be received and the way in which Victorian England talked about him. In the background, rumors had hardened into judgments—for Thackeray, but also for several others; so that Dickens was saved from ostracization—unlike George Eliot—only because he was a male. Or was it because Dickens so controlled the publicity mills and the major forms of communication that his private life did not become a public impediment?

Tomalin continues with Nelly's life after Dickens's death, a life in which she re-created herself, along the way marrying and bearing children. She went from her invisible role into that of a gentlewoman, the wife of a schoolmaster, serving tea to the ladies of the town; and yet a woman who, despite having remade herself, kept her deepest secrets from her son. When he discovered she had been an actress and the rest, he was mortified, this proper young military man who served in some of the sleaziest areas of the world. Yet compelling as Nelly's turnaround is in this portion of her life, compelling as is her still invisible life, without Dickens in the background the story sags. Nelly's husband is, unfortunately, a poor creature compared with his predecessor; but the problem goes deeper than his limitations. It goes into the very nature of the biography Tomalin has written, in which the invisible Dickens has a virtually godlike power; and when *he* vanishes, the magic of "invisibility" vanishes with him. So, too, Nelly becomes ordinary to the degree that she salvages her life: heroic in one sense, in her refusal to succumb, but ordinary and conventional in another. What had created the magic and the extraordinary dimension was her role in handling Dickens — what little we know and all the rest we probably cannot ever know. In those gaps lies the "story," Tomalin's real subject.

Victoria Glendinning's *Anthony Trollope* is the most sure-handed biography of the writer. She uses the fiction to support aspects of the life; she uses the life to show how it led into the fiction; she understands how the historical and social/political context for Trollope's life and fiction must be resurrected for the contemporary reader. Yet Glendinning's very success with what she set out to do raises troubling questions about biography in general and Trollope biography in particular. After John Hall's solid work of only a few years ago, and R. H. Super's study, Glendinning's was bound to have in it some sense of déja vu. She approaches her material freshly, and she explores something which Hall only touched upon — the interpenetration of life and work. Yet it is in that very area that Glendinning is somewhat unsatisfactory — perhaps the most significant part of biography. I am speaking of the biographer's need for acute critical awareness when he or she is writing about a major or near major literary figure; the biographer's task must overlap here with the critical task. They are not separate, any more than psychological and social issues are.

Glendinning has a habit of stating as facts some matters which must be conjectural. For example, she states unequivocally that in the 1850s George Eliot — whom Trollope knew and revered — had "been the mistress of the handsome, philandering editor of the *Westminster*, John Chapman" (324). This is precisely what we do not know. We do know that Eliot, then Marian Evans, moved into the Chapman household on the Strand, where the publisher lived with his wife and mistress. Chapman did pay especial attention to Eliot, but how far they went is shrouded in mystery, and will probably never be known. If Glendinning knows, she must reveal evidence. In a different but somewhat related area, she writes very well about Trollope's relationship with Kate Field, the attractive American many years younger than he. But because she eschews any psychological probing, Glendinning does not trace through what effect this younger woman had on Trollope — besides his repetitive use of such a situation in his fiction. Also, since she can be so sure Eliot was Chapman's mistress, how can she be certain Trollope and Kate Field were *not* intimate? In each instance, conjecture enters, with different results, and yet the evidence for each is somewhat similar.

There are other areas which make the biography feel incomplete, or unargued. Glendinning sidesteps Trollope's anti-Semitism, which, like that of many nineteenth-century English writers, was not virulent but nevertheless there, in early Dickens and Eliot, for instance, in Thackeray and others. It was certainly part of a "scene," in which anti-Semitism was a given, and those who shared in it comprised the establishment point of view. Since Jews do turn up in Trollope, not least in *The Way We Live Now*, this is not an area to be disregarded. But Glendinning also sidesteps how Trollope's retrograde social and political views, his typical racism and sense of English ethnic superiority, limited his fictional outlook; even while she chides him in distinctly politically correct late twentieth-century terms. She fails to create the dialectic or tensions which would show Trollope fighting through retrograde social views in order to create fictions which move creatively beyond his own limited outlook. We see in Dickens and Eliot, for instance, their efforts to deal with contradictory impulses, and the richness of their fiction is the consequence of their struggle between self-limits and imaginative re-creation. We get little sense of this in Trollope, perhaps because Glendinning has no overarching view of the writer, no level to which she holds him. We sense her hesitation when she must go back to the life after discussing the fiction, for she finds the life so limited and halting in its outlook. She cannot satisfactorily answer how that man could have written those novels.

Finally, a writer with forty-seven novels to his credit inevitably becomes a mechanical subject. One reason Trollope biography is so difficult is that the subject was turning out books more rapidly than the biographer can prepare the reader for them. With the best intentions in the world, the biographer finds the subject a machine. Dickens's output was under control, as were Eliot's and Thackeray's, but Trollope had novels backed up, written well before publishers were prepared to issue them. Such traffic affects every aspect of the biography, and Glendinning is no more effective than Hall in trying to mention each book without sounding like a broken record.

Of all the above points, the most serious is that Glendinning has no overall theory or point about Trollope. She wants us to like his books, even while pointing to some of his attitudes as "quite outrageous" to the modern mind.

A good deal of Dickens was also outrageous, but Peter Ackroyd found the means by which Dickens's views could be perceived as part of an inner struggle, somehow transformed in the fiction. Glendinning with all her research abilities, her readable style, her familiarity with the materials, her diligence, misses, somehow, the implications of her biography. In her introduction — after admitting Trollope's attitudes will not do for the modern reader — she states that by understanding the "complex social and psychological forces" which went into a man like Trollope, we can "better analyse the historical process which has produced our own society" (xxiii). This would only be possible if Trollope was seen as a man in some conflict — socially, religiously, politically, sexually — who was able to dramatize those conflicts fictionally. Then there is some historical overlay. Otherwise, we have a writer whose views don't give us too many clues to what he was writing; or put another way, his legacy of writing does not seem to grow out of the man who did the work. Glendinning wants to make the claim, but without the goods to support it.

Other areas, as well, need more bolstering. Trollope is presented as sexually faithful to his wife, although with a wandering eye — no more. Yet something was amiss in his penchant for older-younger person relationships in his life; "amiss" in the sense that he did not find his marriage fulfilling, and that this yearning for other relationships — whether ever consummated or not — gave him particular insight into the sexual conflicts of his age. Glendinning explains Trollope's mother-daughter penchant, or else his several instances of closeness between a young girl and her father or uncle, as outside the realm of "sexual abuse," which breeds "a self-consciousness unknown to Anthony Trollope and his contemporaries" (462). This is the same as claiming that Freudian ideas did not apply to sexual relations before Freud defined them. In other, more literary, terms, Glendinning ignores the fact that Eliot, admired by Trollope, did not think much of his work. She considered much of the 1860s and 70s as a waste land in fiction — unfairly so, but for her Trollope was part of that waste land. Another area which deserves more comment is Trollope's attitude toward Dickens. Glendinning cites Trollope's early mockery of Dickens as having "simplistic attitudes to human character" (222n.); but this she should have disputed, since Dickens's so-called simplicity masked far greater psychological insight than anything in Trollope.

All of this sounds more negative about Glendinning's earnest book than it should be. Her Trollope, finally, does not cohere. There is too much hit and run, and there is insufficient critical acumen, too little of that coherence which biography must make apparent, or else it serves little purpose.

In John Forster's biography of Dickens, the friendship between Wilkie Collins and Dickens is avoided — not only slighted, but not even indicated.

Collins is the missing man, yet he is the man Dickens acted with in plays, travelled with in England and abroad, and considered his closest social friend. Forster's suspicions of Collins occurred on several levels: he considered him a rival for Dickens's affections; he worried about Collins's dissolute life — even while Forster sidestepped Dickens's own liaison with Nelly Ternan; he felt that Collins's flouting of social conventions would jeopardize Dickens's façade of respectability and decorum; and perhaps most of all, he was jealous of Collins's literary success, while he, Forster, remained without any great achievements.

The "absent" Collins fits well with Catherine Peters's perception of him as "the king of inventors" in her book of that title, for Collins helped remake English fiction, not only with the detective story dimension but with the social grounding of the policier type of fiction. Possibly adding to Forster's hostility was the fact that Collins was an influence on Dickens, in matters of the detective story, doubling of characters, qualities of invention, and the like. Yet in some respects, Forster had the final word, for Collins always seemed to operate in Dickens's shadow, and only recently has begun to emerge in his own right.

Peter's book, in most ways a conventional biography, nevertheless attempts to provide some critical grounding. Repeatedly, she relates Collins's life to his fiction, but lacking a psychological perspective, she fails to read back from the fiction to the life, however precarious that enterprise is. Perilous it may be, but it is necessary, since there is little she can discover in Collins's personal background to explain the unconventional matters he located in his novels and stories. Since nurture does not appear to work, the biographer needs psychological strategies. The most Peters can do is to emphasize that Collins's profligate life was a response to his father's strait-laced and respectable mode. But this is not convincing, since the father was doting, not dictatorial; sympathetic, not authoritarian. Rebellion against someone as benign as the painter William Collins is insufficient inference.

Another area that deserves more intense exploration was Collins's sympathy for the working and disadvantaged classes. Peters quotes a relevant passage in which the writer speaks of how his servant girl has no hopes, dreams, chances or opportunities — no holidays, no expectations, only small wages and bare subsistence living. The question is how Collins, from a middle-class background, came by these feelings. Is it enough to say that because of his general desire to break from Victorian proprieties — from everything Mrs. Grundy represented — he came to see the working classes, not as ennobled, but as experiencing a hellish fate? Further, in his perception of lower-class slavery, he described the shame of England: that "No state of society which composedly accepts this, in the cases of thousands, as one of the necessary conditions of its selfish comforts, can pass itself off as civilised except under the most audacious of false pretences'' (Peters, 166). Where did these views come from? When did they first come to Collins? Are they merely part of his rebellion, or do they reach deeper? And to what degree are his social views part of his sexual makeup, or his sexual anxieties? Peters does not make these connections.

Part of the problem lies in the structuring of the book. For despite the careful research, the intelligent comments, the sifting through of the known facts of Collins's life, Peters has built the book on joints and segments. We find a piece of life, then a summary of the latest novel or play, followed by some linkage of life and work; then the procedure repeats itself with the next work. Withal, the inner life of Collins remains occluded and mysterious, especially with a man who was, as the author writes, "haunted by a second self." To this we might add, his need for doubles and deceptions, for implied or real violence, for "ghostly influences" revealed in his need to carry on several lives beneath the surface of what was already a deceptive one. He was also famous in his fiction for changing or removing identities, or having identities substituted. These are questions of self or ego, of his positioning or repositioning of himself both in and outside his work.

We must not forget to factor in not only plot convolutions, but personal ones, his bigamous "wives" and dual families, his desire to cut through cant, his association with women far beneath him in class and education. We must not ignore his relationship in person and in correspondence with the twelve-year-old Nannie Wynne, when he was entering his sixties. And while no overt sexual move was made, Collins did speak to her in sexual terms and did appear to flirt as though she was eligible to be wooed and won. The entire episode, starting within four years of Collins's death — a relationship that was both literary and intimate — is well noted by Peters; but she cannot fit it into any context. In one respect, that failure to find a context for the episode is linked to the failure to find a context for Collins's other "aberrations," whether personal or fictional.

With elements of the biography seeming to float free of each other, Collins escapes Peters's net. This does not suggest she needed some tight or restricted theory to "explain" him; very possibly, his disguises and deceptions were the outgrowth of inner demons which defied definition. Biography cannot penetrate into the very interstices of the writer's craft, into his or her leaps and regressions. But biography does depend, to a large degree, on the biographer's applying some overall theoretical conception to the material. It should allow the subject to breathe, and should permit margin for error, margin for alternate possibilities. Peters has chosen a method which is popular with most British biographers, which is to steer clear of any psychological orientation beyond the most primitive, what we see in most of the books under discussion here. One of the few exceptions was Peter Ackroyd's *Dickens* (1990), and, not unexpectedly, this magnificent biography received quite lukewarm to hostile reviews in the English press, despite its being very possibly the best biography written in the 1980s. Not unexpectedly, also, is that the blurbs on the American paperback are all from American reviewers.

What could Peters have done, if she so chose? She could have presented a far more conflicted Collins. His relationship with Dickens, so close, and yet so disproportionate — to what degree did it create envy, jealousy, inner conflict in Collins? Did he remain equitable through all of Dickens's successes? — not if we cite his letters after Dickens's death, when he criticized *Dombey*, among others, and then faltered when he attempted to duplicate Dickens's success in his public readings. The entire relationship needs re-examination, not in Peters's terms of Collins's great good humor, but in the way he became savage in his work as a result of demons eating away at him.

Similarly, his reluctance to marry within his circle calls for elucidation. His establishment of two parallel households with women he picked up: what did this signify sexually? what was he rebelling against? how did this affect his writing? And then the work itself — where does Peters discuss the literary tradition of Gothic fiction which Collins fitted into in no small part? I have in mind Mrs. Radcliffe's novels, Matthew ("Monk") Lewis's fiction, Mary Shelley's *Frankenstein*, or, even more, Charles Maturin's *Melmoth the Wanderer*, perhaps the greatest of them all. Collins's literary work is a complicated combination of Gothic elements, a Dickensian sense of social justice, several different personal maladjustments (which need to be defined in the fiction and then brought forth into the life), a nineteenth-century concern with recognizable characters, and the elements of mystery and secretiveness which were part of the subgenre he helped define, the detective-policier novel. In the popular mind, Collins became linked to the so-called "sensation novel," whose most successful practitioner among his contemporaries was Mary Elizabeth Braddon; but his work went far beyond that, into mysteries which penetrated deeply into paranoia, schizoid behavior, behavior that bordered on the psychotic and suggested an "unconscious" such as Freud posited.

Peters does introduce Freud late in her study, but by then Collins had foreshadowed many of the dark elements of the psychoanalyst's world. Another problem, somewhat disconnected from what has been said, is that after Collins published his major fiction in the 1860s (*The Woman in White, The Moonstone*, among others), the life becomes anticlimactic. To maintain interest for another twenty years, when the subject is weakening, slowly dying, and producing work of diminished quality is a chore for the biographer. The last two decades become the drum-call of a writer spinning out novels merely because that is his vocation; the energy and inventiveness are gone. Peters handles this as well as can be expected, but it is the dilemma for the biographer of many writers, Conrad, Faulkner, as well as many contemporaries, such as

Bellow, Mailer, Styron — for whom biographies are in the works or already published. One way around this problem — and not a completely satisfactory solution — is for the biographer to work thematically; so that the later work gets caught up in themes rather than chronology. This works as a disguise, deceiving the reader into ignoring the inevitable letdown of the later years, or at least creating the illusion of a still strong subject. In effect, Collins's letdown coincided with Dickens's death in 1870 — since despite the former's considerable accomplishments, the great figure in his life was Dickens; as much a shadow figure for Collins as he was for Claire Tomalin's Nelly Ternan. Such are the difficulties of biography, when a gigantic figure over-shadows one's subject. In this area, Peters has presented the facts, but what one looks for now is the explanation.

Ian Bell set out to write a particular kind of biography in *Dreams of Exile: Robert Louis Stevenson*, and within those limitations he is successful. His was to be a pared-down life of Stevenson, in which he would touch all the major works, but not use them to mine Stevenson's deeper emotions or mental attitudes. It is clear why Bell's book was nominated in 1992 for the British Nonfiction Book of the Year award, since by eschewing virtually all psycho-logical interpretation, Bell provides that kind of clean, somewhat simplistic biographical study admired by the British. Such biography does have its virtues — and Bell is to be praised for his accomplishment *if* we do not fault his book for failing to respond to any changes in the biographical genre for the last forty years. His work seems caught in a time warp: it could have been written in 1950 as well as in the 1990s.

Stevenson is a goldmine for a biographer, although not for a practical man whose background is in journalism; more than realism is called for. Scottish editor of the *Observer*, Bell writes an admirably clean, unadorned, solid prose, but Stevenson somehow never appears to be the author of numerous contradic-tory and ambiguous works, not the least *The Strange Case of Dr. Jekyll and Mr. Hyde*. One area Bell does describe in some detail — and it is unavoid-able — is the almost constant illness of Stevenson, as he passed through one medical crisis after another, before succumbing to a stroke on the island of Samoa in 1894 at the age of forty-four. His symptoms recall tuberculosis, but he underwent such a variety of physical ills that his condition calls out for more than a listing.

Bell fears to enter this thicket, of what illness meant to the subject, beyond his recovering and moving on; or to ask what the illness meant in terms of resolve, or how it shaped his work. Were Stevenson's "regressive" works, those which appealed to children, such as *The Master of Ballantrae* or *Trea-sure Island*, linked to illness? Was this his effort to get behind it to some period when he could see the end of suffering and medication; to a time when he breathed in air that did not infect his body?

In a related respect, how does the biographer deal with the fact that Stevenson could undergo enormous physical ordeals, at sea and elsewhere, as long as he was removed from his parents, and from Scotland itself? Was he so Scots to the core that his home(land) poisoned him? To what extent did his parents — a powerful, but flexible father, a mother whom the writer did not respect — keep him ill as a way of holding on to their only son? Only in later life did Stevenson break from his father's allowance; for most of his adult life, he depended on a generous outlay from home, in fact a rescue pipeline. Money and illness intertwined.

Bell touches on these matters, but his failure to pursue them into some kind of psychological stance turns his biography into nearly all narrative, even when the life demands some theoretical position on Stevenson's psychological and emotional state. Narrative is all to the good if it can be continued as part of the analysis; if the work can be threaded through, not as heavy criticism, but as psychological narrative. The biographer must recognize that the genre has not remained static.

An additional matter is length. *Dreams of Exile* runs to 265 pages, with an Epilogue of 12 pages. It is true that Stevenson died at only forty-four, but Keats at less than twenty-six requires 600-page books; and other artists of comparable stature to Stevenson gain sizable biographies. This does not necessarily mean a hymn to length, a paean to bulk. A good, clean biography might have served at one time; but at present, for a subject born in 1850, there is the need for historical recreation, for in-depth analysis of political and social trends, for a greater sense of Scotland — although as far as he goes Bell is quite good here — for developments in science, psychology, social thought. Bell mentions Herbert Spencer, but little else that impacted intellectually on Stevenson. Then, related to this, the biographer must pursue how Stevenson came to write those books, especially something as enduring as the Jekyll and Hyde novella, and how that book fitted into a Victorian sense of a schizoid vision. To take only this one example: to explain Jekyll and Hyde — as later to explain, perhaps, Bram Stoker's *Dracula* — the biographer needs heavy doses of social thought, psychological insight, the literary milieu, the awareness of mental illness. He must uncover the qualities which pressured Stevenson and yet allowed him release from what was a bifocal vision. To intertwine that one book, only, with its author, the biographer needed a large apparatus, and here Bell fails us — as we note from the very brief footnotes, no more than a dozen scattered throughout the book.

Inevitably, Stevenson was a much more interesting author and phenomenon than Bell can recreate. Since his aim is to pare down elements, he unfortunately reduces. There is no mystery or variousness to his subject; and yet

Stevenson has retained his rank as one of Scotland's three greatest writers — with Burns and Scott — and in other terms as one of the most compelling of the second-tier writers in English; certainly a Victorian phenomenon who needs a more fleshed-out biography than this, although admittedly a more accurate one than Graham Balfour's two-volume *Life* at the turn of the century.

Jennifer Uglow wants Elizabeth Gaskell to be ranked with the leading Victorian novelists, although she recognizes that her subject lacked Eliot's intensity and Dickens's range. One problem with this extraordinarily well-researched biography, *Elizabeth Gaskell: A Habit of Stories*, is that the claims made for Mrs. Gaskell bury her real talents, which are on a smaller scale than Uglow pretends. Some of this overreach is found early on in her use of the conditional tense — a tense suitable for speculation, for projecting one's subject into possibilities which lack documentation. It is a useful tense for those who want to vaunt their subjects or suggest greater range. Uglow's use at first is quite modest, that at the age of eleven Gaskell "must have missed her home," or that Gaskell's early biographer, Mrs. Ellis Chadwick, "could be right in identifying her with Margaret Dawson" (35–36), a character in *My Lady Ludlow*. These are small surmises, but they characterize much of the enterprise, which is to give us a large-size Gaskell to balance out her ongoing reputation as a charming, socially-oriented, second-echelon Victorian novelist.

But first we should comment on the length. This is a work of over 600 large pages, without including notes, index, and other matters. Uglow wanted to include everything; but a severe drawback is the vacuuming up of materials which are hardly relevant to Gaskell; and, surprisingly, the failure to probe elements which might have proven rewarding. Among the latter is Gaskell's relationship to her husband: a devoted wife, she apparently could not stick around for too long before she felt suffocated. She spent an inordinate amount of time away from the Reverend William Gaskell, himself a very sympathetic man as Uglow presents him — somewhat stiff, but witty, high-minded, learned, socially sensitive and generous. Since separation became such a feature of their married life, we would expect some extended commentary on this; and related to it, some further remarks on how Gaskell — who hewed close to what she knew directly — reshaped this arrangement in her fiction.

Another deficiency: it is unclear in what senses Uglow wants Gaskell to be perceived as a feminist. One of the agons of the biography is between the "Victorian wife" aspect of Gaskell and Uglow's desire to make her into a feminist. This is all to the good, since in some ways Gaskell was a feminist — in the ways that George Eliot also was. But the danger comes in conflating contemporary views of feminism with nineteenth-century ways. It was clear by the middle of the last century that a movement supporting women's rights in marriage and divorce laws, in property rights, in the franchise was essential; for the most part, questions of equality, of full justice for women in the marketplace, of the right to hold certain jobs, were not mainstream feminist ideas. Charlotte Brontë in *Shirley* had touched on several of these, especially the right of women to be sheriffs and admirals; but there was little in the early movement to support this. Uglow muddies the waters, calling *Cranford* and *Ruth* "feminist tracts" — without defining what feminism really meant, either as a movement or as something Gaskell believed in. Much of what the latter came to believe was a sense of justice; but that is quite different from a broader-based movement concerned with jobs, marketplace, equal pay, and the rest. Rightly, Uglow shows that many of Gaskell's friends were involved deeply in the movement, women who were the center of the "Langham Place Group" and the 1850s publication called the *Englishwoman's Journal*. But Gaskell was not a true believer, any more than Eliot, who had her own agenda.

Still another deficiency concerns the mechanical way Uglow has structured her massive study: some narrative, then some discussion of the latest novel or story, one cycle following the other. There is little flowthrough of books and life; Gaskell is segmented and compartmentalized. We observe a failure on the biographer's part to integrate life and work into that seamless web which makes both seem exactly right for each other.

On the plus side, Uglow brings back Gaskell as a short story writer. Gaskell's stories would appear to be the building blocks of her fictional career, even though it was her novels which made her moderately famous. Uglow cites her as an "inventive and innovative short-story writer," what is immediately apparent in "Lois the Witch." But many of Gaskell's so-called stories are really novellas, as Uglow admits; and this form intermediate in length may have allowed her her greatest freedom. Here, in this mode, she established some of her most compelling themes and relationships, especially the presentation of troubled family linkages.

Uglow is also solid in her charting of how Gaskell came to write fiction — at first more as a hobby than as a professional endeavor. In 1850, she felt she had reached a pivotal, even critical, time, when she sensed a real conflict between domesticity and her art. The year was further significant for her first meeting with Charlotte Brontë, whose biography she was to write and which was to cause her considerable grief. Also, in 1850, she started writing for Dickens, who proved a most difficult editor and yet one she, like so many others, was forced to submit to. Dickens's *Household Words* provided an outlet for much of Gaskell's shorter fiction, but it was a relationship fraught with abrasiveness, friction, and subtextual enmity.

One of Uglow's real challenges is to relieve Gaskell from several assumptions about her and her work. One begins with the name, Mrs. Gaskell, which is how she is recalled in most critical and scholarly assessments, as well as in the classroom when her work is taught. The "Mrs." is a compromise, since it suggests she belonged to William when she quietly arranged separations; and Uglow tries out Elizabeth, but even there she falters and often falls back on Mrs. Gaskell. More importantly, however, Uglow has to dispel Gaskell's reputation based more or less on *Cranford*, a small, almost perfectly shaped book which consigns its author to minor-league status amidst Victorian giants. With *Cranford*, Gaskell became the mistress of the miniature, stigmatized a "female writer" and a "charmer." This part Uglow dissipates by emphasizing larger themes of social commentary, political insights, even somewhat aberrant personal behavior. This is all to the good, but it does mask the fact that Gaskell was mainly at home in the moderate center — despite even such a bizarre work as "Lois the Witch."

Overall, we miss a more intense psychological study and the recognition, however painful it would be for Uglow, that Gaskell is outside the major rank of Victorian novelists. Biographical art is not well served when the very artistry of the subject cannot maintain the level her biography credits her with. In biographical terms, purely, Uglow's study combines old-fashioned virtues of solid research, a broad range, a deep knowledge of the subject and her historical context; but it lacks, in other ways, any penetration into the subject's inner life, even though that life seems to be moderate, genteel, and balanced. Even such lives can reveal more, and often what they reveal adds to our knowledge, rather than merely reinforcing what we may already know.

New York University

WORKS CONSIDERED

Bell, Ian. *Dreams of Exile: Robert Louis Stevenson*. New York: Holt, 1992.
DeSalvo, Louise. *Virginia Woolf: The Impact of Childhood Sexual Abuse on Her Life and Work*. New York: Ballantine, 1989.
Glendinning, Victoria. *Anthony Trollope*. New York: Knopf, 1993.
Peters, Catherine. *The King of Inventors: A Life of Wilkie Collins*. Princeton: Princeton UP, 1994.
Tomalin, Claire. *The Invisible Woman: The Story of Charles Dickens and Nelly Ternan*. New York: Vintage, 1992.
Uglow, Jennifer. *Elizabeth Gaskell: A Habit of Stories*. New York: Farrar, Straus and Giroux, 1993.

ART HISTORY: RECANONIZING CANONS

By Joseph A. Kestner

IT IS APPROPRIATE that as the decade and the century move toward the millennium the force of canon revision be conspicuous in nineteenth-century British art historical scholarship. Such periods induce rethinking, but recently the process has been greatly encouraged by a range of new resource materials, monographs, essays, exhibition catalogues, and reprints. All of these indicate that the history of art is prompted by the fin-de-siècle to reinvestigate, recontextualize, and reconfigure the canonical even as heretofore non-canonical artists are given renewed scrutiny.

This entire process has been magnificently galvanized by Oliver Millar's *The Victorian Pictures in the Collection of Her Majesty the Queen*, a two-volume set of crucial importance to historians of nineteenth-century British art. Part of an on-going catalogue raisonné of the pictures in the Royal Collection, the first volume is devoted to Millar's introduction and exemplary annotations and catalogue entries for this vast collection; the second volume, of 886 black and white plates, is one of the most important archives of Victorian art to appear in many years. Altogether, the ramifications of these two volumes are extensive. Beautifully produced, cogently and incisively written, Millar's work will exert a major influence on future art history. These volumes concentrate on oils, with a planned future volume on the Victorian drawings and watercolors in the collection.

The Royal Collection is particularly rich in a number of key kinds of canvases favored by Queen Victoria and the Prince Consort. These include, particularly, family portraits, canvases of rituals and ceremonies like coronations and weddings, animal paintings (especially of dogs), military art, and favorite places, especially Scotland. The Queen's acquisition of portraits was facilitated by the appearance at court of Franz Xaver Winterhalter, who became the Queen's favorite such artist after his arrival in Britain in May 1842. As Millar observes, the Queen decidedly favored foreign portrait painters during her reign, not only because when present they would give her their undivided attention. The influence of the Prince Consort undoubtedly was a factor in such a predilection, but it was also the case that Winterhalter had even given the Queen "practical help" (xxvii) in her own drawing and painting. To Winterhalter belonged the great role of constructing the monarch as both ruler and mother, while he endowed the German Albert with stature, glory, and flair, in both instances of major significance in the imaging of the court. To give an idea of Winterhalter's contribution, one need only note that in 1849 he painted ten canvases of the court, and nine each in 1851 and 1859. As Millar observes, "his are the last consistently accomplished — and indeed wholly credible — portraits in the history of royal patronage in this country" (xxvii). While other artists such as Grant or Landseer contributed memorable images during the reign, it is Winterhalter's portraits of the Queen, the Prince Consort, and their family, cousins, and attendants which remain the indelible record. It is important to stress that such canvases were copied and hung throughout the Empire, thereby providing the visual links that sustained the concept of monarchy in the colonies and dominions. Winterhalter was particularly adroit in his strategizing of drapery, suggestive clouds, and distant lights to confer authority and presence on his royal sitters.

The Royal Collection also contains crucial religious works by such artists as Dyce and Herbert. Dyce's *Madonna and Child* and *St. Joseph* show this artist in his Raphaelite phase. A number of Miltonic, Shakespearean, and Spenserian subjects were painted during the period, including canvases by Frost and Horsley. Frith's *Ramsgate Sands* shows that the Queen was willing to purchase scenes of contemporary life, and even a popular genre canvas such as Emily Osborn's *The Governess* gained her approbation. The military pictures in the Royal Collection, such as Lady Butler's *The Roll Call* or *The Defence of Rorke's Drift*, reveal the Queen's unending devotion to her soldiers, while a painting such as *Home: The Return from the Crimea* by Paton reveals her sympathy for wounded veterans. Such canvases are reminders that the Victoria Cross was the first military decoration to recognize the achievements of unsung rankers in the British army. In all of these enterprises, the Queen relied on the taste, education, and connoisseurship of the Consort. Albert was the President of the Fine Arts Commission which oversaw the frescoes for the new Palace of Westminster. The possession of Osborne House in the spring of 1845 gave him a new residence to supervise and enhance with fine art. His death left the Queen without her most important artistic advisor.

These two volumes should do much to reinstantiate the work of Frost, Woodville (the great battle artist), Winterhalter, Paton, Dyce, and Grant, among others. The extremely fine black and white plates constitute a superb archive for historians of Victorian art. In addition, catalogue entries frequently include support drawings and sketches for major pictures, as well as copious documentation about the commissioning of pictures and the Queen's opinions of paintings, drawn from letters, journals, and documents. Many intriguing elements appear in the midst of this assessment of the collection, such as the almost total disregard of the Pre-Raphaelites, dislike of the work of Watts, and the reservations the Queen had about Leighton becoming a peer. One cannot help but wonder what would have been the course of royal patronage and collecting had the Consort survived as long as the Queen. She wrote in her Journal on 30 June 1863: "How dreadful to be always lacking his advice & working in the dark without his unerring eye & great taste. For me, who am so ignorant about art . . . it is most difficult to decide things" (lviii). Millar's superb volumes, however, demonstrate as nothing else ever will the role of art in the fashioning of both court and Empire. Above all, the inclusion of so many reproductions of the work of Winterhalter will surely catalyze the study of portraiture during the era, with all its political ramifications. *The Victorian Pictures in the Collection of Her Majesty the Queen* is a distinguished achievement, probably never to be superseded.

The emphasis in the Royal Collection on military painting as one facet of its range is given a new context in *British Artists and War: The Face of Battle in Paintings and Prints, 1700–1914* by Peter Harrington, Curator of the Anne S. K. Brown Military Collection at Brown University. Lavishly illustrated with thirty color reproductions and many black and white photographs, Harrington's work is a major contribution to Victorian art history, as it incorporates the work of many painters — such as Giles, Gibb, Crofts, Woodville, Joy, Hillingford, Grant, Gilbert, Charlton, Barker — who have never been studied with the precision accorded them by Harrington. Of his fourteen chapters surveying this genre of painting, nine are devoted to Victorian and Edwardian artists. Of extraordinary scholarly value is the Catalogue of Paintings Harrington includes at the end of his study, listing 943 works, their dimensions, and their current locations. The Bibliography is equally thorough, including books, periodicals, and dissertations devoted to this subject. Like the portraits discussed in Millar, military art was crucial in the construction of ideologies of Empire, masculinity, and race during the era, and Harrington's study will be another key archive to both canonical and particularly noncanonical artists for future investigators.

Harrington locates the origin of battle art in the work of Benjamin West, whose history painting established the pre-eminence of battle scenes, particularly the episode of the "death of the hero" in such works as the famous *Death of General Wolfe* exhibited at the R. A. in 1771. Evoking Christian martyrdom and the pietà, West depicted the dying general in contemporary military dress rather than in classical garb. The advent of the French Wars and Waterloo, spanning 1793 to 1815, was the central catalyst which propelled British battle art to prominence. Above all, the death of Nelson at Trafalgar (painted by West, Devis, Dighton, and others) was to constitute "the most common image of the Napoleonic Wars'' (86), unlike Waterloo, which did not elicit the same contemporary response. As Harrington notes, such painting oscillates between "truth" and "epic imagination" (87), for an artist was obliged not only to record but to commemorate. The Crimean War "heralded a new form of battle painting in which the incident replaced the all-embracing narrative panorama" (133), with a new emphasis on the common soldier rather than the officer. Artists such as Jones, Armitage, and Barker produced images of such contests as Balaclava or Inkerman which constituted the official record for British citizens, even as Louis Desanges began his famous series of Victoria Cross recipients commemorating the heroism of the common man.

The most powerful parts of Harrington's study deal with the ideology of Empire in British battle art. Beginning with the revolt in India in 1857, racialist elements entered battle art to construct a program of British and white supremacy over the darker-skinned Other. As painted by artists such as Hopley, Goodall, Paton, and Abraham Solomon, the "Indian Mutiny" was constructed as a revolt against the legitimate authority of colonial administrators. The Zulu War begun in 1879, with its major battles at Isandhlwana (a British defeat) and Rorke's Drift (a victory), presented on canvas the emerging confrontation of subjugated blacks against white authority in the work of Butler, Moynan, and Fayel. These "colonial small wars" in Afghanistan, the Transvaal, the Sudan, and Egypt were commemorated in canvases by Giles, Woodville, Fripp and many others, constructing heroism in Khartoum and lesser engagements. These paintings serve as reminders that during Victoria's long reign, for only about fifteen years were the British not engaged in some conflict or other in the Empire.

Of particular interest is the practice of late Victorian battle art, in which previous wars were depicted for the late nineteenth century. Ernest Crofts in his recreations of the Civil War and of the Napoleonic campaigns and Lady Butler in her evocations of the Crimean conflict resurrected past glories for the edification of the harassed wardens of Empire. An artist such as Robert Gibb is intensely interesting, as he evokes specifically Scottish military heroism in his paintings of the Crimea while chronicling contemporary campaigns like Dargai. Battle art lost its prominence with the advent of photography, and particularly during the Boer War, where the army was dressed in khaki, color values, so key to any such art, could not be maintained. The ideological blurring during the Boer War also contributed to the demise of battle art, as a conflict of white against white decentered racial conceptions.

British battle art was nevertheless crucial to sustaining imperial ideologies. Through the process of engraving, thousands of prints could be hung on walls throughout the country and in the colonial possessions. As Harrington notes, as times changed, houses with small rooms were not suitable for such displays.

Camouflage during World War I demolished color values, while photography increasingly usurped the role once enjoyed by specials (artist-correspondents in the field) and the battle artist. Harrington's book, however, suggests many avenues for future investigation, such as the role of imprinting masculinity on boys, the reification of imperial agendas, and the role of fine art in politics. Harrington's use of diaries, memoirs, and even interviews with descendants gives his research a compelling immediacy. In terms of bringing to recognition the work of many important but neglected painters, *British Artists and War* is a major investigation of Victorian art history.

The centenary of the status of Leeds as a city prompted the Leeds City Art Gallery to produce a landmark exhibition of another great but ignored artist, John William Inchbold (1830–1888), *John William Inchbold: Pre-Raphaelite Landscape Artist*, with an excellent catalogue by Christopher Newall. It is worth recalling that in the 1984 Tate Pre-Raphaelite retrospective, only one canvas by Inchbold was included. Newall has now rectified this unjustifiable omission, baffling in light of the fact that Tennyson and Patmore owned canvases by him, Swinburne admired him intensely, and of all artists he most exemplifies the influence of Wordsworth on landscape painting. Influenced by Ruskin's *Modern Painters* and for a brief period praised by him, Inchbold is known today for *In Early Spring* and *The Glacier of Rosenlaui*, despite the fact that he sojourned for long periods at Tintagel, Venice, and Spain, producing landscapes of the widest possible range of subjects. In addition, like his more famous associate Rossetti, Inchbold also wrote poetry, publishing a volume, *Annus Amoris*, in 1876. Newall emphasizes Inchbold's achievement by noting the washes of thin color, the achievement of texture, and the "sense of luminosity" (23) attained by this painter in the evolution of his career. As Newall observes: "Inchbold's landscape painting operated in a way that is analogous to the mechanism of Swinburne's later poetry. Each abandons all sense of chronological sequence or topographical significance in favour of purely aesthetic qualities. . . . These works of art . . . appealed to an audience for whom the very process of artistic response was its own justification" (24).

And what a justification! The 24 color plates, essential for an exhibition of work by a neglected master, declare this achievement indisputably. The early *At Bolton* (1855) and *Anstey's Cove* (1853–54) attest to strong Pre-Raphaelite detail of landscape, but even as early as the 1857 *Lake of Lucerne*, the shimmering luminosity of such late works as *Castle of Chillon* (c. 1879–87) is anticipated. One is startled by such revelatory paintings as *Venice from the Public Gardens* or *Venice from the Lido to Giudecca* (both c. 1862–64), which in their thin horizon lines anticipate the work of Whistler, while an oil sketch such as *Peat-burning* of c. 1866 is hallucinatory in its atmospheric effects. Newall's catalogue entries will serve as a guide for future researchers, since this exhibition is the most important analysis of Inchbold since Allen Staley's

The Pre-Raphaelite Landscape of 1973. The teaching of Pre-Raphaelitism will never be the same after this exhibition: Inchbold must now be accorded emphasis equivalent to that bestowed on such practitioners as Dyce, Millais, Brett, or — dare one say it? — Ruskin himself.

This is not to say that Ruskin either is or can be ignored, as a very important exhibition attested. *John Ruskin and Victorian Art*, organized by James S. Dearden of the Ruskin Galleries, Bembridge School, Isle of Wight toured four museums in Japan during 1993. Composed primarily of materials from the so-called Bembridge Collection, now housed at Lancaster University under the direction of Michael Wheeler of the Ruskin Programme, the exhibition comprised a major component of this most significant archive. As such, the accompanying catalogue is of key importance to anyone investigating Ruskin at Lancaster, since, of the 242 works included in the exhibition, 164 were by Ruskin, all illustrated in beautiful color plates.

The plates of Ruskin's drawings are a storehouse of material, beginning with some of his earliest drawings from 1832 and continuing to the late work of 1877. These include facades of buildings both in Britain and abroad, dazzling sketches of landscapes (none more so than the *Chamouni* of 1849), details of cathedrals (as in the figures of the south porch of the Church of St. Wulfran, Abbeville, of 1868), and the splendid Venetian views of the 1870s. In addition, sixty other plates reproduce the work of Ruskin's contemporaries, including the great (Millais, Holman Hunt) and the lesser known (Ward, Severn, Leader, Rooke). Of the major Pre-Raphaelites, the attraction is the inclusion of little-known canvases such as Holman Hunt's *The Past and Present* (1868) or Millais's *The Romans Leaving Britain* (1865). Very striking are landscapes by Arthur Severn and Walter Severn, the former especially manifesting allegiance to Turner, a few of whose works are also incorporated. It is intriguing to see works by Burne-Jones juxtaposed with those of his studio assistant Thomas M. Rooke. The exhibition concluded with two works by W. G. Collingwood, one of them a portrait of Ruskin. The argument of *John Ruskin and Victorian Art* establishes, as have many exhibitions before, the decisive influence of Ruskin's writings on Victorian painters, but for the scholar, the key value of the exhibition (and its catalogue) is the trove of material now located at Lancaster University. Since most plates have a page to themselves, the opportunity to study this collection in its new venue is unparalleled with the aid of these reproductions.

The inclusion of works by Burne-Jones in *John Ruskin and Victorian Art* is both appropriate and necessary, as Burne-Jones was supported by Ruskin during his career and testified on Ruskin's behalf (supposedly under coercion) during the famous Ruskin/Whistler trial in 1878. At Peter Nahum in 1993, an exhibition *Burne-Jones: A Quest for Love*, with a catalogue by Bill Waters displayed work by Burne-Jones as well as by a number of contemporaries.

In this installation, Waters (who published a landmark study of the painter with Martin Harrison in 1973) presented the material as significantly involved with the artist's psychosexual life, notably his affair with Maria (or Mary) Zambaco. For example, he sees drawings for *Souls by the Styx* (1873) as representing the artist's own sense of suffering from erotic experience. As Waters notes apropos of two drawings, *Artist's Dreams*, "they depict a woman as a frightening intrusion" (13) on the male's psyche. Waters considers several male nude studies as "placed in the service of a sensual image" (36), a suggestive notion demanding additional exploration. The most exciting item included in the exhibition was *Belle et Blonde et Colorée*, which John Christian in a special catalogue entry calls "an exciting rediscovery" (43), probably dated around 1860. For scholars of Pre-Raphaelitism, there is something to consider from the exhibition of Spencer Stanhope's *The Winepress* (c. 1864), in which the pose of Christ certainly anticipates that of Christ in Holman Hunt's far more famous *The Shadow of Death* of 1873.

Two recent publications also contribute to the range of material on Burne-Jones's achievement. Russell Ash, in *Sir Edward Burne-Jones*, provides a very useful introduction to the artist's work, covering his achievement in watercolor, oil, stained-glass design, and other arenas. Ash notes that the artist treated watercolor as if it were oil, and vice versa, using watercolor "almost as thickly as" oil (n.p.). The book is replete with excellent color reproductions, and forty works receive full-page reproduction, along with individual commentary on each. Like Waters, Ash links certain canvases to Burne-Jones's erotic life, for example, the *Pan and Psyche* with Maria Zambaco's threat to commit suicide. Ash also emphasizes the backgrounds of some of these works, as in *The Mirror of Venus*, whose landscape evokes Botticelli or Leonardo. (The issue of Burne-Jones's strange landscapes deserves much stronger treatment in a separate essay or monograph.) Many of these works, such as *The Wheel of Fortune* or *The Depths of the Sea*, show women dominating males, signifiers of the artist's sexual anxieties.

While Penelope Fitzgerald produced a useful biography of Burne-Jones in 1973, the key document about his life remains Georgiana Burne-Jones's two-volume *Memorials of Edward Burne-Jones*, published by Macmillan in 1904. Long out of print, the work has now been reissued with an introduction by John Christian, who locates the biography as indicating the high status artists such as Watts, Burne-Jones, or Leighton enjoyed during the late nineteenth century. "The substantial biographies, generally in two volumes, which they tended to inspire is further proof of their contemporary reputation" (vii).

One of the famous Macdonald sisters, Georgiana Burne-Jones was a woman of great intelligence, musical ability, and social awareness, so much so that "the book is almost as much of a monument to herself" (xiii). As Christian notes, "the book is invaluable as a historical source" particularly because the writer knew how "to evoke an atmosphere" (xviii, xix). Her strategy in dealing with the Zambaco affair is simply to drop the year 1869, when the relationship reached a climax, from the book. The greatness of the biography, however, is its vast array of material about Burne-Jones's attitudes, evolution (the famous friendship with Morris), and beliefs. The duality of his nature, his recurring despair, his lifelong feeling of loss at Rossetti's death, his belief that art has no moral, his views of war, his isolationism, all are documented through letters and excerpts from conversations with his studio assistant Rooke. As a chronicle of the famous PRB and other coteries, the biography has no competition. As Christian observes, the book is so fine that it leaves one wishing Georgiana Burne-Jones had included more, for example, about Oscar Wilde or Pater or Albert Moore. Although she "did edit the record where she deemed it necessary" (xvii), Burne-Jones's spouse provided all historians of art with one of the great resources for the study of the artist's work. All of the drawings and photographs in the original 1904 issue have been reproduced in this reprint.

A most important exhibition has again brought to the fore not so much non-canonical artists as a non-canonical subject, the agricultural landscape in the tradition of British art. *Toil and Plenty: Images of the Agricultural Landscape in England 1780–1890* originated at Nottingham University Art Gallery before moving to the Yale Center for British Art. The superb catalogue is by Christiana Payne. Although there have been exhibitions of rural and agricultural subjects in the recent past, and while certain artists have received their own retrospectives, Payne's exhibition is a true rethinking of this genre of painting. Representation of the agricultural world has always been beset by a number of problems, not the least of which is the tendency to idyllic images quite at variance with historical reality. William Hazlitt in 1814 condemned "that masquerade style, which . . . models the features of a milkmaid on the principles of the antique," as Payne cites (49). Payne divides the evolution of this form into three periods: 1780–1815, marked by topographical emphasis and patriotic allusions during the Napoleonic Wars; 1815–1848, characterized by "escapist idylls" expressing "disenchantment with contemporary rural society" (46); and post-1848, when a new form of realism, exemplified by Clausen, began to appear.

The rural world was assailed by all kinds of forces: enclosure, mechanization, rick-burning, repeal of the Corn Laws, poaching laws, education acts, and crop rotation during the period covered by this exhibition. The effect of this social revolution was profound: in 1800, "one-third of all workers were engaged in agriculture . . . and in 1900 it was down to one-tenth" (6). The agricultural landscape was in essence a combination of "two accepted artistic categories: landscape and genre" (2), and this melding provoked a strong tendency to idealization, biblical allusion, and mythmaking about the contented poor, much of which served to reify class hierarchies. With its forty oil paintings, forty-five watercolors and drawings, as well as prints and photographs, the exhibition explored the strategies of a broad range of canonical (Brown, Turner, Constable, Holman Hunt) and non-canonical (Mason, Carmichael, DeWint) painters.

One of the strengths of the exhibition was to realize new contexts for the consideration of major works. For example, the opportunity to view Ford Madox Brown's *Carrying Corn* and *The Hayfield* in the context of a tradition engaging Samuel Palmer's *The Harvest Moon* or Holman Hunt's *Cornfield at Ewell* provoked different responses from what a strictly PRB exhibition might suggest. The visionary tendency of Palmer causes one to recognize this element in Brown's work or in that of Richard Redgrave's *The Valleys Also Stand Thick with Corn* or even John Brett's *The Hedger*. The harvest could be construed as a type of the eventual harvest of souls, and often "agricultural landscape [could be a] substitute for the religious painting that it was difficult to produce in Protestant England" (39). While Disraeli in *Sybil* (1845) and Kingsley in *Yeast* (1848) could denounce the wretched condition of the rural laborer, artists often nourished fantasies of rural idylls for their urban patrons. At the same time, however, painters often were meticulous in depicting exact stages of rural activity, noting specific crops, rotated fields, and atmospheric conditions. By the 1880s, artists such as Clausen with his *Winter Work* could depict the harsh environment Hardy was to acknowledge in novels like *Tess of the d'Urbervilles*. Even in *Winter Work*, however, Clausen was compelled to add a little girl with a hoop to his canvas to relieve its otherwise harrowing misery. Even with this addition, Clausen could not sell it: "uncompromising realism would not attract buyers" (126).

Toil and Plenty is one of a small number of exhibitions which truly revolutionize one's conception of a pictorial form. By including photographs, agricultural implements, illustrated books, and other supporting material in the installation, Payne revitalized this subject. The Bibliography to the catalogue is as fine a compendium of recent thought on the field as one is likely to encounter, although Payne does not record Howard Rodee's important 1975 Columbia University doctoral thesis *Scenes of Rural and Urban Poverty in Victorian Painting* or Christopher Wood's *Paradise Lost* (1988), both of which concentrated on art after 1850. Wood's book includes a stunning array of plates in color (much of Clausen, Birket Foster, La Thangue) which can usefully supplement the thirty-four color plates in *Toil and Plenty*. The effect of this exhibition should be transformative for British art history.

To celebrate its centennial, the Denver Art Museum presented *Glorious Nature: British Landscape Painting 1750–1850*, a stimulating exhibition of 91 paintings and watercolors by 44 British artists, drawn exclusively from collections in the United States, including the YCBA and the Metropolitan Museum. The show, curated by Katherine Baetjer and Timothy J. Standring, was accompanied by an excellent catalogue with essays by scholars dealing with such topics as picturesque sketching, Turner, and the role of landscape as high art. Several artists, such as DeWint and Palmer, represented in *Toil and Plenty*, appeared in this installation as well. Such major figures as Constable, Turner, and Gainsborough anchored the show, which also included some small but exceptional work by Ruskin (a study of a hawthorne in flower from c. 1860), a stunning oil sketch by Edward Lear (*Catania and Mount Etna* 1847), a sketch by Samuel Palmer at the age of fourteen, a beautiful oil by David Roberts of 1852 from the Forbes Collection, and John Linnell's *The Storm* of 1853, confirming his place as a master of the form. Most striking in the exhibition were some of the cloud studies by Constable, not seen to such effect since an inclusion of similar work in the 1987 exhibition *William Wordsworth and the Age of English Romanticism*. In examining such work, one is reminded of the tradition which Victorian landscapists not only responded to but inherited. Landscape as a genre always had a difficult time surmounting the hierarchies of painting established by Reynolds in the eighteenth century. The works included in the Denver installation revealed the long trajectory from Sandby, Wilson, Gainsborough, and Wright of Derby through Turner and Constable to Linnell, Ruskin, and Lear which led to its pre-eminence in British art.

An archival moment of great importance for the study of Victorian art history is commemorated in *Victorian Illustrated Books 1850–1870: The Heyday of Wood-engraving*, an exhibition held at the British Museum in 1994 to celebrate the gift to the Museum by Robin de Beaumont of his outstanding collection of illustrated books, containing some 400 volumes. Of significance to scholars is Paul Goldman's catalogue, which not only discusses such subjects as readership, the role of engravers, the artists involved, and the criticism of illustration, but also includes a complete checklist of the de Beaumont Collection, indispensable for future investigators in the field. The range of material displayed in the exhibit itself was dazzling, including such works as Trollope's *Orley Farm* illustrated by Millais, Millais's *Parables of Our Lord, Poems* by Jean Ingelow with illustration by John William North, the Moxon Tennyson *Poems* which engaged the PRB, Gaskell's *Wives and Daughters* with illustrations by Du Maurier (who also illustrated *Sylvia's Lovers* and *Cranford*), and Christina Rossetti's *Goblin Market* and *The Prince's Progress*, with drawings by Dante Gabriel.

During the 1840s, wood-engraving became increasingly popular, so that by the 1860s the whole status of illustration had been transformed. Many factors contributed to this "golden age of British book illustration," as it has been called: the rise in literacy; the emergence of key illustrated magazines,

Once a Week, Good Words, and *The Cornhill Magazine*; the prevalence of railway bookstalls operated by W. H. Smith; and the dissolution of the dominance of the Booksellers' Association in 1852. The de Beaumont gift includes at least twelve major categories of material, including secular poetry for adults, religious poetry, children's books, novels, gift books, foreign literature in translation, and music books. Represented in the collection are extensive materials illustrated by Arthur Boyd Houghton, Arthur Hughes's illustrations for Christina Rossetti's *Sing-Song*, proofs for Frederic Leighton's illustrations to Eliot's *Romola* in *The Cornhill*. Displayed as well were some of the extraordinary bindings accompanying illustrated books during the 1860s and 1870s, compelling recognition that this art is gone for ever. *Victorian Illustrated Books* as an exhibition was but the primer for scholars who must make this archive a central focus of future research.

Another important archive of material is presented in *The Pre-Raphaelites in Context*, which includes two key checklists, one of Pre-Raphaelite manuscripts in the Huntington Library (by Sara Hodson) and one of Pre-Raphaelite works of art in the collection (by Shelley Bennett). The former includes items by Brown, Burne-Jones, Brett, Collins, Deverell (portion of a diary), Holman Hunt, Morris (much material), Christina Rossetti, Dante Gabriel Rossetti (much material), and Ruskin (vast array of material). The latter includes many studies and sketches by artists such as Crane, Holman Hunt, Burne-Jones, Millais, Morris, and Ruskin. While scholars have known of these materials before, this is the first easily accessible publication of checklists to the collections and as such of primary importance. Some of the Burne-Jones correspondence is transcribed in an essay by Jane Munro, including letters to Ford Madox Brown, Harry Quilter, and Henry Holiday, which is like an encapsulated perusal of Georgiana Burne-Jones's *Memorials*. Included in the volume are two conference papers of note, one by Malcolm Warner on the influence of the National Gallery collections on the Pre-Raphaelites, and the other by Susan Casteras on canons of beauty challenged by PRB artists, both prompting new insights about major PRB canvases like Holman Hunt's *The Awakening Conscience* or Millais's *Christ in the House of His Parents*. These essays, and the checklists, make *Pre-Raphaelites in Context* a useful reference volume.

Another centenary commemorated by an exhibition was that of the first publication of *The Yellow Book* in April 1894, a work distinguished for both its literary and artistic innovation. Margaret D. Stetz and Mark Samuels Lasner curated an exemplary *The Yellow Book: A Centenary Exhibition* for the Houghton Library at Harvard, with a catalogue of 96 items, including signed autograph letters, prospectuses for *The Yellow Book*, photographs, drawings, poetry collections, and volumes of this catalyzing publication which ran from 1894 until 1897. The curators declared that their aim was "to dispel the usual myths about *The Yellow Book* — i.e., that Oscar Wilde was a shaping force

1. John William Inchbold, *At Bolton: The White Doe of Rylstone.*

2. Ford Madox Brown, *Carrying Corn.*

3. Dante Gabriel Rossetti, *The Maids of Elfin-Mere,* from William Alling-ham, *The Music Master* (1855). Courtesy of the British Museum.

behind it (he was not); . . . and that its cultural significance ceased after Aubrey Beardsley's dismissal (it did not)'' (5). Their concise yet fine Preface to the catalogue is mandatory reading for anyone studying Aestheticism and its consequences. In this essay they discuss the role of The Bodley Head, the function of the literary editor Henry Harland, the decision to include pictures *not* related to the literary texts, the fact that Wilde should never be allowed to write for it (a personal not homophobic decision, since lesbian and bisexual women and a large number of gay men were involved in the publication), the relentless promotion of the volumes, the desire to attract ''New Woman'' fiction, the eventual dismissal of Beardsley (which opened opportunities for women artists and illustrators), the pursuit of literary lions like Gissing and James for contributions, the use of the square shape derived from Whistler's *Gentle Art of Making Enemies* (1890), and the strategic use of reviews and self-criticism. Lasner and Stetz are particularly fine in discussing the role of women in the publication history of the volumes, as non-canonical writers like Netta Syrett and her artist sister Nellie gained prominence through their engagement with this publication. Among the many key innovations of *The Yellow Book*, none is more significant than its conferring of status on the short story, ''which [in England] had only been named as a separate genre in the 1880s'' (42). The innovations, such as wide margins, square shape, eccentric catchwords, and aggressive pursuit of *japonaiserie* make *The Yellow Book* one of the great cultural moments of the nineteenth century. The checklist of items in the exhibition, which includes a small number of illustrations, is a good guideline for those undertaking future research. This commemorative exhibition, and the vast material now available in the de Beaumont Collection, assure the strength of research in Victorian illustration.

Lasner has also made an important contribution to the resurrection of the non-canonical with his *William Allingham: A Bibliographical Study*. Allingham, marginalized in Victorian literary history, does not merit this neglect, if for no other reason than that he knew ''everybody,'' including Burne-Jones, Rossetti, the Brownings, and Hughes, as well as being married to the artist Helen Paterson. One should recall that Yeats noted in 1904 to Allingham's wife: ''I am sometimes inclined to believe that he was my own master in Irish verse'' (69), surely a fact that needs much additional exploration by scholars of Irish literature. It is not an understatement to declare that Burne-Jones might never have become an artist had Rossetti not produced the famous wood-engraving ''The Maids of Elfin-Mere'' for Allingham's volume *The Music Master* in 1855. Lasner's annotations of Allingham's known works are crucial for scholars. As a figure in Victorian fairy literature, Victorian drama and poetry, and Irish poetry, Allingham is much neglected, undeservedly. As a final point, one ought to note that it was Allingham's poem *Laurence Bloomfield in Ireland* (1864) that is listed among Leopold Bloom's books in

Ulysses, and as Lasner notes, "one suspects Joyce derived his character's name from its title" (15). The fact that Hughes and Millais, in addition to Rossetti, illustrated *The Music Master*, indicates the importance of Allingham's work for scholars of Victorian illustration.

In *London in the 1890s: A Cultural History*, Karl Beckson surveys many dimensions of the era, including drama, the trials of Wilde, the advent of Zolaism, the influence of Wagner, and the consequences of imperialism. For purposes of art history, several of his chapters provide a useful context for the exhibitions of Victorian illustrated books and of *The Yellow Book* discussed above. In his chapter "Defying the Commercial Periodicals," Beckson examines a number of periodicals devoted to art and literature, including *The Germ, Century Guild Hobby Horse, The Dial, The Yellow Book*, and *The Savoy*. In the *Century Guild Hobby Horse*, for example, writers as diverse as Arnold, Ruskin, Wilde, Symonds, Johnson, and Dowson were included, making it, as Beckson observes, "the significant voice of the late 1880s" (241). Beckson's discussions of *The Yellow Book* and *The Savoy* summarize key material about both periodicals. He notes that *The Savoy* contained a "preponderance of material concerned with the French Symbolists" (251), making it a key locus of cultural cross-fertilization between France and Britain. Beckson stresses Havelock Ellis's role as *The Savoy*'s "polemicist" (252), given his defense of Hardy's *Jude the Obscure* in its pages.

Beckson's chapter on Whistler is a solid summary of this artist's polemical career. He notes that "Whistler deceived the public into believing that he was a frivolous dandy . . . when, in fact, he was intent on directing the academic art of his time to a new sense of painting's visionary possibilities" (256). For Beckson, Whistler's achievement is in his "transposition of the arts" (259) whereby paintings appropriated qualities of music, as in Whistler's famous "nocturnes" and "symphonies." Beckson establishes that poets such as Wilde, Henley, Symons, and Davidson were inspired by Whistler's canvases in their deployment of imagery. In his discussion of the influence of Wagnerism, Beckson concentrates on the figure of Tannhäuser in Beardsley and Swinburne, without noting pictorial manifestations by such artists as Dicksee. The importance of Wagner for figures such as Yeats, Moore, Lawrence, and Comyns Carr is noted, for Wagner stimulated another form of "transposition of the arts" as writers began to construct using leitmotifs. Beckson's book is a series of essays, but it maintains its focus by adroit use of contemporary reviews (as in the chapter on the New Drama) and by its careful consideration of key issues, such as Victorian homosexuality in the chapter on the Uranian sensibility in Symonds, Hopkins, Ellis, and Housman. *London in the 1890s*, with its deft style and illustrations, constitutes a valuable appraisal of the complexities of the era.

The resurrection and revival of the reputations of non-canonical artists is a major project of feminist Victorian art history, which in the past decade has assailed the male-dominant canons constructed by critics, biographers, and memoirists. Among exhibitions, the decisive moment was *The Substance or the Shadow: Images of Victorian Womanhood* curated by Susan Casteras for YCBA in 1982. The Yale exhibition was followed in Britain by *Painting Women: Victorian Women Artists* curated by Deborah Cherry at Rochdale in 1987, *Women's Works* curated by Jane Sellars for the Walker in Liverpool in 1988, and *Images of Women* by Corinne Miller, Lynda Nead, and Griselda Pollock for Leeds City Art Galleries in 1989. A range of critical studies, such as Casteras's *Images of Victorian Womanhood* (1987), Nead's *Myths of Sexuality* (1988), Pamela Nunn's *Victorian Women Artists* (1987), and Jan Marsh and Nunn's *Women Artists and the Pre-Raphaelite Movement* (1989), has confirmed this process of reconstructing Victorian art history. Certainly Nunn's editing of *Canvassing* in 1986 was important for bringing primary documents of recollections by women painters to scholars' attention. Books such as Marsh's *Pre-Raphaelite Women* (1987) have concentrated on specific movements during the era. Two recent works by major critics in this field, Susan Casteras and Deborah Cherry, now supplement and promote feminist art history of the Victorian period.

A Struggle for Fame: Victorian Women Artists and Authors, curated for YCBA by Casteras and Linda H. Peterson advances the study of women as artists by including both pictorial and literary manifestations in its exhibition. Casteras, in her introductory essay to the catalogue, notes the elements which made success in either field so difficult: "the exclusivity of male realms of power" (8), "the issue of male criticism of female work" (8), "the fear of seeming unwomanly" (9), "the notion of fame culturally encoded in favor of masculine talent" (9), the emphasis on accomplishments rather than expertise, and for artists such additional factors as lack of access to nude models, the effect of male Hanging Committees, and the dominance of reviewing by men. Only partially alleviating these cultural disabilities was the existence of "matronage" or the support of female clients for art and the system of support groups (composed of fathers, brothers, other female artists, husbands). Women had to fight against being consigned to lower forms in the hierarchy of painting such as landscape or still life.

As Casteras argues, however, many did surmount these situations to become established as artists or illustrators. Helen Paterson Allingham repudiated Ruskin's advice and pursued her own way. Elizabeth Thompson after her famous *The Roll Call* did not need any man's advice, and the Hayllar sisters (Edith, Jessica, Kate, and Mary) had one another and their father to encourage them. The range of works included in the exhibition attests to the commitment and versatility of women painters: Allingham, the Hayllars, Boyce, Adelaide

Claxton, Evelyn DeMorgan, Annie Lea Merritt, Mary Morris, Emily Osborn, Elizabeth Siddall, Rebecca Solomon (from another family of painters), and Marie Spartali Stillman were among those whose works were presented in the installation. The opportunity to see four works by Osborn or a total of eight works by the Hayllars was especially striking. Works by women writers, drawn from the Beinecke and Sterling Libraries of Yale, presented examples from Charlotte Tonna to Christina Rossetti to Elizabeth Gaskell, encompassing the known and lesser known. Black and white plates are included for most of the exhibited pictures. The presentation of both literary and pictorial materials differentiates this exhibition from its predecessors, suggesting that study of women writers and artists might hereafter be profitably conjoined.

Deborah Cherry's *Painting Women: Victorian Women Artists* deploys the same title as that of the exhibition Cherry curated for Rochdale. Illustrated with over forty black and white plates, the book is a very persuasive appraisal of its subject, covering such issues as female friendship, daughters in artist families, the difficulties of art training, the various societies for women artists, and the pressure of economics in forming a career. To this material Cherry brings a mind theoretically informed by Foucault and Mulvey, emphasizing structures of power and strategies of difference during the nineteenth century. Many of the painters exhibited in *A Struggle for Fame* are examined here: Solomon, Siddall, Ward, Osborn, Walker.

It is in the individual analyses of works that Cherry's study is especially valuable, as with her examination of Havers's *The Belle of the Village* and *The End of Her Journey*, Siddall's *Lady of Shalott*, Henrietta Ward's canvas of Mary Queen of Scotts, Henrietta Rae's *Ariadne Deserted by Theseus*, or Anna Lea Merritt's *War*. Her analysis of Solomon's *The Governess* and Osborn's *The Governess* is the kind of juxtaposed commentary that is illuminating in *Painting Women*. Cherry is sensitive to issues of class, as she demonstrates by the example of Siddall, who was accepted so long as she was contented to be a model and muse. When she decided to be an artist in her own right, a former friend, the painter Barbara Bodichon, wrote: "Miss S. is a genius and very beautiful . . . although she is not a lady . . . She is of course under ban having been a model, . . . ergo do not mention to any one" (189). Cherry raises a number of issues worth further study, for example, the depiction of Mary Queen of Scots and the need for women to find heroines equivalent to Carlyle's heroes. Particularly useful is the "Checklist of Artists" appended to *Painting Women*, a compendium listing a storehouse of future research subjects. Cherry's bibliography and notes constitute fairly complete updated records of existing research.

Thames and Hudson in its World of Art series has kept in print Timothy Hilton's appraisal *The Pre-Raphaelites* and Roger Dixon and Stefan Muthesius's *Victorian Architecture*, books marked by excellent plates and certainly suitable for Victorian cultural history seminars and courses. To these two volumes one might now add *Victorian Painting* by Julian Treuherz, a concise, readable, and accessible survey of art during the period. Teuherz is especially good at noting such elements as the changing nature of patronage, as middle-class industrialists began collecting; the rise in stature of Victorian artists; the role of foreign influences, especially from Japan and France; and the role of international exhibitions in establishing national artistic identities. The decline in status of the power and influence of the Royal Academy, signalled by the presence of such venues as the Grosvenor Gallery or the New Gallery, is also a major component of Victorian art history. Treuherz deftly outlines major movements, such as Pre-Raphaelitism, Aestheticism, realism, landscape, and genre, selecting, for so short a volume, many key works to support his arguments. With its excellent plates (mostly black and white but good and some color) and its useful but brief bibliography, *Victorian Painting* fills the need very well for an accessible, inexpensive, and readable introductory volume on the subject.

University of Tulsa

WORKS CONSIDERED

Ash, Russell. *Sir Edward Burne-Jones*. New York: Abrams, 1993.

Beckson, Karl. *London in the 1890s: A Cultural History*. New York: Norton, 1992.

Baetjer, Katherine and Timothy J. Standring, eds. *Glorious Nature: British Landscape Painting 1750–1850*. New York: Hudson Hills P, 1993.

Burne-Jones, Georgiana. *Memorials of Edward Burne-Jones*. 2 vols. London: Lund Humphries, 1993.

Casteras, Susan. *A Struggle for Fame: Victorian Women Artists and Authors*. New Haven: Yale Center for British Art, 1994.

Cherry, Deborah. *Painting Women: Victorian Women Artists*. New York and London: Routledge, 1993.

Dearden, James S., ed. *John Ruskin and Victorian Art*. Tokyo: Shimbun, 1993.

Goldman, Paul. *Victorian Illustrated Books: The Heyday of Wood-engraving*. London: British Museum P, 1994.

Harrington, Peter. *British Artists and War: The Face of Battle in Paintings and Prints, 1700–1914*. London: Greenhill Books, 1993.

Lasner, Mark Samuels. *William Allingham: A Bibliographical Study*. Philadelphia: Holmes, 1993.

Millar, Oliver. *The Victorian Pictures in the Collection of Her Majesty the Queen*. 2 vols. Cambridge: Cambridge UP, 1992.

Newall, Christopher. *John William Inchbold: Pre-Raphaelite Landscape Artist*. Leeds: Leeds City Art Galleries, 1993.

Payne, Christiana. *Toil and Plenty: Images of the Agricultural Landscape in England 1780–1890*. New Haven: Yale UP, 1993.

Stetz, Margaret D. and Mark Samuels Lasner. *The Yellow Book: A Centenary Exhibition*. Cambridge, MA: Houghton Library, 1994.

Treuherz, Julian. *Victorian Painting*. London: Thames and Hudson, 1993.

Waters, Bill. *Burne-Jones: A Quest for Love*. London: Peter Nahum, 1993.

DEFINING THE *FIN-DE-SIÈCLE:* LOOKING BACKWARDS FROM THE 1990S TO THE 1890S

By Philip E. Smith

AS THE CULTURAL HISTORIAN Hillel Schwartz explains, "Late in 1885 *fin de siècle* made its popular debut as a single phrase, a phrase at first descriptive of personal manner and carriage, then of the manners and carriage of the epoch itself" (159). The phrase entitled a French play of 1888 by H. Micard and François de Jouvenot and a novel of 1889 by Humber de Gallier. Oscar Wilde employed the phrase in *The Picture of Dorian Gray* (1891) and, elsewhere, editorialists, writers, and composers used it as a commonly accepted cultural term to capture the feeling of the times (160). "There was something about the approach of the calendrical '00 that made for an epoch-in-waiting during the 'Nineties,' which were at once an endtime and a betweentime, years of nervousness, decadence, boredom and thrill-seeking, suicide and Ferris wheels, faithlessness and occult philosophies, anarchy and artificiality — all that behavior called by 1902 'manic-depressive' " (161).

Owing partly to a long-term cultural fascination with the numerology of time and certainly because of the rich possibilities for investigating the material or spiritual *Zeitgeist* of the 1890s, academics of the 1990s have begun to look backward at the fin-de-siècle. It provides an appropriately celebratory theme to promote the production of books and papers as well as the organization of seminars and conferences focused on a centennial reconsideration and redefinition of fin-de-siècle literature and culture. The first two international conferences on Oscar Wilde were held during 1993, and one of the books reviewed here collects papers from a 1990 conference which took for its title, *"Fin de siècle/Fin du globe,"* a pair of phrases drawn from Wilde's *The Picture of Dorian Gray.*

Ian Small's *Conditions for Criticism: Authority, Knowledge, and Literature in the Late Nineteenth Century* is the shortest, at 155 pages including an index and bibliography, but also the most ambitious contribution to the study of fin-de-siècle literature and culture reviewed here. Small contends that "profound changes in the nature of critical discourse" were directly connected to "changes in the nature of *intellectual* authority in all disciplines of knowledge at the time, changes which coincided with the wholesale professionalization and institutionalization of knowledge which took place, principally in the universities" in Britain from the 1870s to the 1890s (vii). Small argues persuasively that "Historically criticism has derived its principles of validation and its intellectual authority, its methods of enquiry and its modes of operation, from other — and often quite separate and usually more systematic — disciplines of knowledge. And it has done so covertly, almost illicitly, in so far as the nature of its theoretical dependence and its intellectual debts are rarely apparent from its practices" (19). Small claims that his intellectual history and sociology of knowledge of the wider intellectual context will illuminate the fin-de-siècle critical practices of Pater and Wilde.

This ambitious attempt to contextualize the approaches of the two major critics at the end of the nineteenth century sketches the institutionalization of the social sciences, that is, political economy, historiography, and sociology, in British universities. In a single chapter, Small summarizes the paradigm shift in economics following the publication of William Stanley Jevons's *Theory of Political Economy* (1871); he describes the challenge to traditional historiography from Henry Buckle's British version of "scientific history" based on general laws of abstract causation and the eventual adoption of a more scholarly and empirical German historiography; finally, he describes the conflict in sociology between Spencerian and Comtean theories with the resulting "firm rejection of French analytic thought in favour of empirical sociology" (57). Small argues that all three disciplines experienced debates about "the epistemological assumptions used to underwrite their intellectual authority" resulting in "the virtual marginalization of the non-professional intellectual, and thus of what Oscar Wilde later called 'Individualism' " (64). These accounts of disciplinary formation are all very quick summaries, and to go beyond the assertion that there were changes in disciplinary paradigms and that disciplinary methods and results actually were useful (as, in fact, they were) to critics like Pater and Wilde, Small would need to do considerably more work.

Small contends that developments in the relationships among aesthetics and the sciences of biology and psychology suggested a paradigm of the mind based in "individual perceptions, impressions, and desires . . . of precisely the kind which would attract those working without institutional endorsement or those marginalized within particular institutions" like Wilde and Pater, respectively (64). Summarizing a major debate in the disciplinary formation of psychology, Small recounts James Ward's challenge to the reigning orthodoxy of affective psychology, Alexander Bain's Associationism, itself indebted to the evolutionary theories of Darwin and Spencer. Out of Bain's

Associationism came the validating epistemology for impressionist aesthetics as promulgated and practiced by Pater, Wilde, and Henry James, and popularized by Grant Allen. Small shows the crucial relationships between aesthetics and evolutionary theory in an analysis of Vernon Lee's *Juvenilia* (1887), which, he claims, anticipates the positions of Pater and Wilde in the 1890s by focusing on aesthetic reactions to the art-object: "criticism had become precisely what psychological aesthetics had proposed it inevitably had to be: an affective discipline" (87). True enough; however, Small could have done considerably more presentation and argument to advance his case about the relationship between literary criticism and extra-literary disciplinary authority — not only with biology and psychology but also with comparable paradigm shifts and debates in anthropology, the physical sciences, and in philosophy, especially idealist versus empiricist metaphysics and epistemology.

Small reviews Walter Pater's dilemma in the 1880s and early 1890s as he engaged with and attempted, in *Plato and Platonism* (1893) and in *Marius the Epicurean* (1885), "to redefine many of the forms of intellectual authority" (97). Analyzing Pater's use of quotations and intertextuality, Small concludes that "Authority, for Pater, resides in the individual; the authority of an utterance, whether critical or fictional (and it is interesting in this respect that Pater's writing constantly elides the distinctions to be made between genres and between modes of writing) depends upon the authority of the individual making the utterance, and not upon any consistent or verifiable adducing of 'evidence' " (104). As he argues for a revised understanding of what it meant for Pater to have become his own authority for critical judgment, Small asserts what *kind* of work Pater did — that is, criticism practiced as a form of art rather than as scholarship. Pater's development of individual authority is shown against a very quick account of the formation of Greek studies in British universities that would have benefited, as would Small's earlier sketches of disciplinary histories, from a fuller consideration of scholarly works like Richard Jenkyns's *The Victorians and Ancient Greece* (1980) and especially Frank M. Turner's *The Greek Heritage in Victorian Britain* (1981).

Small reads Wilde as a would-be Victorian sage who paradoxically presented himself "at one and the same time as an enemy of authority *and* as a great teacher" (130); like Pater, Small contends, Wilde appealed to individuality as authority. His strategy, however, had to be a more blatant subversion and rejection of the authority of specialist disciplinary knowledge and scholarly critical writing and a corresponding adoption of the position of the critic as artist. Small argues that "the logic of Wilde's critical practice of course derives from his critical theory. . . . Criticism could become analogous with creation, for it was a creative process which could take its material from art instead of from life'' (127). Small's reading is astute and welcome in regard to the details of Wilde's later critical practice, but I think it is nearsighted in regard to both Wilde's theory and his complicated and dialectical position about the authority of philosophical and disciplinary knowledge. As Michael Helfand and I have argued in *Oscar Wilde's Oxford Notebooks: A Portrait of Mind in the Making* (1989), Wilde's critical theory arose out of a complex revision and synthesis of the positions of disciplinary authorities in the sciences, social sciences, and philosophy. Wilde's Oxford Notebooks and his early essay, ''The Rise of Historical Criticism,'' for example, contain significant evidence of Wilde's many uses of intellectual authority in the construction of the critical theory that empowers his fin-de-siècle essays.

Small concludes *Conditions for Criticism* with a parallel consideration of the structure of nineteenth- and twentieth-century ''crises'' in literary studies: ''the purpose of this book was to describe the crisis in the late nineteenth century in *intellectual* rather than in institutional terms, a characterization equally applicable to the present dilemma in English studies. . . . As I have indicated, a crisis in intellectual authority is always caused by competition between the epistemologies which underwrite that authority'' (133). The attempt to find a structural analogue to the twentieth-century crisis, while valuable in itself, takes up correspondingly too much space in such a short book, which could usefully have told us more about the debates between epistemologies in the nineteenth century. For example, the ways in which idealism, empiricism, and materialism in their various manifestations produced differently significant (and differently verifiable) theories of knowledge was of crucial concern to the critical theories of both Wilde and Pater. Small's insistence upon the significance of the *structural* rather than the *intellectual* consequences of debates surrounding paradigm shifts in the disciplines limits his approach. The intellectual consequences for literary study of changes in other disciplines are not sufficiently attended to; that is, *how* differently Wilde and Pater conceived of the art object because of different epistemologies (and *not* because of their different moments of opposition to professionalism) could be more fully discussed. Reservations and wishes for amplification aside, however, I recommend this thoughtful book as a welcome stimulus to anyone interested in the intellectual background and practice of critical theory in fin-de-siècle English studies and especially to students of Pater and Wilde.

In *Fin de Siècle/Fin du Globe: Fears and Fantasies of the Late Nineteenth Century*, John Stokes collects, introduces, and suggests thematic relationships among papers first presented at the eponymous conference in July 1990 at the University of Warwick. Contributors were invited to participate in ''a reassessment of the eschatological ideas of the 1890s in the light of the critical thought of the 1990s that might reveal a more complex and a more material connection between narrative patterns and historical moment'' (1). The quality of the twelve selections varies widely: about half of the essays are both good in themselves and complementarily refractive of others; but those remaining do not rise to that standard. The volume has a useful index which shows that several figures, including Arnold, Freud, James, Morris, Pater, Symons, Wells, and especially Wilde and Yeats, are mentioned widely across the work of many contributors.

The collection opens with John Goode's illuminating essay on utopian fiction, "Writing Beyond the End," in which he contrasts the narrative teleologies of degeneration and social progress from a Marxist critical perspective. Goode analyzes several utopias which constitute an interesting intertextual cluster: Richard Jefferies's *After London* (1885), W. H. Hudson's *A Crystal Age* (1887), Edward Bellamy's *Looking Backward: 2000–1887* (1888), and William Morris's *News from Nowhere* (1890). His analysis works to disable the "immanentist" positions of Jefferies, Hudson, and Bellamy, and instead to celebrate the utopian drive he finds in Morris and in Oscar Wilde's "The Soul of Man Under Socialism" (1891). Goode relies more on assertive classifying than on argument, but he writes from a well-informed position, taking into account other works by these writers as well as a considerable number of critical stances.

The other worthy essays in the collection include William Greenslade's brief "Fitness and the *Fin de Siècle*," which effectively catalogues how, in late Victorian fiction and journalism, the concept of fitness was adopted by several social Darwinistic ideologies as the positive answer to another ideological concept, degeneracy. Patrick Parrinder's useful *"Heart of Darkness*: Geography as Apolcalypse" returns to "the most over-interpreted literary text of the last hundred years" (85) in a reading of Conrad's narrative next to his journal of 1890, the "Up-River Book," with particular attention to explication of two elements, the omission of Arab involvement in the ambush, and the "notorious description of the cannibal crew" (88). Parrinder finds that Conrad's motivation of Marlow out of "a kind of journalistic parody of real anthropology" produces "a story of the dark angel rampant in human affairs and an extraordinary exercise in fin-de-siècle Satanism" (98–99). Approaching Freud's *Studies on Hysteria* (1895), Jan B. Gordon uses a figure from Conrad to investigate productively the relationships among language, the counter-will, and therapeutic hypnosis in "Freud's 'Secret Agent' and the Fin du Corps."

The collection ends with two strong essays. First, Ian Small's "Literary Radicalism in the British *Fin de Siècle*" outlines the argument of *Conditions for Criticism* and is the most suggestive piece in the volume because it takes on the largest issues and scope of thought. Like Small's book, however, the essay also fails to address significantly late nineteenth-century philosophy and physical science, two of the intellectual foundations for the progress of thought in the social-scientific and literary critical disciplines that Small considers. Second, J. Edward Chamberlin's "Whose Spirit Is This? Some Questions about Beginnings and Endings" surveys fin-de-siècle rational irrationalism and some figures important in mathematics and science, such as J. B. S. Haldane, Ernst Mach, G. D. Birkhoff, and Georg Cantor. Chamberlin remarks upon "how much mathematical and physical scientists at the end of the nineteenth century were speculating in ways that were independent of any specific application, as conceptually troubling, as caught up in contemporary fears and fantasies, as other realms of fin-de-siècle speculation" (235). He argues that poets, philosophers, and aesthetes drew upon the work of these fin-de-siècle thinkers for "laws and principles giving order to life, and meaning to art" well into the twentieth century (222).

Adolescence, a constant of human experience, was named in the fin-de-siècle and has been widely featured in literary representations and criticism during the twentieth century. The title of John Neubauer's useful but limited and inconclusive book, *The Fin-de-Siècle Culture of Adolescence*, suggests much more than this comparative study of themes and texts in European literature and culture actually delivers. Neubauer proposes that the term "adolescence" " 'came of age' in the decades around 1900 . . . because interlocking discourses about adolescence emerged in psychoanalysis, psychology, criminal justice, pedagogy, sociology, as well as in literature" (6). For the purposes of his study, Neubauer defines adolescence as "a middle-class social formation in industrial societies generated by the expansion of secondary education" (6); it is appropriately a non-gendered definition, but most of the texts studied concern male adolescence. There are some telling exceptions to the dominance of male subjects, including the expressionist images of females painted by males and the journals of Karen Horney.

Neubauer briefly acknowledges the impact of poststructuralism and cultural studies and allies himself with New Historicism. However, in contrast to the typical New Historicist approach through unpacking a particular historical event, Neubauer takes a more traditional literary-formalist position, beginning his book with the study of literary structures and narrative modes in the belief that "they encode social and historical issues" (10). Neubauer's analysis leads him to question "two interrelated canonized views of the adolescents around 1900: that they were first and foremost engaged in a generational conflict, and that they were heroic rebels fighting for the individual" (11). Instead, he believes, adolescents were far more concerned with peer-group culture than with parental authority. Likewise, literary depictions of adolescents' struggles for individualism should be doubted because "their heroic and emancipatory posture was largely hollowed out psychologically and socially" (11). Neubauer suggests that, far from fashioning themselves into rebellious individualists, the adolescents he studies were plagued by self-doubt and were likely to be subjected to the discipline of organizations like the Boy Scouts in Britain and the various *Wandervogel* groups in Germany: "The military formations of World War I, in which most of the adolescents ended, are in my view the ultimate symbols of broader, profoundly antiliberal and anti-individualist trends in the preceding decades" (11).

Neubauer divides his study into eleven chapters, accompanied by an introduction, an appendix of "Publications on Adolescence, 1881–1925," and a useful bibliography. The first five chapters are concerned with literary representations and the remaining six take up the theme of adolescence in German and Austrian Expressionist visual arts, Freudian psychoanalysis, psychology, schools, church, court, youth organizations, and in conclusion, the relationship between literature and social group behavior in the Boy Scouts and the *Wandervogel*.

His analysis suggests that "literary adolescence and literary modernism developed in a symbiotic relationship, for characteristic traits of adolescence, such as the blurring of identity, rapid role changing, and the merging of the individual into a group, can only be represented by means of those shifting narrative perspectives that literature had been developing since Flaubert" (10). However, in his survey of mostly early modernist texts ranging from the 1880s to the 1920s, Neubauer cannot help but suggest some of the scope that a truly inclusive (and necessarily monolithic) study would need to have. Too often throughout the book, chapters just end rather than conclude with a retrospective look at the argument or with a gesture towards the materials that Neubauer was unable to account for or include.

Neubauer's first two chapters are concerned with metaphoric identity and the "other" in analyses of James Joyce's *A Portrait of the Artist as a Young Man* (1916), Thomas Mann's *Tonio Kröger* (1903), Robert Musil's *The Confusions of Pupil Törless* (1906), Valery Larbaud's *Fermina Márquez* (1910), Alain-Fournier's *Le Grand Meaulnes* (1913), Hermann Hesse's *Demian* (1919), Jacques de Lacretelle's *Silbermann* (1922) — not one of them from the fin-de-siècle. Chapters three and four revisit some of these texts as well as others to examine the depiction of peer groups and spaces (the garden, the room, the school). Neubauer classifies according to his thematic headings various incidents, episodes, and settings. Throughout these "literary" chapters, there is disappointingly little reference to either fin-de-siècle literary texts or the cultural and social contexts that Neubauer deals with in the second half of the book.

Unaccountably, Neubauer delays until chapter five what should have been chapter one, "Literary Adolescence: An Overview," in which he concedes that "identity crises of youth, generational conflicts, processes of maturation, and initiation rites were traditional themes of literature long before adolescence as we know it emerged'' (75). The overview is cursory, but it might have provided a context for Neubauer's excursions, in the previous four chapters, into formalist narratology and the thematizing of groups and scenes. Neubauer attempts to survey the literature of adolescence in France, Germany, and England, but he shows little concern to account for what is omitted (much literature from the USA and Canada, the Commonwealth, Scandinavia, most of Russian, Italian, and Hispanic literatures, to name but a few that would meet the definition). He briefly entertains ''Questions of Genre'' and dismisses both poetry and drama (''expressionist theater tends to be a partisan glorification of rebellious youth'' [83]) as largely unsuitable for the expression of adolescence; fiction is best because ''the subject demanded portrayals of inner lives and multi-perspectival representations'' (84).

The second half of the book introduces Neubauer's readings of other aspects of adolescence: first, a consideration of visual arts limited mostly to expressionists like Munch, *die Brücke*, and the Viennese *Jungen*. He depends heavily on the work of Carl Schorske and Donald Gordon and contends that ''whereas adolescence remains a literary theme even today, its representation in the fine arts essentially terminated with World War I, in Vienna as well as elsewhere'' (119). Next he contrasts narrative control in Freud's *Dora* and Karen Horney's adolescent diaries to show that ''Like Dora, Karen was the victim of the adolescence of psychoanalysis'' (140). Neubauer's chapter on ''The Psychology of Adolescence'' would also have been better placed earlier in the book because it usefully, if too briefly, surveys several studies such as G. K. Hall's *Adolescence* (1905) and their dissemination of unexamined prejudices (in the name of objective knowledge) regarding adolescence and masturbation, homosexuality, and feminism. Neubauer's three pages on the ''scientific'' examination of female adolescence should be supplemented by Cynthia Russett's *Sexual Science: The Victorian Construction of Womanhood* (1989). In considering ''Adolescence in School, Church, and Court,'' Neubauer again must compress too much information — he tries to account for these institutions in Germany, France and Britain — into too few pages. The generalizations are only tantalizing, while the small mistakes erode the reader's confidence: he has Matthew Arnold debating Julian Huxley, instead of his father, Thomas Henry Huxley, and he misreads Cyril Connolly's ''nostalgic-ironic'' description of public school life (166). This chapter ends inconclusively and abruptly with a brief account of juvenile delinquency and without a summation or any attempt to compare, contrast, or contextualize the information he reports.

The final institutional sites of adolescence Neubauer investigates are youth organizations and movements. He contrasts the absence in France of any organized youth movement with "The Boys' Brigade, the Church Lads' Brigade, and the Boy Scouts in England, the German youth movement (*Jugendbewegung*), and the Woodcraft movement in the United States" (186). Neubauer focuses for most of the chapter on the various German *Wandervogel* groups and texts, seeing in them an adumbration of Nazism in the admiration of power "at the cost of intellectual and moral responsibility" that "typifies a dangerous 'aesthetic' stance in the prewar crusade against individualism in Germany, as well as the rest of Europe" (202).

Neubauer's concluding chapter offers the unremarkable contention that literature and social life are connected and that "specific literary works on adolescence have shaped even social institutions" (207), by which he means that the texts and songs of the *Wandervogel* helped build the foundations of nationalism and political conservatism and prepared the way for the acceptance of war as an expression of German national identity. He also suggests connections between Rudyard Kipling's *Kim* (1901), the 1906 Everyman edition of Malory's *Le Morte d'Arthur*, Arthur Conan Doyle's Sherlock Holmes stories, and Robert Baden-Powell's Boy Scouting handbooks. These potentially fruitful lines of analysis, however, end abruptly with the sentiment that "ideology cannot be eliminated from literature. Like adolescent minds, texts speak with many voices; again and again they also bombard us with saving messages from the soapbox" (219). Here, at the end of the book, as elsewhere, the "saving message" should have been an articulated argument about why the interesting information assembled in eleven chapters *matters*, why these particular texts (instead of many others that will seem obvious to most readers) have been assembled, and what, beyond the various thematic similarities, it all signifies for the understanding of fin-de-siècle culture. Disappointingly, these questions are left to the reader's imagination.

Without foregrounding the fin-de-siècle as a special concern, Mary Jean Corbett's *Representing Femininity: Middle-Class Subjectivity in Victorian and Edwardian Women's Autobiographies* includes several of the literary themes and historical issues touched on by Small, Neubauer, and the essayists collected in Stokes's volume. Corbett works in a burgeoning area of nineteenth-century study, where significant contributions have been made by many scholars, including Linda Peterson, Margaret Homans, Martha Vicinus, Elaine Showalter, Valerie Sanders, Mary Poovey, Deirdre David, and Corbett's teacher, Regenia Gagnier. Corbett's well-organized, clearly written, and carefully documented assessment of nineteenth-century autobiographies and memoirs clearly notes its indebtedness to earlier work and at the same time makes a genuine contribution to "writing a collective women's history" (15). While Corbett's scope of inquiry includes autobiographical writings from throughout the nineteenth century, many of the actresses who are her concern in two lengthy chapters in the second half of the book were central figures during the fin-de-siècle and the turn of the century.

Corbett's chapter on Fanny Kemble, Madge Kendal, and Marie Bancroft demonstrates that these actresses thought of themselves in ways quite different from the portrayal of actresses in fiction by Victorian women novelists, who often represent them as daring and unconventional figures. Corbett's work supplements Tracy C. Davis's *Actresses as Working Women: Their Social Identity in Victorian Culture* (1991), which is an invaluable survey of social and labor history, working conditions, the demography of the professions, public and private representations of actresses' respectability versus their supposed sexual availability, and theatrical conventions inside and outside the playhouses that exploited the reputation of actresses' eroticism. Corbett's subjects are among those Victorian actresses whom Davis classifies as having such "impeccable personal and professional credentials" that they were not implicated in the social prejudice against actresses as immoral or worthless women (Davis 77). As Davis shows and Corbett also argues, despite the reputation of the Victorian stage and the theater district of London as sites for sexual transgressions, "like women writers, actresses, too, work within naturalized gendered conventions for theatrical and textual performance which increasingly conform to middle-class standards for domestic femininity . . . a larger cultural and economic hegemony — the professionalization movement of the Victorian theater — helps to produce this paradoxical effect, for the professionalizing theater takes bourgeois values as its standard at every level of theatrical life" (Corbett 108). Accompanying this professionalization was the development of respectable, middle-class theater, as a class-marked form distinctly different from music hall entertainment. By 1865, when Marie Bancroft's Prince of Wales Theatre mounted plays directed to a middle-class audience, the domestication of the theater for a bourgeois clientele was well underway, and actresses like Bancroft, acting in plays like Tom Robertson's *Society* (1865), anticipated directly the fin-de-siècle society heroines in the plays of Pinero, Jones, and Wilde.

Corbett points out that during the fin-de-siècle, attention shifted from the social mimesis of Robertsonian comedy: "the representation of the 'inner drama' of bourgeois femininity becomes the actress's task on the late Victorian stage; it becomes as well the task of the middle-class actress who writes autobiography" (132). Ellen Terry, Stella Campbell, and Irene Vanbrugh helped shape the representation of women through starring roles in the new psychological dramas of Pinero and Jones. These actresses, especially Ellen Terry, illustrate the way in which "the late Victorian actress comes to be the figure through whom the commodification of personality takes place in public representation" (138). That is, Corbett argues, as members of the public attend theaters to see actresses like Terry, whose power is described as the ability to concentrate the strength and illusion of performance so as to persuade individual spectators that she performs for one observer alone, "the public itself is also simultaneously privatized: Like the Victorian home, the theater is made a space in which one can come to participate on terms of nominal equality in an exchange that appears to transcend the economic, but which necessarily depends on the economic and social subordination of one sex and one class to another" (141). This commodification led to the cultivation, for purposes of representation, in actresses like Terry and Stella (Mrs. Patrick) Campbell of a private self that is at once communicable and enigmatic. It also led all of them, but especially Irene Vanbrugh, to cultivate professional selves that reacted to their location in a theatrical marketplace by adopting "aggressive economic individualism, the 'pursuit of self-interest' that had previously been available only to men" (148). As Corbett notes, Vanbrugh's experience does not encourage others to adopt a cooperative model of work and workplace. So fin-de-siècle actresses, both portraying the dramatic dilemmas of late-Victorian bourgeois heroines and New Women, and establishing themselves as professionals with careers on the stage, mark the 1890s not just as a moment of decadence, aestheticism, the discovery of adolescence, or as a time of fears and fantasies aroused by the numerology of century's end — but also as a prelude to the decisive women's movement at the turn of the century. Corbett's last chapter takes up the autobiographies of women who participated in the suffrage campaign of 1905–14; though it lies outside the nominal scope of this review, it marks a moment of transition of women's subjectivities from the nineteenth-century domestic arena or its professionalized theatrical representation at the end of the century, to the realm of public and political events surrounding British women's campaign to win voting rights.

In one way or another each of the four books reviewed here finds in the fin-de-siècle some important aspects of historical change and, in one of late nineteenth-century thought's favorite metaphors, the progress of art and civilization — understood rather differently from our perspective at the distance of one hundred years than it was in its own time. All four books contribute something worthwhile to that perspective, and all four of them belong in the collections of libraries and interested scholars and critics of the period.

University of Pittsburgh

WORKS CONSIDERED

Corbett, Mary Jean. *Representing Femininity: Middle-Class Subjectivity in Victorian and Edwardian Women's Autobiographies*. New York: Oxford UP, 1992.
Neubauer, John. *The Fin-de-Siècle Culture of Adolescence*. New Haven: Yale UP, 1992.

Schwartz, Hillel. *Century's End: A Cultural History of the Fin de Siècle from the 1890's Through the 1990's*. New York: Doubleday, 1990.
Small, Ian. *Conditions for Criticism: Authority, Knowledge, and Literature in the Late Nineteenth Century*. Oxford: Oxford UP, 1991.
Stokes, John, ed. *Fin de Siècle/Fin du Globe: Fears and Fantasies of the Late Nineteenth Century*. New York: St. Martin's, 1992.

TOUCHING THE BODY: CRITICAL APPROACHES TO VICTORIAN LITERATURE

By Rosemarie Morgan

THE FIRST DETECTABLE signs of a materialist criticism foregrounding the body as a vehicle of representation appear in Virginia Woolf's epistemological determinations of sex: "it is not that men describe battles and women the birth of children, but that each sex describes itself." Subsequent growth of this new discourse, no doubt influenced by the sexual revolution of the 1960s, variously posited the Victorian sexual body as "other," notably in Steven Marcus's pathbreaking work *The Other Victorians* (1967), or simply assumed it to be normative, as in Ronald Pearsall's *The Worm in the Bud* (1969), which provides a "sin" map of London showing the close geographical and numerical connection between those two most popular of Victorian institutions: the church and the brothel.

More recently, this field of scholarship has attained broader ideological, social, and political dimensions with such seminal works as *Suffer and Be Still* (1972), edited by Martha Vicinus. This collection of essays offers historicist accounts of the body acculturated to socio-sexual configurations under Darwinism, prostitution, medical science and art. Fraser Harrison's *The Dark Angel* (1977) carries out a similar project, placing a slightly sharper focus on the institutionalization of the body: "To study Victorian sexuality is, in effect, to trace the evolution of Victorian marriage" (7).

However, it was still a full decade after Alex Comfort's *Sex in Society* (1963) and the renowned Masters/Johnson reports of the Sixties that Seymour Fisher attempted a demystification of the female erotic body in *Understanding the Female Orgasm* (1974) — a title that suggests that "each sex" had not as yet fully "described itself." And notwithstanding Peter Gay's remarkable testimonies to the sexually-educated Victorian in *The Bourgeois Experience* (1984), the same could also be said of the historical body. Consider that proverbial image of the draped Victorian piano leg — the oddity is that such an image can still, today, be invoked by scholars as a paradigm of Victorian prudery. The possibility that such a vested object, taken as an indicator of Victorian sexual codes and practices, may actually bespeak a contrary preoccupation, does not seem to suggest itself to the modern mind. But it certainly did to Victorians, for whom almost anything curvilinear, whether a flounced rotundity or the swell of a convexity flanking a columnar form, evoked a highly suggestive bodily image. If we know of this sensibility at all we know it from that distinguished Victorian "erotomaniac" (to use his word) — Thomas Hardy — for whom Gothic arches were suggestive of an uplifted mouth, or of parted lips, and a *cyma recta* curve in architectural tracery more than evocative of the swollen amplitudes of the erotic female body. Equally, we know it from his censors.

By contrast, the post-Freudian cultural imagination has favored the "andromorph," as embodied not only in twentieth-century rectilinear architectural styles but also in a conterminous cultural idealization of the lean, streamlined female body. In reaction to this androcentric emphasis within the dominant culture, feminist critics of the 1970s, Franco-feminists in particular, evaluated the possibilities of dismantling what had by now become known as "phallocentrism." The feminist imperative, at this point, was to deconstruct the man as both central and dominant in sociocultural authority, and as the primary reference point of language, culture and thought. Thus feminists brought their bodily energies to bear, looking for lost women writers, for women's voices and female perspectives. This project has been likened, by Elaine Showalter, to finding the lost continent of Atlantis rising from the sea; by Adrienne Rich, to finding our lost, ancestral mothers whose gifts are buried or aborted; by Luce Irigaray, to finding the diffuse erotic field that is a woman's body.

For Hélène Cixous, Irigaray and (with modifications) Julia Kristeva, a woman does not write like a man because writing is from the body; a writer's voice is nothing if not a prolongation of the body. And since a "feminine" textual body corresponds to the libido, it will manifest, for example, "fluidity" of style; "diffusion" and "multi-focal" sensibilities; "spontaneity" of thought and feeling; and thematic "pluralism." In sum, the female textual body is not subject to the self-limiting economy of male libido.

Opponents of Franco-feminism and *l'écriture féminine* have raised the problem of biological determinism and the conjectural nature of gender difference, arguing that femininity and masculinity are rendered gender-specific more by culture than by genetics. But productive doubt has not diminished the focus on the body in the wider critical arena. In some cases, the "absented," "silenced," "marginalized" female body is projected back on to the Victorians with a post-Freudian emphasis — Freud's notion of female lack, which itself corresponds to the Victorian theory that woman was undeveloped man. And it is precisely this manner of reverse-projection that Helena Michie adopts in *The Flesh Made Word: Female Figures and Women's Bodies*, where the overriding assumption is that bodies are absent or lacking in the Victorian novel.

Michie disregards the fact that, with or without the means of rhetorical tropes, the body itself is only a representation. Like language, the body absorbs the material world and assumes the power to change it — no less in Victorian figurations than in the modern. And the sexual body, the reproductive body, in the representational forms of Victorian culture, emits no Freudian sign of phallic lack or of castration (the much-cited late Victorian iconic "mermaid," for example, is surely an ambiguous representation with its overextended "tail"). If anything, Victorian bodies are simply exempted from carnality — ethereal not corporeal, spiritual not fleshly — in accordance with the dominant sexual ideology. The power of the pale, alabaster madonna is not, of course, "centerfold" power. Not designed to match carnal appetite with carnal flesh, or genital force with genital display, erotica here lies in the correspondence of feeling to form — of enraptured desire to ecstatic body. The explicitly carnal body had far less ideological power than the implicitly divine — or "eschatological," I should say, since the demonic could also be deeply erotic. In this respect, there is no erasure of the body as Michie contends. The body may appear abstracted, or as "a series of tropes or rhetorical codes that distance it from the reader in the very act of its depiction" (5), but these are simply differences of representation.

There is, of course, the unutterable body. Several generations of Victorian editors cut all references to body parts associated with the erogenous or the reproductive zones ("buttocks," "being with child," and so forth). Similarly, all *literal* references to physical contact between the sexes were erased (just as American television today blots out parts of the sexual body). But inevitably, the unutterable defies invisibility: censored, it remains constantly present.

Bodies, of both sexes, quite plainly assert their physical presence in the Victorian novel. And if, for instance, Oliver Twist articulates his bodily hunger in a manner unlike Jane Eyre, who chokes down her burned porridge in silence, or unlike Miss Matty, who withdraws to the privacy of her room to indulge in sucking oranges, this says more about bodily representation — of eating ravenously, nauseously, voluptuously — than about muting the female body. As Michie does suggest, hunger is dangerous (23). But not, as she claims, just for the victimized female. Young Pip, in *Great Expectations*, for example, knows more than most about victimization, hunger and endangerment. And as Adrienne Rich so rightly says, to read silence is not to read absence. In fact, it may well be that to read silence is to read power — as the shaping force of many an heroic deed in history and mythology.

Michie also usefully points to the Victorian literary method of using a body to describe a body: "Dorothea Brooke's body recedes to the distance as it is

framed first in language, then through a series of comparisons to paintings''
(87). The point is useful, though not for its aspect of de-familiarization. Victorians, after all, were avid art-lovers. It is useful for its point of cultural difference in representation: a Raphaelesque angel-woman is to one age what a
Hollywood dumb-blonde is to another.

Jane Gallop, in *Thinking Through the Body*, makes the most of this cultural
difference in a narrative punctuated with ''"centerfold'' images, salacious anecdotes and sexual puns highly appropriate to her emphasis upon the carnal
body. Shifting among feminist theory, Freudian phallocentrism and the embarrassment of her own parapraxis, Gallop filters ponderous scholarship through
autobiographical narcissism with all the contrived, self-conscious charm of a
sex-kitten. Yet *Thinking Through the Body* does speak to Franco-feminism
in an interesting if lascivious way — for Gallop cannot stop playing with her
body, which all too often results in something desensitized and rather sore.
Here, for example, she recommends a "Lacanian Freud" to feminism and
explains that

> the *phallus* is a very complicated notion in Lacan, who distinguishes it from
> the *penis*. The distinction seems, however, to resist clarification. . . . if it is
> nearly impossible to keep the distinction phallus/penis clear, that may account
> for the constant return of the assumption that men are the enemies of femi-
> nism. (125)

Such a feminism would find, Gallop concludes, "that central, transcendental
phallus particularly hard to swallow" (125). But then, there is rather a lot to
choke upon in *Thinking Through the Body*.

By contrast, *Literature and the Body: Essays on Population and Persons*,
edited by Elaine Scarry, provides excellent fare. The recent spate of "body"
topics in literary criticism is due in part, we are told, to

> a kind of collective regret at the very weightlessness, the inconsequentiality of
> conversation about literature. Contemporary political philosophy has charged
> the liberal democratic state with a progressive "thinning out" of the concept
> of personhood and the individual. (xxi)

A language that "has lost its referential aspirations" to the material world
signifies a displacement of that world, or aspects of it that are now rendered
invisible by non-referentiality. This is not a loss we find in Scarry's book,
which is worth the magnificent introduction alone. As she explains,

> The body gradually comes forward in the course of this book in many capacities
> and attributes; its vulnerability to injury and disease, its erotic powers, its capac-
> ity to enter states of sleep and work, to swim, to flirt, to discard class merely
> by performing calisthenics, its power to absorb the artifacts of culture into its
> own interior matter, its experience of gender and race. (xxi)

Scarry's book is never less than profound, never less than rigorous, and never less than authentic in its critical approach to thinking-through-the-body. And although the Victorianist is slightly under-represented here, there is still much that is relevant to the Victorian period. Frances Ferguson's essay, "Malthus, Godwin, Wordsworth, and the Spirit of Solitude," discusses the impulse towards depopulation in major Romantic texts and thus points to a prelusive consciousness of what the Victorians themselves experienced, with bitter nostalgia, as the emptying out of their verdant, pastoral countryside — so deeply a part of their pre-urban consciousness and ancestral identity. Where Malthus fears, from overcrowding, a possible encroachment upon his consciousness, and where Godwin shrinks from notions of expanding individual consciousness into an identity with society, so "Wordsworth must retreat into the landscape" in order to enlarge the self he experiences as limited (122). In each case, it is a question of taking conscious bearings or bearings of consciousness, whether demographic, social, territorial or spiritual.

Alternatively, there is Jerome Christensen's consideration of Mary Wollstonecraft's configurations of the "lustful prowler" in "Setting Byron Straight: Class, Sexuality, and the Poet." Christensen is particularly good on the "something more" in sexual desire that "attracts as the fascination of signification" in Byron's poetic, erotic, and political organization (128–30). Perhaps what is most precursively Victorian here is the fusion of body and voice as they materialize in Byron's botanical codes, in what Christensen identifies as "that hubristic orientation . . . established by the jocular denomination of boys as 'Hyacinths & other flowers' " (137). Latterly, the Victorians were to elaborate the most comprehensive of body/voice fusions. If we take just a cursory glance, beginning with the merging of human voice and botanical body in Keats's garland-laden Muse or Kate Greenaway's little rhyming "marigold" girls, it is not difficult to map this trend through the pale-lilied bodies of the pre-Raphaelites, or Barrett Browning's fruit-lusting maidens, right on to Ruskin's pedagogic allegories of perfumed gardens and beyond. One could add that the merger of voice and botanical body, now expanding self-identity into the landscape of corporate consciousness, enters the twentieth century with the rise of the great fashion houses of Chanel, Givenchy, Balenciaga, Dior.

Reclamation of the material world, by breathing life into bodies hitherto regarded as buried within it, becomes — at John Wiltshire's hands in *Jane Austen and the Body* — an entire resurrection. No one, to my knowledge, has yet interpreted the Austen body in quite this way before, as a body in restraint so powerfully attuned to complicated codes of decorum and so rigorously disciplined in performance that it can only be read, in effect, in translation. Spurning a long critical tradition that goes back as far as Brontë's deprecation of Austen as a novelist who ignores "what throbs fast and full," Wiltshire takes the body in Austen's fiction to be a monumental signifier, a highly-charged vehicle of representation. The aim is to fill the ideological gap that began with Cardinal Newman's complaint that there is a "want of body" (2) to the Austen story.

Newman, of course, means "lack." Wiltshire immediately rewrites "want" as "desire." The Austen body "wants" and "desires" — intensely. For example, if we read the excitable Marianne Dashwood, in *Sense and Sensibility*, straightforwardly through "currently fashionable" codes of ardor and warmth, through the "transparency of her face and gestures," we should translate the less easily decipherable Elinor through her acts of "tact, diplomacy and judicious silences" (28–36). This means reading her desires through the palimpsest, so to speak, of her body in restraint. If we return to the notion of the codified body and the implications of vesting representative forms, the importance of Wiltshire's thesis becomes clear. Reading, for example, all those activities that come under the rubric of nursing, we read the implied body: "Elinor spends much of the novel guarding or protecting her sister from pain and painful notice" and although her activities are "paralleled and commented upon by a continual comedy of illness-coping" (52), it is this particular investment in forms of tending that provides Elinor with her education in sensibility (53).

In the *Emma* chapter, this becomes an issue of health and power. No one, Wiltshire says, "has yet diagnosed *Emma* to be a novel concerned with health" (110). The health (or otherwise) of the body necessitates discourses of the moral life: " 'Spirits' and 'nerves' are culturally determined modes of understanding and representing the body which the text makes use of" and, in this case, it is Emma's capacity to break out of the invisible network of sickness that typifies her triumph (153). Equally, in attending to material forms such as medical provisions and facilities, we discover the ways in which they mask "the psychological and social divisions which traverse the community" (6). The ambit of health serves to "hide or displace the equally constitutive roles of economic and gendering forces": "If the healthy body is largely passive, unconscious of itself, then the unhealthy body, as a site of anxious self-concentration, is the source of events, of narrative energies" (7–10).

Illness itself becomes a language. Here Wiltshire follows Adrienne Rich and others with the idea of "converting our physicality into knowledge and power" (14). Thus, in Austen, making a short leap from illness to power relations, Wiltshire shows that

> The very indefinability of illness is the source of its potency, its infinite use-fulness as a vehicle of covert manipulations. The ill person (or the person who complains of being ill — which may amount to much the same thing in texts, and even in practice) lays friends and relations under tribute. (19–20)

Such characters thus perpetuate dramas of interpersonal tension that use the body as their vehicle.

The great strength of *Jane Austen and the Body*, and its importance for Victorianists in general, is that it advances beyond Freudian/Lacanian critical theories, beyond phallocentric theoretical abstractions, and moves ahead into the wider material world in which the acculturated body signifies as the site where social, political, philosophical, sexual, and psychological meanings reside. Current masculinist-feminist theorists, for example, who predicate the female hysteric — once diagnosed as pathologically disordered — as rescuing something of her own desire in a masculine mode (Kristeva), would perceive, with Wiltshire, the significance of the cultural, social, and ideological factors which "influence definitions and perceptions" of the disease (120). Like blushing, hysteria often communicates itself ambiguously. If Marianne's hysterical illness in *Sense and Sensibility* (when it is not attention-seeking or exhibitionism) calls into question "the distress that, despite her sister's efforts, she will not, or cannot express in language" (43), and if Emma's nervous behavior signifies a "blockage of energies denied their natural outlet" (144), each woman enlists her body, whether perversely or aberrantly, to express the "energies and powers denied other fulfillments in her world" (144). The rage of the hysteric, her manipulation of power, expenditure of energy and sexual tension, signals — under Austen's use of this topos — a relationship between physiology and culture.

Feminists have already come to this. But not in their treatment of Austen, who evidently knows full well that hysteria is not necessarily gender-determined nor gender-bound but rather just another way of channelling suppressed aggression. Or, as Wiltshire puts it, "The lived experiences of the body are dialectically produced by the interaction of desire and social forces" (18).

As with hysteria, so too with the blush, which might signify shame, anger, desire, confusion and may, in turn, generate narrative surprises or indeterminacy. The blush is a problematic text. And, as Wiltshire demonstrates with such suppleminded ease, so too is the headache. In short, the body does more than utter itself; it also utters social conditions, economic conflicts, power relations and even such social conventions as "coming out." In effect, the Austen body exemplifies the most eloquent text of all.

Perhaps it takes an age of reconstruction — bodily reconstruction — to elicit readings of this kind. Never was the body, in representation, more of a public object than in the present day of surgical engineering and mass manufacture of body parts — from hip replacements to silicone gels, from hair implants to steroid supplements, from body-contouring right down to the ideology and morality of diet. Throughout the media, in particular, the body is modelled and publicly exhibited as the material site of cultural values — every feature a signifying construct.

Paradoxically, or perhaps of necessity, in our individualistic age of bodily anxiety, the heroic force of ideology appears to shape more conflicts of identification than were borne by Victorians. Looking to the Dorotheas of the "Middlemarch" world — bodily distanced only as far as the nearest recognisable painting — George Eliot's readers would not, I think, have experienced the depersonalizing effect in quite the same way as, say, Michie does today. Identification with a remote iconic model has become sufficiently commonplace, these days, to warrant even linguistic adaptation to it, as in a Madonna "wannabe." The paradox is, of course, that such modelling renders the body both uniform and individualized — the "individualized" identity now residing less in the autonomous self than in the adopted body of the other. To this extent, depersonalization is manifest in the manner of identifying against the self's unique identity.

Hardy's Fables of Integrity: Woman, Body, Text, by Marjorie Garson, inadvertently reveals many such conflicts of depersonalization and contra-identification. Projecting self-disgust and a pathological fear of sex on to the erotic body in the Wessex novels, Garson first transfers these anxieties to Hardy himself and then attributes them to his narrator: the castration fears of the one "inform and distort" the "fictional material" of the other (1). Providing a close study in neurosis which (like Gallop's self-reflecting titillations) appears to originate less in her subject than in herself, Garson observes that her thesis "makes considerable sense in the light of this pervasive anxiety" (1). *Hardy's Fables* certainly throws light on this, but only in so far as it reflects back on its author's displacement of as many sexual neuroses as could conceivably be transferred, with noticeable arbitrariness, to such items as a broken cask of cider, an old pair of shoes, a worn cobbler's last or a wintry fungoid swamp.

Perhaps Hardy's thought that there is, assuredly, more in a text than the author consciously puts there (Preface to *Jude*), provides accommodation for readers to "put" in their worst fears and anxieties. Does this allow critics to take Hardy's lifelong fondness for wellworn, time-marked objects as symptomatic of his castration fears? Does it sanction a reading of Tess's erotic "garden" as an expression of the author's "fascinated disgust" with her sexuality (146–47), or of Arabella Donn's "immense bosom" as "particularly threatening" (172) to her sexually fearful creator? I doubt it. Did Hardy fight hard and long against contemporary puritanical attitudes for this? Against the partial reading of those of his critics who, like Henry James and Mrs. Oliphant, felt sexual disgust to be a proper measure of decency which Hardy might, at least, show some small sense of owning? Evidently such disgust still exists today. But one thing is certain. The sexual throbbings, moist emanations, and sticky bodies "bursting pollen at a touch," were not, at any point, threatening to Hardy or his narrator. Not, that is, if his autobiographical writings, his poems, his novels and private readings are anything to go by. And, in fact, with James Gibson's discovery of marginalia in Hardy's own (1890s) copy of *Jude* — where he had amended Arabella's "inflated bosom" to read "breast's superb abundance" — we can be thoroughly assured that, unconsciously or otherwise, Hardy was still happily playing with them some thirty years on — annotatively, so to speak.

It seems to be a hazard of topical focus that sexual disgust or fears of bodily decay and dismemberment shape discourses that are themselves noticeably anxious and neurotic. In its bitterly carping tone and oddly-distorted perspective, Garson's book exudes so much hostility towards the women in the Wessex novels that the sense is less of a threatened Hardy than of a threatened Garson. The notion of contra-identification now recurs. For Hardy's struggling, rebellious women, however closely identified with the great classical models (Athena, goddess of wisdom and warfare; Diana, the huntress; and so forth), seem as monstrous to Garson as they were to Mrs. Grundy. In fact, more so: Tess becomes a "victimiser" (150); Sue Bridehead emerges as "sinister" and destructive (172); Elizabeth-Jane is the "woman who killed Henchard" (126); Eustacia and Mrs. Yeobright become accomplices in their mutual capacity for "damaging sons and lovers" (78); and Grace Melbury (who, in actual fact, disappointed Hardy in her sheer insipidity) takes on the dimensions of a "castrating woman" (88–89). Even that gentle, lightly humorous tale of *Under the Greenwood Tree* now fills up with dismembering, "emasculating" women.

Schematic readings of this kind, which purport to speak against the crass blindness of patriarchy, in this case against works authorized by a sexually neurotic man ignorant of his text's "blindness to its sources" (179), do not always escape blindness themselves. Garson, for example, calls her book "feminist" — scorning Hardy, I suppose, as some kind of pornographer. Yet she evidently remains unaware that her text is plainly drawn to traditional male stereotypes or the mythic figures and paradigms of patriarchy: the Edenic Eve, the Femme Fatale, the Christ-Redeemer figure, and so forth (actually, if Hardy uses these configurations at all it is to subvert them — with parody, absurdism, or sheer irony). At the same time, her thesis remains dependent upon traditional Freudian theories long since revised by such feminists as Juliet Mitchell. Likewise her reliance on traditional male critics: where major female critics, such as Patricia Meyer Spacks or Gillian Beer, are invited in, it is not, I am afraid, to the speaker's platform. The "blindness," in this instance, does not lie in patriarchy.

In an age in which the body private has been extensively assimilated to the body politic, and in which individualism veers towards the indivisibility of self and society, there may be a far more widespread inclination to identify against the self — against the self's identity, class, gender, race and sex —

than hitherto in ages less dominated by mass-media prescriptions. For Victorian liberal feminists, to be sure, there was indeed the very real difficulty of struggling under patriarchy to achieve parity of rights and status and yet, at the same time, to resist identifying with patriarchy itself. For clearly, the power wielded by patriarchy was precisely the power women, themselves, sought to possess.

But if *Hardy's Fables* identifies with patriarchy and remains bereft of feminist power, it does not fail in projecting back on to the Victorian text an enabling discourse for bringing a variety of its own repressed authorial fears to the surface. By contrast, in *Charlotte Brontë and Defensive Conduct: The Author and Body at Risk*, Janet Gezari identifies with each and every aspect of female power, rebellious, wrongheaded, nonconformist or otherwise. Projecting back a very clear sense of female autonomy on to characters not yet subjected to Freudian circumscriptions, Gezari reclaims the force and authority of the representative body in Brontë: the body ''as the site of social conflict and constraint'' (3). To begin with, Gezari turns Freud on his head. Subordinating Sigmund to Anna, she tells us that

> Our modern use of ''defensive'' owes a specific debt to the study of defenses and mechanisms of defense in psychoanalysis... Anna Freud describes the term *defence* as the ''earliest representative of the dynamic standpoint in psychoanalytic theory''.... [and says that such defenses] cannot be ''the main focus of attention of clinical observation'' because they are ''normal, not pathogenic.'' (8)

This refutation of Sigmund Freud's theory of pathogenic ''defensiveness'' is taken up by Gezari, who goes on to explain that ''defensive conduct'' encompasses as many complex behaviors as may be encountered in female and male experiences alike. These range from Fanny Burney's ''honorable... acts of self-defense and self-vindication'' (9) to what Matthew Arnold calls Brontë's ''hunger, rebellion and rage'' and to what Samuel Johnson calls ''aggressive strength'' when speaking of comparable *male* ''energies of resistance, confutation and conflict'' (11).

Taking further issue with Freudian theory, Gezari also examines the so-called ''male gaze'' in the light of Brontë's depiction of Jane Eyre's ''acute pleasure in looking'' at Rochester:

> *Jane Eyre* controverts this idea that a woman finds visual pleasure primarily in being visible or that a woman who gazes takes on masculine qualities. (68)

Similarly, in dealing with the ''castration'' issue, Gezari refuses ''to rewrite Brontë's narrative according to the Freudian'' master code which regards ''Rochester's blindness as merely a symbol of his castration'' (85). As she presents the case, Brontë's treatment of vision, sight, and blindness encompasses subtly complex and interactive issues of invisibility, self-effacement, and psychic separation. Moving on to *Villette*, Gezari follows her argument through by protesting, on Ginevra's behalf, the Freudian notion that "narcissism is a mere strategy or that woman's self-sufficiency is only a pretense to attract her lover's desire" (133). In her discussion of *Shirley* Gezari makes a similar case in favor of Caroline's silence as exemplifying copious powers of psychic accommodation.

Connecting the consummate skill with which Brontë mediates cultural conflicts to acts of self-defense and self-vindication, Gezari shows how these acts are anchored to representations of the body — its organs, senses, and appendages embodying wide-ranging social pressures (3). Like Wiltshire on Austen, Gezari focuses on the body in discomfort and hurt, its modes of expressing and caressing and its submission to inevitable pressures. In Brontë's case, however, the emphasis is upon "defensiveness" as appropriate and suitably confrontational. This is a marvellously unflinching book. And the iconoclasm works. Dismantling Freud could itself collapse into defensive conduct, but Gezari succeeds in matching her own cool, objective vision very satisfyingly to her subject: the quietly defensive power of Brontë's women and their male counterparts.

Although specific issues arise in *Defensive Conduct*, such as gender-identity, or male-identity formation in *The Professor*, or self-masking and self-responsibility in *Villette*, it is Gezari's treatment, more generally, of the body as an organizing motif in Brontë's novels that distinguishes this book as vanguard criticism. For, what she does so consistently and so well is to transcend outmoded or inappropriate critical theories in favor of a highly sensitive reading of subtlety, insight and utmost persuasiveness — at all times rigorously body-conscious.

Whether it is accommodation or rigid resistance to social constraints that shapes the body construct, in imaginative works as in life, the current spate of critical "bodies" seems to have generated something of an ontological dynamic all its own — a reversal, even, of the "Cogito." The causal relation between mind and matter has become virtually transposed. Or, at any rate, it has shifted from its Cartesian position to something better resembling the epiphenomenalism of the Victorians, in which, with T. H. Huxley, the causal influence of mind over body was as "the steam above the factory." Thus, for Virginia Woolf "each sex describes itself" and not just from the head; for the modern critic each body describes itself and not just with words. For Gallop the private body sexualizes — and for Garson it neuroticizes — public discourse. For Scarry bodies, as well as language, absorb the artifacts of culture into their own substance and effect a transformation of matter. For Wiltshire, with Austen, the body utters itself as much through gossip as through illness or a rush of blood to the face. And for Gezari, with Brontë, as for all who grapple with bodily anxieties, the body erotic, injured, laboring, performative, fragile or strong registers the contours, force and weight of the material world and as Brontë puts it in *Jane Eyre*, "what hurts becomes immediately embodied."

Yale University

WORKS CONSIDERED

Gallop, Jane. *Thinking Through the Body*. New York: Columbia UP, 1988.

Garson, Marjorie. *Hardy's Fables of Integrity: Woman, Body, Text*. Oxford: Clarendon, 1991.

Gezari, Janet. *Charlotte Brontë and Defensive Conduct: The Author and Body at Risk*. Philadelphia: U of Pennsylvania P, 1992.

Michie, Helena. *The Flesh Made Word: Female Figures and Women's Bodies*. New York: Oxford UP, 1987.

Scarry, Elaine, ed. *Literature and the Body: Essays on Population and Persons*. Baltimore and London: Johns Hopkins UP, 1988.

Wiltshire, John. *Jane Austen and the Body*. Cambridge: Cambridge UP, 1992.

ROBERT AND ELIZABETH BARRETT BROWNING: AN ANNOTATED BIBLIOGRAPHY FOR 1992

By Sandra M. Donaldson

The following abbreviations appear in this year's bibliography:

BIS   *Browning Institute Studies*
DAI   *Dissertation Abstracts International*
VLC   *Victorian Literature and Culture*
VN   *Victorian Newsletter*
VS   *Victorian Studies*

An asterisk* indicates that we have not seen the item. Cross references with citation numbers between 51 and 70 followed by a colon (e.g., C68:) refer to William S. Peterson's *Robert and Elizabeth Barrett Browning: An Annotated Bibliography, 1951–1970* (New York: The Browning Institute, 1974); higher numbers refer to *Robert Browning: A Bibliography 1830–1950*, compiled by L. N. Broughton, C. S. Northup, and Robert Pearsall (Ithaca: Cornell UP, 1953).

Readers are encouraged to send offprints to Sandra Donaldson, Department of English, Box 7209, University of North Dakota, Grand Forks ND 58202. I especially need articles that have appeared in less familiar journals. I wish to thank David Nelson of the University of North Dakota for his help with translating from German.

A. Primary Works

A92:1.* Browning, Elizabeth Barrett. *Complete Poetical Works of Elizabeth Barrett Browning*. Brighton, MI: Native American Book Publications. x + 548 pp. ¶Reprint of Boston: Houghton Mifflin, 1900.

A92:2. Browning, Elizabeth Barrett, trans. *Prometheus Bound*. Ed. William Alan Landes. Studio City, CA: Players Press. 70 pp.

A92:3. Browning, Elizabeth Barrett. *Sonnets from the Portuguese and Other Poems*. Mineola, NY: Dover Publications, 1992. viii + 55 pp.

A92:4. Dunn, Douglas, ed. *Essential Browning*. Essential Poets series, vol. 13. New York: Ecco Press, 1990. 192 pp.

A92:5. Forster, Margaret, ed. and introduction. *Selected Poems of Elizabeth Barrett Browning*. London: Chatto and Windus. 352 pp. ¶Reprint of A88:4.

A92:6. Impey, Rose, trans. *Der Rattenfänger von Hameln*. Auburn, ME: Ladybird Books.

A92:7. Jack, Ian, Rowena Fowler, and Margaret Smith, eds. *Bells and Pomegranates, VII–VIII*. Volume 4 of *The Poetical Works of Robert Browning*. [See A91:5.] ¶Rev. by Stefan Hawlin, *Review of English Studies* 43 (Nov. 1992): 580–81.

A92:8. Karlin, Daniel, ed. and introduction. *Robert Browning and Elizabeth Barrett: The Courtship Correspondence*. [See A89:4.] ¶Rev. by Kathleen Blake, *Modern Philology* 89.3 (Feb. 1992): 377–86; Philip Drew, *Durham University Journal* 82.1: 123; Kenneth Millard, *English Studies* 73.4 (Aug. 1992): 359–60.

A92:9. Kelley, Philip, and Ronald Hudson, eds. *The Brownings' Correspondence, Volume 7*. [See A89:7.] ¶Rev. by Stefan Hawlin, *Review of English Studies* 43 (Feb. 1992): 128–29.

A92:10. Kelley, Philip, and Ronald Hudson, eds. *The Brownings' Correspondence, Volume 8*. [See A90:8.] ¶Rev. by Stefan Hawlin, *Review of English Studies* 43 (Aug. 1992): 448–49.

A92:11. Kelley, Philip, and Scott Lewis, eds. *The Brownings' Correspondence, Volume 9*. [See A91:8.] ¶Rev. by G. B. Tennyson, *Nineteenth Century Literature* 46.4 (March 1992): 579.

A92:12. Kelley, Philip, and Scott Lewis, eds. *The Brownings' Correspondence, Volume 10: January 1845–July 1845*. Winfield, KS: Wedgestone P, 1992. xii + 422 pp.

A92:13. King, Roma A., Jr., and Susan Crowl, eds. *The Ring and the Book, Books IX–XII*. Volume 9 of *The Complete Works of Robert Browning with Variant Readings and Annotations*. Ed. Jack W. Herring, et al. [See A89:10]. ¶Rev. by Stefan Hawlin, *Review of English Studies* 43 (May 1992): 301–02; Mark Roberts, *Notes and Queries* 39 (Dec. 1992): 516–17.

A92:14.* Kubikowski, Tomasz, trans. "Kaliban o Setebosie (Caliban Upon Setebos)" and "Śmierć na Pustyni (A Death in the Desert)." *Znak* (Oct.-Nov. 1990). ¶In Polish. See below, C92:38.

A92:15. Porter, Peter, sel. and introduction. *Elizabeth Barrett Browning*. London: Aurum; New York: Great English Poets, Clarkson N. Potter. 61 pp.

A92:16. Reynolds, Margaret, ed. Introduction and notes to *Aurora Leigh, by Elizabeth Barrett Browning*. Athens: Ohio UP, 1992. xiv + 692 pp.

A92:17. Weavers, Peter, retell and illus., *The Pied Piper of Hamelin*. London: Hutchinson, 1992. 32 pp. ¶Rev. by Helen Gregory, *School Library Journal* 38 (Oct. 1992): 124.

A92:18. Woolford, John, and Daniel Karlin, eds. *The Poems of Browning*, Volume 2. [See A91:11.] ¶Rev. by G. B. Tennyson, *Nineteenth Century Literature* 46.4 (March 1992): 579.

B. Reference and Bibliographical Works and Exhibitions

B92:1. Blake, Kathleen. "Current Elizabeth Barrett Browning Studies." *Modern Philology* 89.3 (Feb. 1992): 377–86. ¶Considers Mermin (C89:51), Stephenson (C89:70), and Karlin (A89:4); refers as well to Karlin (C85:31), Leighton (C86:34), David (C87:11), and Cooper (C88:13).

B92:2. Cohen, Edward H., ed. "Victorian Bibliography for 1992." *VS* 35.4 (Summer 1992): 542–43.

B92:3. Foot, Mirjam M. *Recent Bindings: Seventeen Bindings, 1979–1987; Sonnets from the Portuguese Bound by Eight Women Binders*. Frenich, Foss, Pitlochry, Perthshire: K. D. Duval, 1990. [32–39.] ¶Catalogue for exhibition of bindings of the Officina Bodoni edition (1925) of *Sonnets from the Portuguese* by Micheline de Bellefroid, Elizabeth Greenhill, Angela James, Denise Lubett, Gemma O'Connor, Sally Lou Smith, Faith Shannon, and Joan Rex Tebbutt.

C. Biography, Criticism, and Miscellaneous

C92:1. Battles, Elizabeth Hildebrand. "Trying the Stuff of Language: Stylistic Experimentation in the Early Works of Thomas Carlyle and Robert Browning." *DAI* 53.05 (Nov. 1992): 1524A. Texas Christian University, 1992. 193 pp.

C92:2. Bidney, Martin. "*The Ring and the Book* and *Light in August*: Faulkner's Response to Browning." *VN* 81 (1992): 51–59. ¶Suggests that RB appealed to Faulkner as "the most novelistic of nineteenth-century psychological explorers in verse." *The Ring and the Book* addresses "the complexity of the motives for violencee, the problematic nature of moral judgment, and the need for a compassionate attempt to probe the causes of criminality" — all of which interest Faulkner in *Light in August*. Echoes of RB may be seen in Faulkner's grotesque imagery, motifs of suffering and light and blackness, Biblical allusion, and the characters of Joe being like both Guido and Pompilia, and Hightower like the Pope.

C92:3. Black, Barbara Joanne. "Fragments Shored Against Their Ruin: Victorian Museum Culture (Richard Owen, Henry Cole, Charles Dickens,

Edith Nesbit, Sara Atkins, Moncure Conway, Robert Browning)." *DAI* 53.02 (Aug. 1992): 501A. University of Virginia, 1991. 304 pp.

C92:4. Bornstein, George. *Poetic Remaking: The Art of Browning, Yeats, and Pound.* [See C88:6.] ¶Rev. by Thomas J. Collins, *VS* 35.1 (Aut. 1991): 104–05.

C92:5. Bristow, Joseph. *New Readings: Robert Browning.* [See C91:8.] ¶Rev. by C. M., *TLS* 7 Aug. 1992: 24.

C92:6. Brooks, Roger L., and Rita S. Humphrey, eds. *Selected Papers from the Centennial Symposium, Robert Browning and Nineteenth Century Culture. Studies in Browning and His Circle,* 17 (1989), 106 pp. ¶Proceedings from a conference held at the Armstrong Browning Library, Baylor University, 20–22 September 1989.

C92:7. Byatt, A. S. "Robert Browning: Fact, Fiction, Lies, Incarnation and Art." *Passions of the Mind: Selected Writings.* London: Chatto and Windus, 1991; New York: Random House, 1992. 21–62. ¶Discusses RB's dramatic monologues, especially "Karshish," "A Death in the Desert," *The Ring and the Book*, and the epilogue to *Dramatis Personae*, as attempts "to embody and contemplate the problems which centrally occupied the nineteenth-century European mind: the problems of the relation of time to history, of science to religion, of fact in science or history to fiction, or lies, in both, and of art to all these." The works of D. F. Strauss, Ernest Renan, J. A. Froude, Tennyson, Jules Michelet, George Eliot, and Ludwig Feuerbach provide a context for these ideas. "The Bishop Orders His Tomb," "Fra Lippo Lippi," "Caliban upon Setebos," and "Mr Sludge, 'the Medium' " are also concerned with the questions, particularly of truth, fiction, and art. Expanded from A91:2. Rev. by Suzanne Berner, *New York Times Book Review* 97 (22 Mar. 1992): 16; Valentine Cunningham *TLS,* 16 Aug. 1991: 6; Doris Grumbach, *Book World* 22 (29 Mar. 1992): 11; Ann Irvine, *Library Journal* 117 (1 Mar. 1992): 90–91; *Kirkus Reviews* 60 (1 Jan. 1992): 26; Michèle Roberts, *New Statesman and Society* 4 (9 Aug. 1991): 38; Merle Rubin, *Christian Science Monitor* 84 (31 Mar. 1992): 13; Stevenson Swanson, (Chicago) *Tribune Books* 15 Mar. 1992: 7; Stuart Whitwell, *Booklist* 88 (15 Feb. 1992): 1082.

C92:8. Campbell, Wanda. "Isabella Valancy Crawford and Elizabeth Barrett Browning." *Canadian Poetry* 29 (Fall-Winter 1991): 25–37. ¶Traces echoes of EBB's "A Drama of Exile" in Crawford's long poem, *Malcolm's Katie*, especially in its themes of "the relationship between humanity and nature, men and women, knowledge and power." Both poems lament the loss of the "wild garden" while also announcing a "new order"; Eve and Katie seek "reconciliation with the natural world that suffers the consequences of the Fall" and both "must emerge from Eden into the adult world of passion and pain."

C92:9. Case, Allison Austin. "Writing the Female 'I': Gender and Narration in the Eighteenth- and Nineteenth-Century English Novel." *DAI* 52.8 (Feb. 1992): 2929A. 199 pp. See also C91:13.

C92:10. Cho-Tak, Byong-Eun. "The Emergence and Development of Browning's Auditor." *DAI* 52.12 (Jun. 1992): 4338A. University of North Texas, 1991. 216 pp.

C92:11. Costello, Julie. "Browning and Pompilia: The Contemplation of the Other in *The Ring and the Book*." *Cresset* 55 (Jan. 1992): 9–12. ¶Argues that each major speaker in RB's poem uses Pompilia "to justify his own standpoint" in a male-centered arena. She is presented "as irreconcilable difference," which is the poem's vision of truth: "that which can never be spoken with one voice." As such, "she reflects both the ambiguous condition of women in oppressive patriarchal societies, and the condition of language itself." Too, she discovers a truth about herself "when she least expects it," understanding "a woman's capacity to contain the other, to be both subject and object." We obtain truth only when we resist the need to claim and dominate it; in the poem, then, "Truth is not contained in the work of art, but opened up by it."

C92:12. Crossan, Greg. "Irresolution and Dependence: The Defeat of Wordsworthian Ideals in Coleridge's 'The Picture' and Browning's 'The Last Ride Together'." Petch and Slinn 30–44. ¶Observes that little connects RB and Coleridge except a similar reaction against Wordsworthian ideals, especially resolution and independence. Irony and scepticism characterize RB's thought, and Coleridge's scepticism as expressed in "The Picture" may be seen to be similar to RB's in "The Last Ride Together." In the context of Romanticism, both RB and Coleridge "dramatize the desire for assurance of purpose and for decisiveness of action, and they dramatize also the rationalization of doubt and defeat."

C92:13. Day, Paula. "Nature and Gender in Victorian Women's Writing: Emily Brontë, Charlotte Brontë, Elizabeth Barrett Browning, and Christina Rossetti." *DAI* 53.03 (Sept. 1992): 816A. University of Lancaster, 1990. 364 pp.

C92:14. DeLuise, Dolores. "The *Sonnets from the Portuguese* as Literary Autobiography: A Reading of Sonnet 1." *DAI* 53:04 (Oct. 1992): 1164A. City University of New York, 1992. 213 pp.

C92:15. Erkkila, Betsy. "Dickinson, Women Writers, and the Marketplace." *The Wicked Sisters: Women Poets, Literary History, and Discord.* New York: Oxford UP, 1992. 55–98. ¶Problematizes the familial metaphors of feminism, suggesting that "women are always at odds with and wickedly in excess of their identity as Woman — and sisters." Women poets used the word to resist "masculine power and dominance in their time," enabled to do so by "sisterly bonds of assistance and resistance." Emily Dickinson authorized her own writing through lyrics to ''the most articulate women writers of her age,'' such as EBB, who challenged traditional notions of gender and entered ''the profession of authorship.'' *Aurora Leigh*'s focus on the ''witchcraft'' of poetic work likely gave her courage; also appealing were EBB's privileged upbringing, conservative politics, and faith in the transformative power of art. Like the young Aurora, Dickinson chose not to marry or ''join her American sisters in the 'noble work' of social reform,'' and EBB's ''critique of the literary marketplace'' may have helped her decide not to publish. EBB herself did seek poetic fame, social change, and heterosexual love.

C92:16. Fabisch, Judith Patricia. ''Religious Perspectives: Ethics in the Poetry of Robert Browning.'' *DAI* 52.10 (April 1992): 3610A. Michigan State University, 1991. 204 pp.

C92:17. Foley, Tricia, and Cathy Cook. ''Walking in a Poet's Footsteps at the Hope End Hotel.'' *Victoria* 6.4 (April 1992): 85–90. ¶Describes Patricia and John Hegarty's hotel at Hope End, EBB's childhood home.

C92:18. Fontana, Ernest. ''Browning and the 'Adventurous Spider'.'' Brooks and Humphrey 32–42. ¶Describes the gossamer tradition as a trope for the human mind. In RB's poetry ''the older and newer metaphoric discourses — cobwebs and gossamer'' — contend and are an analog for two views of mind, one stressing submission to an *a priori* reality and the other seeing mind as capable of generating ''its own reality.'' In *Sordello* he uses the trope of the spider as artist and web as imagination, but in ''Master Hugues of Saxe-Gotha'' and ''Mesmerism'' the spider's effusions are ''expressions of an unrestrained subjectivity.'' ''Two in the Campagna'' is his ''original conception of gossamer as an elusive thought-form, desirable to follow and to submit one's mind to,'' even when overwhelmed by the fullness of the external world.

C92:19. Forster, Margaret. *Lady's Maid*. [See C90:31.] ¶Rev. by *Publishers' Weekly* 239 (6 April 1992): 61.

C92:20. Fraser, Hilary. ''Browning and Nineteenth-Century Historiography.'' Petch and Slinn 13–29. ¶Examines affinities between RB as historical poet and French historian Jules Michelet, ''the acknowledged master of the fictional 'reality effect' in historical narrative.'' Both viewed historians as needing ''to 'resurrect' the deceased inhabitants of the past, and to enable these historical 'actors' to speak for themselves.'' Too, they each constructed a nineteenth-century liberal's ''concept of the Renaissance.''

C92:21. Froula, Christine. ''Browning's *Sordello* and the Parables of Modernist Poetics.'' Gibson 161–85. ¶Reprint of C85:21.

C92:22. Gay, Penelope. ''Desire and the Female Voice in Browning's *Men and Women* and *Dramatis Personae*.'' Petch and Slinn 47–63. ¶Analyzes depictions of love and sexual desire in ''By the Fireside,'' ''James Lee's

Wife," "A Woman's Last Word," "Any Wife to Any Husband," "In a Year," "Two in the Campagna," "Dîs Aliter Visum," and "Eurydice to Orpheus." The female monologues "express most poignantly the problematic nature of desire in their culture, the unspeakable physical fact upon which the superstructure of an idealized man/woman relationship is built."

C92:23. Gibson, Mary Ellis, ed. and introduction. *Critical Essays on Robert Browning*. New York: G. K. Hall, 275 pp. ¶Focuses the collection on "relationships among genre, reading practices, and culture" and surveys the reception of RB's work by his contemporaries and ours. Students of his poetry ask "What is the social significance of art in any particular time? Is a poet's vision central or marginal to his or her culture? What are the responses and the responsibilities of readers?" These essays are indebted to the work of numerous earlier critics and are concerned with "language, representation, gender, and ideology," theoretical concerns raised since poststructuralism. The richness and complexity of RB's poetry is "both a pleasure and a challenge" in teaching both versification and "broader social and cultural questions."

C92:24. Harris, Marlene. "A Browning Scholar's Dream." *Victoria* 6.4 (April 1992): 45–47. ¶Describes the Armstrong Browning Library and its founder, for a popular audience.

C92:25. Harrison, Antony H. " 'Cleon' and Its Contexts." Gibson 139–60. ¶Reprinted from C90:41.

C92:26. Hayter, Alethea. *A Sultry Month: Scenes of London Literary Life in 1846*. London: Clark, 224 pp. ¶Reprint of C65:20. Rev. by Lindsay Duguid, *TLS* 21 August 1992: 4; A. N. Wilson, *Spectator* 269 (21 Nov. 1992): 39.

C92:27. Hodgson, Amanda. "Riding Together: William Morris and Robert Browning." *Journal of the William Morris Society* 9.4 (Spring 1992): 3–7. ¶Considers Morris's avowed admiration of RB and similarities between his "Riding Together" and RB's "The Last Ride Together," which Morris had reviewed. Comparison reveals connections between RB's work and poetic theory and Morris's poetic practice. Most notably, both poets are "objective poets" and fear fixity.

C92:28. Holmes, Alicia E. "Elizabeth Barrett Browning: Construction of Authority in *Aurora Leigh* by Rewriting Mother, Muse, and Miriam." *Centennial Review* 36 (Fall 1992): 593–606. ¶Explores the question of women's authority to write, especially in the scene of Aurora's discovery by Romney in Book 2, and EBB's references to Moses and Miriam as competing powers. In the submerged biblical text of Miriam's singing, Aurora perceives a literary foremother: "she must have sung before to get her little brother and her people to the shores of the Red Sea." The portrait of her dead mother provides her a muse, "a kaleidoscopic catalogue of models."

C92:29. Honan, Park. "Historical Privilege." Brooks and Humphrey 7–14. ¶Revision of C90:48.

C92:30. Honour, Hugh, and John Fleming. *The Venetian Hours of Henry James, Whistler and Sargent.* London: Walker; Boston: Little, Brown, 1991. ¶Refers to RB's and Pen's life in Venice and Asolo, and reprints in part Henry James's *Italian Hours* (C2961). Rev. by Michael Levey, *TLS* 20 Dec. 1991: 16–17.

C92:31. Hornecker, George F. "Robert Browning's *Cleon*: A Natural Man." *University of Mississippi Studies in English* 10 (1992): 67–72. ¶Suggests that the phrase "natural man" in 1 Corinthians 2.14 offers a way of seeing Cleon in the tradition of opposing natural to spiritual as well as to civilized man. In this context, RB juxtaposes Christian and pagan cultures, shows the limits of Cleon's character, and develops the poem's irony more fully.

C92:32. Hughes, Linda K. "Of Parts and Periodicity: Robert Browning and Victorian Serials." Brooks and Humphrey 50–59. ¶Observes that reading literature in parts "was an essential element of mass culture" for Victorians, and RB likely published *Bells and Pomegranates* serially for popular acceptance. Like the uniformitarian framework that "assumed regular, sustained, periodic emergence of material over time," both dramatic monologue and a serial literary work's middle installments "follow upon a past and point toward, without embodying, a continuing story." This "expectation of eventual completeness and wholeness" neatly accords with RB's "doctrine of the imperfect," the implications of which can be seen in "An Epistle . . . of Karshish."

C92:33. Huisman, Rosemary. "Who Speaks and For Whom? The Search for Subjectivity in Browning's Poetry." Petch and Slinn 64–87. ¶Applies to "Meeting at Night/Parting at Morning" and "Fra Lippo Lippi" Emile Benveniste's linguistic and semiotic theories about the construction of subjectivity, analyzing the grammar of the poems in detail. Instead of asking "Who is speaking?" we might better ask "Who are interacting in the discourse situation?" In these terms, the dramatic monologue gives "you" central importance and also creates a "fixed, undramatic relationship of 'I' and 'you'."

C92:34. Ives, Charles. "Ives: . . . Robert Browning Overture" (sound recording). Michel Swierczewski and the Gulbenkian Orchestra. Nimbus: NI5316, 59 minutes. ¶Rev. by David Hall, *Stereo Review* 57.11 (Nov. 1992): 146.

C92:35. Jaidka, Manju. "*Pauline*: Influences and Anticipations." *Aligarh Journal of English Studies* 14.2 (October 1989): 153–63. ¶Places RB's *Pauline* in the traditions of spiritual autobiography and confession, and suggests that it is his first dramatic monologue. A tribute to Dante, the poem also has affinities with Wordsworth's *The Prelude*. Like confessional poetry of the 1960s, "the impulse is autobiographical but there is an attempt to disclaim any direct personal involvement."

C92:36. Kienitz, Gail M. "Notes on Browning's Supreme Fiction: The Efficacy of Ambiguity in 'A Death in the Desert'." Brooks and Humphrey 60–83. ¶Contrasts the reception of RB's poetry late in the century by fervid Christian believers with his own "purposeful ambiguity": "what Browning's readers believed he believed and how the strategies of his poetic discourse validated their exegetical freeplay and accommodated their interpretive enthusiasms." Its pseudo-historical appearance distracted early readers of "A Death in the Desert" from the subversive and ironic layers appealing to modern readers. The poem succeeded because of its "confidence of spirit"; it is emotionally compelling, if not intellectually so. Although St. John does not present the desired "final, clear, distinct testimony to the events he witnessed and the truth he knows," the obfuscations of the poem suggest "the singular, subjective, and indistinct nature of individuals' apprehensions of truth."

C92:37. Knoepflmacher, U. C. "Projection and the Female Other: Romanticism, Browning, and the Victorian Dramatic Monologue." Gibson 100–19. ¶Reprint of C84: 38.

C92:38.* Kubikowski, Tomasz. "Dwa poematy Roberta Browninga (The Two Poems of Robert Browning)." *Znak* 10–11 (Oct.–Nov. 1990). ¶In Polish. See above, A92:14.

C92:39. Langbaum, Robert. "Browning and Hardy." Brooks and Humphrey 15–22. ¶Draws connections between various of RB's and Hardy's poems, noting that their diction, rhythm, and syntax especially appealed to the moderns. Hardy's first-person narratives resemble RB's dramatic monologues in their content. Both employ "sophisticated colloquial style" and question sexual morality. Hardy's interest in "Rabbi Ben Ezra" at his death "remains one of those profound mysteries."

C92:40. Latané, David E., Jr. "Browning's *Strafford* and the History of the Present." Gibson 226–42. ¶Examines "the discourse of contemporary politics" in RB's story of the Civil War, *Strafford*, "an oblique history of the present." Avoiding the obvious choice of Hampden as his hero was perhaps a strategy to force his audience "to engage with the ambiguities of historical mirroring," comparing 1630 and post-Reform 1830. RB's "focus on language, before either character or action," arises from his interest "in discursive conflict rather than physical action, and in the self-propagandizing nature of political rhetoric as much as its meaning."

C92:41. Lawton, David. "Browning's Narrators." Petch and Slinn 88–105. ¶Regards RB's shorter dramatic monologues as "*written* performances," with the term " 'narrator' as the least misleading way of grouping a variety of effects from the stylistic to the psychological.'' The narrative itself may be offstage, ''even only one act or one failure to act'' and often ''a process of past cultural production.'' RB's ''fifty men and women'' are ''almost as many attempts to construct linguistic patterns that pass as an idiolect,'' the volume being ''an anthology of almost every metre available or remotely imaginable''; the poet's authority, however, remains perceptible. The differentiation in meter and style among the poems ''is another kind of intertextuality, another meeting with the past.'' ''Childe Roland to the Dark Tower Came,'' one of the greatest poems ''on the theme of failure itself,'' in several ways reflects Byron's *Childe Harold's Pilgrimage*.

C92:42. Leighton, Angela. '' 'Because Men Made the Laws': The Fallen Woman and the Woman Poet.'' *New Feminist Discourses: Critical Essays on Theories and Texts*, ed. Isobel Armstrong. London: Routledge, 1992. 342–60. ¶Reprint of C89:42.

C92:43. Leighton, Angela. *Victorian Women Poets: Writing Against the Heart*. Charlottesville: UP of Virginia; London: Harvester Wheatsheaf. 321 pp. ¶Examines the conjunction of politics and aesthetics (''this resourceful contradiction'') in poetry by eight women: EBB along with Letitia Elizabeth Landon, Felicia Hemans, Christina Rossetti, Augusta Webster, Michael Field, Alice Meynell, and Charlotte Mew. EBB spent a lifetime developing a ''double vision''; her poetry was ''essentially politicised . . . , not because politics is its dominant subject matter and not because she shows herself in any sense a political radical . . . , but because the tensions between desire and fact, between the individual and the system, can be felt in it'' (87). ''To give offence, even poetic offence (as in some of [*Casa Guidi Window*'s] strained metres), in the cause of truth, was always one of her aims'' (111); her achievement was to transcend ''the merely heartfelt sensibility of her predecessors'' and to incorporate both pain and sweetness (117). Rev. by Gillian Beer, *TLS* 13 Nov. 1992: 24.

C92:44. Lewis, Linda M. ''The Artist's Quest in Elizabeth Barrett Browning's *Aurora Leigh*.'' *Images of the Self as Female: The Achievement of Women Artists in Re-envisioning Feminine Identity*, ed. Kathryn N. Benzel and Lauren Pringle De La Vars. Lewiston, NY: Mellen, 1992. 77–89. ¶Describes EBB's novel-poem ''not as sentimental comedy, but as a remarkable study of the creative spirit of the female artist.'' Aurora's spiritual quest takes her through two female myths: woman as seductress and the creative woman as androgyne. Aurora projects the seductress role onto women she dislikes and fears, and she enacts the androgyne herself. EBB was drawn to ''strong and masculine'' women but regarded the emerging role of nurse as a version of the ministering angel. Metaphors of a broken sphere and of the desire for sexual union with ''the god of artistic inspiration'' characterize her artistic aspiration and final psychic integration.

C92:45. Lewis, Linda M. *The Promethean Politics of Milton, Blake, and Shelley*. Columbia: U of Missouri P, 1992. 192–201. ¶Suggests in an afterword that the Promethean rebellion that inspired the Romantics was adopted by nineteenth-century women writers "as a metaphor for sexual politics." In addition to translating *Prometheus Bound* twice, EBB showed her attraction to the myth in references in "The Battle of Marathon," "An Essay on Mind," "The Tempest," "The Seraphim," "A Runaway Slave at Pilgrim's Point," and most notably in her Miltonic Lucifer (and Adam) of "A Drama of Exile."

C92:46. Lucas, John. *England and Englishness*. [See C91:43.] ¶Rev. by Gerald MacLean, *Modern Philology* 90.1 (Aug. 1992): 122–27.

C92:47. Maclean, Kenneth. "Caliban in Shakespeare and Browning." *Caliban*, ed. Harold Bloom. New York: Chelsea House, 1992. 207–20. ¶Reprint of C87:31.

C92:48. Martin, Loy. "The Divided Subject." Gibson 79–99. ¶Reprinted in part from C85:37.

C92:49. Maxwell, Catherine. "Not the Whole Picture: Browning's 'Unconquerable Shade'." *Word & Image* 8.4 (Oct.–Dec. 1992): 322–32. ¶Examines RB's depiction of the Duchess in "My Last Duchess." Identifying the woman with her image "rebounds on the Duke with startling effect," undermining his intentions to reduce and control her in this "battle for mastery." The poem is thus a type of RB's most successful verse, which avoids "straightforward representationalism for the notion of an evocative outline." The theory is seen as well in painter Alexander Cozens's essay on "artificial blotting": Cozens's blot is like RB's "spot of joy" in the Duchess's cheek. Such "tiny yet significant traces" appeal to the reader to compose her picture, making her "the dominating figure in the poem." In "Childe Roland" and "Epilogue," too, the human face becomes an image "of an unpicturable sublime," implying "both the failure and impossibility" of realism, instead offering glimpses of creativity and the imagination.

C92:50. Maynard, John. "Reading the Reader in Robert Browning's Dramatic Monologues." Gibson 69–78. ¶Reprint of C91:47.

C92:51. Melchiori, Barbara. "Upon 'Caliban Upon Setebos'." *Caliban*, ed. Harold Bloom. New York: Chelsea House, 1992. 95–108. ¶Reprint in part of C68:50.

C92:52. Mermin, Dorothy. "Browning and the Primitive." Gibson 202–25. ¶Reprint of C82:30.

C92:53. Mermin, Dorothy. *Elizabeth Barrett Browning: The Origins of a New Poetry*. [See C89:51.] ¶Rev. by Kathleen Blake, *Modern Philology* 89.3 (Feb. 1992): 377–86; William Whitla, *Modern Language Review* 87.3 (July 1992): 716–18.

C92:54. Millgate, Michael. "Robert and Pen Browning." *Testamentary Acts: Browning, Tennyson, James, Hardy*. Oxford: Clarendon; New York:

Oxford UP, 1992. 6–37. ¶Examines the late efforts of four writers "to reappraise their own past works and deeds" and reconstruct "the entire self-construct." RB destroyed many items but not the courtship letters nor EBB's letters to friends; he never resolved "the opposition between his passionate desire for privacy and his profound reluctance to destroy documents deemed precious on literary as well as on purely personal grounds." RB's will did not provide for the disposition of their literary remains nor describe the responsibilities of their son Pen as literary executor, "whether optimistically or fatalistically." Contention over Pen's will or wills at his death resulted in his property being sold. Kelley and Coley's compilation, *The Browning Collections*, lists and describes every item in the Sotheby sale catalog, an example of the way "the unique difficulties of a given scholarly field can serve to stimulate the particular energies and methodologies necessary to their resolution." Pen conscientiously fulfilled his parents' requirements but felt "the oppression of an extravagantly romanticized past." Rev. by P. N. Furbank, *TLS* 17 July 1992: 3–4; Valerie Purton, *Thomas Hardy Journal* 8 (1992): 94–97; John Sutherland, *London Review of Books* 14 (5 Nov. 1992): 8–9.

C92:55. Mitchell, Domhnall. "Browning's 'My Last Duchess'." *Explicator* 50.2 (Winter 1992): 74–75. ¶Suggests that there's an echo of Genesis in the image of the artist creating life in a day (Gandalf's portrait of the Duchess), "dramatizing the paradox of Renaissance humanism": the elevation of God's creation, man, to the center of the universe and consequent devaluation of the divine.

C92:56. Morison, J. Cotter. " 'Caliban upon Setebos'." *Caliban*, ed. Harold Bloom. New York: Chelsea House, 1992. 13–19. ¶Reprint in part of C830 [1884].

C92:57. Morlier, Margaret M. "She for God in Her: Elizabeth Barrett Browning's New Eve." *Sexuality, the Female Gaze, and the Arts*, ed. Ronald Dotterer and Susan Bowers. Selinsgrove, PA: Susquehanna UP, 1992. 127–44. ¶Regards Eve as betrayed by a culture that denies female spirituality and examines ways EBB transformed "Eve's guilt into a ground for the moral authority of Eve's daughters." EBB first states her project in "Fragment of an 'Essay on Woman'." In "A Drama of Exile," the error Eve must overcome is seeing "herself as an object through Lucifer's eyes," a point repeated tragically in "Bertha in the Lane," "The Romaunt of the Page," and "The Romaunt of Margaret." Aurora Leigh is EBB's new Eve, "who seeks equal naming power" to her male counterpart, shifting from a tragic to epic voice. She resists his demonic attraction and creates instead "idealistic, intimate human love." "Lord Walter's Wife" also is tempted but refuses "to be demeaned into an object of lust or use," resolving the ontological dilemma of the earlier poems.

C92:58. Munich, Adrienne Auslander. *Andromeda's Chains*. [See C89:56.]
¶Rev. by Laura Claridge, *Modern Language Review* 87.3 (July 1992): 711–13;
E. F. Harden, *Choice* 27 (February 1990): 940; G. B. Tennyson, *Nineteenth Century Literature* 44 (March 1990): 582; *TLS* 9 March 1990: 244.

C92:59. Munich, Adrienne Auslander. "Browning's Female Signature."
Gibson 120–36. ¶Reprinted from C89:56.

C92:60. Nelms, Jeff. "Dickens's *A Christmas Carol*: A Possible Source
for Browning's *Christmas-Eve*." Brooks and Humphrey 84–90. ¶Compares
Dickens's *A Christmas Carol* with RB's *Christmas-Eve*, looking at structure,
theme, and detail. Their different conclusions are characteristic, Dickens providing satisfying closure and RB leaving things indeterminate.

C92:61. O'Connor, Lisa. "The Construction of a Self: Guido and Metaphor in Book XI of *The Ring and the Book*." Petch and Slinn 139–58. ¶Exam-
ines Guido's struggles with metaphor, noting two opposing drives: "one
which seeks a freedom in chaos through the destruction of meaning, and one
which seeks order and coherence through the creation, with metaphor, of new,
meaningful relationships and structures." Guido shifts the terms of his self
definition from good and evil to weakness and strength. His final appeal to
Pompilia is "to a woman of his own making"; in redefining himself, he
created her as strong and constant, but she cannot prevent his death nor
save him morally. He understands the fallacy and his dependence on having
constructed it, though finally suppressing this knowledge. The steps in this
process "serve to highlight one of Browning's most pressing questions: 'For
how else know we save by worth of word?' (I.837)."

C92:62. O'Neill, Patricia. "The Painting of Nudes and Evolutionary Theory: Parleyings on Victorian Constructions of Woman." *Texas Studies in
Literature and Language* 34.4 (Winter 1992): 541–67. ¶Argues that RB's
"With Francis Furini" in *Parleying with Certain People of Importance in
Their Day* concerns the morality of painting the nude and includes an attack
on evolutionary science. He juxtaposes "moral conventions with artistic practice, and then scientific knowledge": his "sympathy for the human figure"
convinces him of "the existence of the soul, and creates social authority for
his moral aesthetic." Historicizing the female subject constructed by Victorian
art and science exposes the contradictions of "some inherited master narratives of Western culture and civilization." His defense of the nude demonstrates his belief in the "irreducible variety of human behavior" while it
contradicts "the image of the vulnerable female body wrought by [his] moral
imagination and undermines the masculine bias of his poetics."

C92:63.* Østermark-Johansen, Lene. " 'It's Art's Decline, My Son!' —
John Ruskin and Robert Browning. Two Victorian Views on the Italian Renaissance." *Angles on the English Speaking World* 5 (1991): 35–57.

C92:64. Osterwalder, Hans. "Poet and Persona in 'My Last Duchess'." *REAL: Yearbook of Research in English and American Literature* 8 (1992): 183–93. ¶Uses Jakobson's structuralist categories to define the dramatic monologue, distinguishing "between a metonymic, narrative, context-oriented level of discourse based on contiguity and a metaphoric, symbolic, code- or intertext-oriented axis based on similarity." The structure of "implied author/persona — implied reader/listener" operates in "My Last Duchess": "the implied author encodes a message with a determinate meaning for the reader, . . . giving us a clue to the Duke's rigid, life-denying attitude" in spite of the persona's attempts to direct a reading to the opposite conclusion.

C92:65. Pathak, Pratul. *The Infinite Passion of Finite Hearts: Robert Browning and Failure in Love.* New York: Peter Lang. 208 pp. ¶Reprint of C90:70.

C92:66. Pearsall, Cornelia D. J. "Browning and the Poetics of the Sepulchral Body." *Victorian Poetry* 30.1 (Spring 1992): 43–61. ¶Connects RB's "The Bishop Orders His Tomb" with his concerns over funerary sculpture memorializing EBB, demonstrating his belief that prose and sculpture are highly representational, whereas poetry and painting are allusive, offering "images rather than objects or facts." Ruskin used RB's poem, with its focus on the construction of sepulchres, to criticize excesses of Renaissance art, bringing the poem wider general attention. His own death is not the Bishop's main concern, "but rather its representation." Both RB and the Bishop reject direct representation of the figure of the lover, but both work to evoke her "remembered corporeal presence." The Bishop's sensual imagery and imaginings about his tomb are a kind of transubstantiation, transforming the body of his dead mistress into a tomb of himself.

C92:67. Pearsall, Cornelia Donetta Jean. "Demented Ingenuity: Tennyson, Browning, and the Culture of the Dramatic Monologue." *DAI* 53.03 (Sept. 1992): 820A-21A. Yale University, 1991. 248 pp.

C92:68. Pearsall, Cornelia D. J. " 'Is it Poetry?': The Generic Implications of Browning's Obscurity." Brooks and Humphrey 43–49. ¶Traces the charge of obscurity against RB through the reception of *Men and Women* and connects the charge with questioning if they are poems at all. Eliot reduced the poems to their morals, rendering them "into the essays and novels she imagines"; Wilde suggested that RB "leave off his unintelligibility, and lead the people, through inspirational ballads, into a new era of social justice." In modern times, the opposite sentiment has prevailed as readers began "to associate obscurity with poetry."

C92:69. Petch, Simon. "Browning's Roman Lawyers." Petch and Slinn 109–38. ¶Focuses on the Archangeli (VIII) and Bottini (IX) books of *The Ring and the Book*, where the poem engages the legal arguments in *The Old Yellow Book*. The languages of the poem compete with one another as well as with the "system of references to other books, other texts, other sentences" and its sources. RB's "fictive structure puts legal discourse within the jurisdiction of poetic discourse." In Book I the story is retold according to different discursive practices: law, poetry, then history. The poem's "central question of competing stories and conflicting interpretations is at the heart of the legal process." Too, it imitates an open hearing, it "shows language being made, and remade, under pressure and through performance, and it establishes roles, relations, and voices."

C92:70. Petch, Simon, and Warwick Slinn, eds. *AUMLA: Journal of the Australasian Universities Language and Literature Association* 71 (May 1989), 181 pp. ¶Rev. by Thomas J. Collins, *VS* 35.1 (Aut. 1991): 104–05.

C92:71. Phelan, J. P. "A 'Meeting' Between Clough and the Brownings." *Review of English Studies* 43 (Nov. 1992): 535–41. ¶Examines evidence for a meeting between Arthur Hugh Clough and the Brownings in 1849 cited by RB biographers but not mentioned in Clough's published correspondence. No meeting happened, and so Clough's supposed influence on RB's *Christmas-Eve and Easter-Day* is not so strong; thus the poem can be seen "not as an anomalous element" in RB's work because influenced by Clough but "as an integral part of it."

C92:72. Phelps, Deborah Lynne. " 'Disinherited by Thunder': Female Consciousness in the Poetry of Elizabeth Barrett Browning." *DAI* 52.09 (Mar. 1992): 3295A. University of Delaware, 1991. 271 pp.

C92:73. Rader, Ralph W. "Notes on Some Structural Varieties and Variations in Dramatic 'I' Poems and Their Theoretical Implications." Gibson 37–53. ¶Reprint of C84:50.

C92:74. Raymond, Meredith B. "The Flower and the Root." Brooks and Humphrey 99–106. ¶Suggests some roots of RB's enthusiasm for EBB's *Poems* of 1844: in "Bertha in the Lane," "The Rhyme of the Duchess May," and "The Romaunt of the Page" — poems specifically mentioned by RB — EBB presents "an outspoken Christian ethic," all three characters acting "with freedom and joy." In the fourth poem he mentions, "A Drama of Exile," the creative principle of love is situated in a specifically Christian context.

C92:75. Rice, Thomas Jackson. "Dante . . . Browning. Gabriel . . . Joyce: Allusion and Structure in 'The Dead'." *James Joyce Quarterly* 30.1 (Fall 1992): 29–37. ¶Suggests RB's "Apollo and the Fates," from *Parleyings with Certain People of Importance in Their Day*, as the source of Gabriel Conway's uncited non-quotation in Joyce's "The Dead." Readers fashion meaning "by filling the gaps in texts," a technique Joyce uses abundantly in later works. RB's poem is appropriate in a story about "the livingness of the dead." His covert and autobiographical presences in the poem likely appealed to Joyce, as well as its tragic mythological themes and its allusions to Dante.

C92:76. Riede, David G. "Genre and Poetic Authority in *Pippa Passes.*" Gibson 186–201. ¶Reprint of C89:62.

C92:77. Rigg, Patricia Diane. "Romantic Irony and Reader-Response in the Poetry of Robert Browning." *DAI* ADD X1989. University of Calgary, 1988.

C92:78. Root, Amy L. "Scholar Leaves Victorian Poetry Legacy." *Texas Libraries* 52 (Summer 1991): 31–35. ¶Describes the Armstrong Browning Library at Baylor University and its founder, A. J. Armstrong.

C92:79. Rundle, Vivienne Jill. "Framing the Reader: Interpretation and Design in Victorian and Early Modern Narrative." *DAI* 53.05 (Nov. 1992): 1529A. University of Pennsylvania, 1992. 313 pp.

C92:80. Ryals, Clyde de L. *A World of Possibilities.* [See C91:72.] ¶Rev. by Gary Handwerk, *Nineteenth Century Literature* 47.1 (June 1992): 99–101; Anne K. Mellor, *VS* 35.4 (Summer 1992): 434–35.

C92:81. Scheick, William J. "A Verbal Trace in Browning's 'Pictor Ignotus'." *Victorians Institute Journal* 20 (1992): 39–48. ¶Suggests that the word "bar," which appears early in RB's "Pictor Ignotus," is the verbal trace of the author's disappointment with response to his poetry. Although it appears only once, this "belying verbal trace," by its placement and through multiple meanings, challenges the narrator's reliability. The frustration of the desire for "certain comprehension" and for language to signify absolute meaning "urges the reader to recognize the limits of any effort to comprehend individual consciousness."

C92:82. Sharlow, Gretchen E. "Mark Twain Reads Browning Again: A Discovery in the Langdon-Crane Family Library at Quarry Farm." *Mark Twain Journal* 28.2 (Fall 1990): 24–29. ¶Reinforces Alan Gribben's assertion that Mark Twain "was an accomplished oral interpreter" of RB's poetry who analyzed favorite poems in detail. Volumes 4 and 6 of the 1887 edition of RB's works are annotated in Twain's hand and include "penciled cues for voice inflection, pauses, and emphasis." A friend, Mary Mason Fairbanks, who conducted Browning Society and Browning Circle meetings, encouraged Twain's interest in RB.

C92:83. Shaw, W. David. *Victorians and Mystery.* [See C90:82–83.] ¶Rev. by Ruth apRoberts, *Modern Philology* 89.4 (May 1992): 601–04; James Paradis, *Modern Language Review* 87.3 (July 1992): 713–15; Lawrence Poston, *Clio* 21.1 (Fall 1991): 79–82; Harold L. Weatherby, *Nineteenth Century Literature* 46.3 (Dec. 1991): 399–403.

C92:84. Sherwood, Dolly. *Harriet Hosmer.* [See C91:75.] ¶Rev. by Janet H. Murray, *New York Times Book Review* 96 (29 Dec. 1991): 12–13; Marilyn Richardson, *Women's Review of Books* 9.4 (Jan. 1992): 20.

C92:85. Slinn, E. Warwick. *The Discourse of Self in Victorian Poetry.* [See C91:76.] ¶Rev. by Lee Erickson, *VS* 35.4 (Summer 1992): 435–36; James F. Loucks, *Nineteenth Century Literature* 47.1 (June 1992): 113–16.

C92:86. Slinn, E. Warwick. "From Textual Reference to Textual Strategy: Critical Responses to Browning's Poetry." Petch and Slinn 161–81. ¶Uses critics' responses to RB's "Bishop Blougram's Apology" as an index of a shift of attention to his poetry "from meaning by referent to meaning by textual and contextual interplay." Even early efforts to extract meaning by paraphrasing its arguments indicate that the poem requires the reader's engagement. More recent commentators continue the focus on "the structures and dynamics of subject-centered experience." In RB "the drama of self-representation and social identity" are combined with challenges "to assumptions about human understanding and the authority of the individual mind."

C92:87. Slinn, E. Warwick. "Hegel and Browning." Brooks and Humphrey 91–98. ¶Draws connections between Hegel's *Phenomenology of Mind* and RB's poetry, noting that both critique "the powerful Romantic aesthetic of transcendence and the equally powerful *cogito*." Most useful is Hegel's theory of the subject: it "is constituted through a dialectic which . . . is self-affirming while it is self-dissolving; that is, it presents itself outwardly, for another, while presenting itself inwardly, for itself." The subject "is characterized by acts of self-representation, by mediation, and by continually making distinctions, establishing difference." Hegel's assertion that form is inseparable from content is echoed in RB's development of dynamic form in the monologues, for example in "The Bishop Orders his Tomb."

C92:88. Stephenson, Glennis. *Elizabeth Barrett Browning and the Poetry of Love*. [See C89:70.] ¶Rev. by Kathleen Blake, *Modern Philology* 89.3 (Feb. 1992): 377–86.

C92:89. Stern, Madeleine B. "An Early Alcott Sensation Story: 'Marian Earle; Or, Only an Actress!' " *Nineteenth Century Literature* 47.2 (June 1992): 91–98. ¶Examines Louisa May Alcott's use of not only Marian Erle's story from *Aurora Leigh* but EBB's feminist themes of sisterhood and compassion for unwed mothers, as well as the description of "a sensational wedding scene." Alcott's recently-discovered thriller is here correctly ascribed to her.

C92:90. Stern, Martin. "Zu Hofmannsthals 'Drei kleinen Liedern'." *Basler Hofmannsthal-Beiträge*, ed. Karl Pestalozzi and Martin Stern. Würzburg: Königshausen & Neumann, 1991. 63–73. ¶Discusses "Three Little Songs" by Austrian poet Hofmannsthal, focusing on the first, "Hörtest du denn night hinerin," the source for which is RB's "Serenade at the Villa." In German.

C92:91. Stonum, Gary. *The Dickinson Sublime*. [See C90:92.] ¶Rev. by Mary Loeffelholz, *JEGP* 91.2 (Apr. 1992): 278–81.

C92:92. Sussman, Herbert. "Robert Browning's 'Fra Lippo Lippi' and the Problematic of a Male Poetic." *VS* 35.2 (Winter 1992): 185–200. ¶Investigates feminized poetic identity as one of the anxieties of middle-class Victorian manhood, seeing RB's "Fra Lippo Lippi" as a "manifesto of a male poetic" that identifies "creative power with sexual potency." He then inverts such success "to show that the emergence of the male poet into the supposedly free individualistic activity of capitalism generates new forms for imprisoning male desire." Thus Fra Lippo is as much a "failure" as is Andrea del Sarto.

C92:93. Sutcliffe, Rebecca J. "The Sting and the Crook: A Response to Robert Browning's Sleight of Hand." *Victorian Review* 18.2 (Winter 1992): 63. ¶A poem.

C92:94. Taylor, Beverly. " 'School-Miss Alfred' and 'Materfamilias': Female Sexuality and Poetic Voice in *The Princess* and *Aurora Leigh*." *Gender and Discourse in Victorian Literature and Art*, ed. Antony H. Harrison and Beverly Taylor. DeKalb: Northern Illinois UP, 1992. 5–29. ¶Places EBB's and Tennyson's poems in the context of their contemporaries' debates about female sexuality and intellectual activity. Both make the revolutionary assertion that women can fulfill themselves "intellectually and professionally only when they accept their full identities, including their sexual natures." Their conclusions — both protagonists marry — are not conservative but instead revise the convention, imagining "a new form of partnership." Aurora's poetry is not presented in the poem, but the poem itself, "written after the events it records," is the "text in which she articulates the Victorian world through her own life, her own body."

C92:95. Tigges, Wim. "An Analogue to Bloom's Mythical Potato." *James Joyce Quarterly* 29.4 (Summer 1992): 846. ¶Suggests that mentions in *Ulysses* of a talismanic potato, which has been linked to the moly root, have an intertextual reference to EBB's *Aurora Leigh*, 4:405–06.

C92:96. Tucker, Herbert F. "Dramatic Monologue and the Overhearing of Lyric." Gibson 21–36. ¶Reprint of C85:61.

C92:97. Tucker, Herbert F. "Epiphany and Browning: Character Made Manifest." *PMLA* 107.5 (Oct. 1992): 1208–21. ¶Examines Romantic (Wordsworth) and Victorian (RB) as well as scriptural (Matthew 2.1–12) antecedents of the popular literary concept of epiphany. Epiphany in RB "involves conspicuous narrative and cultural dimensions" not readily evident in Joyce. Dramatic monologists' reactions to epiphanies "compose their lives and constitute their characters," as seen especially in "Karshish," "My Star," and " 'Transcendentalism.' " Too, the "infinite moment" in RB implicates "the reader in the drama of interpretation."

C92:98. Viscusi, Robert. " 'The Englishman in Italy': Free Trade as a Principle of Aesthetics." Gibson 243–66. ¶Reprint of C84:66.

C92:99. Waller, Randall Lionel. "The Poetry of Persuasion: Browning's Apologists and the Art of Rhetoric." *DAI* 53.04 (Oct. 1992): 1168A–69A. Texas A&M University, 1991. 211 pp.

C92:100. Welsh, Alexander. "Stories of Experience." *Strong Representations: Narrative and Circumstantial Evidence in England*. Baltimore: Johns

Hopkins UP, 1992. 197–256. ¶Examines the persuasive power of making "facts speak for themselves" in narrative as "carefully managed circumstantial evidence." In RB's modern text "of high Victorianism," *The Ring and the Book*, he questions even being able to know truth. Testimony (the story of experience) too is interrogated in the poem, underscoring RB's belief "that life itself is a trial." The failure of knowing is counterbalanced by "intuitionism," art in its obliqueness. Rev. by John Bayley, *London Review of Books* 14 (11 June 1992): 17–18; Barbara Hardy, *TLS* 5 June 1992: 24; Robert Newsom, *Nineteenth Century Literature* 47.3 (Dec. 1992): 378–81.

C92:101. Wetherell, Marlene. "Mr. Browning Comes to Call." *Victoria* 6.4 (April 1992): 74–82. ¶Retells the story of the Brownings' courtship and marriage for a popular audience.

C92:102. Woolford, John. *Browning the Revisionary*. [See C87:64.] ¶Rev. by Jack Siemsen, *South Atlantic Review* 57 (1992): 117–19.

C92:103. Woolford, John. "The Influence of Edmund Kean on Browning's *Pauline*." Brooks and Humphrey 23–31. ¶Examines allusions to the actor Edmund Kean in RB's *Pauline*, written shortly after seeing "Richard III." The "*idea* of acting catalysed by Kean's performance" connected with RB's conception "of authorship as a species of *dramatic performance*." In actual performances at that time Kean was "half-dead with disease and alcoholism," however. This action-in-decay offered RB a creative paradigm for his own crisis of identity as a Romantic poet: to "at once write and live a part; to be, and not to be, the language one utters; to confess, and in the same words, to disguise, one's essential self."

C92:104. Yeo, Hongsang. "Browning's Novelistic Discourse in *The Ring and the Book*." *Journal of English Language and Literature* 38.4 (Winter 1992): 683–99. ¶Applies Bakhtin's theories of "dialectical interaction between monologism and dialogism," as well as of polyphony and heteroglossia, and of "comico-satirical" effects. Each dramatic monologue "involves an internal dialogism through which the speaker attempts to persuade his/her audience." The juxtaposition of the monologues "produces a polyphonic struggle of different languages and character-positions": Guido's first using "the 'old' language of aristocratic feudalism," and those of Caponsacchi and Pompilia representing the "language of the future." Caponsacchi is transformed from aristocrat to civil individual, and the illiterate Pompilia voices the female Other, "silenced by the male-dominant discourses of Guido's Italy." Comic figures, motifs, and overall design reveal RB's Utopian impulse, and authorial closure is deferred by the coexistence of different stories in the poem.

C92:105. Zorzi, Rosella Mamoli. "Henry James in a 'Venetian' Diary." *Henry James Review* 11.2 (Spring 1990): 101–14. ¶Describes a two-part diary kept by Ariana and Daniel Sargent Curtis, Americans living in Venice at the end of the century; it is unpublished except for the part recording details about RB in his last years (see A85:7).

BIBLIOGRAPHY INDEX

DATE DUE